Jonas & Kovner's

Health Care Delivery in the United States

James R. Knickman, PhD, is president and chief executive officer of the New York State Health Foundation (NYSHealth), a private foundation dedicated to improving the health of all New Yorkers, especially the most vulnerable. Under Dr. Knickman's leadership, NYSHealth has invested more than $90 million since 2006 in initiatives to improve health care and the public health system in New York state. Central to the foundation's mission is a commitment to sharing the results and lessons of its grantmaking; informing policy and practice through timely, credible analysis and commentary; and serving as a neutral convener of health care leaders and stakeholders throughout New York. Before joining NYSHealth, Dr. Knickman was vice president of research and evaluation, Robert Wood Johnson Foundation, and served on the faculty of New York University's Robert F. Wagner Graduate School of Public Service. He serves on numerous boards, including the National Council on Aging and Philanthropy New York.

Anthony R. Kovner, PhD, is professor of management at New York University's Robert F. Wagner Graduate School of Public Service. He has directed the executive MPA in management, the concentration for nurse leaders, the program in health policy and management, and the advanced management program for clinicians at NYU/Wagner. He was a senior program consultant to the Robert Wood Johnson Foundation's rural hospital program and was senior health consultant to the United Autoworkers Union. He served as a manager for 12 years in all, in a large community health center, a nursing home, an academic faculty practice, and as CEO at a community hospital. Professor Kovner is the author or editor, with others, of 11 books, 48 peer-reviewed articles, and 33 published case studies. He was the fourth recipient, in 1999, of the Filerman Prize for Educational Leadership from the Association of University Programs in Health Administration.

Jonas & Kovner's

Health Care Delivery in the United States

11th Edition

James R. Knickman, PhD
Anthony R. Kovner, PhD
Editors

Steven Jonas, MD, MPH, MS, FNYAS
Founding Editor

SPRINGER PUBLISHING COMPANY
NEW YORK

Springer Publishing Company, LLC
11 West 42nd Street
New York, NY 10036
www.springerpub.com

Acquisitions Editor: Sheri W. Sussman
Composition: Exeter Premedia Services Private Ltd.

ISBN: 978-0-8261-2527-9
e-book ISBN: 978-0-8261-2529-3

For Instructors:
Instructors' Manual: ISBN 978-0-8261-7155-9
Transition Guide for the 11th Edition: ISBN 978-0-8261-2628-3
Test Bank: ISBN 978-0-8261-7159-7
PowerPoints: ISBN 978-0-8261-7157-3
Syllabus: ISBN 978-0-8261-7158-0
Please email textbook@springerpub.com to request these files.

For Students and Instructors:
Visit ushealthcaredelivery.com for additional materials including an update on the Affordable Care Act.

16 17 18 / 5 4 3

The author and the publisher of this Work have made every effort to use sources believed to be reliable to provide information
that is accurate and compatible with the standards generally accepted at the time of publication. The author and publisher shall
not be liable for any special, consequential, or exemplary damages resulting, in whole or in part, from the readers' use of, or reliance on, the information contained in this book. The publisher has no responsibility for the persistence or accuracy of URLs for
external or third-party Internet websites referred to in this publication and does not guarantee that any content on such websites
is, or will remain, accurate or appropriate.

Library of Congress Cataloging-in-Publication Data

Jonas and Kovner's health care delivery in the United States / [edited by] James R. Knickman, Anthony R. Kovner.—11th edition.
    p. ; cm.
  Health care delivery in the United States
  Editors' names reversed on the previous edition.
  Preceded by: Jonas & Kovner's health care delivery in the United States.
  Includes bibliographical references and index.
  ISBN 978-0-8261-2527-9—ISBN 978-0-8261-2529-3 (e-book)
  I. Knickman, James, editor.   II. Kovner, Anthony R., editor.   III. Title: Health care delivery in the United States.
  [DNLM: 1. Delivery of Health Care—United States.   2. Health Policy—United States.   3. Health Services—United
States.   4. Quality of Health Care—United States. W 84 AA1]
  RA395.A3
  362.10973—dc23
                                           2014045558

Printed in the United States of America by Bradford and Bigelow.

Contents

List of Tables and Figures

Foreword

This, the 11th edition of *Health Care Delivery in the United States*, appears at an unprecedented moment in the evolution of the U.S. health care system. After decades of relentless increases in the number of uninsured residents, more Americans today hold health insurance coverage than at any time in the past. In the wake of the Affordable Care Act coverage expansion, which began in January 2014, the share of the population uninsured has fallen to levels last seen more than 30 years ago. On the cost front, real per capita spending over the past 4 years has grown at the slowest rate on record. For the 8th year in a row, the Congressional Budget Office has revised downward its projections of Medicare cost growth. Although the exceptional slowdown of overall health spending is largely due to the effects of the Great Recession, changes to payment policies and levels enacted in the health reform law may claim credit for some of the good Medicare news.

The new law, as well as changes in private insurer practices, also seems to have encouraged the proliferation of novel forms of health care delivery that seek to generate the quality and cost benefits long associated with high-performing vertically integrated health care institutions. Some evidence suggests that these incentives have contributed to reductions in readmission rates and health care-acquired infections.

On the public health front, decades of educational efforts, incentives, and interventions, often based on academic evidence, have also led to significant improvements. Teen and adult smoking rates are at all-time lows, and the teen birth rate has fallen almost continuously over the past 20 years. These improvements are testimony to vibrant and creative efforts in health financing, delivery, and public health.

It is comforting and reassuring to imagine that the U.S. health system has settled into a more sustainable, equitable, and effective path. But that sanguine image belies both the condition of our health system and the history of health reform elsewhere. It is true that uninsurance rates have dropped dramatically in some states—but many others have rejected the coverage expansions. A concerted effort in the courts and in Congress seeks to roll back the gains that have already been made. Slower cost growth offers the system some breathing room, but almost all analysts predict that the changes in payments and organizations will not be sufficient to hold spending at supportable levels. Even under the most optimistic scenarios, as the baby boom generation ages, health care will consume a growing share of the gross domestic product and of the federal budget. Health reform and insurer ingenuity have brought an abundance of new organizational forms, but the jury is out on whether these will actually improve quality and reduce costs. U.S. health outcomes, especially for the most vulnerable populations, remain abysmally low in a comparative perspective, and the evidence suggests that inequality in health outcomes is growing.

Students of health care policy and delivery need to chart a middle course: neither complacently optimistic about the promise of a new regime, nor overly discouraged by the still-dismal U.S. context. Instead, as the experience of other countries suggests, we should recognize that health care system reform is a never-ending task. After all, Chancellor Otto von Bismarck initiated the German health insurance system in 1883—and Chancellor Angela Merkel completed the most recent German health insurance reform, building on Bismarck's model, in 2011. Similarly, even though much has changed, our health care system continues to resemble (quite closely) the system described in the first edition of *Health Care Delivery in the United States*, published in 1977. No doubt a student of the future, scanning this 11th edition in 2050, will recognize many similarities to the health system he or she knows and will also see evidence of the decades of reform that will consume policymakers and delivery system managers between now and then.

Health care managers, practitioners, and students must both operate as effectively as they can within the daunting and continually evolving system at hand and identify opportunities for reform advances. For nearly 40 years—27 of them at least in part under the stewardship of Tony Kovner—*Health Care Delivery in the United States* has been an indispensable companion to those preparing to manage this balance. The present edition demonstrates once again why this volume has come to be so prized. It takes the long view—charting recent developments in health policy and putting them side-by-side with descriptions and analysis of existing programs in the United States and abroad. Novelty gets its due, but so does context. The text recognizes that health is, after all, the ultimate object of health care delivery, and so provides a thorough assessment of population health. It explores the key elements of the health care delivery system, from both the supply and the demand sides. In addition, it recognizes that the delivery system doesn't stand alone and examines the structures and processes—technological, governmental, and organizational—that underpin the system.

Health Care Delivery in the United States profits from the editorship of two highly experienced observers of the health care system: James Knickman and Anthony Kovner. Jim, once a faculty member at Wagner, is now president and CEO of the New York State Health Foundation, which, under his stewardship, has been an important contributor to reform of the New York state health system. Tony is, to my delight, my colleague at the Wagner School. He has been a mentor and guide to generations of health care managers and policymakers, both at a distance, as contributor and editor to this text, and as a classroom teacher and adviser. He has transformed the lives of his students, and they, as leaders in health care institutions around the country, have transformed their institutions and the lives of their patients. Tony inculcates in his students—as he has in me—a conviction that policy and management can, should, and must be founded on the best possible evidence. Founding decisions on evidence is not just a mantra—it means asking the right questions, identifying the appropriate literature, and assessing the applicability and quality of this research. In this volume, Tony and Jim have put that system to work, and it is this foundation in rigorous evidence that allows the text to stand the test of time and to be responsive and useful in addressing current developments.

Sherry Glied, PhD
Dean, New York University
Robert F. Wagner School of Public Service
New York, New York

Acknowledgments

The editors would like to express deep appreciation to the team of people who made this book possible. First, we thank our 29 authors of the 16 chapters that comprise the book. They are all noted experts in their fields, and we appreciate their willingness to translate their knowledge into chapters that introduce future leaders to the workings of the U.S. health system. Second, we wish to acknowledge the superb editorial role played by Sheri W. Sussman and the quality control of production under Joanne Jay's direction at Springer Publishing Company. We appreciate Sheri's insights about how to publish a textbook and have benefited from Joanne's keeping the process moving in creating an effective and enjoyable learning experience for *HCDUS* readers. Christine Kovner frequently helped to strengthen the book, reading various chapters and offering advice from her vantage as one of the leading nursing researchers in the country. At the New York State Health Foundation, Susan Illman, Emily Parker, and Amy Shefrin each provided valued assistance gathering current data to inform the book. Finally, we would like to acknowledge Steve Jonas, who originated this book 11 editions ago.

Organization of This Book

This is the 11th edition of *Jonas and Kovner's Health Care Delivery in the United States*, which, although its title has evolved in the last 35 years, has stayed true to its original purpose: helping instructors and students better understand the complicated, expensive, and ever-changing U.S. health care delivery system and the public health system. It is a privilege to be able to work with instructors around the world to introduce the leaders of tomorrow to the health field.

Our nation is embarked on an ambitious attempt to reshape how we go about taking care of the health concerns of our population. On the one hand, there is a new energy to develop initiatives that focus on keeping people healthy. On the other hand, there is a great deal of experimenting with the organization of the care system that addresses the needs of people who have medical problems associated with injuries and disease. The aim of this experimentation is to improve the quality of medical care and to bring costs in line with what Americans can afford and want to spend on the health sector.

This text is organized to address both the challenge of keeping people healthy (Part II) and the challenge of delivering good medical care that helps people recover from medical conditions that do occur (Part III). In addition, we have included a section that describes the current status of the U.S. health care system and explains the complicated public policy process that has so much influence on the way health care is delivered and financed in this country (Part I). The text ends with a consideration of where the health system might be headed in the years to come (Part IV).

Each chapter starts with a list of key words that are central to the chapter's focus, a list of the learning objectives addressed by the chapter, and an outline of what is to come. Each chapter ends with a list of discussion questions and a case study, encouraging the reader to apply the ideas of the chapter to real-life issues and challenges that face health care leaders focused on management issues and policy issues.

In addition to this text, an online Instructors' Manual, which includes a variety of background materials that teachers will find useful in guiding class discussion, is available. It also offers additional resources and class projects that are useful to students and the learning process. In addition, PowerPoints, Syllabus, Test Bank, and Transition Guide are available to instructors via textbooks@springerpub .com

Students and instructors are encouraged to visit ushealthcaredelivery.com for additional materials including an updated supplementary chapter on the Patient Protection and Affordable Care Act.

We encourage instructors and students to communicate with us about this edition, so that we may make the 12th edition even more useful to you. Please submit any comments or questions to us at knickman@nyshealth.org and anthony.kovner@nyu. edu, and we will get back to you. As always, we appreciate your suggestions.

Anthony R. Kovner, PhD
James R. Knickman, PhD

Contributors

Thad Calabrese, PhD, is an assistant professor of public and nonprofit financial management at New York University's Robert F. Wagner Graduate School of Public Service. Dr. Calabrese is the coauthor of two textbooks on financial management with applications to government and nonprofit organizations, including health care organizations. *Financial Management for Public, Health, and Not-for-Profit Organizations* (4th edition) was written with Steven Finkler, Robert Purtell, and Daniel L. Smith. *Accounting Fundamentals for Health Care Management* (2nd edition) was written with Steven Finkler and David Ward. Dr. Calabrese's research applies the principles of corporate finance to organizations involved in the production or coproduction of public goods and services. He teaches courses on financial management for health care organizations and also for nonprofit organizations.

Elaine F. Cassidy, PhD, is a senior consultant in research and evaluation at consulting firm Equal Measure, where she manages projects related to health promotion, particularly among under-privileged populations. Before joining Equal Measure, Dr. Cassidy served as a program officer in research and evaluation at the Robert Wood Johnson Foundation, where she oversaw research and evaluation activities for the Vulnerable Populations portfolio. Her work and professional interests focus primarily on child and adolescent health and risk behavior, violence prevention, and school-based interventions, primarily for young people living in low-income, urban environments. She is a trained school psychologist and mental health clinician who has provided therapeutic care to children and families in school, outpatient, and acute partial hospitalization settings. She holds an MSEd in psychological services from the University of Pennsylvania and a PhD in school, community, and child-clinical psychology from the University of Pennsylvania.

Susan A. Chapman, PhD, RN, FAAN, is professor in the Department of Social and Behavioral Sciences, University of California, San Francisco School of Nursing, and faculty at UCSF's Center for Health Professions and the Institute for Health Policy Studies. She is codirector of the masters and doctoral programs in health policy at the School of Nursing. Her scholarly work focuses on health workforce research, health policy analysis, and program evaluation. Susan's workforce research focuses on transforming models of primary care to address new and expanded roles for the health care workforce and the long-term care workforce. Susan received a BS from the University of Iowa, MS from Boston College, MPH from Boston University, and PhD in Health Services and Policy Analysis from UC Berkeley.

Carolyn M. Clancy, MD, is Interim Under Secretary for Health at the Department of Veterans Affairs, having joined the VA in 2013 as Assistant Deputy Under Secretary for Health for Quality, Safety and Value. Prior to VA, she was director of the federal Agency for Healthcare Research and Quality (AHRQ) for ten years and also was director of AHRQ's Center for Outcomes and Effectiveness Research. Dr. Clancy, a general internist and health services researcher, is a graduate of Boston College and the University of Massachusetts Medical School. After her clinical training in internal medicine, she was a Henry J. Kaiser Family Foundation Fellow at the University of Pennsylvania. Dr. Clancy holds an academic appointment at the George Washington University School of Medicine and serves as senior associate editor for the journal *Health Services Research*. She serves on multiple editorial boards, is a member of the Institute of Medicine, and was elected a master of the American College of Physicians in 2004. In 2009, she was awarded the William B. Graham Prize for Health Services Research. Dr. Clancy's major research interests include improving health care quality and patient safety and reducing disparities in care associated with race, ethnicity, gender, income, and education. As director of AHRQ, she launched the first annual report to Congress on health care disparities and health care quality.

Catherine K. Dangremond, MPA, is currently an administrative fellow at the Yale New Haven Health System. Her professional interests lie at the intersection of health care delivery and health policy, particularly the effects of this intersection on health system strategy and improvement in the delivery of health care and health outcomes. Ms. Dangremond holds an MPA from New York University's Robert F. Wagner Graduate School of Public Service. She previously worked as a process improvement consultant and business development professional, focused in the health care provider and government sectors.

Cathleen O. Erwin, PhD, MBA, is an assistant professor of health services administration in the Department of Political Science at Auburn University. Before her academic career, she worked for many years in administration, development, and communications for nonprofit organizations in the arts, health care, and higher education. Dr. Erwin received her doctoral degree in administration-health services from the University of Alabama at Birmingham. Her research primarily revolves around strategic management, organizational performance, and governance in health care organizations. Dr. Erwin's teaching portfolio includes courses in health care delivery systems, health insurance and reimbursement, health care quality management, health information technology, and fundraising for nonprofit organizations. She is a past president of the Alabama Healthcare Executives Forum, the state chapter of the American College of Healthcare Executives (ACHE), and is an appointed member of the board for the Health Care Management Division of the Academy of Management.

Irene Fraser, PhD, is a political scientist who has focused her work on Medicaid, private health insurance, and health care delivery. Since 1995, she has been at the Agency for Healthcare Research and Quality, where she is director of the Center for Delivery, Organization, and Markets. Dr. Fraser spent 8 years at the American Hospital Association, as senior policy manager on indigent care, Medicaid, and health care reform, and director of Ambulatory Care. Before that, Dr. Fraser was associate professor of Political Science, director of the public policy program at Barat College, and adjunct faculty to the Institute for Health Law at Loyola School of Law. Dr. Fraser's work has appeared in *Health Affairs, Inquiry, Health Care Financing Review, Medical Care Research and Review, Journal of Healthcare Management, Journal of Ambulatory Care Management, Health Services Research,* and *Journal of Health Politics, Policy and Law.* She has a BA in political science and Spanish from Chatham College, and a PhD in political science from the University of Illinois.

Jacqueline Martinez Garcel, MPH, is vice president at the New York State Health Foundation (NYSHealth). Ms. Martinez Garcel serves as a key adviser to the president and CEO and has a central role in developing the foundation's program areas, identifying emerging opportunities and strategic niches, building partnerships with other foundations, and evaluating the performance of programs and grantees. Before joining

NYSHealth, she served as the Executive Director for the Northern Manhattan Community Voices Collaborative (Community Voices). The mission of Community Voices, funded by the W.K. Kellogg Foundation, is to improve access and quality of care for vulnerable populations. Ms. Martinez Garcel also worked with Dr. H. Jack Geiger at the City University of New York to complete an analysis of racial and ethnic disparities in diagnosis and treatment in the U.S. health care system. She has served as an NIH fellow for the Department of Public Health in the City of Merida in Yucatan, Mexico, and an adjunct professor of sociology at the Borough of Manhattan Community College. She is a board director for the Institute for Civic Leadership and for NAMI-New York City Metro. She holds a MPH from Columbia University and a BS from Cornell University.

Michael K. Gusmano, PhD, is a research scholar at The Hastings Center. Dr. Gusmano's research interests include inequalities in health and theories of social justice. He is one of the associate editors of *Making Difficult Decisions with Patients and Families: A Singapore Casebook*. His previous books include *Health Care in World Cities* (with Victor G. Rodwin and Daniel Weisz), *Healthy Voices/Unhealthy Silence: Advocating for Poor People's Health* (with Colleen Grogan), and *Growing Older in World Cities* (coedited with Victor G. Rodwin). Dr. Gusmano holds a PhD in political science from the University of Maryland at College Park and an MPP from SUNY Albany. He was a Robert Wood Johnson Foundation scholar in health policy at Yale University and is a member of the editorial committee of *The Hastings Center Report* and the editorial boards of *Health Economics, Policy and Law,* and the *Journal of Health Politics, Policy and Law*.

Paul L. Kuehnert, DNP, RN, is the team director for the Bridging Health and Health Care Portfolio at the Robert Wood Johnson Foundation in Princeton, New Jersey. Immediately before coming to RWJ, Paul was the county health officer and executive director for health for Kane County, Illinois, a metro Chicago county of 515,000 people, for 5 years. In this role, Dr. Kuehnert provided executive leadership and oversight to four county departments: Health, Emergency Management, Community Reinvestment, and Animal Control. Before working in Kane County, Dr. Kuehnert served as deputy state health officer and deputy director of the state of Maine's health department. Dr. Kuehnert is a pediatric nurse practitioner and holds a DNP in executive leadership as well as an MS in public health nursing from University of Illinois at Chicago. He was named a Robert Wood Johnson Foundation executive nurse fellow in 2004.

Amy Yarbrough Landry, PhD, is an assistant professor in the Department of Health Services Administration at the University of Alabama at Birmingham. She teaches Introduction to Health Systems and Comparative Health Systems to masters and doctoral students in her department. Dr. Landry's research interests pertain to the strategic management of health care organizations in a variety of contexts, including acute care hospitals, long-term care organizations, Medicaid managed care organizations, and physician organizations. Dr. Landry has also done research surrounding leadership in health care organizations. In particular, she is interested in executive selection, training, and development.

Christy Harris Lemak, PhD, FACHE, is professor and chair of the Department of Health Services Administration at the University of Alabama at Birmingham. Dr. Lemak teaches and conducts scholarship in the areas of health care management and leadership, with an emphasis on how leadership and organizational factors lead to high performance in health care. Her research includes studies of a complex pay-for-performance incentive program for physicians, and relationships among organizational culture, management practice, and surgical outcomes in a multihospital surgical collaborative. Dr. Lemak has extensively studied how Medicaid policy demonstrations affect hospitals, health plans, and relationships among provider organizations. She is currently examining new ways of measuring hospital and health system performance. She holds a PhD in health services organization and policy from the University of Michigan, MHA and MBA degrees from the University of Missouri-Columbia, and a BS in health planning and administration from the University of Illinois.

Laura C. Leviton, PhD, is special advisor for evaluation at Robert Wood Johnson Foundation, Princeton, New Jersey. She has been with the foundation since 1999, overseeing more than 100 national and local evaluations. She was formerly a professor at two schools of public health, where she collaborated on the first randomized experiment on HIV prevention, and later on two large place-based randomized experiments on improving medical practices. She received the 1993 award from the American Psychological Association for Distinguished Contributions to Psychology in the Public Interest. She has served on three Institute of Medicine committees and was appointed by the secretary of DHHS to CDC's National Advisory Committee on HIV and STD Prevention. Dr. Leviton was president of the American Evaluation Association in 2000 and has coauthored two books: *Foundations of Program Evaluation* and *Confronting Public Health Risks*. She received her PhD in social psychology from the University of Kansas and postdoctoral training in research methodology and evaluation at Northwestern University.

C. Tracy Orleans, PhD, is the senior scientist for the Robert Wood Johnson Foundation and has led or coled the foundation's public policy and health care system grant-making in the areas of health behavior change, tobacco control, chronic disease management and prevention, physical activity promotion, and childhood obesity prevention during the past 18 years. During the past 6 years, she has focused mainly on discovering, evaluating, and applying effective policy and environmental strategies for reversing the rise in childhood obesity and reducing the disparities in its prevalence and health tolls. She is now working to develop metrics and research that will help to create a broad culture of health nationwide. Dr. Orleans has authored or coauthored more than 250 publications, served on numerous journal editorial boards, on national scientific panels and advisory groups (e.g., Institute of Medicine, U.S. Preventive Services Task Force, Community Preventive Services Task Force, National Commission on Prevention Priorities, National Collaborative on Childhood Obesity Research), and as the associate policy editor for the *American Journal of Preventive Medicine*. Dr. Orleans has received many awards for her national work in the fields of behavioral medicine, tobacco control, and childhood obesity prevention. Most recently, she was deeply honored, along with Drs. Jim Sallis and Mary Story, to receive the CDC's Weight of the Nation Pioneering Innovation Award for Applied Obesity Research in 2012.

Lourdes J. Rodríguez, DrPh, serves as program officer for the New York State Health Foundation (NYSHealth) in the prevention area, disseminating evidence-based programs, supporting promising prevention strategies, and leveraging additional resources for New York state. Before her current position, Dr. Rodríguez served as associate director of community partnerships for healthy neighborhoods at City Harvest, overseeing community engagement activities. From 2004 to 2012 she was on the faculty at the Columbia University Mailman School of Public Health. She coedited a book examining community mobilization for health and has authored numerous publications on violence prevention, mental health, and active living. Dr. Rodríguez received a BS in industrial biotechnology from the University of Puerto Rico, an MPH from the University of Connecticut, and a DrPH from Columbia University.

Victor G. Rodwin, PhD, MPH, professor of health policy and management at the Robert F. Wagner Graduate School of Public Service, NYU, conducts research and teaches courses on community health and medical care, comparative analysis of health care systems, and health system performance and reform. He has lectured widely on these topics in universities around the world, most recently at Sun Yat Sen University in Guangzhou, Fudan University in Shanghai, Renmin University in Beijing, London School of Economics, London School of Hygiene and Tropical Medicine, and the Institut d'Etudes Politiques in Paris. Professor Rodwin was awarded the Fulbright-Tocqueville Distinguished Chair during the spring semester of 2010 while he was based at the University of Paris–Orsay. In 2000, he was the recipient of a 3-year Robert Wood Johnson Foundation Health Policy Investigator Award on "Megacities and Health: New York, London, Paris, and Tokyo." His research on this theme led to the establishment of the World Cities Project (WCP)—a collaborative venture between Wagner/NYU and the International Longevity Center USA, which focuses on aging, population health, and the health care systems in New York, London, Paris, Tokyo, and Hong Kong, and among neighborhoods within these world cities.

Pamela G. Russo, MD, MPH, is a senior program officer at Robert Wood Johnson Foundation (RWJF) in Princeton, New Jersey. She was recruited to RWJF to lead the Population Health: Science and Policy team in 2000. Before RWJF, she was an associate professor of medicine, director of the Clinical Outcomes Section, and program codirector for the master's program and fellowship in clinical epidemiology and health services research at the Cornell University Medical Center in New York City. Dr. Russo earned her BS from Harvard College, with a major in the history and philosophy of science; her MPH in epidemiology from the University of California, Berkeley, School of Public Health; and her MD from the University of California, San Francisco. She completed a residency in general internal medicine at the hospital of the University of Pennsylvania and a combined clinical epidemiology and rheumatology fellowship at Cornell and the Hospital of Special Surgery. Dr. Russo is a member of the IOM Population Health Roundtable.

Keith F. Safian, MBA, FACHE, served as the president and CEO of Phelps Memorial Hospital Center from 1989 through 2014. His career started as an assistant director at Kings County Hospital in Brooklyn, then assistant, associate, and senior associate administrator at NYU Medical Center. He served as the administrator of St. John's Episcopal Hospital in the Rockaways for 4 years before joining Phelps. During Mr. Safian's tenure, the hospital experienced extraordinary growth: from a $40 million operating budget to $245 million, from an 11% operating loss in 1988 to surpluses in 23 of the last 24 years, from 189 medical staff to 503, from 800 employees to more than 1,700, and from the 50th largest employer in Westchester to the 7th. He has received awards for his work in health care from the Dominican Sisters Family Health Service, the American College of Healthcare Executives, and the Hudson Valley Branch of the Arthritis Foundation. He is a fellow of the American College of Healthcare Executives. Mr. Safian holds an MBA from the Wharton Graduate School of the University of Pennsylvania and undergraduate degrees in industrial engineering and electrical engineering from the University at Buffalo.

Nirav R. Shah, MD, MPH, is the chief operating officer for clinical operations for Kaiser Permanente's Southern California region, a $20B health system with 14 hospitals and more than 3.7 million members. He is a graduate of Harvard College and Yale School of Medicine, was an RWJ Clinical Scholar at UCLA, and is board-certified in Internal Medicine. Dr. Shah has been an attending physician at Bellevue Hospital in Manhattan, associate investigator at Geisinger Health in Pennsylvania, and a faculty member of NYU Medical Center in the section of value and comparative effectiveness. Most recently, he served as commissioner of the New York State Department of Health. Dr. Shah is an elected member of the Institute of Medicine of the National Academy of Sciences, and is a nationally recognized thought leader in patient safety and quality, health information technology, population health, and the strategies required to transition to lower-cost, patient-centered health care.

Michael S. Sparer, PhD, JD, is professor and chair in the Department of Health Policy and Management at the Mailman School of Public Health at Columbia University. Professor Sparer studies and writes about the politics of health care, with a particular emphasis on the health insurance and health delivery systems for low-income populations and the ways in which intergovernmental relations influence policy. He is a two-time winner of the Mailman School's Student Government Association Teacher of the Year award, as well as the recipient of a 2010 Columbia University Presidential Award for Outstanding Teaching. Professor Sparer spent 7 years as a litigator for the New York City Law Department, specializing in intergovernmental social welfare litigation. After leaving the practice of law, he obtained a PhD in political science from Brandeis University. Sparer is a former editor of the *Journal of Health Politics, Policy and Law* and is the author of *Medicaid and the Limits of State Health Reform,* as well as numerous articles and book chapters.

Joanne Spetz, PhD, is a professor at the Institute for Health Policy Studies and in the Department of Family and Community Medicine and the School of Nursing at the University of California, San Francisco. She is the associate director for research strategy at the UCSF Center for the Health Professions and the director of the UCSF Health Workforce Research Center. Her fields of specialty are labor economics, public finance, and econometrics. She has led research on the health care workforce, organization of the hospital industry, effects of health information technology, effects of medical marijuana policy on youth substance use, and quality of patient care. Dr. Spetz's teaching is in the areas of quantitative research methods, health care financial management, and health economics.

Frank J. Thompson, PhD, is distinguished professor of public affairs and administration at Rutgers-Newark and at the Rutgers Center for State Health Policy in New Brunswick, New Jersey. He has published extensively on issues of health policy and implementation, with particular attention to the effect of federalism. In 2008, Professor Thompson received a Robert Wood Johnson Investigator Award to study the evolution of Medicaid policy during the Clinton, G.W. Bush, and Obama administrations. This research has led to several publications in scholarly journals and culminated in a book—*Medicaid Politics: Federalism, Policy Durability, and Health Reform* (2012). His book assesses the policy and political dynamics that fueled the dramatic expansion of Medicaid and established it as a key pillar of the Affordable Care Act. Professor Thompson received his PhD in political science from the University of California, Berkeley. He is a fellow of the National Academy of Public Administration.

Matthew D. Trujillo, PhD, is a research associate in the Research, Evaluation, and Learning unit at the Robert Wood Johnson Foundation. Before coming to the foundation, Dr. Trujillo worked as an adjunct researcher at the RAND Corporation. He received his PhD in psychology and social policy from the Woodrow Wilson School of Public and International Affairs at Princeton University. He specialized in prejudice and stereotyping, and his research examines the relationship between racial and ethnic microaggressions, identity, and policy. Originally from Phoenix, Arizona, he received his bachelor's degree in psychology from Arizona State University.

Elizabeth A. Ward is a program assistant at the New York State Health Foundation (NYSHealth). Ms. Ward supports grantmaking efforts for projects under NYSHealth's diabetes prevention and primary care priority areas. Before joining NYSHealth, she held a variety of positions in the public health and policy arena, including the consumer assistance program at the nonprofit law firm Health Law Advocates and the health care advocacy organization Health Care for All, both located in her home town of Boston, Massachusetts. Ms. Ward also served as one of the inaugural volunteer members of the benefits and community outreach team for the Supplemental Nutrition Assistance Program (SNAP) at the Western MA Food Bank. Ms. Ward earned a BS public health, a BA in political science, and a certificate in public policy and administration from the University of Massachusetts at Amherst.

Kathryn E. Wehr, MPH, program officer, joined the Robert Wood Johnson Foundation in 2010. Ms. Wehr focuses on discovering and investing in what works to promote and protect the nation's health and to achieve the foundation's vision where we, as a nation, strive together to build a culture of health enabling all in our diverse society to lead healthy lives, now and for generations to come. Previously, Ms. Wehr was a graduate research assistant at the University of North Carolina–Chapel Hill Sheps Center for Health Services Research. She has also served as community projects coordinator for the Northeast Florida Healthy Start Coalition and as an AmeriCorps member of the North Florida Health Corps.

Health Policy

This first section of the book presents an overview of how the U.S. health system works and how public policy influences its operations. The section also provides basic statistics outlining the dimensions of the health enterprise and sets the U.S. system in the context of the approaches to delivering health care in other countries. At times, it is easiest to understand one health system by comparing it to what happens in other parts of the world.

Chapter 1, authored by the book's two editors, acts as an overall introduction to the material that will be covered in the other 15 chapters of the book. This chapter starts by reviewing why health is so important to people and how that importance is translated into characteristics of the health care sector. The authors also explain the societal dynamics that have shaped the current state of the health system and explore the roles of seven different types of stakeholders in shaping the system.

Chapter 2 offers a set of charts that provide a statistical overview of the U.S. health system. The charts are organized around the topics that will be covered in the book, with key data displayed in a way that introduces the reader to the scale and scope of the system.

In Chapter 3, political scientists Michael Sparer and Frank Thompson address how the public policy process works at the federal government and state government levels. They review how policy is made and the forces that shape public policy in the United States. The chapter focuses principally on the roles government plays in funding and providing health insurance coverage for parts of the population and why government does not cover the entire population, as happens in many other developed countries around the world. This chapter also reviews the recent major expansion of insurance coverage mandated by the Patient Protection and Affordable Care Act of 2010.

Finally, Chapter 4, coauthored by Michael Gusmano and Victor Rodwin, compares the structure and traditions of the health care system in the United States to the systems in other parts of the world. In addition to reviewing how key aspects of the organization of health care vary across countries, the chapter takes a close look at health care delivery in England, Canada, France, and China as good examples of the diversity of approaches to operating health systems.

1

The Challenge of Health Care Delivery and Health Policy

James R. Knickman and Anthony R. Kovner

KEY WORDS

access to health care	payment systems
behavioral health	population health
health care delivery	public health
interest groups (stakeholders)	value
Patient Protection and Affordable Care Act	workforce

LEARNING OBJECTIVES

- Understand the importance of health and health care to American life
- Understand some defining characteristics of U.S. health care delivery
- Identify major issues and concerns
- Identify key interest groups (stakeholders)
- Understand the importance of engaging a new generation of health leaders

TOPICAL OUTLINE

- Why health is so important to Americans
- Factors that shape the structure of the delivery system
- Seven key challenges facing the health system
- Stakeholders who shape and are affected by how the health system is organized and how it functions
- The organization of the book

■ Context

Our goal in editing this book is to provide a vibrant introduction to the U.S. health care system in a way that helps new students understand the wonders of health care. The book lays out the complexities of organizing a large sector of our economy to keep Americans healthy and to help people get better when they become ill. In addition, the book provides a framework to help professors engage students, with room for each professor to bring his or her perspective to the materials covered.

To introduce students to the many parts of the health system in the United States, we have engaged some of the leading thinkers and "doers" in the health sector to explain the parts of the system in which they are expert. Each author brings a different perspective, and it is not our aim to present one voice on this topic. Rather, we have asked each author to lay out the facts about a given topic and to offer ideas about what he or she thinks must happen to improve a specific aspect of the health system.

In many ways, the text lays out a serious "to-do" list facing our health system and offers individuals beginning a health-related career a guide to the types of challenges that could engage them. The authors explain how the health system works, what its challenges are, and how health professionals can contribute to the process of strengthening our system to make sure it works efficiently and effectively at the task of keeping all of us healthy.

In this first chapter, we explain the importance of the health system, provide an overview of how the system is organized, sketch out some of the challenges facing the overall system that are addressed in the book, and discuss the roles of five types of key stakeholders involved in the health enterprise. We also provide the logic behind the topics the book addresses and explain the book's organization.

■ The Importance of Good Health to American Life

Our nation is built on the idea that society should ensure an opportunity for "life, liberty, and the pursuit of happiness." These words, of course, are from the second sentence of our Declaration of Independence. The aspiration of ensuring "life" is the core goal of the health system. It is obvious that nothing is possible for an individual without life, and most of us would agree that health is among the core needs to live a vibrant, viable life. Good health is essential to participate in the political and social system, to work to support ourselves and our families, and to pursue happiness and a good life.

Our nation has invested a tremendous amount to learn how to keep people healthy and how to restore health when disease, injury, or illness occurs. In the 19th century, researchers and public health experts from the United States and other countries began to understand the role of germs in communicating disease and the importance of basic public health practices, such as ensuring clean water and safe sanitation to maintain health. In the 20th century, the science and art of medicine exploded, creating amazing know-how to treat people who have diseases, injuries, and illnesses.

In response to the emerging know-how for delivering medical care, a large and complex health enterprise developed throughout the 20th century and continues to evolve. The pipeline of new ideas for better treating illnesses is quite full and promises to lead to ever-expanding methods to restore health when Americans have life-threatening medical problems.

We use the word "enterprise" deliberately because the health system is a blend of an altruistic-oriented set of providers and activities mixed with a huge industry that accounts for a sizable portion of all economic activity in our society. The value we put on health has led us to devote just under 20% of our economic resources to medical care and health promotion. Fully 13% of all jobs in America are in the health sector. Each of us spends a sizable share of our income on the health care we need. We spend this money through taxes, which support a good share of the health enterprise, through foregone wages used by our employers to pay for health insurance, and by sizable out-of-pocket health care expenses for which each of us is responsible.

Thus, the "pursuit of life," listed as a core principle in the Declaration of Independence, not only has resulted in a set of social and political norms about the importance of good health to everyone in America but also has spurred a huge industry that affects and is affected by society's economic activity and economic decisions. To understand the health system, we need to understand not only the art and practice of medicine and public health but also the economic, organizational, and management issues that must be addressed to keep the health system effective, efficient, and affordable in our overall economic life. How we go about organizing and managing the health system and changing it over time can hurt or help both our health status and our economic status.

■ Defining Characteristics of the U.S. Health System

It is ironic that most health professionals think of themselves as working within the "health system" when in truth one of the first defining features of what we call a system is that health-related activities are not ordered or organized as a single enterprise. Rather, efforts to improve health and health care involve many types of actors and organizations working independently and with little coordination to make contributions to improving health status. In particular, our current approach to delivering medical care has evolved and keeps evolving in a haphazard way shaped more by economic incentives and opportunities than by a central or logical design.

In recent years, we also have begun to recognize the clear difference between "maintaining health" and "restoring health" to a person who has a medical problem. The medical care system clearly takes charge of restoring health when people are ill. Often the medical care system takes charge of caring for people even if restoring health is impossible; the goal may be to limit the spread of a medical problem, to alleviate the symptoms of a medical problem, or to help a person cope with the pain and suffering and loss of function when major medical problems emerge. Doctors, nurses, technicians of various types, hospitals, nursing homes, rehabilitation centers, pharmaceutical companies, and medical device companies are among the actors who engage in efforts to care for people when they have medical problems.

The goal of "maintaining health" also involves many actors and activities. To some extent, medical providers help with this huge task by providing screening and prevention services that can keep people from becoming ill and help to identify illnesses very early when they might be easier to treat. However, good health among a population also requires a vibrant public health system that works to help people avoid illness. Public health activities include preventing epidemics; making sure food, water, and sanitation are safe; monitoring environmental toxins; and developing community-based initiatives, public awareness initiatives, and education initiatives to help people eat healthy foods, exercise, and not engage in unhealthy behaviors such as smoking, drinking alcohol in excess, and using recreational drugs or abusing prescription drugs.

Adequate family incomes, high-quality educational opportunities, and being socially connected are all key factors that predict the health of a given person.

Increasingly, we also recognize that the health of populations is determined by social and economic factors. Adequate family incomes, high-quality educational opportunities, and being socially connected are all key factors that predict the health of a given person. Social issues such as discrimination, abuse, and social respect all are important determinants of health. To ensure attention to these issues and others like them requires involvement from many sectors of our society as well as political leadership to guide collective action to ensure our society encourages pro-health norms and practices. Some people term this a "health in all" approach to social policy.

We have organized this book so that it addresses both types of health issue: the challenge of keeping the population healthy and the challenge of providing effective medical care when needed. There are other key defining characteristics of the U.S. health care system that guide the organization of this book:

- **The importance of organizations in delivering care.** These include hospitals, nursing homes, community health centers, physician practices, and public health departments.
- **The role of professionals in running our system.** These include physicians, nurses, managers, policy advocates, researchers, technicians, and those directing technology and pharmaceutical businesses.
- **The emergence of new medical technology, electronic communications, and new pharmaceuticals.** New techniques in imaging, electronic communications, pharmaceuticals, surgical procedures, DNA coding, and stem-cell technology are remarkable but often expensive ways of improving health care.
- **Tension between "the free market" and "governmental control."** This tension shapes America's culture but is sharply present in the health care sector. Relative to citizens of other countries, Americans have more diversity of opinion about whether health care, or certain health care services, are "goods" or "rights." How one feels about this issue often determines whether a person thinks the delivery of health care should be done by nonprofit or for-profit organizations and whether health care should be financed by taxes or private payments.
- **A dysfunctional payment system.** The current payment system creates poor incentives for providers to be efficient, to be customer or patient friendly, or to focus on the delivery of high-value services. Also, the payment approach is not transparent for individuals who use health care. For example, patients frequently have no idea what a service costs until after it is delivered. This is rarely true for other goods and services in the U.S. economy.

Addressing the challenges of delivering health care is worth the best effort and thinking of our readers, who are tomorrow's health care leaders.

These defining characteristics make health care delivery a challenging part of U.S. politics and the economy. Addressing the challenges of delivering health care is worth the best effort and thinking of our readers, who are tomorrow's health care leaders.

■ Major Issues and Concerns

Reliable studies have indicated that between 44,000 and 98,000 Americans die each year because of medical errors.

There are many ways in which our health system can be improved. The chapters that follow address a long list of specific concerns. Many of these issues flow, however, from seven overarching themes regarding challenges that each of us in the health sector can address:

- **Improving quality.** Reliable studies have indicated that between 44,000 and 98,000 Americans die each year because of medical errors. Other well-regarded studies show that people with mental health or substance use problems, asthma, or diabetes receive care known to be effective only about half the time. In addition, the health system could do much more to improve the experience of patients receiving care. The system is not always "customer friendly" and has not adopted many practices routinely used in other service sectors to improve the consumer experience. We have a good knowledge base about how to organize care so that high-quality services happen virtually all of the time. The challenge is spreading this knowledge into practice across the nation.

- **Improving access and coverage.** Millions of Americans still lack insurance coverage, and millions more have inadequate coverage for acute care. The new federal health reform, the Patient Protection and Affordable Care Act (ACA), has reduced the number of people who lack insurance coverage. But gaps in coverage persist. For example, undocumented immigrants lack coverage. The new federal health reform has not been fully implemented in many states because of political opposition to components of the new policy that are optional for states to adopt. Most Americans lack adequate coverage for chronic (rather than acute) care. Even when Americans have insurance coverage, access to health care is not always ensured. Many rural areas have shortages of doctors and other providers. Many doctors refuse to see patients with Medicaid coverage because of low payment rates.

- **Slowing the growth of health care expenditures.** Health care expenditures are simply the price of services multiplied by the volume of services. Total expenditures are growing much more rapidly than the rest of the economy because both prices and volume of services have increased relentlessly over the past 50 years. To keep health care affordable for middle-class and low-income residents—as well as for taxpayers and employers—we need to devise ways to moderate the ever-increasing share of our nation's economy devoted to the health sector. The challenge is to determine how to restructure delivery and payment so we can focus on high-value care as we get more efficient.

- **Encouraging healthy behavior.** Healthy behavior can help people avoid disease and injury or prevent disease or injury from getting worse. For millions of Americans, leading healthy lives is not of the highest priority. Changing health-related behavior is a difficult challenge, but we need to identify effective prevention programs and ways to make our social and built environments more encouraging of healthy choices.

- **Improving the public health system.** The governmental public health infrastructure maintains population health and regulates aspects of the health care delivery system. State and local health departments monitor the health of residents, provide a wide range of preventive services, and regulate health care providers and businesses, such as restaurants, that affect population health. The effectiveness and funding of state, municipal, and county health departments vary widely.

- **Improving the coordination, transparency and accountability of medical care.** Problems of quality, cost, and access are caused by fragmentation and lack of coordination at the community level. This fragmentation exists both within and between health care organizations. It is affected by a lack of integrated and electronic record systems and by a lack of cooperative relationships among different types of providers who treat the same patient. For example, primary care physicians, hospitals, and specialty physicians often fail to work as teams or in coordinated ways. Consumers often are not given all of the information they deserve to make adequate medical choices. Providers often refuse to reveal the prices they will charge patients, second opinions are still not encouraged as frequently as they should be, and patients often do not get clear explanations of treatment options or the pros and cons of these options.

- **Addressing inequalities in access and outcomes.** In the United States, medical care and its associated outcomes depend on one's income level, race, and geographical location. We are potentially headed toward a three-tier system of medical care in which the way care is delivered to the poor, the middle class, and the wealthy varies markedly. Such a system might be acceptable if the care received by the poor and middle class were effective and adequate to provide the opportunity for "life, liberty, and the pursuit of happiness." However, most studies show that outcomes vary across the tiers in many ways. Other studies demonstrate that access and outcomes vary by race, even for Blacks, Latinos, and Whites who have the same incomes and education levels. Marked differences also exist in access, quality, and outcomes across different regions of our country. Best practices do not spread easily or quickly. Addressing these inequalities is a major challenge facing the health sector.

■ Key Stakeholders Influencing the Health System

A stakeholder group is a set of people who have a strong interest in how something in our society is done.

A complicated enterprise like the health system includes many types of stakeholders. A stakeholder group is a set of people who have a strong interest in how something in our society is done. In addition, stakeholders generally have some power in shaping what happens. Finally, different stakeholders may have very different goals and views about what should be done and how.

To understand the health system, one needs a good scorecard of the interests and roles of distinct stakeholder groups. Each contributor to this book gives attention to roles of stakeholders. The stakeholders that keep appearing as the story of the health system unfolds include five key groups: (a) consumers, (b) providers and other professionals engaged in the health system, (c) employers, (d) insurers, and (e) public policy makers.

CONSUMERS

Consumers (or patients) should be at the center of the health system. After all, it is their needs and wants that are the reason for this giant enterprise. In some ways, however, consumers sometimes seem like bystanders in health care decisions. Often, physicians and other providers assert that they know best and fail to have a patient co-manage a medical problem or be a full partner in selecting a choice of action. Or, perhaps worse, an insurer decides what is best or "allowed" given a specific health condition.

Consumers are also bystanders in issues about payments. Providers sometimes think that their "customer" is an insurance company because the insurer pays much of the bill. In addition, the same provider (unknown to many customers) may charge astonishingly different prices to different groups and individuals. The usual norm in our economy, unlike in health care, is that the person receiving goods or a service is the customer and the customer has a right to know what the charge will be before purchasing the good or service.

Even so, consumers are influential stakeholders in many ways. For example, when there is widespread dissatisfaction among consumers, change happens. Insurers changed the rules of early managed care payment systems in the 1990s due to consumer complaints. Similarly, a major federal program offering a new form of catastrophic insurance to elders was repealed after sharp dissatisfaction among seniors.

Most experts argue that consumers need to be at the center of health care choices. Additionally, individuals need to understand the crucial role their behavioral choices play in determining their health status. Choosing to eat healthy foods, stay physically active, drink alcohol moderately, and abstain from tobacco products are among the most important choices they make to protect their health.

What do consumers want as key stakeholders? Most importantly, consumers want good access to health care for themselves and their families. Polls indicate that individuals value good-quality care and affordable care. They would also like to be treated well by providers and have a good experience when they need care.

PROVIDERS AND OTHERS ENGAGED IN MAKING THE HEALTH SYSTEM OPERATE

Many professionals work to advance medical knowledge, medical practice, and the business of health care. The vast majority of this workforce is motivated principally by the social goal of keeping people healthy. Medical providers, caregivers, pharmaceutical and medical device companies, and researchers have created an impressive set of interventions that can help people who are sick.

In recent years, however, many members of the broad health workforce have faced great financial pressure to prevent the costs of health care from increasing as quickly as in the past. Payment systems keep lowering the fees paid for goods and services, consumers and payers have been demanding better quality, better outcomes, more value, and better patient experiences. In addition, the organization of services has begun to evolve quickly.

Understanding the views and needs of the health workforce and the organizations dedicated to improving health is crucial to understanding how the system works and how to improve the system.

More and more physicians and other providers are working in large practices compared with the small ones that used to be the norm. Hospitals are merging with other types of medical providers, and the approach insurers use to pay for services is changing rapidly.

Understanding the views and needs of the health workforce and the organizations dedicated to improving health is crucial to understanding how the system works and how to improve the system. The following chapters suggest that providers and professionals engaged in the health enterprise would value simpler rules that govern how care is provided and fair opportunities to earn incomes that reflect their expertise and their large investments in training.

EMPLOYERS

Employers are stakeholders because many firms offer employees private health insurance as a key element of their compensation package. In this sense, the cost of health insurance is a cost of doing business for employers and can greatly affect the profitability of a business. For example, employee health care costs add approximately $1,500 to the cost of producing every automobile manufactured in the United States.

In their role as stakeholders, employers want to see a slowdown in their health care cost responsibility as compared with the last 50 years. In addition, employers want healthy employees who are productive and do not have to take time off from work due to illness. These desires lead some employers to advocate for high-quality health care and for wellness and prevention programs that help employees stay healthy.

INSURERS

Insurance companies act as the intermediary among payers (often employers), providers (who need a system for getting paid), and consumers (who need a system to determine the kinds of health care covered by the employer's insurance plan).

In some cases, insurers take some financial risk: If the payments they make to providers exceed the premiums set for employers, the insurer loses money. Increasingly, however, the insurer leaves the employer to bear the risk and plays the role of a pure intermediary, setting rules to determine when a health service is eligible for reimbursement and other rules to determine what payment is made. Of course, an insurer must negotiate these rules with employers and providers.

As stakeholders, insurers always face pressure. Employers, consumers, and providers often have tense relationships with insurers, who in many ways play the role of referees in health care. Payers often feel that the costs of running the insurance process are too expensive.

New approaches to payment currently exist that could compete with traditional insurance companies. Some health systems are starting their own insurance companies, and it is possible that capitated payment systems (payment of a premium for a person/family for the year regardless of use of covered benefits) could bypass traditional insurance systems and go directly from payers to providers. Insurers want to protect their role in the health sector. They also seek to expand their role by offering analytical services that can support higher-quality and more efficient delivery approaches.

PUBLIC POLICY MAKERS

The final type of stakeholder we consider is policy makers; both appointed public officials and elected politicians are included in this category. However, policy makers do not act as a single stakeholder group. Instead, various components of this group set agendas, which often conflict with one another.

Elected officials differ strikingly in their views about how the health system should work and about the role government should play in health care. At times, differences in views reflect different ideologies. Sometimes, however, different views emerge about how best to manage the extensive responsibilities that have fallen to government over the past 80 years.

Consensus does exist on some policy issues, however, within this stakeholder group. Most elected officials and civil servants working on health issues would like to see slower inflation rates in the health sector. In addition, there is consensus that the U.S. health system should use state-of-the-art medical care and prevention interventions. Finally, there is a common sense that quality and the patient experience should be important concerns of health providers.

■ Organization of This Book

The editors have enjoyed the privilege of working many years as part of numerous efforts to improve health care in the United States. We remain optimistic that pragmatism, flexibility, consensus building, and attention to objective, high-quality evidence can bring about positive change. We remain stimulated by the challenges and pleased that we have worked hard at the local, state, and national levels to create and sustain a viable and effective health care system.

Certainly, we have observed that best practices are now being used to improve health care and health across a wide range of settings in the United States and worldwide. How do we speed up the process of getting more for the money we spend, and how do we engage every type of stakeholder to bring about more effective services by insisting on best practices in everything we do? This book gives the reader the motivation and skills to get engaged.

The book is organized into four parts:

Part I: Health Policy has chapters on the current state of health care delivery, charts depicting key statistics, a discussion of the important role of policy, and a comparative analysis of health care delivery in other countries.

Part II: Keeping Americans Healthy has four chapters on population health, public health, behavioral health, and the health of vulnerable populations.

Part III: Medical Care: Treating Americans' Medical Problems has seven chapters discussing organization of care, workforce, financing, cost and value, quality of care, health care management and governance, and information technology.

Part IV: Futures acts as a summary of key ideas addressed in the book, with a look to the future about how change in the health system might play out.

The future U.S. health care delivery system will see improvements if committed and informed Americans choose to enter the field and engage effectively. Future leaders who are knowledgeable about the health sector and who know how to implement effective change are needed. The system also needs to improve quality, get more value for cost, improve patient participation in self-care, and encourage provider transparency and accountability.

■ Discussion Questions

1. What is the real and perceived performance of the U.S. health care system? How do views differ among different groups of patients, providers, payers, and politicians?
2. Why do we spend so much money on health care?
3. Why isn't the population healthier?
4. How is the Affordable Care Act part of the problem or part of the solution to improving health care delivery in the United States?
5. What are your priorities to improve the value of health care Americans get for the money we spend? What is your rationale for these priorities?

CASE STUDY

You are an aide to the governor of State X. A billionaire has said he will give the governor $3 billion if he comes up with a satisfactory plan to improve health and medical care for the state. Assume the state currently spends $300 billion on health care annually. The goal is ensuring quality of health care, improving the patient experience, improving the overall health of the state's population, and containing the increase in health care costs. Develop the criteria for assessing the success of the plan. Where will the major shifts in resources occur? Give a rationale for your recommendations.

As you consider the case study, you might address the following questions:

1. How might the billionaire evaluate whether the governor's plan is satisfactory?
2. After the money is given to fund the plan, what must happen to improve health care delivery performance substantially in State X?

■ Bibliography

Bradley, E. H., & Taylor, L. A. (2013). *The American health care paradox: Why spending more is getting us less.* New York, NY: Public Affairs.

Christensen, C. M. (2009). *The innovator's prescription: A disruptive solution for health care.* New York, NY: McGraw-Hill.

Gawande, A. (2009). *The checklist manifesto: How to get things right.* New York, NY: Picador.

Griffith, J. R., & White, K. R. (2011). *Reaching excellence in healthcare management.* Chicago, IL: Health Administration Press.

Kenney, C. (2011). *Transforming health care: Virginia Mason Medical Center's pursuit of the perfect patient experience.* New York, NY: CRC Press.

2 A Visual Overview of Health Care Delivery in the United States

Catherine K. Dangremond

Note: The visual overview should be utilized in conjunction with Chapter 1, where key words, learning objectives, and a topic outline have been provided.

■ The U.S. Health Care System: A Period of Change

The U.S. health care system is in a period of significant and ongoing change. Many key provisions of the Affordable Care Act either have recently gone into effect or will be implemented in the near future. Health insurance exchanges began accepting applications in the fall of 2013. In 2014, provisions including prohibition of coverage denial based on preexisting conditions and elimination of annual coverage limits took effect. Yet even though more than eight million people applied for insurance coverage through the health care marketplace as of April 2014, and widespread support exists for certain consumer protections included in the Affordable Care Act, consumer perceptions of the U.S. health care system are mixed (Figure 2.1). Looking forward, varying degrees of optimism exist about the extent to which the Affordable Care Act will be able to bring about fundamental change in the aspects of the U.S. health care system that consumers currently dislike.

FIGURE 2.1

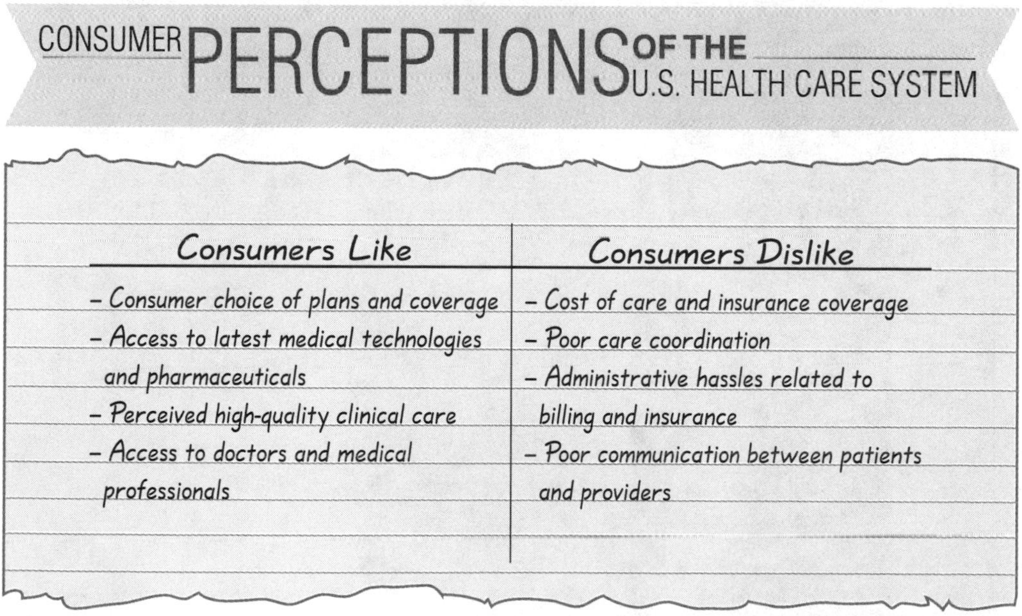

CONSUMER PERCEPTIONS OF THE U.S. HEALTH CARE SYSTEM

Consumers Like	Consumers Dislike
– Consumer choice of plans and coverage	– Cost of care and insurance coverage
– Access to latest medical technologies and pharmaceuticals	– Poor care coordination
– Perceived high-quality clinical care	– Administrative hassles related to billing and insurance
– Access to doctors and medical professionals	– Poor communication between patients and providers

Source: Compiled from information obtained from The Morning Consult, The Commonwealth Fund, Health Affairs.

■ The Shared Responsibility for Health Care

The development of health care policy and provision of health care services is a complex process, with responsibilities shared across all levels of government within the United States (Figure 2.2). The World Health Organization (1948) defines *health* as "a state of complete physical, mental, and social well-being and not merely the absence of disease or infirmity." This makes it quite clear that, within each level of government, the work of many agencies is required in pursuit of the health of the population. For example, within the federal government, responsibilities for health spread far beyond the Department of Health and Human Services (HHS) to agencies that include the Social Security Administration, the Department of Labor, the Department of Veterans Affairs, and the Department of Agriculture, among others.

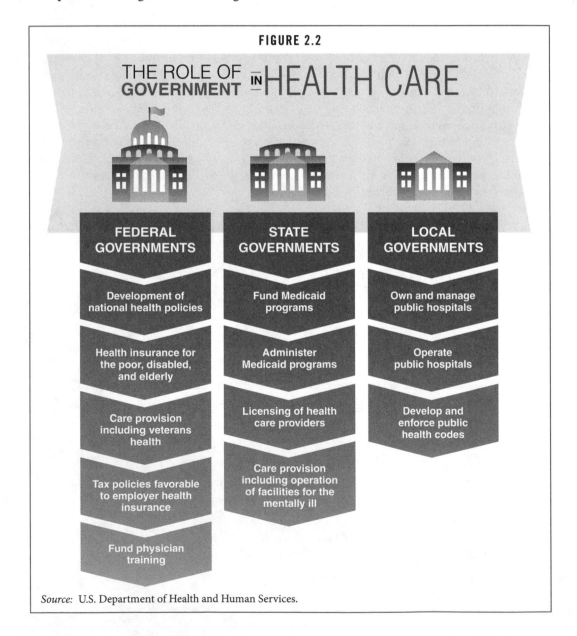

FIGURE 2.2

THE ROLE OF GOVERNMENT IN HEALTH CARE

FEDERAL GOVERNMENTS	STATE GOVERNMENTS	LOCAL GOVERNMENTS
Development of national health policies	Fund Medicaid programs	Own and manage public hospitals
Health insurance for the poor, disabled, and elderly	Administer Medicaid programs	Operate public hospitals
Care provision including veterans health	Licensing of health care providers	Develop and enforce public health codes
Tax policies favorable to employer health insurance	Care provision including operation of facilities for the mentally ill	
Fund physician training		

Source: U.S. Department of Health and Human Services.

The current state of health care delivery in the United States has evolved over time and has been significantly shaped by several key federal policy initiatives implemented since 1965 (Figure 2.3). These initiatives have focused on improving access to care, ensuring affordability of care, protecting patient confidentiality, and controlling the growing cost of health care.

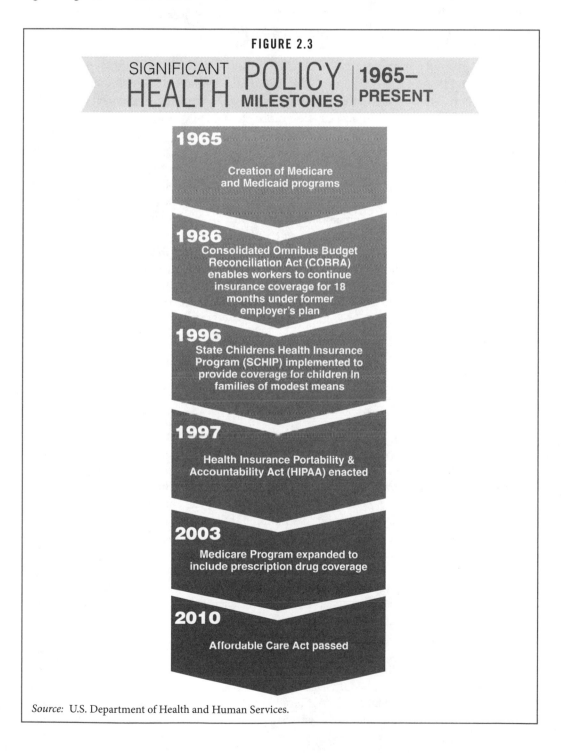

FIGURE 2.3

SIGNIFICANT **HEALTH** **POLICY** MILESTONES | 1965– PRESENT

1965
Creation of Medicare and Medicaid programs

1986
Consolidated Omnibus Budget Reconciliation Act (COBRA) enables workers to continue insurance coverage for 18 months under former employer's plan

1996
State Childrens Health Insurance Program (SCHIP) implemented to provide coverage for children in families of modest means

1997
Health Insurance Portability & Accountability Act (HIPAA) enacted

2003
Medicare Program expanded to include prescription drug coverage

2010
Affordable Care Act passed

Source: U.S. Department of Health and Human Services.

■ Where the Money Comes From, and How It Is Used

Although the rate of growth in health care spending has slowed somewhat in the past few years, such spending continues to account for more than 17% of the U.S. gross domestic product.

In 2012, total health care spending in the United States reached $2.8 trillion. Although the rate of growth in health care spending has slowed somewhat in the past few years, such spending continues to account for more than 17% of the U.S. gross domestic product (GDP), and preliminary data for 2014 indicate that spending may again be trending upward.

The sources of funding for U.S. health care expenditures have changed substantially over time. Most notably, since 1970, total out-of-pocket spending for health care has decreased from 33% to 12% of funds, while spending in public and private insurance programs (Medicare, Medicaid, and private health insurance) has increased from 38% to 68% of funds (Figure 2.4). In recent years, however, out-of-pocket costs have again started to trend upward as cost sharing in insurance plans has increased and consumer-directed health plans have become more common.

In contrast to changes in the sources of health care funding, the use of funds has remained relatively consistent since 1970. Although there has been some transfer away from expenditures on hospital care and growth in long-term and home care, there has not been a sizable shift in how health care spending is allocated in the United States (Figure 2.4).

■ A Comparative Perspective

In 2011, the per capita health care spending in the United States was approximately $8,500. This may not seem particularly troubling, until it is placed in the context of comparison to Organisation for Economic Co-operation and Development (OECD) peers, among whom health care spending averaged approximately $3,300 per capita in 2011. In fact, no other country spent close to the same amount as the United States. Norway and Switzerland ranked a distant second in spending among OECD countries, at approximately $5,600 per capita.

We often perceive that the United States has the best health care system in the world. If this were the case, we could conclude that there is no reason for concern about higher spending rates, assuming such spending results in optimal care and better outcomes. Unfortunately, evidence is not available to sustain this argument and, even as the United States leads the world in spending, it lags behind its peers in health outcomes. Since 1960, for example, Japan has seen an increase of more than 15 years in life expectancy. In comparison, life expectancy in the United States has increased by only 9 years in the same period. In fact, in 1960 life expectancy in the U.S. was 1.5 years *above* the OECD average. Today, it is 1.5 years *below* the OECD average life expectancy of 80.1 years. As illustrated in Figure 2.5, the United States is an outlier in health care spending. Unfortunately, higher levels of spending are not necessarily associated with improved health outcomes.

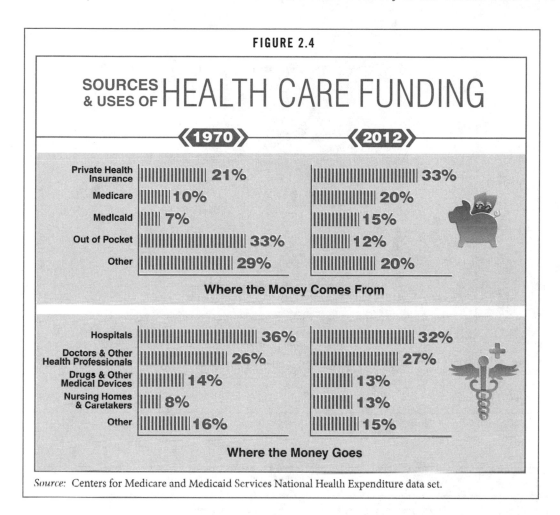

FIGURE 2.4

SOURCES & USES OF HEALTH CARE FUNDING

《1970》 　　　 《2012》

Where the Money Comes From

	1970	2012
Private Health Insurance	21%	33%
Medicare	10%	20%
Medicaid	7%	15%
Out of Pocket	33%	12%
Other	29%	20%

Where the Money Goes

	1970	2012
Hospitals	36%	32%
Doctors & Other Health Professionals	26%	27%
Drugs & Other Medical Devices	14%	13%
Nursing Homes & Caretakers	8%	13%
Other	16%	15%

Source: Centers for Medicare and Medicaid Services National Health Expenditure data set.

■ Population Health: Beyond Health Care

Health is about much more than health *care*—the services provided within the framework of health care institutions. A true assessment of health, an individual's ability to live a long and healthy life, depends on many social and environmental factors beyond health care services, including education, income, racial or ethnic group, genetics, physical environment, and health-related behaviors.

The Population Health Model brings an integrative approach to identifying the influence of the many factors that play a role in the health of the population and to developing strategies for change. This approach takes a broad view, focusing not only on the need for improvement in health *care* delivery, but also on the many determinants of health. For example, the increase in obesity rates worldwide is a significant population health concern (Figure 2.6). A population health approach considers not only medical care interventions to support better prevention and management of obesity by clinicians, but also examines other factors, including health-related behaviors such as diet and exercise and physical environment limitations that may prevent sufficient exercise.

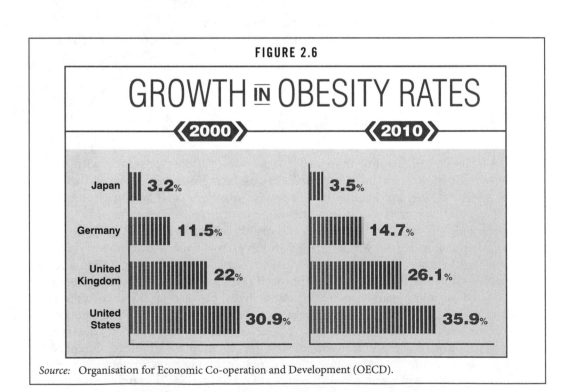

FIGURE 2.5

ASSOCIATION BETWEEN HEALTH SPENDING & LIFE EXPECTANCY

Source: Organisation for Economic Co-operation and Development (OECD). (2013). Health at a glance. OECD Indicators.

FIGURE 2.6

GROWTH IN OBESITY RATES

⟨⟨ 2000 ⟩⟩   ⟨⟨ 2010 ⟩⟩

	2000	2010
Japan	3.2%	3.5%
Germany	11.5%	14.7%
United Kingdom	22%	26.1%
United States	30.9%	35.9%

Source: Organisation for Economic Co-operation and Development (OECD).

■ Access to Care and Variation in Health Outcomes

In 2014, millions of previously uninsured Americans obtained health insurance coverage through the health insurance marketplaces established in accordance with the Affordable Care Act. However, millions of Americans remain uninsured. Economic barriers to care are still present in the forms of uninsurance and underinsurance, whereby an individual may have insurance coverage but copayments and deductibles are unaffordable, thus discouraging the patient from seeking necessary care. At lower income levels, individuals are less likely to have a usual source of care (Figure 2.7).

Wide variation in health status and outcomes exists within the United States by income level, by race and ethnicity, and by education level.

It is also important to recognize that many factors beyond health insurance coverage and income level affect access to care and, ultimately, health outcomes. Well-documented, significant differences in health care utilization and outcomes exist among racial and ethnic groups. Although less well documented, it also has been observed that cultural and language barriers affect health care utilization, potentially for reasons that include the language barrier, differing views on illness and treatment, and distrust of Western medicine. In total, this range of economic and noneconomic barriers to health care access has a significant effect on health outcomes. Wide variation in health status and outcomes exists within the United States by income level, by race and ethnicity, and by education level. Figure 2.8 depicts just one example: Cholesterol levels are more poorly controlled at lower income levels.

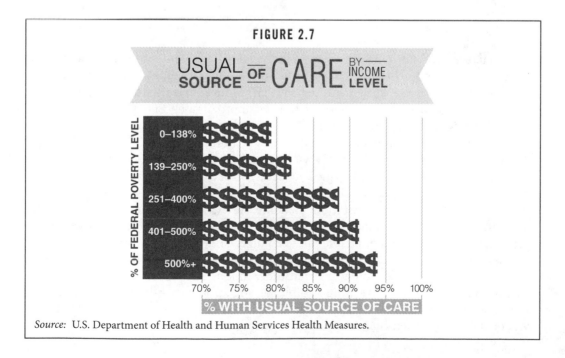

FIGURE 2.7

USUAL SOURCE OF CARE BY INCOME LEVEL

Source: U.S. Department of Health and Human Services Health Measures.

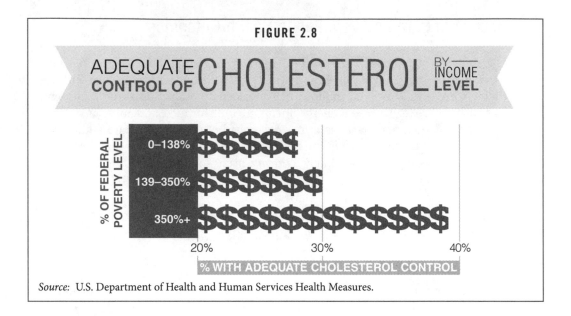

FIGURE 2.8

ADEQUATE CONTROL OF CHOLESTEROL BY INCOME LEVEL

Source: U.S. Department of Health and Human Services Health Measures.

■ Health and Behavior

Behavioral risk factors, including tobacco use, alcohol abuse, unhealthy diets, and sedentary lifestyles, play a fundamental role in poor health.

Many factors combine in determining an individual's health outcomes. Beyond medical care, social and economic factors, and environmental factors, the University of Wisconsin Population Health Institute (UWPHI) Model of Health Improvement indicates that personal health behaviors account for approximately 30% of ultimate health outcomes (Figure 2.9). Behavioral risk factors, including tobacco use, alcohol abuse, unhealthy diets, and sedentary lifestyles, play a fundamental role in poor health. According to the U.S. Preventive Services Task Force, sedentary lifestyles and lack of exercise are associated with type 2 diabetes, stroke, hypertension, osteoarthritis, colon cancer, depression, and obesity. In 2013, the Centers for Disease Control and Prevention (CDC) reported that more than one third (35.7%) of Americans are obese, a significant health risk factor highly associated with behavioral choices. Yet we must recognize that behavior is often difficult to change. Unhealthy behavioral choices may not have a visible health effect for many years. Many approaches to behavioral change exist, but a change in health behavior attitudes among Americans likely will require a continued, concerted effort using a combination of population-based interventions, individual behavioral change approaches, and greater involvement of health care providers and organizations in healthy lifestyle interventions.

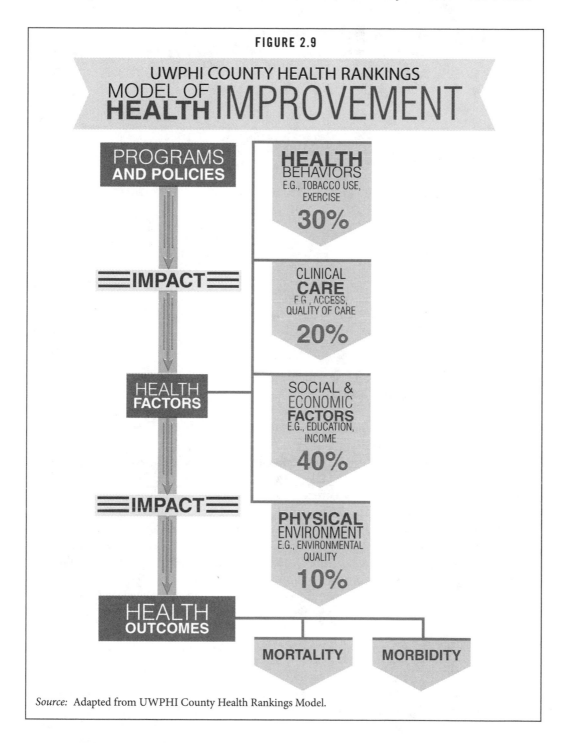

FIGURE 2.9

UWPHI COUNTY HEALTH RANKINGS
MODEL OF IMPROVEMENT
HEALTH

Source: Adapted from UWPHI County Health Rankings Model.

■ The Health Care Workforce

More than 13% of the total U.S. workforce is employed in a health care–related job. From clinical roles, such as nurses, physical therapists, and doctors, to employees fulfilling administrative and support functions, such as environmental services, billing

TABLE 2.1 THE DIVERSE U.S. HEALTH CARE WORKFORCE

	Inpatient Care	Ambulatory Care	Long-Term Care
Delivery	Hospitals	Doctors' offices Hospitals Clinics	Nursing homes Home health care Assisted living
Focus of Services	Acute care	Preventive care Acute care Chronic care	Chronic care
Workforce	Registered nurses (38%) Nursing aides (14%) Technicians (13%) Physicians and surgeons (7%) Licensed practical nurses (6%) Health care services managers (5%) Therapists (5%)	Physicians (17%) Other practitioners (12%) Technicians (12%) Registered nurses, nurse practitioners (11%) Medical assistants (11%) Therapists (5%) Health care services managers (4%)	Nursing and personal care aides (60%) Registered nurses (15%) Licensed practical nurses (11%) Health care services managers (3%) Social workers (3%) Therapists (2%) Technicians (1%)

Source: Adapted from The Partnership for Quality Care.

and finance, and operations management, the health care workforce is both sizable and incredibly diverse. Also, health care workers are employed by many different types of organizations, including hospitals, offices of health care practitioners, nursing homes, and home health agencies, among others (Table 2.1).

The U.S. Bureau of Labor Statistics estimates that the health care workforce could expand by more than 30%, adding an additional four million jobs, by 2020. However, significant challenges exist. The Affordable Care Act and health care reform efforts emphasize increased focus on primary care and coordination of care. It is unclear whether there is an adequate supply of primary care physicians, particularly in certain geographic areas of the United States, to support an increased demand in primary care services. It is clear, however, that change must occur in how health care professionals are trained and incentivized. A move toward more coordinated models of care will undoubtedly require increased focus on communication skills and teamwork. To achieve success, payment and incentive models must move away from siloed, fee-for-service structures and toward payments focused on incentivizing coordination and health outcomes.

■ Variations in Health Care Delivery

It is easy to presume that the quality of health care services and the outcomes achieved should be similar regardless of whether you live in Los Angeles, Dallas, or Boston, and regardless of which hospital or doctor's office in your city you use for services. Research has shown, however, that this is not the case. The Dartmouth Atlas, among others, has shown that where you live, and at which facility you receive care, influence both access to care and the quality of care you receive. Tremendous variations exist among geographic areas, among cities within the same state, and among health care facilities within the same city. The 2012 Commonwealth Fund's *Local Scorecard* has also documented alarming variations including the following:

The rate of potentially preventable deaths before age 75 from health care amenable causes was more than three times as high in the geographic area with the worst (highest) rate than in the area with the best (lowest) rate (169.0 vs. 51.5 deaths per 100,000 population).

The incidence of unsafe medication prescribing among Medicare beneficiaries was four times higher in Alexandria, Louisiana, than in the Bronx and White Plains, New York (44% vs. 11%, respectively).

> *Where you live, and at which facility you opt to receive care, influence both access to care and the quality of care you receive.*

Figure 2.10 provides additional insight regarding some of the types and extent of variation documented by The Commonwealth Fund's *Local Scorecard*. It is evident that significant variation exists in access to care, delivery of care, and health outcomes. The challenge for policymakers and the U.S. health care delivery system is to identify strategies to close these gaps.

■ Health Care Quality

The U.S. health care system is known for being among the most advanced in the world in terms of scientific discovery, equipment, facilities, and training to address complex illness and injuries. However, landmark studies, such as the Institute of Medicine's "To Err Is Human" (1999) and "Crossing the Quality Chasm" (2001), have brought to light the fact that even the most advanced equipment and techniques cannot overcome the system design and team coordination issues that often lead to poor-quality health care outcomes. The Institute of Medicine's research indicates that at least 44,000 Americans die, and hundreds of thousands more are injured, in U.S. hospitals each year due to medical errors. These errors cause unnecessary costs to the U.S. health care system of between $17 billion and $29 billion annually. The Institute developed a road map to achieve better quality, calling for focus on care that is safe, effective, patient centered, timely, efficient, and equitable.

In the years since these studies, many tools, techniques, and measures have been implemented to evaluate and improve quality in the U.S. health care system. Payment systems have also begun to integrate quality measures. Each year since 2003, the Agency for Healthcare Research and Quality (AHRQ) has reported on progress toward improved health care quality and opportunities for ongoing improvement. Although annual improvements have been recognized, the reports also indicate that health care quality and access continue to be suboptimal. Efforts also are underway to ensure that quality health care information is more readily accessible for patients as they make health care–related decisions. The HHS has developed mandatory quality reporting metrics, made publicly available through www.hospitalcompare.hhs.gov. Numerous other public and private sources have begun to provide ratings and information about patient experiences and outcomes. However, many factors other than quality data currently drive decisions when patients select health care providers (Figure 2.11).

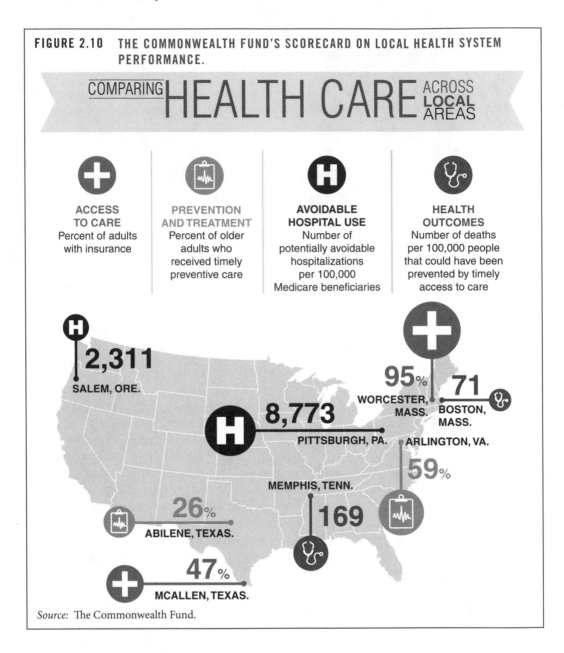

FIGURE 2.10   THE COMMONWEALTH FUND'S SCORECARD ON LOCAL HEALTH SYSTEM PERFORMANCE.

Source: The Commonwealth Fund.

■ Health Care Cost and Value

Just as patients often do not consider quality data in making choices about health care providers, costs typically are not part of the decision-making process. This happens for a number of reasons. For insured patients, focus may be on the required copay amount, as opposed to the total cost of care. In general, the health care system is not designed to allow patients to consider costs and value obtained, as they might when making other purchasing decisions. Yet patients who do attempt to obtain cost information often find that accessing this information is nearly impossible. Costs for the same procedure may vary even within a particular hospital, depending on complexity level and peripheral

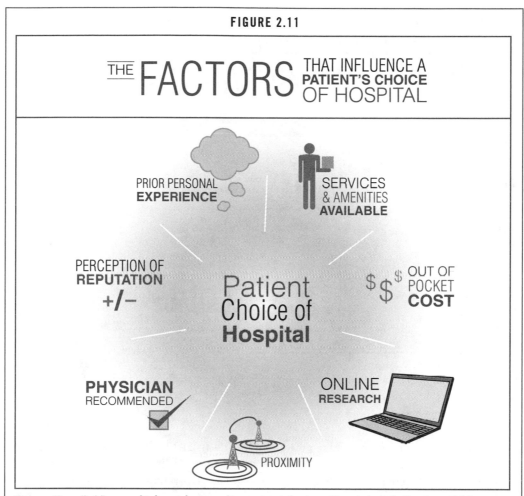

FIGURE 2.11

THE FACTORS THAT INFLUENCE A PATIENT'S CHOICE OF HOSPITAL

PRIOR PERSONAL **EXPERIENCE**

SERVICES & AMENITIES **AVAILABLE**

PERCEPTION OF **REPUTATION** +/−

Patient Choice of **Hospital**

$ $ $ OUT OF POCKET **COST**

PHYSICIAN RECOMMENDED

ONLINE **RESEARCH**

PROXIMITY

Source: Compiled from multiple articles regarding patient selection of hospitals, including Jung, Feldman, and Scanlon (2011).

services. Costs also differ depending on a patient's insurance carrier and the rates that have been negotiated by the insurer. Recent research has shown significant variation in cost for the same service between hospitals, even within the same geographic area (Figure 2.12). It is also clear that a significant disconnect exists between the listed charge for each hospital and the discounted price. Yet, an important question remains unanswered: What is the value of the care received at this price?

> *Recent research has shown significant variation in cost for the same service between hospitals, even within the same geographic area.*

As health care expenditures have continued to grow—and today exceed 17% of the U.S. GDP—there has been increasing pressure for greater transparency regarding health care costs, with the presumption that greater transparency will foster greater

FIGURE 2.12 ADJUSTED CHARGES AND DISCOUNT PRICES FOR UNCOMPLICATED CAESAREAN SECTIONS ACROSS CALIFORNIA HOSPITALS, 2011.

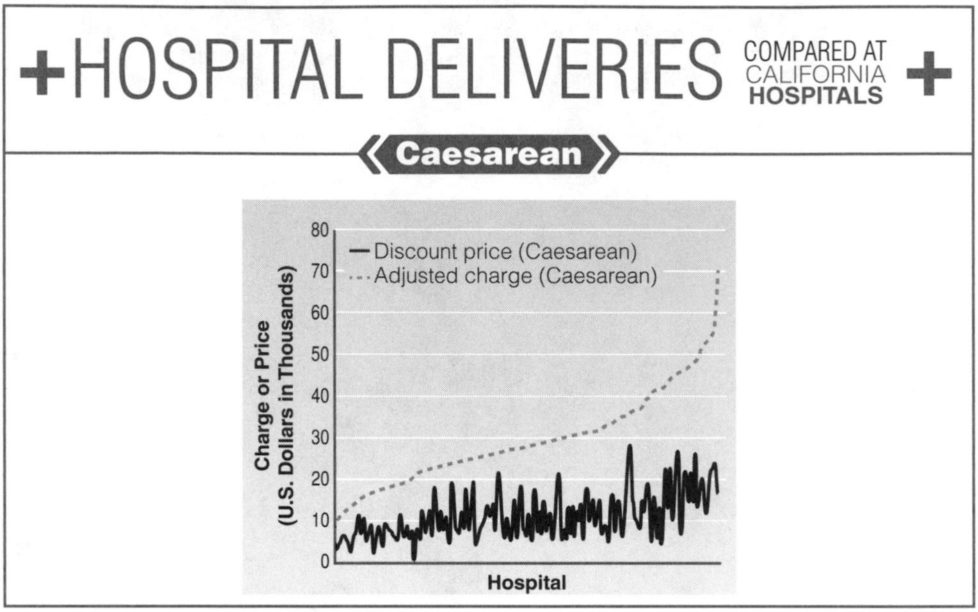

Source: Hsia, Yaa, & Weber (2014).

accountability. In support of this effort, beginning in 2013, the Center for Medicare and Medicaid Services (CMS) began to release certain Medicare provider charge data for public viewing. Although this may be a step toward transparency, given the complexity of the data and the design of health care charge systems, it remains to be seen whether this information will be helpful to patients in decision making or will have any influence on the decisions patients make.

■ The Future of Health Care Delivery

Forecasting the future involves both learning from the past and utilizing current evidence and circumstances to develop a reasonable view of what is likely to happen going forward. Past trends and current evidence make it likely that quality and costs will become an even more central part of the health care delivery dialogue. If implementation of the Affordable Care Act continues to move forward as intended, the focus on coordinated care makes it likely that large health care organizations will become larger and capture a growing segment of the market. An increasing number of physicians are likely to become employed by these large organizations, as opposed to being in private practice.

Health care consumers, however, remain somewhat skeptical about the future of health care delivery. Recent polls have found that Americans remain divided on appropriate next steps for the Affordable Care Act (Figure 2.13). What does seem likely is

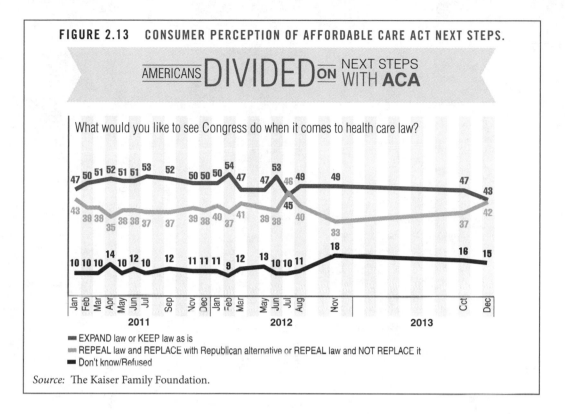

FIGURE 2.13 CONSUMER PERCEPTION OF AFFORDABLE CARE ACT NEXT STEPS.

AMERICANS DIVIDED ON NEXT STEPS WITH ACA

What would you like to see Congress do when it comes to health care law?

- ■ EXPAND law or KEEP law as is
- ■ REPEAL law and REPLACE with Republican alternative or REPEAL law and NOT REPLACE it
- ■ Don't know/Refused

Source: The Kaiser Family Foundation.

that patients will become more actively involved in their health care. As dissatisfaction with the current U.S. system and the cost of care continues to increase, and quality and cost data become more readily accessible, consumers will likely become more active participants in their health care. This alone could prove to be a step in the right direction for the health of the U.S. population.

■ References

Hsia, R. Y., Yaa, A. A., & Weber, E. (2014). Analysis of variation in charges and prices paid for vaginal and caesarean section births: A cross-sectional study. *BMJ Open, 4*(1), e004017. doi:10.1136/bmjopen-2013-004017

Jung, K., Feldman, R., & Scanlon, D. (2011). Where would you go for your next hospitalization? *Journal of Health Economics, 30,* 832–841.

World Health Organization. (1948). Preamble to the Constitution of the World Health Organization as adopted by the International Health Conference, New York, 19-22 June, 1946; signed on 22 July 1946 by the representatives of 61 States (Official Records of the World Health Organization, no. 2, p. 100) and entered into force on 7 April 1948. Retrieved from http://www.who.int/about/definition/en/print.html

3

Government and Health Insurance: The Policy Process

Michael S. Sparer and Frank J. Thompson

KEY WORDS

Children's Health Insurance
    Program (CHIP)
Medicaid
Medicare

Patient Protection and Affordable Care
    Act (ACA) of 2010
policy process

LEARNING OBJECTIVES

- ◉ Review the evolution of government's role in the U.S. health insurance system
- ◉ Describe the roles of public and private stakeholders in the health policy process
- ◉ Explore key issues on the government's health policy agenda, including the enactment and implementation of the Patient Protection and Affordable Care Act of 2010

TOPICAL OUTLINE

- ◉ The government as payer: The health insurance safety net
- ◉ Recent efforts to help the uninsured
- ◉ The ACA and the uninsured
- ◉ Key characteristics of the policy process
- ◉ The dynamics of program expansion: Medicaid

■ Context

Government is deeply entrenched in every aspect of the U.S. health care system (see Chapter 2). The federal government provides tax incentives to encourage employers to offer health insurance to their employees; provides health insurance to the poor, the aged, and the disabled; operates health care facilities for veterans; and supports the training of doctors and other health professionals. State governments administer and help pay for Medicaid, license health care providers, regulate private health insurers, and operate facilities for the mentally ill and developmentally disabled. Local governments own and operate public hospitals and public health clinics and develop and enforce public health codes.

With the enactment of the Patient Protection and Affordable Care Act of 2010 (ACA), government's role has expanded dramatically, especially when it comes to insurance coverage. The law expands eligibility for public insurance, uses federal subsidies to make private coverage more affordable, imposes new rules on insurers and employers to make coverage more accessible, and adds an overarching requirement that nearly all Americans have some form of health insurance (or pay a penalty through the tax code). Most of these provisions took effect in 2014; in that initial year an additional 5 million Americans enrolled in state Medicaid programs, nearly 8 million others received public subsidies for private coverage purchased through newly created insurance exchanges, and private insurers were no longer able to deny coverage based on preexisting health conditions, impose annual or lifetime limits on coverage, or spend excessive amounts on administration or profit.

The goal of this chapter is to provide an overview of the health policy process by looking closely at government's role in the health care system. We do so by focusing on government's role in the health insurance arena and, in particular, on politics and policymaking in the Medicaid program, the nation's public health insurance program for low-income populations. Why focus here instead of on government's role as a regulator or as a provider of care? After all, there is no shortage of interesting and important topics in the health policy arena: As we write this chapter, the Centers for Disease Control and Prevention (CDC) is working to limit the Ebola epidemic, Congress is reviewing claims that the Veteran's Administration has mismanaged its hospital system, the Food and Drug Administration (FDA) is deciding how to regulate e-cigarettes (if at all), and state insurance departments are implementing a host of new and complicated regulations on the private insurance industry.

> *Government's role in the nation's health insurance system provides an important and interesting lens through which to consider the health policy process.*

The short answer is that we (or you) could pick any one of these policy arenas to focus on: Our goal is to provide you with tools for analyzing the policy process that are helpful whether the focus is Medicaid, the CDC, or the FDA. The longer answer is that government's role in the nation's health insurance system provides an important and interesting lens through which to consider the health policy process. In a nation that spends nearly 18% of its gross domestic product on health care, it is important to understand why government provides health insurance to many of those who are not covered by the employer-sponsored private health insurance system and also subsidizes (directly or indirectly) a growing portion of the cost of private coverage. The Medicaid policy process is especially intriguing and unexpected: When enacted in 1965, Medicaid was expected to be a small, welfare-based program for the poorest of the poor; over time, however, Medicaid has evolved into the nation's largest health insurance program, with more than 65 million beneficiaries (at a cost of well over $400 billion annually) and millions more likely to enroll in the next few years. How and why did that happen, and what does that evolution suggest about U.S. health policy?

■ The Government as Payer: The Health Insurance Safety Net

For much of U.S. history, the federal government and the states were minor players in the nation's health and welfare systems. The social welfare system was shaped instead by the principles that governed the English poor law system. Social welfare programs were a local responsibility, and assistance was provided only to those who were outside the labor force through no fault of their own (the so-called deserving poor). National welfare programs were considered unwise and perhaps even unconstitutional. The main exception was the Civil War pension program, which provided federal funds to Union veterans, but even this initiative was administered and implemented at the local level.

Lacking federal or state leadership (and dollars), local governments tried to provide a social and medical safety net. The most common approach was to establish almshouses (or shelters) for indigent aged and disabled people. A medical clinic often provided health care to almshouse residents. These clinics eventually evolved into public hospitals, offering services to the poor without charge. Generally speaking, however, the clinics (and hospitals) provided poor-quality care and were avoided by people who had any alternative. Similarly, the few private hospitals then in operation were charitable facilities that served only the poor and the disabled. These hospitals, like their public counterparts, represented only a small and rather disreputable portion of the nation's health care system.

Most 19th-century Americans received health care in their homes, often from family members who relied on traditional healing techniques. At the same time, an assortment of health care providers—physicians, midwives, medicine salesmen, herbalists, homeopaths, and faith healers—offered their services, as well. Generally speaking, these practitioners charged low fees, which families paid out-of-pocket, much as they would for other commodities.

As the 19th century drew to a close, two developments fundamentally changed the U.S. health care marketplace. First, allopathic physicians (MDs) won the battle for primacy among medical providers. Americans increasingly recognized that medicine was a science and believed that medical doctors were the most scientific practitioners, best able to deliver high-quality care. The status and prestige accorded to MD-physicians grew, whereas the role of alternative medicine providers declined.

The emergence of a physician-dominated health care system was accompanied by a second pivotal factor—the dramatic growth in the size and the status of the U.S. hospital industry. Indeed, the nation's stock of hospitals grew from fewer than 200 in 1873 to 4,000 (with 35,500 beds) in 1900, to nearly 7,000 (with 922,000 beds) by 1930 (Annas, Law, Rosenblatt, & Wing, 1990).

This growth was prompted by several factors. Advances in medical technology (antiseptics, anesthesia, x-rays) encouraged wealthier people to use hospitals, eliminating much of hospitals' prior social stigma. The number of nurses expanded dramatically, as nurses evolved from domestics to trained professionals, and hospital-based nurses worked hard to improve hospitals' hygiene. The growing urbanization and industrialization of American life produced an increasingly rootless society, less able to rely on families to care for their sick at home. Finally, the medical education system began to require internships and residencies in hospitals as part of physician training, which put a cadre of trained doctors to work full time in these facilities.

By the mid-1920s, there was growing recognition that middle-income Americans needed help in financing the rising costs of hospital care and increasingly high-tech medicine.

As the hospital industry grew, so too did the costs of care. By the mid-1920s, there was growing recognition that middle-income Americans needed help in financing the rising costs of hospital care and increasingly high-tech medicine. The onset of the Great Depression made the situation more problematic, as hospital occupancy rates plummeted and numerous facilities went bankrupt. In response to this crisis, the hospital industry created Blue Cross; for-profit insurers soon followed Blue Cross into the health business and the nation's private health insurance industry began to emerge.

The health insurance industry received a major boost from the federal government, first during World War II, when federal policymakers excluded most employer-sponsored health insurance from wage and price controls, and then in the early 1950s when federal officials ruled that premiums paid by employers would not be considered income to the employee (a tax exclusion that now costs the federal government more than $250 billion a year). By the mid-1950s, employer-sponsored private insurance was on its way to becoming the vehicle through which most Americans could afford the rising cost of health care (see Chapter 11 for more on the early history of private health insurance).

At the same time, the demonstrable advances in medical technology after World War II engendered confidence that the medical system would, in time, conquer nearly all forms of disease. This perception prompted the federal government (through the National Institutes of Health) to funnel billions of dollars to academic medical researchers. With federal dollars so readily available, medical schools soon emphasized research, and medical students increasingly chose research careers. Around the same time, Congress enacted the Hill-Burton Program, which provided federal funds to stimulate hospital construction and modernization. The policy assumption was that all Americans should have access to the increasingly sophisticated medical care rendered in state-of-the-art hospital facilities.

Even with the growing employer-sponsored health insurance system, it was soon clear that large portions of the population would not easily have access to such coverage or to the benefits of the new medical advances. Left out of these new systems were the retired elderly, the disabled, the unemployed, the self-employed, the part-time worker, and most of those who worked for small businesses.

To be sure, liberal politicians had argued for many years without success in favor of government-sponsored health insurance that would replace the employer-sponsored private system and would cover all Americans. President Harry Truman had posited that health insurance was part of the Fair Deal to which all Americans were entitled. However, neither Truman nor his liberal predecessors ever came close to overcoming the strong opposition to national health insurance from doctors, businessmen, and others, who viewed it as un-American and socialistic. Doctors feared a government program would lead to greater oversight, requirements to serve indigent patients, and reduced income potential.

By 1949, mainstream Democrats had abandoned their visions of universal insurance and proposed instead that the Social Security (retirement) system be expanded to provide hospital insurance for the aged, reasoning that the elderly were a sympathetic and deserving group and that hospital care was the most costly sector of the health care system.

Conservatives opposed the plan, arguing that it would give free coverage to many people who were neither poor nor particularly needy. They argued instead that government's role is to provide a safety net to the deserving poor who are unable to access employer-sponsored coverage. The result was an amendment to the Social Security Act in 1950 that, for the first time, provided federal funds to states willing to pay health care providers to care for welfare recipients. Interestingly, this "welfare medicine" approach passed with bipartisan support (Sparer, 1996). For liberals, this was an acceptable, albeit inadequate, first step, but at least some poor people finally could obtain services. Conservatives went along because a medical safety net for the poor would undermine arguments for a more comprehensive health insurance program and because responsibility for the program was delegated to state officials.

In 1960, newly elected President John F. Kennedy revived the effort to enact hospital insurance for the aged. Congress responded by enacting the Kerr-Mills Program. This program distributed federal funds to states that were willing to pay health care providers to care for the indigent aged, expanding the welfare medicine model. Congress later opened the program to covering the indigent disabled. These initiatives again deflected support from the president's broader social insurance proposal.

The political dynamic had evolved considerably by 1965. President Lyndon B. Johnson and the Democrats controlling Congress were enacting various laws designed to turn the United States into a "Great Society." This seemed an opportune time to renew the effort to enact national health insurance. Even longtime opponents of health insurance expansions expected Congress to enact a plan far more comprehensive than Kerr-Mills. President Johnson followed the path set by Truman and Kennedy and again proposed hospital insurance for the aged. At the same time, various Republican legislators, citing the nation's oversupply of hospitals and desiring to return to a physician-centered delivery system, recommended that Congress enact physician insurance for the aged. The American Medical Association (AMA), hoping once again to scuttle the social insurance model, urged Congress simply to expand Kerr-Mills.

As Congress debated these various proposals, President Johnson (working behind the scenes) convinced Congressman Wilbur Mills, powerful chair of the House Ways and Means Committee and an aspiring Presidential candidate, to demand that his colleagues enact all three expansion initiatives (Blumenthal & Morone, 2009). The President's proposal for hospital insurance for the aged became Medicare Part A; the Republican proposal for physician insurance for the aged became Medicare Part B. The AMA's effort to expand Kerr-Mills became Medicaid. These government programs, for the first time, became a true health insurance safety net for Americans without employer-sponsored coverage (Marmor, 2000).

MEDICAID

Medicaid is not a single national program, but a collection of 50 state-administered programs, each providing health insurance to low-income state residents but with differing eligibility rules, benefits, and payment schedules. Each state initiative is governed by various federal guidelines, and the federal government contributes between 50% and 78% of its cost (the poorer the state, the larger the federal contribution). In 2012, the various Medicaid programs covered more than 60 million Americans at an annual cost of approximately $415 billion (Kaiser Commission on Medicaid and the Uninsured, 2014).

Given Medicaid's decentralized structure, state officials have considerable discretion. One not-surprising result is that states such as New York have more generous eligibility criteria than do poorer states such as Alabama or Mississippi. Interestingly, however, stark contrasts exist even among the larger states. In fiscal year 2007, New York, for example, spent $8,450 per Medicaid enrollee, whereas California spent only $3,168 (Kaiser Family Foundation, 2010).

During the late 1980s, Congress began imposing rules designed to dramatically increase state coverage. As a result of these mandates, the number of children on Medicaid nearly doubled between 1987 and 1995, and the total number of recipients increased from roughly 26 million to nearly 40 million. Medicaid expansions had become the federal government's main strategy for reducing the ranks of the uninsured.

Concomitantly, Medicaid's annual price tag grew from $57.5 billion in 1988 to $157.3 billion in 1995. State officials blamed this increase on the federal mandates. Federal regulators disputed the claim and suggested that the states themselves were largely responsible for the increase, citing accounting techniques through which states shifted state-funded programs into their Medicaid budget so they could draw down additional federal dollars. This argument produced significant intergovernmental tension (Holahan & Liska, 1997).

During the early 1990s, President Bill Clinton, a former state governor and a critic of Medicaid mandates, stopped considering Medicaid the linchpin in efforts to reduce the number of uninsured. Recognizing that many uninsured people are in families where the husband or wife works full or part time, he proposed instead to require that employers offer health insurance to their employees. The Clinton administration's proposal for national health insurance failed, but the shift away from federal Medicaid mandates persisted (until the recent enactment of the ACA). Instead, federal officials became more lenient in approving state requests for waivers from federal Medicaid rules, giving states additional flexibility and autonomy.

Two trends dominated Medicaid policy during most of the 1990s. First, states used their expanded discretion to encourage or require recipients to enroll in managed care delivery systems. Between 1987 and 1998, the percentage of enrollees in Medicaid managed care increased from less than 5% to more than 50%, from fewer than 1 million people to more than 20 million. Second, growth in the number of Medicaid enrollees ended, and a slow decline began. The most convincing explanation for the decline was federal welfare reform, enacted in 1996. Before then, people receiving Aid to Families with Dependent Children (AFDC, often referred to as welfare) were automatically enrolled in Medicaid. Thereafter, welfare recipients needed to apply separately for Medicaid, as did those no longer entitled to welfare but still eligible for Medicaid. Millions did not know they were Medicaid eligible, the states set steep administrative hurdles that deterred others from applying, and still others were dissuaded by the stigma attached to receiving public assistance. For all of these reasons, between 1995 and 1997, the number of adult Medicaid recipients declined 5.5%, and the number of child recipients declined 1.4%.

During the late 1990s, state and federal officials undertook a major effort to increase Medicaid enrollment. One strategy was to simplify the eligibility process (shortened application forms, mail-in applications, and more eligibility-determination sites). A second strategy was to simplify eligibility rules (eliminating assets tests and ensuring 12 months of continuous eligibility). A third strategy was to expand outreach and education by increasing marketing activities and encouraging community-based institutions to educate and enroll their constituents. These efforts succeeded. Beginning in mid-1998, Medicaid enrollment began to increase again, a trend that has continued.

The growth in enrollment, along with higher costs for prescription drugs, services for people with disabilities, and long-term care, has led to escalating Medicaid costs, and for some years, states' Medicaid expenditures have exceeded what they spend on education. At the same time, state tax revenues declined precipitously in the late 2000s. The ensuing budget crises prompted Medicaid cost-containment efforts in every state. The most popular option was an effort to control the rising cost of pharmaceuticals, either through leveraged buying (purchasing pools) or limits on access (formularies). Other Medicaid cost-containment strategies have included freezing or cutting provider reimbursement, reducing benefits (such as dental and home care), cutting eligibility, increasing copays, and expanding disease management initiatives.

> *The story of Medicaid's growth from a relatively small welfare medicine program to the nation's largest insurance program (with more than 20% of the population enrolled) is a remarkable political story, and one that nicely illustrates several key characteristics of the U.S. health policy process.*

More recently, the ACA contained a significant expansion in Medicaid eligibility, initially requiring all states to expand coverage to 133% of the federal poverty level, though the Supreme Court subsequently converted that mandate into a state option (now in place in roughly half the states). Even with this judicial limit, the story of Medicaid's growth from a relatively small welfare medicine program to the nation's largest insurance program (with more than 20% of the population enrolled) is a remarkable political story, and one that nicely illustrates several key characteristics of the U.S. health policy process. Later in this chapter we review more closely these key characteristics and the policy dynamics of the ongoing growth of the program. First, however, we continue our overview of the nation's health insurance system, starting with Medicare and then focusing on more recent initiatives designed to help the uninsured.

MEDICARE

Like Medicaid, Medicare was enacted in 1965 to provide health insurance to segments of the population not generally covered by the mainstream employer-sponsored health insurance system. Also like Medicaid, Medicare has become a major part of the nation's health care system, providing insurance coverage in 2013 to 43.5 million persons over the age of 65 and to just under 9 million of the young disabled population, at a total annual cost of over $583 billion (The Boards of Trustees, Federal Hospital Insurance and Federal Supplementary Medical Insurance Trust Funds, 2014).

In other respects, however, Medicare differs significantly from its sister program. Medicare is a social insurance program, providing benefits to the aged and the disabled regardless of income, whereas Medicaid is a welfare initiative, offering coverage only to those with limited income. Medicare is administered by federal officials and the private insurers they hire to perform particular tasks, whereas Medicaid is administered by the states following federal guidance. Medicare is funded primarily by the federal government (plus beneficiary copayments and deductibles), whereas Medicaid is funded by the federal government and the states without any beneficiary contribution. Medicare has a relatively limited benefit package that excludes much preventive care, long-term care, and, until 2006, prescription drugs outside of the hospital and the oncologist's office, whereas Medicaid offers a far more generous array of benefits.

For the first 30 years of its existence, Medicare had two separate parts, each with different funding sources and eligibility requirements. *Medicare Part A* covers inpatient hospital care. It is financed primarily by a 2.9% payroll tax: 1.45% paid by the employer and 1.45% paid by the employee, though higher income beneficiaries (post-ACA) pay a higher tax. All beneficiaries automatically receive Part A coverage. *Medicare Part B*, in contrast, is a voluntary program, providing coverage for outpatient care for beneficiaries who choose to pay a $110 monthly premium (though here too individuals with annual income over $85,000 now pay a higher, income-based premium). Some 95% of Medicare beneficiaries choose to enroll in Part B. General federal revenues pay the balance of the Part B bill.

Before 1994, the revenue contributed to the Part A Trust Fund exceeded the program's expenses, and the fund built up a significant surplus. Beginning in 1994, expenses began to exceed revenue; the surplus was used to pay bills, and it began to shrink. Alarmed Medicare experts predicted that the surplus would be gone by the early 2000s, that the Trust Fund would be unable to pay its bills, and that Medicare would slide into bankruptcy. In response to this crisis, Congress in 1997 enacted a broad effort to reduce Medicare costs, mainly by cutting provider reimbursement.

The rapid shift in the economics of Medicare prompted an equally rapid change in its politics (Oberlander, 2003). No longer were politicians claiming that the program was about to go bankrupt. No longer was there talk of greedy providers overcharging and generating excess profits. No longer was there an intense effort to enroll beneficiaries in managed care. There were instead three competing views about how to respond. One camp emphasized the need to undo some of the cuts in provider reimbursement, another focused on the importance of expanding the benefits package, and still another argued against new spending measures, whether on behalf of providers or beneficiaries. This last group—the fiscal conservatives—proposed that any surplus remain in the Trust Fund to be used in years to come.

Faced with these options, Congress chose in 1999 to undo some of the cuts in provider reimbursement. Provider organizations argued that the prior cuts were unnecessarily endangering the financial health of thousands of doctors and hospitals. Even supporters of the cuts conceded that the extent of the reductions was far greater than expected. As a result, Congress reduced the impact of the cuts by $16 billion over the next 5 years and $27 billion over the next 10 years. In 2000, Congress passed another giveback initiative, this time delivering to providers $35 billion over 5 years and $85 billion over 10 years.

Following the provider giveback legislation, newly elected President George W. Bush and Congress took up the issue of prescription drug coverage and enacted Medicare Part D. Under this legislation, beneficiaries can receive outpatient drug coverage through a managed care plan or, if they wish to stay in fee-for-service Medicare, through a private prescription drug plan. In most communities, seniors can choose among dozens of plans, some of which offer limited coverage for a small monthly premium, whereas others offer more generous benefits for a higher premium. The average monthly premium nationwide is $39, in exchange for which the beneficiary has a $310 deductible, after which the plan pays 75% of drug costs up to $2,850 and 95% of the costs beyond $4,550 (the beneficiary pays 100% of the costs between $2,850 and $4,550—the so-called "donut hole," which is slowly being phased out as part of the 2010 health reform legislation).

The Medicare drug legislation was extraordinarily controversial and partisan. President Bush and leading Republicans maintained that the legislation, expected to cost $410 billion over its first 10 years, was the largest public insurance expansion since Medicare was first enacted and that it would provide significant coverage to millions of seniors. Leading Democrats, while supporting the goals of the legislation, complained that the initiative gives too little to needy seniors and too much to health maintenance organizations, big business, and the pharmaceutical industry.

The prescription drug plan was designed, in part, to encourage beneficiaries to enroll in a managed care plan. The managed care program, called Part C and created as part of the 1997 Balanced Budget Act, had only limited success during the early 2000s, largely because of declining health plan interest. Back in 2004, for example, only 4.6 million beneficiaries were enrolled in 145 plans (Kaiser Family Foundation, 2004). Health plans claimed the main barrier to their expanded participation was inadequate reimbursement. However, several studies suggested that Medicare was actually losing money on the managed care initiative because its capitation rates often were set high, based on the health care experience of the average client in a particular community, whereas the typical managed care enrollee was healthier and less costly than average (Kaiser Family Foundation, 2004).

In an effort to reverse the decline in health plan participation and to advance the goals of privatization and competition, the Bush administration proposed that the new drug benefit be delivered exclusively by managed care plans. Although the legislation as enacted does not go so far, it did dramatically increase health plan capitation rates in an effort to encourage plans to get back in the game. Over the next decade, average monthly capitation rates increased dramatically. As a result, plans began aggressively marketing to beneficiaries, and there now are 16 million Medicare Advantage enrollees (Kaiser Family Foundation, 2014).

HELPING THOSE WHO REMAIN UNINSURED: THE EXPANDING PUBLIC SAFETY NET

During the early 2000s, the number of Americans without health insurance grew from roughly 40 million to approximately 46 million—more than 15% of the nation's population. Millions more Americans were underinsured, with high out-of-pocket medical expenses and, often, considerable medical debt. Most of the uninsured (more than 80%) were in families with a full- or part-time worker, and most of these workers were self-employed or employed by small businesses. States with a strong unionized industrial and manufacturing base were likely to have fewer uninsured, whereas states with large numbers of immigrants and a service-based economy were likely to have more. In Iowa, Massachusetts, and Wisconsin, for example, less than 10% of the population was uninsured; whereas in California, Louisiana, and Texas, the percentage hovered between 20% and 25%.

Rather remarkably, the dramatic increase in the nation's uninsured population began in the mid-1990s—an era of unprecedented economic growth, low unemployment, and relatively small rises in health care costs; it then accelerated during the economic downturn of the early 2000s. Much of the increase in the uninsured population also occurred during a time when the Medicaid rolls were expanding dramatically. The best explanation for the rise in the number of uninsured was the decline in the number of Americans with employer-sponsored private health insurance. Between 1977 and

2004, the percentage of Americans under age 65 with employer-sponsored coverage dropped from 66% to 61% (Clemens-Cope, Garrett, & Hoffman, 2006).

The decline in employer-sponsored coverage was due to several factors. Many employers have increased the share of the bill that the employee must pay, prompting some employees to abandon their coverage. Other employers eliminated coverage for spouses and children or phased out retiree health coverage. Still others hired more part-time workers and outside contractors, thereby avoiding the need to offer health insurance. At the same time, much of the recent job growth has been in the service and small business sectors of the economy. These jobs are notoriously low paying and rarely provide health insurance.

In response to these trends and to media and political attention to the problems of the uninsured, state and federal officials tried during the early 1990s to enact new coverage programs (Brown & Sparer, 2001; Sparer, 2003). These proposals generally sought to require employers to provide health insurance to their employees and to use public dollars as a safety net for those outside the labor market. The idea was to retain and reinvigorate the employer-sponsored health insurance system. By the mid-1990s, however, the various employer mandate proposals, including the plan proposed by President Clinton, had disappeared, defeated by vehement opposition from the business community. Business opponents argued that the mandate would be too costly and would force employers to eliminate jobs.

After the collapse of the employer mandate strategy, policymakers (especially at the state level) enacted a host of efforts designed to make health insurance more available and more affordable in the small group and individual insurance markets. These reforms focused on three structural problems in the health care system:

- Employers in the small business community often could not afford to provide health insurance to their employees. These employers lacked the market clout to negotiate a good deal, particularly given the high administrative costs associated with insuring a small group.
- People who are self-employed or employees of small businesses generally earned too little to purchase health insurance in the individual market.
- People with a high risk of catastrophic medical costs were often excluded from the individual insurance market, regardless of their ability to pay.

Many of the state initiatives required insurers to guarantee coverage to segments of the small business community. Others encouraged small businesses to join state-run or state-administered purchasing alliances. Still others allowed insurers to sell no-frills insurance policies, presumably at a lower cost than the more comprehensive packages states often require. Taken together, however, the various state mandates had only a modest effect on the number of uninsured (Robert Wood Johnson Foundation, 2007), while generating significant political controversy, especially from healthy younger workers who complain about paying higher rates to subsidize the older and the sicker and from insurance companies threatening to exit reform-minded states.

By the late 1990s, state and federal policymakers had shifted their focus away from the insurance reforms that had been disappointing up to that point, and toward programs that expanded health insurance for children. Several factors explained the trend. Children are considered a deserving group; there is bipartisan agreement that youngsters should not go without health care services because their parents cannot afford to pay; and children are a relatively low-cost population to insure. In 1993, for example, the average child on Medicaid cost just under $1,000, whereas the typical elderly recipient cost more than $9,200, and disabled recipients' costs averaged just under $8,000.

Child health initiatives also are consistent with the political agendas of both Republicans and Democrats. Republicans, along with many moderate Democrats, support insurance expansions as a counterbalance to other social welfare cutbacks. For example, many families that move from welfare to work continue to need help in obtaining health insurance for their children. At the same time, liberal Democrats, still reeling from the defeat of national health insurance proposals, saw health insurance for children as an incremental step on the path to universal health coverage.

Given this bipartisan support, Congress enacted the State Children's Health Insurance Program (SCHIP; later changed to CHIP in 2009). States can use CHIP funds to liberalize their Medicaid eligibility rules, to develop a separate state program, or to create a combination of the two. The main advantage to using CHIP funds to expand Medicaid is administrative simplicity for both the client and the state. This is especially so for families in which some children are eligible for Medicaid and others for CHIP. At the same time, there are several advantages to creating a separate state program:

- Enrollment can be suspended when the dollars are spent, unlike with Medicaid, which is an entitlement program.
- The state has more discretion when developing the benefits package.
- The state can impose copayments and premiums, which generally are not allowed under Medicaid.
- Beneficiaries and providers may be more likely to participate because the new program lacks the stigma associated with Medicaid.

By all accounts, early efforts to enroll children in SCHIP were disappointing. By the end of 1999, roughly 1.5 million youngsters were enrolled in the program, far fewer than predicted. The low enrollment was due to several factors. Large numbers of eligible families did not know they were eligible. The complicated application processes deterred others. Still others were dissuaded by the stigma often associated with government insurance programs. The premiums and other cost-sharing requirements clearly discouraged others. As a result, by the end of 2000, 38 states had not spent their full allotment of federal CHIP dollars. Funds not expended in these states were reallocated to the dozen other participating states.

Beginning in early 2000, however, CHIP enrollment began to rise significantly. By the end of the year, roughly 3.3 million children were enrolled—nearly double the number from the prior year—and by 2005, there were more than 4 million enrollees. Policymakers attribute the turnaround to improved outreach and education initiatives and to simplified processes for eligibility and enrollment.

As program enrollment grew, bipartisan support began to fade. The political battling was particularly intense during the effort to reauthorize the program in 2007. Congressional Democrats proposed significantly increased funding so as to expand enrollment even further. President Bush and many congressional Republicans opposed the expansion, arguing that expanding enrollment to more middle-class families would undermine the nation's private insurance system, because employers would drop private coverage for children eligible for the expanded public program.

The political battling continued during the last year of the Bush Administration; the president twice vetoed reauthorization legislation. When President Obama took office in late January 2009, one of his first priorities was to sign legislation reauthorizing and expanding the program. He did so on February 4, 2009. As a result, CHIP enrollment continues to increase.

Despite the growth in public insurance programs such as Medicaid and CHIP, the number of uninsured kept rising, leading to an ongoing debate over whether and how government should aid this population. This debate returned to the national agenda during the 2008 presidential campaign, as several Democratic candidates proposed federal legislation to dramatically reduce the number of uninsured, while their Republican counterparts challenged such proposals as both unwise and counterproductive. After the election of Barack Obama and a strong Democratic majority in both the Senate and the House of Representatives, the nation engaged in a fierce and partisan debate over the merits of health reform, a debate that culminated in the enactment of the ACA of 2010.

THE ENACTMENT AND IMPLEMENTATION OF THE ACA

Early in his administration, President Obama decided to push hard for comprehensive health reform legislation. The goals were (a) to reduce dramatically the number of uninsured, (b) to pay for such coverage without adding to the nation's budget deficit, (c) to slow the rising cost of health care more generally, and (d) to encourage a more efficient and higher-value health care delivery system. The president understood, however, that the politics of health reform would be contentious and difficult. Health care is a $2.6 trillion industry, and interest groups (insurers, pharmaceutical companies, employers, hospitals, doctors) would vigorously resist proposals that threatened their share of these dollars.

In addition, reform opponents often characterize comprehensive health reform initiatives as "socialistic" and contrary to our political culture, arguing instead for more incremental reforms that focus on notions of personal responsibility rather than social solidarity or equity. Finally, America's political institutions are designed to make it difficult to enact major new legislation, as the various checks and balances at the heart of the U.S. government provide numerous veto points for those opposed to reform.

In this context, President Obama needed to develop a strategy to overcome the interest group, ideological, and institutional obstacles to reform. By mid-2009, he had developed his strategy. First, he declared health reform to be his top domestic priority (doable during a recession only by declaring that fixing the economy required fixing the health care system). Second, he urged that health reform be enacted during the first year of his term, recognizing that delay was the enemy of reform. Third, he delegated the task of developing a health reform plan to congressional leaders, eschewing the White House–centered approach that ran aground in the Clinton administration, hoping instead to persuade the leadership (especially the Democratic leadership) to be fully invested in the reform initiative. Finally, he encouraged administration officials to negotiate with key interest groups, emphasizing the need to compromise and build incrementally off the current system.

After months of partisan politicking and various unexpected political hurdles (such as the election of Scott Brown to the seat of the recently deceased Ted Kennedy, which meant the Democrats no longer had a 60-vote, filibuster-proof Senate majority), Congress enacted the Patient Protection and Affordable Care Act of 2010. The legislation is long and complex, and covers nearly every aspect of the nation's health care system. At its core, however, is an ambitious effort to provide insurance coverage to more than 32 million of the currently uninsured. There are five key components to this effort:

- The law mandates that nearly all Americans have some form of health insurance or pay a penalty through the tax code. This provision withstood judicial challenge and is now in effect.
- The law requires state Medicaid programs to provide coverage to all persons (and their dependents) with incomes below 133% of the federal poverty level. This provision did not survive judicial challenge and the Medicaid expansion is now an option, not a requirement. By mid-2014, 26 states (plus the District of Columbia) had implemented the expansion, resulting in more than five million new Medicaid enrollees.
- Each state is encouraged to create a so-called insurance exchange, a vehicle through which the uninsured and the small business community could presumably purchase more affordable private coverage. The federal government would then provide subsidies to persons with incomes up to 400% of the federal poverty level to help them afford the more reasonably priced coverage.

  As of mid-2014, however, only 16 states (plus the District of Columbia) had created a state-based exchange; 27 states were relying completely on the newly created federal exchange (healthcare.gov), whereas the remaining seven states have exchanges that operate as state-federal partnerships. During the initial open enrollment period (October 1, 2013 to March 31, 2014), approximately 7 million individuals obtained coverage via these exchanges, more than 80% of whom were receiving federal subsidies.
- The law requires that employers with more than 50 full-time employees either provide coverage to their employees or pay a financial penalty to the federal government. However, the Obama administration has delayed implementation of this provision until 2015 (for firms with more than 100 employees) and until 2016 (for firms with 50–99 employees).
- Private insurance companies are required to comply with a host of federal regulations that seek to eliminate the practice of discriminating against persons with preexisting conditions or who are otherwise likely to incur high medical costs.

■ Government and Health Insurance: The Policy Process

The portraits of Medicare, Medicaid, and the ACA suggest the importance of considering the dynamics of policy processes in the United States more explicitly. We open by highlighting four important characteristics of these processes before turning to the case of Medicaid to illustrate how policy dynamics can stoke program growth.

KEY CHARACTERISTICS OF POLICY PROCESSES

Four observations loom large in considering the policy processes that shape health care programs in the United States. *First, each health program or problem domain typically has a relatively distinct policy subsystem.* These policy subsystems consist of actors from the public and private sectors who are routinely and "actively concerned about a policy problem or issue" and seek to shape what government does about it. These actors include congressional committees, administrative agencies, interest groups, think tanks, specialized news media, and others (Jenkins-Smith & Sabatier, 1993, p. 17). Policy subsystems tend to be fluid and permeable. For instance, a focusing event may occur (e.g., a proposal to restructure Medicare gains visibility), which leads segments of the public and new stakeholders to become active in the subsystem, at least for a while.

> *The fact that states have considerable discretion to shape Medicaid eligibility and services means that 50 policy subsystems at that governmental level help determine who gets what from the program.*

Each policy subsystem tends to be distinctive. Advocates for pediatricians and children are key players in the Medicaid policy subsystem but not in Medicare's. So, too, Medicare has a policy subsystem more exclusively focused on decisions by the federal government, whereas states play a larger role in Medicaid. The fact that states have considerable discretion to shape Medicaid eligibility and services means that 50 policy subsystems at that governmental level help determine who gets what from the program. It means that the National Governors Association and other lobbies for state officials devote much greater attention to federal Medicaid policy than to Medicare.

Second, the fragmented nature of America's governing institutions makes it difficult to translate majority preferences into major policy decisions in the health arena. Two fundamental features of the U.S. Constitution—the separation of powers and federalism—place formidable barriers in the path of those seeking to transform policy. A new law must not only win the approval of the two houses of Congress and the president, it at times must survive a court challenge. (The Supreme Court came within one vote of overturning the entire ACA.) The American electorate's propensity to produce divided government, with different parties controlling the three elected branches, heightens the transaction costs of getting legislation approved. Other features of the policy process also make it hard to translate simple majority preferences into law. By mandating that each state has two senators, the Constitution ensures that less populous states have outsized influence. Moreover, the growing use of the filibuster in the Senate enables a minority of 41 to block legislation. When Congress passes a law that relies on the states to implement it, policymakers at that level of government may decline to participate (e.g., as in the ACA's Medicaid expansion) or otherwise drag their feet.

Given this context, major policy breakthroughs in the expansion of health insurance have occurred during rare and fleeting moments of one-party dominance. When Medicare and Medicaid won approval in 1965, Lyndon Johnson was president and Democrats held a 68 to 32 majority in the Senate as well as a 295 to 140 margin in the House. Similarly, the ACA was passed during a period in which the Democrats controlled the White House, had a 256 to 178 majority in the House of Representatives, and with the help of Independents, had the 60 votes in the Senate needed to surmount a Republican filibuster.

Although America's balkanized institutions have often impeded movement toward universal health insurance, incremental policy changes expanding public coverage have frequently occurred.

Although America's balkanized institutions have often impeded movement toward universal health insurance, incremental policy changes expanding public coverage have frequently occurred. During the last half century, Congress has repeatedly approved amendments to Medicare and Medicaid. At times, federalism has also been catalytic (Brown & Sparer, 2003). When the federal government has failed to expand insurance coverage, several states have acted. Bottom-up policy diffusion has occasionally occurred as policymakers in the nation's capital learn from state initiatives and refashion federal policy. Incremental or other changes in policy depend heavily on the presence of political brokers in Congress who can forge compromises among policymakers and assemble the coalitions needed to legislate. To the degree that partisan polarization occurs and elected officials see compromise as a form of selling out one's principles, the prospects for congressional gridlock increase appreciably.

Third, implementation is a critical part of the policy process, markedly affecting who gets what from federal health programs. Assessments of policy processes have often focused on the dance of legislation—how a bill becomes law. In fact, however, highly discretionary decisions made by administrative agents during the implementation process also shape the outputs and outcomes of federal health programs. These agents include top officials in federal and state bureaucracies, key private contractors, health care providers, and countless others. The importance of implementation partly reflects the propensity of Congress to delegate ever more authority to the executive branch (e.g., Epstein & O'Halloran, 1999). The ACA serves as a case in point. By late 2013, the Obama administration had published more than 70 formal rules related to the ACA under the Administrative Procedure Act and issued scores of interpretive guidelines (Rosenbaum, 2013). These actions did much to fill in the blanks left by the original law, such as whether the federal government or the states would define the exact essential health benefits offered on the insurance exchanges.

Myriad interest groups and other stakeholders employ various strategies to influence administrative decisions. At times implementation becomes a partisan battlefield with heavy congressional involvement. In this vein, Republicans in Congress have repeatedly attempted to defund and otherwise obstruct the implementation of the ACA. Congress, for instance, turned down the Obama administration's request to provide additional funds to help enroll people in the federal insurance exchanges. Secretary of Health and Human Services Kathleen Sebelius responded by seeking grants and contributions from the private sector to support the work of a nonprofit organization called Enroll America. House Republicans denounced her initiative as illegal and called for an investigation. They insisted that navigators working to expedite ACA enrollment take time out to file lengthy reports about their activities. Meanwhile, Republican policymakers in some states enacted certification and training requirements for navigators that hindered their deployment (Thompson & Gusmano, 2014).

Fourth, the establishment of health programs reconfigures policy subsystems and broader political factors in ways that affect program durability. Once enacted, programs vary in the degree to which they become publicly popular and generate political support from interest groups and other stakeholders (Patashnik & Zelizer, 2013). Durability connotes a political strength that allows a health program to resist retrenchment, erosion, or termination. Construed broadly, the concept also characterizes the degree to which a program evinces accretion, growth, and enhanced effectiveness (i.e., provides more high-quality services with improved health outcomes). After enactment, some health programs have eroded or died. In 1988, for instance, Congress passed the Medicare Catastrophic Coverage Act to provide prescription drugs to seniors. The law increased premiums on Medicare enrollees, especially those with higher incomes, to fund the initiative. Many Medicare enrollees objected to these premium hikes, and public support for the new law plummeted. A year later Congress voted to repeal it. In contrast, over time Medicare and Medicaid have generated supportive policy feedback that has helped these programs become major pillars of the American health insurance system. To illuminate expansionary policy processes, we shine the spotlight on Medicaid.

THE DYNAMICS OF PROGRAM EXPANSION: MEDICAID

Medicaid has often been seen as a down-at-the-heels second cousin to Medicare, highly vulnerable to program erosion. In part this pessimism reflected the fact that the program served welfare recipients—a stigmatized, politically weak clientele. It also emanated from the view that states, engaged in interstate economic competition to attract business and keep the lid on taxes, would severely limit spending on a redistributive program like Medicaid. In fact, however, Medicaid expenditures and enrollees have grown by leaps and bounds over the decades. Although many reformers thought the program would fade away with the coming of national health insurance, it instead became a key component of the ACA. The surprising story of Medicaid's rise can be traced through four historical periods, each of which highlights certain policy dynamics.

Welfare Medicine and the Incremental Politics of Long-Term Care (1965–1980)

Working with President Johnson, Representative Wilbur Mills (D-Arkansas) brokered an agreement leading to Medicaid's birth in 1965. Concerned that states might drag their feet in expanding Medicaid coverage to the uninsured, the original legislation required participating states to make a "satisfactory showing" in the "direction of broadening the scope of . . . care" and "liberalizing the eligibility requirements" by 1975 (Rose, 2013, p. 48). As Mills expected, most states did not rush to establish generous Medicaid programs. What Mills failed to anticipate, however, was the degree to which a few states would move apace to extend Medicaid coverage to great segments of their populations (45% in the case of New York). Now concerned about potential runaway costs, Mills and other policymakers moved in 1967 to constrain the number of Medicaid enrollees by prohibiting states from creating income eligibility levels that exceeded 133% of the states' AFDC levels. Hence, Medicaid more explicitly became "welfare medicine" serving the families of unemployed mothers on cash assistance. In 1972, Congress took another step to curb growth by repealing the provision that had required states to expand Medicaid services and eligibility (Rose, 2013, p. 63).

Soon, however, other policy dynamics fueled Medicaid's expansion. From 1968 to 1972, federal and state Medicaid outlays nearly doubled (inflation-adjusted dollars) as

49 states gradually signed up for the program.[1] But Medicaid growth persisted beyond this start-up period, with outlays increasing by nearly 60% in constant dollars from 1972 through 1980. This latter growth substantially reflected an "unchecked" policy incrementalism that greatly enlarged Medicaid's role in providing long-term institutional care for the elderly and people with disabilities (Smith & Moore, 2008, p. 134). This incrementalism featured members of Congress approving a series of amendments, largely in response to lobbying by state officials. Each amendment appeared to be minor and attracted little public attention; minimal consideration was given to its potential cost. But in the aggregate these measures planted the seeds for rapid Medicaid growth.

The original Medicaid statute required participating states to provide skilled nursing home care. Medicaid's founders had envisioned that this care would have a substantial medical component and not extend to those who principally needed "custodial services" (such as the mentally ill and those with intellectual disabilities housed in state institutions). In 1967, however, Congress gave states the option to obtain Medicaid funds to serve people in intermediate care facilities (ICFs), which were more custodial than skilled nursing homes. Subsequent amendments in the early 1970s made ICFs serving the "mentally retarded" and psychiatric hospitals housing the mentally ill eligible for Medicaid payment. Policymakers in many states welcomed these measures as a source of fiscal relief. Whereas in the past states had to spend their own monies to assist people with disabilities, they could now obtain a hefty federal subsidy to do so.

The Triumph of Congressional Entrepreneurship (1981–1992)

This period highlights the role of the *policy entrepreneur* in defending and expanding Medicaid. Policy entrepreneurs can be "in or out of government, in elected or appointed positions, in interest groups or research organizations. But their defining characteristic, much as in the case of a business entrepreneur, is their willingness to invest their resources—time, energy, reputation, and sometimes money—in the hope of a future return" (Kingdon, 1984, p. 129). Few, if any, examples of policy entrepreneurship by a member of Congress exceed that of Representative Henry Waxman (D-California) during this period.

Ronald Reagan's arrival in the White House and the Republican takeover of the Senate in 1981 unleashed a concerted attempt to revamp and retrench Medicaid. Reagan's successor, Republican George H.W. Bush, also sought to pare the program. When the dust settled, however, Waxman not only had fended off these retrenchment initiatives; he had also laid the foundation for substantial Medicaid growth. Throughout the period, Democrats enjoyed substantial majorities in the House of Representatives, with Waxman chairing a subcommittee overseeing Medicaid. In this position, he skillfully exploited his role in the budgetary process to bolster the program. Space does not permit an exhaustive listing of the many Medicaid measures Waxman helped to engineer, but two examples capture the flavor of his efforts. In 1981, when the Reagan administration was laying siege to Medicaid, Waxman played a significant role in establishing Medicaid's Disproportionate Share Hospital (DSH) program (Smith

---

[1] Data on Medicaid expenditure growth primarily come from the Office of the Actuary, Department of Health and Human Services. Calculations are based on constant 2012 dollars. See www.cms/Research-Statistics-Data-and-Systems/StatisticsTrendsReports/NationalHealthExpendData/NationalHealthAccounts.html

& Moore, 2008, pp. 168–169). Under the DSH program, states could direct monies to hospitals that served uncommonly high numbers of the uninsured and Medicaid enrollees. Soon, certain states rushed to obtain subsidies for these hospitals, and DSH program spending grew rapidly to account for over 11% of Medicaid outlays by 1992 (Gusmano & Thompson, 2012, pp. 156, 161). So, too, Waxman worked with southern Democratic governors to expand eligibility for Medicaid. He secured passage of legislation that required all states to cover children younger than age 6 years and pregnant women with incomes up to 133% of poverty, and to phase in coverage for all poor children from 6 to 18 by 2002.

In part reflecting Waxman's policy entrepreneurship, federal and state Medicaid spending grew substantially between 1981 and 1992: by 16% during the first term of the Reagan administration, by 27% in its second term, and by a whopping 66% under President George H.W. Bush (inflation-adjusted dollars).

The Rise of Executive Federalism (1993–2008)

A pattern of executive federalism emerged under which presidents and their appointees, in cooperation with key governors, facilitated a transformation in Medicaid without congressional approval.

Congress continued to play an important role in shaping Medicaid during the Clinton and G. W. Bush administrations. For instance, passage of welfare reform legislation in 1996 and the Children's Health Insurance Program in 1997 further transformed Medicaid into a program for working families rather than those on cash assistance. On balance, however, the surging importance of the executive branch in policy processes stands out as the dominant theme of this period. In essence, a pattern of executive federalism emerged under which presidents and their appointees, in cooperation with key governors, facilitated a transformation in Medicaid without congressional approval (Gais & Fossett, 2005; Thompson, 2012). The soaring use of program waivers abetted the rise of executive federalism.

Waivers are a congressional delegation of authority to the executive branch to permit states to deviate from the ordinary requirements of law. Medicaid waivers assume two basic guises: demonstrations (Section 1115 of the Social Security Act) and more targeted initiatives focused on long-term care (Section 1915c). Demonstration authority gives the federal executive broad discretion to experiment with alternative state approaches to Medicaid. In contrast, the 1915(c) waivers seek to rebalance Medicaid long-term care away from nursing homes and other large institutions toward home and community-based services (HCBS). Before 1993, concerns about the cost neutrality of waivers and other factors undercut federal willingness to approve them. Federal administrators had, for instance, approved about 50 demonstration waivers since Medicaid's inception and seldom renewed them. The Reagan and first Bush administrations had been more willing to sign off on HCBS waivers, but states often found negotiations with the federal bureaucracy over waivers to be arduous and protracted. By 1992, HCBS spending still accounted for only 15% of Medicaid outlays for long-term care.

The arrival of the Clinton administration uncorked an outpouring of Medicaid waivers. Clinton unilaterally initiated administrative measures that made it much easier for states to obtain waivers, and the G. W. Bush administration followed suit. More than 40 states operated some facet of their program under a demonstration waiver by 2008 (Thompson, 2012). Many of these waivers were comprehensive and transformational. For instance, a bevy of states used them to move Medicaid enrollees into managed care while expanding coverage to new adult populations. Of particular note, negotiations between Massachusetts Governor Mitt Romney (R) over a Medicaid waiver yielded a plan for near-universal coverage in that state in 2006. The Massachusetts model became the template for the ACA. HCBS waivers also proliferated, with about 280 in effect by the time the Obama administration took office. Thanks largely to these waivers, HCBS grew to account for nearly 45% of all Medicaid spending on long-term care. Waivers were among the factors leading federal and state Medicaid outlays to more than double during this period (constant dollars).

Health Reform and Contentious Federalism (2009–2015)

The 2008 election gave Democrats control of the presidency and Congress, with substantial majorities in both legislative bodies. As in 1965, this fleeting period of party dominance ushered in a major policy breakthrough. Thus, the story of the policy process is largely about how Congress passed the ACA and why Medicaid became a key component of the law (primarily because it was cheaper than insuring the poor on the insurance exchanges). It is also a story about the courts. Of particular importance, a Supreme Court decision in 2012 effectively made state participation in the Medicaid expansion voluntary rather than required.

Important as Congress and the courts were in this period, themes of executive federalism and unilateral presidential action also persisted. After the 2010 election, gridlock rooted in a three-decade trend toward partisan polarization sidelined Congress from additional legislative action directed at Medicaid. Republicans, who regained control of the House of Representatives, repeatedly attempted to repeal the ACA, derail its implementation, and eviscerate funding for Medicaid. Faced with deeply entrenched Republican hostility in Congress, the Obama administration relied on executive branch action to get the ACA off the ground. In the case of the Medicaid expansion, the White House needed to persuade Republican policymakers in the states to sign up for the expansion. This promised to be a formidable challenge. As 2013 dawned, Republicans controlled the governorship and both houses of the legislature in 24 states. In six of 13 states with divided governments, Republicans occupied the governor's mansion.

The Obama administration pursued several strategies to defuse Republican opposition in the states (Thompson & Gusmano, 2014). As in the prior historical period, waivers loomed large. The ACA provided the executive branch with comprehensive waiver authority starting in 2017. In the meantime, the Obama administration used existing demonstration authority to serve its ends. In this regard, it bent over backward to accommodate states that wanted to enroll new Medicaid enrollees in the insurance exchanges or in other market-based arrangements. These alternative approaches to a traditional Medicaid expansion appealed to Republican policymakers in several states. By July 2014, four Republican-controlled states and seven with divided partisan control had expanded Medicaid. In three of them (Arkansas, Iowa, and Michigan) market-oriented waivers facilitated their participation. Meanwhile, two other Republican states, Indiana and Pennsylvania, indicated they would expand Medicaid if the Obama administration approved their market-flavored waiver requests.

MEDICAID RISING: OVERVIEW AND FUTURE CHALLENGES

Several factors have interacted over four historical periods to fuel supportive policy feedbacks leading to Medicaid's growth (Thompson, 2012). These include Medicaid's open-ended *funding formula,* which allows federal and state governments to leverage money from each other when they enlarge the program. Elected policymakers at the state and national levels can take political credit for expanding Medicaid while paying only part of the tab. So too, state officials, especially governors, became increasingly aware of their stake in the program and, with occasional lapses by Republican governors, formed an *intergovernmental lobby* to support the program. In addition, a panoply of *service providers and other advocates* (such as hospitals, nursing homes, managed care organizations, and disability rights organizations) became increasingly dependent on Medicaid and defended the program. Movement over time toward a *more positive social construction of Medicaid enrollees* has also contributed.[2] Medicaid's image as "welfare medicine" has faded as a shrinking share of its nondisabled enrollees receives cash assistance. Instead, Medicaid has emerged as a program for working people and as a safety net for middle-class individuals who need long-term care for themselves or loved ones due to aging or disability. So too, *skilled policy entrepreneurship* by Democrats in Congress, especially during the 1980s and in the politics triggering the ACA's passage, fueled growth. The *rise of waivers and executive federalism* has also played a role. The increased willingness of the executive branch to grant these waivers has facilitated state eligibility expansions (most dramatically so-called Romneycare in Massachusetts) and kindled the growth of HCBS. In cooperation with key gubernatorial allies, presidents employ waivers to overcome barriers to adaptation and innovation rooted in the supermajority bias of American governance, especially under divided government and intense partisan polarization.

The policy processes that have fueled Medicaid are not, of course, immutable. Changes in the political stream surrounding the program could precipitate retrenchment. This stream includes such factors as the "public mood . . . election results, partisan or ideological distributions in Congress and changes of administration" (Kingdon, 1984, p. 152). In this regard the growth of partisan polarization, especially the movement of the Republican party to the right, could vitiate Medicaid. It could stiffen the resistance of Republican policymakers in the states to the ACA's Medicaid expansion. It could also manifest itself if subsequent national elections leave Republicans in control of the presidency and Congress. After taking control of the House of Representatives in 2011, Republicans for two consecutive years passed budget resolutions that would not only repeal the ACA but convert Medicaid to a capped block grant with massively reduced funding. The Romney–Ryan ticket ran on this anti-Medicaid platform in the 2012 presidential election. After the reelection of President Obama, Republicans in the House persisted in their efforts to retrench Medicaid. In 2014, they approved a budget resolution that would convert Medicaid to a block grant and would slash spending on the program (along with CHIP) by 26% over 10 years. Whether a Republican-dominated government would retrench Medicaid—and the degree to which it would do so—remains an open question. However, the growing federal debt and the rise of partisan polarization heighten the risk of Medicaid falling.

---

[2] Public opinion surveys reveal substantial support for Medicaid (e.g., Rose, 2013, pp. 19–20).

■ Conclusion

The U.S. health system is in the midst of an extraordinary period of transition and transformation. The era of the solo physician is disappearing, replaced by larger and larger health systems. There is increasing debate over the best scope of practice for different groups of providers, as more and more nonphysicians (such as nurse practitioners and physician assistants) take on greater care responsibility. There are new entrants into the health care marketplace, including some of the nation's largest companies, such as Walmart, Apple, and Google. A major effort is underway to change the way we pay for health care services: The idea is to encourage value-based purchasing and pay for performance, rather than the traditional models that provide a preset fee for each service provided. An increased focus on care management especially targets the high-cost medical patient. Meanwhile, nearly every Fortune 1000 company is implementing its own version of an employee wellness program. Tying together all of these changes is a growing use of health information technology in an effort to encourage better communication between newly connected parts of the system.

All of these changes emerge from the ongoing effort to strike a balance among the quality of, access to, and cost of care. Those balancing strategies that are conducted within particular organizations are called *management*. Conversely, those external strategies implemented by government (through laws, regulations, overarching rules) are called *policy*.

This chapter has examined the ways that government sets policy in the health care arena. We began by reviewing government's growing role as a payer for health care services, primarily as an insurer for many of those not covered by the private coverage system, but also as partial financer (through the tax system) of the cost of private coverage itself. We then looked more closely at the policy process itself, emphasizing four key characteristics: (a) Each health program or problem domain typically has a relatively distinct policy subsystem; (b) the fragmented, supermajoritarian nature of America's governing institutions profoundly affects policy processes in the health care arena; (c) implementation is a critical part of the policy process markedly affecting who gets what from federal health programs; and (d) the establishment of health programs reconfigures policy subsystems and broader political factors in ways that affect program durability.

In the case of Medicaid policy, these four characteristics have combined to fuel extraordinary and unexpected program growth. In other issue areas, however, policy outcomes look quite different. Given the extraordinary changes now underway in the nation's health system, the task of the policy analyst and the policymaker could not be more important.

■ Discussion Questions

1. Should the government play a key role in aiding the uninsured, or should market forces reign supreme?
2. How should government finance its efforts to aid the uninsured?
3. How much control should government have over the private health insurance industry?
4. What is the right division of labor between the different branches of government, the private sector, and the individual consumer?

CASE STUDY

You are a staffer for the federal secretary of Health and Human Services. The secretary discusses with you the different ways that states have responded to the Medicaid expansion in the Affordable Care Act: Roughly two dozen states have adopted the expansion without much debate or negotiation; a few states, such as Arkansas, have negotiated special terms for their expanded programs (and are using Medicaid funding to buy private coverage for beneficiaries); and still other states, such as Texas, have simply refused to adopt the expansion. Your assignment is to prepare the secretary for her upcoming visit to Texas (and her meetings with the governor, the Medicaid director, and key interest group leaders) by writing a memorandum summarizing the political and policy dynamics of the proposed Medicaid expansion in Texas. Be sure your memo addresses questions such as the following:

1. Are the political reasons for not supporting Medicaid related to ideology about the role of government in health care, or are they more about potential long-run costs for the state budget?
2. How do the interests of hospitals, which would benefit from the extra revenue if Medicaid expands, affect the political and policy debates?
3. What is the role of public opinion in the choices being made by governors?
4. Will states feel differently about this issue over time and if the new insurance law seems to become a permanent fixture in public policy?

■ References

Annas, G., Law, S., Rosenblatt, R., & Wing, K. (1990). *American health law*. Boston, MA: Little, Brown & Co.

Blumenthal, D., & Morone, J. (2009). *The heart of power: Health and politics in the Oval Office*. Berkeley, CA: University of California Press.

Brown, L. D., & Sparer, M. S. (2001). Window shopping: State health reform politics in the 1990s. *Health Affairs, 20*, 50–67.

Brown, L. D., & Sparer, M. S. (2003). Poor program's progress: The unanticipated politics of Medicaid policy. *Health Affairs, 22*, 31–44.

Clemens-Cope, L., Garrett, B., & Hoffman, C. (2006). *Changes in employee health insurance coverage, 2001–2005*. Washington, DC: Kaiser Commission on Medicaid and the Uninsured.

Epstein, D., & O'Halloran, S. (1999). *Delegating powers: A transaction cost approach to policy making under separate powers*. New York, NY: Cambridge University Press.

Gais, T., & Fossett, J. (2005). Federalism and the executive branch. In J. D. Aberbach & M. A. Peterson (Eds.), *The executive branch* (pp. 486–524). New York, NY: Oxford University Press.

Gusmano, M. K., & Thompson, F. J. (2012). Safety-net hospitals at the crossroads: Whither Medicaid DSH? In M. A. Hall & S. Rosenbaum (Eds.), *The health care safety net in a post reform world* (pp. 153–182). New Brunswick, NJ: Rutgers University Press.

Holahan, J., & Liska, D. (1997). The slowdown in Medicaid growth: Will it continue? *Health Affairs, 16*, 157–163.

Jenkins-Smith, H. C., & Sabatier, P. A. (1993). The study of public policy processes. In P. A. Sabatier & H. C. Jenkins-Smith (Eds.), *Policy change and learning*. Boulder, CO: Westview Press.

Kaiser Commission on Medicaid and the Uninsured. (2014). *Medicaid Moving Forward*. Menlo Park, CA: Kaiser Commission on Medicaid and the Uninsured.

Kaiser Family Foundation. (2004). *Medicare advantage fact sheet*. Menlo Park, CA: Author.

Kaiser Family Foundation. (2010). Medicaid payments per enrollee, FY2007. *Kaiser State Facts*. Retrieved from http://www.statehealthfacts.org/comparemaptable.jsp?ind=183&cat=4

Kaiser Family Foundation. (2014). *Medicare advantage*. Menlo Park, CA: Author.

Kingdon, J. W. (1984). *Agendas, alternatives, and public policies*. Boston, MA: Little, Brown & Co.

Marmor, T. (2000). *The politics of Medicare* (2nd ed.). New York, NY: Aldine de Gruyter.

Oberlander, J. (2003). *The political life of Medicare*. Chicago, IL: University of Chicago Press.

Patashnik, E. M., & Zelizer, J. E. (2013). The struggle to remake politics: Liberal reform and the limits of policy feedback in the contemporary American state. *Perspectives on Politics, 11*(4), 1071–1087.

Robert Wood Johnson Foundation. (2007). *The state of the states*. Princeton, NJ: Author. Retrieved from http://www.rwjf.org/files/publications/bther/StateoftheStates2007.pdf

Rose, S. (2013). *Financing Medicaid: Federalism and the growth of America's health care safety net*. Ann Arbor, MI: University of Michigan Press.

Rosenbaum, S. (2013, August 6). Federal policy implementation under the Affordable Care Act: Six issues whose final resolution awaits, as implementation moves forward [Web log post]. Retrieved from http://healthreformgps.org/resources/federal-policy-implementation-under-the-affordable-care-act-six-issues-whose-final-resolution-awaits-as-implementation-moves-forward/

Smith, D. G., & Moore, J. G. (2008). *Medicaid politics and policy, 1965–2007*. New Brunswick, NJ: Transaction Books.

Sparer, M. S. (1996). *Medicaid and the limits of state health reform*. Philadelphia, PA: Temple University Press.

Sparer, M. S. (2003). Leading the health policy orchestra: The need for an intergovernmental partnership. *Journal of Health Politics, Policy and Law, 28*, 245–270.

The Boards of Trustees, Federal Hospital Insurance and Federal Supplementary Medical Insurance Trust Funds. (2014). *2014 Annual Report of the Boards of Trustees of the Federal Hospital Insurance and Federal Supplementary Medical Insurance Trust Funds*.

Thompson, F. J. (2012). *Medicaid politics: Federalism, policy durability, and health reform*. Washington, DC: Georgetown University Press.

Thompson, F. J., & Gusmano, M. K. (2014). The administrative presidency and fractious federalism: The case of Obamacare. *Publius, 44*(3), 426–450.

4 Comparative Health Systems

Michael K. Gusmano and Victor G. Rodwin

KEY WORDS

health system models

health system performance

national health insurance (NHI)

national health service (NHS)

National Institute for Health and Care Excellence (NICE)

LEARNING OBJECTIVES

- Understand the difference between NHI and NHS systems
- Highlight key features and issues in the health systems of Britain, France, Canada, and China
- View the U.S. health system from an international perspective

TOPICAL OUTLINE

- Looking abroad to promote self-examination at home
- Health system models
- NHS and NHI systems compared with the United States
- The health systems in England, Canada, France, and China
- Provider payment
- Coordination of care
- Workforce and information technology (IT)
- Health system performance
- Lessons

■ Overview

Public opinion polls regularly find that medical professionals and the public are dissatisfied with the system and believe major change is necessary.

Windows can sometimes be mirrors. A look at health systems abroad can enable us to develop a better understanding of our health system in the United States. An international perspective suggests that the United States has the most expensive health care system in the world, but unlike other wealthy countries, we fail to provide universal health insurance coverage and experience large inequities in access to primary and specialty care. Health care costs are often a source of financial strain, even bankruptcy, for people with serious illness (Hacker, 2006), and Americans suffer from high rates of mortality that could have been avoided with timely and appropriate access to a range of effective health care services (Nolte & McKee, 2012). There is also evidence that the U.S. health care system squanders resources and fails to address many of its population's health care needs. Not surprisingly, public opinion polls regularly find that medical professionals and the public are dissatisfied with the system and believe major change is necessary (Blendon, Benson, & Brulé, 2012).

LOOKING ABROAD TO PROMOTE SELF-EXAMINATION AT HOME

International comparisons of health care system performance remind us that there are workable alternatives to our current system. Examining other systems provides "the gift of perspective" and helps us to understand our own system "by reference to what it is like or unlike" (Marmor et al., 2005). As Rudolf Klein (1997, p. 1270) explains:

> Policy learning . . . is as much a process of self-examination—of reflecting on the characteristics of one's own country and health care system—as of looking at the experience of others . . . the experience of other countries is largely valuable insofar as it prompts a process of critical introspection by enlarging our sense of what is possible and adding to our repertoire of possible policy tools. For policy learning is not about the *transfer* of ideas or techniques . . . but about their adaptation to local circumstances. (emphasis in original)

This chapter attempts to provide a better understanding of the U.S. health care system by comparing it to health systems in wealthy countries, which share many characteristics in common, and by contrasting it to China, which is different. Our focus on wealthy nations draws on the experience of those belonging to an organization based in Paris that studies economic trends and policies and collects health data from member nations—the Organisation for Economic Co-operation and Development (OECD). We pay special attention to England,[1] which operates a national health service (NHS), and to Canada and France, which have national health insurance (NHI) systems. Our focus on China is an example of so-called BRIC nations (Brazil, Russia, India, and China) with large populations that have benefited from rapid economic growth over the past two decades and now are demanding access to state-of-the-art medical care.

Although England's NHS is one of the most public systems in the world, it also allows opportunities for private hospitals, private practice, and private insurance for those who prefer such options. Canada is frequently compared with the United States because of its physical proximity and similar political culture; until the mid-1960s, Canada's health care financing and delivery systems were nearly identical to those in the United States (Marmor et al., 2005). France's health system also shares many

---

[1] We focus on England, the largest constituent country within the United Kingdom because there are important differences among the NHS in Scotland, Wales, and Northern Ireland.

features with the U.S. health system. Like the United States, France relies on a multipayer system for financing care and offers a mix of public and private providers for delivering health care services. French citizens also enjoy freedom of choice among providers—to an even greater extent than Americans. The French experience (Rodwin & Contributors, 2006) suggests that it is possible to achieve universal coverage without adopting a single-payer NHI system, such as Canada's, or an NHS, as in England. China offers a more striking contrast to the United States. Despite its rapidly growing economy, China's national investments in public health and medical care are far smaller than those of OECD nations, and out-of-pocket payments represent roughly half of all health care expenditures. We conclude the chapter with some lessons of comparative experience for U.S. policymakers.

■ Health System Models

NHS systems, such as those in the United Kingdom, Sweden, Norway, Finland, Denmark, Portugal, Spain, Italy, and Greece, may be traced back to Lord Beveridge, who wrote the blueprint for the English NHS immediately after World War II. Although such systems are characterized by a dominant share of financing derived from general revenue taxes, this does not preclude other forms of financing. For example, the relative size of private financing and provision is much higher in Italy and Spain than in Sweden or Denmark. In England, 76% of NHS funding comes from general taxation, 18% from a payroll tax, and the remainder from private payments (Thomson, Osborn, Squires, & Reed, 2012, p. 33). Historically, NHI systems have had a more open-ended reimbursement system for health care providers, but this distinction is blurring as NHI systems are increasingly under pressure to operate within budget limits.

NHI systems may be traced back to Chancellor Otto von Bismarck, who established the first NHI program for salaried industrial workers in Germany in 1883. With the exception of Canada, whose dominant share of financing is from general tax revenues, these systems are characterized by payroll tax–based financing. In addition to income taxes, about a quarter of Canada's federal spending on health care comes from corporations. The provinces also supplement income and corporate taxes with additional sources of funding, such as sales, tobacco, and alcohol taxes. As with NHS systems, NHI systems are characterized by significant variation in their financing and organizational arrangements. For example, the share of French health care expenditures financed from general tax revenues has increased beyond 40% (Rodwin & Contributors, 2006).

Whether one's image of a health system is private and market-based, as in the United States and Switzerland; public and government-managed, as in the United Kingdom and Scandinavian nations; or at some intermediary point along such a continuum, as in France and Canada; it is possible to make some useful distinctions with respect to the public versus the private provision of health care and methods of financing of health services. Table 4.1 classifies health systems along these dimensions.

PROVISION OF HEALTH SERVICES

The arrangements for providing health care in Table 4.1 distinguish whether health services are delivered by the public, private not-for-profit, or private for-profit sector. Within these categories, many distinctions may be added. For example, some publicly

TABLE 4.1 HEALTH SYSTEM PROVISION AND FINANCING

Provision	Financing			
	Government A	Social Security/NHI B	Private Insurance C	Out-of-Pocket D
Government Owned A	1	2	3	4
Private Nonprofit/ Quasi-Government B	5	6	7	8
Private For-Profit C	9	10	11	12

capitalized organizations (row A) are national (VHA), others are subnational (state mental hospitals), and many are local (municipal hospitals). Likewise, the not-for-profit category may include a variety of quasi-public organizations, such as hospital trusts in Britain (row B). The for-profit form of provision (row C), a distinctive sub-category in the United States, includes private for-profit hospitals and managed care organizations (MCOs) that sell ownership shares to investors through stock markets. Indeed, the growth of large investor-owned MCOs distinguishes the United States from most other OECD nations.

FINANCING

The four methods of raising revenues to pay for health services correspond to columns A through D:

- A: General revenue financing through the fiscal tax system
- B: Compulsory payroll tax financing through the Social Security (payroll tax) system
- C: Voluntary premiums assessed by private health insurance companies
- D: Individual out-of-pocket payments

There are, of course, other methods and sources of financing, particularly for capital expenditures, such as direct employer contributions and philanthropic funds. But these are no longer dominant sources of health care financing.

Although all countries rely on these four sources of revenue to finance health care services, most developed countries have adopted one of two distinct models for financing care. In NHS systems, the government uses its resources to operate most, if not all, of the delivery system. In NHI systems, revenue is most often raised through payroll taxes to fund a social insurance program that reimburses health care providers for services rather than paying for health care directly through the government's budget.

In contrast to England, Canada, and France, China and the United States rely, to varying degrees, on subnational and local governments to finance health care. In Canada, provinces and territories administer universal health insurance programs and the federal government provides block grants that account for approximately 20% of health care expenditures. To qualify for the federal funds, provincial and territorial health insurance systems must meet five criteria specified by the Canada Health Act of 1984. They must be (a) administered on a nonprofit basis by a public authority; (b) comprehensive in the sense that they must cover most health services provided by hospitals, medical practitioners, or dentists; (c) universal in that all legal Canadian residents are covered; (d) portable so that coverage for all residents in each province or territory is transferable to all other parts of Canada; and (e) accessible, although "reasonable access" is not defined in the law.

In 2009, China adopted a reform that seeks to provide health insurance for all of its population. Although China already provides some minimal health insurance to the majority of its population, coverage remains extremely limited and, as we noted earlier, more than half of all spending on health care still comes from out-of-pocket payments (Table 4.1, column D). In terms of public funding for health care, China relies—to an even greater extent than Canada—on subnational government revenues to finance the country's three national health insurance funds.

Below the national government, China has provincial, regional, and local governments. By the mid-1990s, these subnational government authorities financed 80% to 90% of total government spending on social services, including health care (Hipgravel et al., 2012). The adoption of health reform has increased central government contributions to health care, but local government taxes and out-of-pocket payments from individual patients still represent the two largest sources of revenue. As of 2012, provincial and local government revenues financed 78% of health care expenditures (Fabre, 2013). This approach has exacerbated the large economic disparities between the wealthier coastal provinces and the poorer rural provinces in western China. The national government has attempted to address the country's rural–urban disparities, but with limited success (Jian, Chan, Reidpath, & Xu, 2010).

■ NHS and NHI Systems Compared With the United States

Table 4.1 enables one to highlight key features of NHS and NHI systems and to adopt an international perspective on the U.S. health care system. The most striking difference between the United States and NHS or NHI systems is that the United States—even after passage of the Patient Protection and Affordable Care Act of 2010 (ACA)—includes large elements of financing that are based on actuarial principles whereby private insurance premiums (column C) are set with respect to estimated risk. In contrast, in NHS and NHI systems, most health care financing is based on ability to pay (columns A and B). Ability-to-pay criteria lead to wealthier, younger, and healthier individuals paying disproportionately to finance the care of poorer, older, and sicker individuals. Aside from this important distinction, a look at box 1 through box 12 suggests that most health care systems have elements of many boxes ranging from socialized medicine (box 1) to out-of-pocket payment for private practitioners and hospitals (box 12).

The United States has neither an NHS nor an NHI system. Instead, the U.S. health care system relies on a patchwork of public and private insurance with large gaps in coverage (see Chapter 3). Its enormous pluralism exhibits components of its health system within each of the boxes in Table 4.1. It uses a social insurance system for older people and for those with permanent disabilities (Medicare: columns A and B); a social welfare system for some people with low incomes (Medicaid and CHIP, column B); and a subsidized employer-based private health insurance system for a large, but shrinking percentage of salaried employees in the private and public sectors (column C). Along with its public and private insurance programs, the United States has elements of socialized medicine (publicly funded and provided programs in box 1), such as the military health care system, the Veterans Health Administration (VHA) system, and the Indian Health Service (IHS) for Native American and Alaskan Native people.

■ The Health Systems in England, Canada, France, and China

After World War II, governments have gradually extended their role in the financing and provision of health services.

Beyond the differences we have noted between NHI and NHS systems, these systems have evolved in similar directions. After World War II, governments have gradually extended their role in the financing and provision of health services. What was once largely the responsibility of the family, philanthropy, religious institutions, employers, and local governments has largely been taken over by national and subnational governments—a trend that has accompanied the rise of the welfare state (de Kervasdoué, Kimberly, & Rodwin, 1984). This evolution has affected all wealthy OECD nations and, increasingly, BRIC and less developed nations. The U.S. reliance on employer-based private health insurance—even after the implementation of the ACA—is an important contrast to NHI and NHS systems. Yet even in the United States recent decades have seen an expansion of public insurance and a decline in employer-based coverage.

The growth of government involvement in health systems has characterized OECD nations during the great boom years of health sector growth (1950s and 1960s), when governments encouraged hospital construction and modernization, workforce training, and biomedical research. It continued in the 1970s, when the goals of OECD countries shifted more in the direction of rationalization and cost containment (Rodwin, 1984). In the early 21st century, public and private health insurance has become the dominant source for funding health care, and public expenditure on health care services, along with education and Social Security, has become one of the largest categories of social expenditure as a share of gross domestic product (GDP).

In contrast to these trends in OECD nations, by the end of the 1970s China moved from a health system dominated by public financing to one that is now dominated by private, out-of-pocket payments. Between 1949 and the early 1980s, the Chinese health system was financed largely by the central government and state-owned enterprises (Valentine, 2005). In 1978, Deng Xiaoping called for market reforms. The central government reduced its share of national health care spending from 32% to 15%

(Blumenthal & Hsiao, 2005). It slashed subsidies to public hospitals and introduced market mechanisms in health care, resulting in rapid growth of out-of-pocket payments and income-based inequities.

By the late 1990s, Chinese officials increased investment in public health to address growing disparities between rural and urban areas. Efforts to improve the public health and primary care systems accelerated after the outbreak of SARS in late 2002. By the end of 2003, more than 5,000 people were infected with SARS and 349 people died (Smith, 2006), thus exposing the weaknesses of the public health system. Since 2009, China has continued to expand the role of government through the creation of new public insurance schemes and the adoption of new public health regulations (Wang, Gusmano, & Cao, 2011).

In addition to the growth of government's role in health care, most OECD nations must confront common challenges and exhibit distinct approaches for many issues. We illustrate how this is so by comparing the health systems of England, Canada, France, and China with respect to (a) provider payment, (b) coordination of care, (c) workforce and IT, and most importantly, (d) health system performance.

PROVIDER PAYMENT

All countries rely on multiple methods for paying physicians and hospitals. NHS systems traditionally have relied more on salaried and capitation forms of payment for physicians and budgets for hospitals. In the English NHS, about two thirds of general practitioners (GPs) and dentists work as independent contractors reimbursed through a blended payment system, 75% from capitation payment and most of the rest (20%) from fee-for-service (FFS) payments based on performance. Since 2012, GPs have been placed in charge of clinical commissioning groups (CCGs), which control about 70% of the NHS budget. CCGs are responsible for purchasing hospital and specialty medical care services for their patients. The NHS first introduced a prospective payment system for reimbursing public and private hospitals in 2003 and, in April 2004, phased in a new national tariff system. Since 2012, the NHS has adopted a Payment by Results (PbR) system based on the average cost of providing the procedure or the treatment across the NHS as a whole.

Historically, Canadian primary care physicians have been paid on an FFS basis. The Ministries of Health for all provinces and territories are responsible for negotiating an annual physician fee schedule based on a relative value scale (RVS) for each reimbursable procedure or code. The RVS may be based on a resource-based fee schedule (RBFS), which tries to capture the inputs required to provide the service, or on historical charges. Studies have found wide variation in fee schedules across Canada (Roth & Adams, 2009). In more recent years, some provinces have experimented with blended capitation schemes in family health networks, family health teams, and family health organizations. Blended capitation relies on age- and gender-adjusted payments, coupled with financial incentives to follow "evidence-based" guidelines and FFS when physicians treat nonenrolled patients (HealthForceOntario, 2014).

In France, physicians in the ambulatory sector and in private hospitals are reimbursed on the basis of a fee schedule negotiated among physician associations, NHI funds, and the government. Approximately 15% of all physicians (and 25% of those in private office–based practice) selected the option to extra-bill beyond the negotiated fees that represent payment in full for all other physicians. These figures vary by specialty, with the highest rates of extra-billing among specialists in comparison to GPs. Physicians who have opted to extra-bill may do so as long as their charges are set with "tact and measure," a standard that has never been legally defined but which has been found, empirically, to represent a 50% to 100% increase to the negotiated fees. Physicians based in public hospitals are remunerated on a part-time or full-time salaried basis, and those in private for-profit hospitals may bill the NHI based on the negotiated fees.

Before 1984, public hospitals in France were reimbursed on the basis of a retrospective, cost-based, per diem fee; after that, they were placed on global budgets that were later gradually adjusted for patient case mix in the 1990s. Private for-profit hospitals used to be reimbursed on the basis of a negotiated per diem fee; in the 1990s the per diem payments were also gradually adjusted for their case mix. The basis for case-based adjustment in France is an adaptation of the U.S. Diagnosis Related Group (DRG) categories known in France as GHM (groupes homogènes de malades). The most recent modification was introduced in 2004 (Schreyögg et al., 2006), when activity-based payment (ABP) was introduced to create a level playing field for reimbursement of acute-care services among public and private hospitals. As of 2012, the reimbursement system for public and private hospitals has been completely aligned based on the national ABP tariffs, which take into account each hospital's historical costs. This has resulted in expected activity growth, which in turn, results in downward price adjustments because annual hospital costs are constrained by national and regional hospital expenditure targets (Or, 2010).

In China, the expansion of health insurance is changing the nature of provider payment, but by the end of 2013 about half of physician payments to health care providers still came from FFS payments. Subnational governments in China regulate prices in an effort to make health care affordable and, during the past decade, provincial and local governments, with encouragement from the central government, have introduced such incentives as pay-for-performance based on treatment protocols to improve quality (Yip et al., 2010). Although the central government hopes that the expansion of health insurance will limit hospital reliance on kickback payments from medical device and pharmaceutical companies, such payments continue to be an important source of revenue for Chinese health care providers (Wang et al., 2011).

> *Two of the distinguishing characteristics of the U.S. health care system are that the United States does not operate within a budget and does not negotiate prices with providers as aggressively as other countries.*

In comparison to England, Canada, France, and China, the United States pays significantly higher prices for medical care. Although there is a vigorous debate about the factors that drive U.S. health care spending, consensus is emerging that price is the most important factor in explaining why the United States spends so much more than any other health care system in the world (Anderson, Frogner, Johns, & Reinhardt, 2006). Two of the distinguishing characteristics of the U.S. health care system are that the United States does not operate within a budget and does not negotiate prices with providers as aggressively as other countries.

COORDINATION OF CARE

All countries suffer from problems of coordination among hospitals and community-based services. They differ, nonetheless, with regard to the size and nature of their delivery systems. France, for example, has more practicing doctors per 1,000 population (3.3) than the United Kingdom (2.8), the United States (2.5), Canada (2.4), or China (1.5) (OECD, 2013). France also has more hospital beds per 1,000 population (6.2) than the United States (3.1), the United Kingdom (3.0), Canada (2.8), or China (2.7) (OECD, 2013).

Since its creation in 1948, the NHS has been one of the largest public service organizations in Europe. With more than one million employees, more than 2,500 hospitals, and a host of intermediary health care organizations, the NHS poses an awesome managerial challenge (Klein, 2013). Perhaps because Britain has fewer health care resources than most OECD nations, the British have been more aggressive in weeding out inefficiency than other, wealthier countries. Because the NHS faces the same demands as other systems to make technology available and to care for an increasingly aged population, British policymakers recognize they must pursue innovations that improve efficiency. But numerous obstacles have arisen: opposition by professional bodies, difficulties in firing and redeploying health care personnel, and not least, the tripartite structure of the NHS, which, since its inception, has created an institutional separation among hospitals, general practitioners, and community health programs. This separation is reinforced further by the fact that local authorities are responsible for a great deal of prevention and health promotion, as well as social care, making it difficult to integrate hospital and community-based care.

In Canada less separation exists between physicians and hospitals because specialists are paid FFS and work both in community-based practice and hospitals. Hospitals are largely private nonprofit institutions with their own governing boards, but they are almost entirely publicly financed and subject to tight budget constraints. Most community-based physicians must refer their patients requiring diagnostic procedures and testing, as well as more specialized care, to local hospitals, which can lead to extended waiting times for elective procedures and problems in ensuring optimal coordination between hospital specialists and community-based providers.

France also faces problems with the coordination of care between hospitals and community-based providers. There is inadequate communication between full-time, salaried physicians in public hospitals and solo physicians working in private practice. Although GPs have informal referral networks to specialists and public hospitals, no formal institutional relationships exist to ensure continuity of medical care, disease prevention and health promotion services, posthospital follow-up care, or systematic linkages and referral patterns among primary-, secondary-, and tertiary-level services. Schoen et al. (2012) document that the French health care system is characterized by poor hospital discharge planning and a lack of coordination among medical providers.

In China, before 1978 the health care delivery system in rural areas was organized by communes, which provided housing, education, and social services, as well as basic medical care. An important feature of the communes' Cooperative Medical System was the staff of paraprofessionals known as "barefoot doctors" (Rosenthal & Greiner, 1982). Most of the barefoot doctors were young peasants who received a few months of training and offered basic primary and preventive care, including health education.

If the needs of patients were more complex, the barefoot doctors would refer them to physicians at the commune health centers or, if necessary, to the closest hospital. In urban areas, the health care delivery system relied heavily on so-called first-level hospitals, community clinics with a modest inpatient capacity, to provide ambulatory care.

With the introduction of market mechanisms in the health sector after 1978, the government ended its barefoot doctor program in rural areas, leaving the population in rural China without adequate access to health care services. It also reduced its subsidies to state-owned first-level hospitals; forced to become more self-reliant, these hospitals withdrew public health and primary health care services. Some first-level hospitals went bankrupt, and those that survived turned to profitable medical services rather than emphasize primary care and prevention.

WORKFORCE AND INFORMATION TECHNOLOGY

Primary care vs. specialty care balance. In most OECD health care systems, at least half of physicians are in primary care. The United States stands out, in contrast, because about 70% of physicians are specialists, and only about 30% are in primary care. The situation in China is far more dramatic. Only 57% of cities in China had a community-based primary care organization, and more than 40% of the population reports that it does not have convenient access to a primary care center (Wang et al., 2011). In addition, most general practitioners lack additional training after receiving their undergraduate medical education.

Primary care is important because systems with a higher concentration of primary care practitioners improve coordination and continuity of care. Access to an effective system of primary care appears to result in higher life expectancy projection at birth, lower infant mortality, lower mortality from all causes, lower disease-specific mortality, and higher self-reported health status (Starfield, Shi, & Macinko, 2005).

Workforce shortages/surpluses. Concerns about the adequacy of primary care in the United States are reinforced by discussions about the adequacy of the health and social care workforce in the face of rapid population aging (Carrier, Yee, & Stark, 2011). Increases in Alzheimer's disease and other forms of dementia in particular have raised concerns about the extent to which the health and long-term care systems will have a sufficient number of physicians, nurses, and other medical professionals to address the needs of an aging society (Warshaw & Bragg, 2014).

Although a shortage of clinicians, particularly in primary care, is the major concern in the United States, France, and China, some countries in Europe, particularly England, now wonder whether they may have too many doctors and nurses. Before the global economic crisis began in 2008, many OECD countries adopted policies designed to increase their supply of medical professionals. After the economic slowdown, many countries expressed concern about an "oversupply" of some health care workers (Ono, Lafortune, & Schoenstein, 2013).

Starting in 2000, for example, the English National Health Service adopted a workforce redesign initiative to increase the number of doctors and nurses in the system, expand the roles of existing professionals, and redistribute responsibilities to rely more on teams of health care professionals. As a result, there is now concern that the country may have too many hospital specialists, but there are persistent concerns that it still does not have a large enough supply of well-trained social care workers, particularly for providing home care to older patients (Bohmer & Imison, 2013). Similarly, a recent assessment of health care needs in Ontario, Canada, concluded that there will be an aggregate surplus of GPs and specialists in 20 years, even though some specialties and areas may experience shortages (Singh et al., 2010).

The push for electronic medical records and other forms of health care IT. Throughout the world, policymakers are searching for ways to reduce health care spending while improving the quality of care. The use of electronic health records and other forms of health information technology (HIT) are often touted as solutions to these problems. Harvey Fineberg (2012), the president of the Institute of Medicine, argues that over the long term HIT will improve the quality and efficiency of the health care system. Marmor and Oberlander (2012, p. 1217) dismiss the focus on HIT as a "fad" and suggest that the desire to find a "big fix" to the problems of cost and quality has led policy makers to embrace technical and managerial solutions, including the adoption of HIT, along with various forms of managed care, health planning, and payment reforms designed to align the incentives of providers and patients with public health goals.

This argument supports James Morone's (1993) thesis that the United States tends to search for a "painless prescription" to the major challenges in health care. Indeed, comparative analysis suggests that such technical solutions to the problems of cost and quality as HIT have had little effect on cost or quality in health care and that the United States should focus on more important structural features of other health care systems, such as global budgets, fee schedules, systemwide payment rules, and concentrated purchasing power.

Advocates of HIT argue that newer developments in the use of so-called big data are more likely to transform medical practice because of their capacity to link information among many institutions within a health care system. They also argue that the United States has never adopted HIT on a widespread basis, so the failure of previous efforts to improve quality or lower costs is not sufficient evidence that HIT cannot contribute to these goals in the future.

It seems plausible to suggest that HIT may be a valuable tool for addressing costs and quality in health care, but its value surely depends on the policy context in which it is used. For England, Canada, and France, HIT may further enhance the efficiency of resource allocation by providing administrators, providers, and patients with access to better information. In the United States, however, the effect of HIT within the context of a fragmented, open-ended financing system may be far more limited. Viewed from this perspective, it is easier to understand the arguments of those who remain skeptical of HIT's importance.

HEALTH SYSTEM PERFORMANCE

Policymakers and researchers often want to compare the performance of different systems and identify lessons for health policy. Although these efforts have generated important information, they have often succumbed to the temptation of devising a composite indicator to rank health care systems against one another (Oliver, 2012). This practice encourages lavish attention from the media on the search for the best health care system, the new holy grail of performance assessments. Unfortunately, such an approach lacks any effort to understand, assess, and compare health care systems in relation to the cultural context, values, and institutions within which performance indicators are embedded.

The study of health system performance by the World Health Organization (WHO) is the most prominent example of the composite indicator approach to the comparative analysis of health systems (WHO, 2000). WHO ranked the health systems of 191 member states based on weighted measures of five objectives: (a) maximizing population health (as calculated by disability-adjusted life expectancy, or DALE); (b) reducing inequalities in population health; (c) maximizing health system responsiveness; (d) reducing inequalities in responsiveness; and (e) financing health care equitably.

Although controversial because of its many methodological flaws and missing data, the WHO report generated tremendous discussion about health system performance and the criteria that should be used to assess it (Musgrove, 2003). Some of the controversy generated by the report can be attributed to complaints from countries unhappy with their ranking, but prominent academics also criticized the study for relying on incomplete and inadequate data, as well as on questionable methods (Williams, 2001).

WHO's use of DALE as a measure of health status illustrates the problem of using population health status to assess the performance of health care systems. DALE includes causes of mortality that are amenable to health care as well as a host of social determinants of health. As a result, this measure is not "related directly to the health care system" (Nolte & McKee, 2003, p. 1129). Using DALE, life expectancy at birth and infant mortality are inadequate measures of health system performance because the role of health care in improving population health is small compared with interventions aimed at social and environmental determinants.

As Bradley and Taylor (2013) argue, one reason the United States performs so poorly on such indicators is because it has failed to invest sufficiently in education, housing, employment, and other social programs that help to produce and sustain good health. Between those who emphasize the decisive effect of social determinants of health and those who focus on access to health care, there is a middle ground: attention not only to the consequences of poor social conditions, but also to barriers in access to what we have called effective health care services.

There is a vast literature that measures inequities in access to health care (see Chapter 2). Such studies rely either on comparisons of inputs (e.g., physicians, hospital beds) or on administrative or self-reported survey data to measure service utilization. An alternative approach attempts to capture the consequences of poor access to disease prevention, primary care, and specialty services—in other words, mortality amenable to health care (amenable mortality). Of course, few causes of death are entirely amenable, or not amenable to health care, and as medical therapies improve even more deaths may be classified as potentially avoidable. Nevertheless, based on an OECD study, this summary provides convincing evidence that the United States is not performing well in comparison to other wealthy nations (Gay, Paris, Devaux, & de Looper, 2011).

Crossnational analysis of trends in avoidable mortality indicate that avoidable deaths have declined much faster over the last three decades than other causes of mortality (Nolte & McKee, 2012). This result lends further credence to the validity of avoidable mortality as an indicator for the effectiveness of public health interventions and medical care. We have used this measure to compare the health systems in megacities located within four of the countries we highlight in this chapter: London, New York, Paris, and Shanghai (Gusmano, Weisz, & Rodwin, 2009).

Through accountable care organizations (ACOs) in the United States (see Chapter 11) and various forms of disease management and integrated service delivery proposals in other countries, health care professionals are being encouraged to think about population, as well as individual, health. The effort to shift health systems in this direction is a positive development, but if we hope to understand the performance of health care systems and the relationship between health care inputs and health outputs, it is important to select such indicators as amenable mortality, which are more closely related to the performance of these systems than are broad measures of health such as life expectancy and DALEs.

The extensive criticism of WHO's effort to evaluate health system performance has not discouraged other groups from taking similar approaches. The Commonwealth Fund has a project designed to identify high-performing health systems within the United States and other wealthy nations. It also draws on more dependable data than WHO's for its assessments, in part because its scope is more limited and focuses on nations for which population, health, and health system data are more readily available. For example, the Commonwealth Fund supplements many of the same data sources used by WHO with original surveys of patients and primary care providers fielded by Harris Interactive.

The Commonwealth Fund (2014) uses these survey results, along with a host of other data sources, to compare U.S. national averages on health outcomes, quality, access, efficiency, and equity to "benchmarks," which represent the performance on these measures "achieved by top-performing groups" (Schoen, Davis, How, & Schoenbaum, 2006). In some cases, the "top-performing groups" are other countries. In other cases, they are regions, states, or health plans within the United States. Despite the more reliable empirical analysis and its contribution to stimulating attention to health care systems abroad, this study's use of a single national scorecard to evaluate the performance of the U.S. health system shares many of the same problems highlighted by WHO's effort to rank health systems on the basis of criteria about which policymakers rarely agree.

Access to services across income groups. An important dimension of health system performance is the extent to which a system provides access to health care services by income group. In contrast to the United States, countries with universal or near-universal coverage enjoy a relatively equitable distribution of primary care visits (Van Doorslaer, Masseria, & the OECD Health Equity Research Group Members, 2004). Lower-income residents of Australia, Canada, New Zealand, and the United Kingdom, for example, are less likely to report barriers to health care than people with below-median incomes in the United States (Blendon et al., 2002). Comparative studies that examine hospitalizations for ambulatory care sensitive conditions (ACSC), a measure of access to timely and effective primary care, find that rates are much lower in Canada, England, France, and Germany than in the United States and inequalities in rates of ACSC are smaller in these countries (Billings, Anderson, & Newman, 1996; Gusmano, Rodwin, & Weisz, 2014; Roos, Walld, Uhanova, & Bond, 2005).

A concern often voiced by conservative analysts in the United States is that so-called government-run health care systems, by which they mean both NHS and NHI systems, "ration" care (Goodman, Musgrave, & Herrick, 2004). Because such systems operate within a budget, these analysts claim, they must limit access to specialty and surgical health care services in ways that are unacceptable. This claim is supported by studies that compare access to certain expensive health care services in England and the United States (Aaron, Schwartz, & Cox, 2005). Although there is evidence that some expensive technologies, including revascularization and kidney dialysis, are used less frequently in England than in the United States (Gusmano & Allin, 2011), this is not the case with respect to France or Germany. For example, after controlling for need, the use of revascularization (coronary artery bypass and angioplasty) is comparable in France, Germany, and the United States (Gusmano et al., 2014).

Even among countries that provide universal coverage there are differences in access to specialty services by socioeconomic status. Residents of higher-income neighborhoods in Winnipeg, Canada, a country that strives to eliminate financial barriers to care, receive "substantially more" specialty and surgical care than lower-income residents of the city (Roos & Mustard, 1997). In France, Germany, and England, access to some specialty health care services is significantly worse among residents of lower-income neighborhoods (Gusmano, Weisz, & Rodwin, 2009). Inequalities in access to health care are even greater in BRIC countries and developing nations. Despite remarkable economic growth in recent decades, for example, there are flagrant disparities in access to health care within China.

Cost. As was evident during the debates over the ACA, there is a widely shared belief among American policymakers that a national program providing for universal entitlement to health care in the United States would result in runaway costs. In response to this presumption, nations that entitle all of their residents to a high level of medical care, while spending less on administration and on health care than the United States, are often held up as models. The Canadian health system is the most celebrated example. French NHI is another case in point. England's NHS, although typically considered a "painful prescription" for the United States (Aaron, Schwartz, & Cox, 2005), nevertheless ensures first-dollar coverage for basic health services to its entire population and, as we have seen, spends less than half as much on health care, as a percent of GDP, and approximately one half as much per capita as in the United States (Table 4.2). Huang (2011) expects that China's total health care expenditures will increase rapidly over the coming decade, but its current spending, as a percent of GDP, is far below the OECD average.

Stories in the media often suggest that pressures from population aging will render existing welfare state commitments, including the Medicare and Medicaid programs in the United States, unsustainable. Despite these concerns, most studies

TABLE 4.2 HEALTH CARE EXPENDITURE AS A SHARE OF GDP: SELECTED COUNTRIES, 2011

	Health Expenditure as a Share of GDP, 2011
United States	17.7%
France	11.6%
Canada	11.2%
United Kingdom	9.4%
OECD Average	9.3%
China	5.2%

Source: Organization for Economic Co-operation and Development (2013).

conclude there is no correlation between the percentage of the older population (65 years and over) and health care expenditures as a percent of GDP. The United States, which spends more on health care than any country in the world, is among the OECD countries with the youngest age cohorts. In contrast, Britain, Italy, Sweden, Germany, and France, with older populations than the United States, spend a far lower percentage of GDP on health care. Even if one excludes the United States and examines only the European Union, there is no correlation between population aging and health care spending.

Crossnational analysis of health care expenditure data indicates that, after controlling for income, age has little effect on national health care expenditures. Proximity to death, not age, leads to an increase in health spending (Moon, 1996). An analysis of health spending on older people in Switzerland found that expenditures are concentrated in the last few months of life (Zweifel, Felder, & Meiers, 1999). Although the OECD projects that "age-related spending for the average country will rise by around 6 to 7 percentage points of GDP between 2000 and 2050," they acknowledge that "part of this pressure is a result of cost pressures from advances in medical technologies, rather than ageing per se" (Australian Department of the Treasury, 2007).

Price, volume, and technology diffusion are the most important factors that drive health care costs; as noted earlier, however, high U.S. prices explain why the U.S. health care system is so expensive relative to other nations (Anderson et al., 2006). Although Americans spend more than any other nation, health service use in the United States is actually below the median for the OECD on most measures. A study for the McKinsey Global Institute (Angrisano, Farrell, Kocher, Laboissiere, & Parker, 2007), based on four diseases, provides further support for the role of prices in driving up U.S. health care costs. The study found that in 1990, Americans spent about 66% more per capita on health care than Germans but received 15% fewer real health care resources.

In addition to understanding the factors that drive health care spending, it is important to confront the question: How much spending on health care is too much? Most health economists argue that there is no right amount of money to spend on health care. Cutler (2007) argues that we should focus less on the level of health care expenditure and pay greater attention to whether the expenditures generate more benefits than costs. However, efforts to adopt explicit economic evaluation of health technology provoked controversy in the United States. The ACA forbids federal government agencies from using cost as a criterion for making coverage decisions. Among the countries compared in this chapter, France, Canada, and England, to varying degrees, all use economic evaluations of health technology to make coverage decisions. In France, economic evaluations of new drugs are recommended but not required (Sorenson, 2009). In Canada, these efforts are more decentralized than in England, and "only a handful" of technologies are subject to cost-effectiveness analysis (Menon & Stafinski, 2009). In England, NICE focuses on new technologies only and is reputed to be the leading health technology assessment agency worldwide.

NICE, established in 1999 in response to growing concerns about variations in the use of new technology, is supposed to meet three primary objectives: (a) to reduce unwarranted variation in prescribing patterns across England and Wales, principally through setting practice guidelines; (b) to encourage the diffusion and uptake of effective health technologies; and (c) to ensure value for money for NHS investment by assessing the cost effectiveness of selected interventions. Record increases in NHS expenditures throughout the decade following 2000 were linked to meeting these objectives, particularly in terms of directing spending to facilitate widespread and uniform access to the most cost-effective treatments.

NICE prides itself on its transparency, methodological rigor, stakeholder inclusiveness, consistency, independence from government, and timeliness, all of which appear necessary to secure the legitimacy and effectiveness of its recommendations. Since 2003, it has been mandatory for local NHS purchasers and providers to act on all positive recommendations on technology appraisals (i.e., recommendations that specific health care interventions be made available in the NHS) within 3 months of their publication.

NICE arrives at conclusions about whether interventions are therapeutically beneficial and cost-effective compared with other relevant alternatives by reviewing a range of available evidence, assembled and synthesized by a publicly funded network of academic institutions. The role of social values in the appraisal process is increasingly apparent as NICE reviews complex cases, for instance, on whether select end-of-life cancer drugs be made available to NHS patients despite their offering insufficient value for money with respect to conventionally accepted thresholds of cost-effectiveness.

There is some evidence that widespread adoption of NICE recommendations for specific technologies, particularly cancer drugs and the use of varenicline for smoking cessation, has reduced geographic variations in access to the technologies (Chalkidou, 2009). Also, there is evidence that NICE guidance has increased costs to the NHS, which is not surprising because most cost-effective interventions are more expensive than the alternatives. This does not bode well for those in the United States who hope that economic evaluation of health technology will contain the growth of health care costs, particularly if assessment efforts are disproportionately focused on new, expensive technologies. Chalkidou (2009) estimates that since its creation, NICE's decisions have cost more than £1.5 billion a year. In this context, it should be noted that cost containment was never one of NICE's explicit objectives.

Quality. The focus on quality is a relatively recent phenomenon. For many years, the primary concern of most policymakers, particularly in developed countries, was on overcoming financial barriers to the health care system. In 2002, the OECD created the Health Care Quality Indicators (HCQI) project to develop and implement a set of international indicators. The project includes representatives from 23 of the 30 OECD nations, as well as a number of international partners, including the Commonwealth Fund, the Nordic Council of Ministers Quality Project, and the International Society for Quality in Health Care (ISQua). The project team identified five priority areas for monitoring quality: (a) cardiac care, (b) diabetes mellitus, (c) mental health, (d) patient safety, and (e) primary care and prevention/health promotion. The OECD secretariat asked participating countries to identify expert panelists to review potential indicators (Mattke, Epstein, & Leatherman, 2006). The panels were charged with reviewing existing indicators rather than developing entirely new measures. They used a consensus process and selected 86 indicators on the basis of relevance—including the extent to which the health system can influence the indicator—scientific soundness, and feasibility. Not surprisingly, the project has identified significant variation in quality as measured by these indicators (OECD, 2010).

Even in countries with relatively well-developed health data systems, it is often difficult to link data with unique patient identifiers in ways that allow researchers and policymakers to understand quality of care across different episodes of care and different providers.

Some quality indicators, such as leaving a foreign body inside patients during surgery, follow directly from the literature on medical errors that can be influenced by a health system. The relationships between health system quality and other indicators, however, are controversial. For example, higher rates of 5-year survival among patients diagnosed with breast or cervical cancer may reflect better access to high-quality cancer care. It is possible, however, that these outcomes may reflect more aggressive efforts to diagnose patients with cancer and have little to do with the quality of care patients receive. Beyond these conceptual issues, countries continue to struggle with a lack of relevant data for quality monitoring. Even in countries with relatively well-developed health data systems, it is often difficult to link data with unique patient identifiers in ways that allow researchers and policymakers to understand quality of care across different episodes of care and different providers (OECD, 2010).

In 2010, the United Kingdom's coalition government published a white paper entitled *Equity and Excellence: Liberating the NHS,* which called for the measurement of health outcomes based on a number of specific indicators. To achieve this goal, England has developed the NHS Outcomes Framework (Secretary of State for Health, 2014) with indicators that will be used to evaluate local health care arrangements across five different domains: (a) preventing people from dying prematurely; (b) enhancing the quality of life for people with long-term conditions; (c) helping people to recover from episodes of ill health or after injury; (d) ensuring that people have a positive experience of care; and (e) treating and caring for people in a safe environment and protecting them from avoidable harm.

In France the Haute Autorité de Santé (HAS), or National Authority for Health, was established in 2004 as an independent public organization to promote quality of health services through accreditation, certification, and development of practice guidelines. Today, HAS leads the European Network for Patient Safety (EUNetPaS), which has developed a common agenda to promote patient safety. After a contaminated blood scandal in the early 1990s, the French government established new institutions to conduct disease surveillance and protect the population from unsafe foods, unsafe drugs, and unsafe blood. In addition, France's Ministry of Health recently initiated a small number of aggressive safety campaigns with strong patient involvement, such as one supported by TV spots to improve the use of antibiotics in preventing the appearance of resistant bacteria. Based on a risk-scoring system for surgical wound infections, national prevalence rates of methicillin-resistant *Staphylococcus aureus* (MRSA) in France declined from 2001 (33%) to 2006 (27%). These results are impressive in comparison with other European countries and the United States, where MRSA infections have increased (Degos & Rodwin, 2011).

In 1994, the Canadian government established the Canadian Institute for Health Information (CIHI) to improve its capacity to assess the health care system and to identify standards for health system performance. CIHI maintains 27 databases and clinical registries. The agency receives funding from the federal (80%) and provincial (20%) governments (Marchildon, 2013). In 2004, the federal government adopted a 10-year plan to strengthen health care. The plan increased federal health transfers to the provinces by 6%, and the provinces were supposed to place greater emphasis on reducing wait times and improving quality (Allin, 2012). Some of these funds have been used to track and reduce wait times. The federal government has also encouraged the use of health technology assessment, clinical guidelines, and best practices to enhance patient safety. Critics argue that despite the increase in attention to quality in individual provinces, Canada lacks a "guiding framework that supports" quality improvement in primary care (Sibbald, McPherson, & Kothari, 2013, p. 2).

In China, the issue of quality is also central to recent policy debates, but their starting point is radically different. When the Chinese government reduced its subsidies for health care in the late 1970s, health care organizations and providers often turned to pharmaceutical companies to make up for these lost revenues. Rather than focus on providing primary and preventive care, for example, many first-level hospitals focused on selling drugs to patients (Wang et al., 2011). As a result, these institutions developed a reputation for poor quality, and patients now crowd into larger hospitals and academic medical centers, creating overcrowding problems. Part of the motivation for expanding health insurance in China is to improve the quality of care across the entire health care system (Wang et al., 2011).

Criteria used to evaluate the performance of health care systems—such as access to, cost of, and quality of health care—are often called the "three-legged stool" of health policy. Until recently, however, quality did not receive a great deal of attention. Since the 1970s, researchers, policymakers, and patients have been demanding better information about quality. In the late 1990s, the U.S. Institute of Medicine led the world in calling attention to the importance of this issue, based on a report that uncovered disturbing evidence of problems with safety and quality in the United States (IOM, 1999). In contrast, the SARS epidemic embarrassed the Chinese government and sparked efforts to improve access to and the quality of care. Finding solutions to such problems has been a challenge because stakeholders cling to existing practices and technologies, data limitations make it difficult to measure the quality of care, and fundamental disagreements remain about the meaning of quality and how to measure value for money in health care.

■ Lessons

Based on the experience of NHI and NHS systems in the countries we have examined, we would highlight four lessons for policymakers in the United States:

- Achieving the goal of universal health coverage requires legislation to make such coverage compulsory.
- Financing broader insurance coverage in the United States—beyond Medicare and Medicaid—requires increasing government subsidies based on ability-to-pay criteria.
- Health care systems with universal coverage rely increasingly on economic evaluation of health technology as a criterion for making coverage decisions.
- Containing health care costs has not been achieved without greater reliance than in the United States on price regulation and systemwide budget targets.

The ACA represents the most significant health care reforms since Medicare and Medicaid in 1965, because it is likely to increase significantly the share of the population with health insurance coverage and redistribute the burden of health care financing from those who are wealthier, younger, and healthier toward those who are poorer, older, and sicker (see Chapter 3). We would argue that this legislation draws heavily on the first two lessons of comparative experience (the mandate and the move toward ability-to-pay criteria for financing health care), less so on the third (economic evaluation of health technology), and ignores the fourth (greater price regulation and budget targets). This will bring the United States closer to other wealthy nations in terms of population coverage. Yet the U.S. health care system continues to present some striking contrasts to most other wealthy nations. It remains a patchwork system characterized by a complex combination of institutions that include an enclave of socialized medicine such as the VHA, a social insurance program (Medicare), and social welfare programs (Medicaid and CHIP); tax-subsidized employer-based private insurance for about one half of the population; and heavy reliance on out-of-pocket payment for the population that remains uninsured, similar to the situation in China, India, and most developing nations.

The United States has the highest per capita expenditures; the highest salaries for physicians and other professionals making up the health care workforce; and the highest aggregate prices for hospitals, physicians' services, and pharmaceuticals. Despite our drive to innovate and invest in the latest medical technologies, access to high-technology services, as well as to basic primary care services, is highly inequitable compared with other OECD nations—but not with China, which faces not only the usual inequities among populations of different income and educational levels, but also massive inequities among its urban and rural residents, and, within cities, among its registered and migrant populations.

Another way in which the U.S. health care system differs from that of wealthy OECD nations concerns the vast range of health insurance products we offer to our population, including the option (following the ACA) of not purchasing health insurance, albeit with a financial penalty. Despite the emphasis on choice of insurer many people find themselves confined to obtaining health care within restricted provider networks outside of which payment for services often becomes unaffordable. There is no parallel to this problem in wealthy OECD nations such as England, Canada, and France. In China, choice of too many insurance products is not the problem. The situation there is far worse than in the United States because a large part of the urban migrant population is typically excluded from health insurance coverage. The problem of internal migrants in China is substantial, but not surprising, for a system that spends only 3.2% of its GDP on health care and has only recently set itself the goal of providing universal coverage.

■ Discussion Questions

1. What are some reasons for studying health care systems abroad?
2. How do NHI and NHS systems compare with the health care system in the United States?
3. How do most countries with similar levels of per capita income differ from and resemble the United States with respect to cost, quality, and access to health care?

4. What can the United States learn from other OECD countries about how to extend health coverage while containing health care expenditures?

5. How can health system performance be measured? Compare the approaches adopted by WHO and the Commonwealth Fund.

6. How are the problems and opportunities different for China than for the United States and other OECD countries?

CASE STUDY

You are an employee of a think tank in Washington, DC. The director has been asked to testify before a congressional committee on the following question: In reforming the ACA, what lessons should the United States learn from relevant experience abroad? Your job is to write a memorandum that will help the director answer this question. In writing this memo, you should address the following questions:

1. How can learning from abroad help policymakers engage in a process of self-examination of health policy at home?

2. What is the difference between NHS and NHI systems?

3. What should members of Congress know about China's problems and aspirations in health policy?

4. What lessons from abroad would be most relevant in reforming the ACA?

■ References

Aaron, H., Schwartz, W., & Cox, M. (2005). *Can we say no? The challenge of rationing health care.* Washington, DC: Brookings Institution Press.

Allin, S. (2012). The Canadian health care system, 2012. In S. Thomson, R. Osborn, D. Squires, & M. Jun (Eds.), *International profiles of health care systems, 2012* (pp. 19–25). New York, NY: The Commonwealth Fund.

Anderson, G. F., Frogner, B. K., Johns, R. A., & Reinhardt, U. E. (2006). Health care spending and use of information technology in OECD countries. *Health Affairs, 25*(1), 819–831.

Angrisano, C., Farrell, D., Kocher, B., Laboissiere, M., & Parker, S. (2007, January). *Accounting for the cost of health care in the United States* (Report). San Francisco, CA: McKinsey Global Institute. Retrieved from http://www.mckinsey.com/insights/health_systems_and_services/accounting_for_the_cost_of_health_care_in_the_united_states

Australian Department of the Treasury. (2007). Intergenerational Report. http://archive.treasury.gov.au/documents/1239/PDF/IGR_2007_final_report.pdf. Accessed on January 23, 2015.

Billings, J., Anderson, G. M., & Newman, L. S. (1996). Recent findings on preventable hospitalizations. *Health Affairs, 15*(3), 239–249.

Blendon, R., Benson, J. M., & Brulé, A. (2012). Understanding health care in the 2012 election [Special report]. *New England Journal of Medicine, 367,* 1658–1661. doi:10.1056/NEJMsr1211472

Blendon, R., Schoen, C., DesRoches, C. M., Osborn, R., Scoles, K. L., & Zapert, K. (2002). Inequities in health care: A five-country survey. *Health Affairs, 21*(3), 182–191.

Blumenthal, D., & Hsiao, W. (2005). Privatization and its discontents—The evolving Chinese health care system. *New England Journal of Medicine, 353*(11), 1165–1170.

Bohmer, R. M. J., & Imison, C. (2013). Lessons from England's health care workforce redesign: No quick fixes. *Health Affairs, 32*(11), 2025–2031.

Bradley, E. H., & Taylor, L. A. (2013). *The American health care paradox: Why spending more is getting us less.* New York, NY: Public Affairs.

Carrier, E., Yee, T., & Stark, L. B. (2011). *Matching supply to demand: Address the U.S. primary care workforce shortage* (Policy Analysis No. 7). Washington, DC: National Institute for Health Care Reform. Retrieved from www.nihcr.org/PCP_Workforce

Chalkidou, K. (2009). *Comparative effectiveness review within the U.K.'s National Institute for Health and Clinical Excellence.* New York, NY: The Commonwealth Fund.

Commonwealth Fund. (2014). Retrieved from http://www.commonwealthfund.org/topics/current-issues/international-surveys

Cutler, D. M. (2007). The lifetime costs and benefits of medical technology. *Journal of Health Economics, 26*(6), 1081–1100.

de Kervasdoué, J., Kimberly, J., & Rodwin, V. G. (1984). *The end of an illusion: The future of health policy in western industrialized nations.* Berkeley, CA: University of California Press.

Degos, L., & Rodwin, V. (2011). Two faces of patient safety and care quality: A Franco-American comparison. *Health Economics, Policy and Law, 6*(3), 287–294. doi: 10.1017/S1744133111000107

Fabre, G. (2013). The lion's share: What's behind China's economic slowdown (Working paper). *Fondation Maison des sciences de l'homme, 53.* Retrieved from http://halshs.archives-ouvertes.fr/halshs-00874077

Fineberg, H. (2012). A successful and sustainable health system—How to get there from here [Shattuck lecture]. *New England Journal of Medicine, 366*(11), 1020–1027.

Gay, J. G., Paris, V., Devaux, M., & de Looper, M. (2011). *Mortality amenable to health care in 31 OECD countries: Estimates and methodological issues* (OECD Health Working Papers No. 55). Paris: OECD Publishing. doi:10.1787/18152015

Goodman, J., Musgrave, G., & Herrick, D. (2004). *Lives at risk: Single-payer national health insurance around the world.* Oxford: Rowman & Littlefield.

Gusmano, M. K., & Allin, S. (2011). Health care for older persons in England and the United States: A contrast of systems and values. *Journal of Health Politics, Policy and Law, 36*(1), 89–118.

Gusmano, M. K., Rodwin, V. G., & Weisz, D. (2014). Beyond "US" and "them": Access dimensions of health system performance in the U.S., France, Germany, and England. *International Journal of Health Services, 44*(3), 547–559.

Gusmano, M. K., Weisz, D., & Rodwin, V. G. (2009). Achieving horizontal equity: Must we have a single-payer health care system? *Journal of Health Politics, Policy and Law, 34*(4), 617–633.

Hacker, J. (2006). *The great risk shift: The new economic insecurity and the decline of the American dream.* New York, NY: Oxford University Press.

Health Force Ontario. (2014). *Family practice compensation models* [Web page]. Retrieved from http://www.healthforceontario.ca/en/Home/Physicians/Training_%7C_Practising_Outside_Ontario/Physician_Roles/Family_Practice_Models/Family_Practice_Compensation_Models

Hipgravel, D., Guao, S., Mu, Y., Guo, Y., Yan, F., Scherpbier, R., & Brixi, H. (2012). Chinese-Style decentralization and health system reform. *PLOS Medicine, 9*(11), 1–4.

Huang, Y. (2011, November 1). China's health costs outstrip GDP growth. *The New York Times.* Retrieved from http://www.nytimes.com/roomfordebate/2011/11/01/is-china-facing-a-health-care-crisis/chinas-health-costs-outstrip-gdp-growth

Institute of Medicine (IOM). (1999). *To Err is Human: Building a Safer Health Care System*. Washington, DC: National Academy Press.

Jian, W., Chan, K. Y., Reidpath, D. D., & Xu, L. (2010). China's rural-urban care gap shrank for chronic disease patients, but inequities persist. *Health Affairs, 29*(12), 2189–2196.

Klein, R. (1997). Learning from others: shall the last be the first? *Journal of Health Politics, Policy and Law, 22*(5), 1267–1278.

Klein, R. (2013). *The new politics of the NHS* (7th ed.). London: Radcliffe.

Marchildon, G. P. (2013). Canada: Health system review. *Health Systems in Transition, 15*(1), 1–179.

Marmor, T., Freeman, R., & Okma, K. (2005). Comparative perspectives and policy learning in the world of health care. *Journal of Comparative Policy Analysis: Research and practice, 7*(4), 331–348.

Marmor, T., & Oberlander, J. (2012). From HMOs to ACOs: The quest for the holy grail in U.S. health policy. *Journal of General Internal Medicine, 27*(9), 1215–1218. doi:10.1007/s11606-012-2024-6

Mattke, S., Epstein, A. M., & Leatherman, S. (2006). The OECD health care quality indicators project: History and background. *International Journal for Quality in Health Care, 18*(Suppl 1), 1–4.

Menon, D., & Stafinski, T. (2009). Health technology assessment in Canada: 20 years strong? *Value in Health, 12*(2), S14–S19.

Moon, M. (1996). *Medicare Now and in the Future*. The Urban Insitute.

Morone, J. A. (1993). The health care bureaucracy: Small changes, big consequences. *Journal of Health Politics, Policy and Law, 18*(3), 723–739.

Musgrove, P. (2003). Judging health systems: Reflections on WHO's methods. *The Lancet, 361*, 1817–1820.

Nolte, E., & McKee, M. (2003). Measuring the health of nations: Analysis of mortality amenable to health care. *British Medical Journal, 327*, 1129–1133.

Nolte, E., & McKee, M. (2012). In amenable mortality—deaths avoidable through health care—progress in the US lags that of three European countries. *Health Affairs, 31*(9), 2114–2122.

Oliver, A. (2012). The folly of ranking health systems. *Health Economics, Policy and Law, 7*(1), 15–17.

Ono, T., Lafortune, G., & Schoenstein, M. (2013). *Health workforce planning in OECD countries: A review of 26 projection models from 18 countries* (OECD Health Working Papers, No. 62). Ferney-Voltaire: OCED Publishing. doi:10.1787/5k44t787zcwb-en

Or, Z. (2010). *Activity based payment in hospitals: Evaluation*. Gütersloh, Germany: Health Policy Monitor. Retrieved from http://hpm.org/en/Surveys/IRDES_-_France/15/Activity_based_payment_in_hospitals__Evaluation.html

Organization for Economic Cooperation and Development (OECD). (2010). *Improving value in health care: Measuring quality*. Paris: OECD forum on quality of care.

Organization for Economic Cooperation and Development (OECD). (2013). *Health at a glance 2013: OECD indicators*. Paris: OECD Publishing. doi:10.1787/19991312

Rodwin, V. G. (1984). *The health planning predicament: France, Quebec, England, and the United States*. Berkeley, CA: University of California Press.

Rodwin, V. G., & Contributors. (2006). *Universal health insurance in France: How sustainable? Essays on the French health care system*. Washington, DC: Embassy of France. Retrieved from http://www.frenchamerican.org/sites/default/files/documents/media_reports/2006_fafreport_universalhealthinsurance.pdf

Roos, L. L., Walld, R., Uhanova, J., & Bond, R. (2005). Physician visits, hospitalizations, and socioeconomic status: Ambulatory care sensitive conditions in a Canadian setting. *Health Services Research, 40*(4), 1167–1185. doi:10.1111/j.1475-6773.2005.00407.x

Roos, N. P., & Mustard, C. (1997). Variation in health and health care use by socioeconomic status in Winnipeg, Canada: Does the system work well? Yes and no. *The Milbank Quarterly, 75*(1), 89–111.

Roth, L. S., & Adams, P. C. (2009). Variation in physician reimbursement for endoscopy across Canada. *Canadian Journal of Gastroenterology, 23*(7), 503.

Rosenthal, M. M., & Greiner, J. R. (1982). The barefoot doctors of China: from political creation to professionalization. *Human Organization, 41*(4), 330–341.

Schoen, C., Davis, K., How, S., & Schoenbaum, S. (2006). U.S. health system performance: A national scorecard. *Health Affairs, 25*(6), w457–w475. doi:10.1377/hlthaff .25.w457

Schoen, C., Osborn, R., Squires, D., Doty, M., Rasmussen, P., Pierson, R., & Applebaum, S. (2012). A survey of primary care doctors in ten countries shows progress in use of health information technology, less in other areas. *Health Affairs, 31*(12), 2805–2816.

Schreyögg, J., Stargardt, T., Tiemann, O., & Busse, R. (2006). Methods to determine reimbursement rates for diagnosis related groups (DRG): a comparison of nine European countries. *Health Care Management Science, 9*(3), 215–223.

Secretary of State for Health (2014). *Equity and excellence: Liberating the NHS*. UK Department of Health.

Sibbald, S. L., McPherson, C., & Kothari, A. (2013). Ontario primary care reform and quality improvement activities: An environmental scan. *BMC Health Services Research, 13*(209), 1–11.

Singh, D., Lalani, H., Kralj, B., Newman, E., Goodyear, J., Hellyer, D., & Tepper, J. (2010). *Ontario population needs-based physician simulation model: Final report*. Ontario Ministry of Health and Long-Term Care and Ontario Medical Association.

Smith, R. D. (2006). Responding to global infectious disease outbreaks: Lessons from SARS on the role of risk perception, communication and management. *Journal of Social Science and Medicine, 63*, 3113–3123.

Sorenson, C. (2009). The role of HTA in coverage and pricing decisions: A cross-country comparison. *Euro Observer, 11*(1), 1–12.

Starfield, B., Shi, L., & Macinko, J. (2005). Contribution of primary care to health systems and health. *The Milbank Quarterly, 83*(3), 457–502.

Thomson, S., Osborn, R., Squires, D., Reed, S. J. (2012). *International profiles of health care systems*. New York, NY: The Commonwealth Fund.

Valentine, V. (2005, November 4). *Health for the masses: China's "barefoot doctors"* [Radio broadcast]. Washington, DC: National Public Radio. Retrieved from http:// www.npr.org/templates/story/story.phpstoryId = 4990242

van Doorslaer, E., & Masseria, C. (2004). *Income-related inequality in the use of medical care in 21 OECD countries* (OECD Health Working Papers, 14). Paris: OCED Publishing. doi:10.1787/687501760705

Wang, H., Gusmano, M. K., & Cao, Q. (2011). Review and evaluation of community health organizations in China: Will the priority of new healthcare reform in China be a success? *Health Policy, 99*(1), 37–43. doi:10.1016/j.healthpol.2010.07.003

Warshaw, G. A., & Bragg, E. J. (2014). Preparing the health care workforce to care for adults with Alzheimer's disease and related dementias. *Health Affairs, 33*(4), 633–641.

Williams, A. (2001). Science or marketing at WHO? A commentary on 'World Health 2000'. *Health Economics, 10*, 93–100.

World Health Organization (WHO). World Health Report 2000. Retrieved from http:// www.who.int/whr/2001/archives/2000/en/index.htm. Accessed January 23, 2015.

Yip, W. C. M., Hsiao, W., Meng, Q., Chen, W., & Sun, X. (2010). Realignment of incentives for health-care providers in China. *The Lancet, 375*(9720), 1120–1130.

Zweifel, P., Felder, S., & Meiers, M. (1999). Ageing of population and health care expenditure: A red herring? *Health Economics, 8,* 485–496

Keeping Americans Healthy

An important theme of this book is that the U.S. health system must accomplish two key tasks: It must keep people healthy from birth to death as much as is possible, and it must restore health when people are injured or become ill. Part II focuses on this first challenge: promoting and maintaining good health among the entire population.

In Chapter 5, Pamela Russo introduces readers to the emerging field of population health. It is often said that this field began with a simple question: Why are some people healthy and others are not? The chapter explains how health status is mostly determined by how we live our lives and by how the environment (both social and physical) in which we live supports the ability to lead healthy lives. Russo introduces the concept of the social determinants of health, explaining how income, education, housing, and a range of other such factors contribute to our well-being. The chapter also considers how public policy influences these social determinants of health.

Chapter 6 addresses how the governmental public health system contributes to the health of populations. Although the government plays a key role in financing medical care in the United States, it also is engaged in a wide range of activities focused on preventing illness and promoting healthy living. State governments in particular have important responsibilities for ensuring public health, and in most states there also are public health departments within county or local governments. Laura Leviton, Paul Kuehnert, and Kathryn Wehr explain how public health departments promote health and describe how the public health field is changing, taking on a more active role in ensuring that our communities promote good health among their populations.

Individual choices we make every day have a lot to do with whether or not we maintain our health. Decisions about what and how much we eat, how much we exercise and stay active, how safely we drive, and whether we drink too much alcohol or inappropriately use drugs all shape our health status. Chapter 7, authored by Elaine Cassidy, Matthew Trujillo, and C. Tracy Orleans, explains the range of behavioral choices that affect health and reviews how medical providers, other health professionals, and public initiatives can help people change unhealthy behaviors. The chapter makes clear that the social conditions we face (the focus of Chapters 5 and 6) and the individual choices we make both determine our health status. Also, these two sets of factors interact in that social conditions often affect our behavioral choices.

Chapter 8 focuses on the important issue of addressing the health challenges facing the most vulnerable Americans. This group includes low-income people, who often do not live in places that make it easy to live healthy lifestyles or to have good access to social and health services. What we term the vulnerable population also includes immigrants and people with significant chronic illnesses. Jacqueline Martinez Garcel, Elizabeth Ward, and

Lourdes Rodriguez review emerging ideas for improving how our health system serves the most vulnerable in our society.

Three of the authors in this section are on the senior staff of the Robert Wood Johnson Foundation, the nation's largest foundation focused on the health of Americans. The Foundation has recently refocused its funding and operational priorities to emphasize initiatives that will improve population health across our country. The Foundation's website (www.rwjf.org) is a good source of current information and ideas on this important topic.

5 Population Health

Pamela G. Russo

KEY WORDS

determinants of health

gradient

integrative models

medical model

population health model

population medicine

reverse causality

LEARNING OBJECTIVES

- Understand the differences between the medical and population health models of producing health, including the difference between the concepts of health and health care

- Explain how the two models lead to different strategies for interventions to prevent disease and improve health

- Learn about the differential importance of various health determinants

- Review the evidence regarding social and physical environmental influences on behavior and on health outcomes

- Review the variation in health and life expectancy between counties and between countries

- Describe innovative synergistic approaches that integrate the clinical and population models

TOPICAL OUTLINE

- The population health model

- The medical model

- Comparing the medical and population health models

- The influence of social determinants on health behavior and outcomes

- Leading determinants of health: weighting the different domains

- Health policy and returns on investment

■ Context

The majority of this book concerns what happens *within* the walls of health care institutions—hospitals, clinics, physician offices, and long-term care facilities. The focus in those chapters is on how health care is delivered, financed, managed, and measured for quality and effect, and how access to appropriate and safe diagnostic and treatment modalities varies across populations. In several chapters, disparities in health care and outcomes are shown to exist among insured, underinsured, and uninsured groups, among different races and ethnic groups, between rural and urban populations, among immigrant groups, and even between men and women.

However, having access to high-quality medical care is not the only factor that leads to disparities in *health* between different groups, nor are health care and medical services even the most important factors that determine the overall health of a population. This chapter documents the profound influences on health that occur *outside* of the health care system, where the vast majority of people—or patients—spend the overwhelming majority of the time.

Whether people live long and healthy lives is largely determined by powerful social factors such as education, income, racial or ethnic group, and the quality of environments where they live, learn, work, and play. In fact, the effects of the systematic differences in *health care* are far smaller than the effects of the nonrandom differences in other determinants of health on a population's overall health outcomes. These influences that are *outside* the health care system greatly influence which groups of people are more likely to become ill in the first place, to be injured, or to die early. These influences also help determine people's health care outcomes once they become sick, injured, or disabled.

▣ The Population Health Model

The population health model seeks to explain and intervene in the causes of the systematic differences in health between different groups (Kindig & Stoddart, 2003). To do so, it analyzes the patterns or distribution of health between different groups of people in order to identify and understand the factors leading to poorer outcomes. These factors are often described as "upstream" causes, in the sense that they influence health through a series of pathways that may not be immediately visible (see also Chapter 7).

In addition, population health employs an integrative model, meaning that different factors are highly likely to intersect and combine to produce good or poor health and should be assessed in tandem. Population health scientists use the term "determinants of health" rather than factor or cause, and they use the term "the multiple determinants of health" to describe the determinants that arise from five important domains:

- The social and economic environment—factors such as income, education, employment, social support, and culture (often referred to as the social determinants of health, or SDOH)
- The physical environment, including urban design, housing, availability of healthy foods, air and water safety, exposure to environmental toxins
- Genetics (and, more recently, epigenetics—the study of gene–environment interactions)
- Medical care, including prevention, treatment, and disease management
- Health-related behaviors, such as smoking, exercise, and diet, which in turn are shaped by all of the preceding determinants

Health is therefore conceptualized as the result of exposure to different patterns of these multiple determinants. Although the determinant categories are listed independently, they have substantial and complex interactions over the life course of an individual or group.

Some health care outcomes can, in turn, affect the determinants; that is, they can have a "reverse causality" effect on determinants. For example, whereas social determinants such as income have an effect on outcomes, the outcome of being unhealthy also can have a negative effect on income (Kindig & Chin, 2009).

> *The population health model is that of a web of causation, in which multiple different influences interact to produce good or poor health.*

The population health model is that of a web of causation, in which multiple different influences interact to produce good or poor health (see Figure 5.1). Over the past 40 years, a significant body of knowledge has developed that demonstrates the profound effects of multiple determinants from different domains, as well as the interactions among them, their effects at different stages in the life course from gestation to old age, and their cumulative effects.

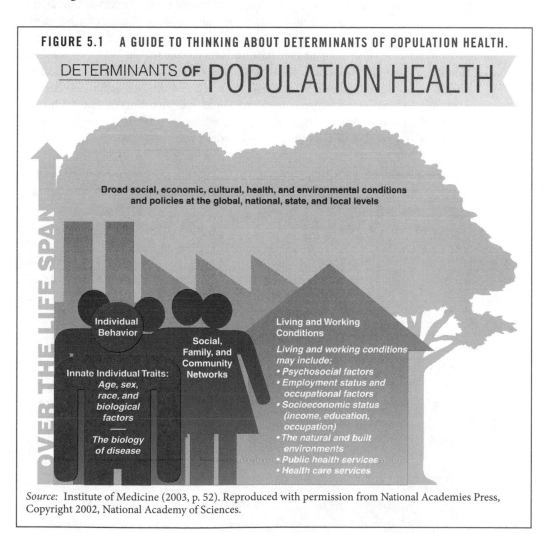

FIGURE 5.1   A GUIDE TO THINKING ABOUT DETERMINANTS OF POPULATION HEALTH.

DETERMINANTS OF POPULATION HEALTH

OVER THE LIFE SPAN

Broad social, economic, cultural, health, and environmental conditions and policies at the global, national, state, and local levels

Individual Behavior

Innate Individual Traits:
Age, sex, race, and biological factors
—
The biology of disease

Social, Family, and Community Networks

Living and Working Conditions

Living and working conditions may include:
• *Psychosocial factors*
• *Employment status and occupational factors*
• *Socioeconomic status (income, education, occupation)*
• *The natural and built environments*
• *Public health services*
• *Health care services*

Source: Institute of Medicine (2003, p. 52). Reproduced with permission from National Academies Press, Copyright 2002, National Academy of Sciences.

■ The Medical Model

In contrast to the population health model, the medical model hones in on individuals, focusing on the factors that are most immediately linked to the pathophysiology underlying a person's disease. It is a reductionist model in the sense that it searches for the mechanisms at the cellular level that explain how specific factors produce illness or act as markers of incipient disease. In turn, the therapeutic goal is to find the "silver bullet" that will stop or reverse those mechanisms and thus cure the current medical problem.

The medical model frames risk factors as working through disease-specific pathways, and typically analyzes risk factors as if they were independent in statistical modeling. The medical model does consider how different biological systems within the individual interact—for example, the endocrine system and the cardiovascular system—but the lens remains focused on the body.

Health care is generally reactive, meaning that it responds to abnormality, disease, or injury, and as a result has been characterized as a "sickness care system" (Evans, Barer, & Marmor, 1994). Health care has traditionally been delivered (and reimbursed) in acute episodes, although the rise of chronic illnesses that require continued care management has led to a more long-term perspective. Historically, the health care system has placed less value on and provided less reimbursement for efforts to promote health or to prevent illness and injury. Although health care has achieved great strides in diagnosing, treating, and in some cases curing illness and injury, and although new knowledge and technology are constantly increasing the capacity to preserve life, relieve suffering, and maintain or restore function, the inexorable increases in U.S. health care spending clearly are not improving Americans' chances for living long and healthy lives, as shown in Figure 5.2.

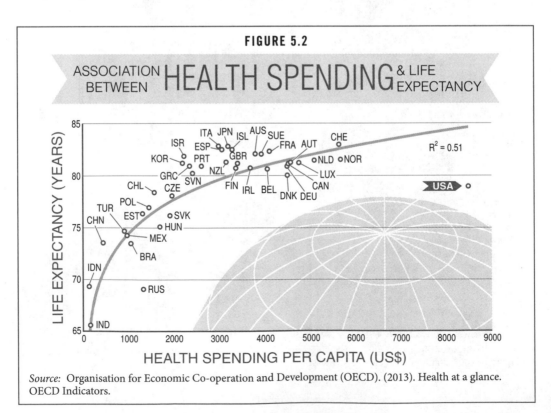

FIGURE 5.2

ASSOCIATION BETWEEN HEALTH SPENDING & LIFE EXPECTANCY

Source: Organisation for Economic Co-operation and Development (OECD). (2013). Health at a glance. OECD Indicators.

The United States is the outlier point on the far right—the highest health care spending—yet Americans' probability of survival to age 80 is lower than that of other developed countries. This marked discrepancy between the highest spending on health care and poorer survival rates is referred to as "the U.S. health disadvantage." The differences between the medical and population health models can help explain the reasons for the disparity between the United States and other developed countries, as well as the severe disparities within the United States among different populations.

■ Comparing the Medical and Population Health Models

Consider two examples, obesity and tobacco use, that illustrate the different explanatory and intervention approaches of the medical model versus the population health model. In the medical model, when an obese adolescent visits a health care provider, the provider will likely take a family history and a diet and physical activity history. These may be followed by laboratory tests to rule out hormonal or other physiological causes for obesity and to check for diabetes and other consequences of extreme overweight. Interventions are likely to include referrals to nutritionists and recommendations for decreasing calories and increasing physical activity, with regular monitoring. In very serious cases (morbid obesity) or with failure to achieve weight loss through these means, the patient may be referred for bariatric surgery.

The medical model does not ask **why** *an epidemic of obesity has occurred over the past 20 years.*

The medical model does not ask *why* an epidemic of obesity has occurred over the past 20 years, or investigate why there are higher rates of obesity in low-income and minority populations, or grapple with the circumstances that make it difficult for many patients to comply with medical recommendations for eating less and exercising more.

In contrast, the population health model has identified a wide variety of causes that have worked synergistically—an unintended conspiracy of causes over time—to produce the epidemic and the differing patterns of obesity observed among population groups. These causes could include the following:

- Higher density in low-income neighborhoods of fast-food restaurants, which offer high-calorie, high-fat, low-nutrient, supersized meals at very low prices
- The presence of vending machines, which sell high-calorie soft drinks as a source of needed revenue, in schools
- Subsidized school lunches with high caloric and fat content—a result of agricultural policies
- The decrease in physical education classes and near-elimination of recess periods, due to shrinking school budgets and a narrow focus on meeting academic test score requirements
- Fewer children and adults walking or bicycling to school or other destinations, due in part to the lack of sidewalks, safe pedestrian crossings, and bicycle lanes

- Few places to play or walk in urban, low-income neighborhoods, due to unsafe playgrounds, crime, and violence
- A lack of grocery stores with healthy food options such as fresh fruit and vegetables in many neighborhoods, due to the higher cost and lower profit margins of these foods

These determinants are all in the social and physical environmental domains, and they strongly limit people's behavioral choices. It is extremely difficult to achieve lasting lifestyle behavioral changes in people who *do* have the economic resources to join gyms, have child care while they exercise, and afford healthier food choices. It is almost impossible to achieve such changes among people for whom healthy choices are out of their financial reach.

Making the healthy choice the easier choice is not always sufficient; programs to change behavior boost the chances that people will make those healthy choices their default choices.

In a population health framework, the relevant interventions could include zoning law changes; menu labeling; working with fast-food industries to provide healthier, but low-cost menu options; educational policies that encourage healthy food choices and increased physical activity in schools and after school; and so on. Such interventions are not traditionally considered part of the health arena by adherents of the medical model. Making the healthy choice the easier choice is not always sufficient; programs to change behavior boost the chances that people will make those healthy choices their default choices. Such programs might include workplace or community programs to encourage physical activity in the form of walking, bicycling, or other exercise, or cooking classes using nutritious, affordable, noncalorie-dense foods.

Tobacco use offers a second example. In the medical model, the focus is on individual patients who smoke or chew tobacco. The solution is framed in individual terms and is geared toward behavioral change through cessation counseling and nicotine replacement options. Success requires having access to providers who support and encourage cessation (see Chapter 7).

In the population health model, the understanding of the problem includes the influences of tobacco production, advertising, distribution, and patterns of use in different groups, and the interventions include smoke-free laws, tobacco taxes, and regulation of advertising and marketing. Without doubt, these populationwide policy changes have changed U.S. social norms regarding the acceptability of tobacco use and prompted a dramatic decrease in the rate of smoking.

As with programs to increase physical activity and healthy eating, policy changes to reduce smoking are usually coupled with increases in access to cessation programs at the community level, such as free quitlines and free nicotine patches, which assist smokers to quit. The population health model also enables targeting policies toward groups with the highest rates of tobacco use, and it responds to tobacco industry actions to redirect their advertising from the more affluent smokers who are able to access cessation programs to new, more susceptible markets, including youth, minorities, and people in developing countries (Kreuter & Lezin, 2001).

■ The Influence of Social Determinants on Health Behavior and Outcomes

The medical model is well accepted and respected by health care providers, laboratory researchers, clinical researchers, and health services researchers. Many people tend to regard medical knowledge as based on the so-called hard sciences, and thus as having greater likelihood of reflecting the "true" nature of human pathophysiology. The population health model, conversely, requires multiple disciplines to collaborate and integrate different social science concepts, methods, and data sources with those of the biological sciences. Although few people may doubt that poverty and lack of education are associated with worse health—as the Australian-born population health researcher John Lynch says, population health is the "science of the bleedin' obvious"—they are not aware of the magnitude of the scientific basis underlying these effects, the gradients in effect, the importance of the interactions, and the biological pathways. They are even less aware of the most effective public health interventions.

Those who follow the medical model are often surprised that the social science disciplines are just as rigorous as the biological sciences—if not more so—in their analysis of data, their reliance on large longitudinal data sets collected under strict criteria, and their coupling of these with work in tightly controlled experimental settings. In fact, significant progress has been made in defining the pathways between the social determinants and health—in other words, how these factors "get under the skin"—using a wide variety of research methods, including animal research, neuroimaging, experimental psychology studies, and a variety of stress-related physiological phenomena involving the cardiovascular, endocrine, neural, and other systems, as well as epigenetics. For a recent, comprehensive review of the research on the interaction between social determinants and human biology, see Adler and Stewart (2010).

Initially, work on health determinants was based on epidemiological findings linking morbidity and mortality to socioeconomic status, defined by education, income, or occupational status or grade. One of the earliest studies to demonstrate the importance of such factors was Michael Marmot's Whitehall study, a longitudinal study conducted over two decades with results reported throughout the 1970s and 1980s (Evans et al., 1994). The British data were especially enlightening because they included a measure of social class, based on occupation, not available in U.S.-based data.

The Whitehall study collected extensive information on more than 10,000 British civil servants, from the lowest rung of the income and rank hierarchy to the highest. Marmot found that the likelihood of death was about *three and a half times higher* for those in the lowest status rank (clerical and manual workers) than for those in the highest administrative jobs. Mortality rates increased steadily with every reduction in rank.

Such a steady increase is known as a "gradient" in the population health model and a "dose-response effect" in the medical model, where it is taken as evidence of a robust relationship between causal factor and outcome. None of the workers in this population were actually poor, and none had high exposure to work-related toxins or other risks in the physical environment. All had access to the British National Health System. The gradient in heart disease mortality continued to be present after adjusting the data for different rates of smoking, high blood pressure, and high cholesterol. In other words, after controlling for the traditional medical model risk factors, the

3:1 difference in death rate by social class could not be explained away. Marmot and others went on to investigate the role of stress associated with occupational rank.

Over the past 20 years, studies on the stress response have rigorously demonstrated its effects on multiple bodily systems in addition to the endocrine system, including the immunological, neural, and cardiovascular systems. These effects have been shown in both laboratory and community situations. A wide variety of stressful stimuli have been studied, including social subordination, lack of job control, discrimination, social isolation, economic insecurity, job loss, bankruptcy, and other situations that provoke anxiety. The proposed pathway is that such situations result in greater stress, which leads to biological dysregulation, adverse physiological responses, and a common pathway of pathology, including the onset and progression of diseases.

Scientists increasingly recognize that the mechanisms by which social determinants act depend on the context in which people encounter stressful events. One area of research focuses on "neighborhood effects," which include the interaction of social and physical environmental determinants; for example, the negative interaction between the physical environment (poor housing, areas of crime and violence, lack of stores with healthy foods, and so on) and social determinants related to poverty.

Recent U.S. data on the links between social factors and health and the wide variations in health among groups come from two reports from the Robert Wood Johnson Foundation Commission to Build a Healthier America (2009), a national, independent, nonpartisan group of leaders who investigated how factors outside the health care system shape and affect opportunities to live healthy lives. The Commission's team of researchers compared average life expectancy by county and found significant variations. For example, the average life expectancy in Bennett County, South Dakota, is 66.6 years, compared with 81.3 years in nearby Sioux County, Iowa—a difference of almost 15 years. The challenge is to understand and address the underlying factors that explain this marked difference in mortality rates.

Two of the most predictive factors of life expectancy are income and degree of education. Examination of the relationship between measures of education and income on U.S. life expectancy showed that:

- College graduates can expect to live at least 5 years longer than those who did not complete high school.
- Upper middle-income Americans can expect to live more than 6 years longer than poor Americans, significant for national life expectancy because 25% of adults nationwide live in poor or near-poor households. (In 2015, the federal poverty level [FPL] was $20,090 for a family of three.)
- Middle-income Americans can expect to live shorter lives than those with higher incomes, whether or not they have health insurance.

The Commission also examined the relationships between health status, educational attainment, and racial or ethnic group. The measure of health status was a self-reported assessment of one's own health as excellent, very good, good, fair, or poor. Self-reported health status corresponds closely with assessments made by health professionals. Indeed, among adults studied by the Commission's research team, those who reported being in less than very good health had rates of diabetes and cardiovascular disease more than five times as high as the rates for adults who reported being in very good or excellent health. Highlights of the Commission's results include:

- Overall, 45% of adults ages 25 to 74 reported being in less than very good health, with rates varying among states from 35% to 53%.
- Adults with less than high school degrees were more than *two to three times* as likely to be in less than very good health than college graduates. There was also a clear gradient in health by educational level.
- Health status varied across racial or ethnic groups; non-Hispanic Whites were more likely to be in very good or excellent health than were other groups nationally and in almost every state. In some states, non-Hispanic Black and Hispanic adults were *more than twice* as likely as White adults to be in less than very good health.
- Analyzing both social factors simultaneously, non-Hispanic Whites had better health status than adults in any other racial or ethnic group *at every level* of education. The gradient in health by educational level within each racial or ethnic group is shown in Figure 5.3.

Educational attainment may influence healthy choices and better health via multiple pathways. For example, people with more schooling may have a better understanding of the importance of healthy behavior, or higher educational attainment may lead to higher-paying jobs with greater economic security, healthier working conditions, better benefits, and increased ability to purchase more nutritious foods and live in a

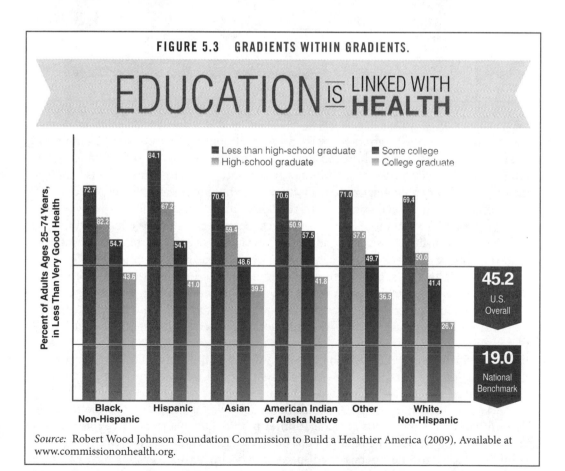

FIGURE 5.3   GRADIENTS WITHIN GRADIENTS.

Source: Robert Wood Johnson Foundation Commission to Build a Healthier America (2009). Available at www.commissiononhealth.org.

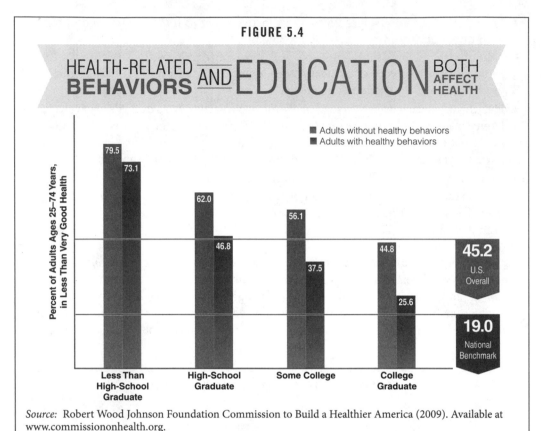

FIGURE 5.4

HEALTH-RELATED BEHAVIORS AND EDUCATION BOTH AFFECT HEALTH

Source: Robert Wood Johnson Foundation Commission to Build a Healthier America (2009). Available at www.commissiononhealth.org.

safe neighborhood with good schools and recreational facilities. Figure 5.4 demonstrates that behavior and education both affect health: At every level of educational attainment, adults who smoke and do not participate in leisure-time exercise are less likely to be in very good health than adults who do not smoke and do get exercise.

Similar to educational attainment, racial discrimination can affect health via multiple pathways. A substantial base of evidence exists regarding the effect of different policies on both discrimination and health. A variety of policies have combined to maintain or worsen Black–White segregation by neighborhood, despite the civil rights legislation of the 1960s. Segregation determines access to educational and employment opportunities and increases the likelihood of unsafe housing, few places to play or exercise, food "deserts" with no access to fresh healthy foods, and exposure to violence. There is strong evidence that elimination of residential segregation would completely eliminate Black–White differences in income, education, and unemployment, in turn reducing racial disparities in health (Williams & Collins, 2001). Exposure to discrimination in and of itself provokes a physiological stress response in the lab, and chronic discrimination results in toxic chronic stress.

As noted earlier, the population health model calls for integration of the multiple determinants of health, with consideration of both negative and positive interactions among different factors. The relationships between socioeconomic status and health are complicated, but the most persistent disparities in health between groups clearly involve the intersection of multiple types of social disadvantages (Adler & Stewart, 2010).

■ Leading Determinants of Health: Weighting the Different Domains

During the 20th century, medical care explained only 5 of the 30-years' increase in life expectancy.

The five different domains or categories of health determinants, described earlier in this chapter, do not make equal contributions to the health outcomes of populations. This is not "new news." In the 1970s, Thomas McKeown (1976) concluded that improved health and longevity in England over the previous 200 years resulted from changes in food supplies, sanitary conditions, and smaller family sizes, rather than medical interventions. In the United States, John Bunker and colleagues (1995) estimated that during the 20th century, medical care explained only 5 of the 30-years of increase in life expectancy, and between 1950 and 1990, when many new therapies were developed for infectious diseases and heart disease, medical care accounted for only 3 of the 7 years of life expectancy increase.

Medical care also can be responsible for *increasing* mortality rates. A 2000 Institute of Medicine (IOM) report publicized the startling finding that medical errors accounted for approximately 2% to 4% of U.S. deaths annually (Kohn, Corrigan, & Donaldson, 2000), which would make medical error the fifth leading cause of death (Bleich, 2005).

There was a period of time in the 1990s during which medical scientists expected that genetics could explain much of the variation in health between groups and individuals; however, experience to date has not borne out this belief. Current estimates suggest that, although many diseases have genetic contributors, only about 2% of U.S. deaths can be explained by genetic factors alone. On a population level, multiple studies of immigrants show that the patterns of disease and death change from those of the original country to those of the new country over a fairly short time period—again suggesting that genetics plays a relatively minor role in preventable deaths (Evans et al., 1994).

Health behavior (smoking, physical activity, substance abuse, sexual activity, diet, and so on) is considered a major determinant of health in both the medical and population health models. Analysis of data from 22 European countries showed that variations in health disparities could be attributed to variations in smoking, alcohol consumption, and access to care, but that the patterns of determinants of inequality were different for men and women, by country, and by which outcome was measured (Mackenbach et al., 2008).

The best weighting scheme to determine the combined effects of determinants from different domains depends on the health outcome of interest. Some outcomes will be more dependent on certain determinants than on others. Researchers have therefore estimated the relative contributions of the multiple determinants of health through what are called *summary* measures of mortality and morbidity; that is, measures that summarize the length and quality of life. Significant progress has been made in accumulating the empirical data that can yield the best approximations of the relative weights of each domain on summary health outcomes.

McGinnis and Foege (1993) reviewed the relevant literature from 1977 to 1993 to analyze the leading causes of U.S. deaths. They concluded that approximately *half* of all deaths in 1990 were due to key nonmedical care factors, led by tobacco use and followed by diet and physical activity. They estimated that about 40% of deaths were caused by behavioral factors, 30% by genetics, 15% by social determinants, 10% by medical care, and 5% by physical environmental exposures. Ten years later, an IOM (2003) analysis revised the 1990 estimate of 50% of all deaths upward to 70% of all deaths being due to key nonmedical care factors. The CDC updated the McGinnis and Foege analysis and concluded that smoking remained the leading cause of preventable deaths, followed by poor diet and lack of physical activity (Mokdad, Marks, Stroup, & Gerberding, 2004).

The *America's Health Rankings* report ranks states in order of overall health status and uses an expert panel to assign weights and attribute causes to four categories of determinants: (a) behavior at 36% percent, (b) community environment at 25%, (c) public and health policies at 18%, and (d) clinical care at 21% (United Health Foundation, 2007). Since 2010, there also has been an annual national *County Health Rankings* report. This report ranks the overall health of every county within each of the 50 states and reports the contribution of the multiple determinants of health on each county's overall health using a population health framework. Health outcomes are viewed as the result of a combined set of factors, and these factors are also affected by conditions, policies, and programs in their communities. The report is based on a model that compares overall rankings on health outcomes with rankings on different health factors (Figure 5.5).

The *County Health Rankings* report estimates the influence on health and longevity of (a) health behaviors at 30%, (b) clinical care at 20%, (c) social and economic factors at 40%, and (d) physical environmental factors at 10%. These rankings demonstrate the dramatic amount of variation between one county and another in health outcomes and in health determinants. This variation is even greater than the variation in health care expenditures and health care outcomes that has been demonstrated over many years by health service researchers. For example, the premature death rate in the least healthy counties was two and one half times greater than in the healthiest counties.

The bottom-line message of the *County Health Rankings* project is that some places are healthy and others are not, so *where* people live matters to their health. The population health framework enables communities to see which factors are contributing the most to their poor or good health outcomes, and thus choose to act to improve the factors affecting health, vitality, and productivity of all community residents.

■ Health Policy and Returns on Investment

In a logical world, the more that is known about the causes of a problem, the more resources would be allocated toward reducing the most important of those causes. In the United States, two thirds of what we spend on health care is attributable to diseases that are preventable. Yet we invest less than 5% of our more than $2 trillion annual health spending on efforts to prevent illness, whereas 95% goes to direct medical care. The population health model shows that only perhaps 10% to 15% of preventable mortality could be avoided by increasing the availability or quality of medical care.

FIGURE 5.5

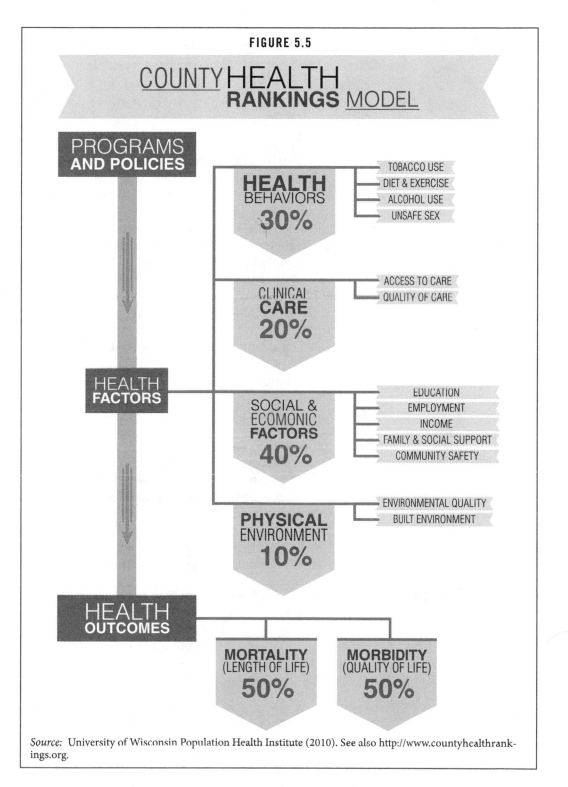

Source: University of Wisconsin Population Health Institute (2010). See also http://www.countyhealthrankings.org.

The population health model suggests that investments and policy decisions in areas that are not traditionally considered the province of health care are more likely to have a significant effect on improving a population's health than will increased spending on medical services.

The population health model suggests that investments and policy decisions in areas that are not traditionally considered the province of health care are more likely to have a significant effect on improving a population's health than will increased spending on medical services. An excellent review of the challenges and effect on health of policies in the areas of education, income transfer, civil rights, macroeconomics and employment, welfare, housing, and neighborhoods is provided in a recent comprehensive text (Schoeni, House, Kaplan, & Pollack, 2008).

Unfortunately, researchers are only beginning to be able to provide the evidence to guide policymakers regarding the comparative effectiveness and costs of specific investment choices across the five categories of health determinants. This lack of cross-sectoral economic evidence stems from complicated issues of interactions among determinants, the latency over time of their effects, and the absence of robust longitudinal data sets.

Nevertheless, this evidence base is growing rapidly, as shown by research such as that which estimates that correcting disparities in education-associated mortality rates would have averted eight times more deaths than improvements attributable to medical advances between 1996 and 2002 (Woolf, Johnson, Phillips, & Philipsen, 2007). Another example comes from a study by the Urban Institute, which calculated the return on investment for prevention and concluded that an investment of $10 per person per year in proven community-based programs to increase physical activity, improve nutrition, and prevent smoking and other tobacco use could save the country more than $16 billion annually within 5 years. This is a return of $5.60 for every $1[invested] (Trust for America's Health, 2008).

In 2009, the Commission to Build a Healthier America delivered a series of evidence-based recommendations to improve health, including the following:

- Provide high-quality early developmental services and support for all children
- Fund and design the Special Supplemental Nutrition Program for Women, Infants, and Children (WIC) and the Supplemental Nutrition Assistance Program (SNAP, also known as food stamps) programs to meet the need of hungry families for nutritious food
- Eliminate so-called food deserts through public-private partnerships
- Require healthy foods and physical activity in all schools (K–12)
- Ensure that decision makers in all sectors have the evidence they need to build health into public and private policies and practices

The last strategy underscores the need to consider the health effects of policies, programs, and projects in sectors that are not traditionally thought of as affecting health. This can be achieved through the use of health impact assessments (HIAs) (www.healthimpactproject.org), which have a long history of use in the same countries that have led the way in developing and acting upon the population health model. HIAs have been used in a wide variety of decisions regarding transportation, housing, zoning, and other aspects of the built environment, and more recently have been used to address social policies related to education, labor, criminal justice, segregation, and other areas. HIAs are one of the tools that can be used to bring a health lens to policy, program, and project decisions made in nonhealth sectors, a practice known as health in all policies (HIAP).

The recommendations for improving health that come from a population health model are very different from the technological breakthroughs and "silver bullets" hoped for in the medical model. With their broad reach across an entire population or community and their focus on the fundamental causes of illness, population health interventions have the potential to create much greater improvements in the health of Americans than further spending increases for medical services. The challenge is to find ways to finance population health interventions. Over the past 5 years, a number of innovative methods have been implemented to direct funding to community prevention addressing social, physical, and economic environments. One model is a wellness trust: a fund set aside specifically to support populationwide interventions or policies. Funds for a wellness trust can come from a number of sources, such as a tax on insurers or hospitals, as was done in Massachusetts in 2013. Another innovation is a variation on social impact bonds as health impact bonds. Capital is raised from private investors to implement community or state prevention interventions, and the resulting health care cost savings are returned to the investors as break-even or profit. There are a number of health impact bonds in progress, including community prevention to reduce the incidence and severity of asthma in Fresno, California; improving birth outcomes through the Nurse-Family Partnership in South Carolina; and reducing recidivism among juveniles in the justice system in New York City.

Another funding mechanism receiving wide attention is community benefits from nonprofit hospitals. Since the 1950s, to keep their tax exempt status nonprofit hospitals have owed certain duties to the community. In large part these duties included providing charity care to the medically indigent, but federal regulations were fairly vague. In 2002, the Congressional Budget Office estimated that the tax savings to nonprofit hospitals were approximately $12 billion, and this brought community benefit under scrutiny. With passage of the Patient Protection and Affordable Care Act (ACA), amendments were made to the Internal Revenue Service code that increased the transparency of hospital reporting, required hospitals to perform a community health needs assessment every 3 years with collaboration from public health experts and the community, and obliged hospitals to conduct community health improvement activities. The last can include community health improvement investments in research, training, and education; certain community-building activities that can be shown to improve health; and community-based health services that are furnished outside of the hospital and are not billable by the hospital. These changes have stimulated increased collaboration by many hospitals with public health and community partners, although the degree to which hospitals are committing funds varies widely. A variety of models are being promoted that show the potential for community benefit to have an effect on population-wide health improvement.

Other innovations include the concept of a health dividend, which refers to the opportunity cost of waste in health care spending, estimated at $750 billion per year. If this waste could be eliminated and the funding recaptured, the money could be used on population health–enhancing improvements in education, job training, or improvement to the built environment.

Other potential population health financing innovations result from the implementation of the ACA. The most significant was the Prevention and Public Health Fund, which is intended to provide stable and increased activities in community health. The fund was designed to build from $500 million in fiscal year 2010 to $2 billion per year by fiscal year 2015. As a result, a number of positive programs to improve population health using place-based strategies have occurred, such as Community Transformation Grants. However, the fund also has been used to fill gaps in the implementation of health care changes under the ACA, and has been a continual target of those opposed to the health reform act.

Other opportunities have resulted from the ACA, including accountable care organizations (ACOs) and Medicaid waivers and innovation grants. ACOs are essentially a network of providers and hospitals that share responsibility for the health care of a set of patients. ACOs provide savings incentives by offering bonuses when providers keep costs down and meet specific quality benchmarks, focusing on prevention and carefully managing patients with chronic diseases. In other words, providers get paid more for keeping their patients healthy and out of the hospital. To do this requires providers and hospitals to work in the community beyond the walls of their institutions to ensure better care coordination—and better social and physical conditions for promoting health. The Texas Medicaid waiver was constructed such that 5% of the billions of dollars in the waiver was earmarked to support public health interventions that would prevent illness or injury and thus save Medicaid money. These innovations, like the ones mentioned previously, must be monitored for their ability to lead to population health improvement interventions and results in order to document their potential as sustainable sources of funding for population health improvement.

■ Conclusion

The population health model has been accepted and used as a basis for health policy decisions in Europe, Canada, Australia, and New Zealand for nearly 20 years, and the World Health Organization Commission on Social Determinants made recommendations for implementation in 2008.

The United States is finally catching up. Recognition of the importance and value of population health science in the United States is demonstrated by numerous types of evidence:

- The very large bibliography of relevant peer-reviewed articles appearing in top U.S. medical and health care journals, as well as books in multiple disciplines
- National Institutes of Health and CDC funding of multidisciplinary population health research and intervention programs
- Numerous IOM review committees and reports on the multiple determinants of health
- The IOM roundtable on population health improvement
- Interdisciplinary population health centers and training programs at premier universities across the country

- The MacArthur Research Network on Socioeconomic Status and Health, a research working group funded by the MacArthur Foundation, which operated from 1998 to 2010
- National commissions on population health and prevention, including the Robert Wood Johnson Foundation's two reports from the Commission to Build a Healthier America
- The annual national *County Health Rankings* report based on a multiple determinants of health framework

The population health model is increasingly accepted as a framework for understanding the multiple determinants of health, with an emphasis on prevention and a strong basis in scientific evidence. However, the same term—"population health"—entered the clinical lexicon in 2007 as part of the Institute for Healthcare Improvement's (IHI) Triple Aim initiative. This initiative's three-part goal is (a) to improve the health of the population, (b) to enhance the experience and outcomes of the patient, and (c) to reduce per capita cost of care for the benefit of communities. The Triple Aim initiative's use of the phrase "population health" has led to some confusion in terminology. Noting this confusion, the IHI stated in 2014 that "population health" refers to the broader determinants of health, whereas the Triple Aim refers to "population medicine" as the management of a discrete population in a health care system, health plan, or accountable care organization to improve outcomes.

There is also a great potential for population health strategies to aid medical care providers in improving the outcomes for their patients. As noted earlier in this chapter, population health is not only about primary prevention; the social, behavioral, and environmental determinants of health also strongly affect patients' ability and likelihood to carry out medical care providers' recommendations about changing lifestyle behaviors to reduce potential complications, or to prevent social crises (such as losing a job or becoming homeless) that in turn trigger serious health crises.

As envisaged in the 2003 IOM report on the future of the public's health, collaboration among those using the medical, governmental public health, and population health models would provide a more coherent national approach to health improvement. Such an approach would include a common, integrated set of metrics for determinants and outcomes, would provide sustainable realigned funding, and would result in more strategic and synergistic planning for the actions best suited for improving the conditions needed for all Americans to have the opportunity to lead healthy lives.

■ Discussion Questions

1. The general public equates the word "health" with "health care." Polls asking people about their health typically result in responses about their health care experiences. How do you define health? How would you assess a population's health if you could ask the people in that population only one question on a survey?
2. Why do some people refer to the health care system as "the sickness care system"? Do you agree or disagree with this term?

3. Cross-sectional research shows that, on average, people with disabilities secondary to illness or injury have lower socioeconomic status than people without disabilities. How could longitudinal research help to explain whether this is because people of lower socioeconomic status are at higher risk of developing disabilities, or because disability leads to loss of income and thus lower socioeconomic status? In a population health model, how might lower socioeconomic status increase the risk of disability secondary to illness or injury?

4. The Commission to Build a Healthier America found that non-Hispanic Whites were more likely to be in very good or excellent health than were other groups nationally and in almost every state. In addition, non-Hispanic Whites had better health status than adults in any other racial or ethnic group at every level of education, but all groups showed a gradient in health by educational level. What are some of the determinants that are likely contributing to this disparity in health between non-Hispanic Whites and other groups after controlling for different educational levels?

5. It is possible that a community's *County Health Rankings* would suggest that the biggest driver of poor health in that community is unemployment. How would you present the case to your nonprofit hospital board that the biggest community benefit contribution the hospital could make would be to join and support an initiative to increase job openings in the community, rather than holding health fairs or offering educational lecture series?

CASE STUDY

Recent data show that Americans consume, on average, more than three times the recommended level of sodium per day in their food and beverages. High salt intake contributes to high blood pressure and its complications—stroke, heart attack, congestive heart failure, and kidney failure. In fact, thousands of lives could be saved if sodium consumption were lowered in people with high blood pressure. Write a memo for the U.S. Secretary of Health and Human Services about what might be done to address concerns about the effect of high sodium intake on health. In preparing your memo, consider the following questions:

1. How might we address this problem in the patient population using the medical model that a health care provider might use versus a population health model that a public health official might use?

2. How far can and should governments go in attempting to create a more healthful environment? Intrinsic to many population health policies is the specter of the so-called nanny state. In this case, is it necessary for everyone to be exposed to lower sodium in their bread, in other common foods, and in restaurants, so as to protect people who have salt-sensitive illnesses?

3. Should manufacturers bear the costs of manufacturing different versions of foods in order to protect the public's health? Should they be required to manufacture healthier foods even if customers prefer the less-healthy versions? Or should they be liable if they don't manufacture healthier foods?

■ References

Adler, N. E., & Stewart, J. (Eds.). (2010). *The biology of disadvantage: Socioeconomic status and health. Annals of the New York Academy of Sciences* (Vol. 1186). San Francisco, CA: MacArthur Network for Socioeconomic Health.

Bleich, S. (2005, July). Medical errors: Five years after the IOM report. *Issue Brief (The Commonwealth Fund)*, 830, 1–15.

Bunker, J. P., Frazier, H. S., & Mosteller, F. (1995). The role of medical care in determining health: Creating an inventory of benefits. In B. C. Amick III, S. Levine, A. R. Tarlov, & D. C. Walsh (Eds.), *Society and health* (pp. 304–341). New York, NY: Oxford University Press.

Evans, R. G., Barer, M. L., & Marmor, T. R. (Eds.). (1994). *Why are some people healthy and others not? The determinants of health of populations.* New York, NY: Walter de Gruyter, Inc.

Institute of Medicine. (2003). *The future of the public's health in the 21st century.* Washington, DC: National Academies Press.

Institute of Medicine. (2013). *Shorter lives, poorer health.* Washington, DC: National Academies Press.

Kindig, D., & Chin, S. (2009, June 18). Achieving "a culture of health": What would it mean for costs and our health status?" *Innovation, health, and equity: Taking a systems approach to health and economic vitality.* Presentation sponsored by Altarum Institute, Ann Arbor, MI.

Kindig, D., & Stoddart, G. (2003). What is population health? *American Journal of Public Health, 93,* 380–383.

Kohn, L. T., Corrigan, J. M., & Donaldson, M. S. (Eds.). (2000). *To err is human: Building a safer health system.* Washington, DC: National Academies Press.

Kreuter, M., & Lezin, N. (2001). *Improving everyone's quality of life: A primer on population health.* Seattle, WA: Group Health Community Foundation.

Mackenbach, J. P., Stirbu, I., Roskam, A. R., Schaap, M. M., Menvielle, G., Leinsalu, M., & Kunst, A. E. (2008). Socioeconomic inequalities in health in 22 European countries [Special article]. *New England Journal of Medicine, 358,* 2468–2481. doi:10.1056/NEJMsa0707519

McGinnis, J. M., & Foege, W. H. (1993). Actual causes of death in the United States. *Journal of the American Medical Association, 270,* 2207–2212.

McKeown, T. (1976). *The role of medicine: Dream, mirage, or nemesis?* London: Nuffield Provincial Hospitals Trust.

Mokdad, A. H., Marks, J. S., Stroup, D. F., & Gerberding, J. L. (2004). Actual causes of death in the United States, 2000. *Journal of the American Medical Association, 291,* 1238–1245. (Correction published 2005, *Journal of the American Medical Association, 293,* pp. 293–294.)

Robert Wood Johnson Foundation Commission to Build a Healthier America. (2009). *Beyond health care: New directions to a healthier America.* Princeton, NJ: Robert Wood Johnson Foundation.

Robert Wood Johnson Foundation to Build a Healthier America. (2014). *Time to act: Investing in the health of our children and communities.* Princeton, NJ: Robert Wood Johnson Foundation.

Schoeni, R. F., House, J. S., Kaplan, G. A., & Pollack, H. (Eds.). (2008). *Making Americans healthier: Social and economic policy as health policy.* New York, NY: Russell Sage Foundation.

Trust for America's Health. (2008). *Prevention for a healthier America: Investments in disease prevention yield significant savings, stronger communities.* Washington, DC: Trust for America's Health. Retrieved from http://healthyamericans.org/reports/prevention08/

United Health Foundation. (2007). *America's Health Rankings: A call to action for people and their communities*. Minnetonka, MN: United Health Foundation.

University of Wisconsin Population Health Institute. (2010). *County Health Rankings model*. Madison, WI: University of Wisconsin Population Health Institute.

Williams, D., & Collins, C. (2001). Racial residential segregation: A fundamental cause of racial disparities in health. *Public Health Reports, 116,* 404–416.

Woolf, S. H., Johnson, R. E., Phillips, R. L., & Philipsen, M. (2007). Giving everyone the health of the educated: An examination of whether social change would save more lives than medical advances. *American Journal of Public Health, 97,* 679–683.

6 Public Health: A Transformation for the 21st Century

Laura C. Leviton, Paul L. Kuehnert, and Kathryn E. Wehr

KEY WORDS

Association of State and Territorial
    Health Officers (ASTHO)

core functions (assessment, assurance,
    policy development)

disease prevention (primary, secondary,
    tertiary)

essential services

health impact assessments

health promotion

National Association of County and City
    Health Officials (NACCHO)

nongovernmental organizations

population health

Public Health Accreditation Board
    (PHAB)

World Health Organization (WHO)
    definition of health

LEARNING OBJECTIVES

- ◉ Contrast defining characteristics of prevention-oriented public health and treatment-oriented health care
- ◉ Describe state, federal, and local authority for public health law, regulation, and services
- ◉ Identify how challenges and opportunities are transforming public health

TOPICAL OUTLINE

- ◉ Who's in charge of public health?
- ◉ A healthy population is in the public's interest
- ◉ Core functions of public health
- ◉ Governmental authority and services
- ◉ A transformation of public health

■ Who's in Charge of Public Health?

This chapter introduces the policies, programs, and practices that constitute public health in the United States. Public health is "what society does collectively to assure the conditions for people to be healthy" (Institute of Medicine [IOM], 2002). It is the science, practice, and art of protecting and improving the health of populations. Historically, public health emphasized regulating and improving community sanitation and monitoring environmental hazards. Over time it greatly expanded its role in documenting and controlling communicable diseases and encouraging healthful behavior. In the late 20th century, many local health departments were the provider of last resort for indigent health care, a situation that is changing with passage of the Patient Protection and Affordable Care Act (ACA) in 2010. As the ACA reorganizes activity and channels resources to prevention, public health champions are working far beyond the health sector to advocate for a broader set of policies and systems changes to improve and protect health.

We first describe the goals and characteristics of public health that differentiate it from medical care treatment, and we outline the core functions of public health. We then describe the complex network of laws, regulations, authorities, and services involved. State, federal, tribal, and local government agencies, often called the *infrastructure*, have legal authority for the core functions. But champions of public health span many public, private, and nonprofit organizations. In the concluding section, we describe forces at work to transform public health in the 21st century.

PUBLIC HEALTH EVERY DAY

Public health activities affect the lives of Americans profoundly, but more often than not these activities are invisible.

Public health activities affect the lives of Americans profoundly, but more often than not these activities are invisible. A thought experiment shows how this works. Imagine waking up and going through your morning routine. You slept 8 hours for a change, because health experts claim that lack of sleep causes stress and other health problems. You wander into the bathroom and brush your teeth—teeth that are still in your mouth and pain-free thanks to regular brushing and flossing, adequate nutrition, the fluoride in your local water supply, and routine dental visits. You rinse your mouth with water that is safe to drink. Before it ever reached your faucet, it was checked for sickness-causing bacteria, heavy metals such as lead (which causes lower intelligence in children), and chemicals such as polychlorinated biphenyls (which cause cancer). When you flushed the toilet, the waste did not get into the water supply where it could kill you.

You get your children ready for school; so far, they have all survived, never having had measles, diphtheria, polio, or other diseases that killed and maimed so many children in bygone days. The kids' breakfast includes cereal and pure pasteurized milk. You looked at the nutritional label on their cereal and saw that the ingredients included whole grains and not too much sugar. You open the newspaper to see that a new influenza strain is spreading, and the authorities have renewed their advisory for hand-washing and travel precautions.

Your sister calls to announce she is going to have a baby! She is not aware that the toast she is eating is fortified with folic acid, the B vitamin that prevents birth defects. The couple can have a baby in part because young people in their town had access to comprehensive sex education and family planning—they never had gonorrhea or chlamydia, which can cause infertility.

The two of you also discuss your father. He's over 70 and not in the best health, so he needs to get his flu and pneumonia shots right away! The last time he had flu, it turned into pneumonia; he went to the hospital and could have died. Both of you are worried about him, because he is overweight, still smokes, and never exercises.

Is a heart attack, diabetes, or stroke in his future? The odds are not in Dad's favor. Quit-smoking programs are available in the community without charge, so you agree that Dad's doctor should try suggesting them again. Too bad there are no sidewalks in Dad's neighborhood; he loves to walk, but there is too much traffic. Does the senior center have an exercise program that might appeal to him?

You buckle the kids into their safety belts. When you get to your job, you see signs that read: "607 days without an accident at this worksite" and "proud to be tobacco free since 2008."

DIVIDED RESPONSIBILITIES AND ISSUE-SPECIFIC ORGANIZATIONS

The responsibility for the public's health and the infrastructure to make it work are divided among many agencies across all levels of government, and many nongovernmental organizations, professional associations, and businesses (see Figure 6.1). In

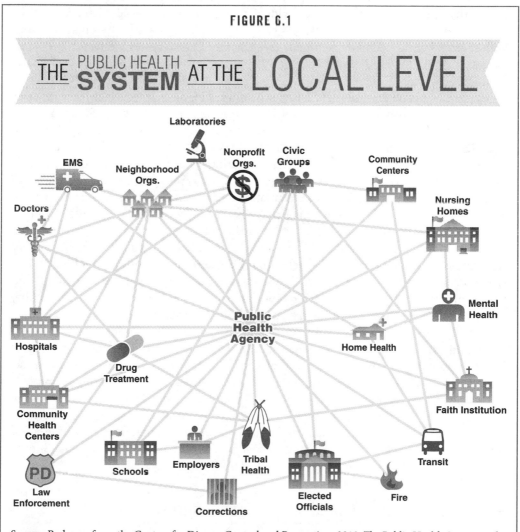

FIGURE 6.1

THE PUBLIC HEALTH SYSTEM AT THE LOCAL LEVEL

Source: Redrawn from the Centers for Disease Control and Prevention, 2013, The Public Health System and the 10 Essential Public Health Services http://www.cdc.gov/nphpsp/essentialservices.html

our thought experiment, for example, municipal authorities handle waste water, but the federal government regulates chemicals in the water supply. The federal government recommends physical activity for older adults, but senior centers, YMCA, private gyms, and city departments of transportation, parks and recreation, and public safety all make it possible to be physically active. The federal government requires seat belts and air bags in cars, but state laws mandate seat belt use and the penalties for violation, and local police generally enforce the laws.

At least four factors account for the complexity and diffuse responsibility for public health in the United States. The first factor is that our government is not centralized; states have authority for public health except where specified by federal and tribal law. How much authority the states in turn share with local government varies a great deal and rests with diverse agencies, boards of health, and municipal and tribal codes (Hodge, 2012; IOM, 2011).

Second is the distinctive American tendency, first recognized by Alexis de Tocqueville in the 1830s, to design laws, policies, and organizations that are problem specific, rather than general. For example, individual diseases receive special legal recognition, and new federal programs, policies, and categorical funding streams are created to deal with them. Diverse federal departments (see Chapter 2) deal with such health problems as assuring pure food and drugs (Food and Drug Administration [FDA] and U.S. Department of Agriculture [USDA]), monitoring and controlling infectious diseases (Centers for Disease Control and Prevention [CDC]), providing guidance to prevent chronic diseases (CDC, National Institutes of Health [NIH]), improving traffic safety (U.S. Department of Transportation, National Highway Traffic Safety Administration [NHTSA]), maternal and child health (Centers for Medicare & Medicaid Services [CMS], Health Resources and Services Administration [HRSA]), and ensuring a healthy place to work (Occupational Safety and Health Administration [OSHA], Mine Safety and Health Administration [MSHA], National Institute for Occupational Safety and Health [NIOSH]).

A third distinctively American approach is the heavy reliance on nongovernmental organizations to achieve public health goals. Yet these organizations also tend to be issue specific: national organizations and their local affiliates such as the American Red Cross, American Heart Association, the Planned Parenthood Federation of America, United Way Worldwide, the Y, various environmental organizations, and many community-based organizations specific to a city neighborhood. With shrinking governments, these organizations take on additional importance.

The fourth cause of diffused responsibility lies in the broad definition of health goals and ongoing debates over what should be done to achieve them. The World Health Organization (WHO) asserts that health is more than the absence of disease, but rather "a state of complete mental, physical, and social well-being" (Green & Kreuter, 1999). Well-being is achieved, for example, when children perform well in school and do not fear neighborhood violence, when physical and mental functioning is maintained well into old age, and when people have a better quality of life. But where, then, do we draw the line between health goals and other societal goals? Should we draw such a line? Who has responsibility, and for which goals?

■ A Healthy Population Is in the Public Interest

Two key assumptions distinguish public health from the health care delivery systems discussed elsewhere in this text: (a) A healthy population is in the public interest, and

(b) working at a societal or community level (outside of what a clinician can do in a medical care setting) we can improve an entire population's health.

THE HEALTH OF POPULATIONS

The goal of public health is to improve the *health status of entire populations,* not just individuals. It is concerned with the incidence, prevalence, and distribution of health problems (see Chapter 5). In using these indicators, public health aims to identify health problems and improve them through action at a community or collective level. This aim is well justified by past successes. Between 1900 and 2000, average life expectancy increased from 47.3 to 76.8 years (CDC, 2011). Medical care treatment did not accomplish this change. Rather, society made pervasive improvements in 10 public health arenas (see Table 6.1). In the present day, health is still most strongly determined by behavioral, community, environmental, and societal forces, not by medical care (see Chapters 5 and 7).

THE PUBLIC INTEREST JUSTIFICATION

Since ancient times, people have taken collective action to protect themselves from plague and environmental disaster. In the 19th century, public health was justified on utilitarian grounds: the greatest good for the greatest number. Healthy people are a more productive workforce and better able to defend the nation. The utilitarian argument is still compelling: For example, a high childhood obesity rate impairs America's economic competitiveness and the combat readiness of youth (IOM, 2012). However, public health today is also justified as a human right and is seen as a means to achieve social justice by addressing social and economic disparities in health (Beauchamp & Steinbock, 1999).

Not everyone agrees with this rationale. Conservatives often reject social justice as a reason for collective action. In truth, most public health services serve both utilitarian and social justice aims. For example, many publicly funded prevention efforts are targeted to poor children, but these efforts also help produce a healthier workforce.

TABLE 6.1 TEN GREAT PUBLIC HEALTH ACHIEVEMENTS: UNITED STATES, 1900–1999

- Vaccination
- Motor-vehicle safety
- Safer workplaces
- Control of infectious diseases
- Decline in deaths from coronary heart disease and stroke
- Safer and healthier foods
- Healthier mothers and babies
- Family planning
- Fluoridation of drinking water
- Recognition of tobacco use as a health hazard

Note: Based on the effect on death, illness and disability in the United States and not ranked by order of importance.
Source: U.S. Centers for Disease Control and Prevention (1999). Ten great public health achievements—United States, 1900 to 1999. Retrieved April 6, 2014 from http://www.cdc.gov/mmwr/preview/mmwrhtml/00056796.htm

Also, libertarians believe public health limits individual liberty (Leviton, Needleman, & Shapiro, 1997). Indeed, public health policy and practice usually balance individual freedoms and collective benefits. For example, health departments have police powers to control infectious disease as a "clear and present danger," but they need to do so without appearing to abuse this power. Finally, some Americans may question whether government should be involved in public health: Can't private or nonprofit organizations play the role that government plays now? In fact, private and nonprofit organizations do play important roles, but without government there is no way to address what economists term "market failures" of health care. For example, private physicians lack the health department's legal authority to monitor, track, intervene, and disrupt the spread of sexually transmitted diseases, food-borne disease outbreaks, rat infestations, lead poisoning among children, and other many other problems.

A COLLECTIVE FOCUS ON DISEASE PREVENTION AND HEALTH PROMOTION

Public health works on prevention at a collective level through health promotion, changes in policy or law, and consensus of professional societies about prevention efforts. Health promotion addresses behavior and lifestyle: "the combination of educational and environmental supports for actions and conditions of living conducive to health" (Green & Kreuter, 1999; see Chapter 7). Health promotion often works through businesses, schools, recreational facilities and community associations, as well as in the health care setting.

The U.S. Preventive Services Task Force (2010) uses three long-accepted categories to describe the full array of potential preventive interventions:

- *Primary prevention:* helping people avoid the onset of a health condition, including injuries
- *Secondary prevention:* identifying and treating people who have risk factors or preclinical disease
- *Tertiary prevention:* treating people with an established disease, in order to restore their highest functioning, minimize negative effects, and prevent complications

These categories, especially tertiary prevention, obviously spill over into the medical treatment of individuals; at a systems level, however, they are public health issues. Providers need guidance and support to carry them out. In Table 6.2 we can see the differences between individual and collective prevention for heart disease and stroke. Notice that successful prevention for an individual (in this case, a person who might have a heart attack or stroke) depends on the widespread availability of prevention services at a *population* level. To understand more about how medical care and public health can support each other, especially since the passage of the ACA, see the Surgeon General's National Prevention Strategy (www.surgeongeneral.gov/initiatives/prevention/strategy/).

Disease prevention and health promotion are rarely completely effective, because there are no "magic bullets" that can prevent 100% of people from becoming sick.

TABLE 6.2 DIFFERENCES BETWEEN THE ROLES OF INDIVIDUAL MEDICAL CARE AND PUBLIC HEALTH

	Individual Medical Care	Public Health
Primary Prevention	Encourages patients to maintain healthy weight, be physically active, and not smoke	Works to establish bike and walking paths and to eliminate transfats from foods, offers smoking quitlines, advocates for smoke-free public spaces and higher cigarette taxes, provides prevention guidelines to medical care providers
Secondary Prevention	Encourages regular checkups for detecting and treating high blood pressure, elevated cholesterol, and other risk factors	Mounts public service campaigns about the importance of controlling blood pressure and "knowing your number" for cholesterol, provides guidelines to medical care providers on diagnosis of blood pressure and hypercholesterolemia
Tertiary Prevention	Treats heart attack to save the heart muscle, treats stroke to minimize nervous system damage, treats atherosclerosis, restores function and prevents recurrence through cardiac rehabilitation and medication	Provides guidelines on treatment to medical care providers, creates widespread awareness of the symptoms of heart attack and stroke and the need to seek help quickly to save the heart muscle, teaches CPR, locates automated external defibrillators in public places and worksites, establishes effective emergency systems, sponsors patient support groups

An important effort of the U.S. Department of Health and Human Services (DHHS, 2013), *Healthy People 2020*, provides a comprehensive review of priority health risks, effective strategies, and public health focus areas for the nation, each with many specific objectives. These areas are updated every 10 years. Progress in meeting the *Healthy People* objectives has been very uneven, because many of the objectives are quite ambitious (Sondik, Huang, Klein, & Satcher, 2010). Disease prevention and health promotion are rarely completely effective, because there are no "magic bullets" that can prevent 100% of people from becoming sick. For example, prevention has greatly reduced the rate of heart attacks, but some heart attacks still occur. Youth smoking has declined, but some youth still take up smoking in spite of all efforts to discourage them. People die in car crashes in spite of lower fatalities and many safety improvements.

Universal prevention means that everyone receives an intervention equally, whereas *targeted prevention* involves identifying and serving people at higher risk. When they are possible, universal approaches are often more effective in improving the health of populations. The case of traffic safety illustrates these approaches. People who drive while intoxicated are clearly at high risk of injury to themselves and others, and targeting drunk drivers improves road safety for everyone. However, universal protections, such as seat belts, air bags, and safer vehicles, contribute much more to reducing traffic fatalities and injuries because they help everyone, even those who never encounter a drunk driver (National Highway Traffic Safety Administration, 2014).

Targeted prevention is an important focus for public health when the risk is prevalent and when there are effective means to identify and treat it. For example, a national campaign in the 1970s led to improved identification and treatment of people with high blood pressure. This, in turn, greatly reduced premature death and disability from cardiovascular disease (CDC, 2011). However, an initial goal was to make sure that providers screened *all* their patients for high blood pressure, a universal strategy with a population focus. Combining universal and targeted strategies can have a cumulative benefit, and a balance of targeted and universal approaches is important to avoid stigma or victim-blaming of people at risk.

■ Core Functions of Public Health

DEFINITION OF CORE FUNCTIONS

Public health serves three core functions—assessment, policy development, and assurance—as seen in Figure 6.2, to solve health problems at a population level (IOM, 2002). *Assessment of public health problems* involves understanding their prevalence, severity, and causes, using various well-tested statistical tools. Although private and nonprofit organizations often do such assessments, public health agencies have the

---

FIGURE 6.2   THE CIRCLE OF PUBLIC HEALTH ACTIVITIES AND 10 ESSENTIAL SERVICES.

THE 10 ESSENTIAL PUBLIC HEALTH SERVICES

The 10 Essential Public Health Services describe the public health activities that all communities should undertake and serve as the framework for the National Public Health Performance Standards (NPHPS) instruments. Public health systems should:

ASSESSMENT
1 Monitor health status to identify and solve community health problems.
2 Diagnose and investigate health problems and health hazards in the community.

POLICY DEVELOPMENT
3 Inform, educate, and empower people about health issues.
4 Mobilize community partnerships and action to identify and solve health problems.
5 Develop policies and plans that support individual and community health efforts.

ASSURANCE
6 Enforce laws and regulations that protect health and ensure safety.
7 Link people to needed personal health services and ensure the provision of health care when otherwise unavailable.
8 Ensure competent public and personal health care workforce.
9 Evaluate effectiveness, accessibility, and quality of personal and population-based health services.
10 Research for new insights and innovative solutions to health problems.

Source: Redrawn from the Centers for Disease Control and Prevention, 2013, The Public Health System and the 10 Essential Public Health Services http://www.cdc.gov/nphpsp/essentialservices.html

primary responsibility for surveillance of population health status, monitoring of disease trends, and analysis of the causes of those trends and points for intervention. The assessment function is undergoing dramatic transformations, both in terms of resources and technology, as seen in the final section.

The second core function, *policy development,* is to create and advocate for solutions to achieve public health goals. Formal policy development includes devising laws and regulations to protect the public, as in the case of environmental protection; funding and reimbursement for specific services such as child immunizations; and setting guidelines or standards for services or practices, such as laboratory testing for infectious diseases. However, policy development can also involve voluntary changes and agreements in communities, business, health care, or nonprofit organizations—for example, locating a supermarket in an underserved area so that people have access to fresh fruits and vegetables.

The third core function, *assurance,* involves enforcement of policy, as with inspection of restaurant sanitation or nursing home safety; monitoring legal compliance, as with smoke-free indoor air laws; ensuring proper implementation of necessary services such as supervision of home visits to new mothers in disadvantaged communities; and adequate crisis response, as when public health plays a role in coping with natural disasters.

In order to fulfill all three core functions, public health departments are highly dependent on other organizations and individuals. For *assessment,* public health relies on medical care providers, first responders, and others to provide the necessary data on births, deaths, reportable diseases, and environmental hazards. For *policy development* it relies on advocates, policymakers, and community collaborators who share a common interest in public health goals. For *assurance* it relies on complementary health care services and voluntary compliance with standards and regulations. Public health agencies do not have the legal authority, financial capability, or personnel to address all health problems by themselves. They need to collaborate with other organizations that have the power, influence, and resources to achieve better public health outcomes—for example, in promoting worker safety, ensuring safe food, or building bicycle- and pedestrian-friendly streets for physical activity.

CORE FUNCTIONS: AN EXAMPLE

The following example, concerning the birth defect spina bifida, illustrates the cyclical problem-solving approach used in public health (see Figure 6.2 and www.cdc.gov/ncbddd/spinabifida/data.html). Different types of assessment, policy development, and assurance issues emerge during this cycle.

1. *Monitor the problem:* Spina bifida is a neural tube defect that develops in the first 3 to 4 weeks of pregnancy, when the neural tube that will form the spine does not close properly. In its most severe form, spina bifida leads to leg paralysis, bowel and bladder control problems, and, without treatment, mental retardation. Spina bifida affects 3.05 out of every 10,000 live births (*assessment*).

2. *Diagnose and investigate:* The CDC projects that 50% to 70% of spina bifida cases can be prevented if women take enough folic acid (a B vitamin) before and during pregnancy. Folic acid is most effective in promoting healthy neural tube

development when taken before pregnancy and during the critical first weeks. For this reason, the CDC recommends that, even *before they become pregnant*, women take a multivitamin with 400 mg of folic acid every day and eat foods rich in folic acid (Centers for Disease Control and Prevention, 2010). (*policy development*).

3. ***Develop policies:*** Unfortunately, women may not know they are pregnant until the defect has developed, as roughly half of all pregnancies are unplanned. Also, foods that naturally contain folic acid may not be readily available to the poor or to individuals eating certain diets (*assessment*). One alternative is to fortify common foods with folic acid (*policy development*).

4. ***Enforce laws and regulations:*** Since 1998, the government has required that enriched cereal, pasta, flour, and bread products include folic acid (*assurance, policy development*).

5. ***Evaluate effectiveness:*** Since the fortification requirement began, the rate of spina bifida in the United States has declined by 31% *(assurance, assessment)*.

6. ***Diagnose and investigate:*** Many scientists believe that we could prevent more cases of spina bifida if new regulations increased the amount of folic acid in grain products *(policy development, assessment)*.

■ Governmental Authority and Services

STATE AUTHORITY FOR PUBLIC HEALTH

State Law
The 10th Amendment to the U.S. Constitution gives states the primary responsibility for public health. (In contrast, the Constitution recognizes tribes as sovereign nations for decision making and designates federal responsibility for their health [Hodge, 2012]). The 50 states vary greatly on how they define and delegate public health authority and responsibility. States enacted public health statutes over time to respond to specific diseases or health threats.

These laws are fragmented and badly out of date, so public health law is emerging as a powerful force to improve effectiveness (IOM, 2011). For example, some state laws have separate sections for specific communicable diseases, instead of standard approaches to address infectious disease in general. This fragmentation leaves them with no standards for addressing new infectious diseases, advances in public health practice, and constitutional law. State laws require updating to permit new multisectoral health promotion efforts—for example, collaborations among public health, transportation, and parks and recreation to encourage more physical activity. State laws may also neglect important safeguards for privacy, due process, and protection from discrimination. The Model State Public Health Act takes a systematic approach to establishing authority, implementing public health responsibilities, and modernizing public health core functions. However, as of 2011 the Model Act did not have much uptake (IOM, 2011).

Although the Model Act addresses inconsistencies within a state, other improvements are needed for problems that cross state lines. Chief among these are problems arising from human-made and naturally occurring events such as the anthrax attacks in the fall of 2001, hurricanes Katrina and Rita in 2005, the 2009 H1N1 influenza pandemic, and Superstorm Sandy in 2012. These events have underscored the need for legal reforms to enhance public health emergency preparedness by addressing a variety of issues including: (a) declaring public health emergencies separate from other types of disasters; (b) expediting public health powers, such as those needed to collect health data, screen, vaccinate or treat exposed people or seize property to abate hazards, isolate or quarantine residents; (c) recruiting and deploying trained health professional volunteers; and (d) providing liability protections to health professionals and entities, among others (Hodge, 2012). Since 2002, 26 states and the District of Columbia have amended their statutes to incorporate the term "public health emergencies" or similar terms (Network for Public Health Law, 2011).

State Health Departments

A state's chief health official directs the department of public health and may report directly to the governor or to an officer in the governor's cabinet. The state health department's position in the chain of command and the governor's priorities affect the authority and power of its director. Medicaid and public assistance programs, being among the costliest state programs, tend to garner most of a governor's attention. At times, this can affect the quality of public health services. The website of the Association of State and Territorial Health Officers (ASTHO, www.astho.org) provides a wealth of detail on the characteristics and financing of state health departments. Twenty-seven state health departments are free standing as separate agencies, whereas 23 states combine public health into umbrella agencies with related programs, such as Medicaid, human services and welfare, mental health and substance abuse, or environmental management. The ways various health-related functions and programs are organized affect how well public health activities can be coordinated. For example, environmental protection is often located outside the health department, in which case conservation, wilderness preservation, or litigation around toxic spills may head that other agency's agenda. This situation often leaves less opportunity for effective interaction with the health department, even though the health department must monitor potential health consequences of environmental exposures.

INTERGOVERNMENTAL RELATIONS

Federal–State Relations

Although the states have constitutional authority to implement public health, a wide variety of federal programs and laws affect their work. Federal law relating to public health preempts state laws, just as state law preempts local laws. (However, tribal governments are sovereign nations, so tribal law supersedes other laws, if they are in place.) Preemption affects public health, because the federal government can require "floor preemptions"—minimum protections below which states cannot go. For example, the Clean Water Act requires a minimum standard for water in all states, although states are allowed to have more stringent standards. But "ceiling preemption" can pose an obstacle to prevention when states and localities are more aggressive than the federal government. For example, the tobacco industry challenged state and local regulation of tobacco in the courts, and more recently, Mississippi passed a law to preempt local efforts to limit the size of sugar-sweetened beverages.

The federal agencies working in public health are described in Chapter 2. States must constantly interact with these federal agencies. For example, the DHHS supports state health departments with block grants for maternal and child health and preventive services; it also supports state agencies for child welfare services, substance abuse treatment and prevention, and mental health. The DHHS also funds the states to train the public health workforce. The CDC provides grants and cooperative agreements to states, cities, and community-based organizations for HIV prevention, chronic disease control, and from 2010 to 2013, for improving state and local infrastructure (see the following). The USDA provides health departments with direct support for food assistance and nutrition education. The Environmental Protection Agency (EPA) provides direct resources to the states for environmental management. Most of these funding streams are *categorical*—that is, the funding is intended for specific categories of people or special purposes. Congress authorizes categorical funding to address a specific health problem, such as preventing AIDS or addressing bioterrorism. However, categorical funding limits states' flexibility to deliver a range of relevant services with available resources.

Delegation of State Authority to Local Health Departments

States vary in terms of the authority they give to local governments and local public health departments. As of 2011, 14 states had centralized public health departments, meaning that employees of the state lead the local health units, and the state retains authority over many decisions relating to the budget, public health orders, and the selection of local health officials. Health departments were decentralized in 27 states: Local governments make many decisions and staff the local health units. Four states shared authority, decision making, and employment with local governments. The remaining five states were mixed, meaning that some features were centralized, whereas others were shared or decentralized.

The National Association of County and City Health Officials (NACCHO) website (www.naccho.org) offers further detail on the wide variety of organizational arrangements, responsibilities, financing, staffing, and authority of local health departments. One reason for this variety is simply historical. The first public health agencies were formed in the early 1800s and were primarily city based. Later in the 19th century, state health agencies began to form. Throughout the 20th century, county health departments developed. One can see the effects by comparing older states with states that were admitted to the union more recently: Massachusetts has 329 local boards of health, whereas Oregon has 34 county health departments. State and local health departments are exploring ways to share services, functions, and staff across jurisdictional boundaries. From "handshake agreements" to more formal memoranda of understanding to consolidations and mergers, these sharing arrangements often seek to balance effectiveness and efficiency concerns (Libbey & Miayhara, 2011).

Local, state, tribal, and federal agencies all have strengths and resources for public health. States and localities usually better understand local problems and how local conditions affect services. Meanwhile, the federal government has greater resources and scientific expertise for tackling large and complex health threats. The CDC, for example, leads the investigation of serious disease outbreaks, such as H1N1, and makes recommendations for both clinical and community prevention. The federal government also steps in when health threats cross state borders or when states cannot comply with federal regulations, offering technical assistance and financial support.

PUBLIC HEALTH SERVICES

State Responsibilities

These generally include disease and injury prevention, sanitation, controlling water and air pollution, vaccination, isolation and quarantine, inspection of commercial and residential premises, food and drinking water standards, extermination of vermin, fluoridation of municipal water supplies, and licensure of physicians and other health care professionals. However, the specific activities and services provided vary widely across states and localities. For example, state and local health departments work to prevent chronic disease but focus to varying degrees on education, social marketing, or policy and environmental changes (see Chapter 7).

Ten Essential Services

In the face of this variation, most public health professionals agree that all health departments should provide the 10 essential services listed in Figure 6.2. Most local health departments are challenged to provide these services on their own, given their serious resource and staffing limitations. Most departments are small and rural: 61% serve fewer than 50,000 people and usually have 15 or fewer full time staff. Staff skills in many health departments are weak, and higher education is not doing enough to provide the appropriate training. Many experienced professionals are on the verge of retirement, and replacements are in short supply given the low salaries and rural location of many local health departments. Many health departments are thinking creatively about how to meet these challenges, the topic of the final section.

Public Health Emergencies

Since the 2001 anthrax attacks, public health agencies have faced the added responsibility of protecting the public against bioterrorism threats and other communicable disease emergencies. Experts agree that we can soon expect another severe flu epidemic, perhaps as serious as the 1918 pandemic that killed an estimated 675,000 Americans. Diseases spread much more quickly than they did in the past because of international travel, urban overcrowding and poverty, climate change, and overuse of antibiotics, which produce multiple drug resistant infections (such as the so-called superbug multidrug-resistant *Staphylococcus aureus* [MRSA]). Interventions include global surveillance networks, stockpiles of vaccines, and better communications to deal with outbreaks. Although preparedness is much better now than in 2001, a 2013 study found that two thirds of the states had inadequate policies and capabilities to protect against threats from communicable diseases (Trust for America's Health, 2013b).

New Training, Competencies, and Accreditation

As of 2011, public health agencies have national voluntary performance standards, with review by an external accrediting body, the Public Health Accreditation Board (PHAB). These standards are a means, not an end, to improve the quality of public health services, including their effectiveness and efficiency. They establish accountability for providing good services, strengthen the credibility of public health agencies, and help to identify areas for improvement (Centers for Disease Control and Prevention, 2004). At the end of 2013, more than 170 state, local, and tribal health departments serving 60% of the U.S. population were accredited or in the accreditation process. The PHAB website gives updates on progress and details of the accreditation standards (www.phaboard. org). PHAB also developed a consensus set of core competencies for public health practice at the entry, supervisory, and executive levels (being revised in 2014). Movement to upgrade the competence of individual public health workers is seen in new management academies, continuing education, and certificate programs (IOM, 2009).

■ Rethinking Public Health for the 21st Century

Champions of the public's health now have a major opportunity to rethink the infrastructure by working in new ways, communicating more effectively with the public, advocating for a wider variety of policies that affect health, and engaging new partners that are vital to achieving public health goals.

Government agencies are important, but they are only part of the public health story, and government is shrinking in the early 21st century. Champions of the public's health now have a major opportunity to rethink the infrastructure by working in new ways, communicating more effectively with the public, advocating for a wider variety of policies that affect health, and engaging new partners that are vital to achieving public health goals.

TRANSFORMING THE INFRASTRUCTURE

Shrinking Government

According to ASTHO and NACCHO, state and local health departments were hard hit by the recession of 2008 to 2010, with job losses totaling about 20% of the total public health workforce. During the recession nearly every health department reported making cuts to programs and services. These staffing and program cuts have continued into the recovery period. How can health departments serve their constituents with high quality and meet new national performance standards? National developments and creative partnerships at the state and local level offer part of the answer.

Federal Action Transforms Prevention

The ACA authorized $15 billion over 10 years for a Prevention and Public Health Fund, and recent stimulus funding, the American Recovery and Reinvestment Act of 2009, provided $650 million. These resources go to state and local governments but also to nongovernmental organizations and community coalitions. Many of the community efforts aim to change policies and environments to prevent chronic disease and promote physical activity, nutrition, and tobacco control (see Chapter 7). However, it has been challenging for the existing systems to absorb these funds quickly and to implement activities at scale (Trust for America's Health, 2013a). Also, the Prevention and Public Health Fund depends on appropriations from Congress; it faced the 2013 federal budget sequester as well as ongoing reductions to pay for other ACA activities such as enrollment in health insurance exchanges. The American Public Health Association (APHA) website (www.apha.org) gives updates on the fund.

Government at all levels aims to encourage more coordinated action across organizations. The ACA and executive orders mandate better planning and coordination of prevention. For example, the White House ordered coordination of childhood obesity prevention efforts across the USDA, CDC, NIH, and Department of Education (IOM, 2012). At the state and local levels, there is a growing realization that public health must rely on the range of partners with power and resources to bring about needed changes.

A New Role for the Health Care Sector

For more than 40 years, many local health departments have provided direct health care to the poor, leaving fewer resources to improve the health of *populations.* The ACA will free up these resources by insuring poor individuals, who may choose providers other than the health department. Some health departments are exploring ways to divest their primary care services while still fulfilling their duties to ensure health care in their jurisdictions, especially for vulnerable populations (Kuehnert & McConnaughay, 2012). Where they continue to provide health care services, health departments are identifying ways to collect third-party reimbursements—collections they have not had to do or been able to do historically. The ACA also alleviates pressure on health departments by giving incentives for providers to work in underserved areas and by reimbursing private plans for essential prevention services, such as vaccinations and screening, if the plans meet federal standards.

New Resources for Assessment

Nonprofit hospitals can satisfy their community benefit obligations under the ACA with community health assessments once every 3 years. These assessments aim to engage multisectoral community stakeholders to identify priority needs (www.cdc.gov/policy/chna/). Also, PHAB accreditation sets health department standards for more consistent, high-quality assessment. New data sources, including electronic health records, shared and linked databases, and techniques such as geographic information systems (GIS), allow rapid response to potential public health emergencies. Equally important, however, they help policymakers and community stakeholders to understand health differently, including opportunities to promote health and reduce health disparities. For example, GIS make it possible to design communities proactively to prevent obesity (IOM, 2012) or to reduce triggers for asthma (http://propellerhealth.com).

Public Health Institutes

The growing number of these institutes is a very positive development for public health. The National Network of Public Health Institutes website (www.nnphi.org) provides details on the 25 institutes, 11 institutes under development, and 7 affiliate organizations. As nongovernmental organizations, these institutes can accept private funds, leverage funding from multiple sources, and serve as fiscal intermediaries for health departments to speed the delivery of services and processes, such as hiring staff and buying supplies or equipment. Institute staff can advocate vigorously for public health programs and funding, whereas government employees have restrictions. Institutes can offer a credible, neutral, third-party voice on issues and can convene all interested parties to address a broad health problem and implement a multisector strategy. In general, health departments support these institutes and recognize their value and complementary roles.

EFFECTIVE COMMUNICATION AND ADVOCACY

Putting the Public Back in Public Health

The public—and policymakers—react to specific problems and crises. They do not see the disease cases, injuries, disabilities, and deaths that have been prevented.

The champions of the public's health need to build a constituency that understands its value, in order to create coalitions, gain allies to solve public health problems, and advocate effectively. The general public does not understand what public health is, often supposing it refers solely to programs for the poor. The public—and policymakers— react to specific problems and crises. They do not see the disease cases, injuries, disabilities, and deaths that have been prevented. And they do not understand why problems are not solved quickly when an eroded infrastructure hinders crisis response—such as when the 2001 anthrax episode overwhelmed many public health laboratories or after Hurricane Katrina, when even such a basic function as handling the dead broke down. In reality, public health is invisible because it is generally so effective. With this in mind, how can public health develop an effective public constituency?

Building and Maintaining Trust

Public health practitioners sometimes can be seen as authoritarian or paternalistic, especially when they stress science and technology ("this is good for you because science says so") while ignoring collaboration, democratic processes, and individuals' preferences. This tendency weakens their connections to grassroots groups and local leadership and limits input from (and active listening to) their constituents. The last years of the 20th century heightened public awareness of the need for a new form of leadership in public health—one that engages people on their own terms in order to engender trust and cooperation. For example, the EPA learned to work with communities affected by toxic contaminants. In its early days, however, the agency did not listen to the public about their concerns, did not provide the information they needed, or gave them incomprehensible techno-babble that enraged community leaders (Leviton et al., 1997). The old bureaucratic ways of doing business were simply not effective when people had legitimate concerns.

The most difficult lesson for public health came from the Tuskegee syphilis experiment (Jones, 1993). In 1932, 600 poor African American men in Macon County, Alabama, unknowingly became syphilis research subjects when the Public Health Service and the Tuskegee Institute began a study of the natural course of syphilis and offered the men "free medical care." Of 600 subjects, 339 had syphilis but were left untreated for up to 40 years, even though a penicillin cure became available in 1947. As many as 100 of the men died of syphilis and many more suffered long-term disabilities before a public outcry and a federal advisory panel's recommendations halted the study in 1972. Along with the Nuremberg Code on medical experiments, this episode led Congress to require new protections for human research subjects. In 1997, President Bill Clinton offered an official public apology to the Tuskegee study's eight survivors and participants' families. However, public health—and the health care system more generally—never fully regained African Americans' trust.

More Effective Voices

ASTHO, NACCHO, and APHA offer important communication tools to increase effectiveness in advocating for policies and resources at state and local levels. Public health also has advocates such as Trust for America's Health (www.healthyamericans. org), an especially vigorous and articulate champion. The Trust draws attention to specific health problems—what Americans generally respond to—tying these issues to the need for better public health infrastructure and investment. The Trust has also been able to bring together diverse stakeholders interested in similar kinds of health protections to amplify the collective message about these issues. County Health Rankings and Roadmaps (www.countyhealthrankings.org) rank the health and well-being of counties within each state. These rankings provide an important new way to convey a snapshot of health, attract the interest of policymakers and the public, and stimulate community discussions and collaborations to improve health.

Advocacy in public health generally has a twofold purpose: It aims to strengthen public health resources and reorganization, but also to make changes that health departments cannot make on their own. For example, advocacy led to increased taxes on cigarettes and smoke-free indoor air laws; now advocacy is generating new state and local policies to increase the school physical education requirement, bring recess back into the school day, and require healthier offerings in school cafeterias (IOM, 2012).

Public health advocacy deals with a wider range of topics today than ever before. Because health is rooted in a wide variety of social and economic conditions, the field has started using an approach called "health in all policies" (HIAP). In this approach, health advocates engage policymakers across various sectors to make sure that decisions will promote, or at least not adversely affect, health. The state of California, for example, has established a Health in All Policies Task Force (sgc.ca.gov/hiap/) to help the state's Strategic Growth Council achieve its goals, including "improving air and water quality, protecting natural resources and agricultural lands, increasing the availability of affordable housing, improving infrastructure systems, promoting public health, planning sustainable communities, and meeting the state's climate change goals"—all tied to the health of the state's residents.

Health impact assessments (HIAs) help policymakers and community stakeholders to identify the health effects of decisions about nonhealth issues, such as economic development or transportation plans. The HIA is a structured process to gather, analyze, and present scientific data, health expertise, and public input to a public policy body so that policy choices can be made that will protect or promote health. HIAs have been used effectively around the world and have become more widespread in the United States over the past 5 years with the development of the Health Impact Project (www.healthimpactproject.org/hia/process).

SHARED INTERESTS AND SHARED RESOURCES

Throughout this chapter, we have attempted to show the many ways in which a wide variety of organizations take on the public health role when they focus on populations. This approach means that other interests can be aligned with the public health mission. For example, walkable communities can appeal to real estate developers, city planners, public health practitioners, and advocates. Across the nation, public health professionals are now working with city planners, police departments, real estate developers, and others to reframe suburban sprawl as an issue that has consequences for people's health. Similarly, employers and public health advocates alike see advantages to having workplace health promotion and disease prevention programs, practices, and policies such as smoke-free campuses.

Local, tribal, and state public health departments and nongovernmental organizations have always connected to grassroots leadership and other public services in order to solve collective problems. However, their leadership abilities for cross-sector collaboration are now being cultivated as never before, in what has become known as the collaborative leadership approach or collective impact. Collaborative leadership means understanding where public health shares common goals with other interest groups and building coalitions based on those common interests. In the same way, public health organizations are now participating more effectively in emergency preparedness and in health reform, because they can show where the public health interest is aligned with national defense and preparation for natural disasters, on one hand, and health care quality and cost containment, on the other. Through coalition building at all levels, public health can leave the sidelines, convene multiple stakeholders, and develop a common vision and shared, measurable goals. Sometimes it must lead, and sometimes it must follow, but most often, we will find public health walking hand-in-hand with its many partners and building on the assets of the communities it serves.

■ Discussion Questions

1. What examples of public health and prevention can you identify in your daily life? How do you believe they have affected your health?
2. Pick two examples from your answer to question 1, from either your own life or the text, and then go to the Internet and find out which federal laws and agencies, state laws and agencies, local health departments, nonprofit organizations, or city and county government units affect this aspect of your health. The more complete your answer, the better your answer is!
3. What is the difference between individual- and population-based prevention efforts? For population-based prevention, what is the difference between universal and targeted strategies?
4. What does a population focus require, in terms of planning, consensus building, and resources for implementation (a) in the case of safety belts and (b) in the case of heart attack prevention?
5. Why can't public health do more to achieve its goals? Name some of the political, legal, logistic, and resource challenges.
6. What should be left to the public sector to do in order to achieve public health goals? Where could other health care delivery systems do more to help? Why?
7. Give some examples of the constituencies that public health will have to reach in order to implement its goals (a) in the case of chronic disease prevention and (b) in the case of HIV/AIDS.
8. How would you personally balance individual liberty, the common good, and social justice in public health? What would have to change to achieve this balance? Give specific examples in the area of public health that you are best acquainted with.

CASE STUDY

You are an analyst for a federal agency. Congress has ordered your agency to come up with policy options to find a cure for birth defects. You recognize that (a) birth defects have many causes, (b) some can be treated, (c) some can also be prevented, but (d) not all of them can be "cured." You analyze this issue using the core functions of public health and the problem-solving process outlined in "Core Functions of Public Health."

Based on the information about spina bifida in that section, you decide it should be the focus for policymaking on birth defects. You decide to propose four options to Congress: (a) more research on treatment of spina bifida, (b) more health education for women about folic acid, (c) more promotion of birth control to reduce the proportion of unplanned pregnancies in the country, and (d) new regulations to increase the amount of folic acid in grain products. You may also see other options, so be sure to discuss them.

In your proposal, take the following questions into account:

1. For each option, what would you need to know to determine effectiveness? Cost-effectiveness?
2. What are the tradeoffs in each course of action?
3. Who would support this option, who would be opposed, and does it matter?
4. Is there a single best option? Why or why not?

■ References

Beauchamp, D. E., & Steinbock, B. (1999). *New ethics for the public's health*. New York, NY: Oxford University Press.

Centers for Disease Control and Prevention. (2011). Ten great public health achievements—United States, 2001–2010. *Morbidity and Mortality Weekly Report, 60*(19), 619–623. Retrieved from http://www.cdc.gov/mmwr/preview/mmwrhtml/mm6019a5.htm

Centers for Disease Control and Prevention. (2013). *The Public Health System and the 10 Essential Public Health Services*. Retrieved from http://www.cdc.gov/nphpsp/essentialservices.html

Green, L. W., & Kreuter, M. (1999). *Health promotion planning: An educational and ecological approach*. New York, NY: McGraw-Hill.

Hodge, J. (2012). The evolution of law in biopreparedness. *Biosecurity and Bioterrorism, 10*(1), 38–48. doi:10.1089/bsp.2011.0094

Institute of Medicine. (2002). *The future of the public's health in the 21st century*. Washington, DC: National Academies Press.

Institute of Medicine. (2009). *HHS in the 21st century*. Washington, DC: National Academies Press.

Institute of Medicine. (2011). *For the public's health: Revitalizing law and policy to meet new challenges*. Washington, DC: National Academies Press.

Institute of Medicine. (2012). *Accelerating progress in obesity prevention: Solving the weight of the nation*. Washington, DC: National Academies Press.

Jones, J. H. (1993). *Bad blood: The Tuskegee syphilis experiment* (New and expanded edition). New York, NY: Free Press.

Kuehnert, P. L., & McConnaughay, K. S. (2012). Tough choices in tough times: Enhancing public health value in an era of declining resources. *Journal of Public Health Management and Practice, 18*(2), 115–125.

Leviton, L. C., Needleman, C. E., & Shapiro, M. (1997). *Confronting public health risks: A decision maker's guide.* Thousand Oaks, CA: Sage.

Libbey, P., & Miyahara, B. (2011). *Cross-jurisdictional relationships in local public health: Preliminary summary of an environmental scan.* Princeton, NJ: Robert Wood Johnson Foundation. Retrieved from http://www.rwjf.org/content/dam/web-assets/2011/01 /cross-jurisdictional-relationships-in-local-public-health

National Highway Traffic Safety Administration. (2014). *Traffic safety facts: 2012 data.* Washington, DC: U.S. Department of Transportation. Retrieved from http://www-nrd.nhtsa.dot.gov/Pubs/811892.pdf

Network for Public Health Law. (2011, August 1). *The model state emergency health powers act: Summary matrix.* Retrieved from https://www.networkforphl.org/_ asset/80p3y7/Western-Region---MSEHPA-States-Table-8-10-12.pdf

Sondik, E. J., Huang, D. T., Klein, R. J., & Satcher, D. (2010). Progress toward meeting the Healthy People 2010 goals and objectives. *Annual Review of Public Health, 31,* 271–281.

Trust for America's Health and the New York Academy of Medicine. (2013a). *A compendium of proven community based prevention programs.* New York, NY: New York Academy of Medicine. Retrieved from http://www.tfah.org/report/110/

Trust for America's Health. (2013b). *Outbreaks: Protecting Americans from infectious disease.* Retrieved from http://www.tfah.org/reports/outbreaks2013

U.S. Department of Health and Human Services (DHHS). (2013). *Healthy people 2020.* Washington, DC: U.S. Government Printing Office. Retrieved from http://www. healthypeople.gov/2020/default.aspx

U.S. Preventive Services Task Force. (2010). *Recommendations.* Washington, DC: DHHS. Retrieved from http://www.uspreventiveservicestaskforce.org/Page/Name/recom-mendations

7 Health and Behavior

Elaine F. Cassidy, Matthew D. Trujillo, and C. Tracy Orleans

KEY WORDS

behavioral risk factors
chronic care model
clinical practice guidelines
community prevention guidelines
health disparities
patient self-management
prevention

quality improvement
social ecological models
social learning theory
social marketing
social media
stages of change

LEARNING OBJECTIVES

- ⊙ Learn about the contributions of personal health practices (e.g., tobacco use, risky drinking, physical activity, diet, obesity) to individual and population health status
- ⊙ Understand how strategies for changing individual and population health behavior have evolved, and identify the targets and characteristics of effective interventions
- ⊙ Learn about the social, policy, and environmental determinants of healthy and unhealthy behaviors and the disparities and inequities in exposure to them
- ⊙ Understand models and prospects for addressing behavioral risk factors through national health care quality improvement efforts and health reform
- ⊙ Describe provider-oriented interventions for changing individual and population health behavior and their influence in achieving national health care quality objectives

TOPICAL OUTLINE

- ⊙ Behavioral risk factors: overview and national goals
- ⊙ Changing health behavior: closing the gap between recommended and actual health lifestyle practices
- ⊙ Changing provider behavior: closing the gap between best practice and usual care

Health care professionals, who live in a world in which often heroic efforts are needed to save lives, can easily believe that medical care is the most important instrument for maintaining and ensuring health. This chapter explains, however, that behavioral choices—and the social, environmental and policy factors that influence them—are key determinants of Americans' health and well-being.

To some extent, the task of helping people adopt healthy lifestyles falls into multiple realms, including behavioral psychology, public health, and even social marketing. However, current models for shaping healthy lifestyles include major roles for medical providers and the health care systems in which they practice. Therefore, clinicians, health care payers, managers of provider organizations, and health care policymakers need to understand and address the powerful behavioral determinants of health and illness.

This chapter begins with a brief overview of the major behavioral risk factors that contribute to the growing burden of preventable chronic disease in the United States—tobacco use, alcohol abuse, and sedentary lifestyle and unhealthy diet, including the joint effects sedentary lifestyle and unhealthy diet have on adult and childhood obesity and overweight. There is now voluminous and incontrovertible evidence for the roles these behaviors and risk factors play in shaping public health.

The chapter then describes the progress that has been made over the past four decades to help adults modify these risk factors by intervening both at the individual level—with behavioral and clinical treatments that can be delivered in health care settings—and at the broader population level—with public health environmental and policy changes and social marketing and media strategies that can prompt and support the development and maintenance of healthy behavior. Theoretical advances (e.g., social learning theory and stage-based and social ecological models) have led to a clear understanding of the need for broad-spectrum, multilevel ecological approaches, and new science-based clinical and community practice guidelines have been developed to guide them.

Multifaceted efforts have been successful in encouraging clinicians to use proven health behavior change protocols in their interactions with patients. Many parallels can be drawn between what we have learned about ways to promote health through individual behavior change and what we have learned about strategies to improve health care quality through provider behavior change. Health reform legislation at the local, state, and national levels increasingly recognizes that the significant progress in both areas holds unprecedented potential for breakthrough improvements in national health status and health care quality.

■ Behavioral Risk Factors: Overview and National Goals

Acute and infectious diseases are no longer the major causes of death, disease, and disability in the United States. Today, chronic diseases—coronary heart disease, cancer, and asthma—are the nation's leading causes of illness and death (Murphy, Xu, & Kochanek, 2013). Given the continued aging of the population, both the prevalence and the costs of chronic illness care will continue to rise. Yet, much of the growing burden of chronic disease is preventable.

More than two decades ago, McGinnis and Foege (1993) estimated that 50% of the mortality from the 10 leading causes of death could be attributed to personal behavior. A more recent analysis by Danaei and colleagues (2009) reinforced this estimate, finding that tobacco use, alcohol abuse, sedentary lifestyle, unhealthy diet, and overweight and obesity together accounted for more than 1 million of the 2.5 million deaths in 2005. Moreover, research findings over the past two decades have established that modifying these behavioral risk factors leads to improved health and quality of life and to reduced health care costs and burden (Orleans, Ulmer, & Gruman, 2004).

Almost 90% of Americans have reported they have at least one of these risk factors, and 52% have reported having two or more, with the highest prevalence of individual and multiple behavioral risks occurring in low-income and racial and ethnic minority groups (Coups, Gaba, & Orleans, 2004). Given these statistics, it is not surprising that many of the leading health indicators tracked by *Healthy People 2020*—which updates the nation's primary objectives for promoting longer, healthier lives and eliminating health disparities—relate to healthy lifestyles. Although recent analyses suggest that our nation had an uneven record in achieving *Healthy People 2010* targets in previous years (see Chapter 6), more well-rounded improvements across multiple health indicators are needed in order to advance quality of life and significantly reduce health disparities (Koh, 2010). Selected indicators for tobacco use, alcohol abuse, physical activity, diet, and obesity are shown in Table 7.1.

The past decade of social science, behavior change, and population health research also has clarified that there are profound sociodemographic inequities in access to community-level and health care supports for healthy behavior and health behavior change (Adler, Bachrach, Daley, & Frisco, 2013). These inequities are powerful drivers of health disparities and threats to the health of the nation. In fact, the Robert Wood Johnson Foundation's Commission for a Healthier America convened in 2013 to emphasize that the nation's health depends fundamentally on ensuring equitable access to the supports and resources needed for making healthy choices in the environments where people live, learn, work, and play.

All Americans do not have the same opportunities to be healthy and to make healthy choices. Sometimes barriers to health and to healthier decisions are too high for individuals to overcome, even with great motivation (Robert Wood Johnson Foundation Commission to Build a Healthier America, 2013).

TOBACCO USE

Tobacco use causes more preventable deaths and diseases than any other behavioral risk factor, including 443,000 premature deaths from several forms of cancer, heart, and lung disease (Centers for Disease Control and Prevention [CDC], 2013b). It accounts for annual health care costs of $96 billion, in addition to an estimated $97 billion in lost productivity costs.

Smoking remains the single most important modifiable cause of poor pregnancy outcomes, accounting for 20% of low birth weight deliveries, 8% of preterm births, and 5% of perinatal deaths. For infants and young children, parental smoking is linked to sudden infant death syndrome (SIDS), respiratory illnesses, middle ear infections, and decreased lung function, with annual direct medical costs estimated at $4.6 billion. Quitting, even after 50 years of smoking, can produce significant improvements in health and less use of health care services.

Although the adult smoking prevalence rate decreased to 19% in 2011, smoking prevalence among adults remains well above the *Healthy People 2020* target of 12% (Ward, Barnes, Freeman, & Schiller, 2012). Nearly one in five adults still smokes, with the highest rates (29%) among members of low-income populations. And even though rates of smoking during pregnancy also have dropped in the past decade, 10% of women reported in 2007 that they smoked during pregnancy.

TABLE 7.1 SELECTED *HEALTHY PEOPLE 2020* OBJECTIVES: BEHAVIORAL RISK FACTORS

	Baseline[a] (%)	2020 Goals (%)
Tobacco Use		
Cigarette smoking		
■ Adults (18 years and older)	24	12
■ Adolescents (grades 9 through 12)	35	16
Exposure to secondhand smoke		
■ Children (6 years and younger)	27	10
Alcohol Misuse/Risky Drinking		
Proportion of adults who exceed guidelines for low-risk drinking	72 (women); 74 (men)	50
Binge drinking		
Adults (18 years and older)	16.6	6
Adolescents (12 to 17 years)	7.7	2
Deaths from alcohol-related auto crashes	5.9	4
Physical Activity		
Regular moderate physical activity		
■ Adults (18 years and older)[b]	15	30
■ Adolescents (grades 9 through 12)[c]	27	35
Vigorous physical activity (at least 3 days per week for 20 minutes)		
■ Adults (18 years and older)	23	30
■ Adolescents (grades 9 through 12)	65	85
Diet and Overweight (Older Than Age 2)		
■ Proportion of people eating at least two servings of fruit daily	28	75
■ Proportion of people eating at least three servings of vegetables (at least one of which is dark green or orange) daily	3	50
■ Proportion of people eating at least six servings of grain products (at least three being whole grains) daily	7	50
Overweight and obesity		
■ Obesity among adults (aged 20 years and older)	23	15
■ Overweight and obesity among children and adolescents (aged 6 to 19)	11	5

[a]Baseline data extracted from sources between 1988 and 1999.
[b]At least 30 minutes per day.
[c]At least 30 minutes 5 or more days per week.
Source: U.S. Department of Health and Human Services. (2011). *Healthy People 2020: Understanding and improving health.* Washington, DC: Author.

Each day, more than 3,000 children and teens become new smokers, and 30% of those young people will become addicted to tobacco. Some 18% of high school students smoke cigarettes and more than 8 million Americans, mostly adolescent and young adult males, report using smokeless tobacco, which is linked to oral cancer, gum disease, and tooth loss (American Cancer Society, 2012; CDC, 2013d). Furthermore, public health and tobacco control experts are concerned that the availability and marketing of electronic cigarettes (e-cigarettes) may reverse recent declines in youth tobacco use initiation and tobacco addiction by reglamorizing smoking and igniting lifelong nicotine addiction (Richtel, 2013). In addition, the most recent survey data from 2009 and 2010 suggest that 42% of children ages 3 to 11 and 28% of adult non-smokers were exposed to secondhand smoke. Socioeconomics may play an important role in influencing smoking behaviors and exposure to tobacco-control policies. A study by Giovino and colleagues (2009) revealed that increasing median household income was associated with decreasing prevalence of smoking, higher cessation rates among smokers, higher state cigarette excise tax rates, and stronger legal protections from tobacco smoke pollution.

ALCOHOL USE AND MISUSE

The millions of Americans who abuse or misuse alcohol include those who are alcohol dependent as well as those who engage in drinking behavior that is risky (e.g., because they drive after drinking alcohol) or harmful (e.g., because they suffer the effects of episodic binge drinking). About 5% of the U.S. adult population meets the criteria for alcoholism or alcohol dependence, and another 20% engages in harmful or risky drinking, defined as drinking more than one drink per day or seven drinks per week for women, more than two drinks per day or 14 drinks per week for men, periodic binge drinking (five or more drinks on a single occasion for men; four or more for women), drinking and driving, or drinking during pregnancy.

The 2013 Monitoring the Future Survey indicates that 22% of high school seniors reported that they engaged in binge drinking in the 2 weeks before the survey (Johnston, O'Malley, Bachman, & Schulenberg, 2013b). Alcohol misuse is most common in young adults, particularly among White and Native American men. And excessive alcohol use among U.S. college students remains a problem with college students, compared with their noncollege peers, reporting more instances of heavy drinking and being drunk (Johnston, O'Malley, Bachman, & Schulenberg, 2013a). It should be noted, however, that low and moderate levels of alcohol use in adults (below those defined as risky) have been linked to modest health benefits, such as lowered risk for heart disease.

Alcohol misuse accounts for approximately 80,000 deaths and more than 2 million years of potential life lost a year (CDC, 2012). The estimated cost of excessive alcohol use was recently estimated at $223 billion (Bouchery, Harwood, Sacks, Simon, & Brewer, 2011). Of this $223 billion, $170 billion was attributed to binge drinking, $25 billion to underage drinking, and $5 billion to drinking during pregnancy (National Institute on Alcohol Abuse and Alcoholism [NIAAA], 2001).

Factors associated with alcohol access, such as alcohol retail density and alcohol-related advertising, can vary by certain neighborhood sociodemographic characteristics. For instance, compared with individuals living in high-income, high-education, mostly White neighborhoods, those living in low-income, low-education, predominantly minority neighborhoods have relatively higher densities of alcohol retail outlets available to them (Berke et al., 2010). Disparities also exist in completion rates for alcohol treatment, with people from minority backgrounds having significantly lower completion rates than their White counterparts (Saloner & Le Cook, 2013).

The health benefits of treating alcohol dependence are well established, and the U.S. Preventive Services Task Force (USPSTF) found that brief behavior change interventions to modify risky drinking levels and practices produced positive health outcomes detectable 4 or more years later.

PHYSICAL ACTIVITY AND SEDENTARY LIFESTYLE

The health risks associated with physical inactivity and sedentary lifestyle are numerous. They include heart disease, type 2 diabetes, stroke, hypertension, osteoarthritis, colon cancer, depression, and obesity (USPSTF, 2003a). Engagement in physical activity helps to maintain healthy bones, muscles, joints, and weight, and it is also associated with positive psychological benefits. Physical activity has been shown to reduce feelings of anxiety and depression and promote feelings of well-being.

In 2011, 48% of adults engaged in at least 75 minutes per week of moderate-to-vigorous aerobic exercise, a proportion that meets *Healthy People 2020* guidelines for recommended physical activity among adults. In comparison, national guidelines recommend at least 60 minutes of moderate-to-vigorous physical activity every day for children and teens, but the majority of young people do not meet this goal (Troiano et al., 2008). Sedentary behavior also has risen for U.S. youth, with the amount of time young people spend in sedentary behaviors, including all forms of screen time, increasing dramatically in recent years (Rideout, Foehr, & Roberts, 2010). Sedentary behaviors are independently linked to a higher risk for obesity, diabetes, and other chronic health problems among adults, even those who are physically active and consume healthy diets (Hamilton, Hamilton, & Zedric, 2007).

The adults, youth, and families most at risk for inactivity include those with lower income and education levels, those living below the poverty line in all racial and ethnic groups, members of several racial/ethnic minority groups (e.g., African Americans, Hispanics), and those with disabilities. Sallis and colleagues (2011) found neighborhood-level income disparities for numerous variables affecting everyday physical activity. For instance, residents of high-income neighborhoods reported more favorable pedestrian and building facilities, safety from traffic, safety from crime, and access to recreation facilities than residents of low-income areas. Furthermore, growing evidence now shows that within the United States, African American and Latino youth and youth living in lower-income communities do not have as many built and social environmental supports for physical activity as White children or those living in middle- and higher-income communities (Taylor & Lou, 2012).

Although the societal costs of physical inactivity are difficult to quantify, the CDC has estimated that nearly $95 billion (adjusted to 2009 dollars) would be saved if all inactive American adults were to become active (CDC, 2013c). In addition to providing objectives for physical activity behaviors, *Healthy People 2020* includes objectives for policies that facilitate physical activity, particularly for children. These policy objectives focus on policies that promote physical activity in childcare settings as well as during recess and physical education classes in schools.

DIET AND NUTRITION

In 2005, unhealthy diet was responsible for just under 350,000 deaths in the United States. Over 40% of these deaths were attributed to either low intake of fruits or vegetables or high consumption of transfatty acids (Danaei et al., 2009). Poor diet and nutrition also has contributed to a surge in overweight and obesity that has reached epidemic proportions over the last 20 years, particularly within low-income and minority populations.

Four of the 10 leading causes of death—coronary heart disease, some cancers, stroke, and type 2 diabetes—are associated with an unhealthy diet. The relationships between dietary patterns and health outcomes have been examined in a wide range of observational studies and randomized trials with patients at risk for diet-related chronic diseases. The majority of studies suggest that people consuming diets that are low in fat, saturated fat, transfatty acids, and cholesterol and high in fruits, vegetables, and whole grain products containing fiber have lower rates of morbidity and mortality from coronary artery disease and several forms of cancer (USPSTF, 2003b). Moreover, dietary change has been found to reduce risks for many chronic diseases, as well as for overweight and obesity.

> *Four of the 10 leading causes of death—coronary heart disease, some cancers, stroke, and type 2 diabetes—are associated with unhealthy diet.*

The 2010 Dietary Guidelines for Americans recommend that Americans reduce their caloric intake from solid fats and added sugars and increase the amount of fruits, vegetables, and whole grains in their diets. Again, as Table 7.1 shows, gaps exist between the recommended guidelines and actual diets of American children and adults. Numerous studies have documented wide racial, ethnic, and socioeconomic disparities in access to healthy food outlets, particularly chain supermarkets (Powell, Han, & Chaloupka, 2010), and that access to healthy food is associated with lower risks of obesity and diet-related chronic diseases. In 2010, PolicyLink and the Food Trust published "The Grocery Gap: Who Has Access to Healthy Food and Why It Matters," a comprehensive review of two decades of food access research. This review found overwhelming evidence that access to healthy food was particularly limited for low-income communities, communities of color, and rural communities.

> *For decades, low-income communities of color have suffered as grocery stores and fresh, affordable food disappeared from their neighborhoods. ... Without access to healthy foods, a nutritious diet and good health are out of reach (Treuhaft & Karpyn, 2010).*

OBESITY

As poor dietary habits and physical inactivity have become endemic, national obesity rates have soared. Nearly 70% of all American adults are overweight or obese—up from 12% just one decade ago. This trend is alarming, given the strong links between obesity and many chronic diseases. Total expenditures related to overweight- and obesity-related problems were estimated at nearly $110 billion, inflated to 2009 dollars (Finkelstein, Fiebelkorn, & Wang, 2003)—a number that will continue to increase until we have effective interventions to teach and reinforce healthy behavior. Even modest weight loss (e.g., 5% to 10% of body weight) over a period of 12 to 24 months can reduce these risks and prevent the onset of diabetes among adults with impaired glucose tolerance.

More alarming is the prevalence of overweight and obesity among children and adolescents (ages 6 to 19), which has increased significantly over the past three decades. Like adults, overweight youth are at risk for coronary heart disease, hypertension, certain cancers, and even type 2 diabetes early in life. The highest and fastest-rising rates of childhood obesity are seen among children and adolescents of African American or Latino descent and children (particularly girls) from low-income backgrounds—making efforts to reach these groups a public health priority (White House Task Force on Childhood Obesity, 2010).

Reducing obesity among adults and children and adolescents represent leading health indicators for *Healthy People 2020*, which set the target rates of adult and child and adolescent obesity at 31% and 15%, respectively. In 2012, the IOM released the report *Accelerating Progress in Obesity Prevention: Solving the Weight of the Nation*, which identified five critical environments in which reform was urgently needed to prevent obesity: (a) environments for physical activity, (b) food and beverage environments, (c) message environments, (d) health care and work environments, and (e) school environments. In a 2013 follow-up report, *Creating Equal Opportunities for a Healthy Weight*, the IOM focused on the research, policies and actions most needed to ensure greater equity in opportunities to achieve a healthy weight and address the pervasive disparities in obesity prevalence and health and economic tolls in the United States.

■ Changing Health Behavior: Closing the Gap Between Recommended and Actual Health Lifestyle Practices

In 1982, the IOM published *Health and Behavior*, one of the first scientific documents to establish convincingly the links between behavioral risk factors and disease and to identify the basic biopsychosocial mechanisms underlying them. The IOM recommended intensified social and behavioral science research to develop interventions that could help people change their unhealthy behavior and improve their health prospects. This section presents a broad overview of the ensuing research—research that has attempted to close the gap between what we know and what we do when it comes to adopting and fostering healthy lifestyles.

A BRIEF HISTORY OF BEHAVIOR CHANGE INTERVENTIONS

Early behavior change efforts in the 1970s and 1980s relied primarily on public education campaigns and individually oriented health education interventions. They were guided by the health belief model and similar theories (the theory of reasoned action, the theory of planned behavior), which emphasized the cognitive and motivational influences on health behavior change and recommended raising awareness of the harms of unhealthy behavior versus the benefits of behavior change as a primary intervention. These cognitive/decisional theories were based on an underlying premise that people's intentions and motivations to engage in behavior strongly predict their actually doing so (i.e., "if you tell them, they will change"). Because raising health risk awareness and motivation was a primary goal, the doctor–patient relationship was seen as a unique and powerful context for effective health education.

Both population-level and individual clinical health education efforts based on these theories achieved initial success. For instance, tens of thousands of smokers quit in response to the publication of the first U.S. Surgeon General's *Report on Smoking and Health* in 1964 and the multiple public education campaigns that followed.

By 2000, hundreds of studies had confirmed that even brief physician advice could be a powerful catalyst for health behavior change—boosting the number of patients who quit smoking for at least 24 hours or who made some changes in their diet and activity levels. But a growing body of research found these successes to be modest— the interventions were important and perhaps *necessary* for changing people's health knowledge, attitudes, and beliefs, as well as broader social norms, but *not sufficient* to produce lasting behavior change. Cumulative findings made it clear that people needed not only motivation but also new skills and supports to succeed in changing deeply ingrained health habits.

These findings spurred the development and testing of expanded multicomponent, cognitive behavioral treatments designed not only to (a) raise perceptions of susceptibility to poor health outcomes and benefits of behavior change, but also to (b) teach the skills required to replace ingrained unhealthy habits with healthy alternatives and to (c) help people make changes in their natural (home, work, social) environments to assist them in successfully establishing and maintaining new behaviors. *Social learning theory*, which emphasized interactions between internal and external environmental influences on behavior, provided the primary theoretical basis for this evolution, and it remains the dominant model for effective cognitive behavioral health behavior change interventions.

Lifestyle change interventions derived from social learning theory combined education and skills development. They included techniques such as modeling and behavioral practice to help people learn not just *why*, but *how*, to change unhealthy habits. For instance, they taught effective self-management and behavior change skills, such as goal-setting, self-monitoring, and stress management skills for people who had relied on smoking, eating, or drinking as coping tactics. They taught skills for reengineering the person's immediate environments, replacing environmental cues and supports for unhealthy behavior with new cues and supports for healthy ones (e.g., removing ashtrays, replacing unhealthy high-calorie foods with healthy alternatives, finding exercise buddies, and avoiding high-risk events, such as office parties at which risky drinking was expected).

The "nudge" principles of modern behavioral economics that, for instance, are used to advocate for replacing soda with water and French fries with apple slices in fast food children's meals have their roots in these approaches. Another principle was that problem-solving should start with helping people set realistic, personal behavior change goals and go on to address the unique barriers and relapse temptations they face. Finally, new social learning theory treatments taught patients to take a long-range perspective, viewing repeated attempts over time as part of a cumulative learning process rather than as signs of failure.

Effective multicomponent treatments were initially delivered and tested in multi-session, face-to-face group or individual clinic-based programs, typically offered in clinical or medical settings and usually led by highly trained (e.g., MD, PhD) professionals. Results were extremely encouraging, with substantial behavior change—for example, smoking quit rates as high as 40%—maintained 6 to 12 months posttreatment. However, participants were typically self-referred or recruited based on high readiness or motivation for change, and thus represented a small fraction of those who could benefit.

The next push was to distill core elements of this treatment approach into lower-cost formats with much wider reach. These formats included paraprofessional-led worksite clinics, self-help manuals and programs, and brief primary care counseling. Absolute treatment effects were smaller—for example, 20% long-term smoking quit rates—but potential population effects were much greater. Only 5% to 10% of smokers might ever attend intensive clinics, whereas 70% of U.S. smokers might receive brief, effective tobacco interventions during visits with their primary care physicians, introducing a context that could double the nation's annual quit rate. Access to telephone quitlines providing free or no-cost counseling and medication proved equally effective and had the benefit of better reaching smokers in sociodemographic populations with limited access to high-quality health care (Schlam & Baker, 2013).

Development of the *stages-of-change model* in the mid-1980s accelerated the shift from individual to population intervention models and has had a profound, lasting effect on the design and delivery of health behavior change programs. Studying how people went about changing on their own, Prochaska and DiClemente (1983) discovered that health behavior change was a multistage process:

- *Precontemplation*: no plans to change behavior; behavior is not seen as a problem
- *Contemplation*: serious plans to change behavior within the next 6 months, weighing the pros and cons, and building supports and confidence
- *Preparation*: plans to change are imminent; small initial steps are taken
- *Action*: active attempts are made to quit smoking, drink less, become more active, or change to a healthier diet and to sustain changes for up to 6 months
- *Maintenance*: change is sustained beyond 6 months
- *Relapse*: the individual returns to any earlier stage and begins to recycle through the earlier stages

Based on these findings, different skills, knowledge and types of treatment were recommended to help people in each stage; motivational and educational interventions were helpful to people in the precontemplation and contemplation stages, and active cognitive-behavioral interventions were needed for those in the preparation, action, and maintenance stages. Many population surveys found that, at any given time, the vast majority of people (80%) are in the precontemplation and contemplation stages, which helped to explain why so few enrolled in weight loss or quit-smoking clinics, even when these were free and accessible.

The stages-of-change model has been successfully applied to numerous behavioral health risks and has helped people with multiple risk factors make progress in changing several at the same time. One of the greatest effects of this model was to propel a dramatic shift away from one-size-fits-all approaches to individualized, stage-tailored strategies that could be applied effectively to entire populations—in communities, worksites, and health care settings—assisting people at *all* stages of change, not just the motivated volunteers in action stages, but also those needing motivation and support to reach action stages. The model stimulated the development and wider use of effective motivational interventions for clinical settings, especially motivational interviewing, which seeks to help people strengthen their determination to change behavior (Emmons & Rollnick, 2001).

Originating as they did in the study of successful self-change, stages-of-change models fueled a burgeoning movement toward low-cost self-help tools and treatment formats. Some tools capitalized on computer-based and interactive communication technologies to design and deliver print and web-based materials, interactive video, and telephone interventions geared to the individual's stage of change. These treatments also addressed many other variables important for tailoring treatment methods and improving treatment outcomes—for example, degree of nicotine addiction, unique behavior change assets, barriers, and cultural norms.

A final force in the evolution from individual to population-based approaches was the emergence of *social marketing strategies,* which apply the concepts and tools of successful commercial marketing to the challenge of health behavior change. Basic marketing principles and methods—including market analysis, audience segmentation, and a new focus on consumer wants and needs—catalyzed the development of culturally appropriate communication and intervention strategies for reaching underserved, high-risk, low-income, and racial/ethnic minority populations for whom the prevalence of behavioral health risks is often highest and access to health-promoting environments and resources is often lowest. For instance, one model program employed social marketing strategies to tailor a no-cost smoking cessation intervention to the needs of African American smokers, using messages on Black-format radio stations to promote culturally tailored quitline counseling and materials. Results included a higher quitline call rate and a higher quit rate among African Americans receiving the tailored intervention versus a generic one.

> *Social marketing strategies apply the concepts and tools of successful commercial marketing to the challenge of health behavior change.*

More recent efforts focus on creating and harnessing the power of social network support for health behavior change (Christakis & Fowler, 2008). Through the Internet, individuals can share and receive health information through open forums, such as those provided through Facebook or Twitter. They can upload health-related apps or access online communities intentionally designed to promote good health. These social media tools have made health interventions more accessible than ever before by delivering strategic, effective, user-friendly messages directly to target audiences, even right into people's hands via their hand-held mobile devices.

Still, more research is needed to assess the effect of social media on health behavior. The practice of using social media tools to promote health has become so widespread in the past decade that the CDC now offers communication guidelines and a social media toolkit for creating social messages in health communications and activities (CDC, 2013a). Furthermore, in 2013, the National Library of Medicine, a division of the Department of Health and Human Services (DHHS), announced its plan to install software that will mine Facebook and Twitter to assess how Tweets and Facebook posts can be used as change agents for health behaviors.

THE ROLE AND IMPACT OF PRIMARY CARE INTERVENTIONS

The progress in health behavior change research and treatment set the stage for the development of brief, individually oriented, primary care health interventions that could be widely offered to all members of a practice, health plan, or patient population.

These efforts were based on a strong rationale for primary care interventions to address behavioral health risks. Patient surveys have repeatedly found that patients expect and value advice from their providers about diet, exercise, and substance use and are motivated to act on this advice. Most primary care providers describe health behavior change advice and counseling as an essential part of their role and responsibilities.

The unique extended relationship that is the hallmark of primary care provides multiple opportunities over time to address healthy behavior in a "string of pearls" approach, capitalizing both on teachable moments—for example, introducing physical activity or diet counseling when test results show elevated cholesterol levels—and on a therapeutic alliance that often extends beyond the patient to include key family members. Moreover, evidence suggests that the health benefits and cost-effectiveness of evidence-based preventive health behavior change interventions rival and frequently surpass those of remedial disease treatments (Maciosek et al., 2006).

In the *minimal contact* primary care counseling interventions that were distilled from the successful multicomponent models, the physician was seen as the initial catalyst for change, providing brief motivational advice, social support, and follow-up, with referral to other staff members or community resources for more intensive assistance. Stage-based and social marketing approaches held the potential to reach and assist entire populations of patients, including those not yet motivated for change and those in underserved and high-risk groups. As social media introduced innovative options to promote health information, computer-based, patient-tailored, and population-targeted interventions provided new ways to reduce provider burden. In fact, in 2013, the Community Preventive Services Task Force added mobile phone–based quit smoking counseling to its roster of recommended tobacco control interventions.

Progress in developing effective minimal-contact, primary care interventions occurred first in the area of smoking cessation, culminating in the development of an evidence-based, practice-friendly intervention model now known as the 5A's: ask, advise, agree, assist, arrange follow-up. The 5A's model was found to be effective when used by a variety of health care providers (physicians, nurses, dentists, dental hygienists), with as few as 2 to 3 minutes of in-office provider time.

The model starts with *asking* about tobacco use, leading to clear and personal *advice* to quit for smokers (or congratulations for quitters), and the offer of help. The *agree* step starts with assessing patient readiness to quit and goes on to establish a goal and quitting plan. For those not ready to quit, *assistance* includes a recommended motivational intervention; for those who are ready to quit, *assistance* combines brief face-to-face or telephone-based behavior-change counseling with FDA-approved pharmacotherapy, such as nicotine gum, patch, nasal spray or inhaler; bupropion hydrochloride (Zyban); varenicline (Chantix); or some combination of these, unless medically contraindicated (e.g., in pregnancy).

Behavioral counseling was effective when provided through multiple formats—self-help materials *and* face-to-face or telephone counseling—and there is a clear dose-response relationship between the amount of counseling and quit rates. Effective follow-up *arrangements* include planned visits, calls, or contacts to reinforce progress, adjust the quitting plan to better meet individual needs, or refer for more intensive help. One-year quit rates for patients receiving these interventions are typically two to three times higher than the 5% to 7% quit rates among people who try quitting on their own. In fact, the CDC and Prevention and Partnership for Prevention found the 5 A's intervention to be one of the most effective and cost-effective of all evidence-based clinical preventive services (Maciosek et al., 2006).

The 5A's model has been formally adopted by the USPSTF as a unifying conceptual framework or guideline applicable to addressing *all* behavioral health risks, including risky drinking, physical activity, diet, and obesity. In most cases, the USPSTF found that counseling interventions could produce clinically meaningful, populationwide health improvements that were sustained for at least 6 to 12 months. Although there are many common elements, the specific intervention components and intensity of recommended strategies vary from behavior to behavior, as does their effectiveness with unselected versus high-risk patients. Primary care providers may intervene more forcefully with healthy patients when they are known to be at high risk for a particular chronic disease, and patients at high risk may feel more vulnerable and motivated to act on the advice and assistance they receive.

The first step is always to *assess*, not only the relevant behavior (using a standard health-risk appraisal or brief screening that can easily be administered in a busy practice setting), but also the individual factors that are helpful in tailoring the intervention, such as medical and physiologic factors, motives, barriers, patient's stage of change, social support, and cultural values. Based on this information, and with reference to the patient's immediate health concerns and symptoms, the clinician provides brief, personalized *advice*, expressing confidence in the patient's ability to change and soliciting the patient's thoughts about the recommended changes.

The next critical step is to negotiate and *agree* on a collaboratively defined behavior-change goal and treatment plan, which commonly includes practical problem-solving to *assist* the patient in addressing personal change barriers, building social support, developing a more supportive immediate social and physical environment, and securing adjunctive behavior change resources and pharmacologic aids, such as nicotine replacement. Adjunctive resources can include evidence-based face-to-face, telephone, or mobile phone counseling; targeted or generic self-help materials; and interactive Internet-based tools that are tailored to a patient's gender, age, racial/ethnic or cultural group, health status or condition, stage of change, and other relevant variables. These resources can be used before, during, and after the office visit.

The final step is to *arrange* follow-up support and assistance, including referral to more intensive or customized help, or to online tools and supports to help the patient maintain behavior change maintenance.

These new guidelines provided unprecedented scientific support for the USPSTF assertion that "the most effective interventions available to clinicians for reducing the incidence and severity of the leading causes of disease and disability in the United States are those that address patients' personal health practices" (1996, p. iv).

However, several important limitations and gaps remain. The greatest limitation is the lack of long-term maintenance after successful behavior change for 12 months or longer. This is not surprising, given that patients return to the environments that shaped and supported their unhealthy lifestyles and choices. Higher maintenance rates are achieved in clinic-based programs that offered extended booster or maintenance sessions, providing ongoing social support and behavior change assistance, or in those that helped patients to create an enduring "therapeutic microenvironment" to shield them from unhealthy influences—for example, implementing an in-home smoking ban, arranging for the delivery of recommended diet foods, or arranging ongoing behavior change buddies.

Researchers and policymakers agree that current research and evidence gaps are the result of too few studies that have developed and tested primary care interventions for children, adolescents, and underserved populations.

MULTILEVEL MODELS FOR POPULATION-BASED HEALTH BEHAVIOR CHANGE

The shift to population-based models of health promotion and disease prevention was prompted by several factors:

- The success of effective, brief, and intensive interventions based on social learning theory, which gave greater prominence to environmental factors in behavior
- The emergence of new stage-based and social marketing models for population-wide interventions
- The disappointing reach and long-term effectiveness of even the most successful cognitive-behavioral treatments

The lackluster performance of individual treatment approaches was especially apparent when contrasted with new evidence from public health research showing far-reaching and lasting health effects from environmental and policy changes that eliminated the need for individual decision making. A prime example is the development of safer roads and more crashworthy automobiles, combined with shifts in laws and norms regarding seatbelt use and drinking and driving, which collectively produced a dramatic decline in auto-related deaths and injuries.

With the stage well set, the final push for a change in approach came in the 1990s with the development of *social ecological models* of health behavior. These models integrate behavioral science with clinical and public health approaches. They redefined what the targets of successful health interventions need to be—not just individuals but also the powerful social contexts in which they live and work. And they emphasized that a person's health behavior is affected by multiple levels of influence: interpersonal factors (e.g., physiologic factors, knowledge, skill, motivation), social factors (e.g., social–cultural norms, supports, and networks), organizational and community factors, broader environmental influences, and public policies.

Proponents of the ecological model recommend multilevel strategies that address all these levels of influence (IOM, 2000, 2012, 2013; Koh, 2010). Specifically, they propose that educational and clinical interventions to improve the motivation, skills, and supports for individual behavior change (e.g., for permanently quitting smoking or risky drinking, or for adopting and maintaining healthier activity and eating patterns) would be more successful when policies and influences in the wider environment prompt and reinforce healthy behavior through, for example, clean indoor air laws and access to safe and attractive places to walk or bike and obtain healthy, affordable foods.

A strong, early proponent of the ecological approach to prevention, McKinlay (1995) proposed a template for more effective population health promotion strategies that linked individual-level, clinical health behavior change strategies with broader, population-level health promotion efforts, including upstream policy and environmental interventions. The model McKinlay proposed (see Table 7.2) recommended interventions across a broad spectrum of factors, linking *downstream* individual clinical approaches with *midstream* interventions aimed at health plans, schools, worksites, and communities with *upstream* macro-level public policy and environmental interventions strong enough to subvert or redirect countervailing societal, economic, and industry forces. In essence, McKinlay was one of the first to argue that success in achieving lasting populationwide health behavior change required a "full court press."

In its landmark review of the past three decades of progress in population health promotion, the IOM's (2000) report, *Promoting Health: Intervention Strategies from Social and Behavioral Research*, recommended individual-level interventions aimed at those who possess a behavioral risk factor or suffer from risk-related disease. For these groups, the emphasis is on changing rather than preventing risky behavior. Population-level interventions that target defined populations in order to change and/or prevent behavioral risk factors may involve mediation through important organizational channels or natural environments. State and national public policy/environmental

TABLE 7.2 THE POPULATION-BASED INTERVENTION MODEL

Downstream Interventions	Midstream Interventions	Upstream Interventions
Individual-level interventions aimed at those who possess a behavioral risk factor or suffer from risk-related disease. Emphasis is on changing rather than preventing risky behavior.	Population-level interventions that target defined populations in order to change and/or prevent behavioral risk factors. May involve mediation through important organizational channels or natural environments.	State and national public policy/environmental interventions that aim to strengthen social norms and supports for healthy behavior and redirect unhealthy behavior.
■ Group and individual counseling	■ Worksite and community-based health promotion/disease prevention programs	■ National public education/media campaigns
■ Patient health education/cognitive behavioral interventions	■ Health plan–based primary-care screening/intervention	■ Economic incentives (e.g., excise taxes on tobacco products, reimbursement for effective primary care, diets, and extensive counseling)
■ Self-help programs and tailored communications	■ School-based youth prevention activities	■ Policies reducing access to unhealthy products (e.g., pricing, access, labeling)
■ Pharmacologic treatments	■ Community-based interventions focused on defined at-risk populations	■ Policies reducing the advertising and promotion of unhealthy products and behavior

Source: From McKinlay, J. B. (1995). The new public health approach to improving physical activity and autonomy in older populations. In E. Heikkinen, J. Kuusinen, & I. Ruoppila (Eds.), *Preparation for aging* (pp. 87–102). New York, NY: Plenum.

interventions aim to strengthen social norms and supports for healthy behavior and redirect unhealthy behavior.

> *(I)t is unreasonable to expect that people will change their behavior easily when so many forces in the social, cultural, and physical environment conspire against such change (Institute of Medicine, 2000).*

The IOM used McKinlay's broad-spectrum, multilevel model for describing the balance needed between the dominant clinical and individually oriented approaches to disease prevention, on the one hand, and the population-level approaches addressing the generic social and behavioral factors linked to disease, injury, and disability, on the other. Observing that many forces in the social, cultural and physical environment often constitute enormous barriers to health behavior change (IOM, 2000, p. 2), the authors recommended population-based health promotion efforts that:

- Use multiple approaches (e.g., education, social support, laws, incentives, behavior change programs) and address multiple levels of influence simultaneously (i.e., individuals, families, communities, nations)
- Take account of the special needs of target groups (e.g., based on age, gender, race, ethnicity and social class)
- Apply a long view of health outcomes, because changes often take many years to become established
- Involve a variety of sectors in society that have not traditionally been associated with health promotion efforts, including law, business, education, social services, and the media

EXAMPLES FROM TOBACCO CONTROL

The last three decades of progress in national tobacco control, hailed by some as one of the greatest public health successes of the second half of the 20th century, is the example most often used to illustrate the power and promise of ecological approaches for health intervention.

Although major disparities in tobacco use and its addiction remain, regressive tobacco tax and price increases have proved especially effective in certain high-risk and underserved populations—including adolescents, pregnant women, and low-income smokers. State telephone quitlines (1-800-QUIT-NOW) offering cost-free counseling and medication have greatly expanded the reach of evidence-based individual cessation treatments to traditionally underserved low-income and minority populations.

Reflecting the growth in research evaluating the population effects of *midstream* and *upstream* interventions for tobacco control, the CDC's Task Force for Community Preventive Services was launched in 1996 to conduct systematic reviews of community-based and policy interventions to change health behavior, similar to the reviews conducted by the USPSTF of *downstream* clinical preventive interventions. Based on its review of evidence for 14 different tobacco control interventions, the CDC makes these recommendations:

- Smoking bans and restrictions to reduce exposure to environmental tobacco smoke
- Tax and price increases and mass media campaigns to reduce the number of youth who start smoking and to promote cessation
- Telephone quitline and mobile phone-based support, as well as a number of health care system interventions, also to increase cessation

Similar ecological models have been described and proposed for each of the other major behavioral risk factors discussed in this chapter—risky drinking, physical inactivity, dietary behavior change, and obesity. These are summarized on the CDC's Community Preventive Services Task Force Community Guide website (CDC, 2013b) and in the Task Force's 2013 *Third Annual Report to Congress,* presenting more than 200 evidence-based recommendations for promoting better health among community members.

EXAMPLES FROM CHILDHOOD OBESITY PREVENTION

A great sense of urgency surrounds the need to identify evidence-based full-court press strategies that can halt the nation's current obesity epidemic, especially among children (IOM, 2010, 2012; White House Task Force, 2010). The dramatic rise in the prevalence of overweight and obesity among youth and adults over the past several decades is primarily due to environmental and economic changes affecting behavior on both sides of the *energy balance equation*; that is, the amount of energy (calories) used versus the amount consumed.

The cumulative effects of technology—such as automobile-dependent transportation and more sedentary jobs—along with changes in lifestyles in typical suburban environments, which limit the places to which adults and children can walk, have reduced the amount of physical activity in everyday life.

At the same time, increased access to low-cost, sugar-laden, and high-fat foods and beverages, increased exposure to marketing for these unhealthy products, larger portion sizes, increased restaurant use, an exodus of grocery stores and other sources of fresh fruits and vegetables from cities to suburbs, and the rising cost of fresh produce relative to soda and snack foods have all played a critical role in promoting excessive caloric intake, especially in low-income and racial/ethnic minority populations. Pervasive racial/ethnic disparities in access to safe places to walk, bike, and play have sparked several studies of socioeconomic differences in access to community sports areas, parks, swimming pools, beaches, and bike paths.

Rapid progress is being made to understand the environmental and policy factors that affect physical activity and identify promising multilevel, broad-spectrum interventions to address the nation's obesity epidemic. The CDC's Community Preventive Services Task Force reviewed research on interventions and found evidence for recommendations spanning the full McKinlay model. These include the following:

- *Downstream* health behavior change programs that increase social supports for physical activity and exercise (e.g., health care provider reminder systems plus provider education)
- *Midstream* requirements for school physical education classes that increase the time students spend in moderate or vigorous physical activity and "point of decision" prompts on elevators and escalators that encourage people to use nearby stairs

- *Upstream* efforts to create, or increase, access to safe, attractive, and convenient places for physical activity, along with informational outreach to change knowledge and attitudes about the benefits of and opportunities for physical activity

Recommendations from the CDC's *Community Guide to Increasing Physical Activity* address transportation and land-use policies, ranging from zoning guidelines to improved federal, state, and community projects for walking and bicycling (2013e). Together, these guidelines have provided a strong, science-based blueprint for multisector efforts by professionals in public health, urban planning, transportation, parks and recreation, architecture, landscape design, public safety, and the mass media to close the gaps between recommended and actual physical activity levels for U.S. children and adults.

Some *upstream* efforts come in the form of federal payments that can help communities create or improve access to healthy options. The Patient Protection and Affordable Care Act (ACA), passed in 2010, provides states and communities with a new stream of funds to promote healthy living by creating and improving multiple factors—such as housing, education, child care, and food outlets—in ways that address health disparities, improve access to behavioral health services, and reduce and control behavioral risk factors.

Other federal and state health-related policy changes have been influential in reducing childhood obesity, particularly among children from low-income families who participate in the Special Supplemental Nutrition Program for Women, Infants, and Children (better known as WIC). A 2008 overhaul of the WIC food package changed the mix of foods covered by the program, making more fruits and vegetables, skim and low-fat milk, and whole grain breads and cereals available to participants. Grocery stores and schools serving WIC children changed their inventories to meet the new standards, which benefitted not only WIC families but also entire communities. In 2013, evidence pointed to declining obesity rates among children from low-income communities in 18 states and one U.S. territory (CDC, 2013c).

Among U.S. cities, Philadelphia set itself apart by reporting a significant decrease in obesity between 2006 and 2010, particularly among schoolchildren in grades K through 12 and adolescents of color. These decreases emerged after the city instituted a decade-long, multipronged effort to combat obesity and influence health behavior. Over those 10 years, Philadelphia implemented the following:

- Nutrition education to public school students whose families are eligible for the federal Supplemental Nutrition Assistance Program
- Financial incentives to attract grocers to open stores in underserved areas
- A school district–wide wellness policy
- Improved nutritional offerings in schools, which included the removal of deep-fried foods, sodas, and sugar-sweetened beverages
- Required calorie postings at chain restaurants

With respect to high-risk populations and environments, systematic surveillance can increasingly monitor the prevalence of behavioral risk factors and related health-promoting programs, resources, and policies. Such surveillance systems, which already exist for tobacco control and are rapidly developing for physical activity, establish a national baseline that makes it possible to assess the effects of specific interventions and to evaluate important local, state, and national intervention efforts (Sallis et al., 2011). Although some events and political changes may create opportunities for rapid change, as did the Tobacco Master Settlement Agreement, a long-term view is essential. Most successful health promotion and social change efforts have required decades of hard work.

As we learned from the success of tobacco control, highly credible scientific evidence can persuade policymakers and withstand the attacks of those whose interests are threatened. Collaboration among public health researchers, advocates, communicators, strategists, and health care providers is needed to ensure that high-quality evidence reaches policy decision-makers at the right times.

The difficulty of implementing effective broad-spectrum approaches should not be underestimated. Powerful political opponents benefit from the sale, promotion, and marketing of unhealthy products. Other barriers include industry lobbying, chronically limited public support for healthy public policies, and inadequate funding for and enforcement of effective policies and programs. Creating a favorable political climate requires advocacy in order to instigate broad public pressure and support for change, clear and well-communicated evidence of public demand and support for change, and evidence of the beneficial health and economic effects of proposed programs and policies.

Changing Provider Behavior: Closing the Gap Between Best Practice and Usual Care

One of the most basic measures of national health care quality is the extent to which patients receive recommended, evidence-based care. Evidence-based guidelines exist for prevention-oriented primary care interventions related to behavioral risks, and putting these guidelines into practice has become an important objective for national health care quality improvement efforts.

More than a decade ago, the IOM's (2001) transformative report, *Crossing the Quality Chasm*, set forth a bold national agenda for improving health care quality across the full spectrum of care, from prevention to acute and chronic illness and palliative care, including health behavior change. A follow-up IOM report (2003) selected health behavior change interventions for tobacco and obesity as two of the top 20 priorities for national action.

These reports and the reviews and recommendations issued over the past decade by the USPSTF and CDC's Community Preventive Services Task Force have had a significant influence on the prevention and public health provisions of the ACA, enacted in 2010. They helped researchers, health professionals, and policymakers understand the need for a multisystemic approach for obesity prevention—one that involved a range of recommendations to build sustainably healthy communities that offer opportunities for everyone to make healthy, productive choices. This strategy was outlined in the IOM's 2012 report, *Accelerating Progress in Obesity Prevention: Solving the Weight of the Nation*, which emphasized the need for targeted health interventions to reduce the inequitable distribution of health promotion and health care resources and risk factors that contribute to health disparities among members of low-income, low-resource communities.

The Institute of Medicine's 2012 Report Accelerating Progress in Obesity Prevention presents an ambitious vision of "a society of healthy children, healthy families, and healthy communities in which all people realize their full potential" made possible through "large-scale transformative changes focused on multi-level environmental and policy changes" (p. 19).

Despite strong evidence for behavioral prevention in primary care, significant gaps persist between recommended and actual care. A landmark study of the quality of outpatient health care found that U.S. adults, on average, receive about *half* the services recommended for people with their specific health problems and even less—only 18%—of the recommended lifestyle screening and counseling services (McGlynn et al., 2003). It is safe to say that most patients who could benefit from health behavior change counseling—particularly those from lower-income and economically disadvantaged racial/ethnic populations, communities, and neighborhoods—are not receiving it. In most studies, patients receive only the first two of the 5A's—*assessment* and *advice.*

- *Tobacco use*: According to national data in 2010, 68% and 19% of visits to office-based ambulatory care settings involved tobacco use screening and tobacco cessation counseling, respectively (DHHS, 2011). These percentages, though higher than those in the baseline year of 2007, are below the *Healthy People 2020* target.
- *Alcohol use*: A 2005 study found that less than one third of individuals who saw a general medical provider were screened for alcohol or drug use (D'Amico, Paddock, Burnam, & Kung, 2005). The probability of problem drinkers in the study's sample being screened for alcohol use was less than 50%.
- *Physical inactivity and unhealthy diet*: National surveys indicate that in 2010 9% of physician visits by children and adults included counseling about exercise (DHHS, 2011). Among patients diagnosed with diabetes, cardiovascular disease, or hyperlipidemia, the percentage of their physician visits that included counseling or education related to exercise was 12%. Survey data also found that in 2010, 14% of physician visits by children and adults included counseling about nutrition or diet. This percentage increases to 19% for patients diagnosed with diabetes, cardiovascular disease, or hyperlipidemia.
- *Obesity*: In 2008, just under half of primary care physicians regularly assessed body mass index for their child, adolescent, and adult patients (DHHS, 2011). Similarly, more recent surveys of family practitioners (Sesselberg, Klein, O'Connor, & Johnson, 2010) and pediatricians (Klein et al., 2010) found that only about half of these primary care providers (45% and 52%, respectively) routinely assess BMI in children over age 2. Among adult patients diagnosed with obesity, the percentage of physician visits that include counseling or education regarding weight reduction, physical activity, or nutrition was 28% (DHHS, 2011).

Systematic evidence reviews beginning in the 1990s have found that most educational approaches, including traditional continuing medical education (CME), had limited effect. More interactive and skills-based educational efforts that used principles of adult learning and social-learning theory (including modeling by respected peer "opinion leaders") were somewhat more effective. Multicomponent interventions that addressed the multiple intrapersonal and environmental barriers to provider adherence, especially system barriers, were most effective.

The limited success of "if you tell them, they will change" provider education strategies drew critical attention to the many system-level barriers to adherence to evidence-based guidelines and recommendations, including the pressure of time (in the face of more urgent medical issues), inadequate office supports, a lack of provider and patient resources, and missing financial incentives.

Follow-up studies confirmed that clinician training was most effective when combined with efforts to create office supports to prompt, facilitate, and reward the delivery of preventive interventions, especially behavioral counseling, and that the most successful interventions were not one-size-fits-all, but tailored to the unique circumstances present in any particular office practice.

MULTILEVEL MODELS FOR IMPROVING DELIVERY OF EFFECTIVE HEALTH BEHAVIOR CHANGE INTERVENTIONS

Collectively, these findings led to a shift in understanding what the targets of interventions to change *provider* health care practices needed to be. Crabtree and colleagues (1998) introduced a *practice ecology model* emphasizing the need to address not just the behavior of individual providers, but also the powerful effects of the health care systems and environments in which providers practice.

They and other proponents of a broader view of health care improvement emphasized the need for *broad-spectrum* strategies addressing multiple levels of influence: *downstream* intrapersonal/individual provider-level factors; *midstream* interpersonal/practice team, office microsystems and health plan influences; and *upstream* macrolevel health care systems and policies (Goodwin et al., 2001) (See Figure 7.1).

Responding to the same evidence, the IOM's (2001) *Crossing the Quality Chasm* report recommended a fundamental reengineering of the nation's health care system—moving from a system designed primarily to support and pay for the delivery of reactive acute and remedial illness care to one that would support and pay for the proactive, preventive, and behavioral care needed to prevent and manage chronic disease.

It has been said that "an ounce of prevention takes a ton of office system change." Until recently, we lacked a coherent model for what this "ton of change" involved. Filling this void, Wagner, Austin, and Von Korff (1996) reviewed the research on effective chronic illness care and prevention and devised a model for the multiple interlocking systems supports required for effective planned, proactive chronic illness care—the chronic care model.

This model applies equally to the *prevention* and to the *treatment* of chronic disease, both of which require helping patients to change the behavioral risk factors that cause or complicate their illnesses. The chronic care model helped to pave the way for the concept of the "medical home" as a means for reorganizing primary care practices to improve health outcomes and reduce health care costs and disparities.

The six key elements of the chronic care model can be implemented at the level of the office practice or larger health care delivery system. Each element includes interventions that are planned rather than reactive, patient-centered and informed

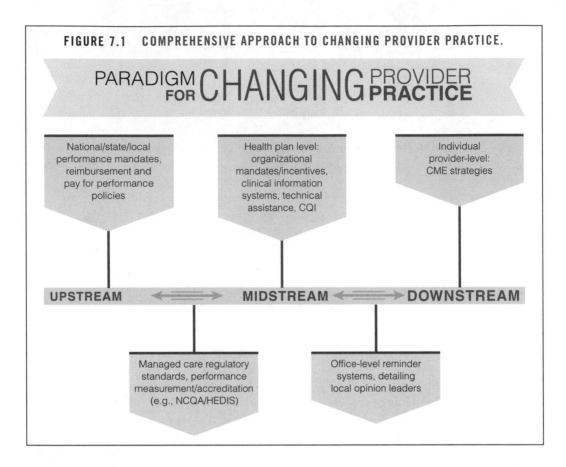

FIGURE 7.1   COMPREHENSIVE APPROACH TO CHANGING PROVIDER PRACTICE.

PARADIGM FOR CHANGING PROVIDER PRACTICE

| National/state/local performance mandates, reimbursement and pay for performance policies | Health plan level: organizational mandates/incentives, clinical information systems, technical assistance, CQI | Individual provider-level: CME strategies |

UPSTREAM ⟺ MIDSTREAM ⟺ DOWNSTREAM

| Managed care regulatory standards, performance measurement/accreditation (e.g., NCQA/HEDIS) | Office-level reminder systems, detailing local opinion leaders |

by individually relevant patient data, proactive, involving scheduled outreach and follow-up, and population-based—that is, focused on an entire panel of patients with a specific behavioral risk factor, disease, or condition and not just on individuals who seek care. Both prevention and treatment of chronic conditions require regular (non-symptom-driven) screening and counseling for health behavior change, involve ongoing planned care with proactive follow-up, depend on active patient involvement in decision making and adherence, and require links to supportive community resources and services.

As an example, the chronic care model proved a helpful heuristic for describing an organization-wide initiative at Group Health Cooperative of Puget Sound that integrates screening and treatment for tobacco use with routine primary care. This successful plan applied all six model elements as follows:

- *Health care organization*: Health plan leaders made reducing tobacco use their top prevention priority, provided financial and other incentives to providers (including hiring dedicated clinic counselors), and eliminated patient copayments for counseling.
- *Clinical information systems* were used to create a registry of the tobacco users enrolled in the health plan, track their use of treatment resources and programs, and generate proactive telephone quitline calls for patients and feedback reports for providers.

- *Decision support tools* included extensive provider training, ongoing consultation, automated patient assessment and guideline algorithms, and reminder tools.
- *Practice redesign* and *self-management support* included self-help materials and a telephone quitline to deliver counseling and pharmacotherapy without burdening the provider.
- *Community resources and policies* included referral to community and worksite quit-smoking clinics and related healthy lifestyle change programs, focused on stress management, exercise, and weight loss, as well as support for worksite smoking cessation. Their efforts also involved campaigns and smoking restrictions and expanded state funding for tobacco prevention and control programs.

The chronic care model has provided a unifying approach to health care quality improvement that cuts across different types of health behavior and chronic conditions with the promise of a more efficient, sustainable, and cost-effective approach to health care quality improvement. This is especially the case given the development of several successful continuous quality improvement (CQI) techniques for putting chronic care model–based system changes into place. Promising midstream CQI techniques have been used to design and test office system changes to find ways to eliminate barriers and strengthen the supports for recommended care, often through a series of "rapid cycle" (plan-do-study-act) improvement efforts.

Successful preventive CQI interventions have been delivered through learning collaboratives involving multiple health care teams from different organizations that meet and work over a 12- to 18-month period with faculty experts in CQI techniques and in the type of care targeted for improvement (e.g., tobacco dependence, obesity, diabetes management). Individual practice-level, chronic care model–based improvements involve planning, implementing, evaluating, and refining changes in individual practices. These efforts have substantially increased the proportion of patients—including the most disadvantaged patients—who receive evidence-based preventive care and for whom individual behavior change plans were developed and implemented.

Effective individual practice consultation models for CQI with a focus on multiple risk behavior change were pioneered in the STEP-UP (Study To Enhance Prevention by Understanding Practice) trial conducted by Goodwin and colleagues (2001). This randomized, controlled trial tested a brief practice-tailored approach to improving preventive service delivery, emphasizing improving rates of health habit counseling and the usage of effective community-based programs and supports for health behavior change.

Intervention practices received a one-day practice assessment, an initial practice-wide consultation, and several brief follow-up visits to assess and address practice-specific barriers. All interventions were delivered by a specially trained nurse facilitator who helped practices to identify promising changes and presented a menu of tools for implementing them (e.g., reminder systems, flow sheets, patient education materials, clinical information systems), including a practice improvement manual. This brief CQI intervention resulted in significant improvements at 6 and 12 months, which were maintained at a 24-month follow-up.

Improvements in behavioral counseling services were especially dramatic. The investigators attributed these lasting results to the maintenance of the practice and system changes that were made—changes that may have been easier to institutionalize because they were tailored to the unique characteristics of each practice.

The success of the STEP-UP trial and similar chronic care model–based primary care practice redesign approaches inspired the Robert Wood Johnson Foundation's Prescription for Health national program. This program funded 27 studies in primary care practice–based research networks to discover and test innovative ways of delivering 5A's interventions for two or more health behaviors: tobacco use, sedentary lifestyle, unhealthy diet, and/or risky drinking.

Projects in round 1 of the program demonstrated that practices could identify at-risk patients and motivate them to make changes. Round 2 projects built linkages between clinical practices and community resources to reduce provider burden and help patients sustain behavior changes. Each project required policy and environmental changes in the practice (e.g., reminder systems, patient registries, performance incentives) to facilitate delivery of evidence-based counseling and related treatments and to facilitate use of needed follow-up support from community resources, such as telephone quitlines. Results showed that primary care providers were able to deliver effective health behavior change interventions when working in supportive health care systems and practices.

In the long run, just as upstream macro-level societal and policy change is needed to sustain individual behavior change, upstream macro-level health system and policy change is needed to improve care in office practices and health plans. Such changes include quality performance measurement and public reporting; "pay-for-performance" initiatives that reward providers based on the quality of care they offer; and improved information technology to drive and support care improvement.

> *Just as upstream macro-level societal and policy change is needed to sustain individual behavior change, upstream macro-level health system and policy change are needed to support and improve care in office practices and health plans.*

Some research has found that providers were more likely to offer health behavior change counseling when a portion of their capitation payment depended on their doing so. Providers in physician organizations were found to be more likely to offer proven health promotion services if their performance measures were publicly reported or they received public recognition or economic benefit, and they had greater clinical information technology capacity (McMenamin et al., 2004).

■ Conclusion

Changing health-related behavior represents a prime target for improving national health and health care. Never have we known more about the importance of addressing the lifestyle factors that pose the most serious threats to Americans' health, produce the greatest demands on our health system, and contribute most to health care costs. The growing burden of chronic disease, a national epidemic of obesity, and escalating health care costs—at a time when health care spending already is growing faster than the U.S. gross domestic product—makes establishing a stronger preventive orientation in the nation's health care and public health systems an urgent priority.

Never have we known as much about how to motivate, support, and assist individuals to make lasting lifestyle changes or how to support and assist health care professionals to deliver evidence-based preventive care aimed at behavior change. The tremendous parallel gains made in what we have learned about how to achieve effective health promotion for individuals and health care quality improvement for providers have created unprecedented potential.

In the ninth edition of this book, published in 2008, we concluded that the stage was set for breakthrough improvements in national health status and health care quality. We recognized, however, that realizing this potential depended on leadership and political will to translate the evidence for health behavior change and health care system change into practice and policy. Recent interest has developed among leaders in health care and public health research, advocacy, practice, and policy to collaborate more effectively in order to assist those in practice and policy to make evidence-informed decisions. These collaborations could significantly help our nation move even closer to maximizing its potential in health and health care quality.

The landmark ACA represents one promising strategy that places prevention at the heart of the efforts needed to improve the nation's health and health care. Its prevention-oriented provisions include (a) full Medicaid and Medicare coverage for all preventive health services recommended by the U.S. Preventive Services Task Force, including those focused on health behavior change; (b) funding for community-based prevention grants to implement programs and policy; (c) environmental changes to improve nutrition, increase physical activity, reduce tobacco use and substance abuse and to reduce health risk disparities; (d) funding for childhood obesity community demonstration projects; and (e) the establishment of a National Prevention, Health Promotion, and Public Health Council to set and track goals and objectives for improving health through federally supported prevention, health promotion, and public health programs.

The law also requires funding for the continuation and greater coordination of the U.S. Preventive Services Task Force and CDC's Community Preventive Services Task Force. Combined, these efforts hold unprecedented potential to capitalize and build on the strong evidence for health-related behavior change created over the past three decades.

■ Discussion Questions

1. Briefly describe the effects of personal health behavior (e.g., tobacco use, risky drinking, diet, and physical activity) on individual and population health status and health care costs in the United States.

2. How have health behavior change programs and interventions evolved over the past 40 years?

3. In order to achieve effective behavioral interventions, most physicians use clinical practice guidelines that are based on the 5 A's model. Briefly describe this model, using tobacco cessation counseling as an example.

4. Describe the parallel shifts that have taken place during the past 30 years in understanding what the essential targets must be for successful interventions (a) to increase patients' adherence to recommended prevention-oriented health behavior and (b) to increase providers' use of recommended clinical preventive behavior change interventions.

5. With reference to McKinlay's population-based intervention model, outline possible coordinated *downstream*, *midstream*, and *upstream* strategies that can be used to achieve one of the following: (a) curb binge drinking on a college campus, (b) increase smoking cessation, especially among pregnant smokers enrolled in a Medicaid managed care plan, or (c) increase physical activity and healthy eating among middle school students in an urban center. Be sure to mention the different sectors that would need to be involved (e.g., public health, law enforcement, local business, school officials, policymakers, community planning, transportation, health plan leaders/providers, and so on).

CASE STUDY

You have just been hired as the director of strategic planning for a health plan that insures 30% of the residents in a metropolitan area of 500,000. Most of those insured by this health plan are employed by large companies in the metropolitan area, and these companies pay for their employees' health insurance. The health plan leaders and the employers both recognize that their business model depends on their success in addressing behavioral risk factors that play a critical role in the prevention and management of chronic diseases, the containment of health care costs, and the enhancement of employee productivity.

In your new role, you are asked to create a comprehensive plan for addressing these behavioral risk factors—by improving both the clinical care provided and the plan's community-based efforts. Specifically, you want to develop strategies to reduce the levels of tobacco use, unhealthy diet, and physical inactivity. In constructing your plan, consider the following questions:

1. What mix of interventions would you need to consider that might change enrollee behavior, provider behavior, and community policies and environments and maximize the cost-effectiveness of this plan?
2. What is the evidence that these interventions would work?
3. What would be the implementation challenges of the plan?

■ References

Adler, N., Bachrach, C., Daley, D., & Frisco, M. (2013). *Building the science for a population health movement* [Discussion paper]. Institute of Medicine, Washington, DC.

American Cancer Society. (2012). *Smokeless tobacco.* Retrieved from http://www.cancer.org/cancer/cancercauses/tobaccocancer/smokeless-tobacco

Berke, E. M., Tanksi, S. E., Demidenko, E., Alford-Teaster, J., Shi, X., & Sargent, J. D. (2010). Alcohol retail density and demographic predictors of health disparities: A geographic analysis. *American Journal of Public Health, 100,* 1967–1971.

Bouchery, E. E., Harwood, H. J., Sacks, J. J., Simon, C. J., & Brewer, R. D. (2011). Economic costs of excessive alcohol consumption in the U.S., 2006. *American Journal of Preventive Medicine, 41*(5), 516–524.

Centers for Disease Control and Prevention (CDC). (2012). *Alcohol related disease impact (ARDI) application.* Retrieved from http://apps.nccd.cdc.gov/DACH_ARDI/Default.aspx

Centers for Disease Control and Prevention (CDC). (2013a). *CDC social media tools, guidelines, and best practices.* Washington, DC: U.S. Centers for Disease Control and Prevention.

Centers for Disease Control and Prevention (CDC). (2013b). *Tobacco: Guide to community preventive services. Reducing tobacco use and secondhand smoke exposure.* Retrieved from http://www.thecommunityguide.org/tobacco/index.html

Centers for Disease Control and Prevention (CDC). (2013c). Vital signs: Obesity among low-income, preschool-aged children—United States, 2008–2001. *Morbidity and Mortality Weekly Report, 62*(31), 629–634.

Centers for Disease Control and Prevention (CDC). (2013d). *Youth and tobacco use fact sheet.* Retrieved from http://www.cdc.gov/tobacco/data_statistics/fact_sheets/youth_data/tobacco_use/#estimates

Centers for Disease Control and Prevention (CDC). (2013e). *The community guide: What works to promote health. Increasing physical activity.* Retrieved from http://www.thecommunityguide.org/about/What%20Works_PA%20INSERT.pdf

Christakis, N. A., & Fowler, J. H. (2008). The spread of obesity in a large social network over 32 years. *New England Journal of Medicine, 357*, 370–379.

Coups, E. J., Gaba, A., & Orleans, C. T. (2004). Physician screening for multiple behavioral health risk factors. *American Journal of Preventive Medicine, 27*, 34–41.

Crabtree, B. F., Miller, W. L., Aita, V. A., Flocke, S. A., & Stange, K. C. (1998). Primary care practice organization and preventive services delivery: A qualitative analysis. *Journal of Family Practice, 46*, 403–409.

D'Amico, E. J., Paddock, S. M., Burnam, A., & Kung, F. Y. (2005). Identification of and guidance for problem drinking by general medical providers: Results from a national survey. *Medical Care, 43*(3), 229–236.

Danaei, G., Ding, E. L., Mozaffarian, D., Taylor, B., Rehm, J., Murray, C. J., & Ezzarti, M. (2009). The preventable causes of death in the United States: Comparative risk assessment of dietary, lifestyle, and metabolic risk factors. *PLoS Medicine, 6*(4), e1000058. doi:10.1371/journal.pmed.1000058

Emmons, K. M., & Rollnick, S. (2001). Motivational interviewing in health care settings: Opportunities and limitations. *American Journal of Preventive Medicine, 20*, 68–74.

Finkelstein, E. A., Fiebelkorn, I. C., & Wang, G. (2003). National medical spending attributable to overweight and obesity: How much, and who's paying? *Health Affairs, W3*, 219–226. Retrieved from http://content.healthaffairs.org/cgi/content/full/hlthaff.w3.219v1/DC1

Giovino, G. A., Chaloupka, F. J., Hartman, A. M., Joyce, K. G., Chriqui, J., Orleans, C. T., . . . Larkin, M. (2009). *Cigarette smoking prevalence and policies in the 50 states: An era of change—The Robert Wood Johnson Foundation impact teen tobacco chart book.* Buffalo, NY: State University of New York at Buffalo.

Goodwin, M. A., Zyzanski, S. J., Zronek, S., Ruhe, M., Weyer, S. M., Konrad, N., & Stange, K. C. (2001). A clinical trial of tailored office systems for preventive service delivery: The study to enhance prevention by understanding practice (STEP-UP). *American Journal of Preventive Medicine, 21*, 20–28.

Hamilton, M. T., Hamilton, D. G., & Zedric, T. W. (2007). Role of low energy expenditure and sitting in obesity, metabolic syndrome, type 2 diabetes, and cardiovascular disease. *Diabetes, 56*, 2655–2667.

Institute of Medicine. (1982). *Health and behavior.* Washington, DC: National Academies Press.

Institute of Medicine. (2000). *Promoting health: Intervention strategies from social and behavioral research.* Washington, DC: National Academies Press.

Institute of Medicine. (2001). *Crossing the quality chasm: A new health system for the 21st century.* Washington, DC: National Academies Press.

Institute of Medicine. (2003). *Priority areas for national action: Transforming health care quality. Quality chasm series.* Washington, DC: National Academies Press.

Institute of Medicine. (2010). *Bridging the evidence gap in obesity prevention: A framework to inform decision making.* Washington, DC: National Academies Press.

Institute of Medicine. (2012). *Accelerating progress in obesity prevention: Solving the weight of the nation.* Washington, DC: National Academies Press.

Institute of Medicine. (2013). *Creating equal opportunities for a healthy weight: Workshop summary.* Washington, DC: National Academies Press.

Johnston, L. D., O'Malley, P. M., Bachman, J. G., & Schulenberg, J. E. (2013a). *Monitoring the future: National results on drug use, 1975–2012* (Vol. 2, College students and adults ages 19–50). Ann Arbor, MI: University of Michigan, Institute for Social Research.

Johnston, L. D., O'Malley, P. M., Bachman, J. G., & Schulenberg, J. E. (2013b). *American teens more cautious about using synthetic drugs.* Ann Arbor, MI: University of Michigan News Service.

Klein, J. D., Sesselberg, T. S., Johnson, M. S., O'Connor, K. G., Cook, S., Coon, M., . . . Washington, R. (2010). Adoption of body mass index guidelines for screening and counseling in pediatric practice. *Pediatrics, 25,* 265–272.

Koh, H. K. (2010). A 2020 vision for Healthy People. *New England Journal of Medicine, 362,* 1653–1656.

Maciosek, M. V., Edwards, N. M., Coffield, A. B., Flottemesch, T. J., Nelson, W. W., Goodman, M. J., & Solberg, L. I. (2006). Priorities among effective clinical preventive services: Methods. *American Journal of Preventive Medicine, 31,* 90–96.

McGinnis, J. M., & Foege, W. H. (1993). Actual causes of death in the United States. *Journal of the American Medical Association, 270,* 2207–2212.

McGlynn, E. A., Asch, S. M., Adams, J., Keesey, J., Hicks, J., DeCristofaro, A., & Kerr, E. A. (2003). The quality of health care delivered to adults in the United States. *New England Journal of Medicine, 348,* 2635–2645.

McKinlay, J. B. (1995). The new public health approach to improving physical activity and autonomy in older populations. In E. Heikkinen, J. Kuusinen, & I. Ruoppila (Eds.), *Preparation for aging* (pp. 87–102). New York, NY: Plenum.

McMenamin, S. B., Schmittdiel, J., Halpin, H., Gillies, R., Rundall, T. G., & Shortell, S. M. (2004). Health promotion in physician organizations: Results from a national study. *American Journal of Preventive Medicine, 26,* 259–264.

Murphy, S. L., Xu, J., & Kochanek, K. D. (2013). Deaths: Final data for 2010. *National Vital Statistics Reports, 61*(4), 1–118.

National Institute on Alcohol Abuse and Alcoholism (NIAAA). (2001). *Economic perspectives in alcoholism research.* (Alcohol Alert No. 51). Washington, DC: Author.

Orleans, C. T., Ulmer, C. C., Gruman, J. C. (2004). The role of behavioral factors in achieving national health outcomes. In T. J. Boll, R. G. Frank, & A. Baum (Eds.). *Handbook of Clinical Health Psychology: Models and perspectives in health psychology* (Vol. 3, pp. 465–499). Washington, DC: American Psychological Association.

Powell, L. M., Han, E., & Chaloupka, F. J. (2010). Economic contextual factors, food consumption, and obesity among U.S. adolescents. *The Journal of Nutrition, 140,* 1175–1180.

Prochaska, J. O., & DiClemente, C. C. (1983). Stages and processes of self-change of smoking: Toward an integrative model of change. *Journal of Consulting and Clinical Psychology, 51,* 390–395.

Richtel, M. (2013, October 26). The e-cigarette industry, waiting to exhale. *The New York Times.* Retrieved from http://www.nytimes.com/2013/10/27/business/the-e-cigarette-industry-waiting-to-exhale.html?adxnnl = 1&adxnnlx = 1388415666-ONxk-wS17kyrjnWucGjHSGg

Rideout, V. J., Foehr, U. G., & Roberts, D. F. (2010). *Generation M2: Media in the lives of 8- to 18-year olds.* Menlo Park, CA: Kaiser Family Foundation.

Robert Wood Johnson Foundation Commission to Build a Healthier America. (2013). *Overcoming obstacles to health in 2013 and beyond.* Retrieved from http://www.rwjf. org/content/dam/farm/reports/reports/2013/rwjf406474

Sallis, J. F., Slymen, D. J., Conway, T. L., Frank, L. D., Saelens, B. E., Cain, K., & Chapman, J. E. (2011). Income disparities in perceived neighborhood built and social environment attributes. *Health & Place, 17,* 1274–1283.

Saloner, B., & Le Cook, B. (2013). Blacks and Hispanics are less likely than Whites to complete addiction treatment, largely due to socioeconomic factors. *Health Affairs, 32,* 135–145.

Schlam, T. R., & Baker, T. B. (2013). Interventions for tobacco smoking. *Annual Review of Clinical Psychology, 9,* 675–702.

Sesselberg, T. S., Klein, J. D., O'Connor, K. G., & Johnson, M. S. (2010). Screening and counseling for childhood obesity: Results from a national survey. *American Board of Family Medicine, 23,* 334–342.

Taylor, W. C., & Lou, D. (2012). *Do all children have places to be active? Disparities in access to physical activity environments in racial and ethnic minority and lower-income communities. A research synthesis.* Princeton, NJ: Active Living Research.

Treuhaft, S., & Karpyn, A. (2010). *The grocery gap: Who has access to healthy food and why it matters.* Oakland, CA: PolicyLink.

Troiano, R. P., Berrigan, D., Dodd, K. W., Masse, L. C., Tilert, T., & McDowell, M. (2008). Physical activity in the United States measured by accelerometer. *Medicine & Science in Sports & Exercise, 40,* 181–188.

U.S. Department of Health and Human Services. (2000). *Healthy people 2010.* Washington, DC: Author.

U.S. Department of Health and Human Services. (2011). *Healthy people 2020.* Washington, DC: Author.

U.S. Preventive Services Task Force. (1996). *Guide to clinical preventive services* (2nd ed.). Baltimore, MD: Williams & Wilkins.

U.S. Preventive Services Task Force. (2003a). Behavioral counseling in primary care to promote a healthy diet: Recommendations and rationale. *American Journal of Preventive Medicine, 24,* 93.

U.S. Preventive Services Task Force. (2003b). Screening for obesity in adults: Recommendations and rationale. *Annals of Internal Medicine, 139,* 930–932.

Wagner, E. H., Austin, B. T., & Von Korff, M. (1996). Organizing care for patients with chronic illness. *Milbank Quarterly, 74,* 511–544.

Ward, B. W., Barnes, P. M., Freeman, G., & Schiller, J. S. (2012, March 21). *Early release of selected estimates based on data from the January–September 2011 National Health Interview Survey* [Online]. Retrieved from http://www.cdc.gov/nchs/data/nhis/earlyrelease/earlyrelease201203.pdf

White House Task Force on Childhood Obesity. (2010). *Report to the President: Solving the problem of childhood obesity within a generation.* Retrieved from http://www.letsmove.gov/sites/letsmove.gov/files/TaskForce_on_Childhood_Obesity_May2010_FullReport.pdf

8 Vulnerable Populations: A Tale of Two Nations

Jacqueline Martinez Garcel, Elizabeth A. Ward, and Lourdes J. Rodríguez

KEY WORDS

behavioral health services

cash (monetary) assistance
    programs

disproportionate share hospitals

dual eligible

Medicaid

Medicare

Patient Protection and Affordable Care
    Act (ACA)

poverty and health

predisposing and enabling factors

safety-net provider

social services

supportive housing programs

LEARNING OBJECTIVES

- ◎ Understand the predisposing and enabling factors that put individuals in vulnerable contexts

- ◎ Explain how the U.S. health care system provides and pays for services to vulnerable populations

- ◎ Identify challenges and opportunities to reduce health care costs and improve health outcomes of vulnerable populations

TOPICAL OUTLINE

- ◎ Understanding vulnerable populations and their context

- ◎ Organization of health care and other services for vulnerable populations

- ◎ Challenges and recommendations for service delivery and payment

- ◎ Opportunities in the ACA to meet health care needs of vulnerable populations

- ◎ Limitations in ACA provisions

Throughout the 20th century, the United States—one of the wealthiest nations in the world—made several strides toward ensuring that all Americans had access to health care. The advent of employer-based health insurance, passage of Medicare and Medicaid in the 1960s, the establishment of community health centers in the 1970s, and the creation of the Children's Health Insurance Program in the 1990s all worked together to connect medically and socioeconomically disadvantaged populations to the U.S. health care system. The passage of the landmark Patient Protection and Affordable Care Act (ACA) in the 21st century was yet another major victory in narrowing the gap between those who have access to health care services and those who have been historically marginalized from them.

All of these efforts have opened the door to health services for millions of Americans who had traditionally been left out—the poor, uninsured, and those without a medical provider. Most of the gains have been made because of the expansion of health insurance. However, progress thus far has barely scratched the surface of a mounting problem—the health and well-being of vulnerable populations in the United States. Positive changes have been slow to come and have not kept up with the growing number of people who fall into the category of vulnerable populations. There remain millions of Americans who have not benefited from these improvements. Moreover, the solutions developed to address the needs of vulnerable populations have been fragmented and categorical, adding to the already heavy burden of those at highest risk for falling through the cracks.

> *Developing solutions that will contain health care expenditures and meet the needs of vulnerable populations is one of the leading challenges facing policymakers in the United States.*

The solutions are also faced with growing price tags. The accelerated spending associated with many of the federal and state programs and policies that were put in place to protect and serve vulnerable populations puts these programs at heightened risk of major funding cuts. Developing solutions that will contain health care expenditures *and* meet the needs of vulnerable populations is one of the leading challenges facing policymakers in the United States. There is a growing awareness that 80% of health care dollars are spent on 20% of the population—of which vulnerable populations make up a large percentage. The United States cannot afford to overlook the needs of vulnerable populations.

This chapter examines the issues affecting vulnerable populations. In the first section, we define and provide an overview of the diverse segments of the population that fall under the category of vulnerable groups. As part of this section, we offer a framework for understanding the factors that enable vulnerability and the domains that affect the well-being of this population. In subsequent sections, we explore the organization and financing of health care for vulnerable populations, examine its limitations, and explore recommendations. In the final section, we discuss opportunities to address the needs of vulnerable populations afforded by the ACA.

■ Understanding Vulnerable Populations and Their Context

DEFINING VULNERABLE POPULATIONS

Whether one lives in a thriving metropolis, a gated suburban community, or a small town in rural America, the presence and realities of vulnerable populations are inescapable. The lives of people in these populations are interwoven into our communities and neighborhoods; their faces greet us at the intersections of our daily routines. They are the single mother of three living next door who just lost her job and who cares for her elderly dad; the young man diagnosed with HIV who sleeps in a makeshift bed at the steps of the local church; the neighbor's daughter who dropped out of high school and has been abusing drugs to self-medicate her untreated bipolar depression; the coworker who has been increasingly withdrawn and depressed after he was diagnosed with diabetes and heart disease; the elderly couple who are home-bound and isolated as a result of decreased mobility.

The term "vulnerable populations" is an umbrella term for all of the individuals who, due to a wide variety of factors, are at a greater risk for poor health status and health care access. Vulnerable groups are categorized by disease status (such as chronic conditions, mental illness, HIV-positive status), demographics (such as socioeconomic status [SES], educational attainment, housing situation, racial/ethnic background, immigration or refugee status), age group (such as children or the elderly), or the ability to access health services (e.g., the uninsured, those who live in a remote rural area, those who lack a regular source of care; Aday, 2001). Regardless of which category or categories a vulnerable individual falls into, the common thread across all groups can be found in the definition of the word "vulnerable." Derived from the Latin verb *vulnerare*, which means "to wound," to be vulnerable means "to be easily hurt or harmed physically, mentally, or emotionally" or "to be open to attack, harm, or damage."

Our humanity, and the range of life experiences we face, puts us all at risk of being vulnerable at different points in our lives. Vulnerability may lead to poor health status and health care access. There are, however, individual and community factors that mediate this risk. For instance, negative or stressful events, such as sudden or chronic illness, unemployment, temporary homelessness, or divorce, may hurt some people more than others. The effect of a stressful life event on a person who lives in a poor neighborhood with limited access to resources is much more adverse than on a person who lives in a wealthy neighborhood with access to a variety of options to ameliorate the problem (Hobfoll, 2001).

> *The intersection of social factors and health problems ultimately predisposes some and not others to fall into the category of "vulnerable populations."*

The intersection of *social factors*—including where we live, income status, education level, job security, and the strength of social networks—and *health problems* ultimately predisposes some and not others to fall into the category of "vulnerable populations."

A FRAMEWORK FOR UNDERSTANDING VULNERABLE POPULATIONS

The common traits and experiences of vulnerable populations provide a comprehensive framework for understanding the underlying determinants and enablers of vulnerability. Models that have emerged within the last decade have begun to recognize the real-life convergence of individual, social, community, and access-to-care risks that lead to vulnerability (Shi & Stevens, 2010). In these models, individual risk factors, such as demographics (age, gender, race/ethnicity, SES), health status, health insurance, and individual belief systems associated with health behaviors, are studied in light of the larger context of a person's life. Environmental (or ecological) risk factors include the geographical location (rural versus urban), socioeconomic status of an entire community (neighborhood income level and unemployment rates), resource inequalities, and the social capital (or social cohesion) of the neighborhood.

Vulnerability to poor health, as posited by this model, is determined by a convergence of predisposing, enabling, and need characteristics at the individual and ecological levels. For example, a man who has hypertension (*health need factor*), is African American (*predisposing factor*), and is uninsured (*enabling factor*) would be considered more vulnerable than an individual who has hypertension alone. In this model, *health needs* directly imply vulnerability, *predisposing factors* indicate the propensity for vulnerability, and *enabling factors* reflect the resources available to overcome the consequences of vulnerability (Shi & Stevens, 2010).

In this chapter, we frame *health needs* using the definition of *health* developed by the World Health Organization (WHO). WHO defines health as a "state of complete *physical, mental*, and *social* well-being" (WHO, 1948). This definition may be understood as follows:

- *Physical* health needs are characterized according to the physiological and physical status of the body. Problems affecting physical health include specific acute or chronic diseases (such as HIV/AIDS, diabetes, asthma) or disabilities.
- *Mental* (or *psychological*) health needs are characterized by emotional and behavioral health—in essence, by an individual's state of mind. Problems affecting mental health include specific mental illnesses, chronic dependence on drugs or alcohol, or a susceptibility to suicidal thoughts.
- *Social* health needs extend beyond the individual and include both the quantity and quality of social contacts with other people. Individuals who have been marginalized or ostracized from their communities (such as homeless individuals, immigrants or refugees, the formerly incarcerated, people living in an abusive home) would be characterized as having social health needs (Aday, 2001).

Poor health along one dimension, for instance physical, is very likely to converge with poor health along others, such as the individual's psychological or social needs. In the earlier example, the African American male who has hypertension and is uninsured would be more susceptible to depression because of the compounding stresses.

The concept of social capital is integral to understanding the enabling factors that can lead to vulnerability. Social capital is measured by the quantity and quality of interpersonal ties among people and groups sharing a community (be it defined geographically or by a common characteristic). Family structure, friendship ties, religious organizations, and neighborhood connections provide social capital to members in the form of social support and associated feelings of belonging, psychological well-being, and self-esteem (Aday, 2001). Social support is critical for mitigating or minimizing the effect of negative life events on health.

A strong social support system is key to making a significant difference in the likelihood of starting—and sticking with—lifestyle changes.

Building on the example of the uninsured, an African American male who has hypertension and begins to suffer from depression: If he is also socially isolated, with little or no social network in his community, it is unlikely that he will succeed in long-term efforts to improve his health, such as establishing healthier eating habits or adhering to a strict medication regimen. A strong social support system is key to making a significant difference in the likelihood of starting—and sticking with—lifestyle changes.

The framework described previously is used throughout this chapter to illustrate best practices; later in the chapter are recommendations for programs and policies that can improve the health outcomes of this population. Before we describe the network of existing services and programs—and their financing mechanisms—that care for the needs of vulnerable populations, we focus in the next section on why the number of vulnerable groups is increasing in the United States. This increase is one of the critical reasons why health care leaders and policymakers must find more effective and efficient ways to address the needs of vulnerable populations than are available in our current systems of care.

■ The Growing Number of Vulnerable Populations

Three leading and concurrent factors have contributed to the growing number of vulnerable populations:

- The rise in prevalence of chronic conditions, such as diabetes and cardiovascular disease
- Shifting demographics of the overall U.S. population, especially the growing income inequality between rich and poor and the graying of the baby boomer generation
- A shrinking and strained sector of supportive services in low-income communities

All three of these factors have affected the American landscape and created fertile ground for the rising number of people and communities who are now considered vulnerable.

PREVALENCE OF CHRONIC CONDITIONS

Chronic illnesses, such as heart disease, diabetes, cancer, respiratory diseases, and arthritis, are ongoing medical conditions that can be treated but not cured. These conditions require constant management, and they significantly alter the daily life of those who suffer from them. In the United States, the rise in chronic conditions has been unprecedented, and these conditions have exacted an enormous human and financial toll. Unhealthy lifestyle behaviors, such as tobacco use, lack of regular physical activity, and consumption of diets rich in saturated fats, sugars, and salt, have greatly contributed to the increase in chronic conditions in the United States. Studies have also shown that people who live in areas of more socioeconomic disadvantage are more likely to take part in these risky health behaviors (Diez-Roux, 2003; Do, 2009; Lang et al., 2009).

The 2010 wave of the National Health Interview Survey estimated that 24.8% of U.S. adults had one chronic condition. The prevalence of *multiple* chronic conditions—comorbidity of any combination of the previously mentioned conditions—makes it even harder to coordinate efforts and address the problems at hand. More than 20% of adults had two or three chronic conditions (Ward & Schiller, 2010). These

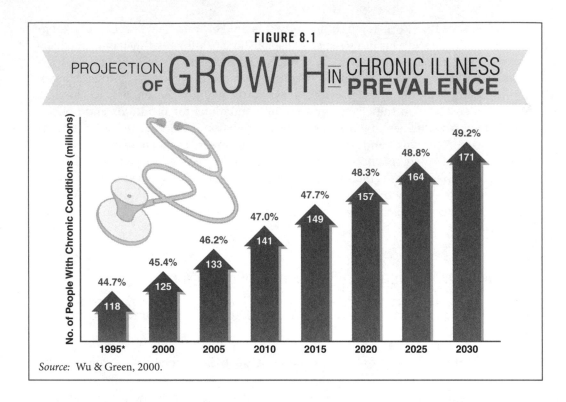

FIGURE 8.1

PROJECTION OF GROWTH IN CHRONIC ILLNESS PREVALENCE

Source: Wu & Green, 2000.

estimates look worse for specific segments of the population, especially racial and ethnic minorities and the poor. If these trends continue unchanged, we can expect the number of adults with at least one chronic disease to reach more than 171 million by 2030 (Figure 8.1; Wu & Green, 2000). Not only is the toll on life high—with 7 out of 10 deaths each year attributed to chronic conditions—but so is the toll on the health care system, because people with chronic conditions account for more than 80% of hospital admissions (Partnership for Solutions, 2004).

Although some individuals with chronic conditions live full and productive lives, for many, one or more of these conditions can be disabling, thereby reducing the quality of life and leading to isolation and depression.

SHIFTING DEMOGRAPHICS IN THE UNITED STATES

Growing Income Inequalities

In 2014, the United States marked the 50th anniversary of President Lyndon B. Johnson's War on Poverty. As a nation, however, the United States has fallen short of the commitment made in 1964 that American citizens would have a fair opportunity to pursue a productive future, earn a decent living wage, and live in a safe community with access to good schools. In 2012, more than 46 million Americans—approximately 15% of the population—were living at or below the federal poverty threshold ($23,492 for a family of four; U.S. Bureau of Labor Statistics, 2012). More than one third of the poor—6.6% of the overall U.S. population—live in deep poverty, earning less than $6,000 a year.

Poverty has persistently affected certain segments of the population more than others. Children under the age of 18 are more likely to live in poverty. In 2012, nearly 22% of children—one out of every five—were living in poverty. Certain racial and ethnic groups are more likely to be poor than others. Poverty rates for Blacks (27%) and Latinos (25%), as well as their children (38% and 33%, respectively), are significantly higher than for White Americans (10%) and their children (20%). To put this in perspective, one out of every three Black children and one out of every four Latino children lives in poverty. Single-parent families are also more likely to live in poverty. Thirty-one percent of female-headed households, for instance, live in poverty, compared with 6% of married couple households. People with disabilities (28%) are more than twice as likely to live in poverty as their counterparts without a disability (12%).

Throughout U.S. history, poverty has been concentrated in cities and in rural communities; there has been a steady increase, however, in the number of people living in poverty in suburban neighborhoods. In 2008, the number of suburban poor exceeded the urban poor in central cities by 1.5 million. Although the rates of poverty continue to be higher in urban areas than in suburbs (18% versus 9.5%), poverty rates are increasing at a faster pace in suburban areas (Allard & Roth, 2010).

Income—or lack thereof—is one of the key enablers of vulnerability. People with financial resources not only have the ability to obtain access to the highest-quality health services, they also have access to other material goods that benefit health and greater opportunities to build the social capital that can serve as a buffer for adverse life events. Income also has a more substantive and complex effect on health when it is considered in the context of a neighborhood. Concentrated wealth has a larger effect on the environment (neighborhood) that shapes a person's position along the socioeconomic gradient, which includes an individual's education level and employment opportunities. In the United States, where you live determines the quality of the education system your children have access to, because the local tax base determines funding for public schools. In communities with concentrated poverty, students have lower average test scores, fewer qualified teachers, fewer interactions with colleges and potential employers, higher levels of teen pregnancy, and higher high school dropout rates than public schools in neighborhoods with more resources (Willms, 1999).

Thus far, we have explored the effect of absolute income and SES status on health and the role of SES as an enabling factor of vulnerability. However, distribution of income is also an important factor in determining the health of a population. Income inequalities are on the rise in the United States; in fact, in 2012 the gap between the richest 1% and the remaining 99% was the largest it has been since the 1920s. According to recent analysis, the 400 richest people in the United States have more combined wealth than the bottom 150 million put together. The relationship between income inequality and health has broader implications in determining health outcomes beyond personal income. Concentrated wealth leads to concentrated poverty, which in turn leads to poor neighborhoods and communities.

People living in neighborhoods with many resources are more likely to engage in healthy behaviors, whether these behaviors are due to the wider availability of primary care services, stores offering healthy food, or environments for safe physical activities.

Myriad studies have shown the correlation between disadvantaged communities and poor health outcomes (Diez-Roux, 2003; Do, 2009; Lang et al., 2009). The widening gap between rich and poor leads to a greater separation between the institutions, organizations, and services that promote and protect health. People living in neighborhoods with many resources are more likely to engage in healthy behaviors, whether these behaviors are due to the wider availability of primary care services, stores offering healthy food, or environments for safe physical activities. An entire population is at greater risk of poor health outcomes when they are persistently exposed to poverty, have limited access to high-quality health organizations, and have major stressors impeding their daily life activities.

The Graying of America

On January 1, 2011, the first baby boomers turned 65 years old. Over the next 5 years, 8,000 people will turn 65 each day. The population aged 65 and over increased from 35 million in 2000 to 41 million in 2011 (an 18% increase). As of 2013, people over 65 represented 13% of the U.S. population, about 1 in every 8 Americans. In 2030, when the entire baby boom generation will have turned 65, seniors will make up one fourth of the population. The segment of the population 85 years and older is projected to increase from 5 million in 2011 to 9 million in 2030 (Knickman & Snell, 2002).

Baby boomers will live longer than previous generations because of improvements in health care, technology, and lifestyles. The elderly of 2030 will also be better educated than the current elderly population, with rates of college graduation two times higher and high school dropout rates one third less than the current elderly generation (Knickman & Snell, 2002). This is good news for the future health of baby boomers because there is a strong association between education and disability. College graduates have a disability rate about half that of high school dropouts (Knickman & Snell, 2002). However, with the aging of America and longer average life spans, the rates of chronic conditions associated with an older population will also grow.

According to the Centers for Disease Control and Prevention (CDC), the average American over the age of 65 has multiple chronic conditions, such as hypertension (72%), arthritis (51%), heart disease (31%), cancer (24%), and diabetes (20%). In 2010, about 13.6 million persons aged 65 or older were discharged from short-stay hospitals. Their rate of discharge is three times the comparable rate for persons of all ages. The average length of stay in a hospital is longer for older people. The average length of stay for persons aged 65 to 74 was 5.4 days; for those aged 75 to 84 it was 5.7 days; and for those aged 85 and over it was 5.6 days. The comparable rate for persons of all ages was 4.8 days.

Health expenditures are a greater financial burden for older people. In 2011, older consumers averaged out-of-pocket health care expenditures of $4,769, an increase of 46% since 2000. In contrast, the total population spent considerably less, averaging $3,313 in out-of-pocket costs. Older Americans spent 12.2% of their total expenditures on health, almost twice the proportion spent by all consumers (6.7%). Health costs incurred on average by older consumers in 2011 consisted of $3,076 (64%) for insurance, $786 (16%) for medical services, $714 (15%) for drugs, and $193 (4.0%) for medical supplies. Considering that the median income of older persons in 2011 was $27,707 for men and $15,362 for women, these health care costs put the elderly at greater risk of financial hardship. Their age (a predisposing factor of vulnerability), coupled with the risk of financial hardship (an enabling factor) and the increased possibility of chronic conditions (another enabling factor), places older Americans—especially those living in impoverished neighborhoods—at highest risk of vulnerability.

A STRAINED SOCIAL SERVICE SECTOR

Between December 2007 and June 2009, the United States experienced an economic recession that was one of the longest and, by most measures, the worst since the Great Depression (Grusky, Western, & Wimer, 2011). This so-called Great Recession began with the bursting of an $8 trillion housing bubble, which was then followed by massive job loss. Between 2008 and 2009, the U.S. labor market lost 8.4 million jobs, or 6.1% of all payroll employment. According to the U.S. Bureau of Labor Statistics, in the months after the recession, the unemployment rate peaked at 10% (in October 2009)—the largest loss of employment in any recession since the Great Depression. To make matters worse, the recovery period after the recession has been sluggish. In October 2010, 16 months after the official end of the recession, the economy still had 5.4% fewer jobs than it did before the recession started. This recession has also seen historic numbers of home foreclosures. Between 2006 and 2009, the number of home foreclosure filings increased from approximately 1.2 million annually to almost 4 million, and have been disproportionately concentrated in Black and Hispanic neighborhoods.

The prolonged economic recession and historically slow recovery have been taking a toll on the average American family. Job loss is a significant source of stress and has been shown to be associated with poor health outcomes, such as increased risk of heart attack, stroke, and psychiatric problems including depression and anxiety. When you combine the rates of unemployment with the unprecedented number of foreclosures, there is no mystery as to why there has been such strain on social and supportive services. Not only are these services serving the millions of Americans who lived in poverty before the economic downturn, they are also serving families who are seeking this type of help for the first time in their lives.

The Brookings Institute reported that 76 metro areas across the United States saw Supplemental Nutrition Assistance Program (SNAP) receipt increase 66%—adding 7.5 million people—between July 2007 and July 2010. In the suburbs, SNAP receipts have increased at an even faster pace: 73% (Garr, 2011). Though not as dramatic, other programs, such as Temporary Assistance for Needy Families (TANF), Medicaid, Supplemental Security Income (SSI), and supportive housing programs, have experienced similar trends in the past 5 years. The agencies that administer these programs are working at full capacity. The problem is not just that the demand for services has grown but that the programs—as well as the agencies that help people connect to them—are experiencing detrimental cuts.

The economic downturn has produced significant gaps between revenues and expenditures in state and local budgets. The decline in revenue and increased demand for state services has resulted in states facing total budget gaps of nearly $300 billion over the 2009 to 2012 period. All levels of government have had to implement a mix of discretionary cuts across the social service sector; in many states these cuts have happened at the same time that governments have cut taxes. In the Brookings Institute study, the researchers looked at three large states and the effect on social services in suburban neighborhoods. Nearly half of the nonprofits surveyed reported a loss in revenue source, and one third of the nonprofits that connect people to social service programs had been forced to lay off staff members because of the cuts (Garr, 2011).

The very same agencies that help to alleviate the economic and social effects on families and communities are being stretched to the limit while experiencing cuts to their own budgets. Even more concerning are the growing threats to cut the financial aid provided by programs such as SNAP. In 2014, SNAP benefits will average less than $1.40 per person per meal (Dean, Rosenbaum, & Foley, 2013). These cuts affect some of the most vulnerable populations that participate in SNAP—including 22 million children (10 million of whom live in "deep poverty," with family incomes below 50% of the poverty line) and 9 million people who are elderly or have a serious disability.

■ Organization and Financing of Health Care and Other Services for Vulnerable Populations

We have defined vulnerable populations and described the pathways through which predisposing and enabling factors lead to vulnerability. We have also described three main reasons why the number of vulnerable groups is projected to grow. In this section, we provide an inventory of the existing resources and strategies set in place to care for the vulnerable. First, we offer a brief description of institutions and structures within the health care system that deliver services for vulnerable populations. Then, we describe financing mechanisms at the federal, state, and private levels that support health care and social services for vulnerable groups. More thorough and general treatments (not specific to vulnerable populations) of some of the topics presented here are offered in other chapters of this book.

PUBLIC HOSPITALS

Public hospitals are core providers of services to America's sickest, poorest, and most vulnerable populations. The mission of a public hospital within the safety-net system is, quite simply, to be the guarantor of health for the public (Gourevitch, Malaspina, Weitzman, & Goldfrank, 2008). Public hospitals focus on providing care to the most vulnerable groups within a community, including the uninsured, the underinsured, the homeless, the disabled, documented and undocumented immigrants, high-risk mothers and infants, and those with limited proficiency in speaking and reading English. Public hospitals also provide services to the incarcerated, respond to disasters within communities, provide trauma care, and administer behavioral health and substance abuse treatment when necessary (Gourevitch et al., 2008). In 2004 alone, public hospitals averaged 405,000 ambulatory visits and 18,000 hospital admissions per site (Gourevitch et al., 2008).

Most patients who receive health care services from public hospitals are low-income and uninsured; they also suffer disproportionately from preventable chronic health conditions. Many of these patients visit the emergency departments (EDs) of public hospitals to receive primary care because they lack a primary care provider. Patients who use the ED for most of their health care, regardless of urgency, are referred to as high utilizers (see Case Study 2).

FEDERALLY QUALIFIED HEALTH CENTERS (FQHCs)

Federally Qualified Health Centers (FQHCs) are systems of safety-net providers that serve predominantly vulnerable groups living in underserved communities. These centers are overseen by the Health Resources and Services Administration (HRSA) of the U.S. Department of Health and Human Services (DHHS).

The FQHC program allocates special Medicare and Medicaid cost-based reimbursement payments to health centers for legislatively specified services. To qualify as an FQHC, a safety-net provider must meet the following criteria:

- Provide services in communities identified as "predominantly medically underserved areas" or provide services to a target population documented to be underserved
- Offer the required primary and preventive health services, meet specific staffing requirements, and offer a sliding-fee payment scale for services rendered
- Participate in an ongoing quality assurance program
- Have a governing board of directors that includes representatives from the populations served

FQHCs include these facilities:

- Community Health Centers (CHCs)
- Migrant Health Centers (MHCs)
- Health Care for the Homeless Centers (HCHs)
- Public Housing Primary Care Centers (PHPCCs)

Community Health Centers (CHCs)
Riding on the successful passage of the 1964 Civil Rights Act and President Johnson's War on Poverty efforts, Tufts University physicians H. Jack Geiger and Count Gibson submitted proposals to the federal Office of Economic Opportunity (OEO) for funding to establish what they called "neighborhood health centers" in inner-city, underserved areas across the United States (Hawkins & Groves, 2011). The Economic Opportunity Act of 1964 provided federal funds for two such centers; both were built in Boston, Massachusetts, in 1965 (National Center for Farmworker Health, n.d.). Building on a community-based health care model already thriving in South Africa, these two CHCs offered comprehensive primary health care that focused on outreach, disease prevention, social support services, and patient education activities, including nutritional education and counseling and sanitation education. Dr. Geiger and Dr. Gibson believed that treating patients with dignity and respect, regardless of age, race, health status, or income level, and engaging them in their own health and health care, were of critical importance and promoted these beliefs as central tenets of CHC care (Adashi, Geiger, & Fine, 2010). As of 2010, there were more than 8,000 designated CHCs throughout the United States, serving as the medical home to more than 20 million Americans—about 5% of the current population (Adashi et al., 2010).

Migrant Health Centers (MHCs)
MHCs serve the migrant and seasonal farm workers who come to the United States each year to harvest, plant, and tend to agricultural crops. Patients pay for care on a

sliding scale (an average visit costs $30). Currently there are 156 MHCs that operate within the CHC system in the United States. In 2011, the federal government spent $166 million to help pay for the care of close to 1 million migrant and seasonal farm-workers (Galewitz, 2012).

Health Care for the Homeless Centers (HCHs)

Although eligible for federally funded health care, approximately 70% of homeless health center patients lack health insurance and face significant barriers to care elsewhere in their communities (National Health Care for the Homeless Council ([NHCHC], 2008). The Health Care for the Homeless program was initially authorized under the Stewart B. McKinney Homeless Assistance Act of 1987. HCHs provide comprehensive medical services to the homeless, including pediatric and adult primary care, screening, health education, referrals for specialty medical care, transportation services, social service outreach, and both long- and short-term rehabilitative care. By statute, the HCH program receives 8.7% of the total health center appropriations for all FQHCs.

Public Housing Primary Care Centers (PHPCCs)

PHPCCs are health centers that provide comprehensive medical care and social support services to individuals who live in public and assisted housing. Currently there are 63 PHPCCs in 25 states and Puerto Rico, and these centers provided services to nearly 171,731 public and assisted housing residents in 2012 (National Center for Health in Public Housing, 2012).

RURAL HEALTH CLINICS (RHCs) AND RURAL HEALTH NETWORKS (RHNs)

Rural Health Clinics (RHCs) were created as a result of the Rural Health Clinic Services Act of 1977. This federal legislation provided reimbursement not just for services provided by full-time doctors but also for preventive and primary care services done by health professionals called mid-level providers (MLPs) such as nurse practitioners (NPs) and physician assistants (PAs) at clinics in underserved rural areas across the United States. This legislation was established both to alleviate the burden on the limited number of full-time doctors and specialists and to cut down on emergency care spending (DHHS Office of Rural Health Policy, 2006).

Rural health networks (RHNs)—also known as rural health alliances, cooperatives, or affiliations—are systems of care in rural areas that include at least one rural hospital and two other separate community health organizations, such as a nursing home or a public health unit. These networks operate by pooling resources in ways such as developing continuing education programs, investing money in electronic medical record systems for easier care coordination between providers, and supporting advocacy activities within the communities served by the RHN (DHHS Office of Rural Health Policy, 2006). These networks were created out of necessity to foster collaboration and discourage reduction in services due to unwarranted competition (Moscovice, Gregg, & Lewerenz, 2003).

INDIAN HEALTH SERVICES (IHS)

Because of the history of oppression and enduring health inequities since Europeans first landed in the Americas more than 500 years ago, Native Americans are considered a special group under the umbrella term "vulnerable populations." The relationship between the U.S. federal government and North American native peoples (that is, Indian tribes) began in 1787 and has evolved ever since with various laws, treaties, and executive orders to protect their status (DHHS Indian Health Services, 2014).

The IHS has an annual budget of about $4 billion (Devi, 2011) and is the primary federal health care provider for approximately 1.9 million American Indians and Alaska Natives who belong to the more than 566 federally recognized tribes in 35 states (DHHS Indian Health Services, 2014). Through a network of 45 hospitals and more than 293 clinics, IHS programs provide Native Americans with preventive, primary, dental, and emergency medical care; mental health and substance abuse prevention and treatment; nutrition education; access to referrals and resources; and social service support, including (but not limited to) assistance in applying for federally designated public housing for Native Americans and other need-based benefit programs such as SNAP, WIC, and TANF.

MENTAL HEALTH AND CHEMICAL DEPENDENCY SERVICES

In 1963, Congress passed the Mental Retardation Facilities and Community Health Centers Construction Act, which provided federal funding for the development and implementation of community-based mental health centers (CMHCs). With the exception of the most severely mentally ill, most previously institutionalized patients were released into their communities and encouraged to seek care at these new CMHCs and other, similar facilities (Unite for Sight, n.d.).

Unfortunately, CMHCs are underfunded and understaffed; as a result, many people living with mental illness or chemical dependence are not receiving the proper comprehensive care they need. Many ultimately end up homeless or in prison. According to the *Journal of Community Mental Health*, the combination of deinstitutionalization and inadequate and underfunded community care has led to "transinstitutionalization," a phenomenon in which prisons, instead of psychiatric or detoxification facilities, become the main providers of highly structured, controlled living environments for the severely mentally ill and chemically dependent (Prins, 2011).

Not only are mentally ill individuals more likely to be incarcerated or homeless, they also contribute significantly to the cost of ED care in hospitals across the country. By one federal estimate, spending by general hospitals to care for these patients will nearly double in one year: from $20.3 billion in 2013 to $38.5 billion in 2014 (Creswell, 2013).

SPECIAL POPULATIONS: HIV/AIDS PROGRAMS

Legislation to address the AIDS epidemic was first enacted in 1990 as the Ryan White Comprehensive AIDS Resources Emergency (CARE) Act. Since then, the legislation has been amended and reauthorized four times to accommodate new and emerging medical and social needs; it is now called the Ryan White HIV/AIDS Program (Henry J. Kaiser Family Foundation, 2013a). HRSA estimates that more than 500,000 individuals receive at least one medical, health, or related support service through a Ryan White program each year (Henry J. Kaiser Family Foundation, 2013a). The multiple parts of the Ryan White Program all emphasize risk reduction and prevention through interventions at both individual and community levels. For those affected, intensive case management in a community-based health care setting is critical to a long life (Aday, 2001).

Despite the delayed response to the HIV/AIDS epidemic in the United States, the wraparound services provided through the Ryan White Program serve as a model for responding to health needs with a whole person approach. No other vulnerable population has been able to advocate as effectively for that level of support.

■ Social Service Needs

Spanish philosopher José Ortega y Gasset posited, "*Yo soy yo y mi circunstancia, y si no la salvo a ella no me salvo yo*" (Ortega y Gasset, 1914), which loosely translates as "I am myself and my circumstance; if I do not help it, I cannot help myself." In that same spirit, social needs are the *circunstancia* that enables the events that lead people with predisposing characteristics to become vulnerable. Toward the end of the 19th century and sporadically throughout the 20th century, the United States made attempts to advance social change. Examples include President Franklin D. Roosevelt's New Deal in response to the Great Depression; the previously mentioned War on Poverty waged by President Johnson; and President John F. Kennedy's work in support of progressive taxation, affordable housing, and extension of social welfare. The existing safety-net of social services is an amalgam of programs that, though not completely infallible, provides some support for vulnerable populations, potentially making the difference between maintaining good health outcomes and succumbing to illness.

In the next section, we highlight three types of social service programs: (a) food assistance, (b) monetary assistance, and (c) housing assistance.

FOOD ASSISTANCE

All food assistance programs listed in this section are administered and funded through the U.S. Department of Agriculture (USDA) Food and Nutrition Service Agency.

Supplemental Nutrition Assistance Program (SNAP)
The first food assistance program was implemented in May 1939 but was shut down in 1943 because "unmarketable food surpluses and widespread unemployment no longer existed" (USDA Food and Nutrition Service, n.d.). It wasn't until President Kennedy came along 18 years later that a second food assistance program was implemented. Kennedy's program eliminated the concept of different stamps for different foods and encouraged beneficiaries to use their stamps to buy healthy food (USDA Food and Nutrition Service, n.d.). In September 2007, the Food Stamp Program was renamed SNAP (Supplemental Nutrition Assistance Program) to decrease the stigma associated with the term "food stamps" and to encourage those who need benefits to apply for them. As of October 2013, more than 47 million individuals were receiving SNAP benefits (Center on Budget and Policy Priorities, 2014).

Women, Infants, and Children (WIC)

The Special Supplemental Nutrition Program for Women, Infants, and Children was authorized by the Child Nutrition Act of 1966 and officially launched in 1974. WIC state agencies receive federal funding to pay for WIC foods, nutrition-related services, and administrative costs (Association of State & Territorial Health Officials, 2010). Pregnant, breastfeeding, or postpartum women, as well as infants and children up to age 5, are eligible for benefits if (a) they meet a predetermined income standard; (b) they already receive SNAP, Medicaid, or TANF benefits; or (c) they have documentation from a medical professional explaining that the mother, her children, or both are at nutritional risk (Kent, 2006). In 2013, WIC had close to 8.7 million participants. The program costs an average of $43.45 per month per participant (USDA Food and Nutrition Service, n.d.).

Other Federal and Private Food Programs

The USDA Food and Nutrition Service administers 11 additional supplemental nutrition programs, ranging from reduced-price or free lunch programs for elementary school children (The National School Lunch Program [NSLP]) to emergency food assistance programs that organize and fund food banks, pantries, and soup kitchens to distribute food items to low-income people (USDA Food and Nutrition Service, n.d.).

The rise in food insecurity since the 1980s has not kept up with federal food program availability. Thus, a network of private food assistance programs has emerged to try to fill the gap between need and federal support. This private food assistance network relies on food donations, at-cost bulk purchasing, and food rescue of perishable, nonperishable, and prepared foods (Daponte & Bade, 2006).

MONETARY ASSISTANCE

Support for vulnerable individuals and families in the form of monetary assistance is aimed at offering both short-term and long-term financial relief to meet basic needs. Several federal agencies administer monetary assistance.

Temporary Assistance for Needy Families (TANF)

Temporary Assistance for Needy Families (TANF) is a monthly cash assistance program for low-income families with children established under the Personal Responsibility and Work Opportunity Reconciliation Act of 1996 as a replacement to the Aid to Families with Dependent Children (AFDC) program. TANF is overseen by the Office of Family Assistance (part of the DHHS Administration for Children & Families), but control over implementation is given to states (Purtell, Gershoff, & Aber, 2012).

Supplemental Security Income (SSI)

President Richard M. Nixon passed the federal Social Security Amendments of 1972 in an effort to centralize the administration of Social Security and reduce inequalities among the state-run adult assistance programs already in existence. Today, the federal SSI program administers cash assistance each month to eligible individuals aged 65 and older, the blind, and mentally or physically disabled children and adults. A preset federal benefit rate determines benefit levels (U.S. Social Security Administration, n.d.).

Unemployment Insurance (UI)

Unemployment insurance (UI) is available to people who have lost their jobs through no fault of their own but as a result of circumstances such as employer cutbacks. Federal funds are distributed through the U.S. Department of Labor to each state; states then administer their UI programs according to state-determined criteria.

HOUSING ASSISTANCE

The first major investment in housing assistance in the United States took place in 1932, when—in the midst of widespread unemployment and homelessness resulting from the Great Depression—Congress passed the Emergency Relief and Construction Act (U.S. Department of Housing and Urban Development, n.d.). This act created the Reconstruction Finance Corporation (RFC), an agency whose responsibility was to make loans to private corporations that were providing housing for low-income families. From 1932 to 1956, four housing acts were enacted; these continued through the 1960s and into the 1970s. Funding included federal investments in new housing construction, the preservation of existing housing resources, and the development of safer, better public housing communities.

The McKinney-Vento Homeless Assistance Act of 1987 established the Supportive Housing Program (SHP) especially for the homeless. The 2009 American Recovery and Reinvestment Act (ARRA) included new housing programs, most notably the Homelessness Prevention and Rapid Re-Housing Program (HPRP). This program allocated $1.9 billion in funding to homelessness housing. Funds allocated for HPRP helped with short-term or medium-term rental assistance and housing relocation and stabilization services, including such activities as mediation, credit counseling, security or utility deposits, utility payments, moving cost assistance, and case management.

This section has not presented an exhaustive list of federal and private social services available for vulnerable populations. For example, in terms of housing, there are services that offer long-term care for elderly and disabled people, such as nursing homes, and supportive at-home services that allow for aging in place, such as home health aides.

The next section offers a more detailed picture of the payment system that covers the health care of vulnerable populations.

■ Federal and State Financing of Care for Vulnerable Populations

There are three main payers for health care for the vulnerable: (a) the federal government, (b) the states, and (c) private sources, including employers, insurers, and philanthropic organizations.

At the federal level, the primary health care payment programs are Medicare, Medicaid, and the Children's Health Insurance Plan (CHIP). These programs are managed by the Centers for Medicare & Medicaid Services (CMS); however, each state has the power to administer its Medicaid program. Medicaid-eligible individuals typically include low-income individuals and families who fall below a certain federal poverty level (FPL) threshold and those receiving SSI.

According to Congressional Budget Office estimates, in 2012 Medicaid provided health coverage for 32 million children, 19 million adults, 6 million seniors, and 11 million persons with disabilities (totaling 68 million low-income Americans) over the course of the year at a cost of $415 billion (Henry J. Kaiser Family Foundation, 2013b).

Individuals eligible for Medicare include the elderly (ages 65 and older), some people under 65 with qualifying disabilities, and people with kidney failure requiring dialysis. The most recent estimate of Medicare expenses in 2009 reported a yearly program cost of $471 billion, with beneficiaries exceeding 49 million people in 2012 (Center on Budget and Policy Priorities, 2013).

Dual eligibles are individuals who qualify for both Medicare and Medicaid and are among the sickest and poorest in the United States. Although they represent a relatively small percentage of the overall Medicare and Medicaid populations, dual eligibles account for $300 billion (approximately 33%) of annual spending between the two programs (Fontenot & Stubblefield, 2011). This population is three times more likely than the Medicare-only population to be disabled and has much higher rates of chronic conditions such as diabetes, pulmonary disease, stroke, mental disorders, and Alzheimer's disease (Fontenot & Stubblefield, 2011). Disproportionate levels of funding for state Medicaid programs means the resources available for dual eligibles vary from state to state.

There is a segment of the vulnerable population that neither qualifies for subsidized care nor receives care through an employer or other private funder. To offset the burden of offering care for the uninsured, federal law offers a modified payment strategy called the Medicaid and Medicare Disproportionate Share Hospital (DSH) program. DSH payments are available to qualifying hospitals that have a high number of Medicaid and Medicare patients and uninsured individuals (Mitchell, 2013).

■ Challenges for Service Delivery and Payment

The systems of care and financing mechanisms currently available in the United States, well intentioned as they are, fall short of their goal of taking care of vulnerable populations. At best, the programs and services are disjointed and, at worst, they offer temporary solutions that deal with isolated problems, and for very targeted populations. For instance, a person's drug or alcohol dependency may preclude him or her from eligibility for supportive housing. Yet, stable housing has been linked to recovery from addictions. The common response by policymakers—and common practice by researchers—is to focus on distinct populations when examining and addressing the needs of vulnerable populations. Disparate and disjointed programs are created to address the needs of children, the elderly, the physically disabled, the chronically ill, the mentally ill, substance abusers, persons with HIV/AIDS, the homeless, residents of rural areas, immigrants, individuals with limited or no English proficiency—the list goes on and on. Yet, the distinctions among many of these vulnerable groups are thin and artificial. Many of these groups share common traits and experience a convergence of multiple vulnerable characteristics. These subpopulations are more likely to live in poor communities, less likely to have access to high-quality health and education, and less likely to have the financial resources to secure adequate, stable, affordable housing.

The programs and services available are not very cost-effective; this puts them at the mercy of critics who would prefer less government involvement in the care of vulnerable individuals and their families. The current market-driven health care delivery and payment system is one that gives providers financial incentives for the volume, not the quality, of services delivered. Some areas for improvement related to delivery and payment are discussed later. In this section, we point out how (and where) the current ways in which care is delivered and payment is structured fall short of their goal to take care of the vulnerable while containing cost. Second, we highlight emerging service delivery models and innovative payment strategies created to reach the Triple Aim—better care for individuals, better health for populations, and lower cost—as it pertains to vulnerable populations.

A FRAGMENTED DELIVERY SYSTEM

Health care initiatives to reduce the barriers created by vulnerability rarely recognize the common overlap of risk factors, and few studies have examined the combined influences of multiple risks on obtaining needed health care services.

Health care initiatives to reduce the barriers created by vulnerability rarely recognize the common overlap of risk factors, and few studies have examined the combined influences of multiple risks on obtaining needed health care services (Shi & Stevens, 2005). The main issues that emerge in a review of delivery systems created to care for vulnerable populations include (a) fragmented and siloed structures and (b) a focus on health and psychological needs that does not always recognize the link between social needs and health.

Fragmentation refers to care that is delivered by different providers who are not co-located or within proximity of each other. Where fragmentation exists, patients must make and manage multiple appointments that may require, for example, more days off from work to attend appointments. *Silo structures* refer to care offered by multiple providers who do not consult with each other. An endocrinologist, for instance, may be unaware of the medications prescribed by a psychiatrist treating a patient's depression—which may have weight gain as a side effect, thus disrupting the patient's diabetes management.

Although there has been budding awareness of the importance of meeting social and other nonclinical needs in relationship to health, the U.S. delivery system has not made the necessary transformation to make this possible. For example, food insecurity would make it hard for a person managing cardiovascular disease to eat more fruits and vegetables, because that person may depend on a local emergency food provider that is unequipped to receive and distribute produce.

VOLUME VERSUS VALUE

A major weakness of our current payment system is that it encourages a *volume-driven* health care system rather than a *value-driven* system. Under fee-for-service (FFS), providers (such as hospitals, physicians, and health centers) gain increased revenue and profit by delivering more services to people. This payment model becomes an enormous barrier to delivering effective and efficient care to vulnerable populations. Providers have little or no incentive to spend the necessary time with an individual who has complex medical, behavioral, and social needs in order to determine a course of action that will address the underlying complexities of the patient's life. Providers are more likely to address the present health crisis affecting the individual—usually by delivering more diagnostic tests, prescribing more medication, or making more referrals to costly specialists. FFS payment systems also reinforce fragmentation of care by paying multiple providers for multiple services or tests for the same patient, regardless of whether the care is coordinated or duplicative.

Behavioral and social services operate in an entirely different realm than medical care; such a vast, complex web of disconnected services is available for vulnerable populations that the time and effort required to coordinate and manage transitions across necessary services are beyond any reimbursement rate set by public or private payer. Instead, there is a perverse payment system that rewards the provider for delivering more health care services, rather than addressing (by connecting patients to critical services) the pressing social and behavioral problems that negatively affect the patient's health outcomes.

REACTIVE VERSUS PREVENTIVE CARE

Only a small fraction of health care spending is devoted to the promotion of healthier behavior, despite the fact that preventable chronic diseases are linked to smoking, obesity, lack of exercise, and drug and alcohol use (DeVol et al., 2007). There are very few incentives in the health care system to promote prevention and early intervention, especially in the case of chronic diseases. Only a small percentage of health care spending is devoted to promoting healthier behavior, despite the fact that preventable chronic diseases are linked to lifestyle behaviors, such as smoking, exercise, and drug and alcohol use, and to social determinants of health (McGinnis, Russo, & Knickman, 2002).

■ Emerging and Tested Ideas for Better Health Delivery

Health care leaders and policymakers are grappling with how to improve our health delivery systems. In this section, we highlight emerging service delivery models created to improve health outcomes for vulnerable groups while containing the cost of care. Definitions and descriptions of these budding models are explained, along with case studies that have implemented these models.

DELIVERY STRATEGIES THAT WORK

Growing evidence shows that three distinct delivery strategies—care coordination, patient engagement and team-based care, and integration of care—help to meet the needs of vulnerable populations. We describe these strategies and discuss the *meaningful* use of data to drive them.

Care Coordination

Creating successful integrated delivery systems for vulnerable populations requires several factors: (a) an emphasis on primary care; (b) coordination of all care, including behavioral, social, and public health services; and (c) accountability for population health outcomes (Witgert & Hess, 2012). The Agency for Health Care Research and Quality (AHRQ) defines care coordination as:

> ...[T]he deliberate organization of patient care activities between two or more participants (including the patient) involved in a patient's care to facilitate the appropriate delivery of health care services. Organizing care involves the marshaling of personnel and other resources needed to carry out all required patient care activities, and is often managed by the exchange of information among participants responsible for different aspects of care. (AHRQ, 2014)

According to a 2011 report published by the American Hospital Association, promising practices that will improve care coordination include (among other practices) conducting periodic home visits, facilitating and encouraging data sharing through the use of integrated health information systems (i.e., electronic medical records [EMRs]), providing non–health care services such as transportation to appointments, employing and incorporating specially trained teams of providers that are aware of each patient's cultural and language backgrounds and can administer guidance and advice as they see fit (Fontenot & Stubblefield, 2011).

Patient Engagement and Team-Based Care

Patient engagement is generally defined as the process of involving individuals in their health care, disease management, or preventive behaviors. Providers can—and do—play an important role in the health outcomes of their patients; however, after a patient has left the doctor's office, the patient's health is largely in his or her own hands. Low income, lack of education, language barriers, and not having a regular source of care are some of the many risk factors that may create significant barriers to accessing necessary health care services (Shi & Stevens, 2005). Patients are expected to follow recommended care management plans, communicate regularly with their providers, and make positive lifestyle changes; however, patients—especially those within vulnerable populations—lack the energy, money, knowledge, and skills needed to navigate successfully their often complex health conditions, regardless of whether they are sick or well (Center for Advancing Health, 2010).

Patient engagement works best when it involves a team that not only possesses clinical expertise, but also considers patients' socioeconomic needs (such as the importance to clinical outcomes of stable housing) and provides coordination (e.g., across multiple providers or between community-based organizations and the health system). The ideal care team includes not only physicians and nurses directing decisions related to medical care, but also psychiatrists, psychologists, or other licensed clinical social workers who support behavioral and mental health, as well as social workers who can provide counseling and access to social services via referrals (Manahan, 2011; Volkmann & Castanares, 2011). More and more, such multidisciplinary teams include outreach specialists and community health workers, especially when addressing the needs of vulnerable populations (Martinez Garcel, 2012; Volkmann & Castanares, 2011). A 2014 report on Bronx Lebanon Hospital's utilization of community health workers (CHWs) showed that CHWs help to reduce the number of ED visits and hospitalizations, thus reducing health care costs and contributing to the management of chronic disease (Findley, Matos, Hicks, Chang, & Reich, 2014). Case Study 1 expands on the Bronx-Lebanon Hospital example (Findley et al., 2014).

CHWs play a critical role in patient engagement. They can explain reasons for their actions in layman's terms and provide a support system that allows patients to feel they have the power to navigate the system and take control of their condition. When care coordination includes the support of individuals such as CHWs, patients have the help they need to think through how to integrate self-management of their chronic conditions into their existing life circumstances and—in the best of cases—are directed to the auxiliary services they need to get a handle on their nonmedical problems, stabilize their routines, and have better health outcomes.

Bringing It All Together: An Integrated System

Populations that are vulnerable due to low income or poor health stand to benefit from the integration of care. Integrated health care delivery systems provide or arrange a coordinated continuum of health care services to a defined population, and these delivery systems hold themselves accountable for the outcomes and health status of their patients (Witgert & Hess, 2012). By ensuring appropriate care, avoiding duplication of services, and reducing fragmentation within a preventive framework, integrated delivery systems seek to promote health care equality while controlling costs.

Use of Data in Improving Care

EHRs (also called electronic health records) and advances in information technology (including geographic information systems) have created new opportunities to improve the effectiveness and efficiency of care—particularly for vulnerable populations. Such technological advances have facilitated the use of large data sets to inform health care delivery and also to conduct comprehensive cost and utilization analysis by population type, geography, and more.

One of the most compelling examples of data-reliant integrated care is the work of New Jersey's Camden Coalition of Healthcare Providers (CCHP), which utilizes the Camden Health Information Exchange (HIE) to track, monitor, and target services for the highest-cost patients across health systems in Camden. Case Study 2 expands on the example of the Camden Coalition.

Case Study 1. Patient Engagement: Bronx-Lebanon Hospital Department of Family Medicine's Patient-Centered Medical Home

The South Bronx is home to a vibrant community, albeit poor, young, and with high rates of every illness now reaching epidemic proportions in the United States: diabetes, asthma, HIV, drug use, and obesity, to name a few. It is also the home of the Bronx-Lebanon Hospital Department of Family Medicine's Patient-Centered Medical Home.

The hospital's chair of family medicine, Dr. Douglas Reich, was grappling with the department's goal of improving health outcomes for the patients with the most complex life contexts. Beyond completing the very important clinical tasks of diagnosis and treatment, Reich's clinicians lacked the time and the skills to conduct meaningful discussions that would help to provide a better context for patients' care: What were the barriers to following a treatment regimen? What was getting in the way of managing illness? Was there room for prevention? An even greater challenge was reaching the hundreds of people who were in need of health care but going without.

In 2007, the Community Health Worker (CHW) program was established. CHWs, supervised directly by the department chair, received extensive training to fulfill their role as care managers. Integration into the care team was achieved by creating opportunities for shared learning and cross-education about team roles, for CHWs and clinical members alike, through continuing education, rounds, staff meetings, and so on.

Achieving CHW program sustainability required additional infrastructure, and protocol changes were necessary, the following among them:

- Recognition of CHW team contributions, including assessments and feedback within the department and hospital administration
- Shared group visits with a CHW and a physician
- Elaboration of the care management process
- Focus of work on interactions with patients

The patients assigned to CHWs demonstrated improvements in medication compliance, increased self-management of chronic conditions, and showing up for follow-up primary care appointments. In several cases, there has been a reduction of ED use and inpatient hospitalization. The CHW program at Bronx-Lebanon Hospital Department of Family Medicine has yielded important lessons for other patient-centered medical homes interested in expanding their care teams to enhance patient engagement.

Case Study 2. Integrated Care: Camden Coalition of Healthcare Providers

Founded in 1828, Camden, New Jersey, was once the center of a thriving manufacturing industry. As with many other U.S. cities, deindustrialization led to high poverty rates that, coupled with political corruption and consistently high rates of violent crime, earned the city the dubious title of poorest city in the country. In addition to high unemployment rates, Camden is home to many Medicaid and Medicare beneficiaries and to others who are uninsured.

Dr. Jeffrey Brenner, a family physician operating a solo practice in Camden, recognized patterns of overspending that did not result in better health outcomes for Camden residents. In 2002, he and a small group of other primary care providers began meeting over breakfast once a month to discuss the issues they faced in their practices. It quickly became evident that all of the providers experienced many of the same barriers. In 2003, Dr. Brenner and colleagues founded the Camden Coalition of Healthcare Providers and set out to convince local stakeholders that an integrated health delivery model, in which patient data were shared and care coordinated, would result in better care for Camden residents (Gawande, 2011).

The coalition showed how vulnerable populations, in absence of a well-integrated and supportive health care system, have higher numbers of ED visits, suffer from more chronic disease, have access to fewer preventive services, and seek more reactive care than their peers living less chaotic lives. The analysis looked at 480,000 records for 98,000 patients by pooling data from the major health care institutions serving Camden for the period between 2002 and 2009. They results showed that 50% of Camden residents used the ED or the hospital in 1 year. Those individuals with the highest number of ED visits and hospitalizations citywide ("super utilizers") accounted for 324 visits in 5 years and 113 visits in 1 year. Thirty percent of costs were incurred by 1% of patients, 80% of costs were incurred by 13% of patients, and 90% of costs were incurred by only 20% of patients. The most expensive patient incurred $3.5 million in health care costs.

For vulnerable populations, *crisis* is the baseline. At the heart of crisis is the confluence of economic, social, geographic, and demographic factors that create the conditions for poor health and make management of illness a difficult task. When conducting a spatial analysis of Camden hospital cost data, the coalition found areas of the city with high concentrations of utilizers. In fact, several buildings each year were responsible for between $1 and $3 million in hospital costs. Furthermore, 6% of city blocks accounted for 18% of patients and 37% of billable visits.

The Camden team created an integrated model of care in response to these findings. Members of the care team check in with individual patients to ask about issues including, but not limited to, their unfilled prescriptions, reasons for missing appointments, and any emerging health issues. All patients have access to the coalition's health care crisis hotline, always staffed by a health care provider who can offer advice in an emergency situation.

Since the coalition formed in 2003, analysis of the data from the first 36 super utilizers has shown a 40% reduction in hospital and ED visits per month, and a 56% reduction in their average combined hospital bills (from $1.2 million to $500,000; Gawande, 2011).

OPPORTUNITIES IN THE ACA TO MEET HEALTH CARE NEEDS OF VULNERABLE POPULATIONS

On March 23, 2010, President Obama signed the ACA into law and altered the landscape of U.S. health care policy. Although much of the law's emphasis has been on the historic expansion of insurance coverage to millions of uninsured people, the ACA also provided major investments to expand federally qualified health centers and initiated efforts to change how health care is delivered and paid for in the United States. Many of these changes will have a direct effect on vulnerable populations. The next section briefly describes several key provisions of the ACA that aim to improve access and quality of care for vulnerable populations.

Improving Access to Community Health Centers

Considering the expanded availability of health insurance, particularly Medicaid, to low-income people, the ACA also included large investments in expanding FQHCs to improve care to this population. For instance, the law appropriated $11 billion in mandatory funding increase for Section 330 grants from 2011 to 2015. The law also boosts funding for FQHCs through increased payment rates for primary care physicians serving Medicaid beneficiaries. As of 2014, Medicaid providers will be paid at 100% of the rate paid to Medicare providers. These provisions will lead to increased access to primary care for vulnerable populations, both by increasing the capacity of this safety net and by creating a financial incentive through increased reimbursement for physicians to accept more people covered by Medicaid.

Advancing Payment and Delivery Reform

With the objectives of improving the quality of care and containing the cost of care, the ACA sets in motion myriad efforts to change how health care is paid for and delivered in the United States. Common underlying themes drive the proposed models of care and payment structures: (a) a move toward value-based purchasing of health services; (b) increased coordination of health, social services, and prevention; and (c) better integration of physical and behavioral health services. The proposed models can potentially have a positive effect on the health outcomes of vulnerable populations while reducing the cost of services delivered to this population.

For example, the ACA encourages state Medicaid programs to develop medical homes, known as Health Homes, for Medicaid patients with two or more chronic conditions or patients who have one serious and persistent mental health condition. The CMS issued specific elements that need to be included as part of a Health Home. These elements include comprehensive care management; intensive care transition services for patients moving out of acute care services (such as hospitals, home-based care, outpatient facilities, and so on); care coordination among physical health, behavioral health and social and community services (such as supportive housing); and individual and family support to patients.

Through better coordination of services through primary care, specialty and hospital care, behavioral health, social service support, and stronger patient monitoring, Health Homes could improve health outcomes and reduce unnecessary care. One study estimated that the U.S. health system would save approximately $175 billion over 10 years if primary care providers shifted to this coordinated system of care (The Lewin Group, 2009).

The ACA has also prompted a move away from the traditional FFS model to payment models that would align reimbursement and incentives to the value of care provided and hold providers accountable for health outcomes. This move toward value-based purchasing of services is central to a major Medicare demonstration supported by the ACA: accountable care organizations (ACOs).

ACOs are groups of doctors, hospitals, and other health care providers who come together voluntarily to give coordinated, high-quality care to their Medicare patients (Bachrach, Bernstein, Karl, Manat, & Phelps & Phillips, 2012). As defined by the ACA, ACOs must manage the health care needs of a minimum of 5,000 Medicare beneficiaries for at least 3 years. The goal of an ACO is to ensure that patients, especially the chronically ill, get the right care at the right time, while avoiding unnecessary duplication of services and preventing medical errors. This approach to care should lead to reductions in the total cost of care for the assigned population of patients. Providers participating in an ACO will share accrued savings with Medicare. In the end, providers get paid more for keeping their patients healthy and out of the hospital—as opposed to getting paid more only for providing more services. If an ACO is unable to save money, it can potentially be at risk for losing money associated with the costs of investments made to improve care, or it may have to pay a penalty if it does not meet performance and savings benchmarks.

Additional payment reform efforts enacted by the ACA include bundled payment demonstrations programs and reduced payments for potentially preventable readmissions and complications. The common goal of all of these efforts is to improve the quality of care and rein in cost of health care, with a special focus on vulnerable populations.

Limitations of the ACA

Even taking the ACA into account, approximately half of the nation's 48 million uninsured could potentially remain without health insurance. The law allowed states to expand Medicaid eligibility to adults with incomes up to 138% of the federal poverty level. However, it is up to each individual state to expand eligibility for Medicaid. As of September, 2013, 26 states have rejected the Medicaid expansion. These 26 states are home to about half of the U.S. population, and nearly 68% of the people living in these states are people living in poverty, uninsured Blacks, and/or single mothers. Because of their income status, many of these individuals do not qualify for federal subsidies to help them buy into the health exchanges. It is estimated that 8 million people will remain ineligible for insurance because they are not poor enough to qualify for Medicaid in its existing form—which has income ceilings as low as $11 a day in several states—yet do not meet the income eligibility for federal subsidies.

Then there are the individuals and families who are undocumented immigrants. The ACA specifically excludes this group from its provisions, leaving out the approximately 11 million undocumented immigrants who reside in the United States. These same individuals and families are likely to live in poverty, experience language and cultural barriers to accessing health care services, and have higher risk factors for chronic conditions.

As a result of these ACA limitations, the safety-net hospitals that provide care to vulnerable populations will experience a significant burden. This is especially troubling in the states with high concentrations of undocumented immigrants and a higher proportion of people who remain ineligible for insurance. Under the ACA, a reduction is scheduled in payments to disproportionate share hospitals, which have helped to absorb the effects of providing uncompensated care. This reduction will add to the strain on the resources of these institutions.

Another important limitation of the ACA that will affect the health and wellbeing of vulnerable populations is its narrow focus on the traditional health care system. Although the law sets in motion delivery system and payment transformations that will help to bridge traditional health care institutions with agencies, programs, and services that address some of the key drivers of poor health (such as housing, behavioral health services, and so on), it falls short of making the necessary investments in the social service sector that will help vulnerable populations get on—and stay on—the path to a healthy life. The United States is one of only three industrialized countries to spend most of its health and social services budget on health care itself (Bradley & Taylor, 2013). For every dollar the United States spends on health care, an additional 90 cents is spent on social services. In peer countries, for every dollar spent on health care, an additional $2 is spent on social services. Researchers who looked at spending across health care relative to social services found that countries with high health care spending compared with social spending had lower life expectancy and higher infant mortality than countries that favored social spending. European countries that have made greater investments in social services relative to health have experienced leaps in life expectancy (well over 80 years) and infant mortality rates that are half those in the United States. Most medical providers concur with this logic. In a Robert Wood Johnson Foundation–funded national survey, four out of five physicians agreed that unmet social needs lead directly to worse health.

If the United States is to make a dent in improving the health outcomes of vulnerable populations, we must go beyond shifting dollars from one part of the health care system to another. Rather, we must make a transformative shift in where the investments are made—and accept that subpar social conditions have a direct consequence on health. As Bradley and Taylor state:

> Homelessness isn't typically thought of as a medical problem, but it often precludes good nutrition, personal hygiene, and basic first aid, and it increases the risks of frostbite, leg ulcers, upper respiratory infections, and trauma from muggings, beatings, and rape. (Bradley & Taylor, 2013)

A program in Boston that tracked the medical expenses of 119 chronically homeless people found that, in a 5-year period, these individuals accounted for 18,834 emergency department visits estimated to cost over $12 million.

■ Conclusion

Vulnerable populations are at greatest risk of poor physical, behavioral, and social health. They have the highest rates of disease burden and mortality. Vulnerable groups have the hardest time accessing timely, high-quality health care and, when receiving care, are more likely to have worse health outcomes than the general population. Despite an extensive body of literature and myriad federal efforts to eliminate these inequities in health and health care between vulnerable groups and the general population, the United States has barely made progress.

> *The prevalence of vulnerable populations is increasing; if we fail to institute policies and programs to improve the health of vulnerable populations, little will be done to contain the cost of care in the United States.*

To some extent, the topic of eliminating disparities has been diluted and overused. It is almost as though the topic of health disparities has become an accepted part of our health literary repertoire. But this issue contains an underlying, explosive problem: The prevalence of vulnerable populations is increasing; if we fail to institute policies and programs to improve the health of vulnerable populations, little will be done to contain the cost of care in the United States. We will continue to spend more on health but have significantly poorer health status compared with other industrialized countries.

In this chapter, we have offered an integrated framework that sets vulnerable groups in the social context of their existence. As opposed to examining the health of discrete vulnerable subgroups, which are not mutually exclusive, the chapter provided a general overview of the predisposing and enabling factors that lead to vulnerability. The approach reflects the co-occurrence of risk factors *and* helps to explain why existing approaches to meet the health needs of this population will continue to fall short. Though well intended, current policies and programs are a patchwork of categorical, fragmented, and uncoordinated attempts that cost a lot of money.

Vulnerability is primarily a social issue created through social forces. It will be addressed adequately only through broader social, communitywide investments. A shift to community-oriented policies and programs that address the social origins of vulnerability can lead to greater improvements in health outcomes. These programs and policies should aim to produce networks of collaboration and integration—rather than wedges of bureaucratic division—across medical care, public health, social and economic solutions, and policies that permanently fix the risks and consequences of vulnerability. Investing time, energy, and resources in improving the health of vulnerable populations as a national priority is more than a social and moral imperative—it is an economic one. The human and financial costs of this problem weigh heavily on the future of the United States to continue as a beacon of justice and equality and a global financial leader. Who are considered vulnerable populations, and what does this tell us about the nature of the problems that predispose and enable vulnerability in the United States?

■ Discussion Questions

1. How have shifting demographics, the rise in prevalence of chronic conditions, and the strained social service sector contributed to the growing number of vulnerable populations?
2. A wide array of medical and social services exists to help meet the complex needs of vulnerable populations; however, the United States has been unable to curb health care costs or improve health outcomes for this segment of the population. What are some of the underlying problems with the current approach to services for vulnerable populations?
3. How does the current payment system fall short in meeting the needs of vulnerable populations?
4. Review the limitations for meeting the needs of vulnerable populations in the ACA provisions. Propose ways in which you would address these limitations using (a) new policies, (b) existing policies and structures, (c) innovative ideas (such as public/private partnerships).

CASE STUDY

The commissioner of health in a large, mostly urban county has secured your services as a consultant to identify strategies to meet the needs of the growing refugee population legally settling in her region. A refugee is a person who has fled from his or her home country and cannot return because of a well-founded fear of persecution based on religion, race, nationality, political opinion, or membership in a particular social group. The commissioner of health has at her disposal both federal and state resources and good relationships with colleagues from other county agencies, such as planning, transportation, education, aging, and so on.

As a consultant, you have been asked to propose a coordinated plan to use existing resources and relationships to better serve the needs of the growing refugee population. When considering your plan, be sure to address the following questions:

1. What type of information would you collect, and how would you use it?
2. Whom else would you engage in developing a plan?
3. How will you ensure that the refugee population has access to existing and new services?
4. Explain how your plan will meet the immediate and long-term needs of this group as part of an improved system of health care and social services.

■ References

Adashi, E. Y., Geiger, J. H., & Fine, M. D. (2010). Health care reform and primary care—The growing importance of the Community Health Center. *New England Journal of Medicine, 362*, 2047–2050. doi:10.1056/NEJMp1003729

Aday, L. (2001). *At risk in America: The health and health care needs of vulnerable populations in the United States* (2nd ed.). San Francisco, CA: Jossey-Bass Publishers.

Agency for Healthcare Research and Quality. (2014). *Care coordination, quality improvement* (Structured abstract). Rockville, MD: Author.

Allard, S. W., & Roth, B. (2010). *Strained suburbs: The social service challenges of rising suburban poverty. Metropolitan opportunity series (Vol. 7)*. Washington, DC: The Brookings Institution Metropolitan Policy Program. Retrieved from http://www.brookings.edu/research/reports/2010/10/07-suburban-poverty-allard-roth

Association of State and Territorial Health Officials. (2010). *MCH technical assistance SNAP & WIC side-by-side comparison*. Retrieved from http://www.astho.org/Programs/Access/Maternal-and-Child-Health/Technical-Assistance/Materials/SNAP-and-WIC-Side-by-Side-Comparison/

Bachrach, D., Bernstein, W., Karl, A., & Manatt, Phelps & Phillips, LLP. (2012). *High-performance health care for vulnerable populations: A policy framework for promoting accountable care in Medicaid* (M. Hostetter, Ed.). New York, NY: The Commonwealth Fund. Retrieved from http://www.commonwealthfund.org/~/media/Files/Publications/Fund%20Report/2012/Nov/1646_Bachrach_high_performance_hlt_care_vulnerable_populations_Medicaid_ACO_v2.pdf

Bradley, E. H., & Taylor, L. (2013). *The American health care paradox: Why spending more is getting us less*. New York, NY: PublicAffairs Books.

Center for Advancing Health. (2010). *A new definition of patient engagement: What is it, and why is it important?* Washington, DC: Author. Retrieved from http://www.cfah .org/file/CFAH_Engagement_Behavior_Framework_current.pdf

Center on Budget and Policy Priorities. (2013). *Policy basics: Introduction to Medicaid.* Retrieved from http://www.cbpp.org/cms/index.cfm?fa=view&id=2223

Center on Budget and Policy Priorities. (2014). *Policy basics: Introduction to the Supplemental Nutrition Assistance Program (SNAP).* Retrieved from http://www.cbpp.org /cms/index.cfm?fa=view&id=2226

Creswell, J. (2013, December 25). E.R. costs for mentally ill soar, and hospitals seek better way. *The New York Times.* Retrieved from http://www.nytimes.com/2013/12/26/ health/er-costs-for-mentally-ill-soar-and-hospitals-seek-better-way.html?_r = 0

Daponte, B. O., & Bade, S. (2006). How the private food assistance network evolved: Interactions between public and private responses to hunger. *Nonprofit and Voluntary Sector Quarterly, 35*(4), 668–690.

Davis, C. (2012). *Q & A: Disproportionate share hospital payments and the Medicaid expansion.* Washington, DC: National Health Law Program. Retrieved from http:// www.healthlaw.org/publications/qa-disproportionate-share-hospital-payments-and-the-medicaid expansion#.VMEVw_nF8yQ

Dean, S., Rosenbaum, D., & Foley, A. (2013). *SNAP benefits will be cut for nearly all participants in November 2013. Center on budget and policy priorities.* Retrieved from http://www.cbpp.org/cms/?fa=view&id=3899

Devi, S. (2011). Native American health left out in the cold. *The Lancet, 377*(9776), 1481–1482. doi:10.1016/S0140-6736(11)60586-2

DeVol, R., Bedroussian, A., Charuworn, A., Chatterjee, A., Kim, I. K., Kim, S., & Klowden, K. (2007). *An unhealthy America: The economic burden of chronic disease.* Santa Monica, CA: Milken Institute. Retrieved from http://assets1b.milkeninstitute.org/ assets/Publication/ResearchReport/PDF/chronic_disease_report.pdf

Diez-Rouz, A. V. (2003). Residential environments and cardiovascular risk. *Journal of Urban Health, 80*(4), 569–589.

Do, D. P. (2009). The dynamics of income and neighborhood context for population health: Do long-term measures of socioeconomic status explain more of the Black/ White health disparity than single-point-in-time measures? *Social Science and Medicine, 68*(8), 1368–1375.

Findley, S., Matos, S., Hicks, A., Chang, J., & Reich, D. (2014). Community health worker integration into the healthcare team accomplishes the Triple Aim in a patient-centered medical home: A Bronx tale. *Journal of Ambulatory Care, 37*(1), 82–91. Retrieved from http://chwcentral.org/sites/default/files/Community_Health_ Worker_Integration_Into_the.10.pdf

Fontenot, T., & Stubblefield, A. G. (2011). *Caring for vulnerable populations. American hospital association 2011 committee on research.* Retrieved from http://www.aha.org/ research/cor/caring/index.shtml

Galewitz, P. (2012, June 6). Migrant health clinics caught in crossfire of immigration debate. *Kaiser Health News.* Retrieved from http://www.kaiserhealthnews.org/stories/2012/june/07/migrant-health-clinics-immigration-debate.aspx

Garr, E. (2011). *The landscape of repression: Unemployment and safety net services across urban and suburban America. Metropolitan opportunity series: Vol. 12.* Retrieved from http://www.brookings.edu/research/papers/2011/03/31-recession-garr

Gawande, A. (2011, January 24). The hot spotters: Can we lower medical costs by giving the neediest patients better care? *The New Yorker.* Retrieved from http://www.newyorker.com/reporting/2011/01/24/110124fa_fact_gawande?currentPage = 3

Gourevitch, M. N., Malaspina, D., Weitzman, M., & Goldfrank, L. (2008). The public hospital in American medical education. *Journal of Urban Health, 85*(5), 779–786. doi:10.1007/s11524-008-9297-4

Grusky, D. B., Western, B., & Wimer, C. (Eds.). (2011). *The great recession*. New York, NY: Russell Sage Foundation.

Hawkins, D., & Groves, D. (2011). The future role of community health centers in a changing health care landscape. *Journal of Ambulatory Care Management, 34*(1), 90–99. Retrieved from http://www.nachc.org/client/documents/The_Future_Role_of_Community_Health_Centers_in_a.11.pdf

Henry J. Kaiser Family Foundation. (2013a). *The Ryan White AIDS program*. Retrieved from http://kff.org/hivaids/fact-sheet/the-ryan-white-program/

Henry J. Kaiser Family Foundation. (2013b). *Total Medicaid spending*. Washington, DC: Urban Institute. Retrieved from http://kff.org/medicaid/state-indicator/total-medicaid-spending/

Hobfoll, S. E. (2001). The influence of culture, community, and the nested-self in the stress process: Advancing conservation of resources theory. *Applied Psychology: An International Review, 50*(3), 337–421.

Kent, G. (2006). WIC's promotion of infant formula in the United States. *International Breastfeeding Journal, 1*(8). doi:10.1186/1746-4358-1-8

Knickman, J. K., & Snell, E. K. (2002). The 2030 problem: Caring for aging baby boomers. *Health Services Research, 37*(4), 849–884. doi:10.1034/j.1600-0560.2002.56.x

Lang, I. A., Hubbard, R., Andrew, M. K., Llewellyn, D. J., Melzer, D., & Rockwood, K. (2009). Neighborhood deprivation, individual socioeconomic status, and frailty in older adults. *Journal of the American Geriatrics Society, 57*(10), 1776–1780. doi:10.1111/j.1532-5415.2009.02480.x

The Lewin Group. (2009). *The Path to a High Performance U.S. Health System: Technical Documentation*. Washington, DC: The Lewin Group.

Manahan, B. (2011). The whole systems medicine of tomorrow: A half-century perspective. *Explore: The Journal of Science and Healing, 7*(4), 212–214.

Martinez Garcel, J. (2012). Casting an A-team to deliver results: Embedding and sustaining the role of community health workers in medical homes. *Medical Home News, 4*(2), 6–7.

McGinnis, J., Russo, P. W., & Knickman, J. K. (2002). The case for more active policy attention to health promotion. *Health Affairs, 21*(2), 78–93. doi:10.1377/hlthaff.21.2.78

McLeod, J. D., & Kessler, R. C. (1990). Socioeconomic status and differences in vulnerability to undesirable life events. *Journal of Health and Social Behavior, 31*, 162–172. Retrieved from http://www.ncbi.nlm.nih.gov/pubmed/2102495

Mitchell, A. (2013). *Medicaid disproportionate hospital share payments*. Congressional research service report. Washington, DC: Government Printing Office. Retrieved from https://www.fas.org/sgp/crs/misc/R42865.pdf

Moscovice, I., Gregg, W., & Lewerenz, E. (2003). *Rural health networks: Evolving organizational forms and functions*. Minneapolis, MN: University of Minnesota School of Public Health Rural Health Research Center. Retrieved from http://rhrc.umn.edu/wp-content/files_mf/formsandfunctions2.pdf

National Center for Farmworker Health (NCFH). (n.d.). *Migrant health center legislation*. Retrieved from http://www.ncfh.org/?pid = 186

National Center for Health in Public Housing (NCHPH). (2012). *Public housing primary care program*. Retrieved from http://www.nchph.org/wp-content/uploads/2013/11/NCHPH-PHPC1.pdf

National Health Care for the Homeless Council (NHCHC). (2008). *The basics of homelessness*. Retrieved from http://www.nhchc.org/resources/general-information/fact-sheets/

Partnership for Solutions. (2004). *Chronic conditions: Making the case for ongoing care, September 2004 update*. Baltimore, MD: Johns Hopkins University. Retrieved from http://www.partnershipforsolutions.org/DMS/files/chronicbook2004.pdf

Prins, S. J. (2011). Does transinstitutionalization explain the overrepresentation of people with serious mental illnesses in the criminal justice system? *Community Mental Health Journal, 47*(6), 716–722. Retrieved from http://link.springer.com/article/10.1007%2Fs10597-011-9420-y

Purtell, K. M., Gershoff, E. T., & Aber, J. L. (2012). Low income families' utilization of the federal "safety net": Individual and state-level predictors of TANF and food stamp receipt. *Children in Youth Services Review, 34*(4), 713–724. doi:10.1016/j.childyouth.2011.12.016

Shi, L., & Stevens, G. (2010). *Vulnerable populations in the United States* (2nd ed.). San Francisco, CA: Jossey-Bass Publishers.

Shi, L., & Stevens, G. D. (2005). Vulnerability and unmet health needs: The influence of multiple risk factors. *Journal of General Internal Medicine, 20*(2), 148–154. doi:10.1111/j.1525-1497.2005.40136.x

Unite for Sight. (n.d.). *Module 2: A brief history of mental illness and the U.S. mental health care system.* Retrieved from http://www.uniteforsight.org/mental-health/module2

U.S. Bureau of Labor Statistics. (2012). *The recession of 2007–2009.* Washington, DC: U.S. Government Printing Office.

U.S. Department of Agriculture, Food and Nutrition Service. (n.d.). *Food and Nutrition Service (FNS) programs and services.* Retrieved from http://www.fns.usda.gov/programs-and-services

U.S. Department of Health and Human Services, Health Resources and Services Administration. (n.d.). *HIV/AIDS programs: Legislation.* Retrieved from http://hab.hrsa.gov/abouthab/legislation.html

U.S. Department of Health and Human Services, Indian Health Services. (2014). *Agency overview.* Retrieved from http://www.ihs.gov/aboutihs/overview/

U.S. Department of Health and Human Services, Office of Rural Health Policy. (2006). *Comparison of the rural health clinic and federally qualified health center programs.* Washington, DC: U.S. Government Printing Office. Retrieved from http://www.hrsa.gov/ruralhealth/policy/confcall/comparisonguide.pdf

U.S. Department of Housing and Urban Development. (n.d.). *HUD historical background.* Retrieved from http://www.hud.gov/offices/adm/about/admguide/history.cfm

U.S. Social Security Administration. (n.d.). *SSI federal payment amounts for 2014.* Retrieved from http://www.ssa.gov/OACT/cola/SSI.html

Volkmann, K., & Castanares, T. (2011). Clinical community health workers: Linchpin of the medical home. *Journal of Ambulatory Care Management, 34*(3), 221–233.

Vulnerable. (n.d.). *Merriam-Webster online.* Retrieved from http://www.merriam-webster.com/dictionary/vulnerable

Ward, B. W., & Schiller, J. S. (2010). Prevalence of multiple chronic conditions among U.S. adults: Estimates from the national health interview survey, 2010. *Preventing Chronic Disease, 2013*(10), 120203. doi:10.5888/pcd10.120203

Willms, D. (1999). *Inequalities in literacy skills among youth in Canada and the United States.* Canada: National Literacy Secretariat.

Witgert, K., & Hess, C. (2012). *Including safety-net providers in integrated delivery systems: Issues and options for policymakers. National academy of health policy.* New York, NY: The Commonwealth Fund. Retrieved from http://www.nashp.org/sites/default/files/Including.SN_.Providers.in_.IDS_.pdf

World Health Organization (WHO). (1948). *Constitution of the World Health Organization.* Geneva, Switzerland: World Health Organization.

Wu, S-Y., & Green, A. (2000). *Projection of chronic illness prevalence and cost inflation.* Santa Monica, CA: RAND corporation. Retrieved from http://www.fightchronicdisease.org/sites/fightchronicdisease.org/files/docs/GrowingCrisisofChronicDiseaseintheUSfactsheet_81009.pdf

Medical Care: Treating Americans' Medical Problems

The subject matter now shifts to introducing readers to how the medical care system works to make people get back to a healthy state or to manage a health problem when they have an illness, a chronic disease, or an injury. Chapter 9, by Amy Yarbrough Landry and Cathleen Erwin, addresses the organization of our large and complex medical care system. The chapter describes the organization of care, examining types of care and types of organizations. The current period is one of substantial change in the way care is being organized. The chapter explains key organizational forms that likely will emerge over the next 5 to 10 years.

In Chapter 10, Joanne Spetz and Susan Chapman focus on the challenges associated with making sure we have the right type of workforce to play the many roles required to deliver services and manage the delivery of services. It is a challenge to make sure we have adequate supplies of service providers and that we support this workforce in its effort to deliver high-quality care. The chapter explains how the composition of the workforce is changing and what the future challenges are in developing a smoothly functioning labor market for health jobs.

The next two chapters turn to the issue of how we pay for medical care in the United States and how we ensure that our resources are being used wisely. In Chapter 11, James Knickman explains the sources of money that pay providers and the methods we use to make the financial transactions that link purchasers and providers. The health care financing system is complicated because most people pay for a good share of their care by purchasing health insurance policies or by relying on insurance policies provided by federal and state governments. Chapter 11 explains why there is dissatisfaction with the current payment system, which relies on fee-for-service payments, and presents the main ideas for reforming how we pay for care.

Thad Calabrese and Keith Safian, in Chapter 12, turn to the question of whether or not the financing system encourages efficiency and high quality among providers. It is a challenge to make sure providers don't have incentives to produce too much care, too little care, or the wrong types of care. The chapter lays out some ideas for how to get providers focused on what is called high-value care: affordable but effective and addressing important health concerns.

Chapter 13, authored by Carolyn Clancy and Irene Fraser, looks at the more technical side of quality improvement and assurance and describes how providers actually go about preventing and responding to mistakes in care and making sure that care leads to the outcomes patients are promised. In Chapter 14, Anthony Kovner and Christy Harris Lemak shift the discussion from managing quality to managing the organization and delivery of care in general. This chapter focuses on how medical care delivery organizations are governed and managed. The chapter makes the case that managers must be sophisticated leaders and should strive to develop evidence about what management practices lead to the most effective organizations and good outcomes.

Chapter 15, by Nirav Shah, turns to the new challenge of making the world of information technology work better in the health system. Medical care organizations have been slow adopters of information technology, but the pace of adoptions has picked up in recent years. The chapter explains how information technology can be used to better manage medical care provision and to improve both the cost and the quality of care.

9 Organization of Care

Amy Yarbrough Landry and Cathleen O. Erwin

KEYWORDS

accreditation

ambulatory care

average length of stay (ALOS)

certification

continuing care retirement community

continuity of care

continuum of care

corporate medical practice

horizontal integration

instrumental activity of daily living (IADL)

long-term care

network

palliative care

patient-centered medical home (PCMH)

primary care

privileges

quaternary care

rehabilitative hospital

same-day surgery

specialty hospital

subacute care

tertiary care

transitional care

urgent care center

LEARNING OBJECTIVES

- Define and distinguish between types of health care services along the continuum of care
- Identify and discuss types of organizations in the U.S. health care delivery system
- Increase awareness of new mechanisms for health system performance improvements
- Understand and discuss future trends in the health delivery system

TOPICAL OUTLINE

- The current organization of the health care delivery system
- Types of health care delivery organizations
- The future of the health care delivery system
- Examples of best practices in the organization of medical care

In the United States, health care is delivered through a complex and multifaceted system of private and public institutions that operate in cooperation with, but largely independent of each other. Unlike many other countries, the United States has no central governmental agency to control the delivery of health care, although delivery is heavily influenced through health care legislation and the government's role as a major purchaser of health care services through Medicare, Medicaid, and other public programs. The continuum of care in the United States encompasses care from the cradle to the grave and includes services focused on both the prevention and the treatment of medical conditions and diseases as well as end-of-life care.

The individuals and organizations that provide care in the United States are faced with increasing pressure and scrutiny from the government, private insurance organizations, and the public to provide the highest quality of care while controlling costs and increasing access to underserved populations. Consequently, health care services and organizational structures are continuously being adapted to meet the demands and mandates of health care policy and to survive and thrive in this dynamic health care environment.

This chapter describes the current health care delivery system in the United States, including services, organizations, health system performance, and new innovations in care delivery.

■ Description of the Current Care Delivery System

By definition, the health system includes all organizations, institutions, and resources that have a primary purpose of promoting, restoring, and/or maintaining health (World Health Organization [WHO], 2015). From a broad, comprehensive perspective it includes clinical care as well as public health. The following sections provide a general discussion of the types of clinical health care services that are available in the United States and the types of organizations through which these services are delivered.

HEALTH CARE SERVICES

> *Health care services are provided for the purpose of contributing to improved health or to the diagnosis, treatment, or rehabilitation of sick people.*

Health care services are provided for the purpose of contributing to improved health or to the diagnosis, treatment, or rehabilitation of sick people (WHO, 2013). Health care services include prevention, cure, rehabilitation, and palliation efforts that are oriented to either individuals or populations.

Prevention
Prevention of disease and maintenance of general good health are the focus of health promotion and preventive services. Health status is affected by a number of factors, including health policy, individual behavior, social determinants, physical determinants, biology and genetics, and availability of health services. Services associated with prevention may be focused on the health of an individual or the health of a population. Although prevention services have always been available in the United States, an even greater emphasis is placed on prevention because of its prominence in the Patient Protection and Affordable Care Act of 2010 (ACA) as an essential component

of health insurance benefits. Most health plans must cover a set of preventive services at no cost to the beneficiary.

The prevention field often distinguishes interventions that are delivered by a health care provider (clinical prevention services) from those delivered by non–health care providers (community-based prevention initiatives). According to the Institute of Medicine (IOM, 2012), a holistic view of community-based prevention incorporates cultural, social, and environmental changes; also, community-based prevention is often more difficult to fund and staff than clinical interventions. Certain preventive services may be offered through a clinical–community relationship that might entail a primary care provider making a connection with a community-based organization to provide specific services (such as a community-based weight-loss program) or collaboration between clinical and community-based organizations to network, coordinate, or cooperate on preventive services delivery. Additionally, the field sometimes distinguishes between prevention initiatives that focus on individuals one at a time and initiatives that are more population-based, working with larger groups of people (e.g., efforts to increase the availability of healthy food in low-income neighborhoods).

Clinical prevention services are often categorized as primary, secondary, or tertiary, based on the stages of the disease they target.

Primary Prevention Services. Primary prevention services are focused on preventing or reducing the probability of the occurrence of a disease in the future. Services are provided through public and private institutions and are often focused on educating the public about the risks associated with individual behaviors that can negatively affect their short- and long-term health.

Examples of primary prevention include immunizations for prevention of childhood diseases, smoking cessation programs to reduce the risk of lung cancer and heart disease, weight loss programs, prenatal and well-baby care, programs to increase workplace safety, and the promotion of hand washing to reduce the spread of influenza or other diseases. The services are provided through a wide variety of institutions, such as public health departments, physician offices, hospitals, places of employment, houses of worship, and broadcast media.

Secondary Prevention Services. These services are focused on the early detection and treatment of disease in order to cure or control its effects. The goal is to minimize the effects of the disease on the individual. Secondary services are largely focused on routine examinations and tests such as blood pressure screenings, pap smears, routine colonoscopies, examination of suspicious moles, and mammograms. Early detection and treatment often increases the probability of a successful outcome.

Tertiary Prevention Services. These services are targeted at individuals who already have symptoms of a disease in order to prevent damage from the disease, to slow down its progression, to prevent complications from occurring as a result of the disease, and ultimately to restore good health to the person with the disease.

Tertiary prevention includes services such as providing diabetic patients with education and counseling on wound care. It also includes institutional practices such as infection control in a hospital facility to prevent illness or injury caused in the process of providing health care.

Acute Care

Acute care is short-term, intense medical care providing diagnosis and treatment of communicable or noncommunicable diseases, illness, or injury. The definition of acute care varies across the scholarly literature and textbooks. Acute care is sometimes defined as being *primary, specialty, tertiary,* or *quaternary* in nature, centered around the care delivered by physicians and other providers in clinical settings (such as physician offices and hospitals). Acute care services may be provided on an *outpatient* basis (i.e., not requiring an overnight hospital or health care facility stay), or on an *inpatient* basis (i.e., requiring an overnight stay).

A more comprehensive definition of acute care includes not only these services but also the emergency services provided in the community given the time-sensitive nature of the need for diagnosis and treatment. One proposed definition of acute care includes the components of the health system where acute care is delivered to treat unexpected, urgent, and emergent episodes of illness and injury that could lead to disability or death without rapid intervention (Hirshon et al., 2013). Based on this definition, acute care encompasses a range of functions including emergency care, trauma care, prehospital emergency care, acute care surgery, critical care, urgent care, and short-term inpatient stabilization (Figure 9.1). The following sections outline the types of acute care based on the framework illustrated in Figure 9.1, although not all of the domains are discussed because of obvious overlaps. The primary, specialty, tertiary, and quaternary care definitions are incorporated into the framework to show where these levels of care best fit within the acute care model and to note relationships to other forms of care.

Emergency and Urgent Care. *Emergency care* is designed to provide immediate care for sudden, serious illness or injury, although it is sometimes utilized for nonemergent care by individuals who are uninsured or underinsured. A medical emergency is defined by what is known as the *prudent layperson standard*:

> [A] condition with acute symptoms of sufficient severity (including severe pain) such that a prudent layperson, who possesses average knowledge of health and medicine, could reasonably expect the absence of immediate medical attention to result in–(i) placing the health of the individual (or unborn child) in serious jeopardy, (ii) serious impairment of bodily functions, or (iii) serious dysfunction of any bodily organ or part. (Social Security Act § 1867)

Emergent types of care (such as trauma) can be classified by the triage level, that is, by the emergency severity index (ESI). The ESI is a five-level triage algorithm that clinically stratifies patients into groups based on immediacy of the need to be seen, which includes the following levels:

1. Immediate (less than 1 minute)
2. Emergent (1–14 minutes)
3. Urgent (15–60 minutes)
4. Semiurgent (61–120 minutes)
5. Nonurgent (121 minutes–24 hours)

In 2010, 1.1% of emergency department (ED) visits were classified as immediate, 10.2% as emergent, and 43.4% as urgent; the remaining 45.3% were either semiurgent

FIGURE 9.1

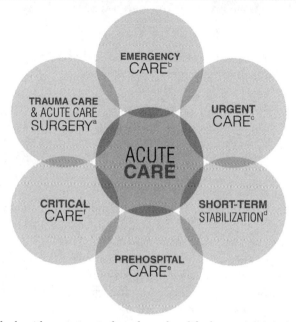

DOMAINS IN ACUTE CARE

[a]Treatment of individuals with acute surgical needs, such as life-threatening injuries, acute appendicitis. or strangulated hernias.

[b]Treatment of individuals with acute life- or limb-threatening medical and potentially surgical needs, such as acute myocardial infarctions or acute cerebrovascular accidents, or evaluation of patients with abdominal pain.

[c]Ambulatory care in a facility delivering medical care outside a hospital emergency department, usually on an unscheduled, walk-in basis. Examples include evaluation of an injured ankle or fever in a child.

[d]Treatment of individuals with acute needs before delivery of definitive treatment. Examples include administering intravenous fluids to a critically injured patient before transfer to an operating room.

[e]Care provided in the community until the patient arrives at a formal health care facility capable of giving definitive care. Examples include delivery of care by ambulance personnel or evaluation of acute health problems by local health care providers.

[f]The specialized care of patients whose conditions are life-threatening and who require comprehensive care and constant monitoring, usually in intensive care units. Examples are patients with severe respiratory problems requiring endotracheal intubation and patients with seizures caused by cerebral malaria.
Source: Hirshon et al., 2013. Used with permission.

or nonurgent or were not triaged (Centers for Disease Control and Prevention [CDC], 2010).

The Emergency Medical Treatment & Labor Act of 1986 (EMTALA) requires that all patients who present themselves for treatment at an ED must be screened and evaluated, provided the necessary stabilizing treatment, and admitted to the hospital when necessary, regardless of ability to pay.

Urgent care is used for an illness, injury, or condition that is serious enough for a reasonable person to seek care right away but not so severe as to require ED care. It is considered *ambulatory* care, which means that the person in need of care can walk (or ambulate) into the facility. However, a patient in need of "ambulatory" care may need some assistance entering the facility depending on the nature of the illness or injury (e.g., severe ankle sprain). Services are provided by physicians and physician extenders (such as nurse practitioners or physician assistants) typically on a walk-in basis without a previously scheduled appointment because of the immediacy of the need. Urgent care services may be provided through a traditional physician practice or an urgent care center.

Prehospital Care. Prehospital care includes medical services provided in the community, such as stabilization by emergency services before or during transportation to a health care facility. It also includes evaluation and treatment provided through local, community-based providers, as in a private physician practice setting.

Primary care. Primary care is the first and most general source for routine treatment of illness and disease. Primary care providers may be physicians, physician assistants, or nurse practitioners who have trained in family medicine, internal medicine, pediatric medicine, gerontology, or other primary care "specialties," such as obstetrics and gynecology. In the managed care environment, primary care delivery plays an important role in the coordination of care to help control costs and ensure that the appropriate level of care is sought for the health concern. Primary care providers are involved in delivering both acute care and preventive care.

Specialty care. Specialty care refers to care delivered through providers who are trained as specialists or subspecialists in the field of medicine. This type of care sometimes requires a referral from a primary care physician. Specialists focus on a particular body system or on a specific disease or condition; they have the knowledge and expertise to handle medical conditions that are beyond the realm of primary care. For example, cardiologists diagnose and treat conditions involving the heart, endocrinologists focus on hormone systems and may specialize in a disease such as diabetes, and neurologists are trained to diagnose and treat disorders associated with the nervous system—brain, spinal cord, and so on. Similarly to primary care, specialty care may be utilized to address both acute and preventive care needs.

Chronic care. Chronic care is the continual treatment and monitoring of conditions that can be controlled but not cured; it includes both physical and behavioral conditions. Examples of chronic conditions include diabetes, hypertension, and depression. As the life expectancy of the population has increased, so have the incidence and prevalence of chronic conditions. It is estimated that more than one fourth of all Americans and two out of three older Americans have at least two chronic conditions, and approximately 66% of the nation's health costs are attributable to the treatment of people living with multiple chronic conditions (Agency for Healthcare Research and Quality, 2013).

The management and treatment of chronic conditions may be delivered by primary and/or specialty care providers. By definition, chronic care is not considered acute care; however, chronic conditions can cause or exacerbate acute episodes of illness. Chronic care also fits within the category of preventive services, which include services that focus on the early detection and management of chronic conditions.

Tertiary Care. Tertiary care typically involves hospitalization for specialty care that requires highly specialized equipment and expertise and involves more complex therapeutic interventions, such as coronary bypass surgery, neurosurgery, advanced neonatal intensive care, or treatments for severe burns or injuries. Some tertiary care services may be provided on an outpatient basis, such as same-day surgeries. Patients are admitted to a tertiary facility through a *practitioner order* from a qualified provider who has been granted admitting privileges by the facility.

Quaternary Care. Quaternary care, an extension of tertiary care, entails providing the most complex medical and surgical care for highly specialized and unusual cases. It may involve experimental procedures, experimental medications, or very uncommon surgeries or procedures. Examples of quaternary care are advanced trauma care and organ transplantation. Quaternary care is not offered by every hospital or medical center; it is more likely to be found in academic medical centers.

Subacute Inpatient Care. Subacute care is a level of inpatient care needed by a patient immediately after or instead of hospitalization for an acute illness, injury, or exacerbation of a disease process. This level of care centers on providing one or more active medical conditions or administering one or more technically complex treatments. It requires more intensive skilled nursing care than is provided to the majority of patients in a skilled nursing facility (i.e., nursing home).

The term "subacute care" has been applied to a broad range of medical and rehabilitative services and settings that provide care to patients after an acute care episode. It combines rehabilitation and convalescent services for patients who typically need 10 to 100 days of treatment, and is provided in settings other than in acute care hospital beds. Subacute care is delivered in facilities licensed to provide the appropriate level of care, which includes special units established by acute care hospitals and skilled nursing facilities.

Rehabilitative Care

Rehabilitative health care services are aimed at restoring a person to his or her original state of health (or as close as possible). Rehabilitation services help a person keep, regain, or improve skills and functioning for daily living that have been lost or impaired because of illness or injury. Services include physical therapy, occupational therapy, speech–language pathology, and psychiatric rehabilitation. Rehabilitative services are offered in a variety of inpatient and outpatient settings.

Long-Term Care

Long-term care encompasses a range of services and support provided to meet personal care needs on a long-term basis, most of which is not medical care. It encompasses an array of services provided in a variety of settings for people who have lost some independence because of a medical condition, injury, or chronic illness. Long-term care is often used to provide assistance with *activities of daily living (ADLs)*, such as bathing, dressing, using the toilet, transferring to or from a bed or chair, and eating, among others. Other common services and support assist with *instrumental activities of daily living (IADLs)*, which are everyday tasks, such as housework, taking medication, preparing meals, shopping, and responding to emergency alerts, among others.

The duration and level of long-term care needed by individuals varies and often changes over time. Long-term care services may be provided in an individual's home or in a community setting or institution.

End-of-Life Care

End-of-life care is provided in the final hours or days of an individual's life. This type of care includes physical, mental, and emotional comfort, as well as social support, for people who are living with and dying of terminal illness or a condition that is advanced, progressive, and incurable. End-of-life care requires a range of decisions. These decisions may include preparing advanced directives to make end-of-life wishes clear to family and providers, as well as determining the types of treatment and care that will be utilized.

Palliative care is the treatment for discomfort, symptoms, and stress of serious illness, providing relief from pain, fatigue, nausea, shortness of breath, loss of appetite, or problems with sleep. Palliative care can be received at any stage of an illness but is always included in hospice care.

When the focus shifts from cure to care, a patient moves to hospice care. *Hospice care* is end-of-life care utilized when a patient is expected to live 6 months or less. It is provided by a team of health care professionals and volunteers in the home, a hospice center, a hospital, or a skilled nursing facility. Hospice programs also provide services to support a patient's family. The interdisciplinary hospice team usually consists of the patient's personal physician; hospice physician or medical director; nurses; hospice aides; social workers; bereavement counselors; clergy or other spiritual counselors; trained volunteers; and speech, physical, and occupational therapists, if needed.

HEALTH CARE DELIVERY ORGANIZATIONS

This section discusses the wide range of organizations that exist to deliver health care services, including hospitals, health systems, physician offices, specialty hospitals, long-term care facilities, rehabilitation hospitals, home health agencies, and other health-related organizations.

Hospitals

By definition, a hospital (other than psychiatric) is an institution that is primarily engaged in providing, by or under the supervision of physicians, to *inpatients*, diagnostic and therapeutic services for medical diagnosis, treatment, and care of injured, disabled, or sick persons; or rehabilitation services for injured, disabled, or sick persons. *Outpatient* services are optional but have been growing in importance over time as more and more medical interventions can be done in an outpatient setting and as the field sees growing importance to integrating primary care, specialty care, and inpatient care for reasons of both quality and efficiency.

According to the American Hospital Association (AHA, 2013), the United States has approximately 5,724 registered hospitals, which include all community, federal, psychiatric, long-term care, hospitals and hospital units located in institutions (such as prison hospitals, college infirmaries, and so on). Hospitals can be categorized in a number of ways, such as by purpose, size, ownership, location (urban or rural), teaching status, or system affiliation (Table 9.1). Most hospitals in the United States provide general medical and surgical services on a short-term basis. The four primary categories for hospitals according to the AHA are (a) *community*, (b) *special*, (c) *rehabilitative* and *chronic disease*, and (d) *psychiatric*.

Hospitals are subject to federal and state regulations. A hospital must be *licensed* to operate; licensing is handled at the state level by the agency or entity that has been

TABLE 9.1 REGISTERED HOSPITALS IN THE UNITED STATES BY TYPE AND OWNERSHIP STATUS

Type/Ownership Status	Number of Hospitals
Community hospitals	4,973
Not-for-profit community hospitals	2,903
Investor-owned (for-profit) community hospitals	1,025
State and local government community hospitals	1,045
Federal government hospitals	208
Nonfederal psychiatric hospitals	421
Nonfederal long-term care hospitals	112
Hospital units of institutions (e.g., prison hospitals)	10

Source: American Hospital Association, 2013.

designated with such authority for the state. Licensure focuses on physical plant requirements, sanitation, personnel, and equipment. In order to receive reimbursement for services provided to Medicare and Medicaid patients, hospitals must receive *certification* from the federal government. Hospitals may choose to pursue *accreditation* by The Joint Commission, an independent, nonprofit organization that accredits hospitals and other types of health care institutions. This voluntary participation in accreditation is a symbol of quality that indicates the organization has met certain performance standards. The Centers for Medicare & Medicaid Services (CMS) recognize accreditation as suitable proof that a hospital has met the minimum requirements to receive certification.

Patients are referred to the hospital for services on the authority of a member of the medical staff (i.e., a physician) who has been granted admitting *privileges* in accordance with state law and criteria for standards of medical care established by the facility. Hospitals provide both *inpatient* (requiring an overnight stay) and *outpatient* services (not requiring an overnight stay). Outpatient services are sometimes referred to as *ambulatory care*, which means the patient is able to walk (ambulate) into the facility to receive diagnostic or therapeutic treatment. However, in actuality not all patients who receive outpatient services can ambulate (e.g., patients brought to the ED by ambulance).

Community Hospitals. By AHA definition, community hospitals are all nonfederal, short-term *general*, and other *special* hospitals that are accessible by the general public. General hospitals provide patient services, diagnostic and therapeutic, for a variety of medical conditions; the *average length of patient stay (ALOS)* is less than 25 days. Hospitals also provide diagnostic x-ray services, clinical laboratory services, and operating room service with facilities and staff for a variety of procedures. Services are provided on both an *inpatient* and an *outpatient* basis. Traditionally, hospitals primarily have delivered care on an inpatient basis, but over the past three decades more services have been moved to an outpatient, or *ambulatory* basis to contain costs. In addition to cost containment, medical practices have advanced enabling many procedures that previously required an overnight stay to become less invasive and therefore require a shorter recovery period that can be achieved at a patient's home without nursing care.

Special hospitals provide diagnostic and treatment services for patients who have specified medical conditions, both surgical and nonsurgical. These hospitals must provide the services that are deemed appropriate for the specified medical conditions for which services are provided.

Community hospitals are grouped by ownership in three categories:

- Voluntary, not-for-profit (nonprofit)
- Investor-owned (for-profit, proprietary)
- Public (state or local government owned and managed)

Some community hospitals operate as free-standing single hospital entities, whereas others are part of a health system. A *system* is defined as either a multihospital or diversified single hospital system. Community hospitals may also be classified as participating in a *network*, which is defined as a group of hospitals, physicians, other providers, insurers, and/or community agencies that work together to coordinate and deliver a broad spectrum of services to the community (AHA, 2013).

Hospitals may also be classified by teaching status—teaching hospitals are affiliated with medical schools and provide clinical education, residencies, and internships for medical and dental students. These teaching hospitals (along with other hospitals that are not affiliated with a medical school) also provide clinical education and training for nursing and allied health professions students. Teaching hospitals are typically voluntary, not-for-profit or public, government-sponsored hospitals. Some teaching hospitals operate as part of an *academic health center*, which comprises an allopathic or osteopathic medical school, one or more health professions schools (e.g., allied health, dentistry, nursing, pharmacy, public health, veterinary medicine), and one or more owned or affiliated teaching hospitals or health systems. Academic health centers are heavily involved in clinical research and high-level tertiary and quaternary care, in addition to providing advanced training and education for clinicians in primary and specialty care.

Rehabilitation Hospitals. Rehabilitation hospitals specialize in providing therapeutic interventions to help patients regain functional ability to the highest possible level after an injury or illness that has caused some loss of ability. By Medicare definition, 75% of a rehabilitation hospital's patients must require intensive (at least 3 hours per day) rehabilitative services to treat conditions related to stroke, spinal cord injury, major trauma, brain injury, or other debilitating disease or injury. Rehabilitative services provided within these facilities include physical therapy, occupational therapy, and speech-language therapy. Other services may also be provided to assist patients with psychological, vocational, or social needs related to their condition.

Psychiatric Hospitals. The primary function of a psychiatric hospital is to provide diagnostic and treatment services for patients who have a psychiatric-related illness. Some facilities specialize in short-term or outpatient therapy, whereas others may specialize in temporary or permanent care of residents who require routine assistance, treatment, or a specialized and controlled environment as a result of a psychological disorder. General hospitals may also operate psychiatric units within their organizations.

Psychiatric hospitals are required to provide clinical laboratory and diagnostic x-ray services in addition to psychiatric, psychological, and social work services. Psychiatric hospitals have written agreements with general hospitals for the transfer of patients in need of medical or surgical services not available at the psychiatric institution (AHA, 2013).

Other Hospitals. The federal government operates approximately 208 hospitals that are not accessible to the general public. Included among these hospitals are those that are operated by the Veterans Administration (VA) for the nation's military veterans, the Department of Defense (DOD) for active duty military personnel, and the Indian Health Service (IHS) for American Indians and Alaska Natives.

Physician Organizations

In the United States, physicians have traditionally been self-employed, working in private medical practices that they own either solely or in partnership with other physicians. Hospitals establish relationships with physicians by granting them admitting privileges to provide inpatient and outpatient procedures and services to their patients that cannot be delivered within the physician practice setting. This is still the predominant model, although there has been a trend in recent years toward the employment of physicians by hospitals and other health care organizations. This trend has been attributed to a number of reasons, including stagnant reimbursement rates, a desire for better work-life balance for physicians, and efforts by hospitals to increase market share (American Medical Association [AMA], 2013). The results of a physician practice benchmark survey in 2012 conducted by the AMA indicate that 53.2% of physicians were full or part owners of their practices, 41.8% were employed, and 5% were independent contractors. Ownership had decreased by 8% from a prior study conducted in 2007. The 2012 survey indicated that having an ownership stake was less common among women physicians than men, and less common among younger physicians than older physicians (Kane & Emmons, 2013).

As mentioned, physicians may be employed by others (e.g., hospitals, government, medical schools) or be self-employed (i.e., in *private practice*). A variety of physician practice settings are utilized in the United States, which include *solo practice, single specialty group practice, multispecialty group practice, corporate medical practice*, and *urgent care centers*, among others.

Solo Practices. A physician practice operated by one physician is known as a solo practice. Approximately 20% of physician practicing in the United States are in solo practices, compared with 40.5% in 1983 (AMA, 2013). According to the AMA (2013), a majority of physicians in solo practices own their practice.

Single Specialty Group Practices. The most common type of physician practice is the single specialty group practice: a practice with two or more physicians that have the same medical specialty, such as internal medicine or cardiology. Forty-five percent of the physicians in the United States are in a single specialty group practice (AMA, 2013).

Multispecialty Group Practices. A multispecialty group practice consists of two or more physicians who practice different medical specialties. Approximately 22% of physicians in the United States are in a multispecialty group practice (AMA, 2013).

Corporate Medical Practices. Corporate medical practices are physician practices that are owned by business corporations or entities. This is commonly known as the *corporate practice of medicine (CPOM)*. CPOM is prohibited in some states: The types of prohibitions vary by state and may be found in various laws, regulations, or court rulings. A typical exception allows hospitals and health maintenance organizations (HMOs) to employ physicians because these businesses were established for the purpose of providing treatment to patients and are licensed entities. Most states allow physicians to provide services through a *professional service corporation (P.C.)*, which is a business entity formed for the purpose of providing professional services, such as medical services. Some states have CPOM laws but do not enforce them. Such laws were established in an earlier era when concern about the commercialization of medicine led to great efforts to ensure that medicine would be practiced only by licensed professionals.

Urgent Care Centers. Urgent care centers offer walk-in, extended-hour access to individuals with acute illness and injuries that aren't bona fide emergencies. In addition to services found in the typical physician's office, urgent care centers usually can treat minor fractures and provide IV fluids as well as perform on-site x-rays and laboratory test processing. These centers are typically staffed by physicians and other providers and operate 7 days a week, including holidays, from 8 or 9 a.m. until 7 or 9 p.m. This is a growth area in the health care delivery system, with more than 9,000 centers operating nationwide and approximately 300 new centers opening each year.

Community Health Centers. Community health centers (CHCs) provide health care services, focusing on primary and preventive care, to medically underserved and indigent populations. Approximately 22 million people are served by more than 1,200 CHCs in the United States (National Association of Community Health Centers, 2013). In order to receive care at a CHC, an individual must be a resident of the state in which the center is located, be uninsured, and be poor as defined by federal poverty guidelines. CHCs contract with the state or local health department to provide services to eligible individuals; they also help to provide linkages to social services and government-sponsored health insurance programs, such as Medicaid and the Children's Health Insurance Program (CHIP). CHCs may be organized as part of a public health department or another health service organization, or as a nonprofit organization.

Ambulatory Surgery Centers

Ambulatory surgery centers (ASCs) are facilities that provide surgical services for procedures that are done on an outpatient basis. This is sometimes referred to as *same-day surgery*. ASCs are not physician offices, although physicians have taken the lead in their development.

The first ASC was established in 1970 by two physicians. Today, physicians have some ownership in approximately 90% of the licensed ASCs in the United States. Community hospitals have also partnered with physicians to open and operate ASCs, and a small percentage of ASCs are entirely hospital owned.

Patients treated at an ASC have already been diagnosed by a physician and have elected to have an outpatient surgical procedure. All ASCs must have at least one dedicated operating room and the appropriate equipment to perform surgery safely and provide quality patient care. The most prevalent specialties served by ASCs are ophthalmology, orthopedics, gastrointestinal, pain management, plastic surgery, and urology (Ambulatory Surgical Center Association, 2013).

Long-Term Care Organizations

Long-term care organizations operate facilities for individuals who are not able to manage independently in the community. The services provided in these facilities vary depending on the level of assistance needed; services may range from custodial care and chronic care management to short-term rehabilitative services. Long-term care facilities (LTCFs) may be owned by government entities, nonprofit organizations (including churches), or investor-owned corporations. LTCFs may be independent facilities that are either freestanding or operated within a *continuing care retirement community*. LTCFs may be part of a multifacility organization (that is, a chain) or may be hospital-owned as either an attached or a freestanding facility.

Independent Living Facilities. Independent living facilities are multiunit housing developments that may provide support services such as meals, transportation, housekeeping, and social activities. These facilities are typically utilized by active senior adults who do not require assistance with ADLs.

Independent living facilities are sometimes operated as part of a *continuing care retirement community*, which provides a full range of long-term care facilities and services—an assisted living facility and a skilled nursing facility. This arrangement enables seniors to make a transition into a residence that meets their physical needs as they begin to require more medical assistance. Independent living facilities that do not provide many services beyond a residence are sometimes referred to as senior apartments.

Assisted Living Facilities. Assisted living facilities are available for individuals who are basically able to care for themselves but may need some assistance with some daily activities. Assisted living facilities are residential facilities that provide services that may include meals, laundry, housekeeping, medication reminders, and assistance with ADLs and IADLs.

Most states require licensure for assisted living facilities, and the exact definition of what constitutes an assisted living facility varies among states. Approximately 90% of assisted living services in the United States are paid through private funds, although a few states allow payment for assisted living through Medicaid waivers.

Skilled Nursing Facilities. A skilled nursing facility (or nursing home) is licensed by the state in which it operates to provide 24-hour nursing care, room and board, and activities for convalescent residents and residents with chronic or long-term illnesses or conditions. Special populations served by skilled nursing facilities include physically or mentally challenged children and adults, and children and adults with debilitating diseases and/or conditions. Regular medical supervision and rehabilitation services must be available. The facilities are staffed by health care professionals including a physician as medical director, registered nurses (RNs), licensed practical nurses (LPNs), and trained nursing assistants. Skilled nursing facilities are reimbursed through a variety of mechanisms, including private funds, long-term care insurance, Medicare (for short-term rehabilitation or subacute care), and Medicaid. Medicaid is the source of payment for about 70% of the residents in skilled nursing facilities.

Rehabilitation Organizations

Rehabilitative services are provided in a variety of inpatient and outpatient settings, including inpatient rehabilitation hospitals, rehabilitation units in acute care hospitals, skilled nursing facilities, outpatient rehabilitation centers and units, and other medical rehabilitation providers.

Inpatient Rehabilitation Facilities. An inpatient rehabilitation facility is either a freestanding inpatient rehabilitation hospital or a unit of an acute care hospital. Intensive acute rehabilitation services are provided and generally include at least 3 hours of therapy per day for 5 to 7 days each week. Therapy may include physical, occupational, speech, or recreation therapy.

Patients who cannot tolerate intensive therapy in an acute rehabilitation setting may be transferred to a *transitional care, long-term care,* or *subacute* care facility, where less intensive rehabilitation services are provided along with other medical services (e.g., 24-hour skilled nursing care) needed for convalescence and recovery.

Outpatient Rehabilitation Providers. Rehabilitation services may be provided on an outpatient basis—that is, the patient lives at home and visits the facility for therapy. Therapy plans are developed on an individual basis and typically include 2 to 3 days of treatment per week. Nursing services are usually not included in the outpatient setting. *Centers of care* are facilities that provide outpatient rehabilitative services for patients with a particular, specific illness, such as multiple sclerosis, Parkinson's disease, or stroke.

Three types of providers may qualify for reimbursement for outpatient rehabilitation services by Medicare:

Rehabilitation agencies are organizations that provide integrated, multidisciplinary programs designed to upgrade the physical functions of handicapped and disabled individuals through a specialized team of rehabilitation personnel.

Rehabilitation clinics are facilities that are established primarily to provide outpatient rehabilitative services by physicians. To meet the definition of a clinic, medical services must be provided a group of three of more physicians practicing rehabilitation medicine together, and a physician must be present in the facility at all times during the hours of operation to perform medical services.

Public health agencies are official agencies established by state or local government that provide environmental health services, preventive medical services, and, sometimes, therapeutic services.

Integrated Delivery Systems

An integrated delivery system (IDS) is an organized, coordinated, and collaborative network that links various health care providers to provide a *continuum of care* to a particular patient population or community and to be clinically and fiscally accountable for the clinical outcomes and health status of the population it serves. Many believe that integrated delivery systems can help to address some of the problems associated with the fragmented delivery system in the United States and move toward the goals of improving the quality and accessibility of care while containing or reducing costs (Enthoven, 2009).

Integrated delivery systems have existed since the early 1900s, but it was in the 1990s when interest in the IDS concept began to spread as hospitals and physician practices consolidated through mergers and acquisitions in the face of changing reimbursement methodologies from public and private insurers. Interest in IDSs has surged in recent years during the national health reform debate as experts have suggested that the IDS approach to health care delivery can improve quality and reduce costs. Research has shown that integrated delivery systems have a positive effect on quality, but there is little evidence of an effect on costs or health care utilization (Hwang, Chang, LaClair, & Paz, 2013).

Two types of integration—horizontal and vertical—are used to create an IDS. *Horizontal integration* involves linking organizations that provide the same level of care, such as a multispecialty group practice. *Vertical integration* involves linking organizations that provide different levels of care, for example, preventive, primary, secondary, tertiary, and long-term care. One of the goals of an IDS is to provide *continuity of care* for the patient, which includes continuity of information (e.g., shared medical records), continuity across primary and secondary care (e.g., discharge planning from specialist to generalist care), and provider continuity (e.g., seeing the same provider each time).

Emergency Medical Services

An emergency medical service (EMS) provides acute care for medical emergencies that take place outside of the hospital setting. EMS is utilized within a community to treat those in need of urgent medical care or to stabilize and transport patients with illness or injuries who are unable to transport themselves to the appropriate medical facility. It is a system of coordinated response and emergency medical care involving multiple people and agencies.

EMS is regulated by federal and state governments, and may be provided by paid professionals or, in some communities, by volunteers. The organization of EMS varies from community to community, based on state regulation, population density, and topography, and may be provided via public institutions, private institutions, or a public–private configuration. Prehospital EMS can be based in a fire department, a hospital, an independent government agency (such as a public health agency), a nonprofit corporation (such as a rescue squad); EMS may also be provided by commercial for-profit companies. The essential components of an EMS system are the same regardless of the provider.

Home Health Care Organizations

Home health agencies and organizations provide medical services in a patient's home. Services are typically provided for elderly or disabled patients, or for patients who are unable to visit a hospital or physician's office because of weakness after surgery or other reasons. Care provided in the home may be acute, long-term, or end-of-life. Home health primarily involves the provision of skilled nursing services and therapeutic services (e.g., physical, occupational, and/or speech and hearing). A home health agency may be a public, nonprofit, or proprietary agency and may be a subdivision of a larger organization. The agency must be licensed by the state in which it operates or receive approval that it has met all standards and requirements to operate. These agencies are also subject to certification requirements by CMS and may also seek accreditation from an independent accrediting organization. Home health agencies and organizations must have policies established by a governing body that must include at least one physician and one RN, and the services it provides must be overseen by a physician or a registered professional nurse.

Hospice and Palliative Care Organizations

Palliative care services are available for anyone with a serious illness as well as for patients who are terminally ill. Palliative care may be provided in a hospital, outpatient clinic, long-term care facility, or hospice facility. It is delivered by a team of specialists, including physicians, nurses, and social workers, and may include other professionals, such as massage therapists, pharmacists, and nutritionists. Each facility where palliative care is provided typically has its own palliative care team; these professionals work in partnership with a patient's primary physician and others involved in treating the individual.

Hospice care is provided to terminally ill patients either in their homes (*hospice residential care*) or in a health care facility (*hospice inpatient care*) owned and operated by a hospice organization or health system. According to the National Hospice and Palliative Care Organization (2013), hospice care programs were first established in 1974 and have grown in number to more than 5,500 programs, including both primary locations and satellite offices, as of 2012. The majority of hospice programs are offered by freestanding, independent agencies (57.4%), and the remainder are part of a hospital system (20.5%), home health agency (16.9%), or nursing home (5.2%). Hospice programs range in size from small organizations serving fewer than 50 patients on an annual basis to large, corporate chains operating programs on a national basis and caring for thousands of patients each year. In 2012, 32% of hospice programs registered with Medicare were nonprofit organizations, 63% were for-profit organizations, and about 5% were government owned and operated.

Pharmacies

Medication is an integral part of health care delivery, and pharmacists play a significant role in ensuring the safe and effective use of medication to achieve desired health outcomes. The role of the pharmacist has traditionally been to dispense medication; that role is now expanding into the direct care of patients as the use of medication has grown and new technologies are employed in the medication dispensing and utilization processes.

Licensed pharmacies include retail pharmacies in the community setting and hospital or other institutional pharmacies. Community pharmacies include chain pharmacy organizations (e.g., CVS, Walgreens), pharmacies located within other large retail organizations (e.g., Walmart, Kroger), and independent, locally owned and operated pharmacies. The community pharmacy provides the public with access to medication, including administering flu shots, and serves as a source of advice on health issues. Approximately 6 out of 10 licensed pharmacists work in the community setting. Institutional pharmacies control drug distribution within the facility, and help to ensure that each patient receives the appropriate drug and dosage. Institutional pharmacies are involved in highly specialized areas, including nuclear medicine, intravenous therapy, and drug and poison information. A hospital or health system may also operate a retail pharmacy within its facilities in addition to its clinical pharmacy operation.

Pharmaceutical Companies and Medical Device Manufacturers

Another integral part of the health care delivery system are the pharmaceutical companies and medical device manufacturers that develop and supply medications, medical supplies, durable medical equipment, and medical devices to health care organizations and sometimes directly to the public. Not only do these organizations supply materials needed for the direct care of patients, but they also play an important role in helping ensure safe and effective care.

Medical device manufacturers provide essential products for modern medical care, including devices that range from CT scanners and surgical robotic devices to blood pressure cuffs and thermometers. Under the ACA, medical device manufacturers are required to pay a 2.3% excise tax on gross sales. This legislation, along with other health policies, is having a large effect, especially on the smaller companies that employ fewer than 50 people that make up about 80% of the medical device industry. Many medical device manufacturers have become vulnerable to takeover by large pharmaceutical companies, and some manufacturers are moving their operations out of the United States to countries with more favorable tax and regulatory climates.

The biopharmaceutical industry comprises the pharmaceutical and biotechnology industries. Biopharmaceutical companies develop, manufacture, market, and distribute drugs and vaccines used to prevent and treat diseases. It is made up of four sectors: (a) pharmaceutical and medicine manufacturers, (b) pharmacy wholesalers, (c) research and development services, and (d) management of companies and enterprises. Biopharmaceutical companies spend up to $135 billion annually on research and development, and it is estimated that it takes up to 15 years to develop a medicine or vaccine. The biopharmaceutical industry accounts for nearly 20% of all research and development investment in the United States, where new drugs must be approved by the Food and Drug Administration (FDA) as safe and effective.

The industry is sometimes referred to as "Big Pharma" because of its size, its influence over health care legislation, and its effect on the cost of health care delivery. Thirty-six of the largest pharmaceutical companies comprise the membership of the industry's professional association, the Pharmaceutical Research and Manufacturers of America (PhRMA), and invest more money in lobbying than any other industry in the United States.

Other Delivery Organizations

Telemedicine. Telemedicine uses electronic communications to exchange medical information between sites to improve a patient's clinical health status. Telemedicine services may include primary care and specialist referral services, remote patient monitoring, consumer medical and health information, and medical education. Hospitals, specialty clinics, home health agencies, and physicians' offices all use telemedicine. The services may be offered within a single health care organization or between health care organizations. Emerging models of telemedicine delivery include offering specialty consultation services through membership associations that match people in need of services with providers, and independent businesses that are organized to provide telemedicine consultation services but are not health care providers. These independent businesses recruit appropriately licensed specialists to provide telemedicine services and then market these services, handling contract negotiations and all legal and technical aspects of delivery.

Retail Clinics

Retail clinics are medical clinics located in pharmacies, grocery stores, and "big box" stores such as Target. These clinics provide routine care for acute conditions (e.g., bronchitis) as well as preventive care. Retail clinics began emerging in 2000; by 2010 there were approximately 2,100 clinics in operation. Retail clinics are often open extended hours and on weekends, offering a convenient alternative for routine care, particularly when conventional physician offices are closed. A study by the Rand Corporation indicated that young adults (ages 18–44) account for 43% of patient visits, although the utilization of retail clinics by seniors is increasing (Rand Health, 2013). In 2010, 73% of the retail clinics in the United States were operated by three companies—CVS, Walgreens, and Target (Rand Health, 2013). Retail clinics are also operated by hospital chains and physician groups, accounting for about 11% of the market. It is anticipated that the full implementation of the ACA could lead to growth in retail clinics in order to meet the demand for primary care by the newly insured.

HEALTH SYSTEM PERFORMANCE

Although the United States spends more money per capita on health care than any other nation in the world, we are lagging behind other countries on a variety of quality indicators, including average life expectancy and infant mortality rates. The Institute of Medicine (IOM) estimates that more Americans are killed every year by medical errors than in automobile accidents. As a response to these staggering statistics, the IOM released *Crossing the Quality Chasm* (2001), a landmark report that issued a mandate for improvement in U.S. health system performance. Additionally, a portion of the ACA is dedicated to improving quality and health system performance through funding research, aligning financial incentives with performance outcomes, and identifying a national quality strategy. Although marginal improvements in quality and performance have been observed in the past decade, we still have a long way to go to achieve a high-performing health system.

Organizations such IOM, the Institute for Healthcare Improvement (IHI), and the National Committee for Quality Assurance (NCQA) are leading the health system improvement movement through initiatives including patient centeredness, The Triple Aim, and the *patient centered medical home* (PCMH). The CMS is financially incentivizing the "meaningful use" of electronic health records (EHR) by health care providers to promote quality improvement in health care. Quality improvement efforts of this type promote collaboration among health care providers, payers, the government, and other stakeholders with the goal of achieving real health system change. In the next section of this chapter, we provide an overview of some of the quality improvement initiatives that demonstrate the most promise in improving U.S. health system performance.

The Triple Aim

The idea behind the Triple Aim is that to improve the delivery of health care in the United States, organizations must simultaneously pursue three dimensions: (a) improve the patient experience of care, (b) improve the health of populations, and (c) reduce the per-capita cost of health care.

The IHI is a not-for-profit organization that is dedicated to improving health and health care worldwide. The IHI (2013) promotes a learning initiative and a framework called the Triple Aim for health care organizations and communities. The idea behind the Triple Aim is that to improve the delivery of health care in the United States, organizations must simultaneously pursue three dimensions: (a) improve the patient experience of care, (b) improve the health of populations, and (c) reduce the per-capita cost of health care.

Achieving this triple aim is difficult, because one organization is rarely accountable for all three dimensions. However, the IHI has identified five system components that are necessary for fulfillment of the Triple Aim:

- *Focus on individuals and families*: Care should be customized at an individual level utilizing families and caregivers as partners.
- *Redesign primary care services/structures*: A team of professionals must be established that can deliver the majority of necessary care.
- *Population health management*: Partnerships within the community are necessary to promote prevention and wellness.
- *Cost control platform*: Cooperative relationships with provider groups must be in place to control costs.
- *System integration and execution*: Services across the continuum of care must be coordinated.

Although the Triple Aim initiative is ambitious, a few health systems have taken on the challenge and have succeeded. A strong focus on primary care, coupled with community alignment, is necessary to achieve positive patient experiences and improvement in population health. Additionally, active physician participation is crucial to reduce costs. A model of care centered around physician partners is one way to approach the Triple Aim. Genesys HealthWorks provides a good example of this physician-centered strategy.

Genesys HealthWorks represents a unique model of care developed by Genesys Health System in Flint, Michigan, with the goals of improving the patient experience of care and population health while controlling costs. Genesys employed three key approaches to achieve this triple aim (Klein & McCarthy, 2010):

1. Genesys created a physician–hospital organization that engaged community-based primary care physicians. The goal of this organization is to facilitate care coordination, emphasize primary care and prevention, and ensure the efficient use of specialty care services.
2. Genesys deployed health navigators. The role of these navigators is to assist patients in the prevention and management of chronic diseases through healthy lifestyles.
3. Genesys partnered with community stakeholders in an attempt to extend their model to the entire community.

The Genesys HealthWorks model has demonstrated success among patients receiving care within the Genesys Health System and affiliated physician groups. This model has reduced utilization and cost of care while simultaneously improving physician quality indicators. Additionally, the model has improved the health behaviors of other patients within the community. Genesys has extended the health navigator program to serve low-income patients enrolled in a county health plan. These patients have improved their health status and decreased utilization as a result of the program.

Patient Centeredness

The IOM identified patient centeredness as one of six domains that define quality care. Patient-centered care is "care that is respectful of and responsive to individual patient preferences, needs, and values and ensures that patient values guide all clinical decisions" (IOM, 2001). Six dimensions to patient-centered care have been identified (Gerteis, Edgman-Levitan, & Daley, 1993):

- Respect for patients' values, preferences, and expressed needs
- Coordination and integration of care
- Information, communication, and education
- Physical comfort
- Emotional support
- Involvement of family and friends

Providing patient-centered care means giving patients the information they need to participate actively in decision making about their care with the goal of obtaining the most desirable outcome. If a patient is incapacitated or unable to participate in decision making regarding his or her care, then a family member or caregiver should be engaged. When a health care intervention cannot provide a cure, it should aim to alleviate the patient's suffering. The likelihood that an outcome desired by a patient can be achieved is increased by actively involving patients and family members in decision making regarding the provision of care.

Although we are making progress in this direction, research suggests that certain patient-centered practices are still rare. Movements toward the PCMH and patient-centered research are continuing to shift the momentum in the right direction; however, there is still a long way to go. The achievement of a truly patient-centered health system will require the participation of patients, family members, physicians, nurses, and other health care providers involved in the provision of care.

■ The Future of the Delivery System

Recent years have seen the introduction of several innovative new models of care that have potential to realign incentives and improve overall health system performance in terms of cost, quality, and access. The ACA has encouraged the adoption of these new models, and a variety of new organizational forms have emerged from the private sector. Renewed interest in physician employment models also demonstrates potential for increased integration and more closely aligned clinical and financial incentives between physicians and other providers.

INNOVATIVE MODELS OF CARE DELIVERY

Patient-Centered Medical Homes

The *PCMH* is a model of primary care that emphasizes communication and care coordination. Patient centeredness is an important goal of PCMHs. Physician practices must meet certain standards to be designated as PCMHs. The National Committee for Quality Assurance (NCQA) released revised standards for PCMHs in 2011 (see Table 9.2). Evidence suggests that the PCMH is effective at improving health care quality and reducing costs.

> *Evidence suggests that the PCMH is effective at improving health care quality and reducing costs.*

Group Health Cooperative (GHC) in Seattle, Washington, provides an example of a successful PCMH model. GHC is a nonprofit health system that consists of physician groups, medical facilities, and health plans that serve Washington and Northern Idaho. In 2006, the system decided to pilot test a PCMH practice. GHC's pilot practice

TABLE 9.2 STANDARDS FOR PATIENT-CENTERED MEDICAL HOMES

Standard	Content
Enhance Access/ Continuity	▪ Patients have access to culturally and linguistically appropriate routine or urgent care and clinical advice during and after office hours ▪ Practice provides electronic access ▪ Patients may select clinician ▪ Practice focuses on team-based care with trained staff
Identify/Manage Patient Populations	▪ Practice collects demographic and clinical data for population management ▪ Practice assesses and documents patient risk factors ▪ Practice identifies patients for proactive reminders
Plan/Manage Care	▪ Practice identifies patients with specific conditions including high-risk or complex care needs ▪ Care management emphasizes previsit planning, assessing patient progress, addressing patient barriers to treatment goals ▪ Practice reconciles medications ▪ Practice uses e-prescribing
Provide Self-Care Support/Community Resources	▪ Practice assesses patient and family self-management abilities ▪ Practice works with patient and family to develop a self-care plan ▪ Practice clinicians counsel patients on healthy behaviors ▪ Practice assesses and provides/arranges for mental health or substance abuse treatment
Track/Coordinate Care	▪ Practice tracks, follows-up, and coordinates tests, referrals, and care at other facilities ▪ Practice manages care transitions
Measure/Improve Performance	▪ Practice uses performance and patient experience data to continuously improve ▪ Practice tracks utilization measures (e.g., hospitalizations, ED visits) ▪ Practice identifies vulnerable patient populations ▪ Practice demonstrates improved performance

Adapted from NCQA's *Patient-Centered Medical Home (PCMH) 2011 Standards* (National Committee for Quality Assurance, 2011).

expanded staffing and emphasized the use of care teams. The ratio of patients to primary care providers was reduced for the pilot practice, and their enhanced staffing model included physicians, medical assistants, LPNs, physician assistants/nurse practitioners, RNs, and pharmacists. The idea behind this increased staffing was to facilitate patient relationships and to allow for comprehensive coordinated care. Additionally, patient encounters with clinical staff increased from approximately 20 minutes to 30 minutes in duration, and time was set aside each day for teams to create coordinated care plans. After 2 years, the GHC's PCMH pilot practice demonstrated improved patient experiences, improved quality, and reduced physician burnout compared with other GHC clinics (Reid et al., 2010).

Health Homes

Health homes were created by the ACA to give states an option for providing patient-centered, medical home–type services to Medicaid beneficiaries suffering from severe or multiple chronic conditions. The purpose of health homes is to create a system of care that facilitates and coordinates access to primary care, acute care, behavioral care, and long-term community-based services. Medicaid beneficiaries with (a) at least two chronic conditions, (b) one chronic condition and high risk for another, or (c) a serious mental health condition are eligible for health home services.

> *Promoting care for the whole person, care that is individually tailored to each patient and family, is a goal of health homes.*

Health home services are offered by designated providers, teams of health professionals that link to a designated provider, or a health team. Physicians, group practices, community health centers, home health agencies, or any other provider deemed appropriate by the state is considered a designated provider. Health teams consist of a physician and other health care professionals such as nurses, social workers, and other appropriate professionals. Health homes provide care management, care coordination, health promotion, transitional care from inpatient to other settings, individual and family support, follow-up care, and referral to community social support services. Additionally, health homes use health information technology to coordinate such services. Health homes must provide quality driven, cost-effective, culturally appropriate care. Promoting care for the whole person, care that is individually tailored to each patient and family, is a goal of health homes.

Accountable Care Organizations

Accountable care organizations (ACOs) are groups of providers that share responsibility and financial accountability for providing high quality, coordinated care to Medicare patients. The goal of ACOs is to ensure that patients get the right care at the right time in the most efficient way. ACOs are organized around primary care providers, and the high level of care coordination provided by ACOs is particularly important for the chronically ill. If ACOs are successful at meeting quality and cost savings targets, these organizations qualify for financial incentives or shared savings from the Medicare program.

The ACA has facilitated the creation of ACOs for the Medicare program. Even though most are in the early stages of development, they demonstrate a promising approach to managing the health of particular patient populations. Additionally, provider groups are creating "ACO-like" organizations that strive to facilitate comprehensive care coordination for patient populations beyond Medicare beneficiaries.

Organizations with experience providing patient-centered, coordinated care were eligible to participate as Medicare Pioneer ACOs. First-year results for the Pioneer ACOs were mixed. Although all 32 participating Pioneer ACOs improved quality, only 13 achieved results worthy of shared savings with the CMS. In fact, nine organizations are either transferring to the shared savings program or dropping out of the pilot all together (CMS, 2013b).

Banner Health Network (BHN) in Arizona, is an example of an ACO with promising first year results. Banner Health is a nonprofit health system that consists of a variety of provider organizations, including acute care hospitals, clinics, home health, hospice, behavioral health facilities, and a Medicare Advantage Plan. Banner made the decision to participate as a Pioneer ACO because this designation is congruent with its desire to deliver the triple aim of great patient experience, improved population health, with low costs.

BHN was created with three goals in mind:

- First, BHN wanted to define and deliver value-based care. This includes identifying appropriate participants, aligning incentives, and relying on delivery models such as PCMN that will support the care continuum.
- Second, BHN wanted to leverage technology to facilitate information sharing and enhance care management.
- The third goal of BHN was to align the financial incentives of stakeholders, including providers, payers, and patients.

In its first year, BHN was able to achieve shared savings of over $13 million and reduce hospital admissions, hospital lengths of stay, and hospital readmissions for its ACO members. Because of its success, BHN has developed ACO-like relationships with other payers, including Blue Cross Blue Shield of Arizona, Aetna, UnitedHealthcare, and Cigna (Nguyen, 2013).

Community-Based Solutions

The ACA has initiated community-based programs designed to keep Medicare beneficiaries out of an inpatient hospital setting and in their communities. One program is the Community-based Care Transitions Program (CCTP), which tests models for improving care transitions to reduce avoidable readmissions. A transition in care occurs when a patient moves from one health care delivery setting to another. Among the Medicare population, it is very common for patients discharged from the hospital to be readmitted within the next 30 days. These readmissions may occur because of inadequate care management resulting from a bumpy transition in care. The CCTP program provides support for community-based organizations (CBOs) to provide care transition services for Medicare patients in their communities who are at high risk for hospital readmission (CMS, 2013a).

The Northwest Triad Care Transitions Community Program (NTCTCP) is a pilot CCTP that is designated to address care transition needs of the patients of North

Carolina. Seven acute care hospitals and four community-based organizations have partnered to try to reduce the number of avoidable hospital readmissions and keep patients in their homes. This collaborative effort is focused primarily on Medicare patients with a diagnosis of heart failure, pneumonia, heart attack, or chronic obstructive pulmonary disease (COPD). NTCTCP is attempting to reduce readmissions through a case management approach, with a heavy emphasis on information sharing and data management. Additionally, patient navigators facilitate transitional care by visiting the homes of participating patients to determine whether medical and social needs are met. Ensuring that prescriptions are filled, transportation to medical appointments is in place, and meal preparation is available are examples of issues patient navigators strive to address.

CLINICAL INTEGRATION

Physician–Hospital Alignment

Identifying ways to align the incentives of physicians and hospitals is vitally important to maximize the clinical quality of care while minimizing costs.

The alignment of physician and hospital goals and incentives is a critical success factor in the era of health reform. Traditionally, both types of provider have been reimbursed based on volume or productivity. However, reimbursement mechanisms are becoming more focused on quality and efficiency. Identifying ways to align the incentives of physicians and hospitals is vitally important to maximize the clinical quality of care while minimizing costs.

Different economic levels and approaches to physician–hospital alignment involve a variety of organizational arrangements. Loosely aligned physician–hospital arrangements involve a traditional independent practice model, in which physicians are still "volunteer" members of a hospital's medical staff and alignment is sought through contractual arrangements to secure medical directors and physician administrators. In this traditional alignment model, economic integration is not achieved. Closer alignment might be achieved through more strategic approaches, such as joint ventures or co-management agreements between physicians and hospitals with some level of shared economic interests. The ultimate level of physician–hospital alignment is achieved through employment relationships with full economic integration. With this level of alignment, physicians are truly employees and are required to comply with hospital policies and share goals (Sowers, Newman, & Langdon, 2013).

A well-regarded example of an integrated health system is Scripps Health (www.scripps.org), which includes acute care hospitals, outpatient centers, and home health and hospice services in the San Diego, California, area. Scripps employs more than 13,500 workers, and approximately 2,600 affiliated physicians provide care at Scripps facilities. Scripps Health is a success story in the area of physician–hospital alignment. In 1999, Scripps was losing millions of dollars a year and physician and employee confidence was at an all-time low. A new CEO created an organizational turnaround by aligning physician and hospital interests more closely through a co-management approach. Although California law makes direct physician employment difficult, closer alignment was achieved through an integrated foundation model that empha-sizes transparency and open communication between physician and administrative leadership. The CEO was able to regain physician trust and leverage close alignment with physicians to achieve financial and quality improvements. Since the turnaround, Scripps Health has been well positioned for growth, and the system has received numerous awards and accolades, including becoming one of *Fortune* magazine's "100 Best Hospitals to Work For" (Scripps Health San Diego, 2013).

Physician Employment Models

More complex reimbursement systems are emerging from health reform and the quality movement. Physician payment is moving from a primarily fee-for-service or volume-based methodology to a model more dependent on quality and clinical out-comes. As a result of this shift, many physicians are no longer interested in private practice models. Instead, they are seeking affiliation and employment opportunities with health systems and hospitals. Physician employment models free up clinician time so that they can focus on providing patient care rather than the business of run-ning a practice. Employment can be advantageous for hospitals and health systems by increasing their level of alignment with physician providers. Physician employment models often tie compensation to quality and productivity metrics.

The Mayo Clinic (www.mayoclinic.org) is one successful model of physician employment. Physicians work together with other clinic staff to care for patients, and their work is centered on the philosophy that "the needs of the patient come first" (Mayo Clinic, 2013). The culture of Mayo is unique, rooted in the values of its found-ers: teamwork, collegiality, professionalism, mutual respect, and commitment to progress for the organization and individuals. Care is provided by integrated teams of physicians, health care professionals, and scientists. The Mayo culture emphasizes team success over individual success. Although physician employees are provided with a vast array of resources and support, they are compensated with a salary. This salary structure eliminates any incentives to perform tests or procedures for financial gain. Treatment is purely focused on what is best for the patient (Mayo Clinic, 2013).

■ Best Practices

INNOVATIVE APPROACHES TO IMPROVING CARE DELIVERY

So far in this chapter we have described several organizations that are using innovative approaches to delivering high-quality health care. Health care delivery organizations must continue to innovate if they hope to deliver high-quality care while controlling costs. This section highlights two organizations that have strong reputations as long-term innovators.

Intermountain Healthcare—Salt Lake City, Utah

Intermountain Healthcare (www.intermountainhealthcare.org) fosters a culture of innovation. Intermountain is a nonprofit health care system comprising 22 hospitals, more than 185 physician clinics, and an affiliated insurance company. The system has more than 33,000 employees, who serve patients in Utah and southeastern Idaho. The mission of Intermountain Healthcare is "to provide clinically excellent medical care at affordable rates in a healing environment that's as close to home as possible" (Intermountain Healthcare, 2013). In addition to pursuing the typical health care delivery activities of an integrated health system, Intermountain has several programs that nurture a learning environment and culture of innovation.

Intermountain has recently associated with technology partners to create a Healthcare Transformation Lab. The purpose of this lab is to bring innovation and technology to the patient's bedside at a rapid pace. In addition to working with external technology partners, Intermountain's Healthcare Transformation Lab also provides opportunities for Intermountain employees to develop ideas into new technology. The lab provides a place for clinicians to work with technology experts in developing innovative ideas that will improve the delivery of health care. Examples of projects targeted by the lab include designing the patient room of the future, creating a hand-washing sensor for providers, 3D printing of medical devices for clinical purposes, and creating a "Life Detector" to notify caregivers of changes in vital signs of patients.

Intermountain also houses the Institute for Health Care Delivery Research. As a leader in health care, Intermountain hopes to affect change in the delivery of health care through providing educational opportunities and conducting research throughout the system. The Institute offers courses to Intermountain employees and to others hoping to advance their skills in leadership, quality improvement, or other related areas. Additionally, through its research the Institute aims to facilitate evidence-based practice through the generation and dissemination of evidence (Intermountain Healthcare, 2013).

The Cleveland Clinic—Cleveland, Ohio

The Cleveland Clinic (www.clevelandclinic.org) is a multispecialty academic medical center with a focus on clinical care and research. It houses more than 1,400 hospital beds at its main campus and works with more than 3,000 physicians and scientists. The Cleveland Clinic's mission is "to provide better care of the sick, investigation into their problems, and further education of those who serve" (Cleveland Clinic, 2013). Quality and innovation are among its core values, and the clinic is consistently named in *U.S. News and World Report's* "America's Best Hospitals" survey.

Cleveland Clinic is innovating care delivery by negotiating directly with self-insured employers as part of its Program for Advanced Medical Care (PAMC). The idea behind PAMC programs is to allow employers to provide their employees with access to world-class health care at a reasonable price. Bundled payment programs and transparency in quality outcomes make the Cleveland Clinic a natural choice for large employers interested in securing greater value in their health care purchases. PAMC's first agreement of this kind began with Lowe's Companies in 2010 to provide heart care for their more than 200,000 employees. The clinic recently expanded its cardiac program by contracting with Walmart and is now focusing on marketing packages of orthopedic procedures to large employers. Promoting this form of "domestic medical tourism" may change the way care is delivered, or at least promote transparency among health care providers in terms of quality and pricing (Cleveland Clinic, 2013).

■ Looking Forward

The U.S. health care delivery system can look forward to many changes on the horizon. The implementation of the ACA will push providers to continually improve quality and manage costs. Innovative new forms of delivering health care will continue to emerge to meet the demands of both patients and purchasers of health care. Health care delivery organizations that fail to evolve and learn will face a difficult road. Those organizations that focus on innovation and knowledge creation will be well positioned for the future.

■ Discussion Questions

1. The U.S. health system is shifting its focus to wellness and prevention. Give an example of the three forms of prevention. How should emphasis on prevention alter the delivery of health services in a particular community?

2. The baby boomer generation, which represents a significant portion of the U.S. population, is reaching an age when its utilization of health services will most likely increase. Additionally, life expectancy continues to improve with advancements in medicine and community health. Discuss how this aging of such a large segment of the population will affect specific health care delivery services and organizations.

3. Most health care in the United States is delivered in traditional settings such as hospitals, physician organizations, and long-term care organizations. However, access to new delivery settings is becoming more readily available, and demand for care delivery through telemedicine and retail clinics is increasing. Give an example of an application for telemedicine. Discuss how the utilization of telemedicine might affect cost, quality, and access to care in the U.S. health care system.

4. Although the United States spends more money per capita on health care than any other country in the world, its performance has much room for improvement. How can ideas such as the Triple Aim initiative or patient centeredness help to improve performance in the U.S. health system?

5. Discuss why coordinated care delivery approaches, such as PCMHs or ACOs, might improve care for patients. Discuss barriers and opportunities for implementation of such coordinated care delivery approaches.

CASE STUDY

You have just been promoted to work as the assistant to the CEO of a large, partially integrated health care delivery system. Your first assignment is to identify several innovative ways to improve health system quality, control costs, and maximize access to care for citizens in your community. Opportunities exist to improve physician-hospital alignment and to provide more integrated care across health system entities. Draft a memo to your CEO that answers the following questions:

1. What are five innovative ideas that your health system could implement to meet improvement goals around cost, quality, and access?
2. What innovation or innovative idea is the most critical to ensure the health system achieves its goals?
3. What innovation will be the most difficult to achieve? Why?
4. Why will the implementation of these innovative ideas improve health system performance?

■ References

Agency for Healthcare Research and Quality. (2013). Retrieved from www.ahrq.gov

Ambulatory Surgical Center Association. (2013). *What is an ASC?* Retrieved from www
.ascassociation.org/AdvancingSurgicalCare/aboutascs/industryoverview

American Hospital Association (AHA). (2013). *Fast facts on U.S. hospitals.* Retrieved
from www.aha.org/research/rc/stat-studies/fast-facts.shtml

American Medical Association (AMA). (2013). *Policy research perspectives.* Retrieved
from http://www.nmms.org/sites/default/files/images/2013_9_23_ama_survey_prp
-physician-practice-arrangements.pdf

Centers for Disease Control and Prevention (CDC). (2010). *National hospital ambulatory
medical care survey: 2010 emergency department summary tables.* Retrieved from
http://www.cdc.gov/nchs/data/ahcd/nhamcs_emergency/2010_ed_web_tables.pdf

Centers for Medicare & Medicaid Services (CMS). (2013a). *Community-based care transitions program.* Retrieved from http://innovation.cms.gov/initiatives/CCTP/

Centers for Medicare & Medicaid Services (CMS). (2013b). *Pioneer accountable care
organizations succeed in improving care, lowering costs.* Retrieved from http://www
.cms.gov/Newsroom/MediaReleaseDatabase/Press-Releases/2013-Press-Releases
-Items/2013-07-16.html

Cleveland Clinic. (2013). *Facts & figures.* Retrieved from http://my.clevelandclinic.org/
about-cleveland-clinic/overview/who-we-are/facts-figures.aspx

Enthoven, A. C. (2009). Integrated delivery systems: The cure for fragmentation.
American Journal of Managed Care, 15(10 Suppl), S284–S290.

Gerteis, M., Edgman-Levitan, S., & Daley, J. (1993). *Through the patient's eyes: Understanding and promoting patient-centered care.* San Francisco, CA: Jossey-Bass.

Hirshon, J. M., Risko, N., Calvello, E. J. B., de Ramirez, S. S., Narayan, M., Theodosis, C.,
& O'Neill, J. (2013). Health systems and services: The role of acute care. *Bulletin of
the World Health Organization, 91,* 386–388.

Hwang, W., Chang, J., LaClair, M., & Paz, H. (2013). Effects of integrated delivery systems
on cost and quality. *American Journal of Managed Care, 19*(5), e175–e184.

Institute for Healthcare Improvement (IHI). (2013). *The IHI triple aim initiative.*
Cambridge, MA: Institute for Healthcare Improvement. Retrieved from http://www
.ihi.org/offerings/Initiatives/TripleAim/Pages/default.aspx

Institute of Medicine (IOM). (2001). *Crossing the quality chasm: A new health system for
the 21st century.* Washington, DC: National Academies Press.

Institute of Medicine (IOM). (2012). *An integrated framework for assessing the value of
community-based prevention.* Washington, DC: National Academies Press.

Intermountain Healthcare. (2013). Retrieved from http://intermountainhealthcare.org/
Pages/home.aspx

Kane, C. K., & Emmons, D. W. (2013). *Policy research perspectives: New data on physician
practice arrangements: Private practice remains strong despite shifts toward hospital
employment.* Chicago, IL: American Medical Association. Retrieved from http://www
.ama-assn.org/resources/doc/health-policy/prp-physician-practice-arrangements.pdf

Klein, S., & McCarthy, D. (2010). *Genesys HealthWorks: Pursuing the Triple Aim through
a primary care-based delivery system, integrated self-management support, and community partnerships.* New York, NY: The Commonwealth Fund. Retrieved from
http://www.commonwealthfund.org/~/media/files/publications/case-study/2010/
jul/triple-aim-v2/1422_mccarthy_genesys_triple_aim_case_study_v2.pdf

Mayo Clinic. (2013). *The Mayo culture.* Retrieved from http://www.mayoclinic.org/
physician-jobs/culture.html

National Association of Community Health Centers. (2013). Retrieved from http://www
.nachc.com

National Committee for Quality Assurance. (2011). *Standards and guidelines for NCQA's Patient-Centered Medical Home (PCMH) 2011*. Washington, DC: National Committee for Quality Assurance.

National Hospice and Palliative Care Organization. (2013). Retrieved from http://www.nhcpco.org

Nguyen, T. (2013). *Banner Health Network: The path to greater value in health care* [Presentation]. Retrieved from http://www.acmq.org/natlconf/2013/presentations/Nguyen%20-%20MQ2013%20Presentation.pdf

Rand Health. (2013). *Retail clinics play growing role in health care marketplace* [Special feature]. Retrieved from http://www.rand.org/health/feature/retail-clinics.html

Reid, R., Colman, K., Johnson, E., Fishman, P., Hsu, C., Soman, M., . . . Larson, E. (2010). The group health medical home at year two: Cost savings, higher patient satisfaction, and less burnout for providers. *Health Affairs, 29*(5), 835–843.

Scripps Health San Diego. (2013). *About us*. Retrieved from http://www.scripps.org/about-us__executive-team__chris-van-gorder

Social Security Act, 42 U.S.C. § 1867(e)(1)(A).

Sowers, K., Newman, P., & Langdon, J. (2013). Evolution of physician-hospital alignment models: A case study of comanagement. *Clinical Orthopaedics and Related Research, 471*(6), 1818–1823.

World Health Organization. (2015). Retrieved from http://www.who.int/healthsystems/hss_glossary/en/index5.html

10 The Health Workforce

Joanne Spetz and Susan A. Chapman

KEY WORDS

demand and supply
health professionals
interprofessional education
job training
labor markets

licensure
maldistribution
need-based demand
scope of practice
workforce planning

LEARNING OBJECTIVES

- ⊙ Understand the importance of the entire health workforce in delivering health care services
- ⊙ Critically assess the reasons for shortages of health care providers
- ⊙ Review new models and new roles of deploying health workers
- ⊙ Assess the effects of health reform on the health workforce

TOPICAL OUTLINE

- ⊙ Components of the workforce
- ⊙ Workforce planning to ensure adequate supplies of providers
- ⊙ Approaches to educating the workforce
- ⊙ Issues and challenges related to the workforce
- ⊙ Future trends related to workforce quality and adequacy

The health care workforce is essential to the delivery of health care; essentially all types of health services require the contributions of individual workers. The health care workforce includes well-known professionals such as nurses, pharmacists, and dentists; it also includes many other, less obvious professions that encompass a wide variety of technicians, therapists, assistants, administrative personnel, and managers. In 2011, there were approximately 14 million jobs in the health care industry in the United States, and compensation for these jobs accounted for nearly half of total health care spending—$846 million of the $1.7 billion spent on health care (U.S. Bureau of Economic Analysis, 2011). The health workforce's central role in all aspects of health care and its significant contribution to total health care costs guarantee that any policies intended to change how health care is financed or delivered will be fundamentally shaped by their interactions with the workforce. This fact becomes more complex when one recognizes that the health workforce plays an important role in economic development and income distribution. Health care jobs often pay well and are stable, and they are frequently filled by people living where the health care is provided (Gitterman, Spetz, & Fellowes, 2004; Zacker, 2011). As health reform reshapes the system of health care in the United States, we will continue to see major changes in the size, composition, and practice of health professionals. Such changes will be complicated by the broader role of health care employment in our economy and society.

■ Who Is Part of the Health Workforce?

The health workforce includes all health professionals and workers who contribute to the delivery of health care. The determination of who falls into this definition can involve some debate. Many occupations are consistently classified as being within the health workforce, such as physicians, radiation technologists, dental assistants, and nurses. Health occupations also include people who do not work in health care delivery settings but instead provide health services in homes, educational institutions, and other places, such as home care aides, personal care assistants, and school nurses (Bipartisan Policy Center, 2011; Matherlee, 2003). In 2012, these and related health care occupations included more than 13 million people, accounting for more than 1 in 12 workers in the United States (U.S. Bureau of Labor Statistics, 2013).

The largest health care occupation is registered nurses (RNs), of whom about 2.6 million were employed in 2012 (U.S. Bureau of Labor Statistics, 2013). Registered nurses work in nearly all health care settings; at least 60% work in hospitals (U.S. Bureau of Health Professions, 2010). Unlicensed nursing assistants are the second-largest health care occupation, with about 1.4 million workers employed. Unlicensed nursing assistants usually work in hospitals and long-term care facilities. About 620,000 certified nursing assistants work in skilled nursing facilities (U.S. Bureau of Labor Statistics, 2013). Licensed practical/vocational nurses are the third-largest occupation, representing 718,000 workers, although it should be noted that there are more personal care aides (985,230) than licensed practical/vocational nurses. There were about 611,650 physicians employed in the United States in 2012.

Other large occupations in health care include home health aides, medical assistants, dental assistants, pharmacy technicians, and emergency medical technicians/paramedics. The health care occupations also include licensed alternative and complementary providers, such as chiropractors and acupuncturists. Table 10.1 presents the 16 largest health care occupations in the United States.

The broadest definition of the health workforce includes anyone who works in a health care occupation or the health care industry, even if that worker is not directly involved in providing health care services—for example, insurance billing specialists, facilities managers, accountants, and other occupations. Within the health care industry, about 2.7 million people are employed in office and administrative occupations, such as secretaries and administrative assistants, information and records clerks, food preparation and food service workers, and education and training workers.

TABLE 10.1 LARGEST HEALTH CARE OCCUPATIONS IN THE UNITED STATES

Occupation	Number of Workers, 2012
Registered nurses	2,633,980
Nursing assistants	1,420,020
Personal care aides	985,230
Home health aides	839,930
Licensed practical nurses/vocational nurses	718,800
Physicians and surgeons	611,650
Medical assistants	553,140
Pharmacy technicians	353,340
Dental assistants	300,160
Pharmacists	281,560
Emergency medical technicians and paramedics	232,860
Radiological technologists	194,790
Physical therapists	191,460
Dental hygienists	190,290
Medical records and health information technologists	182,370
Medical and clinical laboratory technologists	160,700

■ Traditional Approaches to Health Workforce Planning

Approaches to health workforce planning vary across countries. Countries with national health care systems often closely manage the employment of health professionals, as well as the pipeline of new graduates from education programs. Many countries, including the United States, do not have a highly centralized health care system and engage in limited national health workforce planning efforts. Planning is left primarily to the private sector and local government agencies.

The traditional supply-and-demand approach to workforce planning compares the number of working health professionals to estimates of the demand for health workers. Projections of supply are typically built from data about the current number of workers, the number of new entrants per year, the number leaving the profession per year, and the share that is employed. In some cases, supply estimates account for other factors that may affect supply, such as the loss of health professionals to international migration. However, supply estimates rarely can estimate changes in overall supply that might arise due to the development of new health care occupations.

Projections of demand are usually based on current approaches to providing health care services. Some demand projections attempt to establish a targeted number of providers in order to deliver a desired level of services to the population. However, this "ideal" need-based demand may not align with budgetary realities, and thus not match the demand we actually see in the labor market. For example, during economic recessions the demand for health workers usually drops even though demand for health services may remain stable, because employers have less money for hiring. If the amount of money available in the health system is not sufficient to recruit workers and pay salaries, need-based demand and economic demand will diverge.

A growing body of research argues that new, integrated primary care delivery models, increased use of information technology, and expanded roles for nonphysician health professionals could solve shortages of primary care physicians.

Two fundamental shortcomings of workforce planning are that (a) it is usually tied to current care delivery models and (b) it treats each health professional independently. Innovative approaches to care delivery and team-based care could address many reported shortages of health professionals. For example, a growing body of research argues that new, integrated primary care delivery models, increased use of information technology, and expanded roles for nonphysician health professionals could solve shortages of primary care physicians (Auerbach et al., 2013; Bodenheimer & Smith, 2013; Rosenthal, 2014). In order to leverage such innovative approaches, policies and regulations that limit the functions (scope of practice) that can be performed by some health workers may need to be reformed. In addition, health professional education needs to focus on interprofessional collaboration rather than reinforce professional silos.

■ Health Workforce Education

Educational and training requirements vary significantly across health care occupations: Some health workers enter the field without a high school diploma, whereas others complete many years of postgraduate education. Many occupations, such as personal care aides and medical secretaries, require no formal preparation, and training occurs on the job. In other occupations, such as medical assistants and pharmacy technicians, there is variation in employers' preferences for formal education programs versus longer-term, on-the-job training.

Most technical health care occupations require some formal postsecondary education but not a degree; such occupations include surgical technicians, licensed practical/vocational nurses, and emergency medical technicians. A large share of education in these occupations occurs in private vocational schools; for example, about 90% of medical assistants are trained in private and for-profit schools (U.S. National Center for Education Statistics, 2012a). These schools often lack program-specific accreditation and standardized curricula. Some technical professions, such as dental hygienist, respiratory therapist, clinical laboratory technician, and radiology technician, require at least an associate degree. Registered nursing requires a minimum of an associate degree in most states, but many RNs complete baccalaureate education before becoming licensed. Finally, professions such as medicine, pharmacy, physical therapy, and optometry require postgraduate education, typically at the doctoral level.

Postsecondary education is available from many institutions: private vocational schools, public adult school programs, community colleges, and public and private colleges and universities. The costs of educational programs vary significantly. Private education is generally much more expensive than public education; in the 2011 to 2012 academic year, annual costs for public postsecondary education institutions averaged $14,292, whereas these costs averaged $33,047 for private institutions (U.S. National Center for Education Statistics, 2012b). Although prospective students might prefer to attend public institutions, these often have many fewer admission spaces than applicants. Health worker education is relatively expensive to deliver because it often requires the use of laboratories and involves closely supervised clinical training. Many public colleges and universities receive a fixed amount of funding per student, regardless of the major field of study. Thus, these schools face a financial loss if they expand their health professions programs rather than expanding less-costly programs. Moreover, because most health care jobs have relatively high pay, it can be difficult for colleges to recruit faculty.

Differences in the costs of educational programs affect the choices made by students, especially when cost is compared with expected earnings.

Differences in the costs of educational programs affect choices made by students, especially when cost is compared with expected earnings. For example, the education of a primary care physician requires 4 years of post-graduate medical school education, followed by three or more years of residency. Preparation for a specialized field of medicine such as cardiology typically requires more time; for example, a postresidency fellowship. Some research has demonstrated that medical students' choice of specialty is influenced by potential earnings compared with medical school debt, and that the lower earnings of primary care physicians do not compare favorably, even though other fields of medicine require more years of residency and fellowship training (Bodenheimer, Berenson, & Rudolf, 2007; Hauer et al., 2008). A mismatch between the cost of education and expected earnings can be found in other health occupations. For example, medical assistant wages averaged $14.12 per hour in 2012 (U.S. Bureau of Labor Statistics, 2014a), yet some medical assistants attend private training programs that charge tuition and fees of over $10,000 for a program of less than one year.

NEW APPROACHES TO HEALTH WORKFORCE EDUCATION

Health workforce education is traditionally focused on single professions. Physicians attend medical schools, nurses study in nursing schools, and dentists attend dental schools. These siloed education programs rarely offer opportunities to learn together either in the classroom or through clinical experience. Alternative health care professionals, such as chiropractors, are rarely educated alongside physicians or other professionals. However, a growing body of evidence finds that interprofessional education (IPE) and subsequent interprofessional practice, can improve the ability of health care professionals to provide high-quality patient-centered care (Barr, Koppel, Reeves, Hammick, & Freeth, 2005), including mental health care (Richards et al., 2013). Although the rapid emergence of initiatives to promulgate interprofessional education seems recent, their roots date back to more than 40 years ago, when the Institute of Medicine (IOM) published "Educating for the Health Team" (1972). The IOM's second report on this subject, "Health Professions Education: A Bridge to Quality," (2003) brought more attention to the imperative to revamp health workforce training. The report's authors argued that the silo approach to educating health professions contributes to continuing problems in the health care system.

Many private foundations, advocacy groups, and educational institutions are now actively developing and implementing IPE programs to address future health care needs. The Interprofessional Education Collaborative—a consortium including national organizations representing educators in allopathic and osteopathic medicine, dentistry, nursing, public health, and pharmacy—has made specific recommendations regarding the competencies required for successful interprofessional collaborative practice (Interprofessional Education Collaborative, 2011). The competencies fall under four domains: (a) values and ethics for interprofessional practice, (b) roles and responsibilities for collaborative practice, (c) interprofessional communication, and (d) interprofessional teamwork and team-based care. The National Center for Interprofessional Practice and Education, established through a cooperative agreement between the federal government and four private foundations, is leading, coordinating, and studying the advancement of interprofessional collaboration, with a particular focus on the effect of IPE on quality, patient outcomes, and costs.

■ Critical Issues for the Health Workforce

> *For nearly 15 years, it has been recognized that significant changes are needed to improve the quality of care, increase the health status of the U.S. population, and control health care costs.*

The implementation of the Patient Protection and Affordable Care Act (ACA) and a growing focus on the affordability of health care have brought new urgency to the need to reform the delivery of health care in the United States. For nearly 15 years, it has been recognized that significant changes are needed to improve the quality of care, increase the health status of the U.S. population, and control health care costs (IOM, 2000, 2001). These changes, however, may be difficult to implement in the face of ongoing and worsening shortages of health professionals. The most critical issues facing the health workforce now, in addition to the educational reforms described earlier, include ongoing shortages; changes in health care financing, which are rapidly spurring changes in the organization of care delivery; the role of new technologies in changing health professionals' work; the increasing importance of health care labor unions and labor–management partnerships; and the need to revamp regulations so that health professionals can meet health care needs more efficiently and effectively.

HEALTH PROFESSIONAL SHORTAGES

The implementation of the ACA has been accompanied by concerns that there is not an adequate workforce to meet the health care needs of the population, especially those people who will become newly insured (Ormond & Bovbjerg, 2011). It has long been known that people who are uninsured—or whose insurance is inadequate—face greater difficulty accessing care (Doescher, Skillman, & Rosenblatt, 2009; Shipman, Lan, Chang, & Goodman, 2011). The extension of insurance may lead to a surge in the demand for health services, as was observed when Massachusetts implemented health insurance reform. In that state, about 340,000 people gained health insurance in 1 year, and widespread shortages of primary care providers were reported (Sack, 2008). It has been widely expected that there will be a shortage of primary care providers as the ACA is implemented, along with longstanding shortages of other health professionals, which have been reported for at least 15 years (Bodenheimer & Pham, 2010; Colwill, Cultice, & Kruse, 2008; Cooper, Getzen, McKee, & Laud, 2002; Cooper, Laud, & Dietric, 1998; Dill & Salsberg, 2008; Nicholson, 2009; U.S. Bureau of Health Professions, 2008; Whitcomb & Cohen, 2004).

As discussed previously, shortages exist when demand is greater than supply. The economic response to a shortage is an increase in wages, which leads to greater supply (because compensation is more lucrative) and lower demand (because labor costs employers more). However, this normal economic response does not always occur in the labor markets for health professionals. First, wages may not change. The historic fee-for-service (FFS) reimbursement system favors specialized, complex, and procedurally oriented services. Because standard office visits receive lower payment, total compensation for primary care providers is lower. Significant changes in payment methods will be needed to rectify this differential.

The second reason health care labor markets might not follow standard economic behavior is that their supply is constrained by licensure and educational requirements. The time required to prepare a new health care professional for entry into the workforce can be many years. As noted earlier, for example, the education of a primary care physician requires 4 years of medical school education, followed by three or more years of residency. Interest in primary care among medical school students has been dropping for years, with particularly little interest in family medicine (Council on Graduate Medical Education, 2010; McGaha, Schmittling, DeVilbiss Bieck, Crosley, & Pugno, 2010). Registered nurses, who also must be licensed by any state in which they practice, must complete at least 2 years of postsecondary education before they are qualified to take a licensing examination (Buerhaus, Staiger, & Auerbach, 2009). Many other health professions, including physical therapists, medical technologists, and respiratory therapists, face similar licensing and education requirements. Several professions, such as physical therapy, occupational therapy, laboratory medicine, and speech therapy and audiology, have moved toward a clinical doctorate as the recommended or required entry-level education. This degree is not a PhD but is an advanced clinical degree that increases the number of years of education required to begin practice. There is controversy over the value of clinical doctorates in some of these professions and whether the added costs to students and the added years of education will be valued in the health care delivery system (Siler & Randolph, 2007; Dickerson & Trujillo, 2009).

Further constraining the supply of health professionals are limits on educational capacity. Allied health educational programs exemplify some of the challenges in producing an adequate number of health professionals. Educational programs can be expensive to operate, with small class sizes and the cost of supplies for clinical practicums. This is true for many occupations, including radiologic technicians, imaging specialties, and medical laboratory technologists. Many allied health professions education programs are taught in community college settings, where financial resources may be more limited than in universities and private colleges.

The aging of some health professions has been a major concern, including in the allied health workforce (California Hospital Association, 2009, 2014) and registered nursing (Buerhaus et al., 2009). In a survey conducted by the California Hospital Association, hospitals reported that even a few vacancies of very specialized allied health workers affect patient care services (California Hospital Association, 2014).

In addition to the challenge of educating enough health professionals, there is often a problem with the geographic distribution of those workers. In the United States, it has historically been difficult to recruit professionals into rural and poorer urban areas, particularly when jobs are plentiful elsewhere (Bourgueil, Mouseques, & Tajahmadi, 2006; Buchan & Calman, 2004). Despite direct government interventions in the form of academic stipends and loan forgiveness programs, access to primary care in particular remains a problem in many states and in specific regions of some states. Several analyses of health workforce needs for the ACA have reported that the maldistribution of professionals is a critical problem across professions (e.g., Bates, Blash, Chapman, Dower, & O'Neil, 2011). These and other studies have reported that training and retaining allied health workers in rural areas is also a challenge (California Hospital Association, 2009). For this reason, many rural health care programs use a "grow your own" approach recruiting and training students from rural areas to increase the likelihood they will stay to work in the area (IOM, 2011).

The problem of inadequate supply was anticipated to persist even before the ACA was passed. Population growth, the aging of the U.S. population, and increased rates of chronic illness are expected to increase the workloads of primary care providers over the next 15 years (Colwill et al., 2008; IOM, 2008). The proportion of the U.S. population over age 65 is rising rapidly, from 12.8% in 2012 to a projected 20% in 2030 (U.S. Census Bureau, 2012). This is important for the health care workforce for several reasons:

> Health care for older Americans costs more than for other age groups. Data from 2006 show average annual costs ranging from about $11,000, for those ages 65 to 74, to nearly $24,000 annually, for those over age 85 (Federal Interagency Forum on Aging-Related Statistics, 2010, p. 50). Those costs rise even more when one adds the cost of chronic conditions: Costs average $5,100 for those with no chronic conditions to over $25,000 annually for those with more than five chronic conditions.

> Older adults use more services from health professionals. Those over age 65 account for about 26% of all physician visits, 35% of all hospital stays, 34% of prescriptions, and 90% of nursing home use (IOM, 2008).

> Many health professions' curricula do not contain significant content in caring for older adults. At a time when we will most need generalists and specialists in geriatric care, the U.S. workforce is ill-prepared for these challenges.

> Members of the workforce that provides the bulk of long-term care in the home, community, and nursing homes are poorly paid, lack recognition for their work, and have high rates of job dissatisfaction and turnover (IOM, 2008).

The growth of health information technology also has implications for the workforce. With electronic health records, some occupations, such as medical transcriptionist, have become obsolete, whereas others, such as health information technician, are projected to add 41,000 new jobs in the next decade—representing a higher-than-average growth rate of 22% (U.S. Bureau of Labor Statistics, 2014a). Another effect of information technology is the increased opportunity to use telehealth for remote treatment and referrals (Courneya, Palattao, & Gallagher, 2013; Green, Savin, & Lu, 2013). For example, photos of skin lesions can be sent to dermatologists for diagnosis and psychiatrists may provide psychotherapeutic services at a distance using video teleconference technology.

CHANGES IN HEALTH CARE FINANCING AND THE ORGANIZATION OF CARE

Some provisions of the ACA are intended to increase the efficiency of health care delivery and are likely to affect the mix of health workers demanded. Performance-based payment programs, for example, will give health care organizations a financial incentive to focus on implementing models of care that can increase the quality of care at a reasonable cost (Davis & Guterman, 2007). For example, many studies have found that higher RN staffing levels in hospitals are linked to better patient outcomes (e.g., Aiken, Clarke, Sloane, Sochalski, & Silber, 2002; Kane, Shamliyan, Mueller, Duval, & Wilt, 2007; Lang, Hodge, Olson, Romano, & Kravitz, 2004; Needleman, Buerhaus, Mattke, Stewart, & Zelevinsky, 2002). Historically, however, hospitals have had little financial incentive to increase nurse staffing because higher-quality nursing care is not rewarded and nursing wages are expensive. Performance-based payment may lead hospitals to reconsider the value of increasing nurse staffing because there could be a financial gain in improving quality (Kurtzman & Buerhaus, 2008).

Bundled payments, which provide a single payment for hospital services during both initial hospitalization and any subsequent hospitalization for a fixed period of time, are anticipated to lead hospitals to invest in services to prevent rehospitalizations.

Two other innovations in health care financing are Medicare's bundled payment and accountable care organization (ACO) programs, both of which create financial incentives for health care providers to take full responsibility for an episode of care. This is a significant change from the FFS approach and will allow health care organizations to retain financial savings from delivering care efficiently, as long as quality is improved or maintained. The potential for financial gain will give health care providers an incentive to reassess their processes for providing care. Employing care managers, for example, may prove to be a good investment if their coordination of services leads to better outcomes and improved efficiency. Bundled payments, which provide a single payment for hospital services during both initial hospitalization and any subsequent hospitalization for a fixed period of time, are anticipated to lead hospitals to invest in services to prevent rehospitalizations. Postacute care services, such as nursing case management, home care visits, continued monitoring, and expanded patient education, may receive more emphasis, and the IOM (2010) anticipates that the role of RNs in this area will expand.

The ACA also includes provisions to support the patient-centered medical home (PCMH) model of care. A PCMH engages a team of providers in the delivery of care, typically including physicians, nurse practitioners (NPs), RNs, medical assistants, health educators, and pharmacists. Ideally, behavioral and mental health services are integrated into the PCMH (Bates et al., 2011). This and similar team-based approaches to providing primary care services may help to address anticipated shortages of primary care providers by increasing the roles of other health care professionals (Auerbach et al., 2013; Bates et al., 2011). In order for these models of care to be fully successful, however, educational programs need to be realigned to focus on interprofessional teams.

INFORMATION TECHNOLOGIES AND THE WORKFORCE

The rapid expansion of information technology in health care is changing the work of health professionals, as well as the way they communicate with each other and with family members. Electronic health records enable health workers to exchange information rapidly and to engage patients more actively in care. Recent research found that in one integrated health system there was a 25% decrease in primary care visits after the establishment of an electronic health record that facilitated greater use of telephone communication with patients (Chen, Garrido, Chock, Okawa, & Liang, 2009). Even though the expanded use of electronic health records shows promise to improve efficiency, enhance quality, and increase patient engagement in health care, the implementation of such technologies demands notable changes in skills and workflow. Electronic health records organize information differently than do traditional paper charts, and health professionals need to navigate through structured menus to enter information, rather than rely on simple templates and free text. Many organizations have found that in the short term these systems disrupt workflow, and workers with poor typing and computer skills are challenged to use them (Spetz, Phibbs, & Burgess, 2012). To make the best use of these systems, health workers need enhanced computer skills, and health care organizations must carefully redesign workflow to take best advantage of what electronic health records offer.

Telemedicine also is rapidly changing the capacity of the health care workforce, particularly in rural areas. Early use of telemedicine was limited largely to telephone communication, but high-resolution digital imaging, real-time two-way video communication, and rapid transmission of electronic health records make it possible for remote clinicians to access enough information to engage in complex consultations remotely. Rural communities are increasingly using electronic consultations to give patients access to specialists without traveling. Widespread adoption of these technologies in both urban and rural settings could greatly expand the capacity of the current workforce to meet health care needs (Weiner, Yeh, & Blumenthal, 2013).

HEALTH CARE UNIONS AND LABOR–MANAGEMENT PARTNERSHIPS

Growing numbers of health care workers are represented by unions; this trend dates to the 1970s when regulations permitted employees of nonprofit organizations to become unionized and eased the unionization of public-sector workers. About 14% of health practitioner and technical workers are represented by unions, as are 10% of health care support occupations (U.S. Bureau of Labor Statistics, 2014b). Unionized health workers tend to receive higher wages than those not represented by unions. Unions also have sought other concessions from employers, particularly hospitals, such as establishment of fixed nurse-to-patient ratios, preferred shifts based on employment tenure, and improved health and retirement benefits. Health care workers have engaged in highly visible strikes and labor actions; they are politically active, supporting legislation and candidates.

Some employers have developed good working relationships with their unions. For example, in 1997 the Service Employees International Union, which represents multiple health occupations, and 10 other unions partnered with Kaiser Permanente in a landmark agreement. The partnership focused on multiple goals, including improving quality of care for members, making Kaiser Permanente more competitive in its markets, making Kaiser Permanente an "employer of choice," and providing Kaiser Permanente employees with the "maximum possible employment and income security" (Kochan, McKersie, Eaton, & Adler, 2009). Since then, the unions and Kaiser Permanente have worked closely together to establish internal training programs, scholarships and grants for pursuing advanced education, and job transition programs. When Kaiser Permanente established a systemwide health information technology system, it worked with the union to ensure that employees received training and to find new roles for workers, such as clerks, whose jobs would be obviated by the electronic records. Although this partnership has not been without challenges, it has served as one model of a collaborative labor–management approach, rather than an adversarial relationship.

THE NEED FOR REGULATORY REFORM

The growth of team-based models of care, such as the PCMH, and continuing concerns about shortages of physicians have led many researchers and policy analysts to argue that nonphysician providers can and should play a larger role in the delivery of primary care. For example, about 65% of nurse practitioners provide primary care services (American College of Physicians, 2008). Many studies demonstrate that the quality of care delivered by NPs is at least equivalent to that of physicians, and some research has found that NPs have stronger patient communication skills (Horrocks, Anderson, & Salisbury, 2002; Lenz, Mundinger, & Kane, 2004; Newhouse et al., 2011). However, NPs face scope-of-practice laws that require them to work under physician supervision and limit their ability to prescribe medications (Sekscenski, Sansom, Bazell, Salmon, & Mullan, 1994; Wing, O'Grady, & Langelier, 2005). Removal of these barriers would enable NPs to practice to their fullest potential to meet health care needs (IOM, 2010). Regulations also limit the work of other health professionals, such as licensed practical nurses (LPNs) and medical assistants (Seago, Spetz, Chapman, Dyer, & Grumbach, 2004).

The often-stated purpose of scope-of-practice regulation across the professions is consumer protection: safeguarding consumers who cannot independently evaluate the skills or competence of health practitioners. State regulations, including licensure requirements, are meant to outline the basic education, skills, and competency of a health care professional. Sometimes these regulations outline what practitioners of a particular profession can do safely, and in some cases the regulations focus on what members of the profession are not allowed to do. Both the breadth of work permitted and prohibitions can be found in some state regulations.

The effect of NP scope-of-practice regulations has been studied more than those of other professions. There is substantial variation in the scope of practice permitted across states (Christian, Dower, & O'Neil, 2007). In 22 states, NPs are permitted to provide care independently, but in other states NPs are not permitted to practice without physician collaboration or supervision, often requiring written practice protocols, and sometimes including restrictions on the number of NPs with whom a physician may collaborate (Christian et al., 2007; National Council of State Boards of Nursing, 2013). Even when NPs can practice independently, they may be required to have a collaborative or supervisory relationship with a physician to prescribe medications. Restrictive scope-of-practice regulations for NPs have been linked to lower utilization of primary care services (Stange, 2013) and higher costs in retail health care clinics (Spetz & Parente, 2013). At the same time, several systematic reviews have concluded that primary care services provided by NPs are of similar quality as physician care (Horrocks et al., 2002; Lenz et al., 2004; Newhouse et al., 2011). In order to fully leverage the capacity of the health workforce and align care processes to emerging financial incentives, scope-of-practice regulations may need to be reconsidered.

■ Conclusion: Building the Future Health Care Workforce

The health workforce is central to the health care system, and changes in its deployment and utilization will have significant effects on health care quality and costs. The ACA and rising concerns about the efficiency of health care delivery are bringing renewed attention to the importance of team-based care models, interprofessional education, and scope-of-practice regulations. At the same time, concerns and ongoing and emerging shortages of health workers persist. The U.S. Bureau of Labor Statistics estimates that the number of people employed in health occupations will rise to over 15 million by 2022, accounting for more than 1 in 11 jobs. The importance of this workforce to both health care and the overall economy will keep the health professions in the policy spotlight for the foreseeable future.

■ Discussion Questions

1. What are advantages of need-based models of demand? What are disadvantages of this approach to estimating demand?
2. If changes to scope-of-practice regulations could help to abate health worker shortages, why are such changes not made?
3. What are the potential risks in relying more on telemedicine and electronic communication to help meet the need for health care services?

CASE STUDY

You are the newly hired director of human resources (HR) for a large inner-city health care organization. The CEO has asked you to develop a strategic response to numerous HR problems. The main problem has been the inability to recruit new physicians and registered nurses. This problem is compounded by a lack of team work among clinicians and between service departments, and a high rate of turnover of some of the best workers while less able workers remain employed.

In writing your strategic response, consider the following questions:

1. What strategies could be undertaken in the short term to address these problems?
2. What approaches could be taken in the long term?
3. Which of these approaches can be undertaken by the HR department on its own, and which require collaboration with employee groups and/or HR directors at neighboring employers?
4. Choose three short-term priorities and defend them. How might they segue into a long-term strategy?

■ References

Aiken, L., Clarke, S., Sloane, D., Sochalski, J., & Silber, J. (2002). Hospital nurse staffing and patient mortality, nurse burnout, and job dissatisfaction. *Journal of the American Medical Association, 288*, 1987–1993.

American College of Physicians. (2008). *How is a shortage of primary care physicians affecting the quality and cost of medical care?* Philadelphia, PA: Author. Retrieved from www.acponline.org/advocacy/where_we_stand/policy/primary_shortage.pdf

Auerbach, D. I., Chen, P. G., Friedberg, M. W., Reid, R., Lau, C., Buerhaus, P. I., & Mehrotra, A. (2013). Nurse-managed health centers and patient-centered medical homes could mitigate expected primary care physician shortage. *Health Affairs, 32*(11), 1933–1941.

Barr, H., Koppel, I., Reeves, S., Hammick, M., & Freeth, D. (2005). *Effective interprofessional education: Argument, assumption and evidence.* Oxford, UK: Blackwell Publishing.

Bates, T., Blash, L., Chapman, S., Dower, C., & O'Neil, E. (2011). *California's health care workforce: Readiness for the ACA era.* San Francisco, CA: Center for the Health Professions at the University of California.

Bipartisan Policy Center. (2011). *The complexities of national health care workforce planning.* Washington, DC: Bipartisan Policy Center. Retrieved from http://bipartisanpolicy.org/wp-content/uploads/sites/default/files/Workforce%20study_Public%20Release%20040912.pdf

Bodenheimer, T. S., & Smith, M. D. (2013). Primary care: Proposed solutions to the physician shortage without training more physicians. *Health Affairs, 32*(11), 1881–1886.

Bodenheimer, T., & Pham, H. H. (2010). Primary care: Current problems and proposed solutions. *Health Affairs, 29*(5), 799–805.

Bodenheimer, T., Berenson, R. A., & Rudolf, P. (2007). The primary care-specialty income gap: Why it matters. *Annals of Internal Medicine, 146*(4), 301–306.

Bourgueil, Y., Mouseques, J., & Tajahmadi, A. (2006). *Improving the geographical distribution of health professionals: What the literature tells us. Health economics letter.* Paris, France: Institute for Research and Information in Health Economics.

Buchan, J., & Calman, L. (2004). *The global shortage of registered nurses: An overview of issues and actions.* Geneva, Switzerland: International Council of Nurses.

Buerhaus, P. I., Staiger, D. O., & Auerbach, D. I. (2009). *The future of the nursing workforce in the United States: Data, trends, and implications.* Sudbury, MA: Jones and Bartlett Publishers.

California Hospital Association. (2009). *Allied health: The hidden healthcare workforce.* Retrieved from http://calhospital.org/general-information/allied-health-hidden-health-care-workforce

California Hospital Association. (2014). *Critical roles: California's allied health workforce follow-up report.* Retrieved from http://www.calhospital.org/critical-roles

Chen, C., Garrido, T., Chock, D., Okawa, G., & Liang, L. (2009). The Kaiser Permanente electronic health record: Transforming and streamlining modalities of care. *Health Affairs, 28*(2), 323–333.

Christian, S., Dower, C., & O'Neil, E. (2007). *Overview of nurse practitioner scopes of practice in the United States.* San Francisco, CA: University of California Center for the Health Professions. Retrieved from http://futurehealth.ucsf.edu/Content/29/2007-12_Overview_of_Nurse_Practitioner_Scopes_of_Practice_In_the_United_States_Discussion.pdf

Colwill, J. M., Cultice, J. M., & Kruse, R. L. (2008). Will generalist physician supply meet demands of an increasing and aging population? *Health Affairs, 27*, w232–w241.

Cooper, R. A., Getzen, T. E., McKee, H. J., & Laud, P. (2002). Economic and demographic trends signal an impending physician shortage. *Health Affairs, 21*(1), 140–154.

Cooper, R. A., Laud, P., & Dietric, C. L. (1998). Current and projected workforce of nonphysician clinicians. *Journal of the American Medical Association, 280*, 788–794.

Council on Graduate Medical Education. (2010). *COGME 20th report: Advancing primary care.* Rockville, MD: Health Resources and Services Administration. Retrieved from http://www.hrsa.gov/advisorycommittees/bhpradvisory/cogme/Reports/index.html

Courneya, P. T., Palattao, K. J., & Gallagher, J. M. (2013). HealthPartners' online clinic for simple conditions delivers savings of $88 per episode and high patient approval. *Health Affairs, 32*(2), 385–392.

Davis, K., & Guterman, S. (2007). Rewarding excellence and efficiency in Medicare payments. *Milbank Quarterly, 85*, 449–468.

Dickerson, A. E., & Trujillo, L. (2009). Practitioners' perceptions of the occupational therapy clinical doctorate. *Journal of Allied Health, 18*(1), e47–e53.

Dill, M. J., & Salsberg, E. S. (2008). *The complexities of physician supply and demand: Projections through 2025.* Washington, DC: Association of American Medical Colleges.

Doescher, M. P., Skillman, S. M., & Rosenblatt, R. A. (2009). *The crisis in primary care.* Seattle, WA: Rural Health Research Center. Retrieved from http://depts.washington.edu/uwrhrc/uploads/Rural_Primary_Care_PB_2009.pdf

Federal Interagency Forum on Aging-Related Statistics. (2010). *Older Americans 2010: Key indicators of well-being* [Forum]. Washington, DC: U.S. Government Printing Office.

Gitterman, D., Spetz, J., & Fellowes, M. (2004). *The other side of the ledger: Federal health spending in metropolitan economies.* Washington, DC: The Brookings Institution. Retrieved from http://www.brookings.edu/research/reports/2004/09/labormarkets-gitterman

Green, L. V., Savin, S., & Lu, Y. (2013). Primary care physician shortages could be eliminated through use of teams, nonphysicians, and electronic communication. *Health Affairs, 32*(1), 11–19.

Hauer, K. E., Durning, S. J., Kernan, W. N., Fagan, M. J., Mintz, M., O'Sullivan, P. S., . . . Schwartz, M. D. (2008). Factors associated with medical students' career choices regarding internal medicine. *Journal of the American Medical Association, 300*(10), 1154–1164.

Horrocks, S., Anderson, E., & Salisbury, C. (2002). Systematic review of whether nurse practitioners working in primary care can provide equivalent care to doctors. *British Medical Journal, 324,* 819–823.

Institute of Medicine. (1972). *Educating for the health team.* Washington, DC: National Academy of Sciences.

Institute of Medicine. (2000). *To err is human: Building a safer health system.* Washington, DC: National Academies Press.

Institute of Medicine. (2001). *Crossing the quality chasm: A new health system for the 21st century.* Washington, DC: National Academies Press.

Institute of Medicine. (2003). *Health professions education: A bridge to quality.* Washington, DC: National Academies Press.

Institute of Medicine. (2008). *Retooling for an aging America: Building the health care workforce.* Washington, DC: National Academies Press.

Institute of Medicine. (2010). *The future of nursing: Leading change, advancing health.* Washington, DC: National Academies Press.

Institute of Medicine. (2011). *Allied health workforce and services: Workshop summary.* Washington, DC: National Academies Press.

Interprofessional Education Collaborative. (2011). *Core competencies for interprofessional collaborative practice.* Washington, DC: Association of American Medical Colleges.

Kane, R. L., Shamliyan, T. A., Mueller, C., Duval, S., & Wilt, T. J. (2007). The association of registered nurse staffing levels and patient outcomes. Systematic review and meta-analysis. *Medical Care, 45,* 1195–1204.

Kochan, T., McKersie, R., Eaton, A., & Adler, P. (2009). *Healing together: The labor-management partnership at Kaiser Permanente.* Ithaca, NY: Cornell University Press.

Kurtzman, E., & Buerhaus, P. (2008). New Medicare payment rules: Danger or opportunity for nursing? *American Journal of Nursing, 108,* 30–35.

Lang, T. A., Hodge, M., Olson, V., Romano, P. S., & Kravitz, R. L. (2004). Nurse-patient ratios: A systematic review on the effects of nurse staffing on patient, nurse employee, and hospital outcomes. *Journal of Nursing Administration, 34,* 326–337.

Lenz, E., Mundinger, M., & Kane, R. (2004). Primary care outcomes in patients treated by nurse practitioners or physicians: Two-year follow-up. *Medical Care, 61*(3), 332–351.

Matherlee, K. (2003). *The U.S. health workforce: Definitions, dollars, and dilemmas.* Washington, DC: National Health Policy Forum. Retrieved from http://www.nhpf.org/library/background-papers/BP_Workforce_4-03.pdf

McGaha, A. L., Schmittling, G. T., DeVilbiss Bieck, A. D., Crosley, P. W., & Pugno, P. A. (2010). Entry of US medical school graduates into family medicine residencies: 2009–2010 and 3-year summary. *Family Medicine, 42*(8), 540–551.

National Council of State Boards of Nursing (NCSBN). (2013). NCSBN's APRN Campaign for Consensus: State progress toward uniformity. Implementation status map. Retrieved from https://www.ncsbn.org/5397.htm

Needleman, J., Buerhaus, P., Mattke, S., Stewart, M., & Zelevinsky, K. (2002). Nurse-staffing levels and the quality of care in hospitals. *New England Journal of Medicine, 346,* 1715–1722.

Newhouse, R. P., Stanik-Hutt, J., White, K. M., Johantgen, M., Bass, E. B., Zangaro, G., . . . Weiner, J. P. (2011). Advanced practice nurse outcomes 1990-2008: A systematic review. *Nursing Economics, 29*(5), 1–21.

Nicholson, S. (2009). *Will the United States have a shortage of physicians in 10 years?* Princeton, NJ: Robert Wood Johnson Foundation.

Ormond, B. A., & Bovbjerg, R. R. (2011). *Assuring access to care under health reform: The key role of workforce policy.* Washington, DC: The Urban Institute.

Richards, D. A., Hill, J. J., Gask, L., Lovell, K., Chew-Graham, C., Bower, P., . . . Barkham, M. (2013). Clinical effectiveness of collaborative care for depression in UK primary care (CADET): Cluster randomised controlled trial. *British Medical Journal, 347,* f4913.

Rosenthal, T. C. (2014). The medical home: Growing evidence to support a new approach to primary care. *Journal of the American Board of Family Medicine, 21*(5), 427–440.

Sack, K. (2008, April 5). In Massachusetts, universal coverage strains care. *The New York Times.* Retrieved from http://www.nytimes.com/2008/04/05/us/05doctors.html

Seago, J. A., Spetz, J., Chapman, S., Dyer, W., & Grumbach, K. (2004). *Supply, demand, and use of licensed practical nurses.* Rockville, MD: Bureau of Health Professions, Health Resources, and Services Administration.

Sekscenski, E., Sansom, S., Bazell, C., Salmon, M. E., & Mullan, F. (1994). State practice environments and the supply of physician assistants, nurse practitioners, and certified nurse-midwives. *New England Journal of Medicine, 331*(19), 1266–1271.

Shipman, S. A., Lan, J., Chang, C., & Goodman, D. C. (2011). Geographic maldistribution of primary care for children. *Pediatrics, 127,* 19–27.

Siler, W. L., & Randolph, D. S. (2007). A clinical look at clinical doctorates. *Audiology Today, 19*(1), 22–23.

Spetz, J., & Parente, S. T. (2013). Nurse practitioner scope of practice and cost savings from retail clinics. *Health Affairs, 32*(11), 1977–1984.

Spetz, J., Phibbs, C. S., & Burgess, J. F. (2012). What determines successful implementation of inpatient information technology systems? *American Journal of Managed Care, 19*(3), 157–162.

Stange, K. (2013). How does provider supply and regulation influence health care markets? Evidence from nurse practitioners and physician assistants. *Journal of Health Economics, 33,* 1–27.

U.S. Bureau of Economic Analysis. (2011). *Gross-domestic-product-(GDP)-by-industry data.* Retrieved from http://www.bea.gov/industry/gdpbyind_data.htm

U.S. Bureau of Health Professions. (2008). *The physician workforce: Projections and research into current issues affecting supply and demand, IV: Adequacy of physician supply.* Rockville, MD: Health Resources and Services Administration. Retrieved from http://bhpr.hrsa.gov/healthworkforce/reports/physwfissues.pdf

U.S. Bureau of Health Professions. (2010). *The registered nurse population: Findings from the 2008 National Sample Survey of Registered Nurses.* Rockville, MD: Health Resources and Services Administration.

U.S. Bureau of Labor Statistics. (2013). *Occupational employment statistics.* Retrieved from http://www.bls.gov/oes/current/oes_stru.htm

U.S. Bureau of Labor Statistics. (2014a). *Occupational outlook handbook.* Retrieved from http://www.bls.gov/ooh/Healthcare/Medical-assistants.htm

U.S. Bureau of Labor Statistics. (2014b). *Union members—2013.* Retrieved from http://www.bls.gov/news.release/pdf/union2.pdf

U.S. Census Bureau. (2012). *National population projections: Summary tables.* Retrieved from http://www.census.gov/population/projections/data/national/2012/summary-tables.html

U.S. National Center for Education Statistics. (2012a). *Integrated postsecondary education data system.* Retrieved from http://nces.ed.gov/ipeds/

U.S. National Center for Education Statistics. (2012b). *Digest of education statistics.* Retrieved from http://nces.ed.gov/programs/digest/d12/tables/dt12_381.asp

Weiner, J. P., Yeh, S., & Blumenthal, D. (2013). The impact of health information technology and e-health on the future demand for physician services. *Health Affairs, 32*(11), 1998–2004.

Whitcomb, M. E., & Cohen, J. J. (2004). The future of primary care medicine. *New England Journal of Medicine, 351*(7), 710–712.

Wing, P., O'Grady, E., & Langelier, M. (2005). Changes in the legal practice environment of nurse practitioners. *American Journal for Nurse Practitioners, 9*(2), 25–39.

Zacker, H. B. (2011). Creating career pathways for frontline health care workers. *Jobs to careers: Transforming the front lines of health care.* Retrieved from http://beltlineorg.wpengine.netdna-cdn.com/wp-content/uploads/2013/07/J2C_CareerPathways_011011.pdf

11 Health Care Financing

James R. Knickman

KEY WORDS

accountable care organizations (ACOs)
consumer-driven health care
diagnosis-related groups (DRGs)
health maintenance organizations
   (HMOs)
individual insurance market
payer mix

preferred provider organizations
   (PPOs)
private insurance
public insurance
safety-net provider
third-party payers

LEARNING OBJECTIVES

- Understand trends in U.S. health care spending over time
- Explain the flow of funds into the health system (who pays) and the flow of funds through the system (how providers are paid)
- Understand the major categories of services purchased
- Differentiate between public and private spending and purchasing in addition to the categories of health plan types within the public and private systems
- Explain how 2010 federal health reform legislation is changing the health care financing system
- Describe the major reimbursement mechanisms for health care services
- Understand current policy issues in health care financing

TOPICAL OUTLINE

- General overview of health care financing
- What the money buys and where it comes from
- How health insurance works
- How health reform may affect the financing system
- Reimbursement approaches
- Current policy issues in financing

No matter what role an individual or an organization plays in the U.S. health care system, the complex way that we pay for health services in this country influences what is done and how it is done. Almost every aspect of how we organize health care services and how we manage them is shaped by how services are paid for. Most attempts to improve quality or to shift resources from one type of health care to another (e.g., from hospital care to primary care or from acute care services to preventive services) also are shaped by how these services are funded.

This chapter explains the processes used to pay for health care in the United States. Over the past 5 to 10 years, there has been substantial flux in our national approach to paying for care. The Obama administration's ambitious Patient Protection and Affordable Care Act (ACA) of 2010 has extended health insurance coverage to large numbers of Americans—perhaps as many as 24 million people—affecting both individuals and providers. In addition, ongoing national concern about the affordability of medical care has led to much activity among payers—especially government payers—to find new payment approaches that moderate expenditure growth trends.

This chapter considers the types of care that are paid for, how individuals go about paying for care, and how providers are paid. The chapter also explains the types of insurance and how each works, how the 2010 federal health reforms changing financing, and how reimbursement systems have evolved for paying providers and creating incentives for quality and efficiency. Finally, it describes emerging approaches for limiting the growth of health expenditures in the years to come.

■ General Overview of Health Care Financing

If we think of health care as a service that people need to purchase, we find that the approach used to purchase this service is far different from the typical approach for purchasing other kinds of services or commodities in our economy.

What do we mean by the "financing of health care"? This overarching question includes not only how we pay for care, but also who pays for care, how transactions between users and providers are handled, and how many total dollars are spent on care. If we think of health care as a service that people need to purchase, we find that the approach used to purchase this service is far different from the typical approach for purchasing other kinds of services or commodities in our economy.

For most goods and services other than medical care (such as an automobile or a massage), we use a simple payment system: If you want an item, you pay money for it directly. Suppliers of goods and services set prices they think make sense; if a purchaser is willing to pay the price (sometimes there may be a bit of haggling) the transaction happens, and the purchaser buys the service. In the U.S. market-based economy, the consumer needs only to have enough money to make the purchase, and the transaction occurs with little intervention from the government or anybody else.

Health care is not a normal commodity or service, however, because of two features:

- The need for health care varies starkly from one individual to another: 20% of Americans use 80% of all health care dollars expended in any given year.
- The cost of health care is very high, and many people could not afford it if they had to pay cash each time they needed a service. For example, in 2011 a typical 5-day

stay in a hospital could cost well over $25,000. An MRI to diagnose the presence of a tumor could cost anywhere between $1,000 and $12,000, depending on where it is done and who is paying for it.

To overcome the obstacle of high costs, the United States has developed an insurance system that allows us to pay for services collectively. Put most simply, we pool our risks for needing health care. In essence, each individual pays an insurance company the average annual costs of health care across the group of people covered by the insurance company. When these premiums are pooled across a population of people (often employees of a company), there is enough money to pay the expenses of the minority of people who need costly health care. Most of the time, people pay for health insurance but never use many (or any) of the dollars they put into the pool. In a year when someone has high health care needs, however, that person benefits from being able to tap many more resources from the insurance pool than he or she contributed.

This description greatly oversimplifies how the financing system really works across a range of dimensions. In fact:

- There are many types of health insurance; some are publicly paid for through taxes, some are paid for by employers, and others are paid for by individuals directly.
- Insurance does not pay for the entire costs of an individual's health care. Usually, insurance pays only a share of the costs and the individual pays the rest. How this copayment arrangement is structured varies greatly from insurance plan to insurance plan and can be quite complex.
- When insurance becomes involved in the transaction between a service provider and a user of the service, there are rules regarding which services the insurer will pay for and how much it will pay for them. These insurance reimbursement rules also can become incredibly complex and confusing.
- When people do not directly and fully pay for services, economists worry that they will use more services than they need or that a provider will deliver more care than needed. An insurance system must create incentives to avoid overuse and oversupply, or systemwide expenditures could skyrocket.

The U.S. health care financing system has evolved since World War II, when the first health insurance products began to be marketed. In the 1960s, wide-scale public insurance programs were enacted: Medicare, which is insurance for the elderly and the permanently disabled, and Medicaid, which is an insurance-type system for low-income Americans (see Chapter 3).

The U.S. system of financing health care is quite distinct from those used in other developed nations (see Chapter 4). Most other developed countries have a system that involves a set of services to which every citizen is entitled, which is paid for by the central government. In these situations, private insurance companies either help to manage the government-financed system or offer supplementary or alternative coverage.

The emergence of insurance in the United States in the 1940s occurred as new, more effective types of health care technology and practices were being developed. The combination of insurance and rapidly expanding clinical advances led to an expenditure explosion in the 1970s, which has continued ever since. In 1970, U.S. health expenditures totaled $74.9 billion and represented 7.2% of the nation's gross domestic product (GDP)—that is, 7.2% of all goods and services purchased in our economy

TABLE 11.1 NATIONAL HEALTH EXPENDITURES (IN $ BILLIONS), SELECTED CATEGORIES AND YEARS, 1970–2020

	Actual		Projected
Type of Expenditure	**1970**	**2013**	**2020**
Total National Health Expenditures	$74.9	$2,914.7	$4,416.2
Total of All Personal Health Care	63.1	2,452.3	3,717.8
Hospital Care	27.2	929.0	1,397.4
Physician and Clinical Services	14.3	588.8	890.4
Prescription Drugs	5.5	262.3	397.9
Program Administration and Net Cost of Private Health insurance	2.6	217.1	339.1

Sources: 2005–2015 data (Centers for Medicare & Medicaid Services, 2007); 1970 and 2000 data (Levit, Smith, Cowan, Sensenig, Catlin, & the Health Accounts Team, 2004).

were health related. By 2020, health expenditures are expected to reach nearly $4.4 trillion, or 19.2% of GDP (see Table 11.1 and Figure 11.1).

■ What the Money Buys and Where It Comes From

If we consider all types of expenditures in the health system, the total national bill in 2013 was $2.9 trillion dollars. The overwhelming share of this money ($2.5 trillion, or 86%) paid for personal health care services to individuals, whereas the balance paid for public health services, research, and administrative costs associated with running the

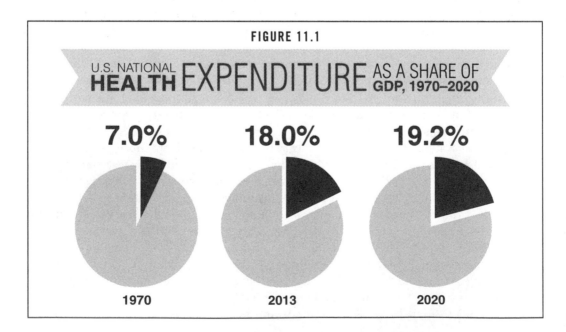

FIGURE 11.1

U.S. NATIONAL HEALTH EXPENDITURE AS A SHARE OF GDP, 1970–2020

| 7.0% | 18.0% | 19.2% |
| 1970 | 2013 | 2020 |

delivery and financing system (see Table 11.1). Among personal health care services, 73% of expenditures focus on three types of care: (a) hospital care, the largest type by far; (b) physician and other clinical services; and (c) prescription drugs. Administrative costs associated with running the health insurance and other regulatory systems represent 9% of expenditures for personal health care services.

HOW INDIVIDUALS PAY FOR HEALTH CARE

We begin with basics, considering how individuals pay for health care when they become ill or injured. In essence, there are two main ways an individual pays for a service: (a) through the person's insurance coverage or (b) out-of-pocket from income or savings. For people who are uninsured and have no money, there is a third option: They can attempt to obtain the service free, as a charity case, through a *safety-net provider*. States have various laws about when providers must give charity care, and the insurance system—especially public insurance—gives providers some money to help reimburse them for the charity care they deliver.

People who have either a public or a private insurance policy usually can receive services after showing their insurance card. The provider then bills the insurance company directly, although some providers demand that the individual pays the bill when the service is provided, in which case the individual must seek reimbursement from the insurer. If a person's insurance will pay for only part of the bill, the individual is usually responsible for paying the balance at the time services are delivered.

■ How Health Insurance Works

A range of insurance types cover different subsets of the U.S. population. The first key differentiation among them is *public programs* versus *privately sponsored insurance products*.

Public insurance programs include Medicare, for the elderly and disabled; Medicaid, for low-income individuals; and other public insurance systems for low-income individuals, such as the Children's Health Insurance Program (CHIP), which covers children who are ineligible for Medicaid. Other public insurance programs cover veterans, public employees, members of the armed services and their families, and Native Americans.

Private insurance coverage varies depending on who pays for it. Small employers can purchase coverage for their workers through commercial companies (such as Blue Cross plans or insurance companies like UnitedHealthcare, Aetna, or Kaiser Permanente). Individuals who work for employers that offer no coverage or who are self-employed or unemployed also may buy insurance through commercial companies. Individuals also can buy insurance through the insurance exchanges that were established by the ACA. These exchanges link individuals to a range of commercial insurance offerings, and the federal government subsidizes the premiums charged within the exchange for families with earnings between 138% and 400% of the federal poverty level (FPL). Large employers can buy coverage from commercial companies, or they can self-insure. Large employers often can save substantial costs by self-insuring, which they can do because they have so many employees that the risks balance out. When an employer does self-insure, it usually engages a commercial insurance company to manage the plan and enforce its rules.

PUBLICLY FINANCED PROGRAMS

Medicaid

Medicaid originally was designed to assist recipients of public assistance—primarily single-parent families and low-income people who are aged, blind, or disabled (see Chapter 3). Over the years, Medicaid has expanded to include additional groups and now covers poor children, their parents, pregnant women, the disabled, and very poor adults (including those 65 and older). Much public attention is given to Medicaid's role in covering children's care; in reality, however, 64% of its expenditures support care for the 35% of enrollees who are elderly or disabled (see Figure 11.2).

Medicaid is administered by the states, and state and federal governments both finance the program. Except for minimum mandatory benefits, the federal government gives states flexibility in implementing and administering Medicaid to best meet the needs of their residents. As a result, there are many seemingly arbitrary differences in eligibility and coverage across states.

The ACA has provisions to expand the range of services covered by each state through the Medicaid program. The ACA also uses federal funds to expand the income eligibility for Medicaid to all individuals living in families with incomes below 138% of the FPL. However, court challenges to this provision have led to allowing states to opt out of accepting federal funds to expand coverage. In 2014, 22 states had chosen not to expand Medicaid eligibility (Kaiser Family Foundation, 2015).

A major change in Medicaid occurred when many states adopted a managed care approach in the early 1990s. In this payment strategy, the state usually pays a fixed, or "capitated," payment to an insurer, who then is responsible for keeping average costs for Medicaid patients below this fixed payment level. It has been difficult, however, for many states to accrue savings using a managed care approach. In most states, Medicaid already paid providers rates that were below (sometimes significantly below) commercial levels, and it was difficult for managed care insurers to reduce them further. Additional reductions would have squeezed safety-net providers, which largely depend on Medicaid revenues, jeopardizing their financial viability.

Medicare

Administered by the federal government, Medicare originally targeted people 65 and over, but it was quickly expanded to cover people with disabilities and severe kidney disease. To qualify, an individual must be a U.S. resident for a specified number of years and pay the Federal Insurance Contributions Act (FICA) payroll tax for at least 10 years. The entitlement was expanded in 1972 to allow people who did not meet the latter requirement to pay a premium for coverage. Even though enrollment in Medicare has doubled since its passage, annual expenditures have increased about 40-fold, making the federal government the nation's single largest payer of health care expenses.

Medicare has two parts: Part A, which is hospital insurance, and Part B, which is supplemental medical insurance covering physician services and outpatient care. The Balanced Budget Act of 1997 established the Medicare+Choice program,

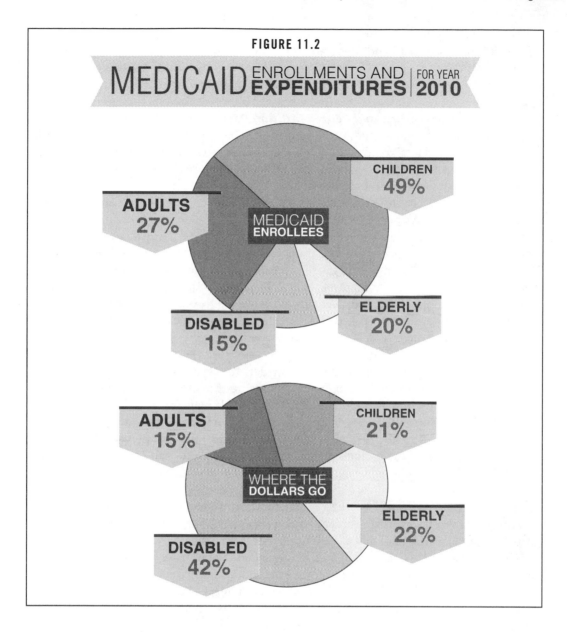

FIGURE 11.2

MEDICAID ENROLLMENTS AND EXPENDITURES FOR YEAR 2010

MEDICAID ENROLLEES

CHILDREN 49%
ADULTS 27%
ELDERLY 20%
DISABLED 15%

WHERE THE DOLLARS GO

CHILDREN 21%
ADULTS 15%
ELDERLY 22%
DISABLED 42%

designed to build on existing Medicare managed care programs and expand options under Part B.

In the 1980s and 1990s, Medicare experienced a series of changes to its payment mechanisms, which appear as dips in the overall growth rate of national health expenditures. In the 1980s, Medicare started paying hospitals under a payment system that set fixed prices (varying by region and the intensity of service required) for each stay in a hospital by a Medicare-covered patient. By the 1990s, Medicare also had started paying physicians differently using fixed payment schedules for different types of physician services.

The George W. Bush administration added pharmaceutical coverage to Medicare through the Medicare Modernization Act, passed in December 2003. This coverage was expanded for Medicare enrollees as a part of the ACA of 2010.

Other Public Programs
In addition to Medicaid and Medicare, the United States has a patchwork of govern-ment health care programs for special populations: active duty and retired military personnel and their families, Native Americans, and injured and disabled workers.

Programs for Active Duty and Retired Military Personnel. Historically, most health care needs of active duty military personnel have been handled in military facilities, where retirees and families also could receive free treatment on a space-available basis. U.S. Department of Defense spending on medical care more than tripled from 1988 to 2005, rising from $14.6 billion to $49 billion.

The Veterans Health Administration, the health care system of the Department of Veterans Affairs (VA), operates the largest integrated health care system in the United States, providing primary care, specialized care, and related medical and social sup-port services to U.S. veterans and their dependents. In recent years, the VA has faced stiff criticism for its waiting lists for services due to a large number of returning vet-erans from the Iraq and Afghanistan conflicts as well as the aging of many veterans who served during the Vietnam War. There have been expanded initiatives to allow veterans to use community-based services when they find it difficult to gain access to services provided directly by VA-run health care facilities.

The Indian Health Service. In 1921, the Snyder Act established a program of health services for Native Americans, known today as the Indian Health Service (IHS) and administered by the U.S. Department of Health and Human Services (DHHS). Eligible are members of federally recognized Indian tribes and their descendants. The pro-gram's budget is approximately $3 billion to $4 billion annually, and it serves approxi-mately 1.9 million of the nation's estimated 3.3 million American Indians and Alaska Natives (DHHS, 2010).

Workers' Compensation. Workers' compensation is an insurance system intended to protect workers against the costs of medical care and loss of income resulting from work-related injuries and, in some cases, illnesses. Underlying workers' compensation is the premise that all job-related injuries, regardless of fault, are a result of the risks of employment, and the employer and employee should share the burden of loss. Work-ers' compensation programs are operated by the states, each with its own authorizing legislation and requirements. The first such law was enacted in New York in 1910; by 1948, all states had a workers' compensation program.

PRIVATELY FINANCED HEALTH CARE

The private share of health care expenditures is made up of direct payments by indi-viduals (representing 18% of total expenditures) and payments made by private insur-ance companies (representing 35% of expenditures). Public payments represent the balance at 47%.

Employer-Based Insurance
During the Great Depression, hospitals found that most Americans could not afford to pay their bills. The hospital industry, through the American Hospital Association,

supported the growth of the first major health insurers: the Blue Cross plans in each state that pay for hospital care and the Blue Shield plans that pay for physician and other outpatient services. Over time, these nonprofit insurers had to compete with for-profit insurance companies, which emerged during World War II when unions began fighting for medical insurance to be part of employee benefits packages.

Growth in the health insurance market was a by-product of wartime wage and price controls; because wages couldn't be increased, enhanced benefits packages were one way unions and employees could obtain increased compensation. Growth accelerated after a decision by the Internal Revenue Service that employers could take a tax deduction for the cost of employee health insurance. The growing costs of health care would have led to increased private or public insurance coverage eventually.

During the next several decades, the employer-based health insurance system became increasingly entrenched. By the end of 2002, more than 64% of Americans received health insurance through their employer (Glied & Borzi, 2004). Since then, the percentage of Americans obtaining employer-based health insurance has slowly but steadily decreased, reaching 61% in 2008 and 56% in 2012.

The Individual Insurance Market

Although employer-based insurance dominates the private health insurance sector, a significant number of people must arrange and pay for health insurance on their own. The Employee Benefit Research Institute found that, in 2008, even though more than 160 million nonelderly Americans were covered by employment-based health benefits, about 16 million purchased coverage for themselves and family members in the individual market (Fronstin, 2009). As implementation of insurance exchanges supported by the ACA began in 2014, however, individual coverage grew quickly, totaling 8 million people the first year of the exchanges—with an expectation that this number could grow to 24 million by 2024. This growth is due in part to the substantial premium subsidies supported by the ACA and also to a mandate that imposes tax penalties on individuals who meet the criteria for purchasing individual policies.

As described later in this chapter, the ACA offers substantial subsidies for many Americans to purchase insurance as individuals. Almost 14 million people purchased subsidized private insurance after the law was implemented in 2014 and the number is expected to grow to at least 16 million.

COBRA

The Consolidated Omnibus Budget Reconciliation Act (COBRA) of 1985 attempts to reduce gaps in insurance coverage for individuals who are between jobs. The act requires employers to extend health insurance benefits to former employees for up to 18 months. Depending on qualifying circumstances, coverage may be extended for a spouse or dependent children for up to 36 months. Employees generally pay the entire premium for the coverage.

COBRA coverage can be expensive because many employers offer insurance that is generous in scope. It is likely that policies offered by the insurance exchanges will be less expensive than COBRA for many people, so COBRA might represent a diminishing share of insurance coverage over time.

■ How Providers Are Paid for the Health Services They Deliver

INSURANCE PAYMENTS

> *In recent years, as public insurance rates have either decreased or not increased as fast as health care inflation, a number of providers have stopped serving Medicare or Medicaid patients.*

Most services delivered by medical care providers are paid for through the complex insurance system described in the previous section. In the case of public payers (mostly Medicare and Medicaid), payment rates for providers are fixed by a complex set of rules and formulas that are set in place by public policy. The rates are in essence a "take it or leave it" offer from the federal government. In recent years, as public insurance rates have either decreased or not increased as fast as health care inflation, a number of providers have stopped serving Medicare or Medicaid patients.

Private insurers go through a negotiation process with hospitals, physicians, and other providers to establish what will be paid by the insurer for each type of service. These negotiations can be quite complex and quite heated as both the payer and the provider seek rates that are favorable to them. Physicians often have less clout in these negotiations than hospitals unless they are organized into large groups or are in communities with physician shortages. In most areas, there are enough physicians to give insurers the upper hand in bargaining. The difficulty of negotiating good rates is one factor driving physicians to either join *preferred provider organizations* (PPOs) or to take salaried positions within hospital systems or in large corporate medical practices.

The various approaches to paying physicians used by Medicare, Medicaid, and private insurers have resulted in decreased payments to many physicians and falling or static incomes for many types of physicians over the past 5 to 10 years. In addition to tighter payment approaches, the recession of 2008 to 2010 decreased the demand for physician services. More people were uninsured and very price sensitive during the difficult economic times, and volumes have not recovered since that period.

Hospitals, by contrast, often have good negotiation positions because there are fewer hospitals in each community and many people insist on having access to hospitals they perceive as high in quality. Smaller hospitals or community hospitals that are not academic medical centers sometimes have substantially less negotiating power. Just like physicians, however, hospitals have felt intense pressure on revenues since the recession of 2008 to 2010.

Any provider that does not negotiate rates with an insurer through a contract is considered an out-of-network provider by that insurer. Often, insurers do not reimburse patients who use out-of-network providers, or they provide only a specified amount and make the patient responsible for the difference between this amount and a hospital's charges.

In general, actual payment rates vary markedly across types of payers. Private insurers often pay the best rates because of the negotiation process; Medicare pays the second-highest rates generally, and Medicaid payment rates tend to be lowest. One exception to this pattern is Federally Qualified Health Centers, which often care for low-income people and have high reimbursement rates paid by public payers. These high rates reflect a priority to ensure access to care for low-income people and to compensate for what is often higher-than-average health care complexity for populations served by community health centers.

The financial viability of any given hospital, physician, or other provider often is crucially associated with the payer mix among the provider's patients. Providers that do not have a healthy share of patients covered by private insurance sometime have a difficult task covering costs.

PAYMENTS MADE DIRECTLY BY PATIENTS

In recent years, more and more physicians have decided to be out-of-network providers, putting more payment responsibility on individual patients.

The other key source of reimbursement in health care comes directly from payments made by individuals. Individuals without insurance must pay cash for services, and individuals who use out-of-network providers also must pay cash and then seek reimbursement from their insurers. In recent years, more and more physicians have decided to be out-of-network providers, putting more payment responsibility on individual patients. This is particularly the case for specialty physicians in urban markets who serve wealthy patients, and even more so for physicians who have reputations for high quality.

On the payer side, insurers also are contributing to the growth in out-of-network providers as insurers move to so-called narrow networks of providers with whom they contract. Insurers are finding that they can offer lower rates if they concentrate their business among a small set of providers. Increasing numbers of consumers and employers seem willing to trade access to a large network of providers for the opportunity to pay less for insurance. Most notably, the first few years of the insurance products offered in the insurance exchanges set up by the ACA have offered narrow networks.

The prices charged by providers, especially hospitals, have become increasingly controversial. Many hospitals set very high rates for the relatively few patients who pay out of pocket for hospital care. In addition, these rates are rarely transparent; most patients are not told what care will cost until after they have received the care. Such practices have spurred a movement pushing for more transparency of prices charged by hospitals and more logic to the basis for setting prices.

■ Specialized Payment Approaches Used by Payers

Over the past 20 years, a range of new payment approaches has been developed in the attempt to achieve two goals: (a) reduce the high rate of year-to-year cost inflation in health care and (b) create incentives for providers to deliver higher-quality care and to use more efficient practices to manage patient care.

MANAGED CARE

The biggest change in the privately financed portion of the U.S. health care system over the last three decades is the shift toward various forms of managed care: prepaid health plans, preferred provider organizations, accountable care organizations, and consumer-driven health care. Large businesses and government payers steered this shift in an attempt to reduce their health insurance costs.

Prepaid Health Plans

Managed care plans structure and reimburse care differently than conventional insurance does. Very strict managed care plans, such as health maintenance organizations (HMOs), use *capitated payments* and control which providers participate in their network. Capitated payments are fixed annual payments for each person for whom the provider is responsible to provide care, regardless of the amount and kinds of services eventually needed. HMOs also require primary care physicians to be gatekeepers to other types of services, by requiring referrals for diagnostic tests and specialty care.

> *The theory was that capitation would encourage providers to think more carefully about the necessity of costly tests and procedures and discourage unnecessary referrals to expensive specialists.*

The theory was that capitation would encourage providers to think more carefully about the necessity of costly tests and procedures and discourage unnecessary referrals to expensive specialists. Despite capitation's limits on reimbursement, providers were expected to participate because they would have a captive audience of patients—in other words, they could make up any reimbursement shortfall by having increased numbers of patients. Patients, in return for giving up the freedom to use whichever physician or hospital they chose, would receive more organized care, with specialist and primary care more effectively coordinated.

HMOs generally act as both the insurer and the provider of services. However, HMOs use a range of approaches to providing services. Some employ physicians and own hospitals, whereas others contract with networks of physicians and with local hospitals. The best known HMO, Kaiser Permanente, uses a defined network of physicians and owns its hospitals.

In the late 1990s, after a period of high cost inflation, the less organized approaches to managed care began to spread widely. Consumers began to dislike these approaches, however, because they perceived many features as overly restrictive. They wanted to choose their own physicians, resented specialty care gatekeeping and other managed care hassle factors, and demanded more plan options. Consumers complained loudly to employers, who eventually moved toward offering less tightly controlled plans, which were not capitated for providers. This trend was in stark contrast to Medicaid managed care, which enrolls about two thirds of Medicaid recipients nationwide into capitated programs in order to control spending. Similarly, some states are moving toward using managed care plans exclusively for Medicaid recipients.

Today, most consumers do not choose to enroll in HMO plans. Only in California and, to a lesser extent in the other west coast states, do HMOs represent a significant share of the insurance and service delivery market. In many areas of the country—including most of the eastern half—HMO penetration is minimal.

Preferred Provider Organizations

At the liberal end of the managed care spectrum are PPOs, rapidly growing organizations that encourage plan members to use a list of physicians with whom they have negotiated discounts. Plan members are rewarded with lower out-of-pocket costs (deductibles, copays, and co-insurance). Patients who use an out-of-network provider often must pay the difference between the insurer's reimbursement rate and whatever the physician charges.

Accountable Care Organizations

Despite the dislike of managed care in the 1990s, the 2010 national health reform law and many private insurers are again promoting a new version of managed care, called accountable care organizations (ACOs; see Chapter 12). Why the reconsideration? Quickly rising health costs and the prospects of sharply rising direct copayments (deductibles and coinsurance) suggest that consumers may be more amenable to trading freedom of provider choice for more coordination of care and lower copayments. In addition, in some versions of the ACO model, the consumer remains free to choose providers outside the ACO.

An ACO has strong financial incentives from insurers to enroll a high percentage of eligible people. If most eligible people do not use ACO services, the ACO is much more likely to lose money based on its contract with an insurer.

Consumer-Driven Health Care and High Deductibles

An approach to insurance that focuses on making consumers sense price signals when they purchase health care is often called *consumer-driven health care*. This approach generally involves setting a high deductible that individuals must pay before they receive insurance benefits. In some cases, costs of care during a deductible period can be paid by a savings account that employers or employees set up for health-related costs.

In many ways, consumer-driven health care—which puts individuals at risk to pay the bulk of everyday health care and pharmaceutical needs—offers a stark alternative to the managed care option. Consumers have very free choice but face sizable personal financial risk. This financial risk is particularly difficult for people with chronic health conditions.

Another feature of consumer-driven health care is a set of efforts to make health care costs more transparent to the user of the services and to improve access to medical care. For example, in some cases this type of plan insists that payers set fixed prices, which enrollees can be made aware of, before a service is provided. Other features include greater use of e-mail and phone calls to facilitate patient-provider interaction and walk-in hours that allow patients to see a provider on the same day they become ill.

DIAGNOSIS-RELATED GROUPS AND PROSPECTIVE PAYMENT FOR HOSPITAL CARE

In 1983, the federal government introduced a new hospital reimbursement system that dramatically altered the way it pays for Medicare beneficiaries' hospital care. The diagnosis-related group (DRG) system set rates prospectively—that is, a payer said up-front that it would pay a fixed amount for the hospital stay of a patient with a specific diagnosis and no more (with some outlier exceptions), no matter how much the patient's care eventually cost or how long the hospitalization turned out to be. Fixed payments give hospitals a powerful incentive to increase efficiency, minimize unnecessary tests and services, and shorten patients' hospital stays.

In concept, the early idea of DRGs is being expanded by the emerging concept of bundled payments, which pay both the physician and the hospital a fixed amount to provide an episode of care or, in the case of patients with chronic conditions, a specified time period of care. Various provisions of the ACA encourage use of bundled payments and capitated payments in the health system.

PROSPECTIVE RATES FOR PHYSICIAN PAYMENTS

A companion idea to DRGs as a basis of reimbursing hospitals for patients with varying needs is the federal government's approach to using standardized principles to set rates for different specialists and for patients with different medical needs. The system is called the resource-based relative value scale (RBRVS; Hsiao, et al., 1988). Rates are determined through detailed research measuring the expected time and other resource inputs that physicians need to deliver a specific service.

Each state's Medicaid program also developed physician reimbursement rates, generally adopting the federal approach of using formulas to set rates rather than negotiate with physicians. Medicaid rates are often much lower than Medicare rates for the same services. The ACA mandates that state Medicaid programs raise physician reimbursement rates to at least 60% of the rates paid by Medicare. This provision is designed to increase the number of physicians willing to care for Medicaid patients.

■ Issues Shaping the Future of Health Care Financing

The years between 2015 and 2020 will likely be dominated by attention to ongoing implementation of the wide-ranging features of the ACA. When passed, the main feature of the Act seemed to be the ambitious expansion of insurance coverage through subsidized private policies and through expanded Medicaid eligibility. However, the law also provided funding to spur changes in the way health care is organized and financed, with an aim of slowing the growth rate of health care expenditures.

For example, the ACA set aside $11 billion over a 5-year period to support expansions of community health centers around the country; these centers would be eligible for generous reimbursement rates as FQHCs. The logic of this funding is to expand primary care access so that the newly insured can see physicians and receive services that would keep them from ending up in emergency departments or acute care hospitals.

The ACA also mandates demonstrations to test the concept of ACOs, which could lead to greater use of capitated payments, instead of fee-for-service payments, for service delivery. The act also funds $10 billion of demonstrations and experiments through a new Center for Medicare & Medicaid Innovation to help providers learn how to integrate and coordinate services across provider organizations and how to use care management approaches for patients with the most chronic and complex medical challenges.

We focus attention on three key issues that will affect the future of health care financing as stimulated by the ACA: (a) the challenge of encouraging new delivery systems that can better manage quality and costs of care, (b) the challenge of rethinking how health care is actually reimbursed by public and private insurers, and (c) the challenge of implementing smoothly operating insurance exchanges.

ENCOURAGING NEW DELIVERY SYSTEMS

Delivery system reform is a recent "big bet" to achieve a health system that delivers more affordable medical care. The general idea is to make medical care more forward looking, meeting the needs of people before they become so sick that they require expensive care in hospitals.

In the past, physicians and hospitals have been set up to be reactive, waiting for patients to seek care when they feel in need of it. However, a more proactive approach involves keeping in touch with patients through care managers to make sure patients are doing self-management of their health problems between provider visits; this is particularly important for people who are dealing with difficult chronic conditions such as diabetes or heart disease. Ideally, a care manager working with a physician or an advanced practice nurse can help to meet the broad set of needs that a chronically ill patient might face: taking the right medications regularly, making appointments with specialty physicians when appropriate, and perhaps getting social services that could help to mitigate their illnesses.

A second strategy for being proactive in the care of patients is to have close ties with a wide range of medical care providers. Care providers that are integrated across service types may be able to better manage and coordinate the needs of patients with complicated medical conditions. Thus, outcomes might be better if hospitals have close ties to primary care physicians, as well as to specialty physicians and other providers such as home care service organizations, laboratories and testing centers, mental health providers, and substance abuse service professionals.

The simplest example of why this is important is what happens when a person leaves the hospital. If the hospital does not make sure the patient is linked to a specialist or primary care physician or to a home care agency (depending on the patient's postdischarge needs), that person likely will not continue to recover and may require readmittance when a medical setback occurs.

The public payment system—especially the Medicaid program—uses a range of incentives to encourage providers to establish integrated networks of different types of providers who can develop protocols for working together in a smooth, effective manner. The federal Center for Medicare & Medicaid Services, for example, is initiating programs in many states to offer substantial financial rewards to integrated sets of providers that meet one or more of these goals: (a) achieve an agreed-upon goal related to improving medical outcomes for a set of individuals, (b) improve the overall health of the entire population in the community where the providers work, or (c) lower the expected costs of medical care. One major program, called the Delivery System Reform Incentive Payments (DSRIP) program, makes large supplemental payments to provider systems that achieve a specified goal related to health system improvement.

In New York, for example, the state government is overseeing a DSRIP program that can support up to $8 billion in initiatives across New York to achieve cost and outcome goals associated with system reform; these goals focus primarily on creating networks of providers that can work cooperatively to meet all of the needs of complex patients. This is called a pay-for-performance approach to encouraging improvement: The costs of implementing the improvement are paid for if the health system achieves the goal it sets. In the long run, both government payers and providers can save resources if the initiative is successful.

Private payers also are experimenting with structures such as ACOs. These initiatives often involve establishing a group of patients covered by the payer and served by the ACO. Concrete reimbursement incentives are established if the providers involved with the ACO achieve quality and efficiency goals.

The present is marked by incredible energy to transform the organization of health care in the United States. Much of the current activity involves trying ideas about care management and integration as approaches to improve quality, outcomes, and efficiency that have not been thoroughly tested through demonstration initiatives. When demonstration initiatives have tested these ideas, the findings have been mixed. Evolution of the organization of care likely will happen slowly but surely, with many changes along the way. There is consensus that the current approach is not optimal, but there is no consensus about which changes will work.

THE CHALLENGE OF CHANGING HOW WE REIMBURSE HEALTH CARE PROVIDERS

Almost every person who interacts with the U.S. health care system (whether as an expert or a patient) comes to an awareness that our payment approach makes little sense. Hospitals post incredibly high prices for services that are charged only to a tiny fraction of people who fall into loopholes in the payment system. Every payer bargains or dictates different payment rates, forcing hospitals and physicians to cross-subsidize different types of patients and often penalizing those whose practices focus on the most needy and poor patients. Providers are overpaid for some of the things they do and sharply underpaid for other, important services, such as counseling patients. This creates incentives to focus on services that lead to high revenues.

The core problem seems to be the use of fee-for-service payments that reward the *volume* of services delivered rather than the *value* of the services or the *outcomes* associated with the services. Despite broad dissatisfaction with the current payment system, it is difficult to design a new system that creates logical incentives encouraging valuable services and good outcomes yet does not financially hurt any of the three principal parties in health care: patients, providers, and payers.

It is useful to begin the payment reform process by establishing a set of principles to guide the reform:

- New payment approaches should encourage primary care and preventive care. These are important services because, when done well, they frequently can avoid the need for more expensive services. Despite our perception that primary care and prevention can help people avoid uncontrolled chronic conditions, we currently spend only about 5% of all health care dollars on primary care.
- Any new payment approach should encourage high-quality care and attention to optimizing the patient experience. Providers that achieve quality and service amenities should be rewarded.

- Payment approaches should discourage duplication and waste by not letting providers benefit financially when these occur. Too frequently patients have unnecessary or duplicated tests because providers are not coordinating care with one another.
- The large variations across localities in how people are treated and in the cost and outcome of care must be reduced. A payment system must encourage providers in different locations to learn from one another and to adopt efficient practices that lead to good outcomes.
- Payment systems also should encourage investments in population health that support a range of community-based and prevention-oriented activities focused on keeping people healthy. In the long run, this strategy is what best leads to good health outcomes and lower costs of medical care.

What types of payment system meet these principles and should be candidates for payment reform efforts? Five candidates have emerged, and each works in a different context:

- *Reference pricing:* This system involves a payer exploring the range of prices charged by different providers for a specific service in a given community. The payer then identifies a subset of providers that charge a fair price and have good health outcomes. The payer can set this price as the reference price and establish a rule that the people covered by the insurance plan receive no more than the reference price as a reimbursement, even if they choose a provider that charges more than the reference price. The aim of this system is to force high-price providers to rethink how they manage the procedure in question and how they can reduce the costs of providing the service. Providers that cannot do this will lose business to the lower-cost providers—as happens in most markets for goods and services in our economy.
- *Bundled or episodic payments:* This payment approach moves away from paying a fee for every discrete activity a provider performs for an individual patient. Instead, a specified health condition for a patient is associated with a fixed price and/or a fixed period of time. This bundled payment is designed to pay for the range of services a patient is likely to require. The approach encourages efficiency and good outcomes; across a panel of patients, physicians will do well financially when they operate efficiently.
- *Pay for performance:* As discussed earlier in this chapter, this approach involves offering extra payments when providers achieve very good health outcomes at affordable prices.
- *Capitation:* This approach—which has been used by HMOs for many years and is on the rise again nationally—gives a provider an annual fixed payment to provide all of the care a specific person needs during the year. Again, providers who are efficient in caring for the person will do well financially across a panel of patients. However, this approach requires a covered person to agree to receive services from a single provider group during the year.
- *Global budgets:* This is the most aggressive approach; it involves a set of providers agreeing to meet the health care needs for an entire community or a large subset of a given community. In return, providers receive a budget that is designed to support the services needed across the entire covered group. This approach very much encourages population health initiatives to keep a population healthy. The best way to manage a global budget is to keep people healthy and to use primary care to decrease the need for high-cost emergency department care and inpatient hospital care.

The effort to transform payment approaches has been happening piecemeal across the United States. The federal Medicare program has been aggressively developing pay-for-performance and capitation approaches, which often are implemented as a voluntary option. Private insurers also have been experimenting with a wide range of alternative payment approaches, including bundled payments, reference pricing, and various forms of capitation.

Some states, however, have been working to develop more comprehensive payment reforms that attempt common incentives for providers no matter which payer is covering an individual. One example is Massachusetts, where a law passed in 2012 mandates that health care expenditures should not grow any faster than overall spending in the Massachusetts economy. The law encourages global budgets for large provider systems to care for specified groups of people and established a state commission to monitor expenses and quality of care and to make recommendations if targets are not met.

In 2014, state-level reform efforts were also underway in Vermont, Maryland, Oregon, Arkansas, and California. Many lessons must be learned before these reforms are fully implemented. These state-level approaches will continue to evolve, along with the range of other piecemeal approaches to payment reform.

However, key ingredients for success seem to be emerging from the activities in the early adopter states. It is important to success that a state has experience in negotiating state-based efforts to improve the quality, organization, and financing of medical care. Local champions in government, private industry, and medical care must emerge to forge consensus and the compromise needed to bring about meaningful reform. State legislators must pass legislation that drives reform. Finally, collaboration across sectors seems to be a common attribute of all successful state-level initiatives toward payment reform.

IMPLEMENTING EFFECTIVE INSURANCE EXCHANGES

A key feature of the ACA is the creation of insurance exchanges that offer private insurance policies with premium rates subsidized by federal dollars. Families with incomes below 400% of the FPL (in 2014, an income of $95,400 was 400% of the poverty level for a family of four) are eligible for insurance subsidies on a sliding scale. In addition, everyone is required to buy some form of insurance policy, as long as at least one offering by a private insurer meets affordability tests for that person or family.

The exchanges are intended to play at least three key roles: (a) calculating the amount of the subsidy for a given family, (b) explaining the features of each private insurance offering, and (c) linking each family to the insurance option the family selects. Exchanges determine which insurance offerings meet federal qualifications to be offered on the exchange; they also have the power to limit the number of insurers offering policies on the exchange. In addition, some states choose to have their exchanges facilitate enrollment in public insurance plans, such as Medicaid.

These are difficult roles to play for new organizations with significant challenges and few organizational precedents. Complicated consensus-building processes that involve insurance companies, consumer groups, and policymakers are necessary to accomplish this in a timely way. A large task has been the development of new eligibility information systems that can translate income levels into subsidy amounts, verify the accuracy of reported incomes, and explain the insurance offerings available to a specific individual or family. Most states also needed new laws to bring state insurance regulations in line with federal requirements and to set governance rules and financing approaches to pay for the operation of the exchanges.

> *Perhaps the greatest challenge in establishing the insurance exchanges under health reform is to ensure seamless enrollment.*

Perhaps the greatest challenge in establishing the exchanges is to ensure seamless enrollment in unsubsidized private policies, subsidized private policies, and the publicly supported Medicaid program. A family that has a change in income status may also have a change in the type of insurance it qualifies for: When income exceeds 400% of the federal poverty level, an unsubsidized policy is required; in most states, income between 133% and 400% of the poverty level require purchase of a subsidized policy; and when income is below 133% of the poverty level, individuals are eligible for free Medicaid insurance (in states that have accepted the federal financing available to support most of this Medicaid expansion).

If enrollment and income documentation systems vary from one insurance category to another, many families will have difficulty making transitions among insurance types. In particular, people who become eligible for Medicaid coverage may fail to comply with complex enrollment processes. A successful integration of differing enrollment requirements could result not only in increased private coverage but also in better take-up rates for the Medicaid program. This would represent an impressive achievement for the ACA.

The initial launch of the exchanges demonstrated how difficult these tasks are to achieve. In many states and in the exchanges run by the federal government in states that did not develop a state-based exchange, the enrollment systems did not work well initially, with some unable to enroll individuals for many weeks. Some of the electronic enrollment systems could not handle the capacity of demand, and the complex software developed to manage enrollments often failed to work. Making the exchanges work more smoothly is a task that will be a priority throughout the period of 2015 to 2020.

◼ Conclusion

The ACA represents the largest change in the nation's health care financing system since the initiation of Medicare and Medicaid in the mid-1960s. If implemented as expected, the Act will likely lead to changes in reimbursement approaches for nearly all providers and dramatically expand the number of Americans with health insurance. In addition, the ACA will require many currently uninsured middle-income Americans to purchase subsidized private policies.

However, the law will endure only if health care costs can be contained. If costs continue to increase year after year—especially at a pace exceeding that of the overall economy—either subsidized insurance will become unaffordable or the federal government will be forced to increase the subsidies. The latter course may not be feasible at a time when federal budget deficits already are considered burdensome and state resources to cover Medicaid costs are threatened. Cost increases also will put pressure on reimbursement rates and the generosity of private insurance coverage. This, in turn, will make it increasingly difficult for health care providers to remain financially viable.

One hope is that emerging reimbursement reforms and new incentive payment schemes will soon slow the growth rate of health care costs. We have been through a period of early experimentation with various incentive payment schemes and have many viable approaches to try. However, firm evidence that they will work is not yet available.

Another hope is that, as a nation, we will make progress on the public health and prevention tasks of helping people to live healthier lives and avoid the health and medical care cost consequences of chronic diseases such as diabetes, heart disease, and asthma. The best way to slow the rate of growth of health care is to reduce the incidence of chronic disease. Helping people to eat better, exercise more, use alcohol responsibly, and avoid the use of tobacco and addicting drugs is crucial to both population health and the economic health of our country.

One final challenge for the U.S. health system is to care for the 5% of people living in America who will not have insurance coverage, even if insurance reform is fully and effectively implemented. Our health system will continue to require a safety-net for the vulnerable and the uninsured. A world of tight reimbursements will make it increasingly difficult for hospitals and other providers to pay for safety-net care by shifting dollars from other payers and revenue sources.

What will happen if federal health reform does not achieve the anticipated expansions of access and control over the growth in health care costs? One of two radical options will most likely emerge: (a) collapse of the private approach to health care financing, which would lead to a single-payer public system like those in most other parts of the developed world (see Chapter 4), or (b) the emergence of a three-tiered system of care that maintains great access to care for wealthy Americans with comfortable incomes but restricts access moderately for middle-income Americans and rations care brutally for low-income Americans. Either option goes against fundamental principles engrained in U.S. history and politics: free enterprise on one hand, and equality and equity on the other. The task of implementing a 21st-century financing system that will endure must engage new thinkers, new leaders, and new researchers who can reinterpret these principles in light of current realities.

■ Discussion Questions

1. What complications does our current financing system cause for providers of care?
2. What complications does our insurance system cause for individual consumers?
3. What are some of the promising new approaches to changing our health system so that it has incentives to provide more efficient care?
4. Some people view increases in health care spending as a response to consumer demand, whereas others see these increases as potentially wasteful spending. When other industry sectors consume a rising share of GDP, it is viewed as a positive development. Should we be concerned about the rising cost of health care and its share of our GDP? What types of health care spending might be classified as valuable? As wasteful?

CASE STUDY

You are the chief executive officer of a large, technology-intensive hospital in a community of 200,000 people. The community includes two other, smaller community hospitals and a wide range of physicians and other providers working in private practice. Currently, you are paid a fixed amount by Medicare—the federal insurance program for the elderly—for every eligible admission to your hospital, based on the severity of the patient's needs. Physicians and other providers in your community are paid fee-for-service.

The federal government has offered to form an ACO in your community that could accept a capitated annual payment for each person eligible for Medicare. Answer the following questions:

1. How would you go about deciding whether to accept the government's offer?
2. Would you want to lead the ACO or just be a part of it?
3. Would you argue for or against accepting the federal offer? Why?
4. If you wanted to proceed and lead the effort to form an ACO, how would you coordinate with the other local hospitals and providers?
5. How might you change the way care currently is organized in your community, given the new financial incentives embedded in a capitated rate?

■ References

Fronstin, P. (2009). *Sources of health insurance and characteristics of the uninsured: Analysis of the March 2009 Current Population Survey* (Issue Brief No. 334). Washington, DC: Employee Benefit Research Institute.

Glied, S. A., & Borzi, P. C. (2004). The current state of employer based health care. *Journal of Law, Medicine, and Ethics, 32,* 404–409.

Hsiao, W. C., Braun, P., Becker, E. R., Causino, N., Couch, N. P., DiNicola, M., . . . Douwe, B. Y. (1988). *A national study of resource-based relative value scales for physician services: Final report to the Health Care Financing Administration* (Publication 17-C-98795/1-03). Boston, MA: Harvard School of Public Health.

Hurley, R., & Somers, S. (2003). Medicaid and managed care: A lasting relationship? *Health Affairs, 22,* 77–88.

Kaiser Family Foundation. (2015). Status of state action on the Medicaid expansion decision. *Kaiser State Health Facts.* Retrieved from http://kff.org/health-reform/state-indicator/state-activity-around-expanding-medicaid-under-the-affordable-care-act/

Levit, K., Smith, C., Cowan, C., Sensenig, A., Catlin, A., & The Health Accounts Team. (2004). Health spending rebound continues in 2002. *Health Affairs, 23,* 147–159.

U.S. Department of Health and Human Services Indian Health Service. (2010). *IHS fact sheets, IHS Year 2010 Profile.* Washington, DC: Author.

12 Health Care Costs and Value

Thad Calabrese and Keith F. Safian

KEY WORDS

accountable care organization (ACO)
centers of excellence (COE)
defensive medicine
electronic medical records (EMRs)

medical malpractice
overconsumption
rationing
value-based purchasing (VBP)

LEARNING OBJECTIVES

- Understand potential contributing factors to the growth in health care costs in the United States over the past 60 years
- Explain value in terms of health care
- Recognize conflicts embedded within the health care delivery system that drive up costs and reduce value
- Identify why attempts at cost control have not succeeded

TOPICAL OUTLINE

- Why health care spending is a national concern
- The concept of value in the health sector
- The challenge of reducing costs but not value
- Technology as a driver of expenditures
- The issue of the prices of inputs in the health sector
- Initiatives to address expenditure/value tradeoffs

This chapter focuses on health care costs and value—concepts that are inextricably linked yet routinely analyzed separately. In 2015, Americans will spend nearly $3.2 trillion on health care, nearly one fifth of all economic activity in the United States and equal to nearly $9,000 per person. If we as a society perceived that we were extracting value at least equal to this spending, it is unlikely that concerns about the "crisis" in health care spending would be so commonplace. For example, in other sectors, such as cable television and Internet service, the United States also has seen huge growth in expenditures. But, in this case growth is based on individual consumers deciding that these expenditures have value that is worth the cost. In the case of health care, this assessment is more difficult to make because of the role of insurance in paying for medical care. As a result, there is a growing sense that our massive spending on health care is not leading to value worth this spending. This chapter explores the relationship between costs and value and considers ways to improve the payoffs from our health spending.

■ The Issue of Health Care Spending Growth

In 1963, before the implementation of our major public insurance programs (see Chapter 3), national spending on health care totaled about $261 billion in current dollars. (Actual spending in 1963 was $34.7 billion, but there has been natural inflation in the economy over time. At today's inflation-affected prices, this $34.7 billion is equivalent to $261 billion. We present the inflation-adjusted figures when referring to 1963 expenditures in order to focus on "real" changes in spending.) On a per capita basis, this 1963 spending equaled $1,440 per person in inflation-adjusted dollars. Per capita spending grew more than 550% in real terms between 1963 and 2012, reaching nearly $9,000 per person in 2012. Importantly, the average annual growth in health care spending between 1963 and 2012 was nearly 9.5%, whereas nominal gross domestic product (GDP) growth during this period was 6.8%—meaning that health care spending grew faster than other economic activity over the past five decades. The implication of these trends is that health care is an increasing share of all spending in the economy. Trying to understand why this is occurring is important.

Figure 12.1 shows how expenditure growth follows the pattern of GDP growth but health expenditure growth relentlessly exceeds GDP growth (U.S. GDP changes come from the Bureau of Economic Analysis). Interestingly, the only time this was not true was between 1993 and 2000, when there was a substantial effort to change the organization and financing of health care during the Clinton administration. After these efforts had failed, expenditure growth spurted back up.

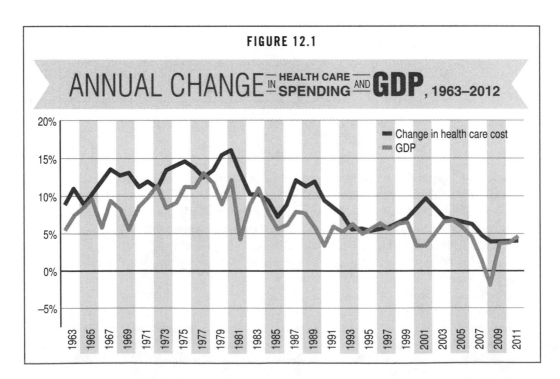

FIGURE 12.1

ANNUAL CHANGE IN HEALTH CARE SPENDING AND GDP, 1963–2012

Why is there so much concern about the growth in health care expenditures in the United States? The important reason is that a great deal of health care expenses are paid by government and employers—and the growth greatly affects these two key sectors of our economy.

The federal government, each state government, and many local governments spend a great deal of their tax revenues on health care. The federal government finances (a) the Medicare program, which provides insurance for elderly Americans; (b) more than half of the Medicaid program, which pays for health care received by low-income Americans; (c) Veterans Affairs and Department of Defense health care expenses; and (d) the costs of extensive research, public health, and training activities. State governments pay for as much as half of the Medicaid program directly, as well as for extensive activities in public health and regulation. Local governments generally support public health expenditures and some safety-net medical care.

The large share of tax dollars allocated to health care is crowding out expenditures on other important needs in our economy, such as expenditures on education and infrastructure.

In 1963, federal, state, and local governments financed only about $6 billion (equivalent to about $46 billion today) of total health care spending. This spending represented about 3% of total public spending. By 2012, governments were spending nearly $1.2 trillion (of the $2.8 trillion total) on health care, comprising more than 19% of total public spending. There are two key concerns with this growth in government costs. First, these costs are putting a great strain on taxes paid by workers and employers, and this strain is seen by many as decreasing the vibrancy of our economy. Second, the large share of tax dollars allocated to health care is crowding out expenditures on other important needs in our economy, such as expenditures on education and infrastructure. This is especially true at the state and local levels, where government spending on health has increased by 154% over the past 40 years but expenditures on education have been "crowded out" and increased by just 74% over the same period.

Health care costs are not purely a public finance issue, however. Private businesses—which purchase health insurance for employees and their families—frequently cite increasing costs as problematic. For example, the cost of health insurance was cited as the top concern of small business owners in 2008 and 2012 (Wade, 2012). As a result, as health insurance costs have increased, employers provide fewer salary increases because resources are instead devoted to increased health insurance costs (again, health expenditures are "crowding out" expenditures on salaries). Additionally, fewer employers continue to offer group health insurance to employees—or they limit dependents of employees who can access coverage. For example, in August, 2013, United Parcel Service began excluding health insurance coverage for spouses with access to health insurance at their own places of employment. Buchmueller, Carey, and Levy (2013) found that even though employers offered health insurance to more than 112 million employees in 2000, this number had declined to 108 million employees in 2011, or 4% fewer workers covered in one decade.

Beyond simple financial costs, studies find that increasing health insurance costs decreases full-time employment and also decreases hours worked for employees that work part time (Baicker & Chandra, 2005; Sood, Ghosh, & Escarce, 2009). Health care costs are implicitly part of national discussions about unemployment and job creation.

Of course, health spending also is a burden on American families, which—despite the large expenditures by government and employers—also pay a sizable amount for health care in their family budgets.

Table 12.1 analyzes how a typical family allocates its income across different types of expenditures. In 2012, total health care spending actually paid by the typical family was $3,556, which ranks it only the sixth largest item consumed, behind housing, transportation, and food costs (see Table 12.1). According to the Bureau of Labor Statistics, the average household spent more on gasoline purchases in 2012 ($2,549) than on health insurance ($2,061). But, the typical family is not every family. Families without insurance coverage and families that include someone with a chronic disease tend to spend a much larger share of after-tax income on health care.

These expenditure patterns explain a large part of the difficulty in making sure we, as a nation, are not spending too much on health care. A typical American might not realize how much he or she ultimately pays for health care (or the protection against health care costs afforded by insurance) because so much of this cost is paid by government and employers. In the end, however, these government and employer payments markedly affect the total after-tax incomes of families.

A final consideration related to American health care spending is that our health care spending far outpaces other western developed nations (see Chapter 4). In 1980, the United States devoted more of its GDP to health care spending (9%) than other western developed nations, but the difference was not extraordinary. By 2011, however, U.S. spending as a share of GDP far exceeded other comparable nations (see Table 12.2). Certainly other nations have experienced increased health care spending,

TABLE 12.1 AVERAGE ANNUAL AFTER-TAX EXPENDITURES BY CONSUMER UNITS/HOUSEHOLDS, 2012

	Average Annual Expenditures in Dollars, 2012	Change from Previous Year
Housing	16,887	0.5%
Transportation	8,998	8.5
Personal Insurance and Pensions	5,591	3.1
Food, at Home	3,921	2.2
All Other Expenditures	3,557	5.2
Health Care	**3,556**	**7.3**
Food, Away From Home	2,678	2.2
Entertainment	2,605	1.3
Cash Contributions	1,913	11.2
Apparel and Services	1,736	−0.2
Total	51,442	

Source: U.S. Department of Labor, Bureau of Labor Statistics.

TABLE 12.2 HEALTH CARE SPENDING AS A PERCENTAGE OF GDP FOR OECD COUNTRIES

	1980	2011	Increase	Rank
United States	9.0%	17.7%	8.7%	1
Sweden	8.9	9.5	0.6	21
Denmark	8.9	10.9	2.0	19
Germany	8.4	11.3	2.9	14
Ireland	8.2	8.9	0.7	20
Netherlands	7.4	11.9	4.5	4
Austria	7.4	10.8	3.4	11
Switzerland	7.3	11.0	3.7	10
Norway	7.0	9.3	2.3	18
France	7.0	11.6	4.6	3
Canada	7.0	11.2	4.2	7
Japan	6.5	9.6	3.1	13
Iceland	6.3	9.0	2.7	16
Finland	6.3	9.0	2.7	16
Belgium	6.3	10.5	4.2	6
Australia	6.1	8.9	2.8	15
New Zealand	5.9	10.3	4.4	5
Greece	5.9	9.1	3.2	12
United Kingdom	5.6	9.4	3.8	9
Portugal	5.3	10.2	4.9	2
Spain	5.3	9.3	4.0	8

Sources: 1980 data (Chandra & Skinner, 2012); 2011 data (OECD, year).

but the United States is unique in the degree of its increase—far outpacing even the nation with the second largest growth.

To return to the primary issue—if the United States spent significantly more on health care and received significantly better health outcomes, then health care cost growth might not be considered problematic. However, according to the Organisation for Economic Co-operation and Development (OECD), the United States ranks 26th out of 36 member countries for life expectancy, and just below the OECD average for life expectancy (see Figure 2.5 in Chapter 2). When fatal injuries are removed, U.S. life expectancy rankings improve dramatically, but they are still only comparable with other OECD nations. Further outcomes (such as infant mortality) are also at best only comparable with other nations, despite our spending. On these measures of outcomes, therefore, it does not appear the U.S. system is getting results for its increased spending.

A more nuanced view of U.S. health care spending, however, is to consider that our increased costs are related to quality of life issues rather than just to life extension. For example, in the United States it is not uncommon for patients in their 70s to have expensive surgeries (such as knee or hip replacements) so that they can maintain or return to physical activities, whereas such procedures would not be as common abroad. Hence, health care value relative to outcomes largely tied to longevity in these international comparisons is frequently defined in a very limited way.

THE VALUE OF HEALTH CARE SPENDING

One major problem with discussions about health care spending is that *value* is difficult to define, let alone measure. Very often, people mistakenly think that cutting cost is the central way of producing value. Third-party payers often argue that the "value" they add is reducing payments to health care providers, thereby reducing the cost of health care to the employer, taxpayer, or individual who is the actual payer. Many health care professionals who think and work on quality issues, by contrast, focus on ensuring that consumers get the best treatment available at the correct time (Robert Wood Johnson Foundation, 2013).

> *Value is best defined as the best patient outcomes relative to the amount of money we as individuals or as a society are able and/or willing to pay to stay healthy or to recover from illness.*

Yet value is not just about cost or just about patient outcomes; rather, value is best defined as the best patient outcomes relative to the amount of money we as individuals or as a society are able and/or willing to pay to stay healthy or to recover from illness. This conception of value focuses on results and not merely on the inputs used to achieve these results. It is possible to increase value by improving the quality, outcomes, and patient experience of medical care, and it is possible to increase value by achieving the same quality, outcomes, and experience at a lower total cost by improving efficiency.

So what has been our experience with improving value? Across some dimensions, the quality of medical care and outcomes are improving markedly in the United States (see Chapter 13). Deaths associated with stroke and heart disease are down substantially, and most would agree this is due to improvements in medical know-how, pharmaceuticals, and emerging technology. Cancer mortality also is improving due to better treatment approaches. Longevity after age 75 is higher in the United States than in many other countries, again perhaps due to the health services associated with medical care. Disparities in health outcomes between people of color and White Americans decrease after age 65, and most experts associate this with the near-universal accessibility of medical care that happens when people become eligible for Medicare.

In addition, beginning around 2008, health care expenses did increase more slowly than in previous years. This trend seems to have started with the deep recession at the beginning of this period but also seems to be related to a flurry of efforts among health care providers to restructure their approaches to health care delivery (see Chapter 11).

This slowdown, however, may be temporary. Health care costs increased significantly at the end of 2013 (increasing nearly 6% in the final quarter) and at the beginning of 2014 (increasing nearly 10% in the first quarter).

In other dimensions, there are serious concerns about the value of medical care. Most importantly and as mentioned earlier, despite our spending vast sums of money on medical care, the health of Americans is not very good compared with that of residents of other developed countries. If we are not getting health and longevity as outcomes associated with our large medical care investment, why are we spending so much on medical care?

The best answer to this question from a value perspective is that Americans seem to strongly value "getting better" after they become seriously ill, even at advanced ages and even when the value of treatments is highly uncertain—or when treatment has a chance of ending up hurting more than helping a condition. However, we cannot really prove that Americans value medical care as much as it appears because—as economists emphasize—we can only really be sure that value exceeds costs when people actually pay the costs to get a service.

What must be kept in clear focus is that spending on medical care does not address the key determinants of the overall health of a population. The best way to keep people healthy is through public health initiatives, prevention initiatives, and social policies that make healthy choices possible and likely. These strategies are not what the medical care enterprise is about; medical care restores health more than it ensures that a population is healthy over its life span. A key question for public policy is to think through how much should be spent to create population health and how much should be spent on recovery-oriented medical care (see Chapter 5).

Emerging data show that many other developed countries spend more per capita than the United States on social programs that encourage health and well-being and less per capita on medical care. These developed countries end up with higher health status over the life cycle than the United States.

ADDRESSING THE CHALLENGE OF REDUCING HEALTH CARE EXPENDITURES THAT DO NOT HAVE VALUE

A first step in efforts to increase the ratio of value to costs in medical care delivery is to consider what expenditures do not create value and what steps might eliminate or reduce these expenses. We consider three broad categories of expenses: (a) waste in production, (b) overconsumption of services, and (c) high prices of labor and inputs.

Waste

A large part of what leads to high health care costs in the United States is caused by the uncoordinated approach we use to take care of people with medical problems and the lack of attention to efficiency in producing care to make people better. "Waste" in this context is most frequently defined as those health care services that do not benefit patients. For example, Berwick and Hackbarth (2012) estimate that 20% of all health care expenditures are wasted. They identify several primary sources of waste, including overtreatment, lack of care coordination (which may lead to hospital readmission, medical complications, or duplicate tests), failure to execute best practices (which might lead, for example, to less than optimal outcomes), administrative complexity (such as incompatible health information systems, third-party payers requiring different insurance forms for similar procedures, and so on), and outright fraud and abuse (which includes money devoted to determining and stopping such efforts). The Institute of Medicine (IOM; 2012) estimates waste at one third of all health care spending, citing unneeded procedures that actually reduce the quality of life. If these estimates are correct, the United States wastes between $560 billion and $950 billion (or between $1,700 and nearly $3,000 per capita) annually on health care—waste that could be eliminated with no harm to consumers. The IOM estimates that administrative complexity alone costs in excess of $360 billion annually.

Statistics suggest that the lack of coordination of care for patients with the most complex medical conditions affects our health care spending significantly. Just 5% of the total population incurs half of all costs, and 20% of the total population is responsible for 80% of total spending (Commonwealth Fund, 2013). Chronically ill patients might have heart conditions, mental health issues, or diabetes (as some examples)—and frequently have multiple diagnoses. As these patients move among various specialists, hospitals, outpatient providers, long-term care facilities, home care, and so on, there often is not an effective way to make sure these services are all needed or delivered efficiently.

Emerick and Lewis (2013) cite overscreening and treatment as a fundamental aspect of waste in health care. As advances in technology and medical condition diagnoses have made detection of potential health problems easier and less invasive, the likelihood of detecting nonthreatening medical conditions, which pose little risk to the patient, also increases. For example, screenings may find lesions or potentially cancerous cells on organs—leading the medical provider to treat the patient (with surgery, medicine, and so on). Yet, these medical conditions may not be problematic or lead to health complications. As such, they lead to increased costs with no certainty of an accompanying increase in value. As one example, U.S. patients receive heart surgeries and angioplasties at more than twice the rate of patients in other countries, yet our health outcomes are identical (OECD, 2013). Hospital visits for chronic health conditions are far more frequent in the United States, as well; hospitalization rates for diabetes and asthma, for example, are nearly twice as high as those in other nations (OECD, 2013).

Overconsumption

In a normally functioning marketplace, the costs of these additional services would be borne by consumers. Hence, if the consumer valued the services, he or she would choose to purchase them. Health care spending, however, is not like other goods or services bought and sold in a competitive marketplace. Importantly, consumers in health care do not make most of the decisions about which services to consume—doctors do. Most doctors want to do everything to help a patient, which increases the health care services consumed. In addition, because third-party insurance programs cover the vast majority of consumers (patients), the goods and services consumed by patients are largely financed by these insurers. As a result, patients may consume more health care than is optimal because they do not face the total cost of the good or service. This moral hazard (as economists refer to it) leads to overconsumption of health care or to patients not taking sufficient care to prevent incurring health care costs—because they do not bear the costs.

Defensive Medicine. If overdiagnosis and treatments drive up health care spending with uncertain increase in health benefits, why do they occur? Although these practices may not improve health outcomes, health care providers may want to protect themselves from medical malpractice claims that they did not do enough to help patients. One study estimates that malpractice and defensive medicine cost approximately $56 billion annually—or less than 3% of total health care spending (Mello, Chandra, Atul, Gawande, & Studdert, 2010), whereas another estimates that it costs between $120 billion and $216 billion—or 5% to 9% of total spending (Kessler & McClellan, 1996). These costs include not just the insurance premiums paid by doctors and health care providers, but also the legal fees, settlements, and judgments of such suits. However—and what the monetary figures fail to capture—is that even the hint of malpractice is enough to ruin the careers of medical providers and the reputations of health care institutions. For most health care providers, the fear of a lawsuit is greater than the fear of lost revenue for providing a noncovered service or test. Providers will default to increasing services as a result. Hence, defensive medicine may be perfectly rational from the perspective of a provider.

Given the potential for malpractice lawsuits, it seems logical for primary care physicians to refer patients to specialists to protect themselves professionally from malpractice exposure and also to ensure patient health outcomes. This referral itself drives up health care spending. Furthermore, we have a system in place that pays these specialists more than primary care physicians—even for the same services. The Relative Value Scale Update Committee (RUC) is an American Medical Association (AMA) panel that recommends to Medicare the relative values of health procedures. The federal government (through the Centers for Medicare & Medicaid Services [CMS] and, in the past, through the Health Care Financing Administration) uses these recommendations in the setting of payments for Medicare patients; however, these rates also influence non-Medicare payers and, as a result, have a large effect on payments to physicians. The RUC has largely advocated for (and the federal government has accepted) payment increases to specialists. Thus, referrals to specialists lead to patient visits that are more costly compared with primary care physician visits, driving up health care spending as a result.

Fee-for-Service Rather Than Fee-for-Value. Providers and institutions are largely paid on a fee-for-service basis. Hence, more procedures lead to more revenue. When third-party insurers—especially public insurers—reduce or limit the price they will pay for procedures—which has become an almost annual ritual for Medicare and Medicaid—providers can partially offset this constraint (a declining or flat price) by increasing volume. Again, as costs will tend to increase over time (due to salary increases, the need to replace fixed assets, and so on), the need to increase revenues is rational to ensure financial sustainability. As a result, increasing procedures is an avenue providers can take to maintain their own fiscal health.

These explanations focus on the health care provider making decisions for patients. Because of the complicated decisions to be made in health care, this may be true much of the time—and as a result, health care providers might make decisions in the best interests of themselves rather than the patient (the so-called principal-agent problem). In many cases, however, patients may advocate strongly for specific treatments, and so a health provider supplies them. For example, drug companies in the United States advertise expensive prescription drugs directly to consumers, hoping such advertising leads patients to ask for and receive the drugs, thereby driving up sales.

Demographics. In 2008, nearly 34% of the U.S. population was defined as obese; other OECD nations had obesity rates of between 4% and 27%. Finkelstein, Trogdon, and Cohen (2009) estimate that obesity costs the U.S. health care system $147 billion annually; obese patients are estimated to cost the health care system 42% more than patients of normal weight—with prescription drug costs making up the largest amount of this increase. Treating the diseases associated with obesity (such as diabetes) is a huge health care cost driver, and obesity rates are not evenly distributed through the U.S. population.

Well-intentioned government mandates also increase costs in many ways. For example, with increasing diversity comes the reality that health care providers need to communicate with an increasingly diverse population. Health care providers are required to provide certified medical translators for patients so that staff may communicate with patients; providers must also have forms and consents available in patients' languages. Certainly such government-mandated services are important to make sure that patients are fully informed about their health care, but the cost of translators is frequently not reimbursable from insurance companies despite the public mandate to provide them. This is but one example of regulations that drive up hospital costs but may not be applied equally to physician-owned or corporation-owned facilities.

End-of-Life Care. A final factor affecting our health care spending patterns bears discussion. End-of-life care is costly, with estimates pegging nearly 32% of Medicare spending to those patients in their last 2 years of life suffering from chronic illnesses (Dartmouth Atlas, 2014). This fraction of spending represents over $170 billion annually. Furthermore, Hagist and Kotlikoff (2006) show that health care spending in the United States increases significantly after age 65. Just as variation exists across the country in Medicare spending, end-of-life care spending by Medicare is not evenly distributed across the country. Patients receiving more aggressive end-of-life care (and, by extension, spending more resources) do not have improved survival or better quality of life than others. For example, many terminal cancer patients choose to undergo chemotherapy during the last 10 to 30 days of life, which is expensive and only marginally extends the patients' lives (see, for example, Harrington and Smith [2008], who note that 43% of terminal lung cancer patients in the United States receive chemotherapy in the last month of life, compared with just 23% in Italy). However, patients, families, and doctors likely feel more satisfied that they tried everything.

The Role of High Input Prices in Driving Health Expenditure Levels

A popular health policy article has the provocative title, "It's the Prices, Stupid: Why the United States Is so Different From Other Countries" (Anderson, Reinhardt, Hussey, & Petrosyan, 2003). In addition to the complexity of costs and value calculations in U.S. health care is this simple fact: Almost every actor in the health sector has managed to command very high prices for the role he or she plays. U.S. physicians earn higher salaries than in almost every other country (Laugesen & Glied, 2011), pharmaceutical prices are much higher in the United States than in other countries, hospital prices are much higher, and hospital administrators earn more in the United States than elsewhere. Even professors in health policy and management programs tend to have higher salaries than professors of history or English literature.

> *Because of the high stakes involved in medical care, patients often find price to be an irrelevant consideration.*

Why have actors in the health system been able to charge such high prices for their services? Because of the high stakes involved in medical care, patients often find price to be an irrelevant consideration. In addition, insurance and extensive government contributions to financing medical care mean that consumers (i.e., patients) have not exerted market power as usually happens for other goods and services in the U.S. economy.

Another factor is the barriers to entry in health care. Because of federal regulations, there are a limited number of slots in medical schools and residency training programs, which helps maintain high input prices. Even if building more hospitals were possible and could drive down prices through increased competition, federal reimbursements are already below costs. For most of the past 20 years, Medicaid and Medicare reimbursements have been below hospital costs; as these public payers make up an increasing share of providers' revenues, the implication is obvious—private payers must make up the difference. In 2012, Medicaid paid about 89% of hospital costs to treat its beneficiaries, whereas Medicare paid only 86% (American Hospital Association, 2012). Private insurers must make up the difference through increased payments, which drives up costs further.

It is more difficult to explain why employers who pay for their employees' health insurance do not bargain more for lower prices through the insurance companies they use. To date, employees have placed a great deal of value on having access to all or most providers in a community so that they have as much choice as possible. This preference, however, impedes the ability of their employers to negotiate prices with local health care providers. Employers have spent more energy in recent years adding copayments and premium sharing for employees to attempt to address their ever-rising costs for insurance.

TECHNOLOGICAL COSTS AS A DRIVER OF HEALTH CARE SPENDING

Not all of the rising expenditures on health care are due to overspending on items that do not create value. In fact, new pharmaceuticals, new technology, and ever-emerging new medical know-how are constantly identifying better ways to address illness and disease. These inventions and innovations are impressive and the United States (both the private and public sectors) has been a leader in sponsoring the research that has expanded our ability to solve more and more medical challenges. With emerging understanding of genes and bioengineering and new ways of using big data to test new approaches in medical procedures, it is likely that more and more possibilities for expanding the tools we have to address illness and disease will continue to grow for the foreseeable future (see Chapter 16).

Most of these new possibilities in treating medical conditions, however, are expensive and will add to the burden of health care in our economy. We will be drawn to spend more and more on health care as new possibilities emerge. Some of the new approaches will have value that exceeds costs, and some will not. Deciding how to measure the value of new approaches relative to cost will be key.

Our experience to date in making choices about what new procedures to cover and what not to cover has been troubling. In many ways, we often seem to allow almost unlimited access to new technologies and procedures. For example, studies find that the United States has more magnetic resonance imaging (MRI) machines, computed tomography (CT) scanners, positron emission tomography (PET) scanners, and mammographs than other developed countries; importantly, the United States utilizes these more expensive technologies relative to other nations, which increases costs (Squires, 2012).

Although referring doctors do not receive any revenues from referring patients to specialists, fear of malpractice claims (discussed earlier) is a potential driver of this increased usage. Furthermore, patients in many cases request these tests even though doctors might not otherwise order them, leading to consumer-driven waste.

Chandra and Skinner (2012) developed a typology of medical technology based on average cost-effectiveness:

- *Category I technologies* are "home runs" that are cost-effective for nearly every relevant patient. Examples of Category I technologies include antibiotics, improved health behaviors (surgeons washing hands, for example), and most vaccines.
- *Category II technologies* are potentially cost-effective, but the benefits vary by patient. For example, angioplasty is beneficial to some, but not to other patients; imaging technologies may not be cost-effective for all patients, and so on.
- *Category III technologies* have modest or uncertain effectiveness. Examples include surgeries designed to treat quality of life rather than acute health conditions.

Unsurprisingly, most studies find that Category II and III technologies have spread through the U.S. system more widely than in other countries. This helps explain why the United States spends more—on technology and health care in general—but some outcomes are no better, because we tend to adopt ineffective technologies (from a cost-effectiveness perspective) more frequently than many other countries.

ATTEMPTS TO CONTROL HEALTH CARE COSTS

Most agree that attempts to control health care costs too often have either modest or no success. The current system tends to reward increased volume of services, but the services may not be justified when one examines the value-added of the service. This issue ties back to Emerick and Lewis's (2013) discussion about overscreening and overdiagnosis by providers; it also relates to employers paying for an increasing amount of health insurance benefits for employees that may not add health value but do add costs.

Other countries have managed to control costs by limiting or rationing some services. Although the United States will treat "marginal" patients who are ill, Europe rations such treatments based on age, gender, and other health factors. For example, the U.S. health care system accepts twice as many end stage renal disease (ERSD) patients for treatment as Europe and 40% more than Canada (USRDS, 1999). With dialysis treatments costing more than $70,000 annually per patient, the U.S. health care system spends significantly more on this service than other nations simply because we do not ration care. Limitless care becomes expensive, and Americans are uncomfortable limiting such care.

Other attempts to control costs involve reducing payments to doctors and providers. As Medicaid has exploded as a share of state budgets, public officials have increasingly turned to limiting reimbursements as a means of controlling public spending. As a result, some doctors have begun refusing new Medicaid patients. This is especially true among more expensive specialist doctors (Jackson Healthcare, 2012). As a result, many patients do not have access to medical professionals despite expensive public insurance, which does not pay enough for practitioners to take on new patients. These patients either end up using the more expensive option of the emergency department or fail to get treatment for treatable chronic conditions. In both cases, the ultimate costs of health care increase. A recent study finds that people in Oregon who received Medicaid benefits did use doctors more than those without health insurance, but these same people also used the emergency department more—thereby driving up health costs (Taubman, Allen, Wright, Baicker, & Finkelstein, 2014).

Finally, attempts to address demographic factors have had mixed success at best. Although public health campaigns and increased taxation have reduced tobacco consumption in the United States, we still have a significant population that smokes; furthermore, public efforts to address obesity through diet restrictions (such as New York City's attempt to limit sales of "supersize" sodas) or increased exercise have not been very successful because obesity rates continue to increase nationally. This is even as health insurance coverage has frequently added wellness programs (and, as a result, added costs) designed to change unhealthy behaviors. However, such programs are used by only a fraction of the covered populations or often are not cost-effective. It is estimated that less than half of eligible employees partake in offered wellness programs and, even though health outcomes apparently improve, cost savings do not seem to materialize as expected (Huang, Van Busum, Khodyakov, & Shier, 2013).

REDUCING COSTS AND INCREASING VALUE

So far, this chapter has explained why health care costs have increased significantly over time without producing the better outcomes and more value that one might expect from our investments in the health system. We now turn to some options that might address this ongoing dilemma.

Reforming Medical Malpractice

Medical malpractice reform could result in providers reducing the level of defensive medicine, leading to fewer tests and consultations, which would in turn reduce costs. Furthermore, malpractice insurance costs would not decrease evenly for all medical providers. Capping noneconomic damages is estimated to reduce insurance premiums by more than 25% for obstetrics doctors, 21% for general surgeons, and nearly 18% for internal medicine doctors (Robert Wood Johnson Foundation, 2007). To the extent that that these specialists are more expensive service providers, reducing mal-practice costs will reduce health care spending.

Choosing Less Costly Treatments

One option that is frequently discussed as a source of savings is a move from more expensive procedures to less expensive treatments that do not negatively affect health outcomes. However, determining what these expensive procedures are and what the equally effective cheaper alternatives are is not easy (if it were, we would have done it already). For example, new beta blocker drugs are frequently as effective as stents for treating chronic heart disease; physical therapy frequently leads to superior out-comes over back surgery. Many health care providers disagree that these alternative treatments, however, are equally effective.

Importantly, both of these examples rely on patients following a medical protocol whereas the more expensive options put the doctor in control of ensuring that a pro-tocol is followed. To the extent that less expensive options rely on patients following through on tasks, we risk not getting value or cost savings because patients are noto-rious for failing to follow doctors' orders. Furthermore, the cost-effective nature of stents (and other treatments for that matter) usually rests on a limited number of stud-ies (Rosenbaum, 2013). Medical trials—with free medications and services, dedicated medical providers, and close monitoring of patients—do not resemble the day-to-day realities of health care practice. In other words, despite the apparent ease of control-ling overtreatment or expensive treatment, achieving this control is in fact difficult.

Paying Fixed Amounts for Procedures

Another option is for insurers to pay only a certain fixed amount for a procedure. This fixed amount might be the average cost in an area, perhaps controlled for qual-ity. If the cost of the procedure exceeds the amount the insurer will pay, the patient (the insured) pays the difference. The insurance company provides the insured with a list of providers who charge at or below the fixed amount. In doing so, the insured is more likely to choose the less expensive providers with no negative implications for quality. In fact, such a program was implemented in California for public employees; as a result, health care costs were reduced by 19%. By providing consumers (patients) with information and giving them incentives to keep costs down (fewer out-of-pocket costs), such an approach could potentially reduce health care costs.

Using Electronic Medical Records

Electronic medical records (EMRs) hold promise for reducing duplicate tests and improving the quality of care. National policy currently expects savings from EMRs. However, one study (McCormick et al., 2012) actually found that physicians were *more* likely to order additional tests in the presence of EMRs. This study focused on office-based doctors, whereas most other studies that found cost savings focused on large medical centers. The cost outcome for EMRs is likely to be mixed, based on the type of provider.

However, if EMRs can push the overall health care system toward greater standard-ization of computer interfaces, part of the administrative complexities that cost hun-dreds of billions of dollars annually might also be saved. The federal government could incentivize such standardization through the Affordable Care Act (Cutler et al., 2012).

Using Value-Based Purchasing

> *Unlike fee-for-service payments, which effectively reward volume regardless of cost or quality, value-based purchasing is meant to encourage specific quality and cost outcomes based on agreed-on performance measures.*

Value-based purchasing (VBP) might also help to generate savings while increasing value. In VBP, payers (including governments) hold providers accountable for cost and quality of care. For example, a physician group might share generated savings with payers if spending growth is kept below some agreed-upon threshold; or a hospital might receive bonus payments for high-quality or increasing quality performance. Unlike fee-for-service payments, which effectively reward volume regardless of cost or quality, VBP is meant to encourage specific quality and cost outcomes based on agreed-on performance measures. One way to accomplish this, advocates argue, is to bundle payments so that outcomes rather than volume drives reimbursements to health care providers. Furthermore, VBP should publicize provider performance so that patients may select high-value providers.

However, VBP requires systems to measure and report performance—that is, it requires spending to achieve future cost reductions and value improvements. The key to whether VBP can be successful is whether we can achieve value from this spending or, alternatively, whether we can reallocate current health care spending to VBP and get more value. One option is to replace Medicare's sustainable growth rate (SGR) formula with a value-based formula (Guterman, Zezza, & Schoen, 2013; Schroeder and Frist, 2013). Given the difficulty in measuring performance in health care, VBP is not an easy solution, despite its obvious appeal.

Reducing the Cost of End-of-Life Care

Changing how we spend on end-of-life care is also critical. One reform is to increase the use of hospices to provide low-cost, high-quality end-of-life care. Currently, most patients and families do not avail themselves of hospices; however, even though a majority of patients say they would prefer to die at home, most actually die in hospitals—suggesting that less aggressive treatments and hospice care at life's end might be possible for and even preferred by patients.

Taking Responsibility for One's Own Health

Personal responsibility to maintain one's health is a critical factor to controlling health care costs. Citizens should exercise, avoid tobacco products, receive proper vaccinations, and maintain healthy body weights. Personal choices such as using tanning beds—which are known to increase incidents of skin cancer—should be discouraged. The U.S. health care system suffers from these self-inflicted costs that are, in many respects, reflective of our nation's economic success. This is perhaps the greatest source of savings, and the hardest to deliver.

Some employers have begun to take matters into their own hands. For example, the Cleveland Clinic will no longer hire workers who smoke tobacco and monitors employees' blood levels; Proctor & Gamble, United Parcel Service, and several state governments (such as Wisconsin and Washington) charge smokers if they do not complete a smoking-cessation program (Kingsbury, 2013). As health costs continue to climb, employers apparently are determined to bring these costs under control.

The Cost of Value

One potential problem with any attempt to control costs, however, is whether the intervention lowers costs simply by lowering standards. If quality controls are eliminated, costs will decline but quality will suffer. If we make consumers more aware of prices and more responsible for their choices in consuming health care services, will they choose lower-quality health care now that simply drives up health care costs later? For example, if MRI costs are greater at a particular hospital because two radiologists read the same film, will patients choose to have MRIs at private practices where only a single radiologist reads the film? This option would certainly be cheaper, but will quality suffer as a result of losing the second radiologist's evaluation?

Ensuring quality and value costs money. Popular press accounts of markups by health care providers are increasingly common. Rosenthal (2013) notes, for example, that a California health care provider charges nearly $37 for Tylenol with codeine when the market price of each pill is only 50 cents. In the case of dispensing a simple over-the-counter medicine to patients, the following steps occur:

1. A doctor orders the patient pain reliever.
2. A registered nurse (RN) receives the order from the doctor.
3. The RN forwards the pain reliever order to the pharmacist.
4. The pharmacist enters the order into the electronic information system.
5. The pharmacist then analyzes the patient's drug profile to reduce the likelihood of drug interactions and complications.
6. A pharmacy technician retrieves the pain reliever drug.
7. The pharmacist verifies it is the correct drug and scans it into an electronic information system.
8. The technician delivers pain reliever to patient's medication drawer and delivers it to the RN.
9. The RN retrieves the drug and brings it to the patient.
10. The RN verifies the patient's identity to ensure the correct patient is receiving the drug.
11. The RN scans the drug so information is captured by the electronic information system.
12. The RN verifies the order in the electronic system.
13. The RN administers the drug to the patient.
14. The RN records and documents drug administration in the electronic system.

In this very simple example, if each step takes on average 4 minutes, nearly 1 hour of labor is consumed simply to dispense a simple pain reliever. If average labor costs are approximately $50 per hour, this 50 cents' worth of drugs can actually cost $50 to dispense—in large part due to (valid) quality and value concerns of patient treatments.

■ Conclusion

Over the past several decades, health care spending in the United States has increased faster than general economic growth. Part of this trend is attributable to our system of health care financing, in which third-party payers, rather than consumers, pay the bulk of the costs. This upward trend is also influenced by citizen demand for limitless health care services and well-intentioned but costly regulations on providers. Furthermore, personal behavioral choices (poor diet, lack of exercise, drug abuse, and so on) also drive up health care costs.

Attempts at slowing cost growth have largely focused on reducing payments to providers or on restraining services covered by insurance companies. These attempts ultimately end up being undone or result in patients' being unable to use their insurance because providers opt out of accepting it.

There are no easy structural fixes—or large pot of money to be found—that will solve the issue of health care cost growth. Importantly, we need to gather data on ongoing programs designed to address the issue. Whether it is accountable care organizations (ACOs), company-sponsored Centers of Excellence (COEs), or the use of technology to reduce unnecessary treatments and procedures, data can provide insights into what saves money without sacrificing value and what does not. Organizations such as Kaiser Permanente, in which the provider is the employer and the insurer, have led to cost reductions and improved outcomes for patients; such models of care should be analyzed for sustainability and scalability. New models of care could be phased in over a 5-year period, gradually replacing traditional fee-for-service reimbursement with more value-based reimbursements (Schroeder & Frist, 2013). Such efforts take time and cannot be implemented rapidly. But research and data will move us closer to aligning providers' and payers' incentives—something the current system still fails to do.

Much potential cost saving comes from changing individuals' behaviors, or perhaps from rationing care given in certain cases (at the end of life, for babies born very prematurely with significant health problems, for health problems brought on by obesity, and so on). Americans have a strong aversion to such limits on health care, however, and such changes are not amenable to public policy options or acceptable to our culture at large. Finding a way to change our culture of health and finding transformative approaches to rethinking our health care system remain key challenges facing the health sector and those who lead it.

■ Discussion Questions

1. Is the growth in health care costs a real concern for the United States? Why or why not?

2. Comment on the claim that "the U.S. health care delivery system is the finest in the world."

3. If obesity and the inability or unwillingness of patients to follow good health protocols are two drivers of health care costs, what are the implications of shifting more costs to consumers who are obese or who do not follow medical protocols? Would such a shift be ethical? Would this shift change behavior, or would it simply make these populations seek less medical treatment (potentially driving up future health costs)?

4. Recent legislation requires insurance companies that offer coverage for mental health or substance abuse to provide the same level of benefits as they do for medical treatments. What are the implications of this requirement for health care costs? What are the implications for value?

5. Pharmaceutical companies frequently advertise drugs to the public that require a doctor's prescription. Consider how such advertising might affect drug costs and utilization of services by patients.

6. An August 4, 2013, a *New York Times* article described the role of nonmedical costs in driving up health care. European health care centers are described as "Spartan"—for example, a Belgian clinic was described as having metal folding chairs, bland wall colorings, and no gift shop. This was contrasted with a U.S. hospital that had a comfortable waiting room, a fancy lobby, and even newsstands to sell conveniences to patients and visitors. Discuss these differences in light of cost and value. What barriers might the United States face in making a transition to a more European-style system?

7. In India, doctors are usually consulted only for very difficult and complicated procedures. Routine procedures are typically handled by lower-skilled health care workers such as nurse practitioners, nurses, or paramedics. What barriers might the United States face in making a transition to a more Indian-style system?

8. Discuss three interventions at the provider level and at the state level (where much regulation occurs) that will increase value for costs in health care. Explain why the interventions will work. If they will work, why haven't we implemented them already?

CASE STUDY

You are a senior manager at a major health care provider in a competitive environment. The CEO of the medical center informs you that the board of directors has asked that monthly reporting not be limited to financial projections and budget-to-actual reports. Rather, they are becoming concerned with evaluating the medical center's performance on value. The board still has a fiduciary responsibility to ensure the financial health of the organization, but members are increasingly concerned with value provided and not just cost. The CEO asks you to advise her on what she should propose to the board for such monitoring of value.

As you draft your recommendations, consider the following questions:

1. Why might the board of directors want to monitor value?
2. What indicators would you recommend to the CEO?
3. How would you gather data and evidence that might suggest increasing value for cost?
4. How would you measure success in these value-for-cost efforts?

■ References

American Hospital Association. (2012). *Avalere Health analysis of American Health Association Annual Survey Data*. Table 4.4, page A-35. Retrieved from http://www.aha.org/research/reports/tw/chartbook/ch4.shtml

Anderson, G. F., Reinhardt, U. E., Hussey, P. S., & Petrosyan, V. (2003). It's the prices, stupid: Why the United States is so different from other countries. *Health Affairs, 22*(3), 89–105.

Baicker, K., & Chandra, A. (2005). *The labor market effects of rising health insurance premiums* (Working paper no. 11160). Cambridge, MA: National Bureau of Economic Research. Retrieved from http://www.nber.org/papers/w11160

Berwick, D. M., & Hackbarth, A. D. (2012). Eliminating waste in US health care. *The Journal of the American Medical Association, 307*(14), 1513–1516.

Buchmueller, T., Carey, C., & Levy, H. G. (2013). Will employers drop health insurance coverage because of the Affordable Care Act? *Health Affairs, 32*(9), 1522–1530.

Chandra, A., & Skinner, J. (2012). Technology growth and expenditure growth in health care. *Journal of Economic Literature, 50*(3), 645–680.

Commonwealth Fund. (2013). *Better care at lower cost: Is it possible?* Retrieved from http://www.commonwealthfund.org/~/media/Files/Publications/Health%20Reform%20and%20You/Health_reform_and_you_COSTS_11_22_2013_web_final.pdf

Cutler, D., Wikler, E., & Basch, P. (2012). Reducing administrative costs and improving the health care system. *New England Journal of Medicine, 367*, 1875–1878.

Dartmouth Atlas of Health Care. (2014). Retrieved from http://www.dartmouthatlas.org/keyissues/issue.aspx?con=2911

Emerick, T., & Lewis, A. (2013). *Cracking health costs: How to cut your company's costs and provide employees better care.* Hoboken, NJ: Wiley.

Finkelstein, E. A., Trogdon, J. G., & Cohen, J. W. (2009). Annual medical spending attributable to obesity: Payer- and service-specific estimates. *Health Affairs, 28*(5), w822–w831.

Guterman, S., Zezza, M. A., & Schoen, C. (2013). *Paying for value: Replacing Medicare's sustainable growth rate formula with incentives to improve care.* New York, NY: The Commonwealth Fund.

Hagist, C., & Kotlikoff, L. J. (2006). *Health care spending: What the future will look like* (Policy report no. 286). Washington, DC: National Center for Policy Analysis.

Harrington, S. E., & Smith, T. J. (2008). The role of chemotherapy at the end of life: "When is enough, enough?" *Journal of the American Medical Association, 299*(22), 2667–2678.

Huang, C. Y., Van Busum, K. R., Khodyakov, D., & Shier, V. (2013). *Workplace wellness programs study: Final report.* Santa Monica, CA: RAND Corporation. Retrieved from http://www.rand.org/pubs/research_reports/RR254

Institute of Medicine (IOM). (2012). *Best care at lower cost: The path to continuously learning health care in America.* Washington, DC: Author.

Jackson Healthcare. (2012). *A tough time for physicians: 2012 medical practice and attitude report.* Retrieved from http://www.jacksonhealthcare.com/media/137811/physiciantrendsreport_ebook0712-final.pdf

Kessler, D., & McClellan, M. (1996). Do doctors practice defensive medicine? *Quartely Journal of Economics, 111*, 353–390.

Kingsbury, K. (November 13, 2013). How your company is watching your waistline. *Reuters.* Retrieved from http://in.reuters.com/article/2013/11/13/usa-healthcare-benefits-idINDEE9AC0BY20131113

Laugesen, M. J., & Glied, S. A. (2011). Higher fees paid to US physicians drive higher spending for physician services compared to other countries. *Health Affairs, 30*(9), 1647–1656.

McCormick, D., Bor, D. H., Woolhandler, S., & Himmelstein, D. U. (2012). Giving office-based physicians electronic access to patients' prior imaging and lab results did not deter ordering of new tests. *Health Affairs, 31*(3), 488–496.

Mello, M. M., Chandra, A., Gawande, A. A., & Studdert, D. M. (2010). National costs of the medical liability system. *Health Affairs, 29*(9), 1569–1577.

OECD. (2013). *Health at a Glance 2013: OECD Indicators*. Retrieved from http://www .oecd.org/els/health-systems/Health-at-a-Glance-2013.pdf

Robert Wood Johnson Foundation. (2007). *Insurance Premiums Decline in States Capping Malpractice Payouts, Alabama University Study Finds*. Retrieved from http://www .rwjf.org/content/dam/farm/reports/program_results_reports/2007/rwjf20381

Robert Wood Johnson Foundation. (2013). *Finding value in health care: How providers are addressing rising costs*. Retrieved from http://www.rwjf.org/content/dam/farm/ reports/issue_briefs/2013/rwjf405299

Rosenbaum, L. (2013, October 23). When is a medical treatment unnecessary? *The New Yorker*. Retrieved from http://www.newyorker.com/tech/elements/when-is-a-medical-treatment-unnecessary

Rosenthal, E. (2013, December 2). As Hospital Prices Soar, a Stitch Tops $500. *The New York Times*. Retrieved from http://www.nytimes.com/2013/12/03/health/as-hospital-costs-soar-single-stitch-tops-500.html

Schroeder, S. A., & Frist, W. (2013). Phasing out fee-for-service payment. *New England Journal of Medicine, 368*, 2029–2032.

Sood, N., Ghosh, A., & Escarce, J. J. (2009). Employer-sponsored insurance, health care cost growth, and the economic performance of U.S. industries. *Health Services Research, 44*(5), 1449–1464.

Squires, D. A. (2012). *Explaining high health care spending in the United States: An international comparison of supply, utilization, prices, and quality*. New York, NY: The Commonwealth Fund.

Taubman, S. L., Allen, H. L., Wright, B. J., Baicker, K., & Finkelstein, A. N. (2014). Medicaid increases emergency-department use: Evidence from Oregon's health insurance experiment. *Science, 343*(6168), 263–268. *doi*:10.1126/science.1246183

USRDS. (1999). Annual Data Report. *Chapter XII: International Comparisons of ERSD Therapy*, 173–184. Retrieved from http://www.usrds.org/chapters/ch12.pdf

Wade, H. (2012). Small business problems & priorities, 2012. Nashville, TN: The National Federation of Independent Business. Retrieved from http://www.nfib.com/Portals/0/ PDF/AllUsers/research/studies/small-business-problems-priorities-2012-nfib.pdf

13 High-Quality Health Care

Carolyn Clancy and Irene Fraser

KEY WORDS

outcomes

pay-for-performance (PFP)

performance measurement

process

statistical process control

structure

value-based purchasing (VBP)

LEARNING OBJECTIVES

- ⊙ Explain why quality promotion is important in health care
- ⊙ Explain why quality assurance is difficult in the health sector
- ⊙ Understand methods used to improve quality
- ⊙ Review how economic incentives can influence quality improvement
- ⊙ Describe recent trends in quality improvement

TOPICAL OUTLINE

- ⊙ Defining quality in health care
- ⊙ The current state of quality in the United States
- ⊙ Approaches to improving quality
- ⊙ Creating incentives for providers to improve quality
- ⊙ The role of managers in promoting quality
- ⊙ Recent developments and trends in the quality improvement field

TG is a 55-year-old man with diabetes, high blood pressure, and arthritis in both knees. As one knee becomes increasingly painful (and sometimes buckles), he is advised to have a total knee replacement. Surgery goes well, but TG develops a serious infection. For months, he's unable to put any weight on the operated leg, and for weeks he is forced to take antibiotics and miss work. TG then has a second surgery to remove the joint replacement and have a new one placed. This time, the operation and recovery both go smoothly. TG's spouse and family are delighted that their long odyssey is over, but they wonder: Could we have done something differently? Should we have searched for information on quality and safety for the physician and hospital, and would doing so have made a difference?

The views expressed in this chapter are those of the authors and are not intended to represent official policy of the Department of Health and Human Services, the Department of Veterans affairs, or the U.S. government.

The authors gratefully acknowledge the expert assistance of Louise Arnheim and Brent Sandmeyer.

Historically, an individual having surgery relied on a physician's recommendation —or that of a family member or friend—regarding a surgeon and/or hospital. Today, there are numerous sources of online information regarding performance for hospitals and other health care organizations. Websites also provide condition-specific information to help people understand what a diagnosis means, the options for treatment, and questions to ask when exploring those options. This plethora of information, however, is not easy to navigate, and many areas have yet to be addressed.

As a result of numerous studies, prestigious reports, and media accounts, Americans now know that high-quality, safe care is not automatic. Furthermore, the past 20 years have been marked by widespread efforts to assess and improve health care quality. Most recently passage of the 2010 Patient Protection and Affordable Care Act (ACA) and the American Recovery and Reinvestment Act of 2009 (ARRA) have created greater momentum toward ensuring quality care by (a) accelerating interest in linking payment for services to results, and (b) creating multiple provisions that put providers on a path to high-quality, affordable health care.

This chapter describes the current state of health care quality (including avoidable harms from care); reviews selected efforts to conceptualize, measure, and improve quality; describes how measures are used to guide improvements in care; addresses promising initiatives to improve care; and predicts how the health care landscape will evolve in the coming years.

■ Defining Quality

Quality is defined by the Institute of Medicine (IOM) as "the degree to which health services for individuals and populations increase the likelihood of desired health outcomes and are consistent with current professional knowledge" (Lohr & Schroeder, 1999). Implicitly, this definition covers both individuals and patient groups, including those who seek care and those who do not. Furthermore, the definition was intended to focus on outcomes or end results important to individuals and to recognize that medical knowledge evolves. The IOM identifies six dimensions of quality: Health care should be safe, effective, patient-centered, timely, efficient, and equitable (IOM, 2001). A frequently used shorthand definition of quality is "the right care for the right patient at the right time."

■ How Are We Doing?

Throughout the 20th century impressive successes in biomedical science and public health—including dramatic reductions in cardiovascular diseases, the transition of HIV from a death sentence to a highly manageable chronic condition, and significant reductions in the percentage of Americans who smoke—resulted in substantial increases in life expectancy by as much as 30 years.

However, multiple studies indicate that there is much room for improvement, especially in the care of chronic illnesses. Multiple studies during the past decade confirm a sizable gap between best possible care and that which is routinely provided. In addition, international studies comparing health and health care in the United States with other countries are sobering. A recent Commonwealth Fund study (Davis, Stremekis, Schoen, & Squires, 2014) of 11 countries (Australia, Canada, France,

Germany, Netherlands, New Zealand, Norway, Sweden, Switzerland, the United Kingdom, and the United States) found that the United States ranked dead last—as it did in the 2010, 2007, 2006, and 2004 editions of the study. The World Health Organization's (WHO) analysis of 191 countries found that the United States spent a higher proportion of its gross domestic product on health than any other country but ranked 37th in performance (WHO, 2000).

> *Numerous studies examining the processes and outcomes of care have shown substantial variations in clinical practice and have resulted in a movement to develop better methods for determining the relationship between care processes and outcomes.*

Numerous studies examining the processes and outcomes of care have shown substantial variations in clinical practice (itself an indicator of questionable quality) and have resulted in a movement to develop better methods for determining the relationship between care processes and outcomes. These efforts also revealed underuse, overuse, and misuse of services, as well as the substantial time lapse for new scientific findings to be translated into practice—a problem that persists to this day. In addition, the past 15 years have witnessed increased attention to avoidable harms that occur as a result of receiving care, such as health care–associated infections (HAIs), surgical complications, and errors in prescribing and dispensing medications. There also has been increasing recognition of how factors external to direct care—including reimbursement, organizational structure, and leadership—influence safety and quality.

The U.S. Agency for Healthcare Research and Quality (AHRQ), which is mandated by Congress to report annually on the state of health care quality and health care disparities, has found statistically significant increases in quality across all settings and populations since 2003. However, the magnitude of improvement has most often been modest, and disparities in care associated with individuals' race, ethnicity, age, education, income, and other factors remain pervasive.

■ How Do We Improve Quality?

Health care quality in the United States is not optimal; in fact, it varies considerably across communities, across providers, and even across departments in the same facility. So how do we improve it? There is no easy, simple answer, no switch that can be flipped. Figure 13.1 provides a framework for identifying the intersection of several major factors in quality improvement. For starters, we know there are several critical steps that providers or administrators can take:

- Measure what you are doing, and with what result.
- Know what works clinically, and make sure you are doing it.
- Look at how care is organized and delivered, and what process improvements might be made.
- Prioritize quality and safety. (This is especially important for those in leadership positions.)

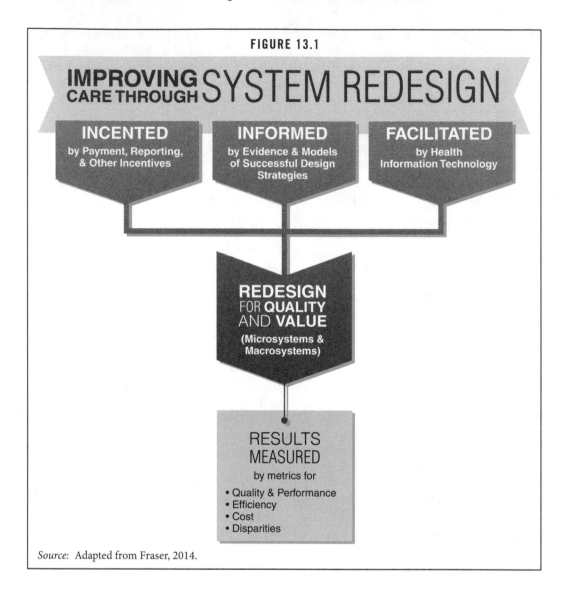

FIGURE 13.1

Source: Adapted from Fraser, 2014.

MEASURE WHAT YOU ARE DOING

Human beings are fascinated with measuring things. This fascination starts at an early age. We give first-grade students a ruler and tell them to go home and measure the length of the kitchen table, the height of their parents, or the size of their television. The children do this with great enthusiasm and usually go beyond the basic instructions to measure things beyond the teacher's list. As we grow older, many of us remain fascinated with measuring things, especially if they are important to us. Golfers, runners, bowlers, and cyclists, for example, frequently keep meticulous records on the events in which they have participated, often so they can track their own improvement.

Similarly, health care providers or leaders who seek to improve the quality and safety of their care start by measuring what they are doing, and with what effect. Obviously, health care is more complicated than running or bowling—and it is growing increasingly more complex. As a result, determining *what* to measure is no easy task. (And, as discussed later in this chapter, the provider is not the only one doing the measuring.)

A good starting point is with the definition of quality provided by Avedis Donabedian (1988). According to Donabedian, quality consists of three important dimensions: structure, process, and outcomes.

- *Structure* refers to facilities and health care professionals providing care.
- *Process* refers to the set of services provided.
- *Outcomes* refer to the end results people experience and that they care about.

The earliest efforts to ensure quality focused on structure, such as urging hospitals to update equipment and check the credentials and training of all health care workers. As Donabedian consistently emphasizes, however, although these three dimensions clearly are interrelated, little is known about their causal linkages.

One way to think about the distinctions among the three dimensions would be to consider the need for regular hand-washing as a way to prevent hospital infections (WHO, 2009). In this case, a *structural* measure would be whether there were sinks in, or by, each patient's room. A *process* measure would be the frequency with which providers entering the room actually did wash their hands before touching a patient. An *outcome* measure would be the frequency of HAIs.

As this example illustrates, structural measures are the easiest to conduct and can measure important elements. However, structural measurements are most remote from the outcome. Having even 10 sinks in the room will not prevent an infection unless the provider uses one of them. Measuring process can bring you closer to the outcome—for example, measuring hand-washing is an effective infection prevention strategy—but does not guarantee the outcome. One could imagine all sorts of scenarios (unsterilized instruments, infected visitors, and so on) in which perfect processes could couple with unsatisfactory outcomes. As this example also illustrates, external factors may come into play (such as the infected visitors). To improve quality, it is critical that providers measure outcomes as well as processes (and structure, where pertinent); in addition, they must identify any external factors that may imperil the outcome and seek ways to exercise some influence over these.

> *Ideally, process measures derive from strong evidence that a specific service results in an improved outcome.*

Ideally, process measures derive from strong evidence that a specific service results in an improved outcome. These measures typically are derived from clinical research that shows a particular act or intervention—for example, giving a beta blocker to patients who have had a heart attack—will, *all things being equal*, achieve better outcomes.

Process measures are commonly expressed as a percentage of eligible patients who received a particular service or action—the beta blocker or the washed hands. Monitoring process measures very closely can be critical to quality improvement. But it is equally important to monitor outcomes to make sure that there are no other, unmeasured factors intervening to produce poor outcomes, even with good process scores. As noted later, consumers and payers are particularly interested in outcomes, and policymakers also are moving in the direction of outcome measures.

> *What a patient cares about is the quality of the entire treatment plan, not just how well each individual piece was done.*

Accompanying this greater interest in outcomes is a growing interest in measuring the quality of an entire episode of care rather than each individual service. After all, what a patient cares about is the quality of the entire treatment plan, not just how well each individual piece was done. Payers moving from fee-for-service to some type of bundled payment or capitation system will also want to measure the whole, rather than just the sum, of the parts. Achieving evidence-based, credible, and reliable measures that cut across services and even sites of care is a major challenge, but one that must be met in order to move the quality agenda forward.

Even though good measures are important, they are meaningless without good data. The definition of what constitutes good data varies depending on the purpose the data will serve. For quality improvement, data ideally are (a) readily available as a byproduct of the care process itself, (b) recent enough to permit analysis and improvement in close to real time, and (c) detailed enough to enable the posing and testing of hypotheses about which factors were responsible for current levels of quality or recent changes in quality. External benchmarks and, especially, examples of high performers can also be useful as a way to prod continuous improvement and guard against complacency.

Just as measures are meaningless without good data, however, the utility of both is limited by poor communication. It is often said that health care is data rich, but information poor. In other words, every encounter involves information collection, yet the information is not easily shared by the multiple providers involved in a patient's care. Indeed, most physicians effectively fly blind, with little (if any) information about how their practices compare to their peers' and with limited capacity to quickly identify all patients in their practice with a specific condition or treatment. Important clinical details are most often recorded on paper, whereas billing is almost universally electronic.

Major data sources for quality assessment include billing data, medical charts (which are more detailed, but expensive and laborious to review), and patient surveys. Provisions in the ARRA requiring broad adoption of electronic health records that can be shared among providers should make the task of data collection easier. These provisions should also facilitate more timely feedback to providers in order to accelerate improvements in care where needed (see Chapter 16).

Fundamentally, at the front lines of care delivery, the process of measurement itself remains very much a work in progress. The heterogeneity of the U.S. health care system means that most hospitals experience separate demands for information on quality from states, public payers, private sector payers, accreditors, and others. Advances in measurement science have enhanced our capacity to assess dimensions of care and identify opportunities for improvement. For example, various tools, such as AHRQ's State Snapshots, allow care providers to compare their quality scores with other providers in their region or state and allow states to compare themselves on numerous quality measures with other states (AHRQ, 2014). Overall, coordination of priorities for quality measurement among multiple payers will be required.

Measurement of care is the first practical step toward improving care. But determining *what* to measure and *how* to measure are critical to gathering the right information that will help to improve organizational processes of care and transform health care delivery for the better.

KNOW WHAT WORKS CLINICALLY

At its core, health care quality is the sum of multiple individual interactions between clinicians and patients; hence, most widely used process measures derive from scientific evidence about which treatments work best, and for whom. In practical terms, valid measures reflect both strong evidence and professional endorsement—a specific treatment or approach represents what should be done for most individuals with a specific condition. The usual approach occurs when clinical professional organizations develop and disseminate practice guidelines, from which measures are derived; these, in turn, are recognized by independent private sector organizations. This supply chain is highly dependent on scientific funding, the capacity of professional organizations to conduct technical work and to update both guidelines and measures to reflect scientific advances, and the degree to which data can be obtained to apply the measure. Policy efforts to promote adoption of electronic health records and other applications of health information technology should be a game changer, making it easier to collect requisite data and to include reminders and decision support that help to improve care in real time.

Since publication of the IOM report *To Err Is Human*, which identified avoidable harms to patients as a result of medical care as a leading cause of mortality, there has been increased emphasis on identifying what works clinically to prevent avoidable harms (IOM, 1999). For example, hospitalized patients who are immobilized for long periods due to injury, surgery, or other factors, are at increased risk of blood clots. Anticipating this risk and administering prophylactic blood thinners reduces the risk dramatically. Similar strategies have been developed and implemented for common preventable harms. The IOM report also directed health care organizations to establish and nurture environments that encourage all staff to speak up with concerns about actual or potential patient harms to minimize these harms.

IMPROVE ORGANIZATION AND DELIVERY

Although it is critical to perform those services with proven effectiveness, doing so will not ensure quality or good outcomes. Human bodies are complex, and health care organizations are also complex. In the past, health care mostly consisted of a visit between one patient and one doctor or other provider. Today, most health care is delivered by very complex, increasingly large organizations. High-quality health care requires that all providers—physicians, nurses, receptionists, technicians, and so on—do excellent work as individuals, as well as in collaborative teams at all organizational levels.

One way to think about this organizational component is to consider a set of concentric circles with the patient and physician (or other provider) at the center. There, at the bedside or in the exam room, it is obviously essential that there be a correct diagnosis and appropriate treatment. Much recent research and quality improvement effort has been directed toward improving safety and quality at this micro level. As noted earlier, however, clinicians seldom act in a vacuum. Outside the clinician–patient circle is a "team" circle. This team might include, for example, a surgeon and others in the intensive care unit, or one or more primary care clinicians and their other staff, such as nurses, nutritionists, receptionist, and so on. A patient's quality of care depends on the talents of individual team members and also on the quality of the members' interactions as a team. Based on early research related to teams, there are now sophisticated tools and training materials to help improve team performance. For example, TeamSTEPPS, developed jointly by the Department of Defense and AHRQ, includes modules on primary care, nursing homes, and care for patients with limited English proficiency (see teamstepps.ahrq.gov).

When looking at ways to improve quality, it is also important to look at the care processes themselves, both at the team level and across teams—at the so-called meso level of the organization—that might be involved in the care of a particular patient. This meso level is the next circle out in the set of concentric circles. Many industries have spent years working to improve their production processes by closely examining each of the steps involved, seeing how they fit together or do not fit together, and then asking whether those processes can be improved to reduce the number of defects or the range of variations. As noted in the final section of this chapter, however, health care has come late to this type of analysis and improvement.

Finally, to truly achieve quality of care for a patient, it is important to look at the macro level—that is, how different health care organizations relate to each other and to the external environment. A patient can experience safety and quality problems even when being treated by a talented and coordinated care organization because multiple organizations can be involved in the care of any particular patient.

For example, the patient "handoff" (e.g., hospital discharge) is a time of particular vulnerability at the macro level. The time surrounding discharge frequently is a difficult and confusing one for all concerned. Patients and their families have a lot of conversations, receive a lot of paperwork, and then go home or to a postacute care facility; they may have few or no follow-up conversations with hospital staff. However, consider the patient who has limited English proficiency or health literacy: Any number of gaps can prove troublesome. For example, the discharge planner may not ask the right questions; the patient may have no regular source of primary care or social support; the patient may even be homeless. A patient with these issues may develop complications or require hospital readmission. Although some readmissions might be planned or result from an unrelated problem, many readmissions result from complications of care during a recent hospital stay, a problem with discharge planning, problems with postacute care, or a lack of necessary follow-up care. Recognition of these issues has led to development of discharge planning toolkits which have had much success in reducing readmission rates.[1] A nationwide public-private partnership—the Partnership for Patients—has used such toolkits as part of a nationwide campaign to reduce readmission rates (see partnershipforpatients.cms.gov).

---

[1] For an example of a discharge planning training program, see AHRQ's Project RED (www.ahrq.gov/professionals /systems/hospital/red/index.html).

Recently, there has been considerable experimentation with efforts to improve care through other macro-level interventions as well. One prominent example is the emergence of primary care medical homes (PCMHs; also called patient centered medical homes) as a way to achieve coordination of care for patients across multiple organizations, with the primary care provider playing an essential role. The growth of accountable care organizations (ACOs), in which a single entity is held accountable for care across the spectrum, provides another example of a macro-level approach. Finally, some organizations—for example, safety-net providers—go even broader by encompassing many nonmedical services in their mix—services such as nutrition counseling, transportation, even housing—recognizing that in the final analysis these nonmedical services can play an even greater role in health than medical care.

Of all of these approaches, micro-level quality improvement is undoubtedly the easiest and the closest to most clinicians' comfort zone. Improvements in care are most dramatic for services under the direct control of a clinician or a health care organization, such as ordering the right tests for patients with diabetes or heart disease. Control of cholesterol or diabetes or asthma, on the other hand, may require changes not only in patients' lifestyle choices but in their communities as well, and achieving these improvements requires coordination with multiple external organizations.

PRIORITIZE QUALITY AND SAFETY

As the earlier discussion makes clear, achieving safety and quality is not easy and requires that everyone involved look outside the box of their own job description, continually seeking ways to achieve more systemic improvements. The single most important determinant of that happening is whether organizational leadership deems quality top priority. Every day, leaders of health care organizations, including their boards, convey their priorities to staff by the questions they ask, the outcomes they reward, and so on. Effective leaders nurture a culture of safety and quality, which lays the groundwork for quality improvement (Jiang, Lockee, Bass, Fraser, & Norwood, 2009). Furthermore, organizations differ substantially in terms of scores on safety culture surveys, such as those compiled by AHRQ at http://www.ahrq.gov/professionals/quality-patient-safety/patientsafetyculture/.

■ How Do We Incentivize Quality Care?

The health care environment is replete with financial, policy, and other drivers that influence provider behavior. Improving the quality of health care, therefore, means finding ways to harness these drivers to maximize and align positive incentives to the provision of quality and to eliminate perverse incentives. Because these incentives occur within the complex human and organizational environment in which care is provided, the effect of particular incentives varies from institution to institution, over time, and within institutions. To complicate matters further, for most potential incentives we lack strong evidence of when, how, how much, and why they will be effective in achieving their intended outcomes while avoiding unintended ones (e.g., manipulating metrics to achieve expected results).

As a starting point, five drivers are discussed: professionalism, public reporting, payment and finance, consumerism, and regulation.

PROFESSIONALISM

Professionalism refers to the conduct, aims, or qualities that characterize members of a given profession. People choose health care over banking or manufacturing for a reason. It is important to recognize that most clinicians strive to provide the right care to the right patient at the right time and take great pride in doing so. In addition, most measure developers recognize the importance of using metrics that are credible with clinicians for their scientific content and recognition by the profession as important. Similarly, when health plans, employers, and community quality collaboratives use private performance reports as a way to encourage quality improvement, it is important that they use measures that resonate with physicians and other providers (Shaller & Kanouse, 2012). In short, efforts to improve quality that build on current science and clinicians' desire to do well by their patients are far more likely to succeed than those perceived as "counting the countable" but overlooking the important aspects of care.

> *Efforts to improve quality that build on current science and clinicians' desire to do well by their patients are far more likely to succeed than those perceived as "counting the countable" but overlooking the important aspects of care.*

Virtually all licensed professionals are required to document a commitment to continuing medical education, an enterprise that is increasingly linked to the challenges confronting clinicians in daily practice. In other words, whereas in the past continuing education focused almost exclusively on knowledge (what to do in specific circumstances), currently far more attention is being paid to expanding the focus to include specific skills (how to provide specific services). In addition, the medical boards that certify physicians based on their knowledge similarly have shifted their process to include an explicit link to quality improvement processes, thereby establishing a direct link between knowledge and actual performance.

An early example of this approach focused on pediatric practices in North Carolina. Practices were randomized to receive focused coaching to improve the delivery of clinical preventive services; all clinicians received continuing education credits in exchange for participation (Margolis et al., 2004). These can and do include medical record reviews, patient surveys, and a new requirement that maintenance of certification is a process of lifelong learning.

Major specialty boards are now partnering with large health care organizations to encourage and support physicians to continually refresh their skills and knowledge. A clear and tangible connection between pride in one's work and the tools for assessing quality can be a potent nonfinancial driver of high-performing organizations.

PUBLIC REPORTING

Another potential driver for quality is creation and dissemination of comparative public reports for consumers. Smith and colleagues (2012) noted that "transparency of process, outcome, price, and cost information, both within health care and with patients and the public, has untapped potential to support continuous learning and improvement in patient experience, outcomes, and cost and the delivery of high-value care."

Reports comparing the quality—and sometimes the cost—of individual facilities or providers have proliferated in recent years. Part of the rationale is philosophical, based on consumers' right to know about their own care. However, the growing impetus behind publication of public reports comes from the premise that the availability and use of this information can be a force for improving quality.

Public reports have the potential to improve quality in two ways. First, public reports theoretically enable consumers to comparison shop for health care, just as they do for other products, selecting those with higher quality, and/or lower costs, more convenience, and so on. At the very least, an effective public report could help an individual consumer identify a hospital or physician practice or nursing home with higher quality and/or better value. If enough informed consumers make these choices, the theory goes, the cumulative effect of individual informed decisions potentially could improve quality across the community, as high-quality providers gain more business and low-quality providers lose business.

Second, public reports enable health care providers to compare their performance with the performance of their peers. For reasons both professional and business-related, providers do not want to be perceived poorly.

Public reports for consumers have proliferated in the past several years, driven by state mandates and national legislation, as well as by regional quality improvement efforts and private transparency efforts such as HealthGrades, Consumer Reports, and so on. As Figure 13.2 shows, reports comparing hospital quality are the most common mandate, but, increasingly, states are requiring quality reports for health plans, nursing homes, and physicians as well. At the national level, the Centers for Medicare & Medicaid Services (CMS) report publicly on the quality of hospitals, nursing homes, physicians, and other providers. Additionally, the ACA ushered in a greater emphasis on public reporting. In particular, sections 3014 and 3015 of the ACA call for increased U.S. Department of Health and Human Services (DHHS) activity in quality measurement and public reporting.

What do we know about the effects of such reports? The evidence is fairly clear about the potential effect on provider behavior. Even though some providers undoubtedly ignore some reports, when there is a clear message providers often take notice and take action (AHRQ, 2012a). A classic study in Wisconsin showed that hospitals with public reports were significantly more likely to initiate quality improvement activities than those with private reports (scores shared only with the individual hospital) or no reports. This finding was particularly the case for low-scoring hospitals and in the areas in which they had scored poorly (Hibbard, Stockard, & Tusler, 2003). Moreover, making data public brought actual improvements in the clinical areas reported (Hibbard, Stockard, & Tusler, 2005).

On the other hand, there is less evidence that public reports significantly change consumer behavior (AHRQ, 2012a). There are several reasons for this finding, and some of those reasons have nothing to do with the reports themselves:

■ Consumers often are not in a position to choose between two providers. Their employer may offer only one health plan, or their plan may restrict their choice of hospital or medical group.

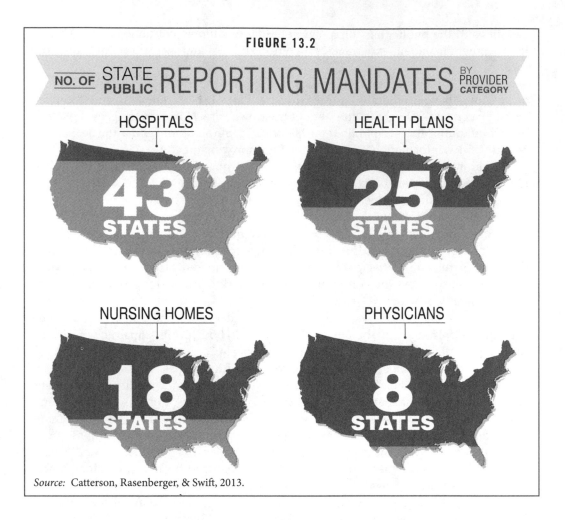

FIGURE 13.2

NO. OF STATE PUBLIC REPORTING MANDATES BY PROVIDER CATEGORY

HOSPITALS
43 STATES

HEALTH PLANS
25 STATES

NURSING HOMES
18 STATES

PHYSICIANS
8 STATES

Source: Catterson, Rasenberger, & Swift, 2013.

- Circumstances may not permit a choice: A patient suffering a heart attack is not in a position to research options for a hospital.
- Patients often rely on physicians for referrals and are not accustomed to seeking information from public reports.

In addition, several factors related to the reports themselves may account for this consumer behavior:

- *The measures:* Most of the information in public reports has not been developed in response to expressed consumer interest, but rather in response to what measure developers and report producers think should interest consumers and patients.
- *Competing reports:* With policy interest in transparency growing and public reports on quality proliferating, confusion reigns regarding scores. Furthermore, the number of competing reports has resulted in tremendous discrepancy.
- *Information overload:* Consumers prefer to start with simple summary measures and icons and then drill down in accordance with their interests. Many report cards are designed as online versions of paper reports, with page after page of detailed tables.

- *Clunky format:* Increasingly, consumers rely upon websites and social media for information. These venues support and link to sophisticated, fast search engines where consumers can prioritize their own preferences as part of the search process. For the most part, public reports on provider quality lag behind this technology trend.

In an effort to assess the state of public reporting, AHRQ partnered with The Commonwealth Fund to convene a summit. The Summit on Public Reporting brought together major stakeholders and experts, including researchers, consumers, payers, providers, and policymakers. The summit's goal was to discuss the current state of the art in public reporting and to identify major gaps and an agenda for the future. In preparation for the summit, a contractor surveyed experts and stakeholders for their take on the current state of public reporting. The results were rather daunting: 81% said that even the best existing reports needed substantial improvement and redesign (AHRQ, 2011).

As a follow-up to the summit, AHRQ partnered in 2012 with the CMS to launch a Science of Public Reporting initiative. The initiative's goal is to build the science and to accelerate adoption of proven improvements by the CMS, states, and others who are developing public reports for consumers. To build the evidence base, AHRQ funded 17 grants in (a) effective design and presentation, (b) effective dissemination, and (c) strengthening the underlying data, measures, and methods (AHRQ, 2012b).

On the dissemination side, AHRQ produced a special journal issue (*Medical Care Research and Review* Supplement, 2014), working directly with some of the major report developers, including the CMS, to ensure that findings are put to effective use as soon as possible after the evidence is available. To bolster this take up and dissemination of findings, AHRQ has accelerated evolution of My Own Network Powered by AHRQ (MONAHRQ, available at MONAHRQ.ahrq.gov), a free, evidence-based website-builder that enables a state or other reporting entity to download free software from AHRQ, including Hospital Compare data, add locally available data (state hospital discharge data) to populate reporting fields, and create an almost instant public reporting website. As of this writing, 13 states are using MONAHRQ to generate public reports.

Public reporting faces several future challenges:

- *Linking cost information (ideally consumer price information) to quality.* With the growing use of high-deductible health plans, consumer interest in price is likely to grow. Some health plans now produce reports for members that show out-of-pocket costs, and some states provide these data more widely, as well.[2] One important caution from research to date is the need to display cost and quality information together; otherwise, a consumer is likely to draw the erroneous conclusion that the higher-cost service is better (Hibbard, Greene, Sofaer, Firminger, & Hirsh, 2012).
- *Incorporating social media.* With so many consumers, particularly younger ones, relying on social media to compare products, and so much of social media working to incorporate health care services, finding ways to incorporate the growing evidence base into these outlets will be an important challenge.

---

[2] See, for example, the All-Payer Claims Database (www.apcdcouncil.org).

- *Increasing the timeliness and clinical robustness of public reports.* Consumers are becoming more and more accustomed to being able to access near real-time information, and providers are rightfully concerned about being judged based on old information. Although there is hope that electronic health records may eventually solve these problems, it is critical in the short term to take advantage of electronic capabilities to add clinical detail and speed to existing reports.

PAYMENT AND FINANCE

Payment and finance are another set of powerful drivers in the quality landscape. Any base payment structure brings inevitable incentives. The typical, traditional payment system for most providers in the United States has been fee-for-service, a system that typically has rewarded providers for more services rendered or longer hospital stays. In the 1980s, the Medicare program moved hospitals to a diagnosis-related groups (DRG) system, in part as a way to reduce incentives for prolonging hospital length of stay. Under capitation, in which a health plan has responsibility for the care of a defined population and is paid a fixed fee per member per month, the incentive is to reduce the number of high-cost services such as hospitalization.

In recent years, public and private payers have sought ways to create deliberate, targeted incentives—usually as an overlay on top of fee-for-service or other payment systems—to reward hospitals, physicians, and others for achieving particular quality or efficiency goals. This array of strategies, which variously are called *pay-for-performance* or *value-based purchasing*, builds on the growing measurement enterprise, often using measures used in public reporting. One recent survey showed that 10.9% of current payments are value-oriented (i.e., tied to performance or designed to cut waste), with traditional fee-for-service, bundled payment, capitation, and partial capitation making up the remaining 89.1% (Catalyst for Payment Reform, 2013). The CMS is moving rapidly in the direction of value-based purchasing, with initiatives such as the Hospital Value-Based Purchasing program, performance bonuses for Medicare Advantage (MA) programs, and the Physician Value-Based Payment Modifier. In the private sector, insurers sometimes reward higher quality (and/or lower cost) by selectively contracting with only some providers in the marketplace, or tiering providers, offering consumers lower copayments for some than for others.

Tracking the effect of such strategies is not easy for several reasons:

- *Incentive size:* The incentive is often relatively small compared with the overall volume of business—and especially compared with the cost of making the improvements required to reap the reward. Consequently, if there is no effect, it is hard to tell whether a larger incentive might have worked.
- *Incentive confusion and fatigue:* The CMS itself has many incentives applied to the same institutions. Hospitals, for example, have incentives related to readmission rates, adoption of "meaningful use" of certified electronic health record technology, and incidence of major patient safety events, in addition to more targeted incentives such as those in the Hospital Value-Based Purchasing program. In any particular market, these incentives may or may not be aligned with the incentives from private payers or even Medicaid. In addition, sorting out the relative effects of public reporting and incentives is no easy matter.

- *No pure controls:* The ubiquity of differing incentives, coupled with public reporting efforts, makes it very difficult to find a control for purposes of evaluation.
- *Context and implementation:* The effect of payment incentives is likely to vary not only by provider (hospitals versus nursing homes versus physician groups), but also depending on how providers pass incentives along within the organization.

There has been a good bit of evaluation of the effect of financial incentives, but the results to date are mixed. Studies show, at most, a small positive effect on quality, and in particular on improvements in process. For the most part, however, improvements in process have not led to improvements in outcome (Shih, Nicholas, Thumma, Birkmeyer, & Dimick, 2014; Jha, Joynt, Orav, & Epstein, 2012; Ryan, 2009). On the other hand, the Medicare program recently has been ramping up its move to value-based purchasing in ways that the market has not seen before, so it is possible that future evaluations may show stronger and broader impact.

Finding a way to hold all providers to high standards for all patients, while accounting for the greater challenges some face, is a continuing goal.

With the proliferation of new, and in many cases stronger, payment incentives, it will be critical that research address the complex question of what *form* of incentives, in what *magnitude* and under what *circumstances*, have the power to produce *which* intended consequences, while *avoiding unintended consequences*. One critical unintended consequence is exacerbation of disparities. Safety-net providers, often financially fragile, care for many patients with medical and nonmedical (such as homelessness) problems that cannot yet be adequately incorporated into risk-adjustment methodologies. Finding a way to hold all providers to high standards for all patients, while accounting for the greater challenges some face, is a continuing goal.

CONSUMERISM

In the past 20 years there has been a gradual but marked change in the public's expectations of health care. Many people are more interested in health and health care, but also more skeptical about advice that doesn't feel right for them. Advances in communications technologies, which have reduced asymmetries in health information between health professionals and patients, have surely accelerated this trend. Moreover, surveys of Americans in the baby boomer age group have consistently demonstrated less trust in authority in multiple areas, including medicine, compared with older cohorts.

As noted in the discussion of public reporting, consumers or patients also can play an important role in quality. Just as consumers want to buy a car or a refrigerator that is reliable, they are even more motivated to receive good health care and to stay healthy. Even though the stakes are so high in health care, the consumer incentive works differently in the health care market than in other markets. There are several reasons for this:

- Because of the private and public insurance system, the purchaser of care is generally not the actual consumer of that care.

- Consumers and patients often lack the information they need to act in their own interests.

- Consumers often do not feel empowered to question their medical care team on recommended services or drugs in the way they would question, for example, a car mechanic or a roofer. Shortened medical visits do not make it any easier for patients to ask questions.

- Medical care services are only one factor that affects health. Lifestyle factors (such as obesity, low activity levels, bad diet, and smoking) have a larger effect on health than medical care.

- Even though consumers have an incentive to be healthy, good health is a more distal goal that often cannot compete well with immediate gratification.

To improve quality and outcomes, it is important to activate and align the incentives of patients and consumers, as well as providers. In the past few years, several developments have created steps in that direction, as these examples illustrate:

- Increased transparency in quality and price is starting to provide some of the information needed for consumers to make better choices, and the increased availability of clinical information on the Internet and social media is also making useful information more accessible to patients.

- Higher copays and deductibles are creating an environment in which consumers are motivated to choose a better-value provider, and also to question services they will purchase out of pocket. Unfortunately, past research (Chernew & Newhouse, 2008) has shown that increasing out-of-pocket payments lead patients to reduce their use of both necessary and less necessary services.

- One recent effort to be more strategic in the use of consumer financial incentives is value-based insurance design, in which copays for services of questionable utility are high and copays for critical services are low or nonexistent.

- Another path for incentivizing consumers is to alter the price of insurance based on health habits—for example, by charging smokers more or providing a reward to smokers who successfully quit. This is a very common approach for employers.

REGULATION

Periodic inspections of health care facilities through accreditation, combined with explicit processes for verifying the credentials and skills of clinicians (often referred to as *credentialing*), have been mainstays of the regulatory approach to health care quality. The application of performance measures to assess quality, however, has shown there is a gap between capability or competence and actual performance—in other words, accreditation and credentialing are necessary but far from sufficient to guarantee provision of high-quality care. No site visit or process can guarantee that care will be of high quality. However, regulatory standards do establish a floor, or minimum set of competencies, that all health care organizations must meet. In addition, these processes are thought to offer a clear framework for health care leaders to understand critical interdependencies as the delivery of care becomes more complex.

■ What Are Major Recent Developments Affecting Quality?

Achieving high-quality health care is a high priority for many stakeholders. For patients, quality can be a life-or-death matter. Some of the initiatives described earlier, such as public reporting and payment incentives, have been deliberate efforts to affect quality. In recent years, passage of the ACA has been the single most important development affecting quality. However, other new forces are also at work.

THE PATIENT PROTECTION AND AFFORDABLE CARE ACT (ACA)

The ACA, signed into law in 2010, is primarily recognized for its effects on health care coverage. The ACA has already expanded access to health insurance to millions of Americans. It also has provided patient and consumer protections—for example, by eliminating use of preexisting condition limitations and lifetime caps on covered expenses.

Far less attention has been paid to the law's explicit recognition that sustaining the promise of expanded health care coverage demands efforts to promote and incentivize high-quality, affordable care. Numerous provisions in the law address many aspects of quality, such as improving measure selection, testing new models of care, and supporting research about which treatments work for patients. In addition, the ACA requires the development and annual update of a first-ever National Strategy for Quality Improvement (www.ahrq.gov/workingforquality/). Selected examples are described here:

- *Building on current efforts:* In the past decade, there have been incremental policy steps encouraging or requiring performance transparency in selected domains. Starting with voluntary efforts, progressing through what has been termed "pay for reporting" (a small percentage of annual update tied to reporting on quality), to linking achievement of selected quality goals to reimbursement (value-based purchasing), this journey also has included expansion in the number and types of metrics, including surveys to assess patients' experiences of care. The ACA requires that this approach be expanded to other settings, including rehabilitation and skilled nursing facilities, and that the incentives be increased over time.

- *Testing new approaches:* The ACA created a new Center for Innovation at the CMS, which is supporting the development and application of new approaches to financing linked with quality requirements. Examples include bundled payments, in which one payment is made for a broad array of services provided within one discrete episode of care, as well as support for ACOs, which integrate services and payments across multiple settings and establish virtual integrated organizations. A unique feature of the ACA allows successful demonstrations or models to be continued and possibly incorporated into future policy updates.

- *Patient-centered medical homes:* PCMHs are part of a professional movement to revitalize and reinvent the delivery of primary care. The ACA includes multiple provisions to support and evaluate this new approach to primary care, which includes a strong focus on care organized around the patient's needs and preferences, a reliance on care teams rather than on individual clinicians, integration of mental health services, and reliable after-hours care. These models are very much in progress, but they are important because the combination of increased needs associated with an aging population and expanded access to insurance is expected to place high demands on the primary care sector.

ROLE OF NONGOVERNMENTAL ORGANIZATIONS

Many nongovernmental organizations also play a significant and evolving role in quality and quality improvement, by developing and endorsing measures, accrediting health care organizations, conducting research on quality improvement at the micro and macro levels, using market power to encourage change, and facilitating use of emerging evidence to bring about transformation. Here are some examples:

- *National Quality Forum (NQF).* The NQF, a not-for-profit, membership-based organization, has a major role in *quality measurement.* It endorses standards for performance measurement; in particular, it reviews and endorses measures for use in public reporting and payment.
- *The Joint Commission:* The Joint Commission, another not-for-profit organization, *accredits and certifies* health care organizations and programs. This accreditation is critical to hospitals and other organizations, because the CMS requires accreditation as a condition of participation in the Medicare program.
- *National Committee for Quality Assurance (NCQA):* The NCQA also *accredits and certifies* health care programs, with a particular initial focus on health plans and now including disease management organizations, primary care medical homes, and accountable care organizations. It also originated and maintains and updates Healthcare Effectiveness Data and Information Set (HEDIS) *measures* of health plan performance.
- *University research programs:* Research programs at major universities around the country, funded by the National Institutes of Health, AHRQ, and private foundations, develop *measures* of quality and safety, as well as *evidence* on how to improve quality and safety at both the micro and macro levels.
- *Employers and employer organizations:* Large employers and employer organizations, such as the National Business Group on Health and the National Business Coalition on Health, have a stake in both employee health and health care costs. Individually and as a group, they seek to *incentivize higher quality and value.*
- *Institute for Healthcare Improvement (IHI):* The IHI, a not-for-profit organization based in Cambridge, Massachusetts, seeks to *organize and mobilize quality improvement* and transformation by organizing learning networks and collaboratives in projects to drive and sustain improvement.
- *Quality improvement organizations (QIOs):* QIOs are groups of health quality experts, clinicians, and consumers who work under the direction of CMS to (a) improve care for Medicare beneficiaries and (b) review quality concerns. (CMS, n.d.) As a result of recent legislation, QIOs doing quality improvement will be separate from those doing review.
- *Community quality collaboratives:* These multistakeholder regional collaboratives around the country take an active role in *public reporting, encouraging community engagement*, and *facilitating quality improvement* at the regional level.

LEAN

Lean, a tool developed by the automotive industry in Japan, is receiving increasing interest as a way to improve health care quality and efficiency in the United States. Lean provides this 5-step process for improving quality:

1. Specify value from the standpoint of the end customer by product family.
2. Identify all the steps in the value stream for each product family, eliminating wherever possible those steps that do not create value.
3. Make the value-creating steps occur in tight sequence so that the product will flow smoothly toward the customer.
4. As flow is introduced, customers pull value from the next upstream activity.
5. As value is specified, value streams are identified, wasted steps are removed, and flow and pull are introduced, begin the process again and continue it until a state of perfection is reached in which perfect value is created with no waste. (Lean Enterprise Institute, n.d.)

Lean has been used successfully to redesign health care. For example, Denver Health implemented a Lean system redesign in 2005, and between 2006 and 2008 achieved a 50% lower registration time in eight Federally Qualified Health Centers, lower patient cycle times and no-show rates, 25% higher provider productivity in clinics, $14 million in cumulative savings, and increased clinic revenues by $3.5 million (AHRQ, 2007).

Even though examples such as this show promise, there has been little systematic evaluation of whether, and under what circumstances, interventions such as these can achieve similar success across a wide variety of systems. There have been some reviews of publications on Lean in health care, but these reviews and most of the underlying studies concentrate on a narrow band of project outcomes, such as quality or efficiency. Although it is clear from this work that Lean *can* be successful, less is known about the factors necessary for such success: the organizational processes supporting implementation, characteristics of implementing organizations, or interactions between Lean and other features of the organizational context. A recent study by AHRQ (Harrison et al., 2014) provides an understanding of how context shapes Lean implementation.

PATIENT AND FAMILY ENGAGEMENT

Many local and regional efforts to promote transparency in quality performance have developed through the establishment of multistakeholder coalitions, including consumers, employers, health care providers, insurers, and other parties. In a similar vein, an increasing number of health care organizations have sought the experiences of patients and families to inform their efforts to deliver services focused on patients' needs and preferences. Studies also have revealed that patients and families often observe aspects of care not immediately visible through other sources; capturing those observations and experiences can provide important insights about the care experience through the patient's eyes. Some observers have labeled patient engagement the "blockbuster drug" of the 21st century.

Even though many governing boards have long included at least one public representative, Massachusetts now requires all hospitals to have a formal patient and family advisory council. AHRQ also has supported an effort to develop and evaluate a survey tool that builds on patient and family experiences of care to improve patient safety. At this writing, it is too early to know the collective effect of these efforts, but it is clear that the patient's voice represents a vital component of current and future efforts to continuously improve health care delivery.

■ Core Competencies for Health Administrators

Until recently, administrators have not necessarily made assessing and improving the quality of care a top priority. Yet, increasingly, the bottom line for all health care facilities—and therefore the priority for administrators—will include an explicit focus on care quality: quality that is transparent and verifiable, rather than reputed. As a result, health care administrators need a solid grounding in quality measurement and in the design and evaluation of interventions and programs to improve quality (Lloyd, 2010a, 2010b).

Pragmatically, the function and structure of quality improvement has evolved considerably in the past 20 years in response to policy, regulatory, and other initiatives. It is also fair to acknowledge, however, that the constellation of disciplines, skills, and triggers for action is still quite dynamic. One fundamental consideration is the extent to which functions are centralized (e.g., a quality department) or distributed (quality is everyone's job); focused on improvement versus minimizing or avoiding risk; and internal to a health care organization versus external to it (e.g., payers writing requirements into contracts).

The steady expansion of policy initiatives, especially growing requirements for performance transparency and value-based purchasing, has resulted in formal activities and initiatives, but external factors remain important as well. The latter might occur in response to adverse publicity about an avoidable adverse event, for example, or as a consequence of insurers' increasing focus on buying value rather than only services.

One health care problem that has galvanized considerable attention is that of health care–associated infections (HAI). In 2007, investigators from Johns Hopkins reported the substantial successes of a deceptively simple approach to reducing infections associated with central line infections (Pronovost et al., 2006).[3] The problem is self-evident: Central line infections have a mortality rate of 25%, and the approaches deployed are straightforward: rigorous attention to hand hygiene and sterile technique, as well as avoidance of the lines when feasible. Yet rates of these infections appeared for many years to be persistently high. The research team partnered with BlueCross in Michigan; all Michigan hospitals, including their CEOs; and the Michigan Hospital Association. They coupled a straightforward set of practices with empowerment strategies (e.g., any worker could "stop the line" if procedures were not followed), involvement of senior leadership, and modest data collection to facilitate rapid feedback. All hospitals in Michigan achieved dramatic reductions; the approach has subsequently spread to hospitals across

---

[3] Central lines are used to administer treatments that frequently destroy peripheral veins, such as chemotherapy or high-dose nutrition for patients unable to eat. They are also used to monitor heart and lung function in severely ill patients.

the country in collaboration with the American Hospital Association. The combination of identifying an important problem (HAIs are easy to understand—and to fear), engaging senior leadership, facility with data, and using practical strategies for applying data was enormously successful. The relevant organizational structures were quite different, depending on hospital size and complexity, but the intervention was highly adaptable.

It is eminently clear that a health administrator's facility with performance data, including the capacity to present the information in different ways to different audiences (e.g., standardized infection rates versus days since we have had an infection in this unit) is and will continue to be a core competence. Note that this implies a full grasp of the application of data to identify and solve problems rather than simply conducting the requisite analyses, though a grounding in statistics is also imperative (e.g., how often should we assess hand-washing rates?). Nurses have arguably led the way in monitoring compliance with regulations and policies as a core component of quality assessment, but the full team required now includes clinicians from multiple disciplines. The ability to motivate, persuade, and communicate effectively is also a clear prerequisite.

Since these results were published, an increasing number of payers now require reporting of different HAIs. Improving quality from the payer side requires many of the skills described earlier, but because the specific actions are one step removed from actual delivery, improvement from this side also requires the ability to specify requirements, communicate results to customers to inspire them to choose high-quality care, and recognize when reported results don't add up.

Addressing near-term challenges specified by the ACA, including the prevention of HAIs, avoidable hospital readmissions, and avoidable patient harms, also requires a new vision for understanding how individual health care facilities relate to others in the community or region.

For example, policies that promote decreased payments for higher-than-average readmission rates will motivate hospitals to work with community partners in very different ways to address the cause of the poor performance—limited primary care capacity, limited after-hours care, poor health literacy among patients in the community, or something else. Similarly, the act's provisions to promote health (i.e., addressing the upstream causes of disease and illness) will also blur traditional hospital boundaries. In other words, the hospital administrator's job will no longer be confined within hospital walls but will require working with community partners, perhaps via health education and disease prevention programs.

In short, a focus on improving quality and safety cannot be outsourced to the quality department or team. To succeed and thrive, every department within a health care organization must make improving quality and safety a strategic imperative. The success of current and future health administrators will likely depend on their willingness and skill to engage clinical colleagues to achieve shared goals.

■ Conclusion

Success in the years ahead will depend on the ability of administrators to implement change and continuously enhance environments that meet these goals: (a) promote excellence in response to individual patient needs and preferences, (b) promote effective teamwork, and (c) celebrate efforts to identify innovations that make the right thing to do the *easy* thing to do. In short, one hopes that today's status quo will be unrecognizable in a few short years, as health care delivery overall responds to public and policy incentives for superb care and links that response closely to broad efforts aimed at promoting health and reducing the need for high-intensity services. The public should expect no less.

■ Discussion Questions

1. Why is it important to measure both process and outcomes? What are the opportunities and challenges of each type of measure?
2. What is the range of factors beyond the patient–physician (or other clinician) dyad that can affect quality of care for the patient?
3. What are the most promising new developments likely to improve health care quality?
4. How do public reporting and payment incentives affect the quality of care by hospitals, physicians, and others?
5. How can a health care leader best mobilize the power of professionalism as a force for quality? How can such strategies align with other incentive systems such as public reporting and payment?

CASE STUDY

You are the CEO of a 200-bed community hospital and have heard that Medicare hospital payments will continue to be trimmed for patients who experience harms considered to be largely preventable, such as blood clots, surgical infections, ventilator-associated pneumonias, and others. You want to make sure that your hospital prevents all possible avoidable harms to patients.

Your assistant summarizes the issues for you: Denied payments focus exclusively on additional care required to treat the injury, such as when a second procedure is required to retrieve a surgical instrument. To date, the denied payments are for hospital care only, but some analysts have recommended that the same policy be applied to physician payments.

One measure your hospital already has taken is to require that all workers who interact with patients wash their hands in order to prevent hospital-acquired infections. Although this would seem a simple and obvious initiative, it has met with limited success. In response to additional queries, you learn that the patient safety department does not track the kinds of events for which the hospital may be financially penalized.

You also know that the ACA affects hospital payment in another way: trimming reimbursements for potentially avoidable hospital readmissions. Your hospital serves an older population, and many patients currently have multiple admissions for acute exacerbations of chronic illnesses, such as congestive heart failure and diabetes. In the future, these multiple admissions may be very costly.

Your hospital's margin last year was razor thin; the combination of the economic downturn and any decreased reimbursements could result in closure.

Consider how you would address these leadership challenges. Be sure to address the following questions:

1. Who on your senior team should lead this effort?
2. Who else should be involved?
3. What precisely are you charging the team to do?
4. Who will help to communicate this effort to all front-line staff?
5. What kinds of systems need to be created to track progress?
6. What external resources could be utilized?

■ References

Agency for Healthcare Research and Quality. (2007). *Managing and evaluating rapid-cycle process improvements as vehicles for hospital system redesign: Continued.* Rockville, MD: Author. Retrieved from http://archive.ahrq.gov/research/findings/final-reports/rapidcycle/rapidcycle1.html

Agency for Healthcare Research and Quality. (2011, March 23). *National summit on public reporting.* Washington, DC.

Agency for Healthcare Research and Quality. (2012a). *Public reporting as a quality improvement strategy: A systematic review of the multiple pathways public reporting may influence quality of health care.* Rockville, MD: Author.

Agency for Healthcare Research and Quality. (2012b). *Building the science of public reporting: Research grants.* Rockville, MD: Author. Retrieved from http://www.ahrq.gov/professionals/quality-patient-safety/quality-resources/tools/sciencepubreport/index.html

Agency for Healthcare Research and Quality. (2014). *State snapshots.* Rockville, MD. Retrieved from http://www.ahrq.gov/research/data/state-snapshots/

Catalyst for Payment Reform. (2013). *National scorecard on payment reform* [PowerPoint slides]. Retrieved from http://www.catalyzcpaymentreform.org/images/documents/NationalScorecard.pdf

Catterson, R. S., Rasenberger, A., & Swift, E. (2013). *Public reporting of health quality and efficiency data: Current and upcoming statutory requirements.* Report prepared for the U.S. Department of Health and Human Services, Office of the Assistant Secretary for Planning and Evaluation, Office of Health Policy.

Centers for Medicare & Medicaid Services. (n.d.). *Quality improvement organizations.* Retrieved from http://www.cms.gov/Medicare/Quality-Initiatives-Patient-Assessment-Instruments/QualityImprovementOrgs

Chernew, M. E., & Newhouse, J. P. (2008). What does the RAND health insurance experiment tell us about the impact of patient cost sharing on health outcomes? *American Journal of Managed Care, 14*(7), 412–414.

Davis, J., Stremekis, K., Schoen, C., & Squires, D. (2014). *Mirror, mirror on the wall, 2014 Update: How the U.S. health care system compares internationally.* New York, NY: The Commonwealth Fund.

Donabedian, A. (1988). The quality of care: how can it be assessed? *JAMA, 260*(12),1743–1748.

Fraser, I. (2014, April 21). *The role of measurement and data in improving health care quality.* Paper presented to Institute of Medicine Conference on Health System Innovation for Effective Universal Health Coverage: Sharing the Experience of the United States and Mexico. Mexico City, Mexico.

Harrison, M. I., Paez, K., Carman, K., Stephens, J., Devers, K., & Garfinkel, S. (2014, August). *Effects of organizational context on Lean project implementation in five hospital systems.* Paper presented at the annual meeting of the Academy of Management, Philadelphia, PA.

Hibbard, J., Greene, J., Sofaer, S., Firminger, K., & Hirsh, J. (2012). An experiment shows that a well-designed report on costs and quality can help consumers choose high-value health care. *Health Affairs, 31*(3), 560–568.

Hibbard, J., Stockard, J., & Tusler, M. (2003). Does publicizing hospital performance stimulate quality improvement efforts? *Health Affairs, 22*(2), 84–94.

Hibbard, J., Stockard, J., & Tusler, M. (2005). Hospital performance reports: Impact on quality, market share, and reputation, *Health Affairs, 24*(4), 1150–1160.

Institute of Medicine. (1999). *To err is human – Building a safer health system.* Washington, DC: National Academies Press.

Institute of Medicine. (2001). *Crossing the quality chasm: A new health system for the 21st century.* Washington, DC: National Academies Press.

Jha, A. K., Joynt, K. E., Orav, E. J., & Epstein, A. M. (2012). The long-term effect of premier pay for performance on patient outcomes. *New England Journal of Medicine, 366*(17), 1606–1615.

Jiang, H. J., Lockee, C., Bass, K., Fraser, I., & Norwood, E. P. (2009). Board oversight of quality: Any differences in process of care and mortality? *Journal of Health Care Management, 54*(1), 15–30.

Lean Enterprise Institute. (n.d.). *Principles of Lean.* Retrieved from www.lean.org/what-slean/principles.cfm

Lloyd, R. (2010a). Helping leaders blink correctly: Part 1. *Health Care Executive, 25*(3), 88–91. Retrieved from http://www.ache.org

Lloyd, R. (2010b). Helping leaders blink correctly: Part 2. *Health Care Executive, 25*(4), 72–75. Retrieved from http://www.ache.org

Lohr, K. N., & Schroeder, S. A. (1990). A strategy for quality assurance in Medicare. *New England Journal of Medicine, 322,* 707–712.

Margolis, P. A., Lannon, C. M., Stuart, J. M., Fried, B. J., Keyes-Elstein, L., & Moore, D. E., Jr. (2004). Practice based education to improve delivery systems for prevention in primary care: Randomised trial. *British Medical Journal, 328*(7436), 388. Retrieved from http://www.ncbi.nlm.nih.gov/pubmed/14766718

Pronovost, P., Needham, D., Berenholtz, S., Sinopoli, D., Chu, H., Cosgrove, S., . . ., Goeschel, C. (2006). An intervention to decrease catheter-related bloodstream infections in the ICU. *New England Journal of Medicine 2006, 355,* 2725–2732

Ryan, A. M. (2009). Effects of the premier hospital quality incentive demonstration on Medicare patient mortality and cost. *Health Services Research, 44*(3), 821–842.

Shaller, D., & Kanouse, D. (2012). *Private "performance feedback" reporting for physicians: Guide for community quality collaboratives.* Rockville, MD: Agency for Healthcare Research and Quality.

Shih, T., Nicholas, L. H., Thumma, J. R., Birkmeyer, J. D., & Dimick, J. B. (2014). Does pay-for-performance improve surgical outcomes? An evaluation of phase 2 of the Premier Hospital Quality Incentives Demo. *Annals of Surgery, 259*(4), 677–681.

Smith, M., Saunders, R., Stuckhardt, L., & McGinnis, J. M. (Eds.). (2012). *Best care at lower cost: The path to continuously learning health care in America.* Washington, DC: National Academies Press.

World Health Organization. (2000). *World Health Organization assesses the world's health systems.* Geneva, Switzerland: Author. Retrieved from http://www.who.int/whr/2000/media_centre/press_release/en

World Health Organization. (2009). *WHO guidelines on hand hygiene in health care.* Geneva, Switzerland: Author. Retrieved from http://whqlibdoc.who.int/publications/2009/9789241597906_eng.pdf

Managing and Governing Health Care Organizations

Anthony R. Kovner and Christy Harris Lemak

KEY WORDS

accountability

evidence-based management

governance

management

organizational performance

stakeholders

LEARNING OBJECTIVES

- ◉ Understand how performance of health care organizations is evaluated
- ◉ Understand mechanisms of accountability for performance
- ◉ Learn what managers and board members do
- ◉ Understand the evidence-based process for evaluating strategic interventions

TOPICAL OUTLINE

- ◉ Governance and management matters
- ◉ Governing boards and owners
- ◉ What boards do
- ◉ Challenges boards face
- ◉ Management work
- ◉ Challenges managers face
- ◉ Challenges to the field of management

This chapter describes how health care organizations (HCOs) are governed and managed and how leadership is held or not held accountable for performance. We start by defining these terms. *Governance* is the process of how strategic decisions are made in HCOs, such as whether and how to finance a new hospital wing, evaluate the quality of patient care, and decide whether to hire nurse practitioners to provide primary care. *Stakeholders* are individuals and groups with an interest in the decisions HCOs make. *Management* shapes and implements governance decisions. *Accountability* is being called into account for decisions that affect health outcomes and processes of care at a given level of quality and a given level of cost. Managers can be called into account by governing boards, by owners, and by stakeholder groups. HCO *stakeholders* include, among others, regulators and accrediting bodies, payers and financers, clinicians and support staff, local community leaders and donors, patients and their families, members and taxpayers, beneficiaries and vendors, and local and state politicians.

■ Governing Boards and Owners

HCOs function under nonprofit, public, or for-profit ownership. Commonly in a nonprofit organization, the organization is "owned" by the nonprofit board. Most nonprofits are chartered and regulated by the state in which the organization was founded. Public HCOs, such as a state-owned medical school, are accountable to elected public officials or to boards appointed by elected public officials. For-profit corporations are accountable to investors, who are typically stockholders. Boards may be subject to ultimate control by remote owners who appoint board members.

HCO governing boards/owners include physicians, cooperatives, government, religious organizations, investors, employers, unions, and philanthropists.

The goals of these groups differ. For example, a union owning a hospital places a higher priority on keeping jobs for its members than a high rate of return on investment. Investor owners may place reverse priorities on these objectives.

WHAT BOARDS DO

According to Bowen (2008), nonprofit boards have eight principal functions:

- Select, encourage, advise, evaluate, compensate, and, if need be, replace the CEO
- Discuss, review, and approve strategic directions
- Monitor performance
- Ensure that the organization operates responsibly as well as effectively
- Act on specific policy recommendations and mobilize support for decisions taken
- Provide a buffer for the president or CEO and "take some of the heat"
- Ensure that the necessary resources will be available to pursue strategies and achieve objectives
- Nominate suitable candidates for election to the board and establish and carry out an effective system of board governance

Most board members are not employees of the organization, and many have limited experience in making important HCO decisions. Together as a board, directors must exercise the duties of care (acting as prudent persons), obedience (to the mission of the organization), and loyalty (have no conflicts of interest.) The board is considered the conscience of the organization and is ultimately accountable for protecting and achieving the mission.

Board members are not liable for bad business decisions as long as it can be shown that a (hypothetical) "prudent board member" could have made the same decisions in the same situation. Fundamentally, board members' decisions must serve their HCO's mission. For example, a board of a nonprofit nursing home should not invest in a race track. They also must be attuned to potential conflicts of interest. For example, when a board is considering a banking relationship, a board member who works for the local bank must acknowledge that interest and be absent from the discussion.

Little is known about the relationship between what nonprofit boards do and organizational performance. Most organizations have no formal accountability mechanisms for their board. Board members elect themselves, and they may or may not have limited terms of office.

What is the value of the board relative to its cost to the organization? There are certain costs in having a board, such as the time the managers must spend caring for the board—organizing meetings, listening to board members' views inside and outside of meetings, negotiating priorities and accountabilities. On the benefit side, boards add energy and considerable resources, have a more balanced view of the context of situations compared with the CEO, and can take a longer-term view in accomplishing the organizational mission. The board can ensure that "the main thing is the main thing," whether this means accomplishing the mission, making money, or ensuring jobs and access to care for low-income populations.

The governing board selects the chief executive officer (CEO), who usually selects the other managers. The board may or may not delegate decision making to the CEO, reserving the power to review or overturn management decisions. Managers are agents of the board, and they work full-time (unlike board members). Board members are not commonly paid, and many have full-time jobs in other organizations. Traditionally, the board's role was defined as policymaking and the manager's role as implementation. This may still be the view in some organizations. Sometimes the manager wants a "rubber stamp" board. Sometimes board members wish to micromanage the implementation of policy. At issue is the board's accountability for achieving the mission and for changing the mission, as circumstances the organization faces change over time. For an example of a mission, vision, and values statement approved by the board, see Exhibit 14.1.

EXHIBIT 14.1 MISSION: VISION AND VALUES: 2013 STATEMENT UCHealth

UCHealth was created through the partnership of the University of Colorado Hospital and Poudre Valley Health System.

Mission: We improve lives. In big ways through learning, healing, and discovery. In small ways through human connection. But in all ways, we improve lives.

Vision: From health care to health.

Values: Patients first, integrity and excellence.

CHALLENGES THAT BOARDS FACE

Boards must respond to many organizational challenges, which vary from institution to institution and over time. Some relatively constant challenges, however, are making sure the organization has revenues that cover operating costs, ensuring that services are delivered with high quality, and making sure that health outcomes among patients served are excellent. In order to do its job addressing these challenges, a board must make sure the executive staff tracks metrics that allow the board to evaluate the organization's performance in these areas. (For an example of how the customer can determine "which hospital is best" see Exhibit 14.2.) The field of measuring the performance of health care delivery has become more and more sophisticated in recent years. Increasingly, comparative data are being made available by payers and government regulators that allow the board to assess performance accurately. (For an example of improving coordinated care, see Exhibit 14.3.)

EXHIBIT 14.2 WHICH HOSPITAL IS BEST?

Assume a grandmother has asked you to help her select a hospital for her hip replacement surgery. For a location you know well, evaluate the local hospitals and make recommendations. What measures are most important? Is there a single "best" hospital? Why is this so difficult?

Tools to use include:

Hospital Compare
(Medicare, http://www.medicare.gov/hospitlcompare/)

Why not the best?
(The Commonwealth Fund://www.whynotthebest.org/)

Leapfrog
(http://www.leapfroggroup.org/)

Of course, there are other organizational goals that a delivery organization and its board can set. For example, the board might push the organization to improve the health of the community's population, rather than just focusing on patients who use the services of the organization. (For an example of linking performance to values, see Exhibit 14.4.) Or the board might set a goal of growing the size of the organization if the community is growing in size or shrinking the size of the organization if demand across the community is decreasing.

EXHIBIT 14.3 COORDINATION OF CARE

The Medical Home Network (MHN) was established as a public–private partnership to better coordinate care for the uninsured and underinsured in southwest Chicago.

A new initiative electronically links hospital emergency departments to local clinics. Patients in the Medicaid program are each assigned to a primary care physician or "medical home." Each time a patient is seen in any of the participating hospital emergency departments, a notification is immediately sent electronically to the medical home. In this way, the clinic can contact the patient the next day, get the patient in for a visit immediately, and discuss ways of managing his or her disease. A small financial award is provided to the medical home each time the patient is seen in the medical home within 7 days of an emergency department visit. The program has achieved important results in financial savings, improved quality of care, and patient satisfaction.

> **EXHIBIT 14.4 LINKING PERFORMANCE TO VALUES**
>
> Concentra, a subsidiary of Humana, Inc., is a national health company with 320 medical centers in 38 states (www.concentra.com).
>
> Managers at Concentra link performance in each of its clinics to values of being Welcoming, Skillful, and Respectful. Measures of performance are tracked and monitored relative to goals and benchmarks, such as metrics for Welcoming (e.g., clinic appearance), Respectful (e.g., follow-up calls made), and Skillful (e.g., wait times, communication, and patient satisfaction). Clinics and staff who consistently achieve benchmark performance receive bonuses and other rewards.

A key responsibility of a board of a community-based delivery organization is to understand the needs of the community and be proactive in meeting these needs.

A key responsibility of the board of a community-based delivery organization is to understand the needs of the community and be proactive in meeting these needs. Increasingly, boards may feel pressure to think in terms of broader outcomes—such as maintaining the health of a community—rather than the narrower outcomes of technical quality and outcome improvement. These changes are driven by changing approaches to reimbursing delivery organizations and increased integration of organizations within a community (e.g., see Chapter 11 on Financing and Chapter 13 on Quality Improvement).

Boards can have a tremendous influence on HCO performance by setting and overseeing strategy for an institution. They can decide to close or merge hospitals or mental health clinics. They can hold managers accountable for improving quality and transparency. They can drive organizations to cooperate with other community organizations to improve health. They can ensure that managerial incentives systems are aligned with strategy.

The challenges are daunting for a board to be effective in its job to make sure a delivery organization is performing well. To be effective, board members must spend enough time to learn how the organization operates and what drives effectiveness.

Healthy relationships between a board and senior staff at the organization, clear goals and objectives, and timely measures of outcomes related to goals and objectives all are essential for good board governance. Finally, to be effective, boards must understand what they should *not* do. Key among the list of things not to do is to meddle in ways that do not allow managers to manage and execute.

■ Management Work

The first thing that comes to mind in thinking about health care delivery is a clinician: a doctor, a nurse, or an aide. But managers, who are often behind the scenes (and who are sometimes clinicians) often make it possible for appropriate medical care to happen. Managers create and maintain the environment that supports clinicians in their work.

Managers create and maintain the environment that supports clinicians in their work.

To understand this crucial part of the health sector workforce, we consider the wide range of roles managers play, the factors that make a manager effective and successful, and some of the key challenges that managers face to keep delivery organizations operating smoothly, efficiently, and in a manner that allows the organization to achieve its goals.

Every manager plays multiple roles in an organization. Managerial work varies from directing health information technology to managing diabetes prevention activities. Managers oversee accounts payable, fund-raising and development, support operations in clinical departments, and labor relations. Commonly managers function in interactive environments, working collaboratively with other managers and clinicians to achieve organizational goals. Managers typically are held accountable for the accomplishment of team or organizational goals.

Three useful ways of looking at what managers do are to consider (a) what functions managers perform, (b) what responsibilities managers are accountable for, and (c) what choices managers make in how they spend their time and effort and with whom. According to Longest (1990) basic managerial functions include:

- *Planning:* determination of goals and objectives
- *Organizing:* structuring people dollars, services, and equipment to accomplish objectives
- *Directing:* motivating workers to meet objectives
- *Coordinating:* assembling and synchronizing diverse activities and participants
- *Controlling:* comparing actual results with objectives

In 2014, a young manager told one of the authors that in his large health system, key managerial functions include:

- Managing performance in areas managers are responsible for
- Coaching and mentoring associates who work with them
- Promoting employee and physician engagement[1]

Stewart and Fondas (1992) view managerial work in terms of choices that managers make in prioritizing their time, responding to:

- *Demands:* claims on managers to which they must respond (e.g., develop a budget)
- *Constraints:* what managers are not allowed to do (e.g., fund raisers are not allowed to make patient care decisions)
- *Choices:* areas over which managers have discretion (e.g., how much time the manager should spend coaching excellent, good, and mediocre members of the team)

---

[1] Engagement is internalization of team and organizational mission, as the employee takes "ownership" of his or her job rather than merely carrying out what the boss tells him or her to do.

The manager's scarcest resource is often his or her own time. Managers may choose whether to do tasks themselves, delegate work or not to do the work (e.g., not respond to memos from other departments). This last is often what occurs, given the large number of claims on the manager's time.

An "effective" manager meets his or her goals. A "successful" manager is perceived, internally or externally, as being effective. (Cynics would add a "successful" manager keeps his or her job.) Being effective includes helping the team or organization accomplish goals and share expectations with key stakeholders. Some HCOs have ineffective managers who fail to adapt to changing circumstances, such as a new CEO. Sometimes managers succeed, but teams and organizations fail to attain their objectives because of external competitive pressures or new governmental regulation.

Goleman (1998) suggests that the most effective managers (he calls them "leaders") have a high degree of "emotional intelligence," which is more important than technical skills and IQ for managerial effectiveness. Goleman's five components of emotional intelligence are self-awareness, self-regulation (e.g., the ability to reflect before acting), motivation, empathy, and social skills.

Although effective managers vary a great deal in their backgrounds, experiences, styles, and extent and nature of formal education, researchers have tried, largely unsuccessfully, to identify underlying factors that lead to successful performance. Boyatzis (1995) has developed a model that describes three sets of managerial competencies (skills that are measureable):

- Primarily "people skills": efficiency orientation, planning, initiative, attention to detail, self-control, flexibility, empathy, persuasiveness, networking, negotiating, self-confidence, group management, developing others, and oral communication
- Use of concepts, systems thinking, pattern recognition, theory building, technology, quantitative analysis, and social objectivity
- Written communication and analytical reasoning

There must be a good fit between the manager's competencies and what the organization is seeking for a particular position. The same manager will be effective in one position and ineffective in another. When successive managers turn over in a particular position, this may mean there are problems in the way the position is designed rather than that the HCO has made a succession of bad hires. Joining an ineffective organization may paradoxically be an excellent opportunity for a new, focused manager who can remove obstacles that prevent team members from working effectively.

An important trait of an effective manager is an ability to work collaboratively with clinicians and to understand the needs of clinicians to deliver high-quality, effective, and efficient medical care. Although delivery organizations are more complex than they were 100 years ago, the traditional view was that a function of a hospital or clinic is really the work space of the clinician. It is still helpful to a manager to understand this view and the day-to-day demands on the busy clinician.

In the United States, more than 200,000 persons are employed as HCO managers. This does not include a large number of people who spend some time doing managerial tasks, such as clinicians who chair a quality committee or head a clinical department. Managerial work increasingly requires data analysis and an ability to collect relevant data to guide practices. Such analysis is extensively used by senior

---

EXHIBIT 14.5   LINKING CEO SALARIES TO PERFORMANCE

CEOs at large hospitals and health systems typically earn large salaries. A recent study* found that the average nonprofit hospital CEO earns about $600,000 annually, and some CEOs earn well into the millions (an average of $1.66 million for the highest 10%). The study examined whether CEO pay was associated with hospital quality, financial performance, technology, and community benefit provided by the facility.

Researchers found that higher pay was associated with running larger organizations, with having more technology available, and with higher levels of patient satisfaction. CEO salaries were not, however, associated with improved clinical quality or financial performance.

*Joynt, K. E., Le, S. T., Orav, E. J., & Jha, A. K. (2013). Compensation of chief executive officers at nonprofit U.S. hospitals. *JAMA Internal Medicine*, 174(1), 61–67.

---

managers, consultants and auditors, marketing analysts, strategic planners, and compliance department heads, as well as by managers of clinician departments (Friedman & Kovner, 2013).

Managers contribute enormously to the functioning and health of an organization. (See Exhibit 14.5 on linking CEO salaries to organizational performance.) A key responsibility of senior managers is to recruit, train, and develop managers reporting to them. In well-run organizations, the process of recruiting and overseeing managers is facilitated by a rigorous approach to evaluating the managerial effectiveness. This can be done by setting management objectives and using metrics to assess performance, just as the board does for higher-level objectives of the organization.

CHALLENGES MANAGERS FACE

Managers of delivery organizations face a multitude of challenges, and many managers are responding adequately to those challenges. Primary external challenges for the manager include obtaining sufficient resources to support the clinicians who provide services and satisfying the customers upon whom resource generation depends. More directly under the control of the manager are three internal challenges:

- Measuring processes and outcomes to allow for continual improvements in operations
- Creating an environment that supports excellent clinical care
- Motivating and supporting staff reporting to the manager

Stakeholders agree that it is the manager's job to measure the operational processes, supply needed support to clinicians given the resources available, and communicate with staff who are direct reports.

Delivering services effectively depends on agreeing upon standards of performance. (See Exhibit 14.6 for a discussion on specifying benchmarks for measuring performance at Mercy Health System.) For example, what is and what should be the waiting time for patients? This includes waiting time to contact a receptionist,

---

EXHIBIT 14.6   BENCHMARKS AT MERCY HEALTH SYSTEM (MHS)

MHS is an integrated health care organization providing health care services in southern Wisconsin and northeastern Illinois.

MHS was establishing goals and measures for its House of Mercy, a 25-bed homeless shelter that provides short-term emergency shelter and access to housing, job placement, and child care services. At first MHS leaders were unsuccessful in locating available measures of "benchmark" or "best practice" for homeless shelters. The CEO insisted, however, that benchmarks be found.

House of Mercy staff held meetings with clients and volunteers and determined that other industries could supply proxy measures of performance. Stretch goals were set from benchmarks in the hotel industry, including volume of services, demand (wait list), facility conditions (cleanliness, comfort), client satisfaction, and availability of services needed by their clients.

---

waiting time for an appointment with the clinician, waiting time in the doctor's office, and waiting time for all of the steps of the patient visit to be completed. These data should be collected routinely, arrayed and analyzed, and discussed with staff providing the services, so that continuous improvement can be implemented and results compared with those of organizations providing similar services. This approach to monitoring and improving waiting time can be repeated for each task and administrative process that is the responsibility of the manager. An activist attitude and a continuous improvement perspective are two key attributes of an effective management team.

Providing a supportive environment for clinicians involves establishing what the dimensions of that environment consist of. This involves observations of working conditions at local and peer environments, communicating with clinicians about their views and feelings, and learning from the field and the literature what works and what does not work and why. Managers have limited time and must focus on priorities. Two obstacles to making the needed interventions are: (a) the lack of effectiveness of care delivery teams, and (b) the lack of effectiveness of performance evaluation systems and human resources workforce planners. A workforce that hasn't been trained to work together cannot be expected to function effectively as a team providing high-quality care to patients.

Often the manager of the team lacks the authority, and sometimes the knowledge, to change procedures and processes as they have been traditionally performed by members of various occupations. The division and coordination of tasks must be changed as work changes, often in response to new technology.

Supervising and motivating staff is a third challenge for every manager. It is most efficient to hire staff with required skills and experience who have already internalized HCO culture. Managers should be spending most of their time removing obstacles for new hires rather than spending a lot of time and energy motivating and supervising the new hire. A popular book on leadership emphasizes that one of the most important tasks of a leader is to "get the right people on the bus." Once the manager has hired the right staff, supervision and motivation become much easier.

A related challenge for the manager is sufficiently communicating to members of the team. There is a big distinction between talking and communicating. A fundamental aspect of human nature is that we often hear what we want to hear rather than what is said. Communication involves connecting with a colleague and making sure he or she understands what is being said and what behavior needs to follow. Often, finding ways to repeat messages in different ways is one approach to communicating clearly. And giving an entire message—even when some of it is not good news to the employee—is crucial.

CHALLENGES TO THE FIELD OF MANAGEMENT

Management performance can be improved by HCOs investing in management training and research. Managers need better evidence about what drives organizational performance, quality of care, and efficiency. Similarly, in a health system that is constantly changing, there is as critical a need to train the people who are already managing in HCOs to ensure that new managers have appropriate skills as they enter.

There is a wide variation in the investment that HCOs make in management training and development (including employee, physician, and governing board). Some organizations provide for perhaps 1 or 2 weeks of paid time for professional development and training activities each year. Other HCOs organize short courses and lectures on site and also pay for part-time or full-time educational opportunities for their employees.

Most employees and even senior managers would agree that continuing education and professional development deserve more investment and further improvements (managers need to be involved in training and development) in terms of quality, content, and accessibility. The challenge is paying for employee development and finding the time to allow it to happen. This will probably be facilitated if progress on learning and professional development is one factor considered in the performance appraisal process, as all managers and their direct reports discuss what they know and can do and what they wish to learn and how this might be accomplished.

Undergraduate students who choose health care management as a career can reasonably start on this path in their junior year of college. Arguments for not pursuing management education until graduate school are based on the opportunity costs to individuals of not pursuing education in other areas—such as government, biology, philosophy, languages, or the arts. An undergraduate can also pursue specializations in the social sciences and quantitative methods, which might have a direct application to management. Upon graduation, the future HCO manager can seek employment or matriculate part time or full time to graduate school.

As of 2014, there is much discussion among educators and HCO managers about the appropriate graduate school curricula in health care management, including the content covered and competencies required. Topics include statistics, microeconomics, management, financial management, health economics, management information systems, process variation, conflict management, human resources, and ethics. Arguments also are made for more effective learning of written, verbal, and interpersonal communications skill sets, statistical analysis and application, financial and market analysis, quality improvement, leadership, managing population health, and career management, among others. Educators debate how and where such topics and competencies are best learned, and to what extent learning should take place when in classes, internships, residencies, fellowships, and when online.

Scant evidence correlates successful coursework in these topics and competencies and success at various management positions. Experts disagree as to whether all or some of these competencies and topics should be required for graduates and for what management jobs.

EVIDENCE-BASED MANAGEMENT

Management decisions should be made based on the best evidence available. All managers make decisions based on evidence. It is shocking to observe the low quality of some of this evidence. Major decisions, such as merging two hospitals, are often based on latest trends or gut instinct rather than on solid evidence that the merger will include quality outcomes and financial viability. Day-to-day management interventions, such as increasing space in the emergency department waiting areas, are often based on anecdotal data rather than a systematic look at the pros and cons and approaches to expanding waiting room space.

A new field of inquiry, called evidence-based management, is emerging to bring systematic data and information together to guide organizational improvements. Evidence-based management has been defined as "the systematic application of the best available evidence to the evaluation of management strategies for improving organizational performance" (Hsu et al., 2006). Steps in the evidence-based management process include translating a specific management challenge into research questions, acquiring relevant research findings and other evidence, assessing the validity, quality, applicability, and adequacy of the evidence, presenting the evidence in a way that will be useful, and including all important stakeholders in the decision-making process (Kovner, Fine, & D'Aquila, 2009).

Traditionally, HCOs have not invested substantially in management research, seeing this as the responsibility of government or philanthropy. Many hospitals have invested in analytical capacity to assess financial decisions and reimbursement decisions, but have often ignored analysis to improve day-to-day operations. Of course, there are exceptions to this, such as the Mayo Clinic and Intermountain Healthcare. Here are a few examples of important questions HCO management research can address:

- How can hospital emergency services be best organized to reduce patient waiting time?
- How can hospital administrators be organized to facilitate working better as teams?
- What are financially viable approaches to expanding hours at ambulatory care clinics?
- How can transport services resources be best organized to minimize wait times for moving patients from rooms to procedure rooms?

Deciding whether to invest in management research involves similar considerations to deciding how much to invest in management training and development. The returns on improved information for decision making must be compared with the costs of obtaining the information. The field needs to determine when analysis to support evidence-based management should be done within a specific HCO and when it could best be done on a collaborative basis through a professional association or through joint funding with a university or a consulting firm.

Managers who do not follow a process of evidence-based management often fail to investigate a sufficiently broad range of alternative strategic initiatives or to test assumptions under which alternatives are proposed. Of course, evidence usually plays the role of informing management decisions. There is plenty of room for managerial judgment in weighing evidence, experience, and logic to make a good decision.

HCOs are more likely to practice evidence-based management when external incentives for performance are strong, such as when payers pay for better performance with penalties for bad performance, when an HCO has a "hard-wired" questioning culture rather than a more hierarchical decision-making structure, when there is focused accountability for management decision making linked to the quality and timeliness of the process, and when managers participate actively in management research.

■ Conclusion

The current drivers of the health care enterprise are demand for improved outcomes and increased value. Consolidation is occurring within the health sector—both vertically in terms of integrated health systems, and horizontally in terms of mergers. Larger HCOs are better able to standardize work processes, install new measurement systems, and develop special processes of communication with key stakeholders, including employees and physicians, about performance and expectations for results.

Under these conditions, the role of managers trained in the necessary skills and provided with the necessary experience increases in value. The emerging health system will require more sophistication of managers who understand how to work in teams, how to manage workers playing various roles, and how to use information to make decisions. This increased sophistication has emerged rapidly in other fields, such as communications, banking, Internet applications, and entertainment.

■ Discussion Questions

1. What are some of the ways to measure performance of HCOs?
2. What are the advantages and disadvantages of public, nonprofit, and for-profit ownership of HCOs?
3. What skills and experience are required to govern and manage HCOs?
4. How should governing boards of HCOs be selected, and how should they be educated?
5. What mechanisms of accountability are most effective for nonprofit HCOs?

CASE STUDY

What follows is a summary of an Academic Medical Center's strategic plan:

- *Mission:* To care, cure, teach, and advance the health of the communities served
- *Vision:* To be a premier academic medical center that transforms and enriches lives
- *Values:* Humanity, innovation, teamwork, diversity, and equity
- *Strategic Goals:*
  - Advance the partnership with the University College of Medicine
  - Create notable centers of excellence in heart and cancer care
  - Build specialty care broadly
  - Develop an effective delivery system with superior access, quality, safety, and patient satisfaction
  - Maximize the effects of community service
- *Organizational Goals:*
  - Create a culture of high performance, motivation, and fulfillment
  - Sustain strong financial health
  - Invest in state-of-the-art facilities and technology
  - Build an aligned and interconnected organization
  - Foster supportive partnerships and alliances

The board of directors engages you as a consultant and asks that you prepare a report addressing the following questions:

1. How should organizational performance of Academic Medical Center be measured?
2. How can the board operate to make sure the plan is implemented?
3. How can top management be held accountable for accomplishing the plan?

■ References

Bowen, W. G. (2008). *The board book.* New York, NY: WW Norton & Co.

Boyatzis, R. E. (1995). Cornerstones of change: Building the path to self-directed learning. In R. E. Boyatzis, S. S. Cowan, & D. A. Kolb (Eds.), *Innovation in Professional Education* (pp. 50–94). San Francisco, CA: Jossey-Bass.

Friedman, L., & Kovner, A. R. (2013). *101 careers in healthcare management.* New York, NY: Springer.

Goleman, D. (1998). What makes a leader? *Harvard Business Review, 76*(6), 93–102.

Hsu, J. L., Arroyo, I., Graetz, E., Neuwirth, E. B., Schmittdiel, J., Rundall, T. G., . . . Curtis, P. (2006). Methods for developing actionable evidence for consumers of health services research. In A. R. Kovner, D. D. Fine, & R. D'Aquila (Eds.), *Evidence-based management in healthcare* (pp. 83–95). Chicago, IL: Health Administration Press.

Kovner, A. R., Fine, D. J., & D'Aquila, R. (Eds.). (2009). *Evidence-based management in healthcare.* Chicago, IL: Health Administration Press.

Longest, B. B. (1990). *Management practices for the health professional* (4th ed.). Norwalk, CT: Appleton & Lange.

Stewart, R., & Fondas, N. (1992). How managers can think strategically about their jobs. *Journal of Management Development, 11*(2), 10–17.

15 Health Information Technology

Nirav R. Shah

KEY WORDS

all payer database (APD)

clinical decision support

e-prescribing

electronic health record (EHR)

health information exchange (HIE)

patient portal

telehealth

Triple Aim

LEARNING OBJECTIVES

- Define health information technology (HIT) and describe what the government has done to spur its adoption
- Examine the role of HIT in the nation's evolving health care system
- Explore the reasons why the health care industry has been slower than other industries to embrace information technology
- Demonstrate how HIT and health data can improve patient care
- Discuss how HIT and health data can improve population health
- Examine the ways in which HIT can reduce health care costs
- Introduce and explore examples of successful HIT adoption and use
- Discuss what is needed in the future as HIT takes on a bigger role in health care

TOPICAL OUTLINE

- Why HIT is so important in health care
- How HIT has the potential to transform our current system
- Using HIT to improve the patient experience
- How HIT can improve overall population health
- The economic effects of HIT through reduced health care costs and new business opportunities
- The role of the government in HIT
- The future of HIT

In the days before her primary care doctor created a patient portal, Linda[1] often had a hard time making an appointment during her busy work day. If her cardiologist didn't send her lab results to her primary care doctor, that doctor would have to call the

---

[1] Names used in this chapter are not the patients' real names.

cardiologist and then wait for the results to come by fax. If Linda got a blood test from her rheumatologist, she often couldn't remember the name of the test to discuss it with her primary care doctor. These issues and others can be addressed by a patient portal, a website that is easy to navigate and allows for communication among providers and the patient in a manner that ensures privacy.

These days, Linda takes a few minutes late at night to log on to make her appointments through an online patient portal. She taps an app on her smartphone to show her doctor her lab results. And she doesn't need to memorize any complex blood tests—or medication dosages or health history, for that matter—because they're all listed on her patient portal. "I'm really pleased with the technology," says the mother of two. "I would love it if my pediatrician had the same."

In some health care circles, information technology (IT) is slowly but surely starting to have a direct effect on the lives of patients and the practice of medicine. In others, it has yet to be adopted, installed, or implemented. The wide array of experiences reflects the diversity of approaches in the health care system's thinking about health IT (HIT). Even though it has taken longer, been more difficult, and cost more than expected to move from a world of paper records to electronic records, there is little doubt that HIT will play a significant role in the future of our health care system and in the health and well-being of our citizens.

Of particular interest is the potential for HIT to help achieve the goals of the Triple Aim: improved patient care, improved population health, and reduced health care costs. The excitement surrounding HIT—with help from the federal government's financial incentives—has spawned the widespread adoption of various health care technologies in physician offices and hospitals across the country. In the last 5 years, that momentum has resulted in significant growth in the implementation and use of different forms of HIT.

In this chapter, we'll explore the promise of HIT, how its emergence is starting to make a difference in our health care system, and the numerous challenges that still remain, including the sociocultural barriers that have made adoption and implementation a lingering challenge. Most experts agree that it is no longer a matter of whether HIT will become an integral part of the health care system; it's a matter of when. With the push for accountable care organizations (ACOs), and the drive to create patient-centered medical homes and health homes, all of which rely on HIT to succeed, the groundwork is laid for widespread use of these various health technologies. If the technology is properly implemented, we are on the cusp of radical changes in our nation's health care system. These changes are long overdue. Almost all would agree that the health care system has lagged behind other industries—such as travel and banking—in its use of technology.

■ HIT Defined

When Donna's doctor created patient portals for all of his patients, Donna was delighted. She finally had a way to keep tabs on her aging parents, who saw the same doctor but didn't enjoy discussing their health issues with their daughter. Thanks to the portal, those discussions have been averted. Donna can go online and see when her parents went to the doctor, what their concerns were, and any medications they were prescribed. "I didn't have to hover or cramp their style," she says. "It also avoided the 'What did the doctor say?' question where the answer inevitably would be 'I forgot.' They hated that as much as it drove me crazy." The portals also help Donna keep track of her family's medications that needed refilling.

Donna and Linda are patients at a Manhattan practice owned by Sal Volpe, MD, a family physician who has not only adopted electronic health records but is also connected to a regional health information organization. In addition, the doctor has set up a patient portal that enables his patients to keep track of their health information, schedule appointments, and check results of lab tests and screenings. The technology enables Dr. Volpe to run a National Committee for Quality Assurance (NCQA) level-3 patient centered medical home (PCMH), a model of care coordinated by a primary care doctor such as Dr. Volpe, with specialists linked into the same network.

HIT is not one specific product. Rather, the term refers to various components, including computers, software, and devices, that function in a larger sociotechnical system, including hardware and software, working together in an organization that involves people, processes, and workflows. Most often, HIT refers to electronic health records (EHRs). Individual components of EHRs can vary and often include:

- *e-Prescription.* When a provider sends a patient's prescription directly to a device using special software to access electronically patient prescription benefit information and patient pharmacy, it is known as e-prescribing. Providers use a computer or handheld device to access medication history and to transmit prescriptions directly to a patient's pharmacy of choice. E-prescribing is considered a significant improvement in patient safety and care quality because it reduces errors caused by inscrutable handwriting by directly delivering the prescription to the pharmacy.

- *Computerized physician (or provider) order entry (CPOE).* Physicians provide a lot of instructions in the course of a work day. CPOE allows providers to directly place their orders and instructions electronically, whether an order is for medication, a lab test, or an imaging exam. Like e-prescribing, CPOE avoids problems created by sloppy handwriting. CPOEs can also avoid dangerous and deadly drug interactions if the entry is incorporated with the patient's medical information, such as allergies and other drugs the patient currently takes. It can also provide information about whether the drug is on the patient's health plan's formulary. After the information has been entered, subsequent providers also will know what medications the patient has been prescribed and what tests he has already had.

- *Clinical decision support (CDS).* CDS monitors and alerts clinicians and health care staff to a patient's specific conditions, prescriptions, and treatments. Used appropriately, CDS has the potential to increase the quality of care, enhance health outcomes, prevent errors and adverse events, and improve efficiency. CDS is considered a sophisticated component of the HIT system and is most often a part of a comprehensive EHR system. These tools combine person-specific data with biomedical knowledge to generate useful medical information at the point of care without disrupting the provider's workflow. The information allows the user to make an informed decision quickly and take action. The technology helps to improve clinical decision making by filtering out excessive amounts of information and zeroing in on what is best for the patient at the point of treatment. CDS systems provide a platform for integrating evidence-based knowledge into care delivery. Tools in CDS include clinical guidelines, condition-specific order sets, focused patient data reports, and summaries.

■ *Patient engagement tools.* With the rise in chronic conditions, encouraging patients to assume greater responsibility for their health has become a bigger priority. The Meaningful Use program of the Office of the National Coordinator for Health Information Technology (2013) has made the engagement of patients and their families the second of their five health policy priorities. EHRs that meet this goal often include tools for patients to use such as patient portals, smartphone applications, emails, and interactive kiosks. These tools enable individual patients to be more proactive in their care. The patient portal, for instance, allows patients to schedule appointments, request medication refills, and readily access test results and health records.

Engaging patients in their own care—as well as engaging the support of their families—is important on many levels. For one, educated patients typically have better health outcomes. They can take an active role in their health care decision making and often are better at managing their chronic health conditions. Involved patients are more likely to comply with their doctor's recommended treatments and lifestyle suggestions. Patients who are involved in their health care can also lower health care costs. A patient who has access to his or her medical records can easily show them to a provider to avoid duplicating tests or procedures that were previously ordered by another physician.

Having EHRs is not enough, however. To maximize the use of electronic records, providers must participate in health information exchanges (HIE). In an HIE, the patient's clinical data—allergies, lab results, diagnoses, and so on—are shared on a regional network, so that a patient's health information follows the patient from one setting to the next. Experts agree that a robust HIE is essential to improving the quality and efficiency of care. It helps ensure that tests are not needlessly repeated and are readily accessible to help with diagnoses, and the information from one visit is consistent and immediately available at the next (Adler-Milstein, Bates & Jha, 2013).

> *Health information exchanges allow doctors in a network to retrieve information about patients across providers and settings, in real time, creating coordinated or integrated care.*

HIEs allow doctors in a network to retrieve information about patients across providers and settings, in real time, creating coordinated or integrated care. The goal is to have that information available to teams of doctors, nurses, and care coordinators in a way that is private and secure, so that the patient's care can be coordinated among providers. Research shows that transitions between providers are a common occurrence, especially among people who have complex and chronic conditions. When the information is shared in a timely fashion, it can improve diagnoses, reduce duplication of testing, prevent readmissions, and avoid medication errors.

Another essential component of HIT is interoperability, which is the ability of different systems to communicate with each other. This is necessary because the United States' private health system has allowed for market competition in the development of EHRs. This has resulted in a wide array of vendors designing IT systems that are not compatible.

Having HIT that is not interoperable is similar to having dinner guests who do not speak the same language: No information is shared or transferred.

Having HIT that is not interoperable is similar to having dinner guests who do not speak the same language: No information is shared or transferred. Interoperability allows providers and insurers to share EHRs and HIEs. The issue of interoperability is of vital importance to creating a national HIE, so that EHRs can be shared across the country, a benefit for those who travel frequently or who live in different places at different times of the year. To help that process along, a national Interoperability Workgroup, a coalition of states, and EHR and HIE vendors have been working together to tackle this problem (Whitlinger Testimony, 2013). The group has been charged with leveraging existing standards to develop consistent implementation guides for interoperability between HIE software platforms, and the applications that interface with them. The workgroup's ultimate goal is to create a single set of standards that link the country's various HIEs. Having a single set of standards will eliminate the need to develop custom interfaces with every connection.

A functioning, interoperable HIE is essential to the future of our nation's health care system, but it starts with the individual patient's care.

A functioning, interoperable HIE is essential to the future of our nation's health care system, but it starts with the individual patient's care. Here's how: If a patient named Mrs. Jones goes to see a social worker for depression, all of her providers will know, so they can consider that fact when treating her for something else. If she gets a new prescription from her gastroenterologist, her providers will see it on her EHR through the HIE. If Mrs. Jones is ordered to get a blood test from one doctor, another doctor won't duplicate that test because that information, along with the results, will show up on her EHR. By sharing that kind of health information, Mrs. Jones avoids excessive testing, risky drug interactions, and unnecessary—and often costly—procedures and admissions.

The good news is that HIEs are growing. Between 2010 and 2012, the number of HIEs in the United States that were actively exchanging clinical data grew 60%, from 75 to 119 (Adler-Milstein & Jha, 2013). By 2015, nearly 30% of U.S. hospitals were exchanging data with nonaffiliated providers, as well as approximately 10% of ambulatory care practices. Despite this trend toward more use of HIEs, the vast majority of hospitals and physicians are not engaged in the clinical exchange of data.

■ The Backing of Government

The push for HIT has been brewing for years, but got significant national attention in 2009, when President Barack Obama delivered his inaugural address and challenged the nation to "wield technology's wonders to raise health care's quality and lower its costs." At that time, fewer than 1 in 10 hospitals had an EHR; among ambulatory care physicians, the number was 1 in 6.

Weeks later, President Obama signed the American Recovery and Reinvestment Act (ARRA). ARRA included the Health Information Technology for Economic and Clinical Health (HITECH) Act, which was the federal government's attempt to spur the adoption of and use of HIT and, in particular, EHRs. The act included $30 billion in incentives, as well future punitive measures for failure to adopt EHRs. Eligible hospitals and health care professionals received these incentives by demonstrating "meaningful use" of EHRs—which, in short, means applying the technology to improve care and lower costs. Examples of meaningful use include e-prescribing of medications and providing patients with access to their digital records.

In the years since the passage of this legislation, the numbers of hospitals and physicians using EHRs has soared (CMS, 2013a). When lawmakers drafted the law, only 12% of acute care hospitals had a basic EHR system, compared with 44% in 2012. By 2012, nearly three quarters of office-based physicians had adopted an EHR system. Indeed, the number of physicians using e-prescribing has soared in recent years, from 7% in 2008 to 54% in 2012. Government incentives have clearly had an effect. As of April 30, 2013, the federal government had doled out $16.6 billion in HITECH Act funds.

MEANINGFUL USE

To achieve broad implementation of HIT, the HITECH Act created a set of meaningful use incentives, to be met over three stages in 5 years. Eligible providers and hospitals must purchase certified technology and meet the demands at each stage if they want to qualify for the financial incentives. The stages are as follows:

- 2011 to 2012: capturing and sharing of data
- 2014: advances in clinical processes
- 2016: improved health outcomes

Meaningful use involves using certified EHR technology to (a) improve quality, safety, efficiency, and reduce health disparities; (b) engage patients and family; (c) improve care coordination, population health, and public health; and (d) maintain privacy and security of patient health information. The goal of meaningful use is to achieve better clinical outcomes, improve population health outcomes, increase transparency and efficiency, empower individuals, and provide more robust research data on health systems. Physicians who are not using EHRs meaningfully by 2015 will start to lose a percentage of their Medicare fees.

At the moment, the adoption and implementation of HIT remain inconsistent. A report by the Robert Wood Johnson Foundation found that certain types of medical practices are more likely to have EHRs than others. Primary care doctors, those in large practices with 11 physicians or more, and physicians in rural practices were more likely to have a basic EHR than specialists, solo practitioners, and doctors in large urban settings (Stalley & DesRoches, 2013). The report found that doctors are increasingly adopting more sophisticated EHRs, but ease of use remains a challenge.

■ Transformative Powers of HIT

In this era of the Patient Protection and Affordable Care Act (ACA), many experts believe that HIT is the key to a better health care system. When designed appropriately and implemented properly, HIT holds great promise for improving patient care, enhancing safety and quality, and even reducing the costs of health care, which have soared to astronomical heights in the current $2.9 trillion system (CMS, 2013b). The next sections discuss some of the sweeping benefits of HIT.

BETTER CLINICAL CARE

Many studies show that HIT is improving patient care. One study (Pollak & Lorch, 2007) looked at the effects of EHRs on mortality in patients with end-stage renal disease in three dialysis units. The study found that patient mortality and nurse staffing levels went down by as much as 48% and 25%, respectively, in a 3-year period after the centers implemented EHRs. Another study (Amarasingham et al., 2009) looked at 41 urban hospitals in Texas and found that those with more advanced HIT had fewer complications, lower mortality, and lower costs than hospitals with less sophisticated technologies.

Patients like Vicky who belong to Dr. Volpe's practice, say EHRs are a significant improvement over paper records. Vicky frequently uses the patient portal to manage her care, which involves treatments for multiple sclerosis and frequent gastrointestinal distress. "The patient portal is a self-serve stop to get all the information about you," she says. "I don't have to leave messages, and it relieves my anxiety about missing calls. And I can print out all my information for another specialist. I can see whether my vitals have changed over time."

The portal lays out Vicky's health history, so she doesn't need to recite it every time she sees a new doctor. Neither must she go to pick up lab test results or wait for them to come in the mail. With the new healow app, she can access anything she needs from her portal directly from her smart phone. "Dr. Volpe's portal is able to house all my data," Vicky says. "He's become the hub for my information." Research shows that patients are becoming increasingly aware of the value of EHRs: A study by Accenture (2013) found that 41% of consumers would switch doctors to gain access to EHRs, but that only 36% currently have access to their EHRs.

EHRs also benefit patient care by using data gleaned from these patient records for research. While working at Geisinger Health, I participated in a comparative effectiveness research study that compared the use of angiotensin-converting enzyme (ACE) inhibitors and angiotensin II receptor blockers (ARBs) in reducing rates of death, new-onset diabetes, stroke, chronic kidney disease and coronary artery disease (Roy, Shah, Wood, Townsend, & Hennessy, 2012). The study was a "natural experiment" that looked at the EHRs of thousands of patients taking these medications to treat hypertension.

ACE inhibitors had been around for a while and cost pennies per pill, but ARBs were the new drugs on the block. They cost more and were widely regarded as the better treatment. Our research showed otherwise: Although there was no evidence of any differences in rates of death, stroke, CAD, coronary artery disease or CKS, chronic kidney disease among people using either of these two drugs, we did observe a higher likelihood of developing diabetes for people taking ARBs compared with ACE inhibitors. The findings provided evidence that clinicians needed to exercise more scrutiny when making the decision to prescribe ARBs over ACE inhibitors. The research was possible only because of EHRs.

In another study (Shah, 2009), we looked at EHR data from patients at Geisinger who had been diagnosed with hypertension based on guidelines from The Joint

Committee. Patients were included based on four criteria: (a) having hypertension on the problem list; (b) at least two outpatient encounters with a diagnosis of hypertension; (c) at least one current medication with an associated diagnosis of hypertension; or (d) two systolic blood pressure measures greater than or equal to 140 or two diastolic BP measures of 90 or more. A total of 106,045 patients were included in the study.

The study found that 30% of patients with hypertension were not being properly identified, much less treated. These were patients who had clinical hypertension on two separate encounters with the health care system. But the lack of continuity from one health setting to another made it easy for practitioners to overlook a previous elevation of blood pressure, so it appeared the high blood pressure was a one-time measurement. Regardless of the cause of the clinical inertia, these patients had clinical hypertension and should have been treated.

MORE STANDARDIZED CARE

HIT has the potential to make health care more uniform from one setting to another and across the country, helping to ensure that patients with the same needs and the same presenting factors get care that is known to work. The patient health data in EHRs allow providers to track the outcomes of evidence-based medicine practices, so they can evaluate which treatments work best (Spooner et al., 2012). EHRs also make it possible to track a patient's care and to follow up with reminders as necessary, thereby improving care and avoiding unnecessary procedures and treatments. Over time, EHRs could lead to more standardized care, so that the best practices become the routine ones.

Jeffe, Lee, Young, Sidney, and Go (2013) looked at the effects of a large-scale hypertension program on patients in Kaiser Permanente's hypertension registry. Hypertension is high blood pressure that may damage arteries, the heart, kidneys, and even parts of the brain, leading to a wide array of potentially life-threatening diseases. Patients were enrolled in the study based on information gleaned from their EHRs. A team of hypertension management experts identified practices that were most effective, created a four-step hypertension control algorithm and distributed it to the medical centers, which produced hypertension control reports every 1 to 3 months. During the 8-year study period, the numbers of adults in the hypertension registry almost doubled. More significant, however, was the percentage of patients whose hypertension was controlled. That figure rose from 43.6% to 80.4%. The researchers credited the success in part to the creation of the hypertension registry and the development and sharing of performance metrics, information that is attainable through EHRs.

BETTER VALUE

Lowering the cost of health care is a key component of the Triple Aim. The current system costs $2.7 trillion a year and takes up 18% of our country's gross domestic product (GDP). The health care system is rewarded financially for treating sick patients with the excessive use of medications, surgeries, and hospitalizations. It is not rewarded for keeping people healthy, preventing illness, or avoiding hospitalizations and surgeries. Experts agree that the fee-for-service system is no longer sustainable at its current rate, and that bending the cost curve is absolutely essential to the nation's economy.

HIT is expected to play a significant role in helping to make that happen, especially if the nation's health care system moves toward a total-cost-of-care (TCOC) model of reimbursement. Under a TCOC model, a patient's entire spectrum of health care—from doctor visits and pharmaceuticals to surgeries and inpatient experiences—is covered by a single, risk-adjusted fee. The care is delivered across all types of providers, all different kinds of health settings, and all varieties of health services. All parties in the contract, which include the physicians, hospitals, and insurers, are rewarded for keeping costs below the fee. The goal becomes to keep a patient well by improving the quality of care, which in turn lowers costs. A TCOC model that is applied to a single episode of care such as hip replacement surgery is known as a bundled payment. When the model is applied to a patient in a health plan, it is known as capitation and is set as a predetermined per-member, per-month (PMPM) payment.

In these kinds of financial arrangements HIT has the potential to improve the quality of individual care while promoting population health. If a doctor can see at a glance that a patient has recently had a CT scan to address a neurological complaint, then the doctor is unlikely to duplicate that procedure, especially if elimination of the current fee-for-service structure removes the financial incentive for doing so. If a patient can be effectively managed upon discharge by a care coordinator who can see the patient's health history in an EHR, then the patient is less likely to be readmitted to the hospital. If a doctor consistently refers patients to an orthopedic specialist for back pain but the patients do not get relief, the low-quality care by the specialist will be quickly apparent.

NEW MODELS OF CARE

The adoption of HIT is spurred in large part by the growing importance of three models of integrated health care—ACOs, PCMHs, and health homes—that will grow in coming years as health reforms become more ingrained. All three depend heavily on HIT, and all three are structured to help rein in spiraling health costs.

Accountable Care Organizations (ACOs)

An accountable care organization (ACO) is a contract between a payer and a group of providers that assigns a group of patients to the providers and holds the providers accountable for the quality of the patients' care, the patients' experience of care, and the total costs of the care that the group engenders. The payer agrees to allow the providers to share in any savings generated by the providers when they meet specific quality benchmarks, thereby reining in costs. Having information about each patient's care will help to ensure that services are not duplicated, that more affordable options are considered, and that overuse of expensive health care is avoided. A rush toward underuse of appropriate care can be avoided by keeping the doctor accountable for outcomes.

Patient Centered Medical Homes (PCMHs)

A patient centered medical home (PCMH) is a model of care that takes a patient-centered, team-based, and coordinated approach to a patient's care. At the hub of that care is the patient's primary care doctor. Responsibility for care, however, belongs to a team of caregivers, who are responsible for all physical and mental health care needs, including prevention and wellness, acute care, and chronic care. A PCMH has a commitment to making its services accessible to its patients, as well as a strong emphasis on patient quality and safety. HIT makes a PCMH possible by linking all of the caregivers electronically. When a patient sees a behavioral health specialist for depression but neglects to discuss his emotional well-being with his other doctors, the rest of the team will see that visit on his records. The information helps the endocrinologist better understand why her patient is struggling to manage his diabetes. His primary care doctor will have a possible explanation for this patient's insomnia and recent weight loss. And if the patient is prescribed an antidepressant, all of the providers on the team will know to steer clear of medications that react with this new drug.

Health Homes

A health home has goals similar to the PCMH and targets the 5% of the population who account for 50% of all health care costs—those patients who have multiple health problems, often with accompanying complex behavioral and social issues. These nonmedical issues are addressed as part of the patient's total care. In a health home, HIT can help provide a fuller picture of the patient's life circumstances, not just the patient's medical needs. In addition to listing a patient's multiple medical problems— high cholesterol, hypertension, diabetes, and heart disease, for example—the health home could provide notes about challenging social problems, known as the social determinants of health, that are affecting the patient's well-being such as domestic violence, substance abuse, or unemployment. Like the PCMH, the health home needs all members of the caregiving team to be in regular contact.

For these models to work, all three require electronic linkages among providers and accessibility for patients. Along the health care spectrum, all parties have a vested interest in obtaining the information available via HIT. Providers need the ability to share lab results, referrals, and discharge summaries, as well as the capability to call up the records of a new patient, especially in an emergency department or urgent care setting. Patients need the ability to access their health information—much in the same way they retrieve their financial information—if they are to take part in their own care. Hospitals will want ready access to this information in the quest to avoid penalties for unnecessary admissions or readmissions. In addition, payers are regularly using these data to determine rates.

IMPROVED POPULATION HEALTH

Gathering patient data into one central database creates opportunities to share records and data, which in turn allows researchers and doctors to mine that data for information that could potentially improve the health of entire populations. Doctors can enter and retrieve information about specific populations—by gender, age, and disease condition, for instance—and pinpoint the most effective treatment for a given patient. The information will enable researchers to determine which treatments work best for certain patients and which ones are dangerous. With the right data, it is possible to identify trends in a given community or population, and then use that information to improve care for individuals. The right data can even enable providers to anticipate the kinds of care a patient will require.

Perhaps the best example of how data can improve population health comes from Camden, New Jersey, where Dr. Jeffrey Brenner used patient data to identify the parts of the community that were using the most medical care. That information became the basis of Dr. Brenner's work with the Camden Coalition, an organization he founded that works with the biggest users of health care in Camden. By targeting these super-users, the organization aims to improve care while lowering costs.

■ HIT at the VA

For a good example of how HIT can work, look no further than the Veterans Health Administration of the Department for Veterans Affairs (VA), a government-run health care system for the nation's veterans. Instead of following the approach of the private health care system, which allowed variation in software from provider to provider, the VA uses a single software system, developed in the 1970s and 1980s and called VistA: Veterans Health Information Systems and Technology Architecture. The program is a bundle of nearly 20,000 software programs and was written largely by doctors and other professionals working in VA facilities around the country. It was developed at a time when patients at the VA were aging and beginning to develop more complex and chronic conditions, such as diabetes, high blood pressure, and cardiovascular disease, that required care from dozens of providers as well as greater involvement from the patients themselves. In other words, the VA was confronting a patient population not unlike the population we see in the United States today.

Phillip Longman (2012) offers examples of how HIT is benefiting patients at the VA. He cites the example of an 87-year old veteran from Maryland who agreed to let his physician show Longman his electronic records. The chart revealed a daily record of his weight changes over a period of months. The patient was using a scale that sent his weight via a wireless signal to his medical records. While the patient was recovering from Lyme disease and a hip fracture, he began having shortness of breath. Chest x-rays were inconclusive and showed a problem in one lung. But the chart revealed that his breathing troubles coincided with his weight gain. The doctor suspected a buildup of fluid in the lungs. It occurred in only one lung because the man was sleeping on his side as a way to avoid pain from his hip fracture. Fortunately, the patient received prompt and appropriate treatment for congestive heart failure.

In another example, Longman relates the story of a nurse who tried to get the computer to accept her intention to give an IV to a patient. The VistA system requires all nurses and patients to wear an ID bracelet that must be scanned before administering medication. One nurse, who had been resistant to the new technology, balked when a computer refused to allow her to give a patient an IV. But when she looked at the bag, she realized she had the wrong medication. The technology spared the nurse of a career-ending misstep and the patient of a potentially lethal mistake.

Byrne and colleagues (2010) found that the VA has achieved close to 100% adoption of several VistA components, and the effects on patients has been positive. The study found that patients in the VA got more cancer screenings than their cohorts in private sector health care. Those with diabetes had better glucose testing compliance and control, more controlled cholesterol, and more timely retinal exams. The study concluded that the VA's investments in HIT had yielded $3.09 billion in potential cumulative benefits net of investment costs by 2007. Most of the benefits were the result of reductions in unnecessary care, including the prevention of adverse drug event–related hospitalizations and outpatient visits and the elimination of redundancies.

VistA also allows the VA to monitor its own quality and to develop its own evidence-based protocols of care. Doctors have mined the data to uncover reasons behind medical trends, track down new disease vectors, and identify doctors or surgeons who are not performing well. During natural disasters such as Hurricane Katrina, the patient information on EHRs in VistA allowed doctors tending to evacuees to gain access to their medical records easily and provide treatments.

The VA demonstrates the potential that is inherent in a good HIT system. But its success is not easily transferred to the health care system in the rest of the country. For one thing, the VA is a single-payer system. And it imposed a single technology on all providers across the board. A similar approach would not be viable in our country's multipayer system, where varying needs and finances seem to make it impossible for the government to impose a single IT system.

The VA is also a part of a joint effort with the Department of Defense to create the Virtual Lifetime Electronic Record (VLER) initiative, which uses interoperability to create a vast EHR for members of the military and their families as they make the transition from active duty to retirement. The VLER uses a common EHR platform to link the Department of Defense, the VA, the Social Security Administration, private health care providers, private health information exchanges, and other federal, state, and local government entities. The data being exchanged now include medical conditions, allergies, medications, language spoken, blood test results, and other information that contributes to the provision of care by a team of providers (U.S. Department of Defense & U.S. Department of Veterans Affairs, 2011).

■ The New York Experience

New York state offers an example of how governments are making use of HIT. New York, like a number of other states, has made the adoption of HIT a priority in devising health policies. According to the Health Information Technology Evaluation Collaborative (HITEC), a multiinstitution academic collaborative that is measuring the effects of HIT, New York hospitals have higher rates of EHR and HIE adoption than hospitals in other states (Abramson et al., 2012). Between 2010 and 2012, New York physicians significantly increased their adoption rates, from 46% to 62%. And about half of all New York nursing homes are using some form of EHR, a number that is not even measured in most states (Abramson et al., 2012).

The state's adoption rates have had direct effects on health. HITEC has found that for every 100 patients whose primary care physicians use EHRs, six more with diabetes get their hemoglobin A1C tested, 13 more get screened for chlamydia, four more get screened for breast cancer, and three more get screened for colorectal cancer (Kern et al., 2013). Hospitals that use a community-based HIE have fewer admissions from the emergency department, fewer repeat radiology images, and fewer 30-day readmissions (Vest et al., 2013a). In Rochester, New York, when the HIE was accessed during an emergency department visit, the odds of an admission decreased by 30% (Vest et al., 2013b).

New York's efforts are buoyed by the presence of the Statewide Health Information Network of New York (SHIN-NY). The SHIN-NY is the state's private, secure health network. Linking into it are 11 regional health information organizations (RHIOs), each of which collects health record data from health providers in its region. With the consent of patients, this information is shared among private practices, nursing homes, clinics, and hospitals from across the state.

The SHIN-NY allows providers access to patients' medical records: lab results, images, drug prescriptions, and so on. Any doctor securely connected to the SHIN-NY through the local RHIO has private access to complete and accurate information about a patient's medical history. The patient is spared the task of calling specialists to obtain results of medical tests and remembering to bring them to appointments. Having access to the RHIO frees up both provider and patient from the mundane administrative details of a visit and allows them to spend the appointment discussing more important matters related to health.

The state itself is making use of the data gleaned from patient records. In 2011, the state enacted legislation that created an all-payer database (APD), a repository for health care data that will be used to manage, evaluate, and analyze the state's health care system. The APD has begun collecting claims data from all major public and private payers, including insurance carriers, health plans, third-party administrators, pharmacy benefit managers, Medicaid, and Medicare. The APD will provide information about patients, their diagnoses, services received, and cost of care—information that will enable consumers to compare health services and to compare cost, quality, and efficiency of potential insurers. The information also helps providers improve the quality of the care they provide. Employers may use the information to design insurance products and select providers based on quality, cost, and efficiency. The data will help researchers analyze treatment options, identify gaps in treatment methods, and determine cost variations across regions, so they can influence policy to promote greater equity.

■ Implementing HIT

For providers, adopting and implementing HIT in a practice or hospital is a major endeavor, one that takes time, money, and energy. The investment of resources is significant, which is why adoption so far has been spotty and inconsistent and demands careful planning.

The first step in adopting this technology is to understand exactly why you are purchasing an EHR system (Health IT.gov). Are you trying to cut down on time spent chasing down lab tests and diagnostic screenings ordered by other physicians? Are you trying to improve a specific aspect of patient care? Are you looking to improve the workflow in your office? Also important is an honest assessment of current record-keeping practices, discussions with staff, and anticipation of how the adoption of an EHR system will improve what's being done. To help assess the system's usage, it's a good idea to establish some goals to provide a measurable gauge of how well the system is working for you.

When it comes time to purchase the technology, it's best to choose a system that will support the practice's goals, while steering clear of systems with functions that you do not need or want. Most national medical associations can provide suggestions on the best systems for their members and provide support to doctors going through the adoption process. For example, the American Academy of Family Physicians has a Center for Health IT. The American Academy of Pediatrics has the Child Health Informatics Center. And the American Academy of Dermatology has the Dermatology Electronic Health Record Manual (dEHRm).

According to the U.S. Department of Health and Human Services (2014), implementing an EHR system can be done in two ways: big bang or phased in. The big bang approach is just as the name implies: Most or all of a system is introduced to the entire organization all at once. The phased-in method takes a more gradual approach, introducing different functionalities a little at a time. A phased-in approach generally makes the process easier and is less disruptive to the practice, but this approach requires maintaining multiple workflows and systems. Phasing in is especially useful in hospitals, where functionalities can be launched in a few departments at a time. Even so, many large institutions will experience a drop in efficiency in the first 3 months of having an EHR, a loss that corrects itself and leads to gains in the subsequent 3 months.

Implementing an EHR system isn't easy. It takes time to bring staff on board and to master its usage. But adopting a careful, methodical, and thoughtful approach to this investment can help to ensure a successful transition from paper to electronics.

■ Challenges and Shortcomings of HIT

Despite the momentum in some pockets of health care, we still have a way to go to get all providers on board with HIT. The reasons for this are technical, organizational, and cultural (Jha, 2012). A significant barrier to HIT adoption is the cost of implementing the technology. Making matters more challenging is the question of whether the investment actually pays off as it has in other industries, such as banking and travel. Industries such as retail and manufacturing spend about 20% of their operating budget on IT and recoup that investment many times over. But the same is not true in health care.

For health care providers, the value of HIT varies widely. With approximately 1,000 HIT products still on the market, it's hard to know which system will work best from one setting to the next. And the technology isn't cheap. Most practices need to spend $65,000 to $100,000 to install an entire EHR system. For a hospital, it costs at least $2 million and can be much more than this for a large, academic medical system. Whether it's worthwhile to make that investment depends on several factors, including patient volume and whether administrative efficiencies that can be achieved with HIT or health care services are actually improved by the added technology. Institutions with the capacity to gauge the effects of HIT typically see a drop in efficiency in the first 3 months, but can usually recover and even improve efficiency once the staff learns the system and billing procedures improve.

Achieving the goals of HIT will also require adopting across-the-board standards for all health care providers across the country. At the moment, such standards do not exist. For patients to get coordinated care, however, all doctors taking care of that patient must share that patient's information. Years ago, a similar situation existed in the banking industry when customers could not use an ATM that was not operated by their bank. The industry has since made it so that customers can use any ATM anywhere, even if isn't operated by their bank, as long as they are willing to pay a fee.

Of course, simply having HIT at a physician's office is no guarantee that patients will experience higher quality and safer care, any more than having a medical license guarantees a good doctor. In fact, according to a report by the Institute of Medicine (IOM, 2012), HIT that is poorly designed, implemented, or applied may have the opposite effect and raise the risk for harm. The report notes that poor user interface design can lead to overdosing of patients, whereas unclear information displays may result in failures to detect life-threatening illness. Poor human-computer interactions or the loss of data can delay appropriate treatments.

Like most technology, HIT relies on the people who use it and who must be well-trained for the IT to be applied correctly. The effectiveness and benefits of HIT hinge on the design, implementation, and use of the technology. Applied or used incorrectly, HIT can threaten patient safety and even result in death and injury. But the studies on exactly how HIT can jeopardize patient safety have been limited. For the research to produce "generalizable knowledge about the impact of health IT on patient safety," the IOM recommends understanding the interaction of numerous factors including (a) decisions about implementation strategies, (b) the degree to which users can configure their IT system and their approaches to such configurations, (c) clinician training strategies, (d) the frontline use of HIT, and (e) how is it integrated into and redesign of clinical workflow. Even though experts are well aware that HIT has the potential to do harm, there is actually a lack of quantifiable evidence to support it.

Concerns about patient safety and quality are overshadowed by the overall sluggish adoption of HIT by the health care system, especially when progress is compared with other industries, such as banking, education, and retail. Even though consumers can now go online to transfer funds between bank accounts, check their children's grades, and shop for virtually anything, they cannot routinely access their health records, get lab results, or find out whether their immunizations are up to date.

Most people would agree that having a patient's clinical data travel wherever the patient goes is a good idea, both for the patient and for the provider. The shared information would be consistent, and the patient would be spared the difficulty of keeping track of his or her health information. Despite these good intentions, the adoption of HIEs has been impeded by several factors, including technical issues, legal challenges, and concerns about privacy and security. But the biggest barrier is financial. Most providers see little incentive for participating in an HIE, given the current competitive fee-for-service structure of the health care delivery system that rewards excessive use of services.

Even if these systems are used effectively, challenges remain. Most systems still lack the ability to allow the seamless flow of clinical data between different settings, which inhibits the effective use of EHRs (Jha, 2012). They are also not equipped to generate and report quality data, which is essential to maximizing the full potential of HIT. Although we are certainly on the right path, the potential that can be derived from HIT has yet to be fully realized.

■ Toward the Future

Making care safer in the context of HIT requires recognizing that these products are not used in isolation but, rather, as part of a larger system that also includes people, organizations, processes, and the external environment (IOM, 2012). To that end, the proper use of these products will be essential and will call for a workforce in the future that is skilled in using HIT. According Schwartz, Magoulas, and Buntin (2013), HIT jobs accounted for 2.5% of all health care job openings between 2007 and 2011.

A workforce that is skilled in using HIT will be essential to the future of our health care system. Educational institutions and medical schools will certainly play a key role in teaching aspiring health care workers to use HIT. Meanwhile, professional organizations will most likely need to set standards and create professional development requirements to ensure that the workforce remain abreast of the latest technology, much in the same way doctors receive continuing medical education credits. The ACA has ensured that HIT will become a vital component of a reformed health care system. Mastering its usage will certainly be essential to a career in health care.

Although this chapter has focused mostly on health information systems as a key way IT is used in health care, there also are other IT and electronic approaches to improving the health system. Telehealth represents one such application. Telehealth uses telephone and video connections to link health care providers in one location with patients in remote locations, often rural areas where access to physician services is difficult. Telehealth has been in use for some time, but the technology is rapidly expanding and making it possible to diagnose more and more health problems from a remote location. In some cases, it is possible for nonphysicians at the remote site to implement a treatment plan.

Recently, an initiative called Project ECHO has been taking another approach to using telehealth technology. The Project ECHO approach links specialty physicians at an academic medical center to primary care physicians and other health practitioners in remote areas. This approach allows the specialist physicians to consult with remotely located care providers to guide diagnoses and develop treatment plans.

The first application of Project ECHO was in New Mexico, where it was used to help rural primary care physicians diagnose and treat hepatitis C, a complex medical problem. The linkages with specialists at the University of New Mexico provided essential coaching, advising, and joint problem solving that allowed for more accessible and higher-quality treatment of this chronic and dangerous disease (Arora et al., 2011). The same approach is being used to help primary care providers better manage a range of complex chronic conditions.

A second area of exploration to use electronic technology to improve health has been the development of applications for smartphones, tablets, and computers. An early focus of innovation has been the design of tools to help people track their physical activity levels, sleep habits, and calorie consumption. Large investments are currently being devoted to a wide array of applications that allow individuals to track their health care utilization, a range of physiological indicators of health and medical problems, and reminders to take medications.

The development of applications for consumers to better interact with health care providers and to better monitor and guide health behaviors has become a growing priority among large digital companies such as Apple, Samsung, and Google. Over the next decade, such applications very well could be a major aspect of new uses of digital technology.

■ Discussion Questions

1. Why has the health care sector been slower than other industries to adopt HIT?
2. How should the issue of patient privacy be addressed? What are some approaches you might suggest? Are they "perfectly secure" or "good enough?"
3. What can be done to encourage more people to consider careers in HIT?
4. What can be done for small practices that cannot afford HIT? Do you think the expense of HIT for small practices will lead to fewer small practices and more large group practices? Why or why not?

5. How should we address the resistance and reluctance to adopt HIT?
6. Many providers say they don't have time to learn the technology. How can this issue be addressed?

CASE STUDY

Dr. Ann Smith is a physician in rural New York, where she still keeps all of her patient records on paper, in folders, stored in file cabinets. Lately, she has been receiving a lot of information about HIT systems and is trying to decide what she should do about purchasing the software, how she can afford it, and when she will find the time to learn the program and train her staff.

Dr. Smith has a heavy workload and is the only physician in an 80-mile radius. She has three nurses on her staff. One of them also serves as the administrative assistant, who answers phone calls. She also has a part-time office manager who handles insurance claims and appeals. Dr. Smith is overwhelmed by the thought of switching to electronic records, and yet she knows she has to do it. She is 40 years old and plans to be in practice for many years to come. Money and time are both tight. With the exception of one nurse, her staff is older and was inherited by Dr. Smith from the previous doctor. Dr. Smith wonders how she will take care of her patients while trying to learn a new system. Yet, she knows, she is under pressure to adopt electronic records for her practice.

Keeping Dr. Smith's needs and concerns in mind, answer the following questions:

1. What should be Dr. Smith's first step toward adopting and implementing an EHR in her practice?
2. What are some ways she can work her own training into her schedule?
3. What are some of the key concerns for her staff, and how might they be addressed?

■ References

Abramson, E. L., McGinnis, S., Edwards, A., Maniccia, D. M., Moore, J., Kaushal, R., & HITEC Investigators. (2012). Electronic health record adoption and health information exchange among hospitals in New York State. *Journal of Evaluation in Clinical Practice, 18,* 1156–1162.

Accenture. (2013). *More than forty percent of U.S. consumers willing to switch physicians to gain online access to electronic medical records, according to Accenture survey* [Press release]. Retrieved from http://www.marketwatch.com/story/more-than-forty -percent-of-us-consumers-willing-to-switch-physicians-to-gain-online-access-to -electronic-medical-records-according-to-accenture-survey-2013-09-16

Adler-Milstein, J., & Jha, A. (2013). Health information exchange under HITECH: Progress and challenges. In C. M. DesRoches, M. W. Painter, & A. K. Jha (Eds.), *Health information technology in the United States: Better information systems for better care, 2013* (pp. 44–56). Princeton, NJ: Robert Wood Johnson Foundation.

Adler-Milstein, J., Bates, D. W., & Jha, A. K. (2013). Operational health information exchanges show substantial growth, but long-term funding remains a concern. *Health Affairs, 32,* 1486–1492.

Amarasingham, R., Plantinga, L., Diener-West, M., Gaskin, D. J., & Powe, N. R. (2009). Clinical information technologies and inpatient outcomes. *Archives of Internal Medicine, 169*(2), 108–114.

Arora, S., Thornton, K., Murata, G., Deming, P., Summers, K., Dion, D., . . . Qualls, C. (2011). Outcomes of treatment for hepatitis C virus infection by primary care providers. *New England Journal of Medicine, 364,* 2199–2207.

Byrne, C. B., Mercincavage, L. M., Pan, E. D., Vincent, A. G., Johnston, D. S., & Middleton, B. (2010). The value from investments in health information technology at the U.S. Department of Veterans Affairs. *Health Affairs, 29,* 629–638.

Centers for Medicare & Medicaid Services. (2013a). *A record of progress on health information technology* [Fact sheet]. Retrieved from www.cms.gov/Newsroom/Media ReleaseDatabase/Fact-Sheets/2013-Fact-Sheets-Items/2013-04-23.html

Centers for Medicare & Medicaid Services. (2013b). CMS National Health Expenditures 2013 Highlights. Retrieved from http://www.cms.gov/Research-Statistics-Data-and-Systems/Statistics-Trends-and-Reports/NationalHealthExpendData/downloads/highlights.pdf

Institute of Medicine (IOM). (2012). *Health IT and patient safety: Building safer systems for better care.* Washington, DC: National Academies Press.

Jeffe, M. G., Lee, G. A., Young, J. D., Sidney, S., & Go, A. S. (2013). Improved blood pressure control associated with a large-sale hypertension program. *Journal of the American Medical Association, 310,* 699–705.

Jha, A. (2012). Health information technology comes of age. *Archives of Internal Medicine, 172,* 737–738.

Kern, L. M., Barron, Y., Dhopeshwarkar, R. V., Edwards, A., Kaushal, R., & HITEC Investigators. (2013). Electronic health records and ambulatory quality of care. *Journal of General Internal Medicine, 28,* 496–503.

Longman, P. (2012). *Best care anywhere: Why VA health care would work better for everyone* (3rd ed.). San Francisco, CA: Berrett-Koehler Publishers.

Office of the National Coordinator of Health Information Technology. (2013). *Update on the adoption of health information technology and related efforts to facilitate the electronic use and exchange of health information* [Report to Congress]. Retrieved from http://www.healthit.gov/sites/default/files/rtc_adoption_of_healthit_and_related efforts.pdf

Pollak, V. E., & Lorch, J. A. (2007). Effect of electronic patient record use on mortality in end stage renal disease, a model chronic disease: Retrospective analysis of 9 years of prospectively collected data. *BMC Medical Informatics and Decision Making, 7,* 1–15.

Roy, J., Shah, N. R., Wood, G. C., Townsend, T., & Hennessy, S. (2012). Comparative effectiveness of ACE inhibitors and angiotensin receptor blockers for hypertension on clinical endpoints: A cohort study. *Journal of Clinical Hypertension, 14,* 407–414.

Schwartz, A., Magoulas, R., & Buntin, M. (2013). Tracking labor demand with online job postings: The case of health IT workers and the HITECH Act. *Industrial Relations: A Journal of Economy and Society, 52,* 941–968.

Shah, N. R. (2009, June). *Identifying hypertension in electronic health records: A comparison of various approaches* [Invited Oral Presentation]. AHRQ Comparative Effectiveness Research Methods Symposium, Rockville, MD.

Spooner, B., Reese, B., & Konschak, C. (Eds.). (2012). *Accountable care: Bridging the health information technology divide* (1st ed.). Virginia Beach, VA: Convergent Publishers.

Stalley, S., & DesRoches, C. M. (2013). Progress on adoption of electronic health records. In C. M. DesRoches, M. W. Painter, & A. K. Jha (Eds.), *Health information technology in the United States: Better information systems for better care, 2013* (pp. 7–21). Princeton, NJ: Robert Wood Johnson Foundation.

Testimony. Implementation and Usability Hearing. Office of the National Coordinator. (2013). (Written testimony of David Whitlinger). Retrieved from http://www.healthit .gov/facas/sites/faca/files/iuhearingwhitlinger.pdf

U.S. Department of Defense & U.S. Department of Veterans Affairs. (2011). *Interagency program office annual report to congress 2011.* Retrieved from http://tricare.mil/ tma/congressionalinformation/downloads/FullyInteroperableElectronicPersonal-HealthInformationDoDDVA.pdf

U.S. Department of Health and Human Services. (2014). *Where can we find a step-by-step approach to implementing an EHR and other software systems?* Retrieved from http:// www.hrsa.gov/healthit/toolbox/ruralhealthittoolbox/selection/stepbystep.html

Vest, J. R., Kaushal, R., Silver, M., Hentel, K., Kern, L. M., & HITEC Investigators. (2013a). *Health information exchange usage and repeat medical imaging.* Presented at AcademyHealth 2013 Annual Research Meeting, Baltimore, MD.

Vest, J. R., Kern, L. M., Campion, T. R., Silver, M. D., Kaushal, R., & HITEC Investigators. (2013b). *The association between community-wide longitudinal patient record systems and admissions via the ED.* Presented at AcademyHealth 2013 Annual Research Meeting, Baltimore, MD.

Futures

IV

*T*he last section of the book focuses on the intriguing question of what could happen in our health system in the next 5 years. The book's editors, James Knickman and Anthony Kovner, reflect on what emerges from the 15 previous chapters that allows us to forecast the future of the U.S. health system.

Chapter 16, which comprises this final section, reviews the key dynamics (each described in more detail in earlier chapters) that will shape the future direction of the health sector. The chapter goes on to offer some predictions about important aspects of the system that will change the most by 2020 and forecasts how different stakeholder groups will both influence and be affected by an evolving health system.

The current moment seems like it could support notable changes in how we address health and medical issues in the United States. In 2014, year-to-year expenditure growth seemed to have decreased, and insurance coverage increased markedly due to the expanded coverage offered by the Affordable Care Act. In addition, the current period is marked by new experimentation among health care providers about how they organize themselves to better coordinate care for people, a new and growing interest in population health across many communities, and new and emerging medical treatments and pharmaceuticals that could substantially improve the ability of health care providers to care for the population's medical problems. This section ends with a call for new leaders who can work across the health field to make sure all of this promise for the future leads to a more effective, affordable, and accessible health system.

16 The Future of Health Care Delivery and Health Policy

James R. Knickman and Anthony R. Kovner

KEY WORDS

analytics

insurance exchanges

leadership

outcome

prediction

stakeholders

telehealth

value

volume

LEARNING OBJECTIVES

- Explain why it is important to forecast the future
- Understand the forces in health care that shape change in the health system
- Describe the roles various stakeholders play in shaping the future
- Evaluate predictions about how the health system might evolve over the next 3 to 5 years

TOPICAL OUTLINE

- Why thinking about the future is important in health care planning
- Approaches to predicting the future
- Dynamics shaping change
- Four aspects of the health system likely to experience large changes in the coming years
- How different stakeholders will be affected by change
- The importance of leadership in making sure that change moves us toward improved health and better health care

It is helpful to reflect on where the health system in the United States is headed. Having some sense of how the system is evolving at any point in history is useful for efforts to shape the system, no matter what one's role.

Having some sense of how the system is evolving at any point in history is useful for efforts to shape the system, no matter what one's role.

To an individual planning to work as a health professional, a sense of the future offers insight about what types of employment might be the most meaningful and the most viable. As a health care manager, making choices about how to ensure your hospital, medical practice, public health agency, or health care company is ready for the future requires a base of understanding about the dynamics shaping change. For a policymaker, it is important to understand clearly how the system is evolving, what forces are shaping it, and how different changes in policy might affect future trends.

Of course the science of prediction is not a precise one, and forecast methods vary among experts. Economists and statisticians have developed highly quantitative forecasting approaches. They analyze past data to predict future economic events. They try to establish the relationships between driving forces and outcomes and then predict the future by assuming that the past relationships will continue going forward.

The Delphi method, a more qualitative approach to forecasting, systematically obtains expert opinions with an end goal of achieving consensus. Facilitators poll experts about their forecasts in three or four rounds of questionnaires separated by discussions among participants or the sharing of views in writing. The group completes a Delphi when it reaches a convergence of opinion. Of course, if rounds go on too long, consensus can evaporate as contrarians move away from consensus.

A third, less scientific approach to forecasting is to rely on nationally recognized leaders in a field to apply their experience of the past and the dynamics of the present to make predictions about the future. This is often the approach used in the popular media, where forecasting is common, and it is the one that we use in this chapter.

The predictions presented in this chapter are shaped by our vantage points, working full time at a health care philanthropic foundation and at a major university in the same large city, and by our past experiences as researchers, consultants, board members, and health care managers. We are fortunate to be able to base our forecasts on the analysis and insights presented by the accomplished and thoughtful authors in the 15 previous chapters of this text.

■ Dynamics Influencing Change

The preceding chapters present explanations of the forces shaping the health care system and identify the challenges that are most important to address to improve the value and outcomes of health care. We think there are four key dynamics to keep in mind when developing forecasts for the future:

1. We are relentlessly moving from a volume-oriented health system to an outcomes-oriented system (i.e., a system that achieves what we want, such as good health). We are now able to measure outcomes and compare factors that lead to variation in outcomes. Also, we are developing better ways to encourage providers to produce outcomes rather than just services. Health care is becoming more like the market for other services in America. Most service sectors focus on producing high-quality services that are valued by consumers and achieve the outcomes consumers want. If a service provider does not offer services that have value, people shop for new providers that do meet their needs.

2. Concern about costs is "top of mind" in so much that is happening in health care right now. The fear is that we have created an approach to services that is unaffordable not just for low-income Americans but also for families earning relatively comfortable middle incomes. The unaffordability factor is front and center in public policy debates. The intersection of a very deep economic recession in the years after 2007 with strong antitaxation sentiments among many Americans has shaped government choices in many ways.

3. Health care has become quite politicized at the federal level, with differences of opinion about almost every aspect of how the health system should be organized and financed. The paralysis that has followed disagreements and politicization makes it impossible to make even simple improvements that require public policy solutions. An end to this dynamic does not seem to be in sight.

4. Perhaps because of different opinions about who should have good access to health care and how this should be paid for, we are seeing sharp variation in the functioning of the health system from state to state. The fact that as of 2014 at least 21 states have decided not to expand their Medicaid programs, despite the offer of the federal government through the Affordable Care Act (ACA) to pay for most of the expansion costs, is a good indication of how voters and leaders in different states view strategies to finance and deliver health care. It is possible that this dynamic could lead to health care systems that look quite different from state to state in the future. Of course, it also is possible that state policymakers who refused to broaden Medicaid eligibility will change their minds if hospitals, consumer advocates, and low-income residents exert pressure in the political process.

■ Aspects of the Health System That Are Set to Change by 2020

MEDICINE AND SCIENCE

> *By far, the key driver of potential change in the health system is emerging technology and medical know-how.*

By far, the key driver of potential change in the health system is emerging technology and medical know-how. It is possible—although not a sure bet—that we could experience breakthroughs in medicine more dazzling than the breakthroughs in digital technology that have been occurring over the past 10 to 20 years.

One source of medical progress relates to the sequencing of the human genome at the start of the 21st century. It is now possible to map an individual's personal genome for less than $1,000; in the future, this information could act as the guide to which medical interventions (especially pharmaceutical interventions) will work for a specific person and which ones will have terrible side effects or be ineffective. This knowledge will usher in a world of personalized medicine. Each cancer patient, for example, will have a treatment regimen that is most likely to work for that person based on his or her genome.

Current research efforts could lead to a better understanding of the risks facing each individual at birth related to contracting chronic diseases or specific categories of medical problems later in life. Potentially, preventive interventions will be able to alter the risk for specific conditions such as heart disease or Alzheimer's disease.

Other advances also likely will occur, such as a universal vaccine for the flu or similar illnesses, which a person would need to take only once in his or her life. We hope this will also be the case for HIV.

Another major source of possible treatment improvements is stem-cell research. Stem-cell technologies may make it possible to grow tissue from a specific individual and for a specific organ. This tissue could be used to guide treatment interventions by seeing which interventions cause positive responses on the tissue where the disease is. And, perhaps most dazzling, stem cells could grow new organs that would not be rejected by an individual when transplanted.

Somewhat related to the emerging knowledge from science and medical research is the likely emergence of new technologies to change the way medical providers manage our care. We already are experiencing the rapidly growing role of robotics in helping surgeons perform surgery with less invasive procedures. Also, it is becoming clearer and clearer how the digital revolution of the past 20 years will affect the ability of providers and patients to monitor health care problems remotely and have information relayed back and forth without the need for patients to visit doctors or go to a provider for testing and monitoring.

Some of these technologies could save medical care costs and could markedly expand the lifespan of individuals, but some will be quite expensive, especially when first introduced. What is new is that some interventions associated with applications of genome and stem-cell research and digital technologies will be prevention oriented. Lowering your risk of a heart attack or another life-threatening medical problem 20 years from now by undergoing some preventive intervention may become commonplace—but not necessarily affordable.

Such medical interventions will be a challenge for the U.S. health care financing system. Will public and private payers be willing to fund these innovations? How much should we invest as a nation to fund the research to develop this new knowledge? What share of the research should be paid for by Americans and what share by residents of other countries? Will patients be expected to pay for the prevention-oriented interventions themselves, rather than through insurance? If so, what will that mean for disparities in health outcomes? The changing world of medicine and science will raise many questions and challenges about the future—and our nation will need to address them all.

PAYMENT APPROACHES AND THE ROLE OF HEALTH INSURANCE

Moving from the science and practice of medical care to the actual delivery and payment of services, it is easy to forecast that large changes are in store relating to how we pay for care and the role and organization of health insurance. The dynamic discussed earlier concerning demands for good outcomes as opposed to more volume of services naturally leads to payment reform that changes financial incentives for providers. New finance approaches will focus on paying fixed amounts of money for taking care of a bundle of needs for patients. As reviewed in Chapter 12, this would make health care reimbursement more like the approach for payment used in other sectors. We do not pay a price for each component of a complex machine like an automobile; we pay a fixed price for the finished product that we know will have the expected "outcome," that is, getting us from one place to another.

This is the best possible strategy to create a "win–win" outcome for both payers and providers. Payers benefit because they can better predict costs and are more likely to keep costs of health care from growing faster than the rest of the economy. Also, it is easier to assess the value of a bundle of services (just as it is easier to assess the value of a car compared with the value of a spark plug in a car). Providers benefit because they have more flexibility in how they organize care and how they can change their delivery systems to live within the capitated or bundled payments that are likely to dominate the payment system. It is much easier to manage with a fixed sum of money than to live by the ever-evolving reimbursement rules that keep ratcheting down fee-for-service rates.

As described in Chapter 11, we have seen the beginnings of this payment transformation already in states such as Massachusetts and Maryland. We predict that many more states will move toward new payment approaches based on collaborations among government, insurers, payers, providers, and consumers.

However, payment reform is not the only possible big change in the financing system. Commentators like Ezekiel Emanuel (who worked for the Obama administration while the ACA was crafted) as well as many conservative scholars make the case that employer-based insurance could disappear over the next 10 to 20 years and that the insurance sector as we now know it could itself disappear (Emanuel, 2014).

Employer-based insurance will become more questionable as a large tax is imposed on plans that are overly generous (called the "Cadillac tax"). This tax provision is one component of the ACA that is designed to push for insurance plans that do not encourage overuse of health care and to raise money to pay for the public insurance expansion. The tax is onerous for employers that offer generous coverage.

If the insurance exchanges set up as part of the ACA and private insurance exchanges become more prominent, it may well become advantageous for both employers and employees to set a fixed payment from the employer to the employee to compensate for not providing employer-based coverage. Employees then could purchase insurance on the ACA insurance exchanges (and if their income is low, they could qualify for federal subsidies). Employers would have to pay a different tax for dropping coverage, but this tax often could be substantially less than the Cadillac tax on generous insurance plans. Of course, employers also would benefit from this strategy because the future payments they make to employees in place of providing actual health insurance would not necessarily be tied to the inflation rate for health care services.

Insurance companies as they are structured now could become less relevant in the near future if large integrated networks of providers form and position themselves to accept capitated payments for the people they take care of. There is less need for traditional insurance companies in a world of simplified capitated payments; large provider systems would be more equipped to manage the financial risks this would involve. Already, in 2014, we are seeing a number of large health systems creating internal insurance companies that in essence compete with existing private insurance companies.

THE ORGANIZATION OF HEALTH CARE PROVIDERS

Perhaps the biggest unknown in health care today is whether all of the current efforts to form integrated networks (see Chapters 3 and 11) will happen on a large scale and will improve health outcomes. From the vantage point of early 2015, the best prediction is that the world of health care 10 to 15 years from now will be more consolidated, with larger integrated groups of providers dominating most community health systems around the country. In many parts of the country, a large amount of energy and resources is already being devoted to designing and building these integrated networks.

There is not strong evidence, however, that these integrated systems lead to better outcomes. There is a logic about integration as a strategy for improving efficiency of resource use and outcomes of care, but whether the wide array of provider types function well in this integrated environment and whether these systems are manageable remain open questions. Integrated networks have worked for systems such as the Kaiser HMO, Intermountain Healthcare in Utah, the Geisinger Health System in Pennsylvania, Group Health of Puget Sound, and the Mayo Clinic in Minnesota. However, these systems have consistently been outliers in terms of their management and financing approaches. The challenge is whether the practices of these forward-thinking outliers can become the norm for the health industry.

The other question mark regarding the move toward integration is whether consolidation will weaken competition across providers, leading to price increases even if these networks are more efficient and effective. Economists generally postulate that, in most markets, market power drives prices more than efficiency. It will be a difficult balancing act for federal and state regulators to encourage the efficiency potentially associated with consolidation and the antitrust, anticompetitive side effects of consolidation.

Other organizational changes also will affect the delivery of health care across the country. Centers of excellence that develop great reputations for value and outcomes for specific types of surgeries and procedures may begin to draw patients from wider geographical areas. Insurers could contract with these centers of excellence and convince patients to travel longer distances to use them when they have a major health problem. Urgent care centers that offer expanded, easy access to basic health care services also could continue to grow, taking business away from traditional physician practices.

Telehealth will continue to expand. This approach to linking patients and physicians in different physical locations will become more and more the norm for delivering specialty care to people living in rural areas. New offshoots of the concept of telehealth will be used to link specialty physicians in large academic health systems to primary care providers in rural areas so specialists can coach primary care providers in diagnosing and managing the treatment of a wider array of medical conditions (see Chapter 15). Additionally, the emergence of digital monitoring capability will connect patients to providers through the Internet, allowing ongoing monitoring of health conditions.

In a world of capitated payments, we also may see more efforts to organize and deliver prevention services in communities. Large integrated health providers responsible for the medical care of a population will have incentives to keep people from needing the most expensive types of medical care. If better approaches to prevention emerge, saving more health care dollars than the prevention activity costs, it will be worth investing in these activities (see Chapters 5, 6, 7, and 8). For example, providing lifestyle counseling that helps an overweight person eat better and exercise more is being shown to slow the onset of diabetes significantly, thereby saving substantial health care dollars.

It may even happen that population health experts develop evidence that creating community environments that encourage healthy living by improving access to healthy foods and creating opportunities for more physical activity saves health care dollars in the long run. And, perhaps getting schools to pay attention to teaching students how our bodies work and how we keep ourselves healthy will have payoffs. If so, a future challenge will be developing mechanisms for moving money from the medical care enterprise to an emerging population health enterprise.

■ Future Prospects for Different Stakeholders in the Health Enterprise

One constant in social interactions is that when a stakeholder is affected by a changing environment, the stakeholder reacts and tries to improve its position.

When looking toward the future, it is always useful to consider how different stakeholders could be affected. One constant in social interactions is that when a stakeholder is affected by a changing environment, the stakeholder reacts and tries to improve its position. How will key stakeholders be affected by the changes we predict, and how will they react? We consider the five key stakeholder groups identified in Chapter 1.

PROVIDERS: HOSPITALS, PHYSICIANS, NURSES, AND OTHER CAREGIVERS

Each type of provider is affected by the technology of delivering service, the organizational environment affecting everyday work life, and financial arrangements. In many ways, the core practice of medicine will remain the same while continuing to evolve with emerging technology and know-how. However, organizational change likely will alter the day-to-day experience of some health care professionals. The new world of health care finance could either decrease incomes (as has happened for many types of physicians in recent years) or slow income growth.

How will physicians, hospitals, and other providers react? First, they will be politically active, looking to protect their personal interests that are affected by public policy. Second, they will seek more market power and more organizational power to control what happens to them. Finally, they will adapt and learn how to thrive in a changing health care world. This is what has happened in the past and what happens in most industries that undergo substantial change.

EMPLOYERS

To date, employers have played a relatively passive role, accepting increases in the cost of the insurance they pay and working in small ways to shape insurance offerings that offer incentives to stay healthy and not to overuse health care. If employers continue to offer employees insurance coverage, they will continue these activities to limit their medical care liabilities, and they will continue to encourage wellness activities that help to lower health costs and to increase workforce productivity. They also will continue to add higher deductibles and copays to pass parts of cost increases along to employees.

However, employers also could begin to exit active roles in health care, as described earlier. They will seek ways to limit increases in the health-related costs they have to pay. As the future evolves, this stakeholder will probably do well.

INSURERS

As described earlier, the insurance system could face substantial changes as large health systems find it attractive to start their own insurance companies. However, the large insurance companies in the United States are increasingly diversified corporations that provide a wide range of services and expertise beyond managing risk and making payments. Most companies have sophisticated analytics capability, the ability to manage and use the very large data sets that are becoming important for managing health care systems, and the ability to use information technologies to manage the flow of dollars among players in the health system. Even if health systems start insurance companies, the major insurance corporations likely will provide services related to these insurance operations at health systems.

PUBLIC POLICYMAKERS

Federal policymakers will be preoccupied with the difficult choices that must be made about the growing costs of the Medicare and Medicaid programs. In the case of Medicare, even if the growth of costs per enrollee slows (as occurred in 2013 and 2014), the aging of our population will increase total expenditures. The political dynamics in Washington also suggest that the grand debate about how much responsibility government should have to ensure access to health care for the poor and elderly will endure for the near future. There are sharp divisions between conservatives, who feel government should have as small a role as possible, and liberals, who think government should ensure access to health care services and is the logical entity to organize and fund insurance coverage for elders and the poor.

At the state level, we can continue to expect great differences in approaches to Medicaid services across states. Some states will try to limit the size of Medicaid programs as much as possible, whereas others will use Medicaid to expand services to state residents. Of course, all states will be interested in new organizational and reimbursement approaches that lower the per beneficiary costs of Medicaid. Trying to make this happen will be a major activity at the state government level.

CONSUMERS

Finally, we get to what the possible changes will mean to users of the health system. In the current system, it is amazing that providers and payers and policymakers sometimes seem to view consumers as bystanders. Placing consumers at the center of every health care transaction and decision should be the goal of how the sector operates. It is possible that consumer advocacy groups could become more prominent in debates about how medical care is structured. It is also possible that consumer voices will more actively shape public policy if health issues become central concerns in political elections. Clearly, how consumers react to experiences with the ACA will have large ramifications for the initiative's future status.

Consumers will face many important personal decisions related to how they interact with the health system. They will need to decide whether they are willing to pay more money themselves for access to a wide panel of providers or whether they are willing to use a narrow network in order to lower their out-of-pocket spending. They will need to decide how much risk they want to take in the form of large deductibles and copays that will lower insurance premiums but increase their financial liability when illnesses occur. In addition, as described earlier, there likely will be many more medical interventions that become possible that are not covered by insurance. Consumers will need to determine how much of their wealth they will invest in interventions that could increase their chances of leading longer and healthier lives.

■ Conclusion

We began with a list of key stakeholders who shape the U.S. health care system: consumers; providers of care; insurance, pharmaceutical and medical device companies; payers; and public policymakers. We ended with an assessment of likely effects of changes in our health system on each of these stakeholders.

These stakeholders all play a part in what will happen and in how it will happen. One of the most important requirements for an improved health system, however, is a cadre of motivated, well-trained, thoughtful leaders working throughout the health system. The earlier chapter on governance and management (Chapter 14) explains how good leadership is developed and emphasizes two important traits of effective leaders: (a) they are transparent and (b) they hold themselves accountable. Leaders with these attributes are needed at the policy level and at the private sector corporate level. They are needed to organize the voices of consumers. Perhaps most importantly, leaders are needed throughout our health care service delivery system and our public health system.

Improvements come from the hard work and coordination of many individuals with knowledge and motivation. The readers of this book who are preparing for careers in the world of health care should be prepared for an exciting era of innovation and change in our health system. You should lead as health professionals, as consumers and patients, as citizens, and as payers of health care. The system will not improve without such leadership and the energy that comes from it.

■ Discussion Questions

1. Why is it difficult to forecast the future of health care delivery in the United States?
2. Analyze a forecast about health care delivery. Do you agree or disagree with the forecast and why?

3. What forces do you think will drive the health care delivery system over the next 4 years?

4. What do you think are the most important ways the ACA will be changed in 2020?

CASE STUDY

Discuss what would have to take place in the United States for passage of either a single-payer system or budget caps in total payments to providers under the Medicare program. Address questions such as the following:

1. How will political ideology affect such a consideration?
2. How will out-of-pocket costs affect such a possible change?
3. What would be the transition challenges of making such a change?

◾ Bibliography

Emanuel, E. J. (2014). *Reinventing American health care: How the Affordable Care Act will improve our terribly complex, blatantly unjust, outrageously expensive, grossly inefficient, error prone system.* New York, NY: PublicAffairs.

Silver, N. (2012). *The signal and the noise: Why so many predictions fail—but some don't.* New York, NY: Penguin Press.

Topol, E. (2012). *The creative destruction of medicine: How the digital revolution will create better health care.* New York, NY: Basic Books.

U.S. Department of Health and Human Services. (2011). *Healthy people 2020.* Washington, DC: U.S. Department of Health and Human Services.

Wennberg, J. (2010). *Tracking medicine: A researcher's quest to understand health care.* Oxford, UK: Oxford University Press.

Appendix:
Major Provisions of the Patient Protection and Affordable Care Act of 2010

The following summary of the health reform act passed in 2010 is reprinted with permission from the Henry J. Kaiser Family Foundation, a nonprofit private operating foundation based in Menlo Park, California, and dedicated to producing and communicating the best possible analysis and information on health issues.

The Affordable Care Act (ACA) represents the largest and most complicated piece of federal legislation affecting the U.S. health system perhaps since the passage of the original Medicare and Medicaid programs in the 1960s. The effects of the law are discussed frequently within the chapters of this book, and the law will continue to be a major factor influencing the shape of U.S. health care in the foreseeable future.

The ACA led to a significant legal battle that eventually was resolved in a 2012 Supreme Court ruling. The major change in the law described in the first summary comes from the Supreme Court's ruling that the expansion of Medicaid programs in states, which had been a component of the new law, became a voluntary choice for each state government, rather than a federal mandate.

As of late 2014, 27 states and the District of Columbia have voluntarily expanded their Medicaid programs as supported by the law. The other 23 states chose not to expand their Medicaid programs as of 2014.

The Kaiser Family Foundation makes available a wide range of materials explaining and tracking the implementation of the ACA on its website, available at kff.org/health-reform. Included on the website is a useful summary of the implications of the Supreme Court ruling, along with updates on implementation of the initiative.

■ SUMMARY OF THE NEW HEALTH REFORM LAW

On March 23, 2010, President Obama signed comprehensive health reform, the Patient Protection and Affordable Care Act, into law. The following summary of the new law, and changes made to the law by subsequent legislation, focuses on provisions to expand coverage, control health care costs, and improve the health care delivery system.

	Patient Protection and Affordable Care Act (P.L. 111-148)
Overall approach to expanding access to coverage	Require most U.S. citizens and legal residents to have health insurance. Create state-based American Health Benefit Exchanges through which individuals can purchase coverage, with premium and cost-sharing credits available to individuals/families with income between 133-400% of the federal poverty level (the poverty level is $18,310 for a family of three in 2009) and create separate Exchanges through which small businesses can purchase coverage. Require employers to pay penalties for employees who receive tax credits for health insurance through an Exchange, with exceptions for small employers. Impose new regulations on health plans in the Exchanges and in the individual and small group markets. Expand Medicaid to 133% of the federal poverty level.
INDIVIDUAL MANDATE	
Requirement to have coverage	■ Require U.S. citizens and legal residents to have qualifying health coverage. Those without coverage pay a tax penalty of the greater of $695 per year up to a maximum of three times that amount ($2,085) per family or 2.5% of household income. The penalty will be phased-in according to the following schedule: $95 in 2014, $325 in 2015, and $695 in 2016 for the flat fee or 1.0% of taxable income in 2014, 2.0% of taxable income in 2015, and 2.5% of taxable income in 2016. Beginning after 2016, the penalty will be increased annually by the cost-of-living adjustment. Exemptions will be granted for financial hardship, religious objections, American Indians, those without coverage for less than three months, undocumented immigrants, incarcerated individuals, those for whom the lowest cost plan option exceeds 8% of an individual's income, and those with incomes below the tax filing threshold (in 2009 the threshold for taxpayers under age 65 was $9,350 for singles and $18,700 for couples).
EMPLOYER REQUIREMENTS	
Requirement to offer coverage	■ Assess employers with more than 50 employees that do not offer coverage and have at least one full-time employee who receives a premium tax credit a fee of $2,000 per full-time employee, excluding the first 30 employees from the assessment. Employers with more than 50 employees that offer coverage but have at least one full-time employee receiving a premium tax credit, will pay the lesser of $3,000 for each employee receiving a premium credit or $2,000 for each full-time employee. (Effective January 1, 2014) ■ Exempt employers with 50 or fewer employees from any of the above penalties. ■ Require employers that offer coverage to their employees to provide a free choice voucher to employees with incomes less than 400% FPL whose share of the premium exceeds 8% but is less than 9.8% of their income and who choose to enroll in a plan in the Exchange. The voucher amount is equal to what the employer would have paid to provide coverage to the employee under the employer's plan and will be used to offset the premium costs for the plan in which the employee is enrolled. Employers providing free choice vouchers will not be subject to penalties for employees that receive premium credits in the Exchange. (Effective January 1, 2014)

	Patient Protection and Affordable Care Act (P.L. 111-148)
Other requirements	▪ Require employers with more than 200 employees to automatically enroll employees into health insurance plans offered by the employer. Employees may opt out of coverage
EXPANSION OF PUBLIC PROGRAMS	
Treatment of Medicaid	Expand Medicaid to all individuals under age 65 (children, pregnant women, parents, and adults without dependent children) with incomes up to 133% FPL based on modified adjusted gross income (as under current law and in the House and Senate-passed bills undocumented immigrants are not eligible for Medicaid). All newly eligible adults will be guaranteed a benchmark benefit package that at least provides the essential health benefits. To finance the coverage for the newly eligible (those who were not previously eligible for a full benchmark benefit package or who were eligible for a capped program but were not enrolled), states will receive 100% federal funding for 2014 through 2016, 95% federal financing in 2017, 94% federal financing in 2018, 93% federal financing in 2019, and 90% federal financing for 2020 and subsequent years. States that have already expanded eligibility to adults with incomes up to 100% FPL will receive a phased-in increase in the federal medical assistance percent-age (FMAP) for non-pregnant childless adults so that by 2019 they receive the same federal financing as other states (93% in 2019 and 90% in 2020 and later). States have the option to expand Medicaid eligibility to childless adults beginning on April 1, 2010, but will receive their regular FMAP until 2014. In addition, increase Medicaid payments in fee-for-service and managed care for primary care services provided by primary care doctors (family medicine, general internal medicine or pediatric medicine) to 100% of the Medicare payment rates for 2013 and 2014. States will receive 100% federal financing for the increased payment rates. (Effective January 1, 2014)
Treatment of CHIP	▪ Require states to maintain current income eligibility levels for children in Medicaid and the Children's Health Insurance Program (CHIP) until 2019 and extend funding for CHIP through 2015. CHIP benefit package and cost-sharing rules will continue as under current law. Beginning in 2015, states will receive a 23 percentage point increase in the CHIP match rate up to a cap of 100%. CHIP-eligible children who are unable to enroll in the program due to enrollment caps will be eligible for tax credits in the state Exchanges
PREMIUM AND COST-SHARING SUBSIDIES TO INDIVIDUALS	
Eligibility	▪ Limit availability of premium credits and cost-sharing subsidies through the Exchanges to U.S. citizens and legal immigrants who meet income limits. Employees who are offered coverage by an employer are not eligible for premium credits unless the employer plan does not have an actuarial value of at least 60% or if the employee share of the premium exceeds 9.5% of income. Legal immigrants who are barred from enrolling in Medicaid during their first five years in the U.S. will be eligible for premium credits.
Premium credits	▪ Provide refundable and advanceable premium credits to eligible individuals and families with incomes between 133-400% FPL to purchase insurance through the Exchanges. The premium credits will be tied to the second lowest cost silver plan in the area and will be set on a sliding scale such that the premium contributions are limited to the following percentages of income for specified income levels: Up to 133% FPL: 2% of income 133-150% FPL: 3 – 4% of income 150-200% FPL: 4 – 6.3% of income 200-250% FPL: 6.3 – 8.05% of income 250-300% FPL: 8.05 – 9.5% of income 300-400% FPL: 9.5% of income

	Patient Protection and Affordable Care Act (P.L. 111-148)
	▪ Increase the premium contributions for those receiving subsidies annually to reflect the excess of the premium growth over the rate of income growth for 2014-2018. Beginning in 2019, further adjust the premium contributions to reflect the excess of premium growth over CPI if aggregate premiums and cost sharing subsidies exceed .54% of GDP. ▪ Provisions related to the premium and cost-sharing subsidies are effective January 1, 2014.
Cost-sharing subsidies	▪ Provide cost-sharing subsidies to eligible individuals and families. The cost-sharing credits reduce the cost-sharing amounts and annual cost-sharing limits and have the effect of increasing the actuarial value of the basic benefit plan to the following percentages of the full value of the plan for the specified income level: 100-150% FPL: 94% 150-200% FPL: 87% 200-250% FPL: 73% 250-400% FPL: 70%
Verification	▪ Require verification of both income and citizenship status in determining eligibility for the federal premium credits.
Subsidies and abortion coverage	▪ Ensure that federal premium or cost-sharing subsidies are not used to purchase coverage for abortion if coverage extends beyond saving the life of the woman or cases of rape or incest (Hyde amendment). If an individual who receives federal assistance purchases coverage in a plan that chooses to cover abortion services beyond those for which federal funds are permitted, those federal subsidy funds (for premiums or cost-sharing) must not be used for the purchase of the abortion coverage and must be segregated from private premium payments or state funds.
PREMIUM SUBSIDIES TO EMPLOYERS	
Small business tax credits	▪ Provide small employers with no more than 25 employees and average annual wages of less than $50,000 that purchase health insurance for employees with a tax credit. – Phase I: For tax years 2010 through 2013, provide a tax credit of up to 35% of the employer's contribution toward the employee's health insurance premium if the employer contributes at least 50% of the total premium cost or 50% of a benchmark premium. The full credit will be available to employers with 10 or fewer employees and average annual wages of less than $25,000. The credit phases-out as firm size and average wage increases. Tax-exempt small businesses meeting these requirements are eligible for tax credits of up to 25% of the employer's contribution toward the employee's health insurance premium. – Phase II: For tax years 2014 and later, for eligible small businesses that purchase coverage through the state Exchange, provide a tax credit of up to 50% of the employer's contribution toward the employee's health insurance premium if the employer contributes at least 50% of the total premium cost. The credit will be available for two years. The full credit will be available to employers with 10 or fewer employees and average annual wages of less than $25,000. The credit phases-out as firm size and average wage increases. Tax-exempt small businesses meeting these requirements are eligible for tax credits of up to 35% of the employer's contribution toward the employee's health insurance premium

	Patient Protection and Affordable Care Act (P.L. 111-148)
Reinsurance program	■ Create a temporary reinsurance program for employers providing health insurance coverage to retirees over age 55 who are not eligible for Medicare. Program will reimburse employers or insurers for 80% of retiree claims between $15,000 and $90,000. Payments from the reinsurance program will be used to lower the costs for enrollees in the employer plan. Appropriate $5 billion to finance the program. (Effective 90 days following enactment through January 1, 2014)

TAX CHANGES RELATED TO HEALTH INSURANCE OR FINANCING HEALTH REFORM

| Tax changes related to health insurance | ■ Impose a tax on individuals without qualifying coverage of the greater of $695 per year up to a maximum of three times that amount or 2.5% of household income to be phased-in beginning in 2014.
■ Exclude the costs for over-the-counter drugs not prescribed by a doctor from being reimbursed through an HRA or health FSA and from being reimbursed on a tax-free basis through an HSA or Archer Medical Savings Account. (Effective January 1, 2011)
■ Increase the tax on distributions from a health savings account or an Archer MSA that are not used for qualified medical expenses to 20% (from 10% for HSAs and from 15% for Archer MSAs) of the disbursed amount. (Effective January 1, 2011)
■ Limit the amount of contributions to a flexible spending account for medical expenses to $2,500 per year increased annually by the cost of living adjustment. (Effective January 1, 2013)
■ Increase the threshold for the itemized deduction for unreimbursed medical expenses from 7.5% of adjusted gross income to 10% of adjusted gross income for regular tax purposes; waive the increase for individuals age 65 and older for tax years 2013 through 2016. (Effective January 1, 2013)
■ Increase the Medicare Part A (hospital insurance) tax rate on wages by 0.9% (from 1.45% to 2.35%)
■ On earnings over $200,000 for individual taxpayers and $250,000 for married couples filing jointly and impose a 3.8% tax on unearned income for higher-income taxpayers (thresholds are not indexed). (Effective January 1, 2013)
■ Impose an excise tax on insurers of employer-sponsored health plans with aggregate values that exceed $10,200 for individual coverage and $27,500 for family coverage (these threshold values will be indexed to the consumer price index for urban consumers (CPI-U) for years beginning in 2020). The threshold amounts will be increased for retired individuals age 55 and older who are not eligible for Medicare and for employees engaged in high-risk professions by $1,650 for individual coverage and $3,450 for family coverage. The threshold amounts may be adjusted upwards if health care costs rise more than expected prior to implementation of the tax in 2018. The threshold amounts will be increased for firms that may have higher health care costs because of the age or gender of their workers. The tax is equal to 40% of the value of the plan that exceeds the threshold amounts and is imposed on the issuer of the health insurance policy, which in the case of a self-insured plan is the plan administrator or, in some cases, the employer. The aggregate value of the health insurance plan includes reimbursements under a flexible spending account for medical expenses (health FSA) or health reimbursement arrangement (HRA), employer contributions to a health savings account (HSA), and coverage for supplementary health insurance coverage, excluding dental and vision coverage. (Effective January 1, 2018)
■ Eliminate the tax deduction for employers who receive Medicare Part D retiree drug subsidy payments. (Effective January 1, 2013) |

	Patient Protection and Affordable Care Act (P.L. 111-148)

Tax changes related to financing health reform	▪ Impose new annual fees on the pharmaceutical manufacturing sector, according to the following schedule:
	  – $2.8 billion in 2012-2013;
	  – $3.0 billion in 2014-2016;
	  – $4.0 billion in 2017;
	  – $4.1 billion in 2018; and
	  – $2.8 billion in 2019 and later.
	▪ Impose an annual fee on the health insurance sector, according to the following schedule:
	  – $8 billion in 2014;
	  – $11.3 billion in 2015-2016;
	  – $13.9 billion in 2017;
	  – $14.3 billion in 2018
	  – For subsequent years, the fee shall be the amount from the previous year increased by the rate of premium growth.
	▪ For non-profit insurers, only 50% of net premiums are taken into account in calculating the fee. Exemptions granted for non-profit plans that receive more than 80% of their income from government programs targeting low-income or elderly populations, or people with disabilities, and voluntary employees' beneficiary associations (VEBAs) not established by an employer. (Effective January 1, 2014)
	▪ Impose an excise tax of 2.3% on the sale of any taxable medical device. (Effective for sales after December 31, 2012)
	▪ Limit the deductibility of executive and employee compensation to $500,000 per applicable individual for health insurance providers. (Effective January 1, 2009)
	▪ Impose a tax of 10% on the amount paid for indoor tanning services. (Effective July 1, 2010)
	▪ Exclude unprocessed fuels from the definition of cellulosic biofuel for purposes of applying the cellulosic biofuel producer credit. (Effective January 1, 2010)
	▪ Clarify application of the economic substance doctrine and increase penalties for underpayments attributable to a transaction lacking economic substance. (Effective upon enactment)

HEALTH INSURANCE EXCHANGES	
Creation and structure of health insurance exchanges	▪ Create state-based American Health Benefit Exchanges and Small Business Health Options Program (SHOP) Exchanges, administered by a governmental agency or non-profit organization, through which individuals and small businesses with up to 100 employees can purchase qualified coverage. Permit states to allow businesses with more than 100 employees to purchase coverage in the SHOP Exchange beginning in 2017. States may form regional Exchanges or allow more than one Exchange to operate in a state as long as each Exchange serves a distinct geographic area. (Funding available to states to establish Exchanges within one year of enactment and until January 1, 2015)
Eligibility to purchase in the exchanges	▪ Restrict access to coverage through the Exchanges to U.S. citizens and legal immigrants who are not incarcerated.
Public plan option	▪ Require the Office of Personnel Management to contract with insurers to offer at least two multistate plans in each Exchange. At least one plan must be offered by a non-profit entity and at least one plan must not provide coverage for abortions beyond those permitted by federal law. Each multi-state plan must be licensed in each state and must meet the qualifications of a qualified health plan. If a state has lower age rating requirements than 3:1, the state may require multi-state plans to meet the more protective age rating rules. These multi-state plans will be offered separately from the Federal Employees Health Benefit Program and will have a separate risk pool.

	Patient Protection and Affordable Care Act (P.L. 111-148)
Consumer Operated and Oriented Plan (CO-OP)	▪ Create the Consumer Operated and Oriented Plan (CO-OP) program to foster the creation of nonprofit, member-run health insurance companies in all 50 states and District of Columbia to offer qualified health plans. To be eligible to receive funds, an organization must not be an existing health insurer or sponsored by a state or local government, substantially all of its activities must consist of the issuance of qualified health benefit plans in each state in which it is licensed, governance of the organization must be subject to a majority vote of its members, must operate with a strong consumer focus, and any profits must be used to lower premiums, improve benefits, or improve the quality of health care delivered to its members. (Appropriate $6 billion to finance the program and award loans and grants to establish CO-OPs by July 1, 2013)
Benefit tiers	▪ Create four benefit categories of plans plus a separate catastrophic plan to be offered through the Exchange, and in the individual and small group markets: – Bronze plan represents minimum creditable coverage and provides the essential health benefits, covers 60% of the benefit costs of the plan, with an out-of-pocket limit equal to the Health Savings Account (HSA) current law limit ($5,950 for individuals and $11,900 for families in 2010); – Silver plan provides the essential health benefits, covers 70% of the benefit costs of the plan, with the HSA out-of-pocket limits; – Gold plan provides the essential health benefits, covers 80% of the benefit costs of the plan, with the HSA out-of-pocket limits; – Platinum plan provides the essential health benefits, covers 90% of the benefit costs of the plan, with the HSA out-of-pocket limits; – Catastrophic plan available to those up to age 30 or to those who are exempt from the mandate to purchase coverage and provides catastrophic coverage only with the coverage level set at the HSA current law levels except that prevention benefits and coverage for three primary care visits would be exempt from the deductible. This plan is only available in the individual market. ▪ Reduce the out-of-pocket limits for those with incomes up to 400% FPL to the following levels: – 100-200% FPL: one-third of the HSA limits ($1,983/individual and $3,967/family); – 200-300% FPL: one-half of the HSA limits ($2,975/individual and $5,950/family); – 300-400% FPL: two-thirds of the HSA limits ($3,987/individual and $7,973/family). – These out-of-pocket reductions are applied within the actuarial limits of the plan and will not increase the actuarial value of the plan.
Insurance market and rating rules	▪ Require guarantee issue and renewability and allow rating variation based only on age (limited to 3 to 1 ratio), premium rating area, family composition, and tobacco use (limited to 1.5. to 1 ratio) in the individual and the small group market and the Exchange. ▪ Require risk adjustment in the individual and small group markets and in the Exchange. (Effective January 1, 2014)
Qualifications of participating health plans	▪ Require qualified health plans participating in the Exchange to meet marketing requirements, have adequate provider networks, contract with essential community providers, contract with navigators to conduct outreach and enrollment assistance, be accredited with respect to performance on quality measures, use a uniform enrollment form and standard format to present plan information.

	Patient Protection and Affordable Care Act (P.L. 111-148)
	▪ Require qualified health plans to report information on claims payment policies, enrollment, disenrollment, number of claims denied, cost-sharing requirements, out-of-network policies, and enrollee rights in plain language.
Requirements of the exchanges	▪ Require the Exchanges to maintain a call center for customer service, and establish procedures for enrolling individuals and businesses and for determining eligibility for tax credits. Require states to develop a single form for applying for state health subsidy programs that can be filed online, in person, by mail or by phone. Permit Exchanges to contract with state Medicaid agencies to determine eligibility for tax credits in the Exchanges. ▪ Require Exchanges to submit financial reports to the Secretary and comply with oversight investigations including a GAO study on the operation and administration of Exchanges.
Basic health plan	▪ Permit states the option to create a Basic Health Plan for uninsured individuals with incomes between 133-200% FPL who would otherwise be eligible to receive premium subsidies in the Exchange. States opting to provide this coverage will contract with one or more standard plans to provide at least the essential health benefits and must ensure that eligible individuals do not pay more in premiums than they would have paid in the Exchange and that the cost-sharing requirements do not exceed those of the platinum plan for enrollees with income less than 150% FPL or the gold plan for all other enrollees. States will receive 95% of the funds that would have been paid as federal premium and cost-sharing subsidies for eligible individuals to establish the Basic Health Plan. Individuals with incomes between 133-200% FPL in states creating Basic Health Plans will not be eligible for subsidies in the Exchanges.
Abortion coverage	▪ Permit states to prohibit plans participating in the Exchange from providing coverage for abortions. ▪ Require plans that choose to offer coverage for abortions beyond those for which federal funds are permitted (to save the life of the woman and in cases of rape or incest) in states that allow such coverage to create allocation accounts for segregating premium payments for coverage of abortion services from premium payments for coverage for all other services to ensure that no federal premium or cost-sharing subsidies are used to pay for the abortion coverage. Plans must also estimate the actuarial value of covering abortions by taking into account the cost of the abortion benefit (valued at no less than $1 per enrollee per month) and cannot take into account any savings that might be reaped as a result of the abortions. Prohibit plans participating in the Exchanges from discriminating against any provider because of an unwillingness to provide, pay for, provide coverage of, or refer for abortions.
Effective dates	▪ Unless otherwise noted, provisions relating to the American Health Benefit Exchanges are effective January 1, 2014.
BENEFIT DESIGN	
Essential benefits package	▪ Create an essential health benefits package that provides a comprehensive set of services, covers at least 60% of the actuarial value of the covered benefits, limits annual cost-sharing to the current law HSA limits ($5,950/individual and $11,900/family in 2010), and is not more extensive than the typical employer plan. Require the Secretary to define and annually update the benefit package through a transparent and public process. (Effective January 1, 2014)

Patient Protection and Affordable Care Act (P.L. 111-148)	
	▪ Require all qualified health benefits plans, including those offered through the Exchanges and those offered in the individual and small group markets outside the Exchanges, except grandfathered individual and employer-sponsored plans, to offer at least the essential health benefits package. (Effective January 1, 2014)
Abortion coverage	▪ Prohibit abortion coverage from being required as part of the essential health benefits package. (Effective January 1, 2014)
CHANGES TO PRIVATE INSURANCE	
Temporary high-risk pool	▪ Establish a temporary national high-risk pool to provide health coverage to individuals with preexisting medical conditions. U.S. citizens and legal immigrants who have a pre-existing medical condition and who have been uninsured for at least six months will be eligible to enroll in the high-risk pool and receive subsidized premiums. Premiums for the pool will be established for a standard population and may vary by no more than 4 to 1 due to age; maximum cost-sharing will be limited to the current law HSA limit ($5,950/individual and $11,900/family in 2010). Appropriate $5 billion to finance the program. (Effective within 90 days of enactment until January 1, 2014)
Medical loss ratio and premium rate reviews	▪ Require health plans to report the proportion of premium dollars spent on clinical services, quality, and other costs and provide rebates to consumers for the amount of the premium spent on clinical services and quality that is less than 85% for plans in the large group market and 80% for plans in the individual and small group markets. (Requirement to report medical loss ratio effective plan year 2010; requirement to provide rebates effective January 1, 2011) ▪ Establish a process for reviewing increases in health plan premiums and require plans to justify increases. Require states to report on trends in premium increases and recommend whether certain plan should be excluded from the Exchange based on unjustified premium increases. Provide grants to states to support efforts to review and approve premium increases. (Effective beginning plan year 2010)
Administrative simplification	▪ Adopt standards for financial and administrative transactions to promote administrative simplification. (Effective dates vary)
Dependent coverage	▪ Provide dependent coverage for children up to age 26 for all individual and group policies. (Effective six months following enactment)
Insurance market rules	▪ Prohibit individual and group health plans from placing lifetime limits on the dollar value of coverage and prohibit insurers from rescinding coverage except in cases of fraud. Prohibit pre-existing condition exclusions for children. (Effective six months following enactment) Beginning in January 2014, prohibit individual and group health plans from placing annual limits on the dollar value of coverage. Prior to January 2014, plans may only impose annual limits on coverage as determined by the Secretary. ▪ Grandfather existing individual and group plans with respect to new benefit standards, but require these grandfathered plans to extend dependent coverage to adult children up to age 26, prohibit rescissions of coverage, and eliminate waiting periods for coverage of greater than 90 days. Require grandfathered group plans to eliminate lifetime limits on coverage and beginning in 2014, eliminate annual limits on coverage. Prior to 2014, grandfathered group plans may only impose annual limits as determined by the Secretary. Require grandfathered group plans to eliminate pre-existing condition exclusions for children within six months of enactment and by 2014 for adults. (Effective six months following enactment, except where otherwise specified)

	Patient Protection and Affordable Care Act (P.L. 111-148)
	■ Impose the same insurance market regulations relating to guarantee issue, premium rating, and prohibitions on pre-existing condition exclusions in the individual market, in the Exchange, and in the small group market. (See new rating and market rules in Creation of insurance pooling mechanism.) (Effective January 1, 2014) ■ Require all new policies (except stand-alone dental, vision, and long-term care insurance plans), including those offered through the Exchanges and those offered outside of the Exchanges, to comply with one of the four benefit categories. Existing individual and employer-sponsored plans do not have to meet the new benefit standards. (See description of benefit categories in Creation of insurance pooling mechanism.) (Effective January 1, 2014) ■ Limit deductibles for health plans in the small group market to $2,000 for individuals and $4,000 for families unless contributions are offered that offset deductible amounts above these limits. This deductible limit will not affect the actuarial value of any plans. (Effective January 1, 2014) ■ Limit any waiting periods for coverage to 90 days. (Effective January 1, 2014) ■ Create a temporary reinsurance program to collect payments from health insurers in the individual and group markets to provide payments to plans in the individual market that cover high-risk individuals. Finance the reinsurance program through mandatory contributions by health insurers totaling $25 billion over three years. (Effective January 1, 2014 through December 2016) ■ Allow states the option of merging the individual and small group markets. (Effective January 1, 2014)
Consumer protections	■ Establish an internet website to help residents identify health coverage options (effective July 1, 2010) and develop a standard format for presenting information on coverage options (effective 60 days following enactment). ■ Develop standards for insurers to use in providing information on benefits and coverage. (Standards developed within 12 months following enactment; insurer must comply with standards within 24 months following enactment
Health care choice compacts and national plans	■ Permit states to form health care choice compacts and allow insurers to sell policies in any state participating in the compact. Insurers selling policies through a compact would only be subject to the laws and regulations of the state where the policy is written or issued, except for rules pertaining to market conduct, unfair trade practices, network adequacy, and consumer protections. Compacts may only be approved if it is determined that the compact will provide coverage that is at least as comprehensive and affordable as coverage provided through the state Exchanges. (Regulations issued by July 1, 2013, compacts may not take effect before January 1, 2016)
Health insurance administration	■ Establish the Health Insurance Reform Implementation Fund within the Department of Health and Human Services and allocate $1 billion to implement health reform policies.
STATE ROLE	
State Role	■ Create an American Health Benefit Exchange and a Small Business Health Options Program (SHOP) Exchange for individuals and small businesses and provide oversight of health plans with regard to the new insurance market regulations, consumer protections, rate reviews, solvency, reserve fund requirements, premium taxes, and to define rating areas.

	Patient Protection and Affordable Care Act (P.L. 111-148)
	■ Enroll newly eligible Medicaid beneficiaries into the Medicaid program no later than January 2014 (states have the option to expand enrollment beginning in 2011), coordinate enrollment with the new Exchanges, and implement other specified changes to the Medicaid program. Maintain current Medicaid and CHIP eligibility levels for children until 2019 and maintain current Medicaid eligibility levels for adults until the Exchange is fully operational. A state will be exempt from the maintenance of effort requirement for non-disabled adults with incomes above 133% FPL for any year from January 2011 through December 31, 2013 if the state certifies that it is experiencing a budget deficit or will experience a deficit in the following year. ■ Establish an office of health insurance consumer assistance or an ombudsman program to serve as an advocate for people with private coverage in the individual and small group markets. (Federal grants available beginning fiscal year 2010) ■ Permit states to create a Basic Health Plan for uninsured individuals with incomes between 133% and 200% FPL in lieu of these individuals receiving premium subsidies to purchase coverage in the Exchanges. (Effective January 1, 2014) Permit states to obtain a five-year waiver of certain new health insurance requirements if the state can demonstrate that it provides health coverage to all residents that is at least as comprehensive as the coverage required under an Exchange plan and that the state plan does not increase the federal budget deficit. (Effective January 1, 2017)
COST CONTAINMENT	
Administrative simplification	■ Simplify health insurance administration by adopting a single set of operating rules for eligibility verification and claims status (rules adopted July 1, 2011; effective January 1, 2013), electronic funds transfers and health care payment and remittance (rules adopted July 1, 2012; effective January 1, 2014), and health claims or equivalent encounter information, enrollment and disenrollment in a health plan, health plan premium payments, and referral certification and authorization (rules adopted July 1, 2014; effective January 1, 2016). Health plans must document compliance with these standards or face a penalty of no more than $1 per covered life. (Effective April 1, 2014)
Medicare	■ Restructure payments to Medicare Advantage (MA) plans by setting payments to different percentages of Medicare fee-for-service (FFS) rates, with higher payments for areas with low FFS rates and lower payments (95% of FFS) for areas with high FFS rates. Phase-in revised payments over 3 years beginning in 2011, for plans in most areas, with payments phased-in over longer periods (4 years and 6 years) for plans in other areas. Provide bonuses to plans receiving 4 or more stars, based on the current 5-star quality rating system for Medicare Advantage plans, beginning in 2012; qualifying plans in qualifying areas receive double bonuses. Modify rebate system with rebates allocated based on a plan's quality rating. Phase-in adjustments to plan payments for coding practices related to the health status of enrollees, with adjustments equaling 5.7% by 2019. Cap total payments, including bonuses, at current payment levels. Require Medicare Advantage plans to remit partial payments to the Secretary if the plan has a medical loss ratio of less than 85%, beginning 2014. Require the Secretary to suspend plan enrollment for 3 years if the medical loss ratio is less than 85% for 2 consecutive years and to terminate the plan contract if the medical loss ratio is less than 85% for 5 consecutive years.

	Patient Protection and Affordable Care Act (P.L. 111-148)
	• Reduce annual market basket updates for inpatient hospital, home health, skilled nursing facility, hospice and other Medicare providers, and adjust for productivity. (Effective dates vary)
	• Freeze the threshold for income-related Medicare Part B premiums for 2011 through 2019, and reduce the Medicare Part D premium subsidy for those with incomes above $85,000/individual and $170,000/couple. (Effective January 1, 2011)
	• Establish an Independent Payment Advisory Board comprised of 15 members to submit legislative proposals containing recommendations to reduce the per capita rate of growth in Medicare spending if spending exceeds a target growth rate. Beginning April 2013, require the Chief Actuary of CMS to project whether Medicare per capita spending exceeds the average of CPI-U and CPI-M, based on a five-year period ending that year. If so, beginning January 15, 2014, the Board will submit recommendations to achieve reductions in Medicare spending. Beginning January 2018, the target is modified such that the board submits recommendations if Medicare per capita spending exceeds GDP per capita plus one percent. The Board will submit proposals to the President and Congress for immediate consideration. The Board is prohibited from submitting proposals that would ration care, increase revenues or change benefits, eligibility or Medicare beneficiary cost sharing (including Parts A and B premiums), or would result in a change in the beneficiary premium percentage or low-income subsidies under Part D. Hospitals and hospices (through 2019) and clinical labs (for one year) will not be subject to cost reductions proposed by the Board. The Board must also submit recommendations every other year to slow the growth in national health expenditures while preserving quality of care by January 1, 2015.
	• Reduce Medicare Disproportionate Share Hospital (DSH) payments initially by 75% and subsequently increase payments based on the percent of the population uninsured and the amount of uncompensated care provided. (Effective fiscal year 2014)
	• Eliminate the Medicare Improvement Fund. (Effective upon enactment)
	• Allow providers organized as accountable care organizations (ACOs) that voluntarily meet quality thresholds to share in the cost savings they achieve for the Medicare program. To qualify as an ACO, organizations must agree to be accountable for the overall care of their Medicare beneficiaries, have adequate participation of primary care physicians, define processes to promote evidence-based medicine, report on quality and costs, and coordinate care. (Shared savings program established January 1, 2012)
	• Create an Innovation Center within the Centers for Medicare and Medicaid Services to test, evaluate, and expand in Medicare, Medicaid, and CHIP different payment structures and methodologies to reduce program expenditures while maintaining or improving quality of care. Payment reform models that improve quality and reduce the rate of cost growth could be expanded throughout the Medicare, Medicaid, and CHIP programs. (Effective January 1, 2011)
	• Reduce Medicare payments that would otherwise be made to hospitals by specified percentages to account for excess (preventable) hospital readmissions. (Effective October 1, 2012)
	• Reduce Medicare payments to certain hospitals for hospital-acquired conditions by 1%. (Effective fiscal year 2015)
Medicaid	• Increase the Medicaid drug rebate percentage for brand name drugs to 23.1 (except the rebate for clotting factors and drugs approved exclusively for pediatric use increases to 17.1%); increase the Medicaid rebate for non-innovator, multiple source drugs to 13% of average manufacturer price. (Effective January 1, 2010) Extend the drug rebate to Medicaid managed care plans. (Effective upon enactment)

	Patient Protection and Affordable Care Act (P.L. 111-148)
	▪ Reduce aggregate Medicaid DSH allotments by $.5 billion in 2014, $.6 billion in 2015, $.6 billion in 2016, $1.8 billion in 2017, $5 billion in 2018, $5.6 billion in 2019, and $4 billion in 2020. Require the Secretary to develop a methodology to distribute the DSH reductions in a manner that imposes the largest reduction in DSH allotments for states with the lowest percentage of uninsured or those that do not target DSH payments, imposes smaller reductions for low-DSH states, and accounts for DSH allotments used for 1115 waivers. (Effective October 1, 2011) ▪ Prohibit federal payments to states for Medicaid services related to health care acquired conditions. (Effective July 1, 2011)
Prescription drugs	▪ Authorize the Food and Drug Administration to approve generic versions of biologic drugs and grant biologics manufacturers 12 years of exclusive use before generics can be developed. (Effective upon enactment)
Waste, fraud, and abuse	▪ Reduce waste, fraud, and abuse in public programs by allowing provider screening, enhanced oversight periods for new providers and suppliers, including a 90-day period of enhanced oversight for initial claims of DME suppliers, and enrollment moratoria in areas identified as being at elevated risk of fraud in all public programs, and by requiring Medicare and Medicaid program providers and suppliers to establish compliance programs. Develop a database to capture and share data across federal and state programs, increase penalties for submitting false claims, strengthen standards for community mental health centers and increase funding for anti-fraud activities. (Effective dates vary)
IMPROVING QUALITY/HEALTH SYSTEM PERFORMANCE	
Comparative effectiveness research	▪ Support comparative effectiveness research by establishing a non-profit Patient-Centered Outcomes Research Institute to identify research priorities and conduct research that compares the clinical effectiveness of medical treatments. The Institute will be overseen by an appointed multi-stakeholder Board of Governors and will be assisted by expert advisory panels. Findings from comparative effectiveness research may not be construed as mandates, guidelines, or recommendations for payment, coverage, or treatment or used to deny coverage. (Funding available beginning fiscal year 2010) Terminate the Federal Coordinating Council for Comparative Effectiveness Research that was founded under the American Recovery and Reinvestment Act. (Effective upon enactment)
Medical malpractice	▪ Award five-year demonstration grants to states to develop, implement, and evaluate alternatives to current tort litigations. Preference will be given to states that have developed alternatives in consultation with relevant stakeholders and that have proposals that are likely to enhance patient safety by reducing medical errors and adverse events and are likely to improve access to liability insurance. (Funding appropriated for five years beginning in fiscal year 2011)
Medicare	▪ Establish a national Medicare pilot program to develop and evaluate paying a bundled payment for acute, inpatient hospital services, physician services, outpatient hospital services, and postacute care services for an episode of care that begins three days prior to a hospitalization and spans 30 days following discharge. If the pilot program achieves stated goals of improving or not reducing quality and reducing spending, develop a plan for expanding the pilot program. (Establish pilot program by January 1, 2013; expand program, if appropriate, by January 1, 2016)

	Patient Protection and Affordable Care Act (P.L. 111-148)
	▪ Create the Independence at Home demonstration program to provide high-need Medicare beneficiaries with primary care services in their home and allow participating teams of health professionals to share in any savings if they reduce preventable hospitalizations, prevent hospital readmissions, improve health outcomes, improve the efficiency of care, reduce the cost of health care services, and achieve patient satisfaction. (Effective January 1, 2012) ▪ Establish a hospital value-based purchasing program in Medicare to pay hospitals based on performance on quality measures and extend the Medicare physician quality reporting initiative beyond 2010. (Effective October 1, 2012) Develop plans to implement value-based purchasing programs for skilled nursing facilities, home health agencies, and ambulatory surgical centers. (Reports to Congress due January 1, 2011)
Dual eligibles	▪ Improve care coordination for dual eligibles by creating a new office within the Centers for Medicare and Medicaid services, the Federal Coordinated Health Care Office, to more effectively integrate Medicare and Medicaid benefits and improve coordination between the federal government and states in order to improve access to and quality of care and services for dual eligibles. (Effective March 1, 2010)
Medicaid	▪ Create a new Medicaid state plan option to permit Medicaid enrollees with at least two chronic conditions, one condition and risk of developing another, or at least one serious and persistent mental health condition to designate a provider as a health home. Provide states taking up the option with 90% FMAP for two years. (Effective January 1, 2011) ▪ Create new demonstration projects in Medicaid to pay bundled payments for episodes of care that include hospitalizations (effective January 1, 2012 through December 31, 2016); to make global capitated payments to safety net hospital systems (effective fiscal years 2010 through 2012); to allow pediatric medical providers organized as accountable care organizations to share in cost-savings (effective January 1, 2012 through December 31, 2016); and to provide Medicaid payments to institutions of mental disease for adult enrollees who require stabilization of an emergency condition (effective October 1, 2011 through December 31, 2015). ▪ Expand the role of the Medicaid and CHIP Payment and Access Commission to include assessments of adult services (including those dually eligible for Medicare and Medicaid). ($11 million in additional funds appropriated for fiscal year 2010)
Primary care	▪ Increase Medicaid payments in fee-for-service and managed care for primary care services provided by primary care doctors (family medicine, general internal medicine or pediatric medicine) to 100% of the Medicare payment rates for 2013 and 2014. States will receive 100% federal financing for the increased payment rates. (Effective January 1, 2013) ▪ Provide a 10% bonus payment to primary care physicians in Medicare from 2011 through 2015. (Effective for five years beginning January 1, 2011)
National quality strategy	▪ Develop a national quality improvement strategy that includes priorities to improve the delivery of health care services, patient health outcomes, and population health. Create processes for the development of quality measures involving input from multiple stakeholders and for selecting quality measures to be used in reporting to and payment under federal health programs. (National strategy due to Congress by January 1, 2011)

	Patient Protection and Affordable Care Act (P.L. 111-148)
	▪ Establish the Community-based Collaborative Care Network Program to support consortiums of health care providers to coordinate and integrate health care services, for low-income uninsured and underinsured populations. (Funds appropriated for five years beginning in FY 2011)
Financial disclosure	▪ Require disclosure of financial relationships between health entities, including physicians, hospitals, pharmacists, other providers, and manufacturers and distributors of covered drugs, devices, biologicals, and medical supplies. (Report due to Congress April 1, 2013)
Disparities	▪ Require enhanced collection and reporting of data on race, ethnicity, sex, primary language, disability status, and for underserved rural and frontier populations. Also require collection of access and treatment data for people with disabilities. Require the Secretary to analyze the data to monitor trends in disparities. (Effective two years following enactment)
PREVENTION/WELLNESS	
National strategy	▪ Establish the National Prevention, Health Promotion and Public Health Council to coordinate federal prevention, wellness, and public health activities. Develop a national strategy to improve the nation's health. (Strategy due one year following enactment) Create a Prevention and Public Health Fund to expand and sustain funding for prevention and public health programs. (Initial appropriation in fiscal year 2010) Create task forces on Preventive Services and Community Preventive Services to develop, update, and disseminate evidenced-based recommendations on the use of clinical and community prevention services. (Effective upon enactment) ▪ Establish a Prevention and Public Health Fund for prevention, wellness, and public health activities including prevention research and health screenings, the Education and Outreach Campaign for preventive benefits, and immunization programs. Appropriate $7 billion in funding for fiscal years 2010 through 2015 and $2 billion for each fiscal year after 2015. (Effective fiscal year 2010) ▪ Establish a grant program to support the delivery of evidence-based and community-based prevention and wellness services aimed at strengthening prevention activities, reducing chronic disease rates and addressing health disparities, especially in rural and frontier areas. (Funds appropriated for five years beginning in FY 2010)
Coverage of preventive services	▪ Improve prevention by covering only proven preventive services and eliminating cost-sharing for preventive services in Medicare and Medicaid. (Effective January 1, 2011) For states that provide Medicaid coverage for and remove cost-sharing for preventive services recommended by the US Preventive Services Task Force and recommended immunizations, provide a one percentage point increase in the FMAP for these services. Increase Medicare payments for certain preventive services to 100% of actual charges or fee schedule rates. (Effective January 1, 2011) ▪ Provide Medicare beneficiaries access to a comprehensive health risk assessment and creation of a personalized prevention plan. (Health risk assessment model developed within 18 months following enactment) Provide incentives to Medicare and Medicaid beneficiaries to complete behavior modification programs. (Effective January 1, 2011 or when program criteria are developed, whichever is first) Require Medicaid coverage for tobacco cessation services for pregnant women. (Effective October 1, 2010)

	Patient Protection and Affordable Care Act (P.L. 111-148)
	■ Require qualified health plans to provide at a minimum coverage without cost-sharing for preventive services rated A or B by the U.S. Preventive Services Task Force, recommended immunizations, preventive care for infants, children, and adolescents, and additional preventive care and screenings for women. (Effective six months following enactment)
Wellness programs	■ Provide grants for up to five years to small employers that establish wellness programs. (Funds appropriated for five years beginning in fiscal year 2011) ■ Provide technical assistance and other resources to evaluate employer-based wellness programs. Conduct a national worksite health policies and programs survey to assess employer-based health policies and programs. (Conduct study within two years following enactment) ■ Permit employers to offer employees rewards—in the form of premium discounts, waivers of costsharing requirements, or benefits that would otherwise not be provided—of up to 30% of the cost of coverage for participating in a wellness program and meeting certain health-related standards. Employers must offer an alternative standard for individuals for whom it is unreasonably difficult or inadvisable to meet the standard. The reward limit may be increased to 50% of the cost of coverage if deemed appropriate. (Effective January 1, 2014) Establish 10 state pilot programs by July 2014 to permit participating states to apply similar rewards for participating in wellness programs in the individual market and expand demonstrations in 2017 if effective. Require a report on the effectiveness and impact of wellness programs. (Report due three years following enactment)
Nutritional information	■ Require chain restaurants and food sold from vending machines to disclose the nutritional content of each item. (Proposed regulations issued within one year of enactment)
LONG-TERM CARE	
CLASS Act	■ Establish a national, voluntary insurance program for purchasing community living assistance services and supports (CLASS program). Following a five-year vesting period, the program will provide individuals with functional limitations a cash benefit of not less than an average of $50 per day to purchase non-medical services and supports necessary to maintain community residence. The program is financed through voluntary payroll deductions: all working adults will be automatically enrolled in the program, unless they choose to opt-out. (Effective January 1, 2011)
Medicaid	■ Extend the Medicaid Money Follows the Person Rebalancing Demonstration program through September 2016 (effective 30 days following enactment) and allocate $10 million per year for five years to continue the Aging and Disability Resource Center initiatives (funds appropriated for fiscal years 2010 through 2014). ■ Provide states with new options for offering home and community-based services through a Medicaid state plan rather than through a waiver for individuals with incomes up to 300% of the maximum SSI payment and who have a higher level of need and permit states to extend full Medicaid benefits to individual receiving home and community-based services under a state plan. (Effective October 1, 2010) ■ Establish the Community First Choice Option in Medicaid to provide community-based attendant supports and services to individuals with disabilities who require an institutional level of care. Provide states with an enhanced federal matching rate of an additional six percentage points for reimbursable expenses in the program. Sunset the option after five years. (Effective October 1, 2011)

	Patient Protection and Affordable Care Act (P.L. 111-148)
	■ Create the State Balancing Incentive Program to provide enhanced federal matching payments to eligible states to increase the proportion of non-institutionally-based long-term care services. Selected states will be eligible for FMAP increases for medical assistance expenditures for noninstitutionally- based long-term services and supports. (Effective October 1, 2011 through September 30, 2015)
Skilled nursing facility requirements	■ Require skilled nursing facilities under Medicare and nursing facilities under Medicaid to disclose information regarding ownership, accountability requirements, and expenditures. Publish standardized information on nursing facilities to a website so Medicare enrollees can compare the facilities. (Effective dates vary)
OTHER INVESTMENTS	
Medicare	■ Make improvements to the Medicare program: – – Provide a $250 rebate to Medicare beneficiaries who reach the Part D coverage gap in 2010. (Effective January 1, 2010); – – Phase down gradually the beneficiary coinsurance rate in the Medicare Part D coverage gap from 100% to 25% by 2020: ■ For brand-name drugs, require pharmaceutical manufacturers to provide a 50% discount on prescriptions filled in the Medicare Part D coverage gap beginning in 2011, in addition to federal subsidies of 25% of the brand-name drug cost by 2020 (phased in beginning in 2013) ■ For generic drugs, provide federal subsidies of 75% of the generic drug cost by 2020 for prescriptions filled in the Medicare Part D coverage gap (phased in beginning in 2011); Between 2014 and 2019, reduce the out-of-pocket amount that qualifies an enrollee for catastrophiccoverage; – Make Part D cost-sharing for full-benefit dual eligible beneficiaries receiving home and community-based care services equal to the cost-sharing for those who receive institutional care (Effective no earlier than January 1, 2012); – Expand Medicare coverage to individuals who have been exposed to environmental health hazards from living in an area subject to an emergency declaration made as of June 17, 2009 and have developed certain health conditions as a result (Effective upon enactment); – Provide a 10% bonus payment to primary care physicians and to general surgeons practicing in health professional shortage areas, from 2011 through 2015; and – Provide payments totaling $400 million in fiscal years 2011 and 2012 to qualifying hospitals in counties with the lowest quartile Medicare spending; and – Prohibit Medicare Advantage plans from imposing higher cost-sharing requirements for some Medicare covered benefits than is required under the traditional fee-for-service program.(Effective January 1, 2011)
Workforce	■ Improve workforce training and development: – Establish a multi-stakeholder Workforce Advisory Committee to develop a national workforce strategy. (Appointments made by September 30, 2010) – Increase the number of Graduate Medical Education (GME) training positions by redistributing currently unused slots, with priorities given to primary care and general surgery and to states with the lowest resident physician-to-population ratios (effective July 1, 2011); increase flexibility in laws and regulations that govern GME funding to promote training in outpatient settings (effective July 1, 2010); and ensure the availability of residency programs in rural and underserved areas. Establish Teaching Health Centers, defined as community-based, ambulatory patient care centers, including federally qualified health centers and other federally-funded health centers that are eligible for Medicare payments for the expenses associated with operating primary care residency programs. (Initial appropriation in fiscal year 2010)

	Patient Protection and Affordable Care Act (P.L. 111-148)
	– Increase workforce supply and support training of health professionals through scholarships and loans; support primary care training and capacity building; provide state grants to providers in medically underserved areas; train and recruit providers to serve in rural areas; establish a public health workforce loan repayment program; provide medical residents with training in preventive medicine and public health; promote training of a diverse workforce; and promote cultural competence training of health care professionals. (Effective dates vary) Support the development of interdisciplinary mental and behavioral health training programs (effective fiscal year 2010) and establish a training program for oral health professionals. (Funds appropriated for six years beginning in fiscal year 2010) – Address the projected shortage of nurses and retention of nurses by increasing the capacity for education, supporting training programs, providing loan repayment and retention grants, and creating a career ladder to nursing. (Initial appropriation in fiscal year 2010) Provide grants for up to three years to employ and provide training to family nurse practitioners who provide primary care in federally qualified health centers and nurse-managed health clinics. (Funds appropriated for five years beginning in fiscal year 2011) – Support the development of training programs that focus on primary care models such as medical homes, team management of chronic disease, and those that integrate physical and mental health services. (Funds appropriated for five years beginning in fiscal year 2010)
Community health centers and schoolbased health centers	▪ Improve access to care by increasing funding by $11 billion for community health centers and the National Health Service Corps over five years (effective fiscal year 2011); establishing new programs to support school-based health centers (effective fiscal year 2010) and nurse-managed health clinics (effective fiscal year 2010).
Trauma care	▪ Establish a new trauma center program to strengthen emergency department and trauma center capacity. Fund research on emergency medicine, including pediatric emergency medical research, and develop demonstration programs to design, implement, and evaluate innovative models for emergency care systems. (Funds appropriated beginning in fiscal year 2011)
Public health and disaster preparedness	▪ Establish a commissioned Regular Corps and a Ready Reserve Corps for service in time of a national emergency. (Funds appropriated for five years beginning in fiscal year 2010)
Requirements for non-profit hospitals	▪ Impose additional requirements on non-profit hospitals to conduct a community needs assessment every three years and adopt an implementation strategy to meet the identified needs, adopt and widely publicize a financial assistance policy that indicates whether free or discounted care is available and how to apply for the assistance, limit charges to patients who qualify for financial assistance to the amount generally billed to insured patients, and make reasonable attempts to determine eligibility for financial assistance before undertaking extraordinary collection actions. Impose a tax of $50,000 per year for failure to meet these requirements. (Effective for taxable years following enactment)
American Indians	▪ Reauthorize and amend the Indian Health Care Improvement Act. (Effective upon enactment)

	Patient Protection and Affordable Care Act (P.L. 111-148)
FINANCING	
Coverage and financing	The Congressional Budget Office (CBO) estimates the new health reform law will provide coverage to an additional 32 million when fully implemented in 2019 through a combination of the newly created Exchanges and the Medicaid expansion. CBO estimates the cost of the coverage components of the new law to be $938 billion over ten years. These costs are financed through a combination of savings from Medicare and Medicaid and new taxes and fees, including an excise tax on high-cost insurance, which CBO estimates will raise $32 billion over ten years. CBO also estimates that the health reform law will reduce the deficit by $124 billion over ten years.
Sources of information	www.democraticleader.house.gov/

Glossary

academic medical centers: Hospitals and other types of providers that are affiliated with a medical school and play active roles in training new health care providers, especially physicians, and in clinical research in collaboration with a medical school.

access: An individual's ability to obtain medical services on a timely and financially acceptable basis. Factors determining ease of access also include availability of health care facilities, transportation to them, and reasonable hours of operation.

accountable care organizations (ACOs): An entity—usually a hospital or a physician group—that accepts responsibility for the medical care of a population of people. An insurer or government payer develops some form of financial incentives to motivate the ACO to ensure that health care cost patterns for the covered group are better than the patterns for comparable people not in the group. First initiated by the Medicare program, various versions of the ACO idea are being tried by a range of payers.

accreditation: A decision made by a recognized organization that an institution substantially meets appropriate standards.

activities of daily living (ADLs): Tasks required for a person's normal functioning.

acute care: Medical care of a limited duration, provided in a hospital or outpatient setting, to treat an injury or short-term illness.

advanced practice nurse: Registered nurse, such as a clinical nurse specialist, nurse practitioner, nurse anesthetist, or nurse midwife, with a master's or doctoral degree concentrating on a specific area of practice.

adverse selection: Occurs when a population characteristic, such as age, increases health services utilization and costs above the capitation rate.

advocacy: Actions taken by an individual or group aiming to influence public policy, resource allocation, and other decisions. Activities may include media campaigns, public speaking, funding and publishing research, conducting polls, and lobbying.

alliance: Organizational relationship for specific purposes.

ambulatory care: Health care services that patients receive when they are not an inpatient or home in bed.

ambulatory care sensitive conditions: Conditions for which patients are hospitalized that could have been handled on an outpatient basis.

appropriate care: Care for which expected health benefits exceed negative consequences.

assisted living: Services provided to individuals who need assistance with activities of daily living.

Several of these definitions have been adapted from terms defined in Healthcare Acronyms & Terms for Boards and Medical Leaders, published by the Governance Institute, 6333 Greenwich Drive, Suite 200, San Diego, CA 92122, June 2004.

attending physicians: Doctors who have "privileges" to use a particular hospital for inpatient care of their patients.

average daily census: The number of people who stay overnight in a hospital bed on a typical day at a specific hospital.

avoidable mortality: A count of unnecessary deaths from diseases for which effective public health and medical interventions are available.

Bayes theorem: A formula for determining conditional probability (the likelihood of an event occurring given that another event has occurred) that allows for revising existing predictions or theories given new evidence.

behavioral health services: Clinical and supportive activities intended to treat or manage mental illness and/or alcohol or substance abuse (chemical dependency).

behavioral risk factor: An element of personal behavior—such as unbalanced nutrition, use of tobacco products, leading a sedentary lifestyle, or the abuse of alcohol—that leads to an increased risk of developing one or more diseases or negative health conditions.

benchmark: The best known value for a specific measure, from any source.

beneficiary: Any person, either a subscriber or a dependent, eligible for service under a health plan contract.

benefits: Specific areas of plan coverage, such as outpatient visits, hospitalizations, or prescription drugs, that make up the range of medical services marketed under a health plan.

biotechnology: The use of living organisms and biological systems to develop medical products and medical treatments. Biotechnology also is used in fields such as agriculture, new fuel products, and plastics.

bundled payment: A payment arrangement whereby a provider is paid a fixed amount of money to address a specific medical problem, often for a specific period of time. For example, a surgeon could receive a bundled payment that covers his or her services, the cost of any medical assistants used, the cost of any devices required for the surgery, and perhaps the cost of the surgical suite itself.

capitation: A payment method in which a physician or hospital is paid a fixed amount per patient per year, regardless of the volume or cost of services each patient requires.

carrier: An insurer; an underwriter of risk that is engaged in providing, paying for, or reimbursing all or part of the cost of health services under group insurance policies or contracts, medical or hospital services agreements, membership or subscription contracts, or similar arrangements in exchange for premiums or other periodic charges.

case management: A broadly used term that could describe a range of services directed at coordinating the care a person receives, making sure the person gets the care needed, or making sure the person follows medical advice. Case management is performed by different types of caregiver, ranging from physicians and nurses to community health workers, who often focus on helping a patient get social services he or she needs in addition to medical services.

case manager: An individual who coordinates and oversees other health care workers in finding the most effective methods of caring for specific patients and arranges for necessary services.

cash (monetary) assistance programs: Previously referred to as welfare, provide financial support to qualifying low-income individuals or families. These programs include Temporary Assistance for Needy Families (TANF), Supplemental Security Income (SSI), and Unemployment Insurance (UI).

catastrophic coverage: A type of insurance that pays for high-cost health care, usually associated with injuries and chronic conditions, such as cancer and AIDS.

census: In the United States, refers to the count of members of the national population and their demographic characteristics undertaken by the U.S. Census Bureau every 10 years; in the health care delivery system specifically, refers to the number of patients in a hospital or other health care institution at any one time.

Centers for Medicare & Medicaid Services (CMS): Administers Medicare, Medicaid, and the Children's Health Insurance Program (CHIP). Formerly called the Health Care Financing Administration (HCFA).

certificates of need: Approval for major new services and construction or renovation of hospitals or related facilities, as issued by states.

charity care: Care given to needy patients without expectation of payment.

chronic care: Treatment or rehabilitative health services provided to individuals on a long-term basis (more than 30 days), in both inpatient and ambulatory settings.

chronic care model: Organizing care to be proactive and focused on keeping people as healthy as possible, instead of performing reactively when people are injured or sick. A critical aspect is the focus on patient self-management.

clinical nurse practitioner: Nurse with extra training who accepts additional clinical responsibility for medical diagnosis or treatment.

clinical trials: The testing on patients in a clinical setting of a diagnostic, preventive, or therapeutic intervention, using a study design that will provide for a valid estimation of safety and efficiency.

closed panel: A managed care plan that contracts with physicians on an exclusive basis for services and does not allow those physicians to see patients who are members of another managed care organization.

coinsurance: An insurance provision that limits the amount of plan coverage to a certain percentage, commonly 80%. Any additional costs are paid out-of-pocket by members.

community benefits: Programs and services offered by medical care providers and other health care organizations to improve health in communities and increase access to health care. Hospitals are required to spend money on community benefits based on their tax status and, often, on the public funds they received to build the hospital.

community hospital: A hospital offering short-term general and other special services, owned by a corporation or agency other than the federal government.

community rating: The rating system by which a plan or an indemnity carrier uses the total experience of the subscribers or members within a given geographic area, or "community," to determine a reimbursement rate that is common for all groups, regardless of the individual claims experience of any one group.

comorbidity: One or more disorders or diseases occurring simultaneously or sequentially with a primary disorder or disease.

comparative effectiveness research: Studies that compare two or more health care technologies, products, or services against each other or against the conventional standard of care. Interventions are also compared for their costs relative to their benefits.

competency: The combination of knowledge, skills, personal characteristics, and individual and social behavior needed to perform a job effectively.

complementary and alternative medicine: Diagnostic and treatment interventions that fall outside the realm of state-licensed medical practice as it is defined by the privilege to use certain restricted diagnostic regimens, prescribe drugs, and practice surgery. Such disciplines include chiropractic, acupuncture, homeopathy, herbal medicine, naturopathy, and therapeutic touch.

comprehensive coverage: A health insurance system that pays for a broad range of services.

computerized physician order entry (CPOE): A process of electronically entering medical practitioner instructions for the treatment of hospitalized patients under a physician's care.

Consolidated Omnibus Budget Reconciliation Act of 1985 (COBRA): Federal law (P.L. 99–272) that requires all employer-sponsored health plans to offer certain employees and their families the opportunity to continue, at their personal expense, health insurance coverage under their group plan for up to 18, 24, or 36 months, depending on the qualifying event, after their coverage normally would have ceased (e.g., due to the death or retirement of the employee, divorce or legal separation, resignation or termination of employment, or bankruptcy of the employer).

continuous quality improvement (CQI): A systematic approach to improve processes of health care, such as admission to the hospital or delivery of patient medications.

copayment: A specified amount that an insured individual must pay for a specified service or procedure (e.g., $8 for an office visit).

cost-sharing: A provision that requires individuals to cover some part of their medical expenses (e.g., copayments, coinsurance, deductibles).

cost-shifting: Passing the excess costs of care for one group onto another group. For example, if the rate one group of health plan enrollees pays for services is less than the actual cost of those services, the difference can be made up through higher-than-cost charges to another group.

credentialing: The most common use of the term refers to obtaining and reviewing the documentation of professional providers.

critical pathway: The mapping out of day-to-day recommendations for patient care based on best practices and scientific evidence.

data: In health, an event, condition, or disease occurrence that is counted. In health services, an episode of care, costs of care, expenditures, quantification of human resources and facilities and their characteristics, and the like.

deductible: The amount insured individuals must pay out-of-pocket, usually annually on a calendar-year basis, before insurance will begin to cover their health care costs.

defensive medicine: The practice of physicians recommending a diagnostic test or treatment that is not necessarily optimal for the patient, but which serves to protect the physician against the patient's potentially bringing a lawsuit for insufficient care.

defined contribution plan: Benefits plan that gives employees a certain amount of total compensation to allocate among various benefits, rather than providing employees with the specific benefits, such as hospitalization coverage.

demographic characteristics: Such characteristics of an individual or population group (averages in the latter case) as age, sex, marital status, ethnicity, geographic location, occupation, and income.

denominator: For health care, the total number of people among whom numerator items are being counted.

diagnosis-related groups (DRGs): Groups of inpatient discharges with final diagnoses that are similar clinically and in resource consumption; used as a basis of payment by the Medicare program and, as a result, widely accepted by others.

discharge planning: A part of the patient management guidelines and the nursing care plan that identifies the expected discharge date and coordinates the various services necessary to achieve the target.

disproportionate share hospital (DSH): A hospital that provides a large amount (or disproportionate share) of uncompensated care and/or care to Medicaid and low-income Medicare beneficiaries.

dual eligible: Describes the status of individuals in the United States who qualify to receive benefits from both the Medicare and Medicaid programs simultaneously.

electronic health records (EHRs): Digital records that contain a comprehensive patient medical history, combining information from multiple provider sources. Also called electronic medical records (EMRs).

Emergency Medical Treatment and Labor Act (EMTALA): A portion of the COBRA law setting forth requirements for hospitals participating in Medicare to provide emergency care so that patients who cannot pay are not "dumped" to other hospitals.

emotional intelligence: A person's capacity to perceive, control, express, and evaluate emotions in interpersonal relationships.

Employee Retirement Income Security Act (ERISA): A 1974 federal law (P.I.. 93–406) that set the standards of disclosure for employee benefit plans to ensure workers the right to at least part of their pensions. The law governs most private pensions and other employee benefits and overrides all state laws that concern employee benefits, including health benefits; therefore, ERISA preempts state laws in their application to self-funded, private employer–sponsored health insurance plans.

enabling factors: Skills or physical elements, such as availability and accessibility of resources, that make it either possible or easier for individuals or populations to change their behavior or environment. Examples include living conditions, social support, resources, and skills.

encounter: A patient visit to a provider. The term often refers to visits to providers by patients in capitated health plans.

end-of-life care: Care that helps people with advanced, progressive, incurable illnesses to live as well as possible until they die. Types of care include management of pain and other symptoms as well as psychological, spiritual, social, and practical support.

enrollment: The process by which an individual and family become subscriber(s) for coverage in a health plan. This may be done either through an actual signing up of the individual, or through a collective bargaining agreement, or the employer's conditions of employment. A result is that the health plan is aware of its entire population of eligible beneficiaries. As a usual practice, individuals must notify the health plan of any changes in family status that affect the enrollment of dependents.

entitlements: Government benefits (e.g., Medicare, Medicaid, Social Security, food assistance programs) that are provided automatically to all qualified individuals and are therefore part of mandatory spending programs.

evidence-based management: The use of the best available evidence to make management decisions.

evidence-based medicine (EBM): That portion of medical practice, estimated at much less than 50%, that is based on established scientific findings.

experience rating: A method used to determine the cost of health insurance premiums, whereby the cost is based on the previous amount a certain group (e.g., all the employees of a particular business) paid for medical services.

Federal Employee Health Benefits Program (FEHBP): The health plans made available to federal employees as part of their employment benefits.

fee-for-service: A billing system in which a health care provider charges a patient a set amount for each individual service provided.

fee schedule: A listing of accepted fees or established allowances for specified medical procedures, as used in health plans; it usually represents the maximum amounts the program will pay for the specified service.

fixed costs: Costs that do not change or vary with fluctuations in enrollment or in utilization of services.

food assistance programs: Previously referred to as food stamps, provide financial support to qualifying individuals or families who are food insecure. These programs include the Supplemental Nutrition Assistance Program (SNAP) and the Special Supplemental Nutrition Program for Women, Infants, and Children (WIC).

formulary: A listing of drugs prepared by, for example, a hospital or a managed care company, that a drug plan will pay for.

for-profit hospitals: Those owned by private corporations that declare dividends or otherwise distribute profits to individuals, also called investor-owned; many are also community hospitals.

full-time equivalent (FTE): A way of calibrating the workforce used when some employees work part time and some employees work full time. For example, a person who works 4 hours per day generally would be considered a .5 FTE worker.

gatekeeper: A health care practitioner who makes decisions regarding the type and volume of services to which a patient may have access; generally used by health maintenance organizations (HMOs) to control unnecessary utilization of services.

generic drug: A therapeutic drug, originally protected by a patent, the chemical composition of which meets the standards for that drug set by the Food and Drug Administration, usually manufactured by a different company than the branded drug.

governance: The activity of an organization that monitors the outside environment, selects appropriate alternatives, and negotiates the implementation of these alternatives with others inside and outside the organization.

governing board: A group of individuals who, under state law, own an organization, regardless of whether they can obtain any financial advantage through such ownership.

graduate medical education: The education and training of physicians beyond the 4 years of medical school, in positions that may be termed internships, residencies, fellowships, postgraduate Years 1, 2, 3, and so on. Although one can enter medical school with only an undergraduate degree, in the United States, the 4 years of medical school leading to the MD or DO (doctor of osteopathy) degrees are customarily referred to as "undergraduate medical education."

group model: An HMO that contracts with a medical group for the provision of health care services. The relationship between the HMO and the medical group is generally very close, although there are wide variations in the relative independence of the group from the HMO; a form of closed panel health plan.

group practice: Three or more physicians who deliver patient care, make joint use of equipment and personnel, and divide income by a prearranged formula.

health behavior: An action such as regular exercise, eating a balanced diet, or obtaining necessary vaccinations that people practice to maintain, attain, or regain good health and to prevent illness.

health care delivery: The provision of preventive, treatment, or rehabilitative health services, from short term to long term, to individuals as well as groups of people, by individual practitioners, institutions, or public health agencies.

health care providers: Professional health service workers—physicians, dentists, psychologists—who are licensed to practice independently of any other health service worker; hospitals and other institutions offering health care services.

health care workforce: All of the people, professional and nonprofessional alike, who work in the health care services industry.

health exchange: A government-regulated marketplace of insurance plans with different levels of coverage offered to individuals and small businesses without health insurance.

Health Insurance Portability and Accountability Act of 1996 (HIPAA): Key provisions of this federal law improve health coverage for workers and their families when they change or lose jobs and establish privacy standards for medical information; overseen by the Department of Health and Human Services Office of Civil Rights.

health maintenance organization (HMO): A managed care company that organizes and provides health care for its enrollees for a fixed, prepaid premium.

Health Plan Employer Data and Information Set (HEDIS): A standard set of performance measures of the quality and performance of health plans, sponsored by the National Committee for Quality Assurance (NCQA).

health promotion (personal): The science and art of helping people change their lifestyles to move toward a state of optimal health. Optimal health is defined as a balance of physical, emotional, social, spiritual, and intellectual health.

health systems: Organizations that operate multiple service units under single ownership.

Healthy People 2020: Formal goals and objectives for the nation's health status that aim to be achieved by the year 2020. The Healthy People objectives are updated every 10 years by the federal government.

home health care: Health services provided in an individual's home.

hospice care: Programs that operate in different settings to provide palliative care and comprehensive support services to dying patients, as well as counseling and bereavement support for their family members. Hospice care is reimbursable under Medicare and many state Medicaid programs, as well as by private insurers.

hospitalists: Physicians, usually hospital employees, who practice only in acute care settings to provide inpatient care otherwise provided by attending physicians.

hospitalization: The admission of a patient to a hospital.

hospitalization coverage: A type of insurance coverage for most inpatient hospital costs (e.g., room and board), diagnostic and therapeutic services, care for emergency illnesses or injuries, laboratory and x-ray services, and certain other specified procedures.

human genome: The human genetic code, involving billions of base pairs in the DNA sequence of 26,000 to 40,000 genes in the 23 human chromosomes.

incidence: The number of new events, disease cases, or conditions counted in a defined population during a defined period of time.

indemnity insurance: Benefits paid in a predetermined amount in the event of a covered loss; differs from reimbursement, which provides benefits based on actual expenses incurred. There are fewer restrictions on what a doctor may charge and what an insurer may pay for a treatment, and generally there are also fewer restrictions on a patient's ability to access specialty services.

independent living facility: Housing designed for seniors 55 years of age and older who do not require assistance with daily activities or round-the-clock skilled nursing, but who may benefit from convenient services, a senior-friendly environment, and social opportunities.

independent practice association (IPA): Association of independent physicians formed as a separate legal entity for contracting purposes with health plans. Physicians see fee-for-service patients as well as those enrolled.

infant mortality: The death of a child born alive before 1 year of age.

information technology (IT): Electronic systems that store, retrieve, manipulate, and communicate information. Health care organizations want information technology that is accessible—with privacy safeguards—to multiple users within an organization.

inputs: Resources needed to carry out a process or provide a service. In health care, these resources typically include finances, buildings, supplies, equipment, personnel, and clients.

insurance exchanges: Entities that link individuals to health insurance offerings. The 2010 Patient Protection and Affordable Care Act (ACA) relies extensively on state-specific insurance exchanges to manage the enrollment of individuals in subsidized and nonsubsidized insurance policies offered by private insurance companies. Private insurance exchanges also are emerging to assist people in enrolling in Medicare offerings and other types of insurance products.

integrated delivery system (IDS): A group of health care organizations that collectively provides a full range of health-related services in a coordinated fashion to those using the system.

integration, horizontal: Affiliations among providers of the same type (e.g., a hospital forming relationships with other hospitals).

integration, vertical: Affiliations among providers of different types (e.g., a hospital, clinic, and nursing home forming an affiliation).

international medical school graduate: A U.S. citizen or noncitizen physician who has graduated from a medical school not located in the United States that is also not accredited by the U.S. medical school accrediting body, the Liaison Committee on Medical Education.

investor-owned hospital: A hospital owned by one or more private parties or a corporation for the purpose of generating a profitable return on investment.

length of stay: Days billed for a period of hospitalization.

licensure: A system established by a given state recognizing the achievement of a defined level of education, experience, and examination performance, which qualifies the person or organization meeting those standards to work or operate in a defined area of practice, which is prohibited to any person or organization that has not met those standards.

life expectancy: The predicted average number of years of life remaining for a person at a given age.

long-term care: A general term for a range of services provided to chronically ill, physically disabled, or mentally disabled patients in a nursing home or through long-term home health care.

loss ratio: A term used to describe the amount of money spent on health care. An insurance company with a loss ratio of 0.85, for instance, spends 85 cents of every premium dollar on health care and the remaining 15 cents on administrative costs, such as marketing and profits.

managed care: A system of health care delivery that influences or controls utilization of services and costs of services. The degree of influence depends on the model used. For example, a preferred provider organization (PPO) charges patients lower rates if they use the providers in its preferred network. HMOs, on the other hand, may choose not to reimburse for health services received from providers with whom the HMO does not contract.

mandated benefits: Benefits that a health plan is required to provide by law. This term generally refers to benefits above and beyond routine insurance-type benefits, and it generally applies at the state level (where there is high variability). Common examples include in vitro fertilization, defined days of inpatient mental health or substance abuse treatment, and other special condition treatments. Self-funded plans are exempt from mandated benefits under the Employee Retirement Income Security Act (ERISA).

Medicaid: A joint federal-state program of health care coverage for low income individuals, under Title XIX of the federal Social Security Act. States set benefits and eligibility requirements and administer the program. Medicaid is the major source of payment for nursing home care of the elderly.

medical home: A physician-directed medical practice with a team of providers in which each patient has an ongoing relationship with a personal physician, who coordinates care.

medical model: The set of procedures traditionally used by Western physicians to diagnose and treat illness: complaint, history, physical examination, ancillary tests if necessary, diagnosis, treatment, and prognosis with and without treatment.

medical savings account: Accounts similar to individual retirement accounts (IRAs) into which employers and employees can make tax-deferred contributions and from which employees may withdraw funds to pay covered health care expenses.

medically indigent: Those who do not have and cannot afford medical insurance coverage yet who are not eligible financially for Medicaid.

Medicare: A federal entitlement program of medical and health care coverage for the elderly and disabled and people with end-stage renal disease, governed by Title XVIII of the federal Social Security Act and consisting of several parts: Part A for institutional and home care; Part B for physician care; a managed care component (informally called Part C); and Part D, covering prescription drugs.

Medicare Prescription Drug, Improvement, and Modernization Act (MMA): Federal law signed in 2004 that offers a discount card at a nominal fee to Medicare beneficiaries for drugs and a prescription drug benefit that started in 2006 for those on Medicare who enroll and pay a premium.

medigap: Also known as Medicare supplemental insurance, a type of private insurance coverage that may be purchased by an individual enrolled in Medicare to cover certain needed services that are not covered by Medicare Part A or B (i.e., that fall into "gaps").

moral hazard: Purchasing more of something because someone else's money pays for all or part of it, as in providers and patients utilizing greater medical procedures because health insurance companies shoulder the majority of the cost.

morbidity: An episode of sickness, as defined by a health professional. A morbidity rate is the number of such episodes occurring in a given population during a given period of time.

mortality: Death. A mortality rate is the number of deaths—either the crude rate, which is all deaths, or a specific rate, which is number of deaths by, for example, a specific cause, at a specific location, or within a specific age group—occurring during a given period of time.

multispecialty group practice (MSGP): An MSGP employs primary and specialty care physicians who share common governance, infrastructure, and finances; refer patients for services offered within the group; and are typically affiliated with a particular hospital or hospitals.

natality: A live birth. The natality rate is the number of live births occurring in a given population during a given period of time.

national health insurance: A system for paying for one or more categories of health care services that is organized on a nationwide basis, established by and usually operated by a government agency.

National Health Service (NHS): A comprehensive, government-funded and operated system, such as that found in Great Britain.

network: An arrangement of several delivery points (e.g., a medical group practices affiliated with a managed care organization); an arrangement of HMOs (either autonomous and separate legal entities or subsidiaries of a larger corporation) using one common insuring mechanism such as BlueCross BlueShield; a broker organization (health plan) that arranges with physician groups, carriers, payer agencies, consumer groups, and others for services provided to enrollees.

nurse practitioner (NP): Registered nurses who have been trained at the master's level in providing primary care services, expanded health care evaluations, and decision making, and can write prescriptions, either independently or under a physician's supervision, depending on state law.

office visit: A formal, face-to-face contact between a physician and a patient in a health center, office, or hospital outpatient department.

open enrollment period: A requirement that all possible customers for a particular health insurance policy be accepted and, once accepted, cannot be terminated by the insurer due to claims experience.

out-of-pocket: Health care expenses paid by patients that are not reimbursed by health insurance companies, such as deductibles, copays, and coinsurance.

outcomes: Measures of treatments and effectiveness in terms of access, quality, and cost.

outlier: Under a DRG system of payment, additional per diem payments are made to hospitals for cases requiring extraordinary stays. Such cases are referred to as long-stay outliers.

palliative care: Pain and symptom management and emotional and spiritual support for individuals facing a chronic, debilitating, or life-threatening illness.

patient-centered medical home (PCMH): A widely accepted philosophy (not a destination) of primary care that is patient centered, comprehensive, team based, coordinated, accessible, and focused on quality and safety.

patient portals: Secure websites or applications that give patients access to personal health information and allow them to interact and communicate with their health care providers.

Patient Protection and Affordable Care Act (ACA): The 2010 health reform act that could extend insurance coverage to as many as 32 million Americans. The law also included regulations that affect the quality of coverage insurers must offer. Additionally, the law created a range of initiatives focused on encouraging reform in how medical care is organized and delivered, with a goal of reducing costs and improving quality and outcomes. Finally, other aspects of the law provided funding for expanded primary care capacity and a wide range of other health system improvements.

per diem payment: Reimbursement rates that are paid to providers for each day of services provided to a patient, based on the patient's illness or condition.

performance management: Measuring, monitoring, and enhancing staff performance to improve overall organizational performance.

physician assistant (PA): A specially trained and licensed worker who performs certain medical procedures under the supervision of a physician. Physician assistants are usually not registered nurses.

point-of-service plan (POS): A managed care plan that offers enrollees the option of receiving services from participating or nonparticipating providers. The benefits package is designed to encourage the use of participating providers through higher deductibles or only partial reimbursement for services provided by nonparticipating providers.

policy: Guidelines adopted by organizations and governments that promote constrained decision making and action and limit subsequent choices.

population health: The health outcomes of a group of people and the distribution of outcomes within that group. The field of population health assesses how patterns of health determinants affect health outcomes and develops policies and interventions that link these areas.

predisposing factor: Preexisting characteristics of an individual or his or her context that may influence (encourage or inhibit) a health-related behavior. Some are amenable to change (e.g., knowledge, attitudes) whereas others are not (e.g., genetic or demographic characteristics).

preexisting condition: A physical and/or mental condition of an insured that first manifests itself prior to issuance of a policy or that exists before issuance and for which treatment was received.

preferred provider organization (PPO): A limited group (panel) of providers (doctors and/or hospitals) who agree to provide health care to subscribers for a negotiated and usually discounted fee and who agree to utilization review.

premium: A periodic payment required to keep an insurance policy in force.

prepayment: A method of providing, in advance, for the cost of predetermined benefits for a population group through regular periodic payments in the form of premiums, dues, or contributions, including contributions that are made to a health and welfare fund by employers on behalf of their employees and payments to managed care organizations made by federal agencies for people who are Medicare eligible.

prescription: An order, usually made in writing, from a licensed physician or an authorized designee to a pharmacy, directing the latter to dispense a given drug, with written instructions for its use.

prevalence: The total number of events, disease cases, or conditions existing in a defined population, counted during a defined period of time or at a given point in time (known as point-prevalence).

primary care: The general health care that people receive on a routine basis that is not associated with an acute or chronic illness or disability and may be provided by a physician, nurse practitioner, or physician assistant.

primary care practitioners: Doctors in family practice, general internal medicine, obstetrics/gynecology, or pediatrics; nurse practitioners and midwives; and may also include psychiatrists and emergency care physicians.

privileges: Rights granted annually to physicians and affiliate staff members to perform specified kinds of care in the hospital.

public hospital: A hospital operated by a government agency. In the United States, the most common are the federal Veterans Health Administration hospitals (restricted to certain categories of veterans), state mental hospitals, and county and city general hospitals.

quality assurance: A formal set of activities to measure the quality of services provided; these may also include corrective measures.

quality improvement: Activities undertaken to improve quality relative to accepted standards of care.

quality of care: Measurement of the quality of health care provided to individuals or groups of patients, against a previously defined standard.

registered nurse (RN): A nurse who is a graduate of an approved education program leading to a diploma, an associate degree, or a bachelor's degree who also has met the requirements of experience and exam passage to be licensed in a given state.

reinsurance: Insurance purchased by a health plan to protect it against extremely high-cost cases.

reserves: A fiscal method of withholding a certain percentage of premiums to provide a fund for committed but undelivered health care and such uncertainties as higher hospital utilization levels than expected, overutilization of referrals, and catastrophes.

resource-based relative value scale (RBRVS): As of January 1, 1992, Medicare payments are based on a resource-based relative value scale (which replaced the former "usual, customary and reasonable" charge mechanism) for fee-for-service providers participating in the Medicare program. The objective is for physician fees to reflect the relative value of work performed, their practice expense, and malpractice insurance costs.

reverse causality: When two things are related to one another but the issue of which one causes the other can be unclear. For example, we observe that people with high income are healthier than people with low income and assume that this means income is a determinant of health. It may be the reverse, with good health leading to high incomes.

risk: Any chance of loss, or the possibility that revenues of the health plan will not be sufficient to cover expenditures incurred in the delivery of contractual services.

risk contract: A contract to provide services to beneficiaries under which the health plan receives a fixed monthly payment for enrolled members and then must provide all services on an at-risk basis.

risk management: Identification, evaluation, and corrective action against organizational behavior that would otherwise result in financial loss or legal liability.

safety-net provider: A person or institution that delivers care for free or at a reduced cost to low-income and/or uninsured patients.

Sarbanes-Oxley Act (SOA): The 2002 federal legislation that affects corporate governance, financial disclosure, and the practice of public accounting.

self-insurance: A program for providing group insurance with benefits financed entirely through the internal means of the policyholder, in place of purchasing coverage from commercial carriers. By self-insuring, firms avoid paying state taxes on premiums and are largely exempt from state-imposed mandates.

skilled nursing facility (SNF): Facility providing care for patients who no longer require treatment in the hospital but who do require 24-hour medical care or rehabilitation services.

social determinants: The circumstances in which people are born, grow up, live, work, and age, and the systems in place to address illness that are, in turn, shaped by larger forces, including economics, social policies, and politics.

social marketing: The use of marketing to design and implement programs to promote socially beneficial behavior change.

social services: An amenity or activity offered to promote the welfare (well-being) of individuals or groups. May be offered by the government, charitable organizations, or other groups seeking collective benefits.

socialized medicine: Usually an epithet used by opponents of any type of national government involvement in either the financing or operation of a national health care delivery system, regardless of whether such a government could be defined as socialist.

solo practice: Individual practice of medicine by a physician who does not practice in a group or does not share personnel, facilities, or equipment with three or more physicians.

staff model: An HMO that employs providers who see members in their own facilities. A form of closed-panel HMO.

stakeholders: Persons with an interest in the performance of an organization. Examples of hospital stakeholders are physicians and nurses, payers, managers, patients, and government.

Stark legislation: Federal laws (named after their sponsor, California Representative Fortney "Pete" Stark) that place limits on physicians' referring patients to facilities in which they have a financial interest.

strategic planning: A process reviewing the mission, environmental surveillance, and previous planning decisions used to establish major goals and nonrecurring resource allocation decisions of an organization.

supportive housing programs: A social service that couples medical assistance, supervision, or assistance in activities of daily living with safe and stable living accommodations.

surveillance: Ongoing observation of a population for rapid and accurate detection of events, conditions, or emerging diseases.

sustainable growth rate (SGR): Method used by the Centers for Medicare & Medicaid Services to control public spending on physician services by limiting growth for physician services to some predetermined target growth in spending.

teaching hospital: A hospital in which undergraduate and/or graduate medical education takes place.

telemedicine: The use of telecommunications technology by health care professionals to exchange medical information with physician specialists in other locales to improve the clinical health status of patients who are typically in remote areas, such as underdeveloped countries or rural communities.

tertiary care: Medical care or procedures performed by specialized physicians and teams in specially equipped hospitals. Advanced cancer care, burn treatment, and advanced surgeries are examples of tertiary care. Quaternary care is even more highly specialized, rarely used, and sometimes experimental.

The Joint Commission: Formerly the Joint Commission on Accreditation of Healthcare Organizations, The Joint Commission is a national organization of representatives of health care providers: the American College of Physicians, American College of Surgeons, American Hospital Association, American Medical Association, and consumer representatives. The Joint Commission inspects and accredits the quality of operations for hospitals and other health care organizations.

transparency: Operating in an accountable way by providing health care consumers cost and quality data before treatment so they can choose the best care at the best price.

Triple Aim: The concurrent pursuit of three objectives to improve the U.S. health care system: improving patients' health care experience, improving health outcomes, and reducing health care costs.

underwriting: Bearing the risk for something (i.e., a policy is underwritten by an insurance company); also the analysis done for a group to determine whether it should be offered coverage.

uninsured: In the United States, a person who has no third-party source of payment for health care services.

universal health insurance: A national health insurance system that provides for comprehensive coverage for all permanent residents of a country.

utilization: Quantity of services used by patients, such as hospital days, physician visits, or prescriptions.

utilization review: A system for measuring and evaluating how physicians utilize services for their patients against established standards.

value: Health care that is measured by the outcomes achieved instead of the amount of services delivered.

vital statistics: Numbers and rates for births, deaths, abortions, fetal deaths, fertility, life expectancy, marriages, and divorces.

volunteers: People who are not paid for giving their time and service to a health care organization, their only compensation being personal satisfaction.

vulnerable populations: Groups of people who are likely to be at greater risk for developing health problems because of challenges such as limited access to resources, poverty, marginalized sociocultural status, limited education, chronic mental illness, homelessness, incarceration, or age.

waste: System and organizational inefficiencies that lead to higher health care costs without improved outcomes.

workforce: The people engaged in or available for work in a particular industry, such as health care.

Index